International Family Law Desk Book

Ann Laquer Estin

Co-sponsored by the
Section of Family Law

Defending Liberty
Pursuing Justice

ABA Section of
International Law
Your Gateway to International Practice

Printed in the United States of America.

16 15 14 13 12 5 4 3 2 1

Library of Congress Cataloging-in-Publication Data
Estin, Ann Laquer, 1956–
 International family law desk book / edited By Ann Laquer Estin. — 1st ed.
    p. cm.
 ISBN 978-1-61438-317-8 (print : alk. paper) — ISBN 978-1-61438-318-5 (ebook)
1. Domestic relations. 2. Conflict of laws—Domestic relations. 3. Legal polycentricity. I. Title.
 K670.E845 2012
 346.01'5—dc23

                                                                    2011052207

Discounts are available for books ordered in bulk. Special consideration is given to state bars, CLE programs, and other bar-related organizations. Inquire at Book Publishing, ABA Publishing, American Bar Association, 321 North Clark Street, Chicago, Illinois 60654-7598.

www.shopABA.org

For my parents,
Edward Laquer and Alice Thorn Laquer
with love and gratitude.

Contents

Chapter 6: International Child Abduction 177

Acknowledgments

This book would not have been possible without the generous support of the University of Iowa, including a Global Scholar fellowship awarded by the Office of the Provost and a semester in residence at the Obermann Center. Dean Carolyn Jones and Dean Gail Agrawal of the College of Law provided encouragement as well as financial support for several trips to The Hague for meetings of the Hague Conference on Private International Law, where I served as an observer representing the International Society of Family Law.

For their support in the early stages of this project, I am particularly grateful to Professor William Duncan, Deputy Secretary General of the Hague Conference; Professor Robert Spector of the University of Oklahoma; and Mary Helen Carlson of the U.S. State Department.

Many collegues and friends answered questions and helped in various ways, including Gloria DeHart, Corrin Ferber, Bob Keith, Jack Sampson, and Mary Gay Sprague. All mistakes, of course, are my own. Any comments or suggestions may be sent to me at Ann-Estin@uiowa.edu.

My thanks also to my assistant, Melanie Stutzman, and to the law students who worked with me on different stages of this project, including Kathleen Cerniglia, Tiffany Hill, Rachael Jensen, Brent Liebersbach, Abigail Linn, and Brandon Phillips. As always, I am deeply indebted to Jim Estin, my own partner in international and family adventures.

About the Author

Ann Laquer Estin has been teaching and writing about family law for more than 20 years, and currently holds the Aliber Family Chair at the University of Iowa College of Law. She is an active member of the International Society of Family Law, and has attended numerous meetings of the Hague Conference on Private International Law focused on the four Hague Children's Conventions. She is also a frequent participant in meetings of U.S. State Department's Advisory Committee on Private International Law. Her international work was recognized with a Global Scholar award from the University of Iowa in 2009.

Ann's publications include many law review articles and several other books: *The Multi-Cultural Family* (2008), *Global Issues in Family Law* (with Barbara Stark) (2007), and *Cases and Problems in Domestic Relations* (with Homer H. Clark, Jr.) (7th ed. 2005). Before coming to the University of Iowa in 1999, she taught as the University of Colorado Law School, and practiced law in Denver, Colorado. She is a member of the bar in Colorado and Iowa, and a graduate of Dartmouth College and the University of Pennsylvania School of Law. She edits a blog on international family law issues at www.familiesacrossborders.com.

Introduction

Twenty years ago, it was hardly possible to discuss "international family law" as a field of legal practice. The United States joined the Hague Child Abduction Convention in 1988, but it was several years before the Convention drew much attention or litigation. International adoption was on the upswing in the early 1990s, regulated by a patchwork of foreign and state adoption laws and federal immigration law. Occasional judicial opinions, enough to fill a few footnotes in the RESTATEMENTS OF CONFLICT OF LAWS and FOREIGN RELATIONS LAW, addressed matters such as recognition of foreign divorce decrees or marriages. Some states had begun exploring techniques for international child-support enforcement, but these arrangements fell largely outside the scope of either the domestic child-support system or the international treaties used by other countries. Very few lawyers had reason to be concerned with any of these problems, and there was nothing to connect these disparate pieces into a larger whole.

Today, international family law has emerged as an important subject in its own right. The United States has joined two of the four Hague Children's Conventions and is working toward ratification of the others. Uniform laws in effect in every state provide for recognition and enforcement of foreign-custody and child-support orders. The Office of Children's Issues in the State Department has a staff of nearly 100 people who manage hundreds of international child abduction complaints and thousands of intercountry adoptions every year. State and federal agencies work with their counterparts in more than 25 countries to establish and enforce support orders for children with global families. International issues have become part of the everyday work of family court judges and family law practitioners across the country.

International family law presents many puzzles, especially in the United States. This book takes a broad approach to the subject, bringing together the law applicable to a wide range of cross-border family issues. It is designed to serve as a compact and useful resource and reference tool; the chapters that follow address marriage, divorce, the financial aspects of divorce, parentage and parental rights, custody and child abduction litigation, child support, and intercountry adoption. Each chapter builds on the foundation established by treaties and uniform acts and incorporates case law, the Restatements, and important secondary sources whenever possible. The book includes extensive discussion of the international treaties that have come to form the basis for reciprocal rela-

---

Further Reading: International Family Law

D. MARIANNE BLAIR ET AL., FAMILY LAW IN THE WORLD COMMUNITY: CASES, MATERIALS AND PROBLEMS IN INTERNATIONAL FAMILY LAW (2d ed. 2009).

ANN LAQUER ESTIN & BARBARA STARK, GLOBAL ISSUES IN FAMILY LAW (2007).

DAVID HODSON, A PRACTICAL GUIDE TO INTERNATIONAL FAMILY LAW (2008) (United Kingdom).

JEREMY D. MORLEY, INTERNATIONAL FAMILY LAW PRACTICE (2009).

JOHN MURPHY, INTERNATIONAL DIMENSIONS IN FAMILY LAW (2005) (United Kingdom).

JANET LEACH RICHARDS, CHEN WEI, & LORELLA DAL PEZZO, PRACTICAL GLOBAL FAMILY LAW: UNITED STATES, CHINA AND ITALY (2009).

BARBARA STARK, INTERNATIONAL FAMILY LAW: AN INTRODUCTION (2005).

---

tionships between the United States and more than 85 other nations, but it focuses on the law applied to these transnational family issues in the United States. Although written primarily for U.S. practitioners, it will hopefully also be of use to foreign lawyers and judges with an interest in understanding the U.S. system.

Because family law is primarily a subject of state law, and given the wide diversity in the approaches of different states to many of the core questions in family law, there are important local variations on the subjects discussed here that are not governed by federal statutes or treaties. For this reason, citations to state law are intended as examples to illustrate the points discussed and to assist practitioners in developing an analysis under local law and procedure. The book is not designed to serve as a practice manual or a source of legal advice.

In assembling the rules, statutes, treaties, and cases discussed here, this volume builds on a series of core principles that have shaped public policy and guided the growth of international family law over the past 30 years. The system depends on a *commitment to international comity*, including both respect for legal actors in other countries and implementation of concrete measures to facilitate communication and cooperation across borders. It proceeds from a conviction that *family relationships matter*, in all their rich diversity, and should be sustained and supported whenever possible. International family law also reflects the traditional view that family law serves *protective purposes*, prioritizing the best interests of children, attending to physical and financial risks that may confront children and other family members, and working within the larger framework of protection for international human rights. Finally, the new international family law seeks *pragmatic solutions* that take the circumstances of families into account and are accessible and efficient enough to assist children and families in all parts of the world.

1

Transnational Family Litigation

Lawyers and judges working in family law face complex procedural and conflict-of-laws issues, and these issues are even more pronounced in cases that reach across national borders. International litigation has many unique aspects and traps for the unwary. Besides the usual range of state common law and statutes, these cases may require reference to international treaties, such as Hague Conventions on Service of Process, Taking of Evidence, and Legalisation of Documents. This chapter gives an overview of the special requirements of transnational family litigation, considering questions of jurisdiction and choice of law, international assistance with service of process and obtaining evidence, and recognition and enforcement of judgments.

Determining Jurisdiction and Choice of Law

Judicial jurisdiction for most family law matters in the United States lies exclusively with the state courts. The subject matter jurisdiction of state courts in family cases is largely defined by statute. Personal jurisdiction presents a more complicated problem. Under the prevailing norms in the United States, a divorce decree does not require personal jurisdiction over the respondent spouse. Thus, a court may enter an ex parte divorce decree in the state where the petitioner is domiciled, even if the respondent spouse is not subject to the court's jurisdiction.[1] For litigation over family financial matters, however, courts must have personal jurisdiction over the respondent, as determined by state long-arm statutes and the Due Process Clause of the Constitution.[2] The Uniform Interstate Family Support Act (UIFSA) requires personal jurisdiction for litigation of child support matters.[3] Jurisdiction for custody litigation is defined by the Uniform Child Custody Jurisdiction and Enforcement Act (UCCJEA), which does not require personal jurisdiction.[4]

In the United States, personal jurisdiction in family law matters may be based on consent, residence within the forum state, or tag service on an individual who is physically present within the territory of the state. The Supreme Court upheld a state court's exercise of personal jurisdiction over a nonresident based on tag service in a child-support case in *Burnham v. Superior Court*.[5] Tag jurisdiction is widely criticized in other nations, however, that may not recognize and enforce orders from the United States

entered on this basis.[6] State courts may also exercise jurisdiction under a long-arm statute if the respondent has constitutionally sufficient "minimum contacts" with the state.[7]
Beyond the minimum contacts inquiry, the Supreme Court has held that the exercise of
personal jurisdiction must be reasonable and consistent with "traditional conception[s]
of fair play and substantial justice."[8]

In *Kulko v. Superior Court*, the Supreme Court applied the minimum-contacts
approach to a child-support case in which the children and their mother resided in
California and the father lived in New York.[9] When the mother sought a child-support
award, the Court concluded that the father did not have sufficient contacts with California to sustain the exercise of personal jurisdiction for this purpose. The Supreme Court
has not addressed the question of whether minimum contacts might be required (and
what contacts might be sufficient) to sustain personal jurisdiction over a respondent in
a custody proceeding.[10] State long-arm statutes vary widely in their reach, and this factor
may complicate adjudication of marital-property issues. In family support and parentage
cases, however, the UIFSA includes a long-arm provision extending jurisdiction to its full
constitutional extent.[11]

Federal Court Jurisdiction

International civil litigation often takes place in the federal courts based on diversity of
citizenship. Under 28 U.S.C. § 1332(a)(2), federal district courts have original jurisdiction
in civil actions between "citizens of a State and citizens or subjects of a foreign state"
where the matter in controversy is greater than $75,000. However, most international
family litigation that would meet the diversity and amount-in-controversy requirements
of the statute is excluded from federal courts under the domestic relations exception to
diversity jurisdiction. As reaffirmed in *Ankenbrandt v. Richards*,[12] this exception extends
to suits for divorce, alimony decrees, and child-custody orders, and it applies in both
international and domestic cases.[13] The Supreme Court has also concluded that the jurisdiction of the federal courts in "all Cases affecting Ambassadors, other public Ministers
and Consuls" does not include domestic-relations matters.[14] Diversity actions seeking
enforcement of alimony or child-support decrees that meet the amount-in-controversy
requirement have been heard in federal courts,[15] as have family tort actions for monetary
damages. If filed in state court, an action that meets the requirements for diversity jurisdiction may be removed to federal court by the defendant.[16] When a court concludes that
an action outside the scope of the domestic relations exception is nonetheless "inextricably intertwined" with matters addressed in a state court family law proceeding, it will
abstain from hearing the matter.[17]

International family litigation falls within the federal question jurisdiction of the federal courts under 28 U.S.C. § 1331 in a few situations. Primarily, this occurs with claims
under the International Child Abduction Remedies Act (ICARA),[18] which implements
the Hague Child Abduction Convention, and with several federal criminal statutes.[19] A
number of federal courts have considered whether family law torts can be litigated under
the Alien Tort Statute (ATS), 28 U.S.C. § 1350, which confers federal court jurisdiction
when an alien sues for a tort committed "in violation of the laws of nations." But because
the Supreme Court has narrowly construed that statute, these claims are unlikely to be
allowed.[20]

Parallel Proceedings and Injunctive Relief

Many international family disputes could be heard in more than one forum, based on the parties' ties to different countries. In this circumstance, courts in two different jurisdictions may proceed simultaneously in hearing the case. Comity does not compel one court to defer to another until one of the actions has proceeded to judgment. This principle is illustrated by two decisions in *Bourbon v. Bourbon*, a divorce case litigated simultaneously in France and New York by a French couple who lived in both locations.[21] A week after the wife filed proceedings in New York, the husband began litigation in France. The New York court rejected the husband's challenge to its jurisdiction and declined to dismiss the wife's action on grounds of comity or forum non conveniens. After the French court issued a final divorce decree, however, the New York court dismissed the wife's suit based on comity, res judicata, and collateral estoppel.

In the case of competing lawsuits in different jurisdictions, one of the parties may seek an injunction forbidding the other party from litigating in another forum.[22] Although a court with personal jurisdiction over both parties has authority to take this step, anti-suit injunctions raise complex issues of comity and are rarely ordered in family law cases in either the domestic or international setting.[23] The federal courts are divided as to the proper standard for issuing foreign anti-suit injunctions; several circuit courts take a strict approach, and several others apply more flexible standards.[24] Alternatively, a trial judge may have discretion to stay proceedings under the doctrine of lis alibi pendens, which is closely related to the inconvenient-forum doctrine.[25]

More limited injunctive relief may be requested to secure assets or otherwise preserve the status quo during the pendency of litigation. Prejudgment attachment orders and other measures to freeze assets are common in international litigation and may extend to property both within and beyond the jurisdiction where the injunction is granted.[26] A financial restraining order is a routine consequence of a divorce filing in many states, but in international cases doing so might require the cooperation of authorities in different jurisdictions. For example, on the request of a Guatemalan family court, *Cardenas v. Solis* approved a temporary injunction under Florida law freezing half of the funds in the defendant's bank accounts in the state.[27]

Forum Non Conveniens

A court with personal and subject matter jurisdiction may decline to hear an action based on forum non conveniens, a common law doctrine that allows the court to dismiss or stay the proceeding. In international forum non conveniens cases, state courts often draw on the Supreme Court's analysis in *Gulf Oil Corp. v. Gilbert*,[28] which held that courts should consider (1) the private interests of the plaintiff; (2) the relative ease of access to sources of proof; (3) the availability of compulsory process and the cost for attendance of witnesses; (4) the necessity and possibility of a view of the premises; (5) whether the plaintiff's choice of forum was made solely to vex, harass, or oppress the defendant; and (6) whether, in light of the public interest in having a localized controversy decided where it originated, the state in which the suit was filed has some tangible or intangible relation to the litigation.[29]

Under *Gulf Oil* and other cases, there is a strong presumption that a court should respect the plaintiff's choice of forum unless the balance of these factors weighs strongly in favor of the defendant. In *Piper Aircraft Co. v. Reyno*,[30] the Supreme Court held that a U.S. plaintiff's choice of a U.S. forum was entitled to particularly strong deference, noting, however, that it might not be reasonable to assume that a U.S. forum is convenient when it is chosen by a foreign plaintiff.[31]

In custody proceedings, UCCJEA § 207 provides that a court "may decline to exercise jurisdiction at any time if it determines that it is an inconvenient forum under the circumstances and that a court of another State is a more appropriate forum."[32] The statute includes a list of factors the court must consider and provides that if the court determines another forum is more appropriate, it should stay its proceedings on the condition that another child-custody proceeding be started promptly in another jurisdiction.

Choice of Law and Proof of Foreign Law

Many family law matters require reference to the law of another country. The validity of a marriage or divorce decree is determined by the law of the place where the marriage or divorce took place. Rights of custody in a proceeding under the Hague Child Abduction Convention are determined based on the law of the child's habitual residence. In these and other contexts, proof of foreign law may be a significant challenge.[33]

For courts in the United States, "the rule is that unless the law of a foreign jurisdiction is proved to be otherwise, it will be presumed to be the same as the law of the forum state."[34] A party seeking to have the court apply foreign law must adhere to local rules, which follow several different patterns. The common law required a party intending to rely on foreign law to plead and prove the applicable law as a matter of fact. Under Rule 44.1 of the Federal Rules of Civil Procedure, the pleading requirement was relaxed, and the issue was reframed as a matter of law to be determined by the court.[35]

Rule 44.1 requires reasonable written notice that a party intends to rely on foreign law, and it allows the court to consider "any relevant material or source, including testimony, whether or not submitted by a party or admissible" under the rules of evidence. The court may either carry out its own research or rely on experts appointed by the court or designated by the parties. This is relatively uncomplicated in some circumstances, where the relevant sources are available in English and easily understood.[36] But in other

---

Researching Foreign Law

These web sites provide a useful starting point for research into foreign law.

OAS Internet Treaty Database: http://www.oas.org/DIL/treaties_and_agreements.htm

Library of Congress: Multinational Reference Guide: http://www.loc.gov/law/help/guide/multiref.php

Global Legal Information Network (GLIN): http://www.loc.gov/lawweb/servlet/Glic?home

FindLaw International Resources: Country Listings: http://www.findlaw.com/12international/countries/index.html

LLRX: Comparative and Foreign Law: http://www.llrx.com/comparative_and_foreign_law.html

LLRX: Features: International Family Law: A Selective Resource Guide (Marilyn J. Raisch 2000): http://www.llrx.com/features/int_fam.htm

---

Further Reading: Jurisdiction and Choice of Law

Gary B. Born & Peter B. Rutledge, International Civil Litigation in United States Courts (2007).

Sofie Geeroms, Foreign Law in Civil Litigation: A Comparative and Functional Analysis (2004).

International Litigation Strategies and Practice (Barton Legum ed., 2005).

Ved P. Nanda & David K. Pansius, Litigation of International Disputes in U.S. Courts (2d ed. 2005).

---

cases, there may be difficulty finding sources, or disagreement between the experts on the point of foreign law in question.[37] State rules take a range of different approaches to this problem; some follow the lead of Rule 44.1 and others take the common law approach.[38]

Obtaining International Judicial Assistance

Transnational litigation often requires the cooperation of judicial or other authorities across borders. In many countries, an attempt to serve process or conduct discovery without invoking the assistance of public authorities is viewed as an infringement of national sovereignty and may violate the criminal law.[39] Traditionally, judicial cooperation was accomplished with letters rogatory, which are formal requests for assistance from the courts in one country to the judicial authorities of another country. The process can be time-consuming and cumbersome, and there is no guarantee that it will succeed.[40] Bilateral and multilateral treaties provide an alternative to letters rogatory. These treaties include the 1965 Hague Convention on the Service Abroad of Judicial and Extrajudicial Documents in Civil or Commercial Matters and the 1970 Hague Convention on the Taking of Evidence Abroad in Civil or Commercial Matters. In addition, counsel may make use of the 1975 Inter-American Convention on Letters Rogatory and its Additional Protocol (IACAP).

Judicial Assistance

In the United States, both the State Department and the Justice Department have responsibilities for international judicial assistance. The Office of American Citizen Services, located in the Bureau of Consular Affairs in the U.S. State Department, has detailed, country-specific judicial assistance information at http://travel.state.gov/law/judicial/judicial_2510.html. See also the information circular on Judicial Assistance, available at http://travel.state.gov/law/judicial/judicial_702.html.

The Office of International Judicial Assistance (also known as the Office of Foreign Litigation) in the Civil Division of the Department of Justice, 1100 L St. N.W. Room 11006, Washington DC 20530—phone: (202) 307-0983; fax: (202) 514-6584—acts as the U.S. Central Authority under the Hague litigation conventions. Incoming and outgoing requests for formal service of process are managed by Process Forwarding International (PFI), 633 Yesler Way, Seattle, WA 98104—phone: (206) 521-2979; fax: (206) 224-3410; website: http://www.hagueservice.net.

Service of Process

Constitutional due process norms mandate service of process on the defendant in all litigation in state and federal courts. As construed by the Supreme Court, due process requires notice "reasonably calculated under all of the circumstances" to inform the defendant of the action and give the defendant an opportunity for a hearing.[41] This may be accomplished by personal service, or by some alternative method, including service by publication when the defendant's location cannot be determined. Beyond this notice function, personal service on the defendant within the territory where the court is located may be the basis for obtaining personal jurisdiction over the defendant pursuant to *Burnham*.[42] Personal service on the defendant outside the territory where the court is located may the basis for an assertion of personal jurisdiction over a defendant who has constitutionally sufficient minimum contacts with the forum. Without those minimum contacts, personal service outside the court's territory, even if it is completed according to the rules described below, does not confer personal jurisdiction over the defendant.[43]

Service of process on an individual in a foreign country is subject to the law of the forum where the action has been filed[44] and to any applicable provisions of foreign or international law. Useful information, including country-specific flyers on service of process, is available on the State Department's website.[45] The Hague Service Convention provides a vehicle for service in many foreign countries; if the Convention is not applicable, service by letters rogatory may be required. Service of process on a member of the U.S. armed services who is stationed abroad may be facilitated by military authorities.[46] Foreign defendants who are present within the territory of the United States may be served with process here, provided that service complies with the applicable procedural rules of the forum.[47] If service within the forum state is relied upon to confer personal jurisdiction on the court, counsel should be aware that foreign jurisdictions may not be willing to enforce an in personam decree based only on tag jurisdiction, which is widely rejected outside the United States.

Hague Service Convention

For service of process in civil proceedings, including family law matters, adherence to the Hague Service Convention is mandatory in any of the more than 60 countries where it is in force.[48] As a treaty, the Convention preempts inconsistent provisions of state law, but service must also nonetheless comply with applicable state laws.[49] Service in treaty countries that does not comply with the Convention is ineffective, even if the respondent

---

For assistance with international service, contact Process Forwarding International (PFI), 633 Yesler Way, Seattle WA 98104—phone: (206) 521-2979; fax: (206) 224-3410; website: http://www.hagueservice.net. PFI manages all incoming and outgoing requests for formal service of process under the Hague Service Convention, the Inter-American Convention, and letters rogatory.

The U.S. State Department information circular on Service of Legal Documents Abroad is available at http://travel.state.gov/law/judicial/judicial_680.html, and the circular on Judicial Assistance—Service of Process Abroad is available at http://travel.state.gov/law/judicial/judicial_2513.html.

had actual notice of the proceeding.[50] A party who fails to raise objections to service in a timely manner may be deemed to have waived them, however.[51] Under the Convention, each contracting state designates a Central Authority to receive incoming requests for service of documents.[52] The U.S. Central Authority is the Office of International Judicial Assistance in the Department of Justice, and outgoing requests are managed by a contractor acting on behalf of the Central Authority.[53]

Under Article 5 of the Service Convention, the Central Authority in the receiving country has responsibility to serve the document or arrange to have it served by an appropriate agency, either "(a) by a method prescribed by its internal law for the service of documents in domestic actions upon persons who are within its territory, or (b) by a particular method requested by the applicant, unless such a method is incompatible with the law of the State addressed." The receiving country may require that the document be written or translated into one of its official languages. Article 5 also provides that "the document may always be served by delivery to an addressee who accepts it voluntarily," unless this is incompatible with the law of the state addressed.

In addition to service through the Central Authority under Article 5, the Convention permits other types of service under Article 10. Contracting States may object to this aspect of the treaty, however.[54] Unless there has been an objection in the country where service will be made, Article 10(a) protects "the freedom to send judicial documents, by postal channels, directly to persons abroad," and Articles 10(b) and 10(c) allow requests for service to be sent directly to the judicial officers, officials, or other competent persons of the State of destination.[55] Many Contracting States have made objections to aspects of Article 10; and in these countries, service through the Central Authority may be necessary.[56] Complete information on the types of service accepted in participating countries is available on the Hague Conference website and in the U.S. State Department's country-specific judicial assistance information circulars.

Courts in the United States have held that service need not be made according to the Service Convention when the defendant can be served within the United States. In *Volkswagenwerk AG v. Schlunk*,[57] the Supreme Court affirmed this reading of the treaty in the context of service on a foreign corporation through a domestic subsidiary. The Court held that the question of whether "service abroad" was required should be answered

Caution: Although international registered mail services are available for most countries in the world, this method of service may be prohibited by law in a particular foreign country. Counsel *should not attempt service of process by mail* in the following countries, which have objected to this type of service under Article 10(a) of the Hague Service Convention.

Argentina	Greece	Mexico	Slovak Republic
Bulgaria	Hungary	Monaco	Sri Lanka
China (PRC)	India	Norway	Switzerland
Croatia	Korea, Republic of	Poland	Turkey
Czech Republic	Kuwait	Russian Federation	Ukraine
Egypt	Lithuania	San Marino	Venezuela
Germany	Macedonia	Serbia	

Hague Service Convention

Hague Convention of 15 November 1965 on the Service Abroad of Judicial and Extrajudicial
    Documents in Civil or Commercial Matters, 20 U.S.T. 361, T.I.A.S. 6638, 658 U.N.T.S. 163,
    reprinted in 4 I.L.M. 341 (1965).

The full text and current status information for the Service Convention is available on the Hague
    Conference website at http://www.hcch.net (under "Conventions" and "14"). See also
    Hague Conference on Private International Law, Practical Handbook on the Operation
    of the Hague Convention of 15 November 1965 on the Service Abroad of Judicial and
    Extrajudicial Documents in Civil or Commercial Matters (3d ed. 2006).

---

with reference to the internal law of the state where the action is pending. As the opinion
also noted, however, compliance with the Convention may make it easier to enforce a
judgment abroad, even if the law of the forum state does not require it.

Inter-American Convention

The United States has a treaty relationship with a dozen countries under the IACAP, thus
providing another mechanism for service of documents through a central authority. The
Inter-American Convention is not exclusive, and service under the Convention and Protocol is generally similar to the Hague Service Convention.[58] Currently, the treaty is in
force for purposes of service of process only between the United States and Argentina,
Brazil, Chile, Colombia, Ecuador, Guatemala, Mexico, Panama, Paraguay, Peru, Uruguay,
and Venezuela. Requests from the United States are transmitted by Processing Forwarding International (PFI), the private contractor working with the Office of International
Judicial Assistance in the Department of Justice.

Letters Rogatory

Letters rogatory, the traditional method of securing judicial cooperation across international borders, are typically drafted by counsel and signed by a judge in the United
States.[59] Depending on the country to which they are sent, the letters must be authenticated and translated and then submitted to the Secretary of State for transmittal through
diplomatic channels. Depending on the law of the other country involved, it may be

---

Inter-American Convention and Protocol

Inter-American Convention on Letters Rogatory, OAS Treaty Series No. 43, *reprinted in* 14 I.L.M.
    328 (1975); Additional Protocol, OAS Treaty Series No. 56, *reprinted in* 18 I.L.M. 1238
    (1979).

For the text of the Inter-American Convention and current status information, see the OAS Internet
    Treaty Database at http://www.oas.org/juridico/english/treaties/b-36.html; for the text of
    the Additional Protocol and status information, see http://www.oas.org/juridico/english/
    sigs/b-46.html.

The U.S. State Department information circular on the Inter-American Service Convention and
    Additional Protocol is available at http://travel.state.gov/law/judicial/judicial_5219.html.

The U.S. State Department information circular on Preparation of Letters Rogatory is available at http://travel.state.gov/law/judicial/judicial_683.html.

possible to transmit the letter through local legal counsel. A useful explanation of the process, including country-specific information on what is required, is available on the State Department's website. Transmission of letters rogatory is governed by the Vienna Convention on Consular Relations (VCCR) and various bilateral consular conventions.[60]

Discovery and Taking Evidence

In many foreign countries, there is no equivalent to the wide pretrial discovery permitted in the United States.[61] Particularly in civil law jurisdictions, the practice is for judicial officers—rather than the parties and their counsel—to collect evidence. Failure to follow the laws of the country where evidence is sought is a violation of territorial and judicial sovereignty, and it may be a criminal offense. In some countries, "blocking statutes" prohibit production of evidence for purposes of foreign legal proceedings unless appropriate procedures are followed.[62] Accordingly, counsel should proceed with caution. International judicial assistance in collecting evidence is available under the Hague Convention on the Taking of Evidence Abroad in Civil or Commercial Matters, or through the use of letters rogatory.[63]

To the extent that a court in the United States has personal jurisdiction over the parties or witnesses, discovery in an international case may proceed in largely the same manner as in a purely domestic proceeding. In 1987, a majority of the Supreme Court concluded in *Société Nationale Industrielle Aérospatiale v. United States District Court* that use of the Hague Evidence Convention was optional to the extent that it "did not deprive the District Court of the jurisdiction it otherwise possessed to order a foreign national party before it to produce evidence physically located within a signatory nation."[64] Rather, the Court concluded that lower courts should take considerations of international comity into account in exercising their power to supervise pretrial discovery proceedings. Some state courts have followed this approach, while others have directed litigants to proceed first under the Evidence Convention.[65] To the extent that parties seek discovery within a foreign country, or from an individual who is not subject to the court's personal jurisdiction, this approach is not available.

There is substantial literature on the mechanics of extraterritorial discovery, but the country-specific judicial assistance information assembled by the State Department is a useful starting point.[66] Depositions in foreign countries are addressed in the Federal Rules of Civil Procedure. Under Rule 28(b), depositions may be taken pursuant to any applicable treaty or convention, pursuant to a letter of request or letter rogatory, "on notice before a person authorized to administer oaths in the place where the examination is held," or "before a person commissioned by the court" and authorized "to administer any necessary oath and take testimony."[67] State courts may also issue letters rogatory or commissions for taking depositions according to their rules of procedure and evidence.[68]

Consular officials have an important role in this process. Under federal law, consular officials of the United States can provide notarial services similar to those provided

The U.S. State Department information circular on Notarial and Authentication Services of U.S. Consular Officers Abroad is available at http://travel.state.gov/law/judicial/judicial_2086.html.

by a notary public in the United States,[69] including taking depositions on notice,[70] provided that these functions do not violate the local law of the country where the services are requested. In addition, federal statutes provide for taking evidence from "a national or resident of the United States who is in a foreign country" by authorizing the federal courts to issue a subpoena under 28 U.S.C. § 1783 to require appearance of a witness or production of a document or other thing if the court finds that it is "necessary in the interest of justice." Contempt sanctions are available under 28 U.S.C. § 1784 if the subpoena is ignored.[71]

Hague Evidence Convention

More than 50 countries participate in the Hague Convention on the Taking of Evidence Abroad in Civil or Commercial Matters, and the Convention is in force for the United States in most of these countries.[72] The Convention uses a Central Authority system, which for the United States is the Office of International Judicial Assistance in the Department of Justice. Because participating nations have made different reservations and declarations regarding the Convention, the U.S. Central Authority provides country-specific information on its website.

Under the Evidence Convention, a judicial authority in one contracting state may send a Letter of Request to the competent authorities of another contracting state, requesting that those authorities obtain evidence intended for use in judicial proceedings or perform some other judicial act.[73] Letters of Request are transmitted through the Central Authority of the receiving state. The Convention specifies what must be included in a Letter of Request, and participating countries may also require a certified translation. In executing a Letter of Request, authorities must "apply the appropriate measures of compulsion in the instances and to the same extent as are provided by its internal law for the execution of orders issued by the authorities of its own country or of requests made by parties in internal proceedings."[74] Execution of these requests is mandatory, with a few narrow exceptions specified in the treaty, and must be completed expeditiously and largely without cost. The evidence taken is returned to the requesting authority, and if the request is not executed for any reason, the requesting authority must be informed and advised of the reasons.

Although Article 9 of the Evidence Convention provides that the judicial authority executing a Letter of Request "shall apply its own law as to the methods and procedures to be followed," it also provides that the executing authority "will follow a request of the requesting authority that a special method or procedure be followed," unless this provision is incompatible with its internal law or is impossible to perform "by reason of its internal practice and procedure or by reason of practical difficulties." This allows for the possibility that lawyers from the United States may be able to conduct discovery following U.S. procedures even if those methods would not generally be available in the

---

Hague Evidence Convention

Hague Convention of 18 March 1970 on the Taking of Evidence Abroad in Civil and Commercial Matters, 23 U.S.T. 2555, T.I.A.S. 7444, 847 U.N.T.S. 231, *appended to* 28 U.S.C. § 1781, *reprinted in* 8 I.L.M. 37 (1969).

The full text and current status information for the Evidence Convention is available from the Hague Conference website at http://www.hcch.net (under "Conventions" and "20"). See also Hague Conference on Private International Law, PRACTICAL HANDBOOK ON THE OPERATION OF THE HAGUE CONVENTION OF 18 MARCH 1970 ON THE TAKING OF EVIDENCE ABROAD IN CIVIL OR COMMERCIAL MATTERS (1984).

---

requested country. This may be important in obtaining evidence in a form that is admissible in court. Besides providing for the sending and execution of Letters of Request, the Evidence Convention allows for the taking of evidence by diplomatic officers or consular agents and commissioners under Articles 15, 16, and 17. Generally, this procedure must take place without compulsion, and with the acquiescence of the requested state; it may be used for taking voluntary depositions at a U.S. embassy or consulate. Article 23 of the Evidence Convention permits a contracting state to declare when it joins the Convention that it will not execute Letters of Request "for the purpose of obtaining pre-trial discovery of documents as known in Common Law countries." Many states have made this declaration, either in broad or more limited form.[75] The drafters evidently intended to prevent counsel from conducting U.S.-style "fishing expeditions" that are seen as objectionable in many countries.[76]

When the Hague Evidence Convention is not available for obtaining evidence abroad, the alternative is to use letters rogatory, typically sent through diplomatic channels. The principal difference is that execution of letters rogatory is voluntary, although execution may be subject to bilateral agreements.[77] Letters rogatory are used routinely between courts in the United States and Canada, which has not ratified the Evidence Convention.

Obtaining Evidence in the United States for Use Abroad

Under 28 U.S.C. § 1781, Letters of Request or letters rogatory may either be submitted directly to a court in the United States that is requested to provide assistance or sent through diplomatic or consular channels. Letters received though these channels are typically routed through the Justice Department and the U.S. Attorney's office and filed with the federal district court.[78] The United States also permits direct execution within the United States of a commission for taking evidence issued by a foreign court. In addition, 28 U.S.C. § 1782 authorizes the federal district courts to order any person residing or found within the district to give testimony or produce a document or other thing for use

---

For assistance in obtaining evidence in the United States for use abroad, contact the U.S. Department of Justice, Office of International Judicial Assistance, 1100 L Street N.W., Room 11006, Washington DC 20530—phone: (202) 514-7455; fax: (202) 514-6584.

in a foreign or international tribunal "upon the application of any interested person."[79] In the family law context, this statute has been used to order individuals to provide blood samples for testing in paternity cases.[80]

Legalization and the Apostille Convention

To use foreign documents such as marriage or birth certificates in the United States, it is often necessary to legalize the documents. This process involves two steps: The document must first be authenticated or certified by the foreign ministry of the country where it originated, and then it is legalized by the U.S. embassy or consulate in that country. Traditionally, legalization involved sealing the original document and then attaching an authentication form by grommet. This process has been simplified for documents from countries that have adopted the 1961 Hague Convention Abolishing the Requirement of Legalization for Foreign Public Documents, also known as the Apostille Convention.[81]

Under the Convention, the foreign document is certified by an apostille completed by the appropriate authority according to the terms of the Convention.[82] Once certified in this manner, the document must be accepted as authentic by courts and other authorities in the United States.[83] The Convention applies to a variety of public documents: "documents emanating from an authority or an official connected with the courts or the tribunals of the State, including those emanating from a public prosecutor, a clerk of court or a process server," administrative documents, notarial acts, and "official certificates which are placed on documents signed by persons in their private capacity, such as official certificates recording the registration of a document or the fact that it was in existence on a certain date and official and notarial authentications of signatures."[84] This latter category includes items such as affidavits, wills, and powers of attorney. The Apostille Convention has been widely embraced and is now in effect in more than a hundred countries.

In outgoing cases, public documents produced in the United States that will be used in another Convention country are certified by either state or federal authorities. The clerk of every federal court has authority to issue apostilles for documents from that court, and the State Department Authentications Office issues apostilles for documents certified by federal agencies. State secretaries of state have authority to issue apostilles for documents certified by their state courts and private documents that have been notarized within the state. Listings of the competent authorities, and detailed information on how to obtain an apostille, are available on the Hague Conference and State Department websites noted above. Once an apostille is issued, authorities in all coun-

---

Hague Apostille Convention

Hague Convention of 5 October 1961 Abolishing the Requirement of Legalisation for Foreign Public Documents, 33 U.S.T. 883, T.I.A.S. 10072, 527 U.N.T.S. 189, appended to Fed. R. Civ. P. 44, *reprinted in* 20 I.L.M. 1405 (1981).

The full text and current status information for the Apostille Convention is available from the Hague Conference website at http://www.hcch.net (under "Conventions" and "12").

The U.S. State Department information circular on What Is an "Apostille" is available at http://travel.state.gov/law/judicial/judicial_2545.html; and the circular on Notarial and Authentication Services of U.S. Consular Officers Abroad is available at http://travel.state .gov/law/judicial/judicial_2086.html.

> **For assistance with legalization of U.S. documents,** contact the U.S. Department of State, Bureau of Administration, Office of Authentications, 518 23rd St. N.W. SA-1, Washington DC 20520—phone: (202) 647-5002; fax: (202) 663-3636; website: http://www.state.gov/m/a/auth/.

tries that participate in the Convention have a treaty obligation to accept the certified document.[85]

If a document produced in the United States will be used in a country that is not a party to the Apostille Convention, traditional legalization may be obtained through the State Department. This process typically requires certification up the line, beginning with the notary public or court clerk, then the secretary of state for the state where the document originated, then an authentication officer in the State Department, followed by legalization at the U.S. embassy or consulate in the country where the document will be used. Procedures for authentication by the State Department are governed by federal statutes and regulations, and there is a small fee for this service.[86]

Recognizing and Enforcing Judgments

In the United States, all states have a constitutional obligation to give full faith and credit to judgments entered in other states, but judgments of foreign courts are enforced only on the basis of comity. Courts in the United States are generous in their recognition of foreign court orders, including divorce decrees, support orders, and child custody orders, when these orders have a jurisdictional basis that would be adequate under U.S. law and where the general requirements of due process were observed.[87] In some settings, the requirements for recognition of foreign judgments are defined by statutes, including the UCCJEA, the UIFSA, and the Uniform Foreign Money-Judgments Recognition Act (UFMJRA). For the United States, achieving international recognition and enforcement of state court judgments has been difficult because of the differences between jurisdictional and other rules applied in the United States and those prevailing in other nations, particularly those with civil law systems.[88] In certain specific family law contexts, such as international adoption and international child support enforcement, the United States participates in international treaties that provide for mutual recognition and enforcement of judicial decrees.

Further Reading: International Judicial Assistance

ABA Section of Antitrust Law, OBTAINING DISCOVERY ABROAD (2d ed. 2005).

ABA Tort Trial and Insurance Practice Section, INTERNATIONAL LITIGATION: DEFENDING AND SUING FOREIGN PARTIES IN U.S. FEDERAL COURTS (David J. Levy ed., 2003).

STEPHEN M. FERNELIUS, REBECCA J. COLE, & GRAIG J. ALVAREZ, PRACTICAL GUIDE FOR CONDUCTING EXTRATERRITORIAL DISCOVERY FOR USE IN U.S. LITIGATION (2d rev. & exp. ed. 1999).

BRUNO A. RISTAU, INTERNATIONAL JUDICIAL ASSISTANCE (1995).

> The U.S. State Department information circular on Enforcement of Judgments is available at
> http://travel.state.gov/law/judicial/judicial_691.html.

Comity

Under the classic definition articulated by the Supreme Court in *Hilton v. Guyot*, comity is "the recognition which one nation allows within its territory to the legislative, executive or judicial acts of another nation, having due regard both to international duty and convenience, and to the rights of its own citizens, or of other persons who are under the protection of its laws."[89] In *Hilton*, the Court indicated that a foreign judgment should be given effect in the United States when it meets basic requirements of reliability and fairness:

> When [a] . . . foreign judgment appears to have been rendered by a competent court, having jurisdiction of the cause and of the parties, and upon due allegations and proofs, and opportunity to defend against them, and its proceedings are according to the course of a civilized jurisprudence, and are stated in a clear and formal record, the judgment is prima facie evidence, at least, of the truth of the matter adjudged; and it should be held conclusive upon the merits tried in the foreign court, unless some special ground is shown for impeaching the judgment, as by showing that it was affected by fraud or prejudice, or that by the principles of international law, and by the comity of our own country, it should not be given full credit and effect.[90]

For decrees concerning personal status, *Hilton* articulated a broad recognition principle: "A decree confirming or dissolving a marriage, is recognized as valid in every country, unless contrary to the policy of its own law."[91]

More recent conflict-of-laws authorities in the United States have embraced the formulation of common law comity principles in the Restatement (Third) of Foreign Relations Law.[92] Section 481 sets out a presumptive rule that "a final judgment of a court of a foreign state granting or denying recovery of a sum of money, establishing or confirming the status of a person, or determining interests in property, is conclusive between the parties, and is entitled to recognition in courts in the United States." Section 482 defines two sets of exceptions to this rule. A court in the United States must not recognize a foreign-court judgment if it "was rendered under a judicial system that does not provide impartial tribunals or procedures compatible with due process of law," or if the foreign court did not have jurisdiction over the defendant in accordance with its own laws and consistent with the Restatement's standards.[93] In addition, under the following circumstances a court in the United States is not required to recognize a foreign-court judgment (1) that was entered without subject matter jurisdiction; (2) when the defendant did not have notice and an opportunity to offer a defense; (3) in circumstances of fraud; (4) when the judgment is contrary to the public policy of the United States or of the state where recognition is sought; (5) when the judgment conflicts with another judgment that is entitled to recognition; or (6) if the foreign court proceeding was contrary to an agreement between the parties to submit the controversy to another forum.[94] These broad general principles are regularly applied to foreign-court judgments in divorce, property, support, and custody cases.

In *Hilton*, although the Supreme Court determined that a decree entered by a French court against two New York residents satisfied the general requirements of comity, a majority of the Court concluded that it should not be enforced in the United States on reciprocity grounds, based on evidence that a U.S. decree would not have been enforceable in France.[95] Four justices dissented from this aspect of the ruling. The reciprocity requirement has continued to be problematic and controversial, and courts in the United States have largely, but not entirely, abandoned it.[96] For example, *Nichol v. Tanner*, a case seeking enforcement of a German child support and paternity judgment against a defendant in Minnesota, rejected the *Hilton* reciprocity rule, concluding that "it is not the business of the courts, whose province is the decision of individual cases, to impose rules designed to coerce other nations into giving effect to our judgments."[97]

Currency exchange rates may complicate the international recognition and enforcement of judgments. Under Restatement (Third) of Foreign Relations § 823(2), when a court gives judgment in dollars based on a foreign currency obligation, "the conversion from foreign currency to dollars is to be made at such a rate as to make the creditor whole and to avoid rewarding a debtor who was delayed in carrying out the obligation." For a judgment based on an obligation to make periodic payments, such as a spousal or child support order, the currency conversion may need to be made separately for each payment date. Interest on past-due payments is determined by the law of the forum, including its choice of law rules.[98]

Recognition under Uniform Laws

Comity principles are codified in the 1962 UFMJRA[99] and its successor, the 2005 Uniform Foreign-Country Money Judgments Recognition Act (UFCMJRA).[100] The drafters hoped that a codification of these principles would satisfy the reciprocity concerns of foreign courts, making it more likely that state court judgments would be recognized abroad. The statute provides generally, with some exceptions, for enforcement of foreign money judgments "in the same manner as the judgment of a sister state which is entitled to full faith and credit."[101]

Although the original UFMJRA is sometimes applied to the enforcement of foreign judgments in marital-property cases, the law excludes any "judgment for support in matrimonial or family matters."[102] The amended version of the legislation is more sweeping, excluding "a judgment for divorce, support, or maintenance, or other judgment rendered in connection with domestic relations."[103] According to the official comments, the drafters concluded that recognition and enforcement of domestic relations judgments are more appropriately handled through comity and the provisions of specialized statutes such as the UIFSA. The UFMJRA does not include a reciprocity requirement, but some states have incorporated this consideration into their statutes.[104]

Recognition and enforcement of a foreign country's child custody or visitation orders is available under the UCCJEA,[105] provided that the foreign order must have been

Assistance with international child support enforcement is often available from state child support offices. Contact information for state agencies is available from the federal Office of Child Support Enforcement website at http://www.acf.hhs.gov/programs/cse/ (under "State Child Support Agency Links").

entered under factual circumstances in substantial conformity with the jurisdictional standards of the UCCJEA.[106] Recognition and enforcement of foreign spousal and child support orders can be accomplished using the UIFSA.[107] This act extends to support orders from several categories of foreign nations: those designated as foreign reciprocating countries under federal law, those that have established reciprocal arrangements with a particular state, those that have enacted laws or procedures that are substantially similar to UIFSA, and those where the 2007 Hague Family Maintenance Convention is in effect with respect to the United States.[108] For support orders from foreign nations that do not fall into any of these categories, UIFSA preserves the possibility of recognition and enforcement based on comity.[109] The federal child support enforcement program administered by the Department of Health and Human Services provides support enforcement services without charge for many foreign child-support orders and some foreign spousal support orders.[110]

Foreign Recognition and Enforcement of U.S. Court Orders

Other common law countries apply similar principles of comity when recognizing and enforcing foreign court orders.[111] In these countries, as in the United States, recognition and enforcement may be obtained by bringing an action for enforcement of the foreign court judgment.[112] In civil law countries, a foreign judgment may be recognized and enforced by registration in an exequatur proceeding.[113] The rules and procedure are different in different legal systems; in some, recognition of foreign judgments may depend on proof of reciprocity.[114] Foreign countries may refuse to recognize in personam judgments from the United States that are based on a minimum-contacts theory or on personal service within the jurisdiction (i.e., tag jurisdiction).[115] To present a state court decree in a foreign country for recognition and enforcement, the parties or their counsel may have the decree authenticated by legalization or an apostille.[116]

Further Reading: Recognition and Enforcement of Judgments

ENFORCEMENT OF FOREIGN JUDGMENTS (Dennis Campbell ed., 1997).

ENFORCEMENT OF FOREIGN JUDGMENTS WORLDWIDE (Charles Platto & William G. Horton eds., 2d ed. 1993).

Hague Service Convention Contracting States (as of November 15, 2011)

Albania	Germany	Poland
Antigua and Barbuda	Greece	Portugal
Argentina	Hungary	Romania
Australia	Iceland	Russian Federation
Bahamas	India	Saint Vincent and the Grenadines
Barbados	Ireland	San Marino
Belarus	Israel	Serbia
Belgium	Italy	Seychelles
Belize	Japan	Slovakia
Bosnia and Herzegovina	Korea, Republic of	Slovenia
Botswana	Kuwait	Spain
Bulgaria	Latvia	Sri Lanka
Canada	Lithuania	Sweden
China, People's Republic of	Luxembourg	Switzerland
Croatia	Malawi	The former Yugoslav Republic of Macedonia
Cyprus	Malta	Turkey
Czech Republic	Mexico	Ukraine
Denmark	Monaco	United Kingdom of Great Britain and Northern Ireland
Egypt	Morocco	United States of America
Estonia	Netherlands	Venezuela
Finland	Norway	
France	Pakistan	

Hague Evidence Convention Contracting States (as of November 15, 2011)

*(Accessions of countries marked with * had not yet been accepted by the United States.)*

Albania*	Iceland	Romania
Argentina	India	Russian Federation*
Australia	Israel	Serbia*
Barbados	Italy	Seychelles
Belarus	Korea, Republic of	Singapore
Bosnia and Herzegovina	Kuwait	Slovakia
Bulgaria	Latvia	Slovenia
China, People's Republic of	Liechtenstein	South Africa
Croatia	Lithuania	Spain
Cyprus	Luxembourg	Sri Lanka
Czech Republic	Malta*	Sweden
Denmark	Mexico	Switzerland

Hague Evidence Convention Contracting States—continued

Estonia	Monaco	The former Yugoslav Republic of Macedonia
Finland	Morocco*	Turkey
France	Netherlands	Ukraine
Germany	Norway	United Kingdom of Great Britain and Northern Ireland
Greece	Poland	United States of America
Hungary	Portugal	Venezuela

Hague Legalization (Apostille) Convention Contracting States (as of November 15, 2011)

Albania	Germany	Norway
Andorra	Greece	Oman
Antigua and Barbuda	Grenada	Panama
Argentina	Honduras	Peru
Armenia	Hungary	Poland
Australia	Iceland	Portugal
Austria	India	Romania
Azerbaijan	Ireland	Russian Federation
Bahamas	Israel	Saint Kitts and Nevis
Barbados	Italy	Saint Lucia
Belarus	Japan	Saint Vincent and the Grenadines
Belgium	Kazakhstan	Samoa
Belize	Korea, Republic of	San Marino
Bosnia and Herzegovina	Kyrgyzstan	São Tomé and Príncipe
Botswana	Latvia	Serbia
Brunei Darussalam	Lesotho	Seychelles
Bulgaria	Liberia	Slovakia
Cape Verde	Liechtenstein	Slovenia
Colombia	Lithuania	South Africa
Cook Islands	Luxembourg	Spain
Costa Rica	Malawi	Suriname
Croatia	Malta	Sweden
Cyprus	Marshall Islands	Swaziland
Czech Republic	Mauritius	Switzerland
Denmark	Mexico	The former Yugoslav Republic of Macedonia
Dominica	Moldova, Republic of	Tonga
Dominican Republic	Monaco	Trinidad and Tobago
Ecuador	Mongolia	Turkey

Hague Legalization (Apostille) Convention Contracting States — continued

El Salvador	Montenegro	Ukraine
Estonia	Morocco	United Kingdom of Great Britain and Northern Ireland
Fiji	Namibia	United States of America
Finland	Netherlands	Uzbekistan
France	New Zealand	Vanuatu
Georgia	Niue	Venezuela

Notes

1. *See* Williams v. North Carolina, 317 U.S. 287, 298–99 (1942) ("[E]ach state, by virtue of its command over its domiciliaries and its large interest in the institution of marriage, can alter within its own borders the marriage status of the spouse domiciled there, even if the other spouse is absent."); Williams v. North Carolina, 325 U.S. 226, 239 (1945) (holding that domicile in the state may be challenged). Divorce jurisdiction is discussed in Chapter 3.
2. Jurisdiction regarding financial matters is covered in Chapter 4.
3. Uniform Interstate Family Support Act § 201, 9 (IB) U.L.A. 72 (Supp. 2011) (UIFSA). *See* Chapter 7.
4. Uniform Child Custody Jurisdiction and Enforcement Act § 201(c), 9 (IA) U.L.A. 649 (1999) (UCCJEA). Jurisdiction regarding financial matters is covered in Chapter 5.
5. 495 U.S. 604, 628 (1990).
6. *See* RESTATEMENT (THIRD) OF FOREIGN RELATIONS LAW § 421, Reporter's Note 5 (1987) ("Jurisdiction based on [tag jurisdiction] is no longer acceptable under international law if that is the only basis for jurisdiction and the action in question is unrelated to that state."). *See also* Kevin N. Clermont & John R. B. Palmer, *Exorbitant Jurisdiction*, 58 ME. L. REV. 474 (2006).
7. *E.g.*, Farah v. Farah, 323 N.E.2d 361, 366 (Ill. App. Ct. 1975) (exercising long-arm jurisdiction under Illinois statute).
8. Burger King Corp. v. Rudzewicz, 471 U.S. 462, 464 (1985). This two-prong test was applied in Phillips v. Phillips, 826 S.W.2d 746, 748–49 (Tex. App. 1992) (upholding jurisdiction over nonresident husband living in Kenya based on contacts with wife and children in Texas).
9. 436 U.S. 84, 92 (1978).
10. *But see* May v. Anderson, 345 U.S. 528, 533 (1953) (holding that custody adjudication made without personal jurisdiction over respondent parent was not entitled to full faith and credit in another state). This ruling is in considerable tension with the jurisdictional and full faith and credit requirements of UCCJEA § 202 and the federal Parental Kidnapping Prevention Act, 28 U.S.C. § 1738A (2006) (PKPA), which require that states recognize and enforce custody orders without taking personal jurisdiction into account.
11. UIFSA § 201.
12. 504 U.S. 689, 703 (1992).
13. *E.g.*, Bercovitch v. Tanburn, 103 F. Supp. 62 (S.D.N.Y. 1952) (affirming the dismissal of an action based on the domestic relations exception where plaintiff was a Canadian citizen and defendant was a New York citizen); Buechold v. Ortiz, 401 F.2d 371 (9th Cir. 1968) (affirming the dismissal of a paternity and child-support action filed in federal court by German citizens against California citizens); *cf.* Kirby v. Mellenger, 830 F.2d 176 (11th Cir. 1987) (concluding that when "domestic relations issues are only tangentially present" to the issue in question, the district court has less discretion to refuse jurisdiction).
14. Ohio *ex rel.* Popovici v. Agler, 280 U.S. 379, 382–84 (1930); *but see* Carrera v. Carrera, 174 F.2d 496, 498 (D.C. Cir. 1949).

15. *See* Jagiella v. Jagiella, 647 F.2d 561, 564 (5th Cir. 1981) (affirming diversity jurisdiction in suit by French ex-wife against Georgia resident to collect arrearages of alimony and child support).

16. *See, e.g.*, Ackerman v. Ackerman, 676 F.2d 898, 901 (2d Cir. 1982); *see also* Matusow v. Trans-County Title Agency, 545 F.3d 241, 246–47 (3d Cir. 2008); Norton v. McOsker, 407 F.3d 501, 504–05 (1st Cir. 2005).

17. *E.g.*, Marran v. Marran, 376 F.3d 143, 149–51 (3d Cir. 2004) (affirming dismissal based on the Rooker-Feldman doctrine, which "bars lower federal courts from exercising jurisdiction over a case that is the functional equivalent of an appeal from a state court judgment").

18. 42 U.S.C. §§ 11601–11611 (2006).

19. *Id.* § 11611; *e.g.*, International Parental Kidnapping Crime Act, 18 U.S.C. § 1204 (2006) (IPKCA).

20. *See* Taveras v. Taveras, 477 F.3d 767, 772 (6th Cir. 2007), applying Sosa v. Alvarez-Machain, 542 U.S. 692, 729 (2004); *see also* Adra v. Clift, 195 F. Supp. 857, 865 (D. Md. 1961).

21. Bourbon v. Bourbon, 687 N.Y.S.2d 426, 427 (N.Y. App. Div. 1999), *remanded to* 751 N.Y.S.2d 302 (N.Y. App. Div. 2002).

22. *See* RESTATEMENT (SECOND) OF CONFLICT OF LAWS § 53 (1971). *See generally* GARY B. BORN & PETER B. RUTLEDGE, INTERNATIONAL CIVIL LITIGATION IN UNITED STATES COURTS 521-60 (2007); EUGENE F. SCOLES ET AL., CONFLICT OF LAWS § 24.9, at 1273-76 (4th ed. 2004); Jonathan I. Blackman, *Provisional Measures in Cross-Border Cases, in* INTERNATIONAL LITIGATION STRATEGIES AND PRACTICE 65, 71–72 (Baron Legum ed., 2005).

23. *Cf.* Brown v. Brown, 387 A.2d 1051, 1055 (R.I. 1978) (concluding that the trial court properly issued an injunction prohibiting respondent from instituting any new proceedings for divorce in another jurisdiction). *But see* Verdier v. Verdier, 22 Cal. Rptr. 93, 105 (Cal. Ct. App. 1962) (concluding that an injunction was not proper because "the issues in the two actions were not the same, and there was no former adjudication").

   In U.S. family law, anti-suit injunctions were sometimes issued to prevent an individual domiciled in a state with strict divorce laws from going to another place to procure a divorce. Older cases are collected in E. H. Schopler, Annotation, *Injunction Against Suit in Another State or Country for Divorce or Separation*, 54 A.L.R.2d 1240 (1957 & Supp.).

24. *See* BORN & RUTLEDGE, *supra* note 22, at 540-43 (noting that the First, Second, Third, Sixth, and D.C. Circuits have placed stringent limits on the use of foreign anti-suit injunctions, while the Fifth, Seventh, and Ninth Circuits have applied more flexible standards).

25. *See* BORN & RUTLEDGE, *supra* note 22, at 522.

26. *See* Blackman, *supra* note 22, at 65-70. These issues are considered in Chapter 4.

27. 570 So. 2d 996, 997 (Fla. Dist. Ct. App. 1990); *see also* Marriage of Kosmond, 830 N.E.2d 596, 597 (Ill. App. Ct. 2005) (holding that trial court with personal jurisdiction over the parties had authority to freeze wife's assets held by foreign bank, but that court abused its discretion by failing to consider whether bank's compliance with injunction would require it to violate German law); *cf.* Nasser v. Nasser, 859 N.Y.S.2d 445, 445 (App. Div. 2008) (affirming dismissal of dispute regarding parties' assets filed in New York, during pendency of litigation in Brazil, on basis of inconvenient forum).

28. 330 U.S. 501 (1947). *See generally* SCOLES, *supra* note 22, §§ 11.8-.12, at 492-502.

29. *Gulf Oil Corp.*, 330 U.S. at 508-09.

30. 454 U.S. 235 (1981).

31. Courts have deferred to the plaintiff's choice of forum in the domestic relations context. *See, e.g.*, MacLeod v. MacLeod, 383 A.2d 39, 42 (Me. 1978) (holding that the superior court erred in dismissing suit for forum non conveniens where the record did not indicate the availability of a more convenient alternate forum).

32. UCCJEA § 207(a). Under UCCJEA § 105(a), state courts treat foreign countries as states of the United States for purposes of this provision.

33. *See generally* Susan Van Syckel, *Strategies for Identifying Sources of Foreign Law: An Integrated Approach*, 13 TRANSNAT'L LAW. 289 (2000).

34. Maple v. Maple, 566 P.2d 1229, 1230 (Utah 1977); *see also* Meissner v. Meissner, 707 So. 2d 1040, 1044 (La. Ct. App. 1998) (applying presumption to Brazilian divorce judgment); Hosain v. Malik, 671 A.2d 988, 996-97 (Md. Ct. Spec. App. 1996) (comparing Pakistani and Maryland

law); De Liedekerke v. De Liedekerke, 635 A.2d 339, 343 (D.C. 1993) (applying presumption to Belgian prenuptial agreement).

35. *See generally* VED P. NANDA & DAVID K. PANSIUS, LITIGATION OF INTERNATIONAL DISPUTES IN U.S. COURTS §§ 18:1–:13 (2d ed. 2005 & Supp. 2007).

36. *See* Bodum USA, Inc. v. La Cafetiere, Inc., 621 F.3d 624, 628–29 (7th Cir. 2010); *see also id.* at 631–34 (Posner, J., concurring).

37. *See generally* SOFIE GEEROMS, FOREIGN LAW IN CIVIL LITIGATION: A COMPARATIVE AND FUNCTIONAL ANALYSIS 41–219 (2004) (discussing the process of introducing and ascertaining foreign law); John G. Sprankling & George R. Lanyi, *Pleading and Proof of Foreign Law in American Courts*, 19 STAN. J. INT'L L. 3 (1983); John R. Schmertz, Jr., *The Establishment of Foreign and International Law in American Courts: A Procedural Overview*, 18 VA. J. INT'L L. 697 (1977). *See also* Jeffrey F. Ghent, Comment-Note, *Pleading and Proof of Law of Foreign Country*, 75 A.L.R.3d 177 (1977 & Supp.) (collecting examples).

38. *See, e.g.*, Moustafa v. Moustafa, 888 A.2d 1230 (Md. Ct. Spec. App. 2005) (applying MD. CODE ANN., CTS. & JUD. PROC. § 10-505, which requires notice of intent to rely on a foreign law and proof regarding the content of the foreign law).

39. *See generally* BORN & RUTLEDGE, *supra* note 22, at 815–1007.

40. One case illustrating the difficulty of service using letters rogatory is Hollow v. Hollow, 747 N.Y.S.2d 704, 708 (N.Y. Sup. Ct. 2002), in which the court permitted substituted service by e-mail on husband who had moved to Saudi Arabia. *See also* Porres v. Porres, 428 N.Y.S.2d 428, 431 (N.Y. Sup. Ct. 1980) (permitting substituted service on husband in Italy based on financial hardship; decided before Service Convention came into effect between Italy and the United States).

41. Mullane v. Cent. Hanover Bank & Trust Co., 339 U.S. 306, 314 (1950).

42. *See supra* notes 5–6 and accompanying text.

43. *Cf.* Marriage of Tsarbopoulos, 104 P.3d 692, 694 (Wash. Ct. App. 2004) (vacating property division and child support orders on the conclusion that defendant lacked sufficient minimum contacts with the state). *See generally* BORN & RUTLEDGE, *supra* note 22, at 855–56. The majority opinion in Goldstein v. Goldstein, 494 S.E.2d 745, 748–49 (Ga. Ct. App. 1997), holding that personal service in Switzerland conferred personal jurisdiction on state trial court, is incorrect on this point.

44. *E.g.*, FED. R. CIV. P. 4(f). State rules are often based either on the former Rule 4(i) or the now-withdrawn Uniform Interstate and International Procedure Act. *See generally* BORN & RUTLEDGE, *supra* note 22, at 827 (citing examples); 1 ROBERT C. CASAD & WILLIAM B. RICHMAN, JURISDICTION IN CIVIL ACTIONS §§ 4-6, at 508–17 (3d ed. 1998). The notice requirement of the UCCJEA applies to domestic and international cases. *See also* UIFSA §§ 108 and 205 and Marriage of Tsarbopoulos, 104 P.3d 692 (Wash. Ct. App. 2004).

45. *See* U.S. Dept. of State, Service of Legal Documents Abroad, http://travel.state.gov/law/judicial/judicial_680.html. *See also* Charles B. Campbell, *No Sirve: The Invalidity of Service of Process Abroad by Mail or by Private Process Server on Parties in Mexico Under the Hague Service Convention*, 19 MINN. J. INT'L L. 107 (2010) (service in Mexico).

46. *See* 32 C.F.R. § 516 (service on Army personnel); 32 C.F.R. § 720.20 (service on Navy and Marine Corps personnel). Note that under these regulations a service member may decline to accept voluntary service; *see, e.g.*, Harris v. Harris, 922 N.E.2d 626 (Ind. Ct. App. 2010). *See generally* MARK E. SULLIVAN, THE MILITARY DIVORCE HANDBOOK: A PRACTICAL GUIDE TO REPRESENTING MILITARY PERSONNEL AND THEIR FAMILIES 8–30 (2d ed. 2011).

47. *See* Volkswagenwerk AG v. Schlunk, 486 U.S. 694, 707 (1988) (concluding that when service is effectuated on a domestic agent and is "valid and complete under both state law and the Due Process Clause" the Hague Service Convention does not apply).

48. Hague Convention on the Service Abroad of Judicial and Extrajudicial Documents, art. 1, Nov. 15, 1965, 20 U.S.T. 361, 658 U.N.T.S. 163 [hereinafter Service Convention]; *see* Société Nationale Industrielle Aérospatiale v. U.S. Dist. Court, 482 U.S. 522, 534 n. 15 (1987). *See generally* RESTATEMENT (THIRD) OF FOREIGN RELATIONS LAW § 471 (1987); BORN & RUTLEDGE, *supra* note 22, at 815–96; NANDA & PANSIUS, *supra* note 35, §§ 2.3–.9; Marjorie A. Shields,

When Is Compliance with Hague Convention on Service Abroad of Judicial and Extrajudicial Documents in Civil and Commercial Matters Required? 18 A.L.R. FED. 2d 185 (2007 & Supp.). A list of the contracting states, and information on reservations, declarations, or notifications for each country, is available on the Hague Conference website.

49. *E.g., In re* Alyssa F., 6 Cal. Rptr. 3d 1, 5 (Cal. Ct. App. 2003) (concluding that service by first-class mail in Mexico was not adequate under state law in termination of parental rights case); Estate of Graf Droste zu Vischering, 782 N.W.2d 141 (Iowa 2010) (ruling that service on estate beneficiary in Germany must comply with Convention). *Cf.* Van Den Bosch v. Weinstock, 732 N.W.2d 636, 638–39 (Minn. Ct. App. 2007) (reviewing service in Philippines in action to modify parenting time under state procedural rules).

50. *See, e.g.,* Wood v. Wood, 647 N.Y.S.2d 830, 830–31 (App. Div. 1996) (delivery of summons and complaint to wife at her residence in Germany was improper and ineffective under Convention); Zwerling v. Zwerling, 636 N.Y.S.2d 595, 598–600 (N.Y. Sup. Ct. 1995) (personal service in Israel ineffective under Convention); Ward v. Ludwig, 778 N.E.2d 650, 653 (Ohio Ct. App. 2002) (concluding that service in Germany by registered mail was improper and ineffective); Saysavanh v. Saysavanh, 145 P.3d 1166, 1172 (Utah Ct. App. 2006) (concluding service by mail in Mexico was ineffective).

51. *E.g.,* Bakala v. Bakala, 576 S.E.2d 156, 164 (S.C. 2003) (declining to address issue under the Service Convention that was not raised in the lower court). In some cases, it appears that neither the parties nor the court were aware of the applicability of the Service Convention. *See generally* Marriage of Tsarbopoulos, 104 P.3d 692 (Wash. Ct. App. 2004) (failing to discuss the Service Convention where service was effectuated on defendant in Greece).

52. Service Convention, *supra* note 48, art. 2.

53. There is a fee for this service; information is available from the website of the DOJ contractor, Process Forwarding International, at http://www.hagueservice.net.

54. Article 8 allows service by diplomatic or consular agents, "without application of any compulsion." If the state in which such service would be made has declared that it is opposed to this type of service, then Article 8 applies only to service by consular officials "upon a national of the State in which the documents originate." U.S. consular officials are, however, prohibited from serving process or legal papers unless specifically directed to do so by the State Department. *See* 22 C.F.R. § 92.85. The rule is different for service of subpoenas; *see infra* note 71 and accompanying text. Similarly, although Article 9 of the Service Convention permits indirect service through consular and diplomatic channels, this mechanism is not effectively available for parties in the United States.

55. *See generally* BORN & RUTLEDGE, *supra* note 22, at 869–83 (describing alternative methods of service authorized under the Service Convention). There is divided authority within the United States as to whether sending judicial documents by mail is sufficient to constitute service of process under the Federal Rules of Civil Procedure. *See id.* at 870–71, 877–80.

56. *E.g.,* Collins v. Collins, 844 N.E.2d 910, 913 (Ohio Ct. App. 2006) (noting that Germany "has expressed a specific objection to service by international mail and has asserted that the Hague Convention is the exclusive method for international service of process in Germany). *See generally* Beverly L. Jacklin, *Service of Process by Mail in International Civil Action as Permissible under the Hague Convention,* 112 A.L.R. FED. 241 (1993 & Supp.)

57. 486 U.S. 694 (1988).

58. *See generally* BORN & RUTLEDGE *supra* note 22, at 895–96; NANDA & PANSIUS, *supra* note 35, § 2.10.

59. *See* 22 C.F.R. §§ 92.54, 92.66–.76 (2009).

60. Statutory authority for the State Department to transmit and receive letters rogatory is provided in 28 U.S.C. § 1781 (2006), with regulations published in 22 C.F.R. pt. 92.

61. *See* Société Nationale Industrielle Aérospatiale v. U.S. Dist. Court, 482 U.S. 522, 549–51 (1987) (Blackmun, J., concurring in part and dissenting in part).

62. *See* RESTATEMENT (THIRD) OF FOREIGN RELATIONS LAW § 442, Reporter's Notes 1, 4–9 (1987).

63. *See generally* RESTATEMENT (THIRD) OF FOREIGN RELATIONS LAW § 473 (1987); BORN & RUTLEDGE, *supra* note 22, at 907–94; NANDA & PANSIUS, *supra* note 35, ch. 17.

64. *Société Nationale Industrielle Aérospatiale*, 482 U.S. at 539–40.

65. *See generally* RESTATEMENT (THIRD) OF FOREIGN RELATIONS LAW § 473 (1987); BORN & RUTLEDGE, *supra* note 22, at 980–81. Cases holding that plaintiffs should begin with the Evidence Convention include Umana v. SCM S.p.A., 737 N.Y.S.2d 556 (N.Y. App. Div. 2002), and Husa v. Laboratories Servier SA, 740 A.2d 1092 (N.J. Super. Ct. App. Div. 1999).

66. *See generally* ABA SECTION OF ANTITRUST LAW, OBTAINING DISCOVERY ABROAD (2d ed. 2005) (describing procedures in Belgium, Canada, France, Germany, Italy, Japan, the Netherlands, Switzerland, and the United Kingdom); *see also* ABA TORT TRIAL & INSURANCE PRACTICE SECTION, INTERNATIONAL LITIGATION: DEFENDING AND SUING FOREIGN PARTIES IN U.S. FEDERAL COURTS (David J. Levy ed., 2003); STEPHEN M. FERNELIUS ET AL., PRACTICAL GUIDE FOR CONDUCTING EXTRATERRITORIAL DISCOVERY FOR USE IN U.S. LITIGATION (2d rev. & exp. ed. 1999).

67. FED. R. CIV. P. 28(b); *see also* FED. R. CIV. P. 45(b)(2).

68. *E.g.*, Boatswain v. Boatswain, 778 N.Y.S.2d 850, 853–54 (N.Y. Sup. Ct. 2004) (approving open commission for deposition in Canada).

69. 22 U.S.C. § 4215 (2006); 22 C.F.R. §§ 92.1–92.75 (2009); *see also, e.g.*, Moezie v. Moezie, 192 A.2d 808, 811 (D.C. 1963) (addressing authority of American consul to provide notarial service in divorce case).

70. *See* 22 C.F.R. § 92.55 (2009).

71. *See* 22 C.F.R. §§ 92.86, 92.88 (describing consular responsibility for serving subpoenas on national or resident of the United States who is in a foreign country). *See generally* NANDA & PANSIUS, *supra* note 35, § 17:54.

72. Hague Convention on the Taking of Evidence Abroad in Civil or Commercial Matters, Oct. 7, 1972, 23 U.S.T. 2555, 847 U.N.T.S. 231 [hereinafter Evidence Convention]. Information on ratifications, accessions, and acceptances of accessions is available on the Hague Conference website at http://www.hcch.net. At this writing, the United States had not yet accepted the accessions of Albania, Malta, Morocco, the Russian Federation, and Serbia.

73. Evidence Convention, *supra* note 72, art. 1. " '[O]ther judicial act' does not cover the service of judicial documents or the issuance of any process by which judgments or orders are executed or enforced, or orders for provisional or protective measures." *Id. See generally* NANDA & PANSIUS, *supra* note 35, §§ 17:14-:19.

74. Evidence Convention, *supra* note 72, art. 10.

75. For details of these declarations, see the country-specific information on the State Department judicial assistance web pages or the Hague Conference website at http://www.hcch.net.

76. *See* BORN & RUTLEDGE, *supra* note 22, at 966–68.

77. *See supra* notes 59–60 and accompanying text; *see generally* RESTATEMENT (THIRD) OF FOREIGN RELATIONS LAW § 473 (1987). Although the Inter-American Convention on Letters Rogatory and its Additional Protocol (IACAP) also covers requests to obtain evidence, the United States has made a reservation to this aspect of the treaty.

78. *See* RESTATEMENT (THIRD) OF FOREIGN RELATIONS LAW § 474 (1987); *see generally* NANDA & PANSIUS, *supra* note 35, §§ 17.45-.52.

79. 28 U.S.C. § 1782 (2006). *See generally* Intel Corp. v. Advanced Micro Devices, Inc., 542 U.S. 241, 246–47 (2004) (holding that statute does not require a threshold showing that the information sought would be discoverable in the foreign proceeding).

80. *E.g.*, *In re* Letter of Request from Amtsgericht Ingolstadt, Fed. Republic of Ger., 82 F.3d 590 (4th Cir. 1996); *In re* Letter Rogatory from the Nedenes Dist. Court, Nor., 216 F.R.D. 277 (S.D.N.Y. 2003).

81. Hague Convention Abolishing the Requirement of Legalization for Foreign Public Documents, Oct. 15, 1981, 33 U.S.T. 883, 522 U.N.T.S. 189 [hereinafter Apostille Convention].

82. A model form for the certificate was annexed to the Convention; under Article 4, the certificate must be placed on the document itself or on an allonge attached to the document.

83. Under Article 2, "Each contracting State shall exempt from legalisation documents to which the present Convention applies and which have to be produced in its territory." Apostille Convention art. 2. *See* Peter Pfund, *Legalization of Documents for Use Abroad*, in THE INTERNATIONAL LAWYER'S DESKBOOK 297, 299–300 (Lucinda A. Low et al. eds., 2d ed. 2002).

84. Apostille Convention, *supra* note 81, art. 1.
85. If a U.S. apostille is not accepted, there may be recourse though the Office of Treaty Affairs of the State Department. *See* Pfund, *supra* note 83, at 301.
86. *See* 22 U.S.C. § 2651a; 22 C.F.R. § 131.1 (2009). *See generally* Pfund, *supra* note 83, at 298–99.
87. *See generally* RESTATEMENT (THIRD) OF FOREIGN RELATIONS LAW §§ 484–86 (1987).
88. *See generally* BORN & RUTLEDGE, *supra* note 22, at 1012, 1016–18.
89. 159 U.S. 113, 164 (1895).
90. *Id.* at 205–06.
91. *Id.* at 167.
92. *See* RESTATEMENT (THIRD) OF FOREIGN RELATIONS LAW §§ 481–88 (1987); *see also* RESTATEMENT (SECOND) OF CONFLICT OF LAWS § 98 (1971).
93. RESTATEMENT (THIRD) OF FOREIGN RELATIONS LAW § 421(1) provides that the courts of a state may exercise jurisdiction with respect to a person of thing "if the relationship of the state to the person or thing is such as to make the exercise of jurisdiction reasonable." Under § 421(2), exercise of jurisdiction will generally be reasonable if the person "is present in the territory of the state, other than transitorily," if the person is domiciled in, resident in, or a national of the state, if the person consents to jurisdiction, or if the person carries on business in the state.
94. *See generally id.*; Courtland H. Peterson, *Foreign Country Judgments and the Second Restatement of Conflict of Laws*, 72 COLUM. L. REV. 220 (1972).
95. *Hilton*, 159 U.S. at 228; *cf.* Ritchie v. McMullen, 159 U.S. 235, 242–43 (1895) (recognizing Canadian judgment based on reciprocity).
96. *See generally* RESTATEMENT (THIRD) OF FOREIGN RELATIONS LAW § 481 cmt. d & Reporter's Note 1 (1987); BORN & RUTLEDGE, *supra* note 22, at 1026–34.
97. 256 N.W.2d 796, 801 (Minn. 1976).
98. *See* RESTATEMENT (THIRD) OF FOREIGN RELATIONS LAW § 823 cmt. e (1987). *See also* Hixson v. Sarkesian, 123 P.3d 1072 (Alaska 2005) (computing support obligation of father who was paid in Swiss francs).
99. Uniform Foreign Money-Judgments Recognition Act, 13(2) U.L.A. 43 (1962 & Supp. 2009) (UFMJRA).
100. Uniform Foreign-Country Money Judgments Recognition Act, 13(2) U.L.A. 9 (Supp. 2009) (UFCMJRA). At of the time of this writing, the UFCMJRA had been adopted in 17 states: California, Colorado, Delaware, Hawaii, Idaho, Illinois, Indiana, Iowa, Michigan, Minnesota, Montana, Nevada, New Mexico, North Carolina, Oklahoma, Oregon, and Washington. The original 1962 UFMJRA was still in effect in another group of jurisdictions, including Alaska, Connecticut, the District of Columbia, Florida, Georgia, Maine, Maryland, Massachusetts, Missouri, New Jersey, New York, North Dakota, Ohio, Pennsylvania, Texas, the U.S. Virgin Islands, and Virginia. Current information is available from the Uniform Law Commission website at http://www.nccusl.org.
101. UFMJRA § 3. The exceptions, defined in UFMJRA § 4, are similar to those outlined in RESTATEMENT (THIRD) OF FOREIGN RELATIONS LAW § 482. The UFMJRA does not require reciprocity as a condition to the enforcement of foreign court judgments. *See* UFMJRA § 4 n. 2. Note that the UFMJRA and the UFCMJRA do not apply to nonmonetary judgments such as a foreign divorce decree. *See* Sanchez v. Palau, 317 S.W. 3d 780 (Tex. App. 2010).
102. UFMJRA § 1(2).
103. UFCMJRA § 3(b)(3). Some courts concluded that the earlier language should be read to exclude all domestic relations judgments. *See, e.g.*, Wolff v. Wolff, 389 A.2d 413, 418 (Md. Ct. Spec. App. 1978).
104. *See* BORN & RUTLEDGE, *supra* note 22, at 1032–33 (citing statutes).
105. UCCJEA, 9 (1A) U.L.A. 649 (1999). As of this writing, the UCCJEA had been enacted in every state except Massachusetts. Current information is available on the Uniform Law Commission website at http://www.nccusl.org.
106. UCCJEA § 105(b). *See* Chapter 5.
107. UIFSA, 9 (IB) U.L.A. 159 (2005 & Supp. 2011). UIFSA was originally adopted in 1992, with

significant amendments in 1996, 2001, and 2008. Citations in this book are to the 2008 revision. UIFSA has been enacted in some form in every state. Current information is available on the Uniform Law Commission website at http://www.nccusl.org.

108. UIFSA §§ 102(5), 105.

109. UIFSA § 104(a).

110. Child support enforcement is discussed in Chapter 7.

111. These issues are considered separately in each of the following chapters.

112. *See* RESTATEMENT (THIRD) OF FOREIGN RELATIONS LAW § 481, Reporter's Note 6 (1987).

113. For example, on the procedure in France, see PETER HERZOG & MARTHA WESER, CIVIL PROCEDURE IN FRANCE 598–600 (Hans Smit ed., 1967), describing when an exequatur is necessary and explaining treatment of U.S. divorce judgments. Since 2006, French courts have significantly eased the recognition process for foreign judgments in matrimonial and other matters. *See* Alain Cornec & Julie Losson, *French Supreme Court Restates Rules on Jurisdiction, Recognition, and Enforcement of Foreign Decisions in Matrimonial Matters: A New Chance for Old Cases*, 44 FAM. L.Q. 83 (2010). On the German law, see Kurt Sier, *Private International Law*, *in* INTRODUCTION TO GERMAN LAW 354 (Mathias Reimann & Joachim Zekoll eds., 2d ed. 2005), describing the process of exequatur for non-European foreign decrees.

114. *See generally* ENFORCEMENT OF FOREIGN JUDGMENTS (Dennis Campbell ed., 1997); ENFORCEMENT OF FOREIGN JUDGMENTS WORLDWIDE (Charles Platto & William G. Horton eds., 2d ed. 1993).

115. *See supra* note 6 and accompanying text.

116. *See supra* notes 81–86 and accompanying text.

2

Marriage, Partnership, and Cohabitation

International human rights law recognizes the central position of marriage and the family in human societies. The Universal Declaration of Human Rights states that "the family is the natural and fundamental group unit of society and is entitled to protection by society and the State."[1] In addition, it declares that "men and women of full age, without any limitation, due to race, nationality, or religion, have the right to marry and found a family. They are entitled to equal rights as to marriage, during marriage, and at its dissolution." This right to marry is implemented in the International Covenant on Civil and Political Rights, which the United States ratified in 1992,[2] and the Convention on the Elimination of All Forms of Discrimination Against Women (CEDAW).[3] Other important human rights instruments extend similar protections, including the European Convention on Human Rights, which guarantees the right to respect for family life.[4]

Marriage and domestic partnership laws follow similar patterns in many countries around the world, but the laws of different jurisdictions retain significant diversity. In the United States, marriage is primarily a matter of state law,[5] but marriage recognition questions are frequently important in immigration law and other federal subjects such as income tax, bankruptcy, and public benefits. These laws generally refer to state law to establish a couple's marital status,[6] but federal law currently denies any recognition to same-sex marriages. This chapter considers laws regulating marriage and marriage recognition, as well as civil union, registered partnership, and unmarried cohabitation.

Getting Married

To contract a marriage, most states require a couple to obtain a marriage license and have their marriage solemnized by a public official or member of the clergy.[7] Typically, both parties must appear in person to apply for a license, but they need not be residents of the state in order to be married there. Some states impose waiting periods of one to five days after a license is issued before a marriage can take place, although these requirements may be waived in some circumstances. A small number of states still require premarital blood tests.[8]

The documentation required for a marriage license typically includes a proof of age for each party, such as a birth certificate, and copies of divorce decrees if either was previously married. If these are in a foreign language, certified translations may be necessary. In *Buck v. Stankovic*, a couple challenged a local registrar's requirement that a non-U.S. citizen applying for a marriage license must also present proof of lawful presence in the United States, such as a permanent resident card or a foreign passport with a valid visa.[9] The couple argued that this rule violated their constitutional right to marry, and a federal court granted a preliminary injunction against the rule, finding that there was a reasonable probability that the policy violated the Due Process and Equal Protection guarantees of the Constitution.[10]

State statutes generally require solemnization of the marriage after a couple obtains a license. For example, New York provides that a marriage is solemnized when the parties "solemnly declare in the presence of clergyman or magistrate . . . that they take each other as husband and wife."[11] In most states, both parties must be present to solemnize a marriage, but several permit a marriage by proxy if one cannot attend.[12] After solemnization, the parties or the officiant must return the marriage license or certificate to the appropriate state office for recording.

Designated public officials and religious clergy of all denominations have authority to solemnize marriages.[13] *Persad v. Balram* held that the reference to "clergyman" in the New York marriage statute must be read to include a Hindu priest, noting that it should be "given a broad interpretation so as not to infringe on an individual's constitutional guarantee of religious freedom. . . . Subsumed within this constitutional right is the freedom to be married in accordance with the dictates of one's own faith."[14] Similarly, *Aghili v. Saadatnejadi* concluded that a person competent under Islamic law to perform marriage ceremonies would have authority to solemnize a marriage in Tennessee.[15] The Uniform Marriage and Divorce Act (UMDA) allows solemnization "in accordance with any mode of solemnization recognized by any religious denomination, Indian Nation or Tribe, or Native Group."[16] A few states permit a couple to solemnize their marriage themselves, or allow any person to obtain certification for the purpose of solemnizing a marriage.[17]

A marriage celebrated in another country is subject to the marriage laws of that country, even if the parties are U.S. citizens.[18] U.S. diplomatic and consular officials are not permitted to perform marriages, but may authenticate foreign marriage documents for use in the United States.[19] Procedures for marrying abroad may be lengthy and complex, and they often include a minimum period of residency.[20] A foreign marriage that violates a strong public policy in the United States is likely not to be recognized, even if it was fully valid in the place where it was celebrated.[21]

Statutes and case law in the United States tend to uphold the validity of marriages even when parties fail in some respect to comply with the licensing or solemnization requirements. Courts employ a presumption that a ceremonial marriage is valid, and generally uphold marriages even when the officiant was not properly qualified or the parties failed to return the marriage license or certificate for recording.[22] Some states

The U.S. State Department information circular on Marriage of U.S. Citizens Abroad is available at http://www.travel.state.gov/law/family_issues/marriage/marriage_589.html.

treat a ceremonial marriage as valid even if the parties failed to obtain any license at all.[23] In these jurisdictions, a religious ceremony with no license may be fully binding as a civil matter. Even when the defect with a marriage is one of substance rather than form, doctrines including common law marriage and putative marriage protect the interests of parties who act in good faith by sustaining the validity of their marriage.[24]

Common Law and Putative Marriage

At this writing, couples may validly contract a common law marriage in ten states and the District of Columbia. These are Alabama, Colorado, Iowa, Kansas, Montana, Oklahoma, Rhode Island, South Carolina, Utah, and Texas. Another group of states have abolished common law marriage fairly recently, but common law marriages contracted in those states before the date of abolition remain fully valid.[25] A few states have statutes that define parameters for recognition of a common law marriage.[26] As a general matter, proof of a common law marriage requires a showing that the couple had a present intention to be married, which may be established by direct evidence of their agreement to be married in words spoken in the present tense, or by circumstantial evidence of their constant cohabitation and holding out in the community as a married couple.[27] All states recognize common law marriages, legally valid in the state where they occurred, in some circumstances. Recognition is particularly likely if the couple were domiciled or had a regular residence in the common law marriage state at the time of their marriage.[28]

To enter a common law marriage, the parties must be eligible to marry under the general marriage laws of the state where the marriage took place. Once a couple forms a common law marriage, their marriage has the same incidents and effects as any other legal marriage.[29] The common law marriage continues until it is terminated by divorce or annulment, or by the death of one of the parties. There is no such thing as an informal or common law divorce in any state.

Putative marriage began as a civil law doctrine that protected the community property rights of an individual who married and later discovered a defect in solemnization or an impediment to the marriage. The doctrine is now widely recognized by the states and utilized in many legal contexts, including eligibility for federal Social Security benefits.[30] To qualify as a putative spouse, an individual must have a good-faith belief that the marriage was valid.[31]

Marital Consent

Marriage is often described as a contract, and both parties must have the legal capacity to contract. Accordingly, a marriage entered into by an individual who is mentally incompetent[32] or below the age of consent[33] may be annulled. Annulment is also possible if consent to a marriage was induced by fraud or duress, or based on a jest or dare.[34] State laws typically characterize marriages with these defects as voidable, and they remain fully valid unless successfully challenged.

International law evinces a particular concern with preventing child marriage and forced marriage. This is reflected in Article 16 of the Universal Declaration on Human Rights, which holds that "marriages shall be entered into only with the free and full consent of the intending spouses." This language formed the basis for the United

Nations Convention on Consent to Marriage, Minimum Age for Marriage, and Registration of Marriages in 1962,[35] and the principle was reinforced by Article 16 of the CEDAW in 1979.[36]

Child Marriage: Age Requirements

Most states set the legal age for marriage at 18, and many allow 16- or 17-year-olds to marry with the consent of one or both parents or approval of a court.[37] In some states, teenagers younger than 16 may marry, although this ordinarily requires court approval.[38] Recognizing that legal systems incorporate different marriage ages, the United Nations has recommended that 15 should be the minimum legal marriage age.[39] In addition to state laws that establish a minimum age for marriage as a civil matter, state criminal statutes define a minimum age of consent for sexual relationships and provide for punishment of adults (or older children) who violate these norms.[40] Parental authority is also constrained by the criminal law. In *People v. Benu*, a noncustodial father who arranged a wedding for his 13-year-old daughter was convicted for endangering the child's welfare.[41]

Because of the variation in state marriage laws, many cases have considered couples who traveled from one state to another to take advantage of lower age requirements. Marriage validation policies are important here, and state laws traditionally treat a marriage contracted before the age of consent as voidable rather than void. Parties may confirm a youthful marriage by continued cohabitation after both individuals reach the legal marriage age. When an underage party objects to a marriage, however, there are strong arguments for allowing that individual to have the marriage annulled, particularly when there are facts to suggest that the union was not entirely consensual.[42]

Forced Marriage: Fraud and Duress

Because both spouses must consent to a marriage, annulment is allowed if a marriage resulted from duress or fraud. Annulment is often said to require fraud going to the "essentials" of a marriage, but the case law in many states has expanded this category to include almost any material misrepresentation, particularly when the parties have never lived together as a married couple.[43] Courts regularly grant annulments in cases in which a man or woman entered into a marriage with a U.S. citizen or resident solely to secure a favorable immigration status.[44] Marriage fraud has a particular definition in federal immigration law, discussed below.[45]

A party may establish duress by proof of physical force or threats, and some cases have granted annulment when a marriage was the result of strong parental pressure.[46] For example, in *Hirani v. Hirani*, the Court of Appeal in England granted an annulment in "the classic case of a young girl, wholly dependent on her parents, being forced into a marriage with a man she has never seen and whom her parents have never seen."[47] Forced marriage also violates international human rights laws,[48] and it has been a par-

The U.S. State Department/information fliers on Forced Marriage Prevention are available at http://travel.state.gov/travel/tips/safety/safety-5475.html.

For assistance in cases of possible marriage coercion involving a U.S. citizen abroad, contact the U.S. State Department, Bureau of Consular Affairs, Office of American Citizen Services, at (202) 647-5225 or (202) 647-5226; website: http://www.travel.state.gov. Contact information for U.S. consulates and embassies around the world is available at http://travel.state.gov/travel/travel_1744.html.

ticular concern in the international setting, where marriage to a citizen or permanent resident can secure access to important immigration benefits.[49] Both men and women may be subject to marriage coercion, and the problems extend to children as well as those who are fully of age to marry. In the United Kingdom, after a number of high-profile cases in which women were coerced into marriages by family members, often while in other countries, the Forced Marriage (Civil Protection) Act in 2007 expanded the circumstances in which authorities can intervene.[50]

Concerns regarding marriage coercion abroad involving a U.S. citizen should be directed to the Office of American Citizen Services (ACS) at the State Department,[51] or the appropriate U.S. embassy or consulate.[52] Consular intervention in this area falls within the scope of the Vienna Convention on Consular Relations (VCCR), and the measures that may be taken are addressed in the U.S. Foreign Affairs Manual.[53] Marriage coercion cases within the United States should be referred to local police or child welfare authorities. A marriage that was not based on the full and free consent of both parties may be annulled under state law, and this relief should also be available following a forced marriage in another country.[54]

Marriage Prohibitions

Federal constitutional law and international human rights law[55] protect the right to marry. Since 1967, the U.S. Supreme Court has recognized a fundamental right to marry, protected by the Due Process and Equal Protection clauses of the Constitution. *Loving v. Virginia*[56] held that state laws prohibiting interracial marriage were unconstitutional, and in subsequent rulings the Court struck down laws that effectively prohibited marriage of prisoners or parents who were in default of their child support obligations.[57] In *Buck v. Stankovic*, the reasoning of these cases was extended to prohibit a state from denying a marriage license to an individual who was not legally present in the United States.[58]

Close Family Relationships

All states prohibit marriages between siblings or between parents and their children or grandchildren, and criminal statutes bolster these prohibitions.[59] Beyond this core, there are notable differences between the states, particularly regarding first-cousin marriages and uncle-niece or aunt-nephew marriages.[60] A few states prohibit marriage within a wider range of family relationships, including relationships by marriage such as in-law or stepfamily members.[61] The U.S. restriction on the marriage of first cousins is relatively unusual in international terms, and may cause particular problems for couples with ties to countries or cultures where these marriages are common or even preferred.

Polygamy

Bigamous marriages violate both the civil and criminal law,[62] and federal immigration laws expressly exclude polygamists from entry to the United States.[63] In *Reynolds v. United States*, the Supreme Court rejected the argument that laws criminalizing polygamy violated the constitutional right to free exercise of religion, and the Court has reaffirmed this ruling several times.[64]

Despite the strong statutory policies against bigamy, several doctrines blunt the force of these rules. In many states, a marriage that was initially invalid because one party had a prior undissolved marriage may subsequently become valid if the parties continue to cohabit after the impediment is removed, at least when the parties have acted in good faith.[65] In other cases that appear to involve bigamous marriages, courts apply a presumption that the latest marriage of a series of marriages is valid. These cases often pit two widows against each other, and the burden of proof, placed on the party who seeks to disprove the validity of the later marriage, may be extremely high.[66] *Gomez v. Windows on the World* applied the presumption in a dispute over workers' compensation benefits following the September 11 attack at the World Trade Center.[67] The decedent's first wife, in Colombia, prevailed over his subsequent wife in New York, based on her testimony and evidence of his marital status recorded in the Colombian civil registry.[68] Context is also important here, and the presumption in favor of the later marriage is not sufficient to convict a defendant for bigamy.[69] To establish a valid marriage for immigration purposes, a petitioner will need to offer proof that all previous marriages of both parties were validly terminated, and the presumptions of validity will not apply.[70]

Same-Sex Couples

At the time of this writing, same-sex couples have the right to marry under state law in Connecticut, Iowa, Massachusetts, New Hampshire, New York, Vermont, and the District of Columbia,[71] and under national laws in countries including Argentina,[72] Belgium,[73] Canada,[74] Iceland,[75] the Netherlands,[76] Norway,[77] Portugal,[78] South Africa,[79] Spain,[80] and Sweden.[81] Same-sex marriage is also permitted in Mexico City.[82] Several of these countries make some distinction between the rights of same-sex and opposite-sex married couples. In the United States, most states that do not permit same-sex marriage also refuse to recognize same-sex marriages formalized in other states or foreign countries.[83] At least 40 states have enacted a statutory or constitutional ban on recognition of same-sex marriages.[84]

The federal Defense of Marriage Act (DOMA) provides in 28 U.S.C. § 1738C that no state is required to recognize or give effect to a same-sex marriage that is valid under the law of another state. Beyond the question of recognition across state borders, DOMA also limits the definition of "marriage" and "spouse" for purposes of federal laws to opposite-sex couples.[85] Under the present law, a married same-sex couple is not eligible for joint filing status under the federal income tax laws, for spousal benefits under the Social Security Act, for family preferences under the Immigration and Nationality Act, or any other federally defined rights or obligations.

Annulling a Marriage

Actions for annulment were more common before the spread of no-fault grounds for divorce, and an extensive body of statutory and case law elaborates various grounds for annulment, based on the rules for marital capacity and consent and the substantive requirements of marriage described above. Some state laws refer to annulment as a declaration of invalidity. Courts may or may not make an annulment or declaration of invalidity retroactive to the date of the marriage.[86]

Jurisdiction and Choice of Law

Under *Restatement (Second) of Conflict of Laws* § 76, jurisdiction to annul a marriage exists in the place where the marriage was celebrated if the respondent is subject to the court's personal jurisdiction, or wherever there would be jurisdiction to grant a divorce.[87] Section 283(1) provides that "the local law of the state which, with respect to the particular issue, has the most significant relationship to the spouses and the marriage" should determine the validity of the marriage. While the place of celebration generally has the strongest interest in regulating the formalization of marriage, the place where the parties were domiciled immediately before or after their marriage is likely to have the strongest interest in the substantive qualifications for marriage.[88] In *Singh v. Singh*, a husband brought an action in New York to set aside a marriage performed in India that was "arranged by the respective parents of the plaintiff and the defendant without the consent of either of the parties." The court found jurisdiction based on the petitioner's residence in New York for more than two years, and held that the purported marriage was invalid under the laws of both India and New York because the bride, who opposed the marriage, had refused to participate in two ceremonies required by the Hindu Marriage Act.[89]

Consequences of Annulment

Traditionally, an annulment decree declared that the marriage was invalid from the outset, so the marriage had no legal consequences. If children had been born, those children became illegitimate. Statutes in most states have significantly altered these rules. Most states define children born during an invalid marriage as legitimate, and reforms in the treatment of nonmarital children have substantially eliminated the legal status and significance of legitimacy.[90] In financial terms, annulment may have consequences similar to those of divorce, based on statutes allowing this type of recovery or on the equitable and common law remedies available to unmarried cohabitants.[91] An annulment decree that voids a marriage from the outset may have significant immigration consequences, however.[92]

Marriage Alternatives: Partnership and Cohabitation

In addition to those states and foreign countries that permit same-sex couples to marry, many jurisdictions have established an alternative legal status, such as civil union or registered partnership law, that confers some or all of the legal rights and obligations of marriage. Courts in the United States use a range of legal theories to address the property claims of unmarried couples, of the same or opposite sex, at the end of their cohabitation. In most states, however, cohabitation does not carry with it any of the wider range of rights and obligations that accompany marriage.

Civil Union and Registered Partnership

A growing number of states provide for civil union or domestic partnership as a legal status for same-sex couples fully equivalent to marriage under state law. Delaware, Hawaii, Illinois, New Jersey, and Rhode Island have civil union laws;[93] California, Nevada, Oregon, and Washington provide for domestic partner registration.[94] Generally, this alternative is limited to same-sex couples, although opposite-sex couples may obtain a civil union in Illinois and Hawaii, may register as domestic partners in California if one partner is at least 62 years old, and may register as domestic partners in New Jersey if both members of the couple are 62 or older.[95] Beyond the United States, several countries have national registration schemes that create an alternative status closely equivalent to marriage. This includes civil union in Brazil[96] and New Zealand,[97] and civil partnership in Ireland[98] and the United Kingdom.[99]

In these jurisdictions, the procedure and requirements for forming, annulling, or dissolving a union are closely parallel to those for marriage. The members of the couple may not be closely related, and couples may not contract a civil union or register their partnership if either member has a prior, undissolved marriage or partnership. Divorce or dissolution proceedings are necessary to terminate a civil union or registered partnership.

Other marriage alternatives, available at the national, state, or local level, extend a narrower range of legal rights and obligations to registered same-sex couples. Colorado, Maine, Maryland, and Wisconsin have these types of statutes.[100] Registered partner schemes have been enacted in many European countries including Andorra, Austria, the Czech Republic, Denmark, Finland, France, Germany, Greenland, Hungary, Iceland, Luxembourg, Slovenia, and Switzerland.[101] Civil unions are available in Ecuador[102] and Uruguay.[103] These institutions have widely varying characteristics. For example, the German life partnership law does not include all of the tax and inheritance benefits of marriage,[104] and registered partnerships in Switzerland do not confer the same rights with respect to joint parentage and adoption.[105] In France, a same- or opposite-sex couple may register an agreement known as a *pacte civil de solidarité* ("civil solidarity pact," or PACS) that addresses property rights and provides the some of the tax, insurance, and other public benefits that accompany marriage.[106]

Cohabitation

Case law in many states allows an unmarried cohabitant to seek a financial recovery from his or her partner at the end of their relationship, based on contract or property theories or equitable remedies.[107] Cohabitation status is rarely recognized in other legal contexts, which means that cohabitants in most states have no inheritance rights and no right to the tort recovery or social insurance benefits available to a married partner.[108] For this reason, nonmarital cohabitation must be distinguished from common law marriage, which is fully equivalent to formalized marriage.[109] To the extent that state laws allow cohabitation claims, this recovery is available to both same-sex and opposite-sex cohabitants.[110] In jurisdictions where same-sex couples cannot marry, form a civil union, or register their partnership, legal instruments including contracts, wills, and powers of attorney may be used to accomplish some of the purposes that marriage would otherwise serve.[111]

Express contracts between cohabitants are generally enforceable, unless based explicitly on a meretricious consideration.[112] Restitution remedies are available to compensate for joint financial investments or services provided to property or business interests, but not typically for the mutual services or shared expenses of a life together.[113] In a small group of states, including California, New Jersey, Oregon, and Washington, broader equitable remedies may also be available to cohabitants.[114]

The relative absence of legal protections for cohabitants in the United States contrasts with the legal regimes in a number of countries that provide more systematic protection. Legislation in New Zealand[115] and various states in Australia[116] has addressed the property rights of de facto couples, and many of these jurisdictions extend the same protections to same-sex and opposite-sex couples. Judicial rulings and legislation in many Canadian provinces have extended a range of important protections to cohabitants in marriage-like or "common law" relationships at the federal and provincial level.[117] Civil law countries including France[118] and Mexico[119] have developed the institution of *concubinage*; and in Colombia, a de facto union (unión de hecho) is legally equivalent to marriage after a couple has lived together for two years.[120]

Courts in the United States have consistently refused to treat foreign cohabitation as analogous to common law marriage, unless there is proof that the alternative status is equivalent to marriage under the applicable foreign law.[121] For example, *Estate of Huyot* decided that concubinage in France was not equivalent to marriage, and therefore that a surviving concubine could not claim an elective share in her partner's estate as his spouse under New York law.[122] *Rosales v. Battle* held that a Mexican woman could not sue for her partner's wrongful death in California after he was killed in a car accident there, despite her status in Mexico as his informal partner or *concubina*.[123] Similarly, *American Airlines v. Mejia* concluded that the surviving member of a *unión marital de hecho* in Colombia could not bring a wrongful death action after his partner's death in Florida.[124]

Recognition of Marriage and Partner Relationships

Traditional conflicts principles, incorporated into the statutes of several states, determine the validity of a marriage based on the law of the place of celebration.[125] In some states this rule does not apply to evasive marriages, in which parties who are domiciled in a state that would prohibit their marriage attempt to avoid the prohibition by marrying in another jurisdiction.[126] States also may refuse recognition to a marriage that was valid in the place of celebration if recognition would be contrary to some strong public policy of the forum state.[127] Despite consensus on these broad principles, the wide variation among the formal and substantive requirements for marriage in the different states has produced a substantial body of conflicts law applicable to interstate and international marriage cases.[128]

Courts decide marriage recognition disputes against a strong background policy of sustaining marriage whenever possible. Many common law presumptions reflect this policy. Once a party proves that a marriage ceremony was performed, the marriage is presumed to be valid and continuing, and the burden of proof to rebut this presumption lies with the party challenging it.[129] Another rule presumes the validity of the latest in a series of marriages. In addition, many states have adopted the civil law doctrine of putative marriage to protect the interests of an innocent spouse.[130]

Formal Validity

The traditional marriage recognition rule is relatively easy to apply when the issue concerns marriage formalities. For example, courts regularly recognize a common law marriage or a proxy marriage contracted in a state or foreign country that permits those marriages.[131] As an expression of the marriage validation policy, many courts also uphold marriages when the parties have failed to comply with the formalization requirements of the place of celebration, particularly when the marriage would be valid under the law of another state with a substantial relationship to the parties and the marriage.[132] This was the result in *Donlann v. Macgurn*, which upheld a marriage obtained by an Arizona couple while on vacation in Mexico. Despite evidence that the marriage did not satisfy all the local requirements of Mexican law, the court applied the test in *Restatement (Second) of Conflict of Laws* § 283(1) and concluded that "even if a marriage is invalid where it was contracted . . . [it] can be recognized by another state with a more significant relationship to the parties and to the marriage."[133]

The proponent of a marriage must prove that the marriage took place, usually based on documents or testimony.[134] *Marriage of Akon* concluded that there was sufficient evidence to establish a valid "cultural marriage" in the Sudan based on evidence of a wedding ceremony and a substantial payment toward the dowry owed to the bride's father.[135] Once a foreign marriage is established, courts may extend the presumption of validity to it, imposing a significant burden of proof on the contesting party.[136] Using this presumption, courts have upheld marriages based on the parties' settled expectations despite what appears to have been a clear failure to comply with the formalization requirements of the place of celebration. For example, *Xiong v. Xiong* upheld a marriage celebrated with a traditional Hmong ceremony in Laos near the end of the Vietnam War, despite the couple's failure to comply with the requirements of Laotian law.[137] *Amsellem v. Amsellem* applied a presumption of validity to sustain a religious marriage performed in France without the civil formalities required by French law.[138] In both of these cases, the foreign marriage was followed by a significant period of married life together in the United States.

Courts do not always effectuate the marriage validation policy, however. The court in *Farah v. Farah* considered a Muslim marriage that took place in stages, each in a different place: signing a proxy marriage form, or *nikah*, in Virginia, a proxy ceremony to solemnize the marriage in England, and a wedding reception or *rukhsati* in Pakistan several weeks later. Pointing to England as the place where the marriage was contracted and celebrated, the court concluded the marriage was invalid because it did not comply with any of the English marriage formalities.[139]

Substantive Validity

In disputes concerning substantive marriage requirements, sometimes referred to as the essential validity of a marriage, there are often tensions between marriage validation and other public policies. Contrary policies are most likely to prevail if a marriage violates some strong public policy of the place where the couple was domiciled at the time they attempted to marry.[140] Marriage evasion statutes in some states accomplish this by invalidating any marriage in which an individual domiciled in the state goes to another place to contract a marriage that would be void under the law of the domicile.[141] The policy issues are more difficult when a couple contracts a marriage that is fully valid in the place where they live and then moves to (or visits) a place where their marriage would not be permitted.[142]

Marriage regulations alone are usually not sufficient to establish a "strong public policy" for the purpose of denying recognition to a marriage, particularly in those areas where there is substantial disagreement among the states. For example, courts routinely uphold first-cousin marriages, uncle-niece marriages, or underage marriages that were valid in the place of solemnization unless there is explicit statutory language to prevent this result.[143] In *May's Estate*, the New York Court of Appeals upheld an uncle-niece marriage that was valid in Rhode Island, even though it would have been void if celebrated in New York.[144] In *Catalano v. Catalano*, the Connecticut Supreme Court reached the opposite conclusion, refusing to recognize a valid Italian marriage between a man who lived in Connecticut and his niece who lived in Italy.[145] A court in Louisiana recognized an Iranian marriage of first cousins in *Ghassemi v. Ghassemi*, concluding that although the marriage could not have been contracted in Louisiana, the state "does not have a strong public policy against recognizing a marriage between first cousins performed in a state or country where such marriages are valid." The opinion emphasized that first-cousin marriages are widely accepted around the world, and also noted that sexual relationships between first cousins were not prohibited by the state's criminal incest statute.[146]

State criminal laws, such as laws that define and penalize bigamy and incest, are a much stronger indication of the outside limits of state public policy.[147] On this basis, authorities in the United States generally refuse to give effect to a foreign polygamous marriage, even if this was permitted under the law of the place of celebration.[148] For example, in *Application of Sood*, the court agreed that a potentially polygamous Hindu marriage in India was valid and effective to prevent the husband from being eligible to marry again in New York.[149] *People v. Ezeonu* held that a married defendant charged with statutory rape could not defend against the charge by claiming that the young woman was his "second" or "junior" wife under Nigerian customary law.[150]

Marriage validity may be litigated as an incidental question, by parties other than the married couple, in the context of claims for inheritance rights, public benefits, tort recovery, or immigration status. In these cases, the married couple may have no direct ties to the forum state.[151] When marriage validity is framed as an incidental question, courts may extend limited recognition to marriages that would otherwise be treated as void.[152] In *Dalip Singh Bir's Estate*, the court found that two women living in India, both legally married there to the same husband, were both entitled to share distribution of his estate after his death in California.[153] Federal immigration cases have concluded that children born of polygamous marriages may be legitimate, and therefore entitled to immigration rights based on their fathers' citizenship or residence status, if the applicable law viewed the children as legitimate.[154]

In many states, statutory or constitutional provisions explicitly prohibit recognition of same-sex marriages formalized elsewhere. This is authorized by the federal Defense of Marriage Act (DOMA), 28 U.S.C. § 1738C, which provides that states need not give effect to "any public act, record, or judicial proceeding of any other State, territory, possession or tribe respecting a relationship between persons of the same sex that is treated as a marriage under the laws of such other State, territory, possession, or tribe, or a right or claim arising from such relationship." Another provision of DOMA, codified at 1 U.S.C. § 7, effectively prohibits recognition of same-sex marriages for purposes of federal law including immigration benefits.[155] Courts in states that do not permit same-sex marriage are divided on whether they have jurisdiction to dissolve an out-of-state, same-sex marriage.[156] Although not required to do so, states may recognize a same-sex marriage that the parties validly contracted in another place, particularly when the issue arises as an incidental question.[157] This was the practice in New York, before the law changed to allow same-sex marriage.[158]

Recognizing Civil Union or Registered Partnership

States that authorize same-sex marriage, civil union, or registered partnership generally extend recognition to similar forms of partnership contracted in other states or foreign countries, but this question is complicated by the many different forms of these marriage alternatives.[159] States that do not allow formalization of same-sex unions have generally been reluctant to give legal effect to an out-of-state civil union or partnership, even if the issue arises as an incidental question. This has been the result in wrongful death litigation[160] and when one member of a couple seeks to invoke the court's jurisdiction to dissolve their relationship.[161] In cases involving children, courts are required to recognize adoption or custody orders from courts in other states as a matter of full faith and credit, even when those orders involve same-sex-couple families.[162] In *Debra H. v. Janice R.*, the New York Court of Appeals recognized parental status arising from an out-of-state civil union on the basis of comity.[163]

Marriage and Partnership Recognition in Other Countries

Marriage recognition rules in England and in civil law countries distinguish between the formal and substantive validity of a marriage, looking to the law of the place of celebration to determine issues of form, and to the law of the parties' domicile or nationality on issues of substantive or "essential" validity.[164] The 1977 Hague Convention on Celebration and Recognition of the Validity of Marriages[165] attempts to harmonize these rules, generally extending recognition to marriages that are valid in the place of celebration but authorizing State Parties to refuse recognition on several grounds, including that (1) one of the spouses has a prior marriage, (2) there is a direct lineal or sibling relationship between the spouses, (3) the relationship was not freely consented to or either party was not of age, and (4) the marriage is incompatible with the public policy of the state where recognition is requested.[166] The United States has not joined the Marriage Convention.

As is the case within the United States, the question of recognition for same-sex marriages across international borders is complex and largely unsettled. In *Wilkinson v. Kitzinger*, the High Court of Justice in the United Kingdom applied traditional marriage recognition principles to conclude that a same-sex marriage in Canada of two women who were domiciled in England at the time of their marriage was not valid.[167] England, Wales, Scotland, and Northern Ireland do recognize certain "overseas relationships" within the framework of the Civil Partnership Act, however,[168] and South Africa recognizes U.K. civil partnerships as civil unions under South African law.[169]

In Europe, at least 17 countries, have registration schemes that are available to same-sex couples and in some cases also to opposite-sex couples. including many member states of the European Union.[170] Because there are very significant differences among these regimes, and no European convention or regulation to harmonize them, registered partners and same-sex couples may find that their relationships take on either lesser or greater legal stature when they cross borders.[171] Registered partners or married same-sex couples from the United States and other countries outside Europe face the same difficulty.

Marriage and Immigration

Immigration laws in the United States make special provision for marriages formed across international borders. The spouse of a U.S. citizen is an "immediate relative" who can enter the country without an immigrant visa, based on a petition filed by the citizen spouse.[172] Similarly, a lawful permanent resident (LPR) may obtain a family preference immigrant visa to sponsor the immigration of his or her spouse.[173] An immigrant spouse who is already present in the United States may apply for adjustment of his or her immigration status after being married to a citizen or LPR.[174] If the couple has not yet married, a fiancé (or "K") visa allows an individual to enter the United States for the purposes of marrying a U.S. citizen applicant.[175] The parties must marry within 90 days, and after the marriage occurs the fiancé may apply for adjustment of status.[176]

In each of these categories, the spouse who is already a U.S. citizen or LPR must petition with his or her spouse. In cases involving serious domestic violence or the death of the petitioning spouse, the statutes allow the sponsored spouse to petition alone.[177] The process also provides an important financial protection for the sponsored spouse. Under federal law, the Form I-864 Affidavit of Support, filed by the family member who is sponsoring an immigrant, is a binding contract that may be enforced by the immigrant in state or federal court, including in divorce proceedings.[178]

In immigration cases, a petitioner has the burden of proving that the marriage occurred and that it was legally valid where it took place. The validity of a marriage may be determined by a visa officer in a U.S. consulate or by the administrative authorities within U.S. Citizenship and Immigration Services (USCIS). Marriage recognition for immigration purposes generally follows the rules applied in other settings.[179] Religious, customary, or common law marriages are recognized for immigration purposes if they were legally valid in the place of celebration, but a petitioner may need to produce evidence of applicable foreign law.[180] Generally, a marriage that was valid where it took place, will be recognized for immigration purposes, with certain exceptions: Proxy marriages are not recognized unless they have been consummated,[181] polygamous marriages are subject to specific restrictions,[182] and same-sex marriages are not recognized.[183] For marriages of close relatives or those under age 18, the immigration inquiry sometimes requires a further reference to the law of the place where the couple lives, including its choice of law rules and marriage evasion or validation policies.[184]

Immigration law reflects a special concern with fraudulent marriages. USCIS may deny an immigrant visa petition if it concludes that the petitioner entered into a sham marriage to obtain immigration benefits. Certain factors are treated as red flags that trigger more intensive scrutiny, including substantial disparity in the parties' ages, economic circumstances, or cultural and linguistic background.[185] The federal case law defining a sham marriage focuses on whether the couple intended to establish a life together with the usual rights and obligations of a marriage relationship.[186] The petitioner generally must prove by a preponderance of the evidence that the claimed marriage exists, is legally valid, and the parties did not enter into it solely for immigration purposes.[187]

Due to the 1986 Immigration Marriage Fraud Amendments (IMFA), an immigrant spouse in a marriage of less than two years is limited to conditional permanent resident status. After two years, the spouses must petition jointly to have the condition removed.[188] This is a complex process that may become significantly more complicated if the couple separates or divorces during the period of conditional residence. The immigrant spouse may be able to obtain LPR status based on a showing of extreme hardship or that the marriage was entered into in good faith.[189] Because an immigrant spouse is in a vulnerable position during the period of conditional residence, the IMFA and subsequent legislation have enacted protections including the possibility of a waiver of the joint petition requirement, particularly in circumstances of domestic violence.[190]

The United States regulates international matchmaking organizations under the International Marriage Broker Regulation Act, which requires these organizations to make various disclosures about the U.S. citizen or resident to the potential foreign

---

Further Reading: Recognition of Marriage and Partnerships

IAN CURRY-SUMNER, ALL'S WELL THAT ENDS REGISTERED? THE SUBSTANTIVE AND PRIVATE INTERNATIONAL LAW ASPECTS OF NON-MARITAL REGISTERED RELATIONSHIPS IN EUROPE (2005).

SPECIAL SYMPOSIUM, INTERNATIONAL MARRIAGE AND DIVORCE REGULATION AND RECOGNITION: A SURVEY, 29 FAM. L.Q. 497 (1995).

---

fiancé.[191] There are civil and criminal sanctions for violations of the act. Applying state law, *Ureneck v. Cui* held that a contract requiring payment for international matchmaking services was void and unenforceable as a matter of public policy.[192]

Notes

1. Universal Declaration of Human Rights, art. 16, G.A. Res. 217A, at 71, U.N. GAOR, 3d Sess., 1st plen. mtg., U.N. Doc. A/810 (Dec. 12, 1948).
2. International Covenant on Civil and Political Rights of 1966 (ICCPR) art. 23, 999 U.N.T.S. 171, *reprinted in* 6 I.L.M. 368 (1967). The United States ratified the ICCPR in 1992.
3. Convention on the Elimination of All Forms of Discrimination Against Women (CEDAW), art. 26, G.A. Res. 34/180, at 193, U.N. GAOR Supp. No. 146, U.N. Doc. A/34/46 (opened for signature Mar. 1, 1980), 1249 U.N.T.S. 13, 20, 1989 U.K.T.S. 2, 1982 Misc. 1, Cm. 643, Cmnd. 8444, *reprinted in* 19 I.L.M. 33–45 (1980).
4. European Convention for the Protection of Human Rights and Fundamental Freedoms, art. 8, 213 U.N.T.S. 221 (1950).

5. *See generally* HOMER H. CLARK, JR., THE LAW OF DOMESTIC RELATIONS IN THE UNITED STATES §§ 2.1–.16 (2d student ed., 1988).

6. Thus, state law determines a person's marital status for federal income tax purposes, *see* Rev. Rul. 58-66, 1958-1 C.B. 60, and under the Social Security Act, *see* 42 U.S.C. § 416(h)(1)(A) (2010). *Cf.* Minasyan v. Gonzales, 401 F.3d 1069, 1076 (9th Cir. 2005) (defining "legal separation" for immigration purposes with reference to state law). Federal immigration law includes additional requirements, discussed *infra* at notes 179–87 and accompanying text.

7. *See* CLARK, *supra* note 5, § 2.3.

8. *E.g.*, MISS. CODE ANN. § 93-1-5(e) (2010) (syphilis); MONT. CODE ANN. § 40-1-203 (2010) (rubella); N.Y. DOM. REL. LAW § 13-aa (2010) (sickle-cell anemia).

9. 485 F. Supp. 2d 576 (M.D. Pa. 2007). The local requirement was imposed under 23 PA. CONS. STAT. § 1301(c), which provides that "[p]rior to issuance of the [marriage] license, the person issuing the license must be satisfied as to the identity of both of the applicants." *Id.* at 580.

10. The prospective bride was a U.S. citizen, and the groom an undocumented immigrant from Mexico; the couple had lived together for more than a year and had a child together. The opinion points out that the right to marry is a fundamental right; *see also* notes 56–58 and accompanying text.

11. *See* N.Y. DOM. REL. LAW § 12 (2010), which also provides that "[n]o particular form or ceremony is required." *Cf.* W. VA. CODE § 48-2-404 (2010) (prescribing ritual for civil officials to use in formalizing marriage).

12. *E.g.*, COLO. REV. STAT. § 14-2-109(2) (2010); MONT. CODE ANN. § 40-1-301(2) (2010).

13. *E.g.*, N.Y. DOM. REL. LAW § 11(1) (2010) (marriage may be solemnized by a "clergyman or minister of any religion").

14. 724 N.Y.S.2d 560, 563 (N.Y. Sup. Ct. 2001) (construing N.Y. DOM. REL. LAW § 11(1) and N.Y. RELIG. CORP. LAW § 2). Courts in New York and several other states have held that the "Universal Life Church" is not a bona fide religious organization under state law, and weddings solemnized by Universal Life ministers are therefore invalid. *See* Ranieri v. Ranieri, 539 N.Y.S.2d 382 (N.Y. App. Div. 1989).

15. 958 S.W.2d 784, 787–88 (Tenn. Ct. App. 1997). In both *Persad* and *Aghili*, the parties began living together after the marriage ceremonies but continued negotiating or disputing the terms of premarital agreements.

     In traditions in which betrothal and marriage ceremonies involve multiple steps that occur over a period of time, parties may dispute when, where and whether a marriage was concluded. *See Aghili*, 958 S.W.2d at 786 (Islamic blessing ceremony followed by formal wedding reception two weeks later). *See also* Farah v. Farah, 429 S.E.2d 626 (Va. Ct. App. 1993), discussed *infra* note 139. Estate of Farraj, 886 N.Y.S. 2d 67 (table) 2009 WL 997481 (N.Y. Surr. Ct. 2009) (unreported), applied conflict-of-laws principles to uphold the marriage of a couple living in New York who were married in an Islamic ceremony performed without a license in New Jersey, followed by a reception in New York. Unlicensed marriages are valid in New York but void in New Jersey; *see infra* note 23. The court noted but did not address the argument that under Islamic law a marriage is not final until the reception and consummation take place, *see id.* at n. 4.

16. UNIF. MARRIAGE & DIVORCE ACT § 206(a) (amended 1973), 9A U.L.A. (pt. 1) 182 (1998) (UMDA). The UMDA was adopted in eight states and was later withdrawn and renamed the Model Marriage and Divorce Act. *Id.* at 159.

17. *E.g.*, CAL. FAM. CODE § 401(b) (2010) (deputy commissioners of civil marriages); *see also* COLO. REV. STAT. § 14-2-109 (2010); VA. CODE ANN. § 20-25 (2010).

18. *But see infra* notes 131–39 and accompanying text.

19. Celebration of Marriage, 22 C.F.R. §§ 52.1–.3 (2010).

20. *See id.; see also* EUGENE F. SCOLES ET AL., CONFLICT OF LAWS § 13.6 (4th ed., 2004). Scoles et al. state that the validity of a marriage at sea requires compliance with the law of the nation whose flag the ship is flying. Since there is no general marriage law of the United States, for ships flying a U.S. flag the rule is modified to look to the requirements of state law for the state

where the ship's owner is domiciled. *Id.* at 570. *See also* CLARK, *supra* note 5, at 37–38; 7 U.S. Dep't of State, Foreign Affairs Manual (FAM) § 1457.2, Marriage of U.S. Citizens on High Seas (2005).

21. *See infra* notes 140–58.

22. *See* CLARK, *supra* note 5, at 40–41.

23. *Compare* N.Y. DOM. REL. LAW § 25 (statutes "shall [not] be construed to render void by reason of a failure to procure a marriage license any marriage solemnized between persons of full age"), *applied in* Persad v. Balram, 724 N.Y.S.2d 560, 563 (N.Y. Sup. Ct. 2001), *with* N.J. STAT. § 37:1-10 (failure to comply with the marriage license requirement "shall render the purported marriage absolutely void"), *applied in* Yaghoubinejad v. Haghighi, 894 A.2d 1173, 1174 (N.J. Super. Ct. App. Div. 2006). *See also* Carabetta v. Carabetta, 438 A.2d 109, 112 (Conn. 1980) ("in the absence of express language in the governing statute declaring a marriage void for failure to observe a statutory requirement, this court has held . . . that such a marriage, though imperfect, is dissoluble rather than void"). In California, the marriage license requirement is mandatory; *see* Estate of DePasse, 118 Cal. Rptr. 2d 143 (Cal. Ct. App. 2002). In a common law marriage state, proof of an unlicensed ceremonial marriage should be legally sufficient. *See* State v. Phelps, 652 N.E.2d 1032 (Ohio Ct. App. 1995) (finding that Islamic marriage ceremony constituted a common law marriage).

24. *See also infra* notes 66–70 (courts presume most recent marriage to be valid), notes 143–46 (courts sustaining foreign marriages of close relatives), and notes 151–54 (courts recognize foreign polygamous marriages when issue is incidental to proceeding) and accompanying text.

25. The most recent statutes abolishing common law marriage are GA. CODE ANN. § 19-3-1.1 (effective 1997); IDAHO CODE ANN. § 32-201 (effective 1996); OHIO REV. CODE ANN. § 3105.12 (effective 1991); and 23 PA. CONS. STAT. ANN. § 1103 (effective 2005).

26. *E.g.,* IOWA CODE § 595.11 (2010); TEX. FAM. CODE ANN. § 2.401 (2010); UTAH CODE § 30-1-4.5(2) (2010). *See also* N.Y. DOM. REL. LAW § 11(4) (recognizing marriage contracted by a written, signed, witnessed, and acknowledged document).

27. *See* CLARK, *supra* note 5, § 2.4.

28. *See id.*

29. *See State v. Phelps,* 652 N.E.2d 1032, 1035–36 (Ohio Ct. App. 1995) (recognizing common law marriage for purposes of spousal testimonial privilege and competency in criminal proceeding).

30. *See* 20 C.F.R. § 404.346; *see generally* CLARK, *supra* note 5, at 55–56. *See also supra* note 6 and accompanying text.

31. *E.g.,* Xiong v. Xiong, 800 N.W.2d 187 (Minn. Ct. App. 2011) (Hmong wife had good-faith belief that she was legally married after obtaining marriage license). *Cf.* Marriage of Vryonis, 248 Cal. Rptr. 807 (Cal. Ct. App. 1988) (holding that a woman had no status as a putative wife after a Muslim *muta,* or temporary marriage, which was not a valid form of marriage in California).

32. *See* CLARK, *supra* note 5, § 2.13.

33. *See id.* § 2.10.

34. *See, e.g.,* N.J. STAT. ANN. § 2A:34-1.d, *applied in* Faustin v. Lewis, 427 A.2d 1105, 1106 (N.J. 1981) (wife who married solely to become U.S. permanent resident may have marriage annulled based on "lack of mutual assent to the marital relationship"). *See also* Persad v. Balram, 724 N.Y.S.2d 560, 565 (N.Y. Sup. Ct. 2001) ("This court can imagine a variety of circumstances where a religious union might be considered invalid based on a lack of mutual intent to be wed. For instance, if the ceremony was a prank or the parties were under the influence at the time, a marriage could conceivably be a nullity.").

35. Convention on Consent to Marriage, Minimum Age for Marriage, and Registration of Marriages art. 2, opened for signature Dec. 10, 1962, 521 U.N.T.S. 231 (1962). *See also* ICCPR, *supra* note 2, art. 23.

36. CEDAW, *supra* note 3, art. 16(2) ("The betrothal and marriage of a child shall have no legal effect and all necessary action including legislation, shall be taken to specify a minimum age for marriage and to make the registration of marriages in an official registry compulsory.").

37. *See, e.g.*, UMDA § 203, which allows issuance of a marriage license to parties who are 18 or older, or to parties who are 16 or 17 with either consent of both parents or judicial approval. This section included optional language to allow marriage of an individual under the age of 16 with both parental consent and judicial approval; *see, e.g.*, COLO. REV. STAT. § 14-2-106 (2010).
38. *See, e.g.*, N.H. REV. STAT. ANN. § 457:6 (2010). In a number of states, younger teenagers may obtain permission to marry if one is pregnant. *See, e.g.*, MD. CODE ANN., FAM. LAW § 2-301(b) (2010) (age 15); N.C. GEN. STAT. §§ 51-2 to -2.1 (2010) (ages 14 and 15); OKLA. STAT. tit. 43, § 3 (2010) (under age 16). *See also* MO. ANN. STAT. § 451.090 (2010) (no one under age 15 may be issued a license, except that a judge may issue a license "for good cause shown and by reason of such unusual conditions as to make such marriage advisable"); WASH. REV. CODE ANN. § 26.04.010 (2010) (marriages under age of 17 void except where waived by judge on a "showing of necessity").
39. Recommendation on Consent to Marriage, Minimum Age for Marriage, and Registration of Marriages, G.A. Res. 2018, at 36, U.N. GAOR, 20th Sess., Supp. No. 14, U.N. Doc. A/6014 (1965).
40. *See, e.g.*, State v. Moua, 573 N.W.2d 202 (Wis. Ct. App. 1997) (affirming conviction for second-degree sexual assault after Hmong traditional marriage between defendant and young teenage wife).
41. 385 N.Y.S.2d 222 (N.Y. Crim. Ct. 1976). The conviction was sustained despite a showing that the marriage was voidable rather than void and that neither the daughter nor her custodial parent had taken steps to obtain an annulment.
42. *E.g.*, B. v. L., 168 A.2d 90 (N.J. Super. Ct. Ch. Div. 1961) (annulling Italian marriage arranged by parents of 15-year-old wife). *See generally* Wilkins v. Zelichowski, 140 A.2d 65 (N.J. 1958).
43. *See generally* CLARK, *supra* note 5, § 2.15.
44. *E.g.*, Janda v. Janda, 984 So. 2d 434 (Ala. Civ. App. 2007); Lamberti v. Lamberti, 77 Cal. Rptr. 430 (Cal. Ct. App. 1969); Rubman v. Rubman, 251 N.Y.S. 474 (N.Y. Sup. Ct. 1931); Seirafi-Pour v. Bagherinassab, 197 P.3d 1097 (Okla. Civ. App. 2008); *cf.* Patel v. Navitlal, 627 A.2d 683 (N.J. Super. Ct. Ch. Div. 1992).
45. *See infra* notes 185-190 and accompanying text.
46. *See, e.g.*, Fratello v. Fratello, 193 N.Y.S. 865 (N.Y. Sup. Ct. 1922); Avakian v. Avakian, 60 A. 521 (N.J. Ch. 1905); *but see* Fluharty v. Fluharty, 193 A. 838 (Del. Super. Ct. 1937) ("the mere commands of a father . . . do not show the necessary subjection of one person to another to constitute coercion"). *See also* CLARK, *supra* note 5, § 2.14.
47. Hirani v. Hirani, [1983] 4 FLR 232 (Civ.) (Eng.) The court wrote that "[t]he crucial question in these cases, particularly where a marriage is involved, is whether the threats, pressure, or whatever it is, is such to destroy the reality of consent and overbears the will of the individual." *See also* Kaur v. Singh, [2005] S.C.L.R. 1000 (Sess. 2005) (Scot.). *See also infra* note 89 and accompanying text.
48. ICCPR, *supra* note 2, art. 23.
49. *See infra* notes 172-176 and accompanying text.
50. The British Foreign & Commonwealth Office has established a Forced Marriage Unit that handles 250 to 300 cases a year. Information is posted on this website: http://www.fco.gov.uk/en/travel-and-living-abroad/when-things-go-wrong/forced-marriage/. *See generally* DAVID HODSON, A PRACTICAL GUIDE TO INTERNATIONAL FAMILY LAW 56-59 (2008).
51. *See* 7 U.S. DEP'T OF STATE, FOREIGN AFFAIRS MANUAL (FAM) § 100, Welfare and Whereabouts of U.S. Nationals Abroad (2005), http://www.state.gov/m/a/dir/regs/fam/.
52. For example, the U.S. Embassy in Bangladesh provides this information on assistance for victims of marriage coercion: http://dhaka.usembassy.gov/forced_marriage_home.html.
53. *See* 7 FAM § 1459, Forced and Arranged Marriages of Adults (2005); 7 FAM § 1740, Forced Marriage of Minors (2005).
   See also Catherine Dauvergne & Jenni Millbank, *Forced Marriage as a Harm in Domestic and International Law*, 73 MOD. L. REV. 57 (2010); Alison Symington, *Dual Citizenship and Forced Marriages*, 10 DALHOUSIE J. LEGAL STUD. 1 (2001); Sara Hossain & Suzanne Turner, *Abduction for Forced Marriage—Rights and Remedies in Bangladesh and Pakistan*, 2001 INT'L FAM. L. 15, 15-24 (Apr. 2001).

54. *See also infra* notes 87–89 and accompanying text.

55. *See supra* notes 1–4 and accompanying text.

56. 388 U.S. 1 (1967).

57. Zablocki v. Redhail, 434 U.S. 374 (1978); Turner v. Safley, 482 U.S. 78 (1987). The cases make clear, however, that most marriage laws are not subject to rigorous scrutiny: "[R]easonable regulations that do not significantly interfere with decisions to enter into the marital relationship may legitimately be imposed." *Zablocki*, 434 U.S. at 386.

58. *See supra* notes 9–10 and accompanying text.

59. For criminal incest statutes, see, for example, COLO. REV. STAT. § 18-6-301 (2010); MODEL PENAL CODE § 230.2, 10A U.L.A. 601 (2001).

60. *See generally* CLARK, *supra* note 5, § 2.9. Under UMDA § 207, uncle-niece and aunt-nephew marriages are forbidden except for "marriages permitted by the established customs of aboriginal cultures." In Rhode Island, General Laws section 15-1-4 (2010) specifies that the statutory marriage prohibitions "shall not extend to, or in any way affect, any marriage which shall be solemnized among the Jewish people, within the degrees of affinity or consanguinity allowed by their religion." First-cousin marriages are fully valid in a substantial minority of states and recognized if valid where contracted in many others. *E.g.*, Ghassemi v. Ghassemi, 998 So. 2d 731, 748–49 (La. Ct. App. 2008). *See also* Mason v. Mason, 775 N.E.2d 706 (Ind. Ct. App. 2002) (Tennessee marriage of first cousins recognized in Indiana).

61. *E.g.*, MASS. GEN. LAWS ch. 207 §§ 1, 2 (2010); MISS. CODE § 93-1-1 (2010).

62. For criminal statutes, see, for example, CAL. PENAL CODE §§ 281-284 (2010); COLO. REV. STAT. §§ 18-6-201 to -202 (2010); MODEL PENAL CODE § 230.1, 10A U.L.A. 599 (2001).

63. *See infra* note 182 and accompanying text.

64. 98 U.S. 145 (1878); *see also* Cleveland v. United States, 329 U.S. 14 (1946).

65. CLARK, *supra* note 5, at 52–55. This rule is found in common law marriage jurisdictions, but also in other states. *See, e.g.*, MASS. ANN. LAWS ch. 207, § 6 (2010); WIS. STAT. § 765.24 (2010); Matter of Walls' Estate, 99 N.W.2d 599 (Mich. 1959).

66. *See, e.g.*, Chandler v. Cent. Oil Co., 853 P.2d 649, 655 (Kan. 1993) (to overcome presumption, "every reasonable possibility of validity of that marriage must be negative" by evidence that is "clear, strong, and satisfactory and so persuasive as to leave no room for reasonable doubt"). *See generally* CLARK, *supra* note 5, § 2.7. These cases have involved serial bigamists, rather than individuals who cohabited simultaneously with multiple partners.

67. 804 N.Y.S.2d 849 (N.Y. App. Div. 2005). The story of a migrant who leaves a spouse and children in one place and forms a new family somewhere else is a common one. *See, e.g.*, Ghassemi v. Ghassemi, 998 So. 2d 731, 733–34 (La. Ct. App. 2008); Application of Sood, 142 N.Y.S.2d 591, 592 (N.Y. Sup. Ct. 1955).

68. *Gomez*, 804 N.Y.S.2d at 851–52. The burden of proof in *Gomez* seems less stringent than what was required in the sources cited *supra* in note 66. *Cf.* Cobo v. Sierralta, 13 So. 3d 493 (Fla. Dist. Ct. App. 2009) (evidence insufficient to rebut presumption that prior Venezuelan marriage had been validly terminated). *See also* R.M. v. Dr. R., 855 N.Y.S.2d 865 (N.Y. Sup. Ct. 2008); Guzman v. Alvares, 205 S.W.3d 375 (Tenn. 2006).

69. *See, e.g.*, State v. Rivera, 977 P.2d 1247, 1249 (Wash. Ct. App. 1999) ("The context in which validity of a marriage is questioned determines presumptions and burden of proof.").

70. For this purpose, the immigration practice largely follows the rules for recognition of foreign divorce decrees discussed in Chapter 3. *See, e.g.*, Marriage of Luna, 18 I. & N. Dec. 385 (BIA 1983). *See generally* SARAH B. IGNATIUS & ELISABETH S. STICKNEY, IMMIGRATION LAW AND THE FAMILY §§ 4:7-:14 (Susan Compernolle updating ed., 2010).

71. *See* Goodridge v. Dep't of Pub. Health, 798 N.E.2d 941 (Mass. 2003); Kerrigan v. Comm'r of Pub. Health, 957 A.2d 407 (Conn. 2008); Varnum v. Brien, 763 N.W.2d 862 (Iowa 2009); D.C. CODE § 46-401 (2010); N.H. REV. STAT. ANN. § 457:1-a (2010); N.Y. DOM. REL. LAW § 10-a (2011); VT. STAT. ANN. tit. 15, § 8 (2010). Same-sex marriages were permitted in California for several months in 2008 before the passage of a ballot measure that amended the state constitution to prohibit same-sex marriage.

72. Matrimonio Civil 1054/2010, Law No. 26.618, July 21, 2010 Arg. *See* Cecilia P. Grosman & Marisa Herrera, *Family, Pluralism and Equality: Marriage and Sexual Orientation in Argentine Law*, 2011 INT'L SURV. FAM. L. 27.

73. CODE CIVIL art. 143 (Belg.). *See* Aude Fiorini, *New Belgian Law on Same Sex Marriage and the PIL Implications*, 52 INT'L & COMP. L.Q. 1039 (2003); Kees Waaldijk, *Others May Follow: The Introduction of Marriage, Quasi-Marriage, and Semi-Marriage for Same-Sex Couples in European Countries*, 569 NEW ENG. L. REV. 569, 581–84 (2004).

74. Bill C-38, "An act respecting certain aspects of legal capacity for marriage for civil purposes" (the Civil Marriage Act), STATUTES OF CANADA 2005, ch. 33.

75. Reuters, *Iceland Passes Gay Marriage Law in Unanimous Vote*, June 11, 2010, http://www.reuters.com/article/2010/06/11/us-iceland-gaymarriage-idUSTRE65A3V020100611.

76. *See* Waaldijk, *supra* note 73, at 572–80; *see also* IAN CURRY-SUMNER, ALL'S WELL THAT ENDS REGISTERED? THE SUBSTANTIVE AND PRIVATE INTERNATIONAL LAW ASPECTS OF NON-MARITAL REGISTERED RELATIONSHIPS IN EUROPE 120–21 (2005).

77. Fellesekteskapslov for heterofile og homofile par, OT. PRP. NR. 33 (Nor. 2008). *See* John Aslan & Peter Hambro, *New Developments and Expansion of Relationship Covered by Norwegian Law*, 2009 INT'L SURV. FAM. L. 375.

78. Casamento entre pessoas do memo sexo, Lei no. 9/2010 D.R. No. 105, Série I de 31 de Maio 2010 (Port. 2010).

79. Civil Union Act (No. 17 of 2006) (S. Afr.). *See* June Sinclair, *A New Definition of Marriage: Gay and Lesbian Couples May Marry*, 2008 INT'L SURV. FAM. L. 397.

80. Ley 13/2005 de 1 julio 2005 (B.O.E. July 2, 2005, 157) (Spain).

81. *See* Anna Singer, *Equal Treatment of Same-Sex Couples in Sweden*, in 2010 INT'L SURV. FAM. L. 393.

82. The Legislative Assembly for the Federal District of Mexico (Mexico City) amended the Civil Code in December 2009 to permit marriage of same-sex couples. A subsequent ruling by the Supreme Court of Mexico held that same-sex marriages from Mexico City must be recognized in other parts of the country. *See* David Agren, *Mexican States Ordered to Honor Gay Marriages*, N.Y. TIMES, Aug. 10, 2010.

83. *See infra* notes 156–158 and accompanying text.

84. *See* Andrew Koppelman, *Interstate Recognition of Same-Sex Marriages and Civil Unions: A Handbook for Judges*, 153 U. PA. L. REV. 2143 (2005) [hereinafter Koppelman, *Interstate Recognition*]. The analysis is extended in ANDREW KOPPELMAN, SAME SEX, DIFFERENT STATES: WHEN SAME-SEX MARRIAGES CROSS STATE LINES (2006).

85 *See* 28 U.S.C. § 1738 (full faith and credit provisions); 1 U.S.C. § 7 (definition of "marriage" and "spouse").

86. UMDA § 208(a) and (b) define four types of marriages that may be declared invalid and establish different standing rules for each category. The first three types are based on lack of capacity or consent and are subject to relatively narrow standing rules and limitation periods. The fourth category includes marriages that are prohibited, which term is defined in § 207 to include polygamous and incestuous marriages.

87. *See also* RESTATEMENT (SECOND) OF CONFLICT OF LAWS §§ 70–72 (1971). *See generally* CLARK, *supra* note 5, § 3.2; SCOLES ET AL., *supra* note 20, §§ 15.15–.16. The rules governing jurisdiction over divorce are discussed in Chapter 3 and Chapter 4.

88. *See generally* CLARK, *supra* note 5, § 3.2; SCOLES ET AL., *supra* note 20, § 15.16.

89. 325 N.Y.S.2d 590, 592 (N.Y. Sup. Ct. 1971). The bride refused to participate in the *saptapadi* ceremony that that marks completion of the marriage under § 7 of the Hindu Marriage Act of 1955. The couple never lived together, and the marriage was not consummated. *Id.* at 591. *See also* Moustafa v. Moustafa, 888 A.2d 1230 (Md. Ct. Spec. App. 2005) (applying Maryland law to void bigamous marriage entered into in Egypt).

90. CLARK, *supra* note 5, § 3.3. *See, e.g.*, UMDA § 208(d), *supra* note 16 ("Children born of a marriage declared invalid are legitimate.").

91. *E.g.*, Sclamberg v. Sclamberg, 41 N.E.2d 801 (Ind. 1942) (approving financial award on equitable grounds despite fact that foreign uncle-niece marriage was void). UMDA § 208(e) allows the

court to determine whether or not a declaration of invalidity will be made retroactively and states that "The provisions of this Act relating to property rights of the spouses, maintenance, support, and custody of children on dissolution of marriage are applicable to non-retroactive decrees of invalidity." *See* CLARK, *supra* note 5, § 3.4.

92. *See generally* IGNATIUS & STICKNEY, *supra* note 70, § 4:11.

93. Del. S.B. 30, An Act to Amend Title 13 of the Delaware Code Relating to Civil Unions, 146th Gen. Assembly (May 11, 2011, effective Jan. 1, 2012); Haw. S.B. 232, A Bill for an Act Relating to Civil Unions, 26th Leg. (Feb. 23, 2011, effective Jan. 1, 2012); Ill. S.B. 1716, Religious Freedom Protection and Civil Unions Act (Public Act 96-1513) (Jan. 31, 2011, codified at 750 ILL. COMP. STAT. 75/1); N.J. STAT. ANN. §§ 37:1-2, -6, -29 (2010).

Same-sex couples had access to civil union in Vermont, Connecticut, and New Hampshire before same-sex marriage was authorized in these states. Civil unions in Connecticut and New Hampshire were automatically converted to marriages; civil unions in Vermont remain valid unless couples choose to convert to marriage.

94. CAL. FAM. CODE §§ 297-299 (2010) (domestic partnership); NEV. REV. STAT. §§ 122A.010-.510 (2010); OR. REV. STAT. §§ 106.300-106.340 (2010) (domestic partnership), WASH. REV. CODE §§ 26.60.010-.090 et seq. (2010) (domestic partnership). *See also* D.C. CODE ANN. § 32-702 (2010) (domestic partnership).

95. *See* CAL. FAM. CODE § 297(b)(5)(B) (2010); N.J. STAT. § 26:8A-4 (2010).

96. This follows a unanimous decision of Brazil's Supreme Court on May 5, 2011.

97. Civil Union Act, 2004 S.N.Z. No. 102 (N.Z.) (effective Apr. 26, 2005). *See* Bill Atkin, *Landmark Family Legislation*, 2006 INT'L SURV. FAM. L. 304, 317.

98. Civil Partnership and Certain Rights and Obligations of Cohabitants Act (No. 24 of 2010) (Ir.) (effective Jan. 11, 2011).

99. Civil Partnership Act 2004 (U.K.). The act came into force for England, Wales, Scotland, and Northern Ireland in December 2005. *See generally* MARK HARPER ET AL., CIVIL PARTNERSHIP— THE NEW LAW (2005).

100. *See* COLO. REV. STAT. §§ 15-22-101 to -112 (2010) (Designated Beneficiary Agreement Act); ME. REV. STAT. ANN. tit. 22, § 2710 (2010) (domestic partner registry); MD. CODE ANN., HEALTH— GEN. § 6-101 (2010) (domestic partnership defined; documentation requirements); WIS. STAT. ANN. §§ 770.001-.18 (2010) (domestic partnership).

101. *See* Ian Curry-Sumner, *Interstate Recognition of Same-Sex Relationships in Europe*, 59 J. GENDER RACE & JUST. 59, 61-63 (2009) (citing laws). Other European countries allowed for registered partnerships before legalizing same-sex marriage, including Belgium, Iceland, the Netherlands, Norway, Spain, and Sweden; *see id.* For Austria, the legislation is the Eingetragene Partnerschaft Gesetz [EPG] [Registered Partnership Act] Bundesgesetzblatt [BGB1 I] No. 135/2009 (Austria).

102. Constituciones de 2008, art. 68 (Ecuador). The law in Ecuador limits adoption to opposite-sex couples.

103. Ley No. 18.246 [Unión Concubinaria] Dec. 18, 2007 (Uru.). In Uruguay, same-sex couples must live together for five years before registering their civil union.

104. *See* Stephen Ross Levitt, *New Legislation in Germany Concerning Same-Sex Unions*, 7 ILSA J. INT'L & COMP. L. 469 (2001).

105. Bundesgesetz über die eingetragene Partnerschaft gleichgeschlechtlicher Paare [Federal Law on Registered Partnerships of Same Sex Couples] (Partnerschaftsgesetz, Part G), SR 211.311 2004 (Switzerland); *see* Ingeborg Schwenzer & Anne-Florence Bock, *New Statutory Rules on Registered Partnership and Protection Against Domestic Violence*, 2008 INT'L SURV. FAM. L. 445; CURRY-SUMNER, *supra* note 76, at 159-202.

106. *See* Curry-Sumner, *supra* note 101, at 73-115; Helen Stalford, *Family Law, in* JOHN BELL ET AL., PRINCIPLES OF FRENCH LAW 258-62 (2d ed. 2008); Claude Martin & Irène Théry, *The PACS and Marriage and Cohabitation in France*, 15 INT'L J.L. POL. & FAM. 135 (2001).

107. *E.g.*, Marvin v. Marvin, 557 P.2d 106 (Cal. 1976); *see generally* CYNTHIA GRANT BOWMAN, UNMARRIED COUPLES, LAW, AND PUBLIC POLICY 47-91 (2010); Ann Laquer Estin, *Ordinary Cohabitation*, 76 NOTRE DAME L. REV. 1381 (2001).

108. *See, e.g.,* Elden v. Sheldon, 758 P.2d 582 (Cal. 1988) (no claim for loss of consortium or negligent infliction of emotional distress); Sykes v. Propane Power Corp., 541 A.2d 271 (N.J. Super. Ct. App. Div. 1988) (no wrongful death claim); Peffley-Warner v. Bowen, 778 P.2d 1022 (Wash. 1989) (no inheritance rights). *But see* Lozoya v. Sanchez, 66 P.3d 948 (N.M. 2003) (allowing cohabitant consortium claim).

109. *See supra* notes 26-29 and accompanying text.

110. *See, e.g.,* Vasquez v. Hawthorne, 33 P.3d 735 (Wash. 2001); Whorton v. Dillingham, 248 Cal. Rptr. 405 (Cal. Ct. App. 1988).

111. *See, e.g.,* Posik v. Layton, 695 So. 2d 759 (Fla. Dist. Ct. App. 1997) (enforcing express written contract).

112. *Marvin,* 557 P.2d at 112. Some state courts have refused to enforce cohabitation contracts. *See* Hewitt v. Hewitt, 394 N.E.2d 1204 (Ill. 1979); Rehak v. Mathis, 238 S.E.2d 81 (Ga. 1977).

113. *See* Estin, *supra* note 107, at 1395-1402.

114. *See id.* at 1391-95.

115. *See* Bill Atkin, *The Challenge of Unmarried Cohabitation—The New Zealand Response,* 37 FAM. L.Q. 303 (2003). De facto same-sex and opposite-sex couples have the same rights in New Zealand.

116. Reg Graycar & Jenni Milbank, *From Functional Family to Spinster Sisters: Australia's Distinctive Path to Relationship Recognition,* 24 WASH. U. J.L. & POL'Y 121 (2007). *See also* BOWMAN, *supra* note 107, at 194-201.

117. *See* JULIEN D. PAYNE & MARILYN A. PAYNE, CANADIAN FAMILY LAW 45-63 (2d ed. 2006). *See also* BOWMAN, *supra* note 107, at 186-94.

118. *See* BOWMAN, *supra* note 107, at 206-14. Same-sex cohabitants are not eligible for cohabitation benefits in France.

119. *See* JORGE A. VARGAS, MEXICAN LAW FOR THE AMERICAN LAWYER 573-617 (2009).

120. Under Colombia's 1991 Constitution, a *union de hecho,* or de facto union, is legally equivalent to marriage. In January 2009, Colombia's Constitutional Court ruled that this status was also available to same-sex couples. *See 42 Disposiciones Modificó La Corte Constitucional Para Amparar Derechos De Las Parejas Gay,* eltiempo.com, Jan. 28, 2009.

121. Am. Airlines, Inc. v. Mejia, 766 So. 2d 305 (Fla. Dist. Ct. App. 2000). *Cf.* T.T. v. K.A., 2008 WL 2468525 (N.Y. Sup. Ct. 2008) (unpublished) (recognizing Ghanaian customary marriage as equivalent to common law marriage).

122. 645 N.Y.S.2d 979 (N.Y. Surr. Ct. 1996), *aff'd,* 666 N.Y.S.2d 697 (N.Y. App. Div. 1997); *see also* Estate of Gernold, 800 N.Y.S.2d 329, 330 (N.Y. Surr. Ct. 2005); Estate of Jenkins, 506 N.Y.S.2d 1009 (Surr. Ct. 1986).

123. 7 Cal. Rptr. 3d 13 (Cal. Ct. App. 2003). *See also* Estate of Duval, 777 N.W.2d 380 (S.D. 2010) (holding that concubinage in Mexico is not equivalent to a common law marriage).

124. *Mejia,* 766 So. 2d at 305. *See also* Bansda v. Wheeler, 995 A.2d 189 (D.C. 2010) (unregistered domestic partnership in the Netherlands not equivalent to common law marriage).

125. *See generally* SCOLES ET AL., *supra* note 20, § 13.5. For the contemporary formulation of this rule, see RESTATEMENT (SECOND) OF CONFLICTS OF LAWS § 283(2): "A marriage which satisfies the requirements of the state where the marriage was contracted will everywhere be recognized as valid unless it violates the strong public policy of another state which had the most significant relationship to the spouses and the marriage at the time of the marriage."

126. *See infra* note 141 and accompanying text.

127. *E.g.,* CAL. FAM. CODE § 308 (2010); UMDA § 210, *supra* note 16; *see generally* CLARK, *supra* note 5, at 87.

128. As Koppelman demonstrates, the Full Faith and Credit Clause has not been read to require that states recognize marriages from other states. Koppelman, *Interstate Recognition, supra* note 84, at 2146-47.

129. *See generally* CLARK, *supra* note 5, § 2.7. The presumption is codified in California, *see* CAL. EVID. CODE § 663, *applied in* Estate of DePasse, 118 Cal. Rptr. 2d 143, 155 (Cal. Ct. App. 2002) (executor successfully rebutted presumption by proving that parties never obtained a marriage license). *See also* James v. James, 45 S.W.3d 458 (Mo. Ct. App. 2001) (presuming ceremonial marriage to be valid despite fact that evidence of Mexican law was "not compelling").

130. *See, e.g.,* CAL. FAM. CODE § 2251 (2010); *DePasse,* 118 Cal. Rptr. 2d at 155-56; UMDA § 209. *See supra* notes 30-31 putative marriage and notes 66-70 (presumption of validity of most recent marriage) and accompanying text.

131. *E.g., In re* Valente's Will, 188 N.Y.S.2d 732 (N.Y. Surr. Ct. 1959) (recognizing proxy marriage in Italy); *In re* White, 223 N.Y.S. 311 (N.Y. Surr. Ct. 1927) (recognizing religious ceremony and subsequent cohabitation of parties as valid marriage in Ontario). *Cf.* Farah v. Farah, 429 S.E.2d 626 (Va. Ct. App. 1993) (proxy marriage not valid in England).

132. *See* RESTATEMENT (SECOND) OF CONFLICT OF LAWS § 283, cmt. I (1971). *See generally* SCOLES ET AL., *supra* note 20, § 13.6. Hudson Trail Outfitters v. D.C. Dep't of Employment Servs., 801 A.2d 987 (D.C. 2002), applied the traditional conflicts rule, concluding that an exchange of vows in a religious ceremony in Nicaragua did not establish a valid marriage where the parties did not comply with the necessary civil formalities.

133. 55 P.3d 74, 77 (Ariz. Ct. App. 2002) (finding that marriage would have been valid if solemnized in Arizona). *But see* Estate of Rodriguez, 160 P.3d 679 (Ariz. Ct. App. 2007) (applying Arizona law to find Arizona marriage void despite fact that couple resided in Mexico). An unpublished decision in New York applied the Restatement rule and New York law to uphold an unlicensed marriage of a New York couple in an Islamic ceremony in New Jersey followed by a reception in New York. Estate of Farraj, 886 N.Y.S.2d 67 (Table); 2009 WL 997481 (N.Y. Surr. Ct. 2009) (unpublished).

134. Verma v. Verma, 903 N.E.2d 343, 346 (Ohio Ct. App. 2008), held that the wife had the "burden to prove that the alleged 1994 Hindu marriage ceremony occurred, and that it was valid under the law of India." The dispute in Madireddy v. Madireddy, 886 N.Y.S.2d 495 (N.Y. App. Div. 2009), centered on a 1952 Hindu religious marriage ceremony in India; the court concluded that it could not determine whether this was a valid Hindu marriage based on neutral principles of law.

135. 248 P.3d 94 (Wash. Ct. App. 2011).

136. *E.g.,* Marriage of Ma, 483 N.W.2d 732 (Minn. Ct. App. 1992).

137. 648 N.W.2d 900 (Wis. Ct. App. 2002). At the time of the marriage, the husband was part of a Hmong guerrilla army working with U.S. Central Intelligence Agency. The dispute in *Xiong* followed the wife's accidental death more than 20 years later. The court upheld the marriage and ruled that the husband was a surviving spouse, so that the couple's children could not bring a wrongful death action. The court based its ruling on the putative spouse doctrine, and also discussed the presumption of validity and the possibility that the parties had concluded a common law marriage.

138. 730 N.Y.S.2d 212 (N.Y. Sup. Ct. 2001). *Amsellem* was a divorce case, in which the husband argued that the marriage was not valid. The religious marriage ceremony in France was performed by a rabbi from New York, and the parties returned afterward to live in New York. The court concluded that the defendant had not provided "documentation or facts sufficient to overcome the strong presumption that the parties are married," and noted that "even if the parties' marriage were deemed null and void, this Court would nevertheless have subject matter jurisdiction over the ancillary issues which include custody and visitation of the parties' children, support, distribution of the parties' joint assets, etc." *Id.* at 214-15. *Cf.* Bronislawa K. v. Tadeusz K., 393 N.Y.S.2d 534 (N.Y. Fam. Ct. 1977) (refusing to recognize prior religious marriage celebrated in Poland without civil formalities where that would invalidate wife's current marriage).

139. Farah v. Farah, 429 S.E.2d 626 (Va. Ct. App. 1993). The couple had lived as a married couple for most of a year in Virginia, and the court noted that Virginia law did not recognize proxy or common law marriages. Because it found no valid marriage, the court vacated the divorce decree and equitable distribution order, and left the parties "to seek such other remedies as are appropriate to determine and resolve their property rights." *Id.* at 630.

140. The parties' domicile is usually the state with the most significant relationship to the spouses and the marriage for this purpose; *see* RESTATEMENT (SECOND) OF CONFLICT OF LAWS § 283, cmt. k (1971). *See also* SCOLES ET AL., *supra* note 20, §§ 13.7-.8.

141. *E.g.,* ARIZ. REV. STAT. ANN. § 25-112 (2010); 750 ILL. COMP. STAT. 5/216 (2010); MASS. GEN. LAWS ANN. ch. 207, § 10 (2010); *see also* IOWA CODE § 595.20 (2010). *See generally* CLARK, *supra*

note 5, at 87; Scoles et al., *supra* note 20, § 13.13; Koppelman, *Interstate Recognition, supra* note 84, at 2152–53.

142. *See* Koppelman, *Interstate Recognition, supra* note 84, at 2153–62.
143. *E.g.*, Leszinske v. Poole, 798 P.2d 1049 (N.M. Ct. App. 1990); May's Estate, 114 N.E.2d 4 (N.Y. 1953). *See generally* Scoles et al., *supra* note 20, §§ 13.11–.12.
144. 114 N.E.2d 4 (1953). The marriage was challenged in estate proceedings after the couple had lived together for 32 years.
145. 170 A.2d 726 (Conn. 1961). Although the uncle-niece marriage was prohibited by the Italian Civil Code, the couple obtained legal dispensation for the marriage from Italian authorities.
146. Ghassemi v. Ghassemi, 998 So. 2d 731, 748–49 (La. Ct. App. 2008). The opinion notes that first-cousin marriages were not prohibited by the common law, and are not within the biblical incest restrictions in Leviticus 18. *Id.* at 747.
147. At one time, interracial marriages violated the criminal law of many states, but these restrictions have been unconstitutional since Loving v. Virginia, 388 U.S. 1 (1967). For case law, *see* Scoles et al., *supra* note 20, § 13.10, and Koppelman, *supra* note 84.
148. *E.g.*, Matter of H, 9 I. & N. Dec. 640 (BIA 1962); Matter of Mujahid, 15 I. & N. 546 (BIA 1976). *Cf.* Seth v. Seth, 694 S.W.2d 459 (Tex. Ct. App. 1985) (applying Texas law to conclude that husband's attempted *talaq* divorce of first wife and subsequent remarriage to second wife did not validate second marriage).
149. 142 N.Y.S.2d 591 (N.Y. Sup. Ct. 1955). *See also* Royal v. Cudahy Packing Co., 190 N.W. 427, 428 (Iowa 1922) (finding potentially polygamous Syrian marriage valid for workers' compensation purposes).
150. 588 N.Y.S.2d 116 (N.Y. Sup. Ct. 1992). Defendant argued that the 13-year-old complainant "was his 'second' or 'junior' wife, given to him by her parents in Nigeria pursuant to the laws and tribal customs of that country…[which] allow one man to have multiple wives." *Id.* at 117.
151. *See* Scoles et al., *supra* note 20, § 13.3; Koppelman, *Interstate Recognition, supra* note 84, at 2162–63.
152. *See generally* Scoles et al., *supra* note 20, §§ 13.17–.19.
153. 188 P.2d 499 (Cal. Ct. App. 1948). *See also* Rhona Schuz, *When is a Polygamous Marriage Not a Polygamous Marriage?*, 46 Mod. L. Rev. 653 (1983).
154. *See* Ignatius & Stickney, *supra* note 70, §§ 4.18 and 6.
155. The statute reads:

In determining the meaning of any Act of Congress, or of any ruling, regulation, or interpretation of the various administrative bureaus and agencies of the United States, the word "marriage" means only a legal union between one man and one woman as husband and wife, and the word "spouse" refers only to a person of the opposite sex who is a husband or a wife.

1 U.S.C. § 7 (2010).
156. *Compare* O'Darling v. O'Darling, 188 P.3d 137 (Okla. 2008), Chambers v. Ormiston, 935 A.2d 956 (R.I. 2007), *and* Marriage of J.B. & H.B., 326 S.W.2d 654 (Tex. App. 2010) (denying jurisdiction), *with* C.M. v. C.C., 867 N.Y.S.2d 884 (N.Y. Sup. Ct. 2008), Beth R. v. Donna M., 853 N.Y.S.2d 501 (N.Y. Sup. Ct. 2008), *and* Christiansen v. Christiansen, 253 P.3d 153 (Wyo. 2011) (assuming jurisdiction to grant divorce).
157. Depending on the context, there are strong constitutional arguments to require this limited recognition. Koppelman makes this argument based on federalism grounds and the constitutional right to travel. *See* Koppelman, *Interstate Recognition, supra* note 84, at 2159–62.
158. New York courts have allowed recognition of same-sex marriages from Canada and Massachusetts in cases involving spousal health care or retirement benefits, *see* Godfrey v. Spano, 920 N.E.2d 328 (N.Y. 2009), and for purposes of divorce cases, *see supra* note 156 and accompanying text. For a case involving parental rights of a same-sex couple married in the Netherlands, *see* Adoption of Sebastian, 879 N.Y.S.2d 677 (N.Y. Surr. Ct. 2009).
159. *See, e.g.*, Cal. Fam. Code § 299.2 (2010) (recognizing legal union, other than marriage, of two persons of the same sex validly formed in another jurisdiction that is substantially

equivalent to a domestic partnership under state law); CONN. GEN. STAT. § 46b-28a (2010) (recognizing validity of marriages and other relationships celebrated in other jurisdictions); N.J. STAT. §§ 37:1-34 (2010) (extending recognition to civil union relationships entered into outside the state), 26:8A-6(c) (2010) (extending recognition to domestic partnership, civil union, or reciprocal beneficiary relationships entered into outside the state). *See also* Recognition in New Jersey of Same-Sex Marriages, Civil Unions, Domestic Partnerships and Other Government-Sanctioned, Same-Sex Relationships Established Pursuant to the Laws of Other States and Foreign Nations, N.J. Att'y Gen. Formal Op. No. 3-2007 (Feb. 16, 2007), 2007 WL 749807.

160. *E.g.*, Langan v. St. Vincent's Hosp. of N.Y., 802 N.Y.S.2d 476 (N.Y. App. Div. 2005).

161. *E.g.*, B.S. v. F.B., 883 N.Y.S.2d 458 (N.Y. Sup. Ct. 2009); *see also* Rosengarten v. Downes, 802 A.2d 170 (Conn. App. Ct. 2002) (decided prior to passage of civil union law in Connecticut).

162. *See* Finstuen v. Crutcher, 496 F.3d 1139 (10th Cir. 2007) (holding that Oklahoma's "Adoption Invalidation Law" violates Full Faith and Credit Clause); Miller-Jenkins v. Miller-Jenkins, 912 A.2d 951 (Vt. 2006); Miller-Jenkins v. Miller-Jenkins, 637 S.E.2d 330 (Va. Ct. App. 2006) (Virginia court may not disregard Vermont custody order under the federal Parental Kidnapping Prevention Act).

163. 930 N.E.2d 184 (N.Y. 2010).

164. British marriage recognition rules are discussed in JOHN MURPHY, INTERNATIONAL DIMENSIONS IN FAMILY LAW 33-119 (2005); HODSON, *supra* note 50, at 28-41. For German rules, see Kurt Siehr, *Private International Law, in* INTRODUCTION TO GERMAN LAW 337, 350 (Mathias Reimann & Joachim Zekoll eds., 2d ed. 2005). *See generally* SCOLES ET AL., *supra* note 20, § 13.4; Lennart Pålsson, *Marriage and Divorce, in* 3 INTERNATIONAL ENCYCLOPEDIA OF COMPARATIVE LAW, ch. 16 (Kurt Lipstein ed., 1978). *See also Special Symposium, International Marriage and Divorce Regulation and Recognition: A Survey,* 29 FAM. L.Q. 497 (1995).

165. Hague Convention on Celebration and Recognition of the Validity of Marriages (Marriage Convention), concluded Mar. 14, 1978, Misc. 11 (1977) Cmnd. 6930, *reprinted in* 16 I.L.M. 18-21 (1977), 25 AM. J. COMP. L. 399 (1977).

166. The Marriage Convention has only three contracting states: Australia, Luxembourg, and the Netherlands.

167. Wilkinson v. Kitzinger, [2006] EWHC 2022 (Fam.), [2007] 1 FLR 295.

168. Civil Partnership Act 2004, ch. 33, §§ 212-18 (Eng.). Courts in New York have extended recognition to foreign same-sex marriages without inquiring into the domicile or nationality of the married partners. *See* cases cited *supra* in notes 156 and 158.

169. AC v. CS 2011 (2) SA 360 (WCC) (S. Afr.).

170. *See* Curry-Sumner, *supra* note 101, at 61-62. *See also* CURRY-SUMNER, *supra* note 76; Katharina Boele-Woelki, *The Legal Recognition of Same-Sex Relationships Within the European Union*, 82 TUL. L. REV. 1949 (2008).

171. Curry-Sumner, *supra* note 101.

172. *See* 8 U.S.C. § 1151(b)(2)(A)(i). Other "immediate relatives" include a U.S. citizen's parents and unmarried children under 21. *See generally* IMMIGRATION LAW & THE FAMILY 1-12 (Charles Wheeler ed., 2009).

173. *See* 8 U.S.C. § 1153(a)(1)-(4). There are four family preference categories, subject to different numerical limits and waiting periods.

174. *See* 8 U.S.C. § 1255(a). *See generally* IGNATIUS & STICKNEY, *supra* note 70, §§ 8:1-:53.

175. *See* 8 U.S.C. § 1184(d). This is the K-1 visa; the fiancé may also obtain K-2 visas for unmarried children under the age of 21. *See generally* IGNATIUS & STICKNEY, *supra* note 70, §§ 14:5-:18; Kerry Abrams, *Immigration Law and the Regulation of Marriage*, 91 MINN. L. REV. 1625, 1650-64 (2007); Wheeler, *supra* note 172, at 76-79.

176. An immigrant with a K visa can only adjust status based on a marriage to the citizen who filed the original application. *See* 8 U.S.C. § 1255(d).

177. *See generally* IGNATIUS & STICKNEY, *supra* note 70, §§ 5:39-:59.

178. 8 U.S.C. § 1183a. *See* Shumye v. Felleke, 555 F. Supp. 2d 1020 (N.D. Cal. 2008); Younis v. Farooqui, 597 F. Supp. 2d 552 (D. Md. 2009); *cf.* Schwartz v. Schwartz, 409 B.R. 240 (B.A.P. 1st

Cir. 2008). In the state courts, *see* Iannuzzelli v. Lovett, 981 So. 2d 557 (Fla. Dist. Ct. App. 2008); Marriage of Sandhu, 207 P.3d 1067 (Kan. Ct. App. 2009); Naik v. Naik, 944 A.2d 713 (N.J. Super. Ct. App. Div. 2008).

179. *See supra* notes 125–162 and accompanying text. *See generally* IGNATIUS & STICKNEY, *supra* note 70, §§ 4:2–:26.

180. *See generally* IGNATIUS & STICKNEY, *supra* note 70, §§ 4:3–:4 and 7:22.

181. *See* 8 U.S.C. § 1101(a)(35) (2010). *See* IGNATIUS & STICKNEY, *supra* note 70, § 4:15.

182. *See* 8 U.S.C. § 1182(a)(10)(A) (2010) (barring admission of "[a]ny immigrant who is coming to the United States to practice polygamy." *See* IGNATIUS & STICKNEY, *supra* note 70, § 4:19; *see also* Abrams, *supra* note 175, at 1670–72 (2007) (regarding nonrecognition of incestuous or polygamous marriages).

183. This is a consequence of the Defense of Marriage Act, cited *supra* note 85. *See* IGNATIUS & STICKNEY, *supra* note 70, § 4:18; *see also* Abrams, *supra* note 175, at 1672–78.

184. *E.g.*, Matter of Balodis, 17 I. & N. Dec. 428, 1980 WL 121911 (BIA 1980). *See generally* IGNATIUS & STICKNEY, *supra* note 70, § 4:4.

185. *See generally* IGNATIUS & STICKNEY, *supra* note 70, §§ 4:20–:33.

186. *See* Lutwak v. United States, 344 U.S. 604 (1953); United States v. Rubenstein, 151 F.2d 915 (2d Cir. 1945); Bark v. Immigration & Naturalization Serv., 511 F.2d 1200 (9th Cir. 1975); Damon v. Ashcroft, 360 F.3d 1084 (9th Cir. 2004). *See also* 8 C.F.R. § 216.5(e) (2010), *applied in* Cho v. Gonzales, 404 F.3d 96 (1st Cir. 2005). *See generally* CLARK, *supra* note 5, § 2.16; Abrams, *supra* note 175, at 1682–94.

187. *See* IGNATIUS & STICKNEY, *supra* note 70, §§ 7:22–:26. The burden is higher in some cases; for example, when a marriage occurs after the initiation of exclusion, deportation, or removal proceedings. *See id.* § 7:8.

188. *See* Immigration Marriage Fraud Amendments, 8 U.S.C. § 1186a (2010). *See generally* IGNATIUS & STICKNEY, *supra* note 70, §§ 5:1–:79. Regulations and case law under the IMFA have further elaborated the test of a bona fide marriage.

189. *See* 8 U.S.C. § 1186a(c)(4) (2010).

190. *See* 8 U.S.C. § 1186a(c)(4)(C) (2010); *see, e.g.*, Hernandez v. Ashcroft, 345 F.3d 824 (9th Cir. 2003) (discussing "extreme cruelty"). *See generally* IGNATIUS & STICKNEY, *supra* note 70, § 4:34–:68; Wheeler, *supra* note 172, at 169–90.

191. International Marriage Broker Regulation Act, 8 U.S.C. § 1375a (2010). *See generally* IGNATIUS & STICKNEY, *supra* note 70, § 14:16; Abrams, *supra* note 175, at 1653–64. *See also* European Connections & Tours, Inc. v. Gonzales, 480 F. Supp. 2d 1355 (N.D. Ga. 2007).

192. 798 N.E.2d 305 (Mass. App. Ct. 2003).

3

Divorce and Separation

Most nations of the world permit divorce, and many have adopted some form of no-fault divorce law, yet international divorce remains a challenging field. The grounds, procedures, and consequences of divorce and separation vary widely in different countries, and divorce laws have resisted harmonization even within the United States and Europe. In the United States, international divorce cases proceed on the same jurisdictional basis as interstate divorce cases. The central distinction is that while divorce or separation decrees from other states are entitled to full faith and credit, foreign judgments are given effect only on the basis of comity.

For practitioners in the United States, cross-border litigation is complicated by the doctrine of divisible divorce, which distinguishes the principles of jurisdiction and recognition of judgments applied to questions of marital status from the principles applied to disputes over marital property and support. These issues are also divided here; this chapter focuses on questions of jurisdiction and choice of law in divorce or separation proceedings and interstate and international recognition of divorce decrees. The financial aspects of marriage and divorce are covered in Chapter 4.

Bringing a Divorce Action

Lawyers working with transnational families decide where to commence divorce proceedings based on a range of practical, legal, and strategic considerations. The determination is often driven by complex and important choice of law concerns regarding child custody or the financial aspects of the case. Because jurisdiction to obtain a divorce or separation decree can be obtained more readily than jurisdiction over ancillary financial matters, the proceeding may be divided between different courts in different places. Members of a couple may start competing proceedings in different jurisdictions. The prospect of parallel litigation raises issues of forum non conveniens, injunctive relief, comity, and recognition of judgments.

Jurisdiction

Jurisdiction for divorce or separation proceedings in the United States is based on the residence or domicile of either spouse in the state where the action is brought. A court with jurisdiction based on the petitioner's residence may enter an ex parte divorce decree, even if it has no basis for exercising personal jurisdiction over the respondent. A court must have full personal jurisdiction over both parties, however, to enter orders concerning financial matters including spousal support and marital property division.[1] This distinction is known as divisible divorce. Issues of child custody or visitation as well as child support are also governed by distinct jurisdictional standards.[2]

Residence and Domicile

Although the rules governing ex parte divorce proceedings were developed for interstate divorce disputes in an era before most states had enacted no-fault divorce laws, courts still apply these rules in interstate and international cases. Under *Williams v. North Carolina*,[3] a state court must have jurisdiction based on the petitioner's domicile in the state in order to enter a decree dissolving a marriage that will be entitled to full faith and credit in other states.[4] "Domicile" and "residence" are often used interchangeably in this context.[5] State laws generally allow individuals to establish a domicile relatively quickly; most statutes define the period of time that a petitioner must reside within the state before filing for a divorce.[6] If a divorce decree is entered ex parte, the court's jurisdiction may be subject to a later collateral challenge.[7] When both spouses participate in the proceeding, however, the respondent and any third parties will be bound by the court's jurisdictional determination.[8] Federal courts do not have jurisdiction in divorce or related proceedings.[9]

Because courts base their jurisdiction on domicile, rather than nationality or citizenship, an alien present in the United States who intends to remain indefinitely may petition for divorce in state court.[10] The cases reach different conclusions on the factual question of whether particular individuals residing in the United States on temporary nonimmigrant visas have established domicile,[11] but they agree on the principle that such individuals may establish residence for divorce purposes despite their temporary status. As one court framed the inquiry: "Immigration status is, at most, evidence of domiciliary intent, but not dispositive of the residency issue as a matter of law."[12] This allows for the possibility of concurrent jurisdiction: An individual may be a resident of a state for jurisdictional purposes even if he or she has a domicile in another country.[13] In the tradition of ex parte divorce, an individual who has established residence in a state

---

Overseas Americans

The U.S. State Department information circular on "Divorce Abroad" is available at
http://www.travel.state.gov/law/family_issues/divorce/divorce_592.html.

For divorce issues involving families of U.S. armed services members, see generally MARK E. SULLIVAN, THE MILITARY DIVORCE HANDBOOK (2d ed., 2011).

Information on divorce issues involving U.S. Foreign Service families is available from the website of the State Department's Family Liaison Office at http://www.state.gov/m/dghr/flo/index.htm.

> **Example: Divisible Divorce**
>
> Husband and Wife are living together in Country X when they separate. Wife returns to her original home in the United States, and a year later she files for divorce in state court. The court can enter a decree terminating the marriage, but it cannot order the husband to pay spousal support unless it has a basis for exercising personal jurisdiction over him.

may obtain a divorce there even if the respondent is a foreign citizen, living abroad, who is not subject to the court's personal jurisdiction.[14]

State court jurisdiction to grant a divorce to a U.S. citizen living abroad is more problematic. Expatriate Americans are obligated to pay U.S. federal income taxes,[15] and they retain the right to vote in national elections.[16] Government employees, particularly those in the armed services, retain a domicile in the state from which they entered service, and they may file for divorce on this basis even after long absences.[17] U.S. citizens with an established foreign domicile may seek a divorce abroad if this is permitted by local law, and courts in the United States should recognize this type of foreign divorce.[18] If divorce is not permitted under local law, the citizen living abroad may have to reestablish residency in the United States in order to bring an action for divorce.[19]

Divisible Divorce

Although an ex parte divorce decree must be given full faith and credit in every state, a decree addressing the financial incidents of divorce is not entitled to full faith and credit unless the court entering the decree had personal jurisdiction over the respondent spouse.[20] As a result of this rule of divisible divorce, a divorce decree issued in one jurisdiction may be followed by a second proceeding in a different jurisdiction to determine support and property rights. In international cases, this may mean that a divorce in the United States will address only the question of marital status and leave financial issues unresolved.[21] Or, a court in the United States may give limited effect to a foreign-country ex parte divorce decree, recognizing the decree as effective to dissolve the parties' marriage but not for other purposes, and then take jurisdiction to address those other matters in a separate proceeding.[22] Note that under the law in some states, the support or property rights of a spouse may be cut off by an ex parte out-of-state or foreign-country divorce decree.[23] In these jurisdictions, taking action to protect these financial interests before any divorce decree is entered may be extremely important.

Same-Sex Marriages and Civil Unions

Jurisdiction to divorce a same-sex married couple or dissolve a civil union or registered partnership may present a complex problem. Difficulties arise when same-sex couples obtain a marriage or civil union in their place of residence and then relocate to a state that does not recognize same-sex unions, as well as when same-sex couples reside in a state that does not allow same-sex unions and travel to a state or country that does for the purpose of formalizing their relationship before returning home.[24] Because jurisdiction over divorce in the United States is based on residence or domicile, both situations present the risk that the couple will not have access to a court with jurisdiction to terminate their relationship. Similarly, Canadian law requires that one of the spouses must be ordinarily resident within the province or territory where a divorce is sought for at least a year immediately before the proceeding begins.[25]

Service of Process

Beyond the question of jurisdiction, due process requires that a respondent must be afforded notice and an opportunity for a hearing, even in the context of an ex parte divorce. The same rule applies in international cases.[26] If a state court has a basis for long-arm jurisdiction over a respondent, state law may authorize personal service on that respondent outside the jurisdiction.[27] The question of whether substituted service is permitted is determined by the law of the forum, but the means utilized must also comply with the laws of the country in which service is made. Practitioners should be aware that personal service or service by mail on a respondent located in another country may violate the law of that country.[28] Where the Hague Service Convention is in force, compliance with its terms is mandatory.[29] Where the Convention is not in force, service may be accomplished by letters rogatory. Note, however, that service under the Service Convention does not confer personal jurisdiction over a respondent who does not have the requisite minimum contacts.

Because of the tradition treating divorce actions as in rem proceedings, some forms of substituted service are permitted under state law when the respondent cannot be located or served using conventional techniques. In *Hollow v. Hollow*, the court approved service by e-mail in a divorce action in which the husband had relocated from New York to Saudi Arabia. Finding that the wife had made reasonable though unsuccessful efforts to effect service through an international process server and husband's employer, the court concluded that those methods were impracticable under the New York rule and that substituted service by e-mail would be the best means of providing the husband with notice of the proceedings.[30] Similarly, in *Porres v. Porres* the court concluded that the expense of personal service on defendant in Italy made it impracticable for an indigent plaintiff, and approved service by mail as an alternative.[31] Substituted service permits the court to proceed with the divorce action, but does not confer in personam jurisdiction, even if the respondent has minimum contacts with the jurisdiction.

Choice of Law

Grounds for divorce are defined by state law, and state courts almost always apply their own divorce statutes when determining whether to grant a divorce.[32] Because every state has now incorporated some no-fault divorce ground into its statutes, the old practices of migratory divorce have largely disappeared, and the choice of law question has become much less important with respect to grounds for divorce.[33] Choice of law issues are more significant with respect to marital property and support rights, particularly in international cases. In the common law world, courts routinely look to the law of the forum as to both grounds for divorce and its financial consequences, but divorce courts in civil law countries apply more elaborate choice of law rules.[34] Because of these different rules, and the possibility that several courts may have concurrent jurisdiction over a divorce, the choice of law question is often fought out indirectly in disputes over jurisdiction, forum non conveniens, and the role of comity with respect to a foreign divorce proceeding or decree.

Foreign-Country Divorce Laws

Most legal systems around the world have some form of no-fault divorce law although it may require mutual consent of the parties or a period of separation.[35] Foreign countries base jurisdiction for divorce on connecting factors including residence or domicile and, in some countries, the nationality of the parties to the marriage.[36] In Canada, the federal Divorce Act confers jurisdiction to grant a divorce on the court of a province where either spouse has been "ordinarily resident" for at least a year before commencing proceedings.[37] Divorce is available on grounds of a breakdown of the marriage, which may be established by proof that the couple has lived separately for a year or by proof of adultery or cruelty by the respondent spouse.[38] In Mexico, divorce jurisdiction is based on the parties' domicile.[39] When there is mutual consent, divorce can be accomplished in some cases in an administrative procedure, or alternatively in a voluntary judicial proceeding. When the spouses do not agree, divorce requires proof of fault grounds such as adultery or cruelty in a contested proceeding filed in the place of conjugal domicile.[40]

Substantive divorce laws differ among the member countries of the European Union (EU), but in most of these nations divorce jurisdiction is defined by the Brussels IIA Regulation, also known as Brussels II *bis* or Brussels II Revised.[41] Under Brussels IIA, courts can exercise jurisdiction in divorce, legal separation, or marriage annulment proceedings in the country where either or both spouses are habitually resident,[42] or in a country for which both spouses hold nationality (or, in the case of United Kingdom and Ireland, where both parties are domiciled). In situations in which more than one country within the EU could assert divorce jurisdiction, Brussels IIA gives an almost absolute priority to the first jurisdiction in which proceedings are filed.[43]

Managing Parallel Proceedings

When divorce litigation is begun in two different courts, each with a valid basis for jurisdiction, a party may seek a stay or dismissal of one proceeding on the basis that the other

---

Foreign Divorce Law

These sources provide an introduction to foreign divorce laws:

Australia: Geoff Monahan & Lisa Young, Family Law in Australia (6th ed. 2006).

Canada: Julien D. Payne & Marilyn A. Payne, Canadian Family Law 174–208 (2d ed. 2006).

France: Helen Stalford, *Family Law, in* Principles of French Law (John Bell et al., eds., 2d ed. 2008).

Germany: Dieter Martiny, *Family Law, in* Introduction to German Law (Joachim Zekoll & Mathias Reimann eds., 2d ed. 2005).

Mexico: Jorge A. Vargas, Mexican Law for the American Lawyer 493–571 (2009).

United Kingdom: Nigel Lowe & Gillian Douglas, Bromley's Family Law (10th ed. 2007).

See also 1 European Family Law in Action: Grounds for Divorce (Katharina Beole-Woelki et al., eds., 2003) (surveying divorce grounds in 22 European jurisdictions); Jeremy D. Morley, International Family Law Practice (2009) (surveying divorce grounds in Australia, Canada, Denmark, England and Wales, France, Germany, Greece, Ireland, Japan, Malta, Mexico, Netherlands, New Zealand, Pakistan, Philippines, Sweden, Switzerland, and Thailand); and Janet Leach Richards et al., Practical Global Family Law: United States, China and Italy (2009).

forum is more appropriate.[44] This happens in domestic as well as international divorce litigation, usually in the context of disputes over financial matters or custody, particularly when one forum has more favorable substantive law.[45] The second court has no obligation to defer to the first court to take jurisdiction, and the determination whether a forum is inconvenient lies within the sound discretion of the trial court.[46] When a court has personal jurisdiction over both spouses, one of the parties may seek to have the other enjoined from litigating in another forum. Courts in different jurisdictions sometimes cooperate by entering provisional orders to secure assets pending resolution of the financial issues in the case.

Inconvenient Forum

In *Marriage of Kimura*, the court described the inconvenient forum doctrine as "a self-imposed limit on jurisdictional power that can be used to avoid unfair, vexatious, oppressive actions in a forum away from the defendants' domicile," and noted that it emerged as a response to expansive approaches to jurisdiction under long-arm statutes. As the court summarized its test, "The mere desire of a party for some other forum is not enough to sustain a dismissal on the grounds of forum non conveniens. Nor is a showing that the claim arose elsewhere enough. . . . What the moving party must show is that the relative inconveniences are so unbalanced that jurisdiction should be declined on an equitable basis."[47] The court also enumerated a series of factors to consider in making this determination, many of which are similar to the factors listed by the U.S. Supreme Court in *Gulf Oil Corp. v. Gilbert*.[48]

The *Kimura* court acknowledged that the case involved a choice of law problem. The husband and wife were married in Japan and lived there for more than 20 years before the husband relocated to the United States. When the husband sought a divorce in Iowa, the wife argued that Japan had more significant contacts with their marriage and that the husband would not be entitled to a divorce under Japanese law. The court refused to decline jurisdiction, noting that its jurisdiction extended only to determining the marital status of the parties and concluding that the husband was entitled to the protection of the Iowa no-fault divorce law.[49]

Some courts considering inconvenient forum questions in divorce cases have focused on jurisdictional issues and the fact that one forum may be in a position to exercise jurisdiction over all issues in a case while the other would have jurisdiction only to dissolve the marriage.[50] This may be a particular concern when one spouse's property or support rights could be lost due to a foreign ex parte divorce decree. If no alternative forum is available, the court is unlikely to stay or dismiss the proceeding.[51]

The arguments for a stay or dismissal are strongest in those cases where the jurisdictional ties are weakest. In the case of simultaneous divorce litigation filed both in London and Los Angeles by Bianca Jagger, the California court noted that Bianca and Mick, the lead singer of the Rolling Stones, had few marital contacts with the state, and pointed out that state courts were congested and California had "no substantial interest" in the case. The court found that the balance of factors "weigh[ed] so heavily in favor of establishing inconvenience . . . as to compel trial court action to abate proceedings," noting also that "the probability, if it exists, that the California court may be more generous in its awards" could not be given any weight.[52]

If a court refuses initially to dismiss or stay its proceedings on inconvenient forum grounds, the issue may come up again after a final judgment is entered in the other forum. At this point, the question becomes one of comity and recognition for the foreign court's decree. The litigation in *Bourbon v. Bourbon* illustrates this point. Husband and wife were French citizens who had relocated to New York and lived there together with their children for more than ten years. A week after the wife filed for a divorce in New York, the husband began proceedings in France. When the husband moved for a dismissal or stay of the action on jurisdictional and inconvenient forum grounds, the New York courts refused, pointing out that the parties had extensive contacts with the state and noting that the French court had issued a temporary support order but no final judgment.[53] After the French court issued a divorce decree, however, the husband renewed his motions, and the New York courts concluded that the French decree was entitled to recognition on the basis of comity.[54]

Other common law countries apply a similar inconvenient forum doctrine, including Canada[55] and the United Kingdom.[56] In the regime established by the Brussels IIA Regulation in the European Union, however, the first court seised in a divorce matter is required to proceed, even if another forum within the EU would be more appropriate. Where there is a potential conflict between a divorce court subject to Brussels IIA and one in a country, such as the United States, that is not subject to the regulation, the law is less clear.[57]

Injunctive Relief

A different response to parallel proceedings or the threat of parallel proceedings is to seek an injunction restraining the other party from filing or continuing to litigate in another forum.[58] Courts in the United States view anti-suit injunctions as an extraordinary step, to be ordered only in unusual circumstances.[59] In *Arpels v. Arpels*, the New York Court of Appeals refused to approve an injunction against French divorce proceedings, writing that the injunctive power should be "rarely and sparingly employed, for its exercise represents a challenge, albeit an indirect one, to the dignity and authority of that tribunal. Accordingly, an injunction will be granted only if there is danger of fraud or gross wrong being perpetrated on the foreign court."[60] Canadian courts are similarly reluctant to grant injunctions to restrain foreign litigation when competing proceedings are filed in both a Canadian court and a foreign jurisdiction.[61]

Courts may issue injunctions to protect their jurisdiction and prevent the confusion and complexity of multiple suits on the same issues. The court must have personal jurisdiction over both parties to enter this type of injunction.[62] An injunction against maintaining a divorce action in another jurisdiction is generally not appropriate when the spouse sought to be enjoined has a bona fide domicile in the foreign jurisdiction that was established before the litigation began.[63] Injunctive relief should be more readily available against a party who has filed multiple proceedings or refused to comply with the court's orders.[64] In those states where a spouse's support or property rights would be affected by a foreign ex parte divorce, injunctive relief may be sought to address this risk.

Temporary injunctive measures are often employed in divorce cases to prevent one spouse from transferring, encumbering, concealing, or disposing of financial assets during the litigation.[65] This relief may be available on an ex parte basis, and courts may agree to freeze assets held by banks or other third parties.[66] In international cases, this may require cooperation between authorities in different countries.[67] Asset-freezing injunctions, sometimes with a worldwide scope, are commonly issued by English courts in divorce proceedings.[68]

Dealing with Domestic Violence

Separation and divorce proceedings pose heightened risks of serious domestic violence, and screening for these issues should be part of all divorce representation.[69] Spousal and partner violence pose particularly difficult legal and financial issues in cross-border divorce cases. Safety planning is often complicated by cultural and language barriers and immigration or visa issues. Americans abroad may not have access to resources that are commonly available in the United States, such as civil protection orders or domestic violence shelters. In urgent situations, U.S. consular officials may be able to assist U.S. citizens in returning to the United States. For domestic violence cases in which an alleged abuser is a member of the armed services, a Military Protective Order (MPO) may be issued to protect the victim as an administrative matter by the military commander. An MPO is enforceable by military rather than civilian authorities and remains in place while the allegations are investigated.[70]

In the United States, every state has a process for obtaining civil protection orders, and federal law mandates recognition of these orders across state borders.[71] Some states have enacted the Uniform Interstate Enforcement of Domestic-Violence Protection Orders Act, which provides for enforcement of orders issued in other states and includes an optional procedure for advance registration of civil protection orders.[72] The act does not apply to protection orders issued by tribunals in foreign countries.[73]

A victim of spousal or partner abuse who relocates into a state may seek protection orders or other relief from the local authorities. In many states—but not all—courts have authority to issue protection orders to petitioners who have recently arrived in a state; but these courts will not order affirmative relief without personal jurisdiction over the respondent.[74] Depending on the facts, a court may be able to assert personal jurisdiction in a domestic abuse case under a long-arm statute. For example, in *McNair v. McNair*, a court in New Hampshire concluded that it had long-arm jurisdiction over a woman's ex-husband who lived in Texas based on a series of harassing and threatening phone calls he made to her in New Hampshire.[75]

For assistance in international domestic violence cases, contact the Americans Overseas Domestic Violence Crisis Center (AODVCC) at http://www.866uswomen.org. AODVCC operates an international toll-free crisis line: 866-USWOMEN (879-6636). To call toll-free from outside the United States, begin by dialing the AT&T USADirect access number, available at http://www.usa.att.com/traveler/access_numbers/index.jsp, and then enter the crisis line number at the prompt.

For consular assistance, contact the U.S. State Department, Bureau of Consular Affairs, Office of American Citizens Services, at (202) 647-5525 or (202) 647-5226; http://www.travel.state.gov. Contact information for U.S. consulates and embassies around the world is available at www.usembassy.gov.

Further Reading: International Divorce Proceedings

DAVID HODSON, A PRACTICAL GUIDE TO INTERNATIONAL FAMILY LAW (2008).

JEREMY D. MORLEY, INTERNATIONAL FAMILY LAW PRACTICE (2009).

Various forms of U.S. immigration relief are available to a battered or abused spouse who is married to a U.S. citizen or legal permanent resident. The battered spouse may petition, without the knowledge or consent of the other spouse, for classification as an immediate relative eligible to become a legal permanent resident of the United States. This relief is also available to the children who have been abused. Among other requirements, the battered spouse must show that he or she currently resides in the United States, that the abusive treatment occurred in the United States, or that the abusive spouse is a U.S. government employee or military servicemember.[76]

Spousal abuse has significant ramifications for other aspects of divorce proceedings, including custody and child abduction matters. Screening for domestic violence is especially important in cases where mediation is contemplated. In an international case with a history of family violence, it is important to collect whatever documentary evidence may be available in the other countries involved, including medical records, police reports, prior protection orders, and court records.

Recognition of Divorce and Separation Decrees

There are strong policy arguments for upholding the validity of a divorce obtained in another jurisdiction, including the concern to prevent "limping marriages," terminated in one jurisdiction but still valid in another. These policies are reflected in the 1970 Hague Convention on the Recognition of Divorces and Legal Separations and in the U.S. case law that gave rise to the doctrine of divisible divorce. In view of these policies, recognition for a foreign-country divorce decree presents a different and much easier problem than the question of recognition for foreign-country orders regarding the financial aspects of divorce or child custody and child-support matters.[77] Although the United States has not signed or ratified the Hague Divorce Convention, courts recognize most foreign-country divorce decrees based on principles of comity. An individual seeking recognition and enforcement of a foreign-country divorce or separation decree may file an action for this purpose in a state court in the United States.[78]

Comity

Within the United States, a divorce or separation decree entered in one state is entitled to recognition in every other state based on the Full Faith and Credit Clause of the Constitution. Decrees from foreign nations are not entitled to full faith and credit, but they are often recognized on a discretionary basis as a matter of comity. A divorce obtained in a foreign country based on domicile or habitual residence of one or both parties in that country will generally be recognized in the United States. Two types of foreign divorces have generated problems, however: migratory divorces obtained abroad when neither party had an established residence in the forum,[79] and ex parte divorces obtained by one spouse in a foreign proceeding in which the other spouse did not have notice or opportunity for a hearing.

General principles of comity are elaborated in *Hilton v. Guyot* and the *Restatement (Second) of Conflict of Laws* and the *Restatement (Third) of Foreign Relations Law*.[80] The Supreme Court's opinion in *Hilton* articulated a broad recognition principle for divorce judgments: "A decree confirming or dissolving a marriage, is recognized as valid in every country, unless contrary to the policy of its own law."[81] Under this test, courts sitting in jurisdictions with restrictive divorce laws factored divorce policy considerations into the comity determination; but with the broad expansion of no-fault divorce in the United States, most of the public policy concerns of the older decisions are no longer relevant. Today, the primary inquiry in divorce cases is whether the foreign judgment meets basic due process requirements.

Section 484 of the *Restatement (Third) of Foreign Relations Law* states that "courts in the United States will recognize a divorce granted in the state in which both parties had their domicile or their habitual residence at the time of divorce, and valid and effective under the law of that state." Under Section 484, state courts may—but need not—recognize a migratory or ex parte foreign divorce.[82] This reflects the divergent approaches to migratory and ex parte divorces taken by different states at a time when divorce laws were relatively strict and spouses sought "tourist divorces" in places such as Mexico and the Dominican Republic.[83] Now that all states have adopted non-fault divorce laws,[84] the more important policy concern is whether extending comity to a foreign ex parte divorce would adversely affect the property or support rights of the absent spouse.[85]

In determining whether to recognize a foreign divorce judgment, courts assess the foreign court's jurisdiction based on standards applied in the United States[86] that focus on domicile or residence rather than other possible connecting factors, such as nationality. State courts generally adopt the same approach to international ex parte divorces that they take in interstate cases. When an individual with a foreign residence or domicile obtains a judicial divorce in that country, state courts routinely recognize the foreign decree as effective to terminate the marriage, even if it was entered ex parte.[87] Courts also recognize a foreign divorce decree obtained by one spouse in the country where the other spouse resides.[88] Conversely, courts do not generally give effect to an ex parte divorce obtained abroad by an individual who is domiciled in the United States.[89]

As is true in the domestic context, courts deciding whether to extend comity in international cases require that the respondent must have had notice and an opportunity to be heard. Without proof of notice, the decree is not subject to recognition.[90] If the respondent received notice and chose not to participate, he or she may be foreclosed from challenging the divorce in a subsequent proceeding.[91] When the respondent participated in the foreign divorce litigation, state courts routinely recognize the resulting decree,[92] and a spouse who has participated in a foreign divorce proceeding or relied upon it may be estopped from challenging its validity.[93] In cases of extrinsic fraud, a court may allow a collateral challenge to a foreign divorce decree and deny comity on that basis.[94]

The rules governing comity for foreign divorce decrees must be considered in light of the doctrine of divisible divorce. In the case of an ex parte foreign divorce, state courts

---

Example: Recognition of Foreign Divorce

Husband and Wife are married in the United States, but live together for many years in Country X. When the parties separate, Husband returns to the United States, and Wife relocates to Country Y, where she eventually obtains a divorce. If Husband had notice and an opportunity to be heard in the proceedings in Country Y, the divorce will be recognized in the United States.

---

extend only partial recognition, giving effect to the decree for purposes of terminating the marriage but not with respect to ancillary property or financial matters.[95] If the foreign divorce court had personal jurisdiction over both petitioner and respondent, however, its decree may be given full effect. This is the usual result when the respondent entered an appearance in the foreign proceeding,[96] and it may occur even if the respondent did not participate where circumstances indicate that the foreign court had a basis for exercising personal jurisdiction over the respondent.[97] State courts make this determination based on U.S. standards of due process.[98]

To be recognized in the United States, a foreign divorce order must have been valid and effective under the law of the place where it was entered. A party offering proof of a foreign divorce should be careful to comply with the procedural and evidentiary rules of the forum, including requirements for authentication and translation of foreign documents.[99] Once proved, foreign decrees are presumed valid until evidence is presented to the contrary.[100] Resolving these issues may require pleading and proof of foreign law.[101] As with other aspects of comity, determination of the validity of a foreign divorce is within the discretion of the court asked to recognize the decree. Thus, despite documentary evidence and the testimony of a foreign attorney, the court in *Adams v. Adams* concluded it would not extend comity to a purported Honduran divorce that appeared to contradict the requirements of Honduran law.[102]

Nonjudicial Divorces

Religious or nonjudicial divorces, such as a Muslim *talaq* or Jewish *get*, have no secular legal effect if performed in the United States.[103] Some early cases considered whether to extend comity to foreign nonjudicial divorces that would not have been valid if obtained in the United States; these cases generally concluded that a divorce should be recognized if it was legally valid in the place where the parties were domiciled.[104] State courts and immigration authorities still give effect on this basis to foreign divorces obtained under religious or customary law by parties living in the country where the divorce was obtained.[105] The same recognition is extended to divorces based on tribal custom obtained by Native Americans living in reservation communities within the United States.[106] In these cases, the more substantial problem centers on what evidence will be considered sufficient to prove the fact of a nonjudicial divorce. Proof of civil registration, or an order from a local court confirming the customary or religious divorce, may be necessary.[107] Based on these principles, courts in the United States should also recognize administrative divorces granted in countries that permit this type of procedure.[108]

When asked to recognize a nonjudicial divorce, courts apply the same rules of comity that they apply to other foreign divorces, including the requirements of jurisdiction, notice, and an opportunity to be heard. Courts refuse to recognize a customary or religious divorce obtained unilaterally by one spouse in another country at a time when the married couple was resident in the United States, even if the individuals have ties (such as nationality) to the country where the divorce was obtained that might support its jurisdiction.[109]

Public policy considerations are part of the traditional approach to comity in divorce cases, reflected in the test established in *Hilton v. Guyot*.[110] In *Aleem v. Aleem,* the court cited the state Equal Rights Amendment in holding that enforcement of a talaq divorce, "where only the male, i.e., husband, has an independent right to utilize *talaq* and the wife may utilize it only with the husband's permission, is contrary to Maryland's constitutional provisions and thus is contrary to the 'public policy' of Maryland."[111] The parties in *Aleem* had lived in Maryland for 20 years but were still citizens of Pakistan when the wife filed for divorce in Maryland. While the action was pending, the husband performed *talaq* in a written document executed at the Pakistan Embassy and then asked the state court to dismiss the wife's claims for divorce and division of marital property, including a substantial pension from husband's employment at the World Bank.[112] Similarly, in *Matter of Ramadan* the court found that public policy supported the trial court's decision to retain jurisdiction over divorce proceedings commenced in New Hampshire despite a religious divorce decree that husband subsequently obtained in Lebanon.[113]

An alternative public policy approach focuses on the problem of limping divorces and the complications that result when a couple is divorced in one place yet still married in another. With its traditional emphasis on domicile to the exclusion of other connecting factors, such as nationality, U.S. case law is at odds with the broader approach toward recognition of foreign divorces emerging in international law.[114] Now that unilateral no-fault divorce is almost universally available in the United States, there is little reason to resist recognition of foreign divorce decrees based on residence or nationality. In the context of ex parte decrees, the rule that gives effect to such decrees for purposes of terminating marital status but not for determining the financial incidents of marriage is usually sufficient to protect the important interests of the absent spouse.[115]

Foreign Recognition of Divorce and Separation Decrees

To facilitate the process of obtaining recognition and enforcement of a U.S. divorce decree, the parties or their counsel may have the decree authenticated through either the Hague Apostille Convention or the traditional legalization process.[116] The question whether a divorce decree obtained in the United States will be recognized abroad depends on the law of the country in which recognition is sought.[117] Foreign divorces obtained in the domicile of either party are regularly given effect in England[118] and other common law jurisdictions, including Canada,[119] Australia,[120] and New Zealand.[121]

Obtaining recognition for a foreign judgment concerning civil status is simpler than securing recognition and enforcement of a foreign money judgment, which typically requires the judgment creditor to bring a new action for enforcement of the foreign-court judgment.[122] This is true in France, where foreign judgments concerning civil status and child custody may be recognizable without a court proceeding, while money judgments typically require enforcement through an exequatur proceeding.[123] In Germany, exequatur proceedings are necessary unless both spouses were nationals of the foreign country

---

Hague Divorce Convention

Hague Convention on the Recognition of Divorces and Legal Separations (June 1, 1970), 978 U.N.T.S. 393, *reprinted in* 8 I.L.M. 31 (1969).

The full text and current information for the Divorce Convention is available from the Hague Conference website at http://www.hcch.net (under "Conventions" and "18").

---

where the divorce was ordered at the time of the divorce decree.[124] The rules and procedure for recognition of financial judgments are different in different legal systems; in some, recognition of foreign judgments may depend on proof of reciprocity.[125] Foreign courts commonly refuse to recognize in personam judgments from the United States that are based on jurisdictional grounds that are not accepted in local law. Although this may not present problems for a simple divorce decree, it will complicate recognition of financial or other orders entered by a court based on either a minimum contacts approach or personal service within the jurisdiction ("tag jurisdiction").

The Hague Divorce Convention

Nineteen nations, located primarily in Europe, have joined the 1970 Hague Convention on the Recognition of Divorces and Legal Separations, designed to facilitate international recognition of divorce and separation decrees.[126] The United States participated in negotiations, but it has not ratified the Divorce Convention, which is effective only between its members. The Convention requires that member states give effect to divorce and separation decrees obtained in officially recognized proceedings in any contracting state, if those proceedings were based on one of a series of possible jurisdictional grounds listed in the Convention. The enumerated grounds include nationality and habitual residence. Contracting states may refuse to recognize a divorce under the Convention "when, at the time it was obtained, both the parties were nationals of States which did not provide for divorce and of no other State," or if recognition would be "manifestly incompatible with their public policy."[127] The Convention addresses only recognition of divorces and legal separations, and specifically "does not apply to findings of fault or to ancillary orders" such as "orders relating to pecuniary obligations or to the custody of children."[128]

European Union Principles

For countries within the European Union (EU), different frameworks apply to conflict-of-laws questions involving other member states of the EU and those involving countries outside the EU, such as the United States.[129] Between EU member countries, jurisdictional and conflict-of-laws issues in matrimonial matters are governed by the Brussels IIA

Brussels IIA Regulation

Council Regulation (EC) No. 2201/2003 of 27 Nov. 2003 concerning jurisdiction and the recognition and enforcement of judgments in matrimonial matters and the matters of parental responsibility ("Brussels IIA").

> **Example: Brussels IIA Jurisdiction**
>
> Husband and Wife are French citizens who have been living for several years in England when their marriage ends. Husband relocates to the United States, and Wife remains in England. If Wife begins divorce proceedings in England, the tribunal can exercise jurisdiction based on the couple's habitual residence there. Husband may commence divorce proceedings in France, based on the couple's joint French nationality. If proceedings are commenced in both England and France, the first court to obtain jurisdiction must hear the case, and the second court must stay its proceedings. Alternatively, if Husband were to file for divorce in the United States rather than France, that proceeding would not be affected by Brussels IIA.

Regulation.[130] As is true of the Divorce Convention, Brussels IIA does not address issues such as divorce grounds or ancillary financial matters, but it also addresses proceedings concerning matters of parental responsibility, including measures for the protection of a child, whether or not those matters arise in connection with a divorce proceeding.

Under Brussels IIA, courts of the Member States have jurisdiction over divorce, legal separation, or marriage annulment when one or both spouses have been habitually resident within the territory of that State.[131] In addition, courts have jurisdiction in these cases based on the nationality or domicile of both spouses.[132] Under these tests, courts in EU countries often are able to take jurisdiction in divorce cases involving EU citizens who are habitually resident in non-EU countries, including the United States, and also are able to take jurisdiction in cases involving U.S. citizens who are habitually resident within the EU. Among member states, in cases of concurrent jurisdiction, the Regulation accords a strict priority to the first court seised, and imposes a mandatory stay, or lis pendens, on the other court. The Regulation does not permit a court to decline jurisdiction on the basis of forum non conveniens.[133] Brussels IIA does not address choice of laws issues, which are resolved as a matter of national law in each member country.[134]

Divorce and Immigration

For some individuals, divorce has significant immigration consequences. A person who is present in the United States on a derivative visa, for example as the spouse of a person holding a student or work visa, will lose that status automatically should the couple divorce. This may be an important factor to consider in timing a divorce decree.[135] If the derivative spouse applies for another nonimmigrant visa before the divorce is finalized, he or she will be able to remain in the United States while the application is considered.[136] In cases of domestic violence, a battered spouse with a derivative visa may be able to obtain a "U" visa to remain in the United States; this visa requires showing that he or she is a victim of criminal activity that caused substantial physical or mental abuse and that the individual has been or will be helpful to the investigating or prosecuting authorities.[137]

Divorce also presents risks for an immigrant to the United States seeking lawful permanent residence status based on his or her marriage to a U.S. citizen. A person in this situation who has been married less than two years at the time of application receives conditional permanent residence status for two years, and the couple must file jointly to remove the condition at the end of the two-year time period.[138] The law ordinarily requires proof that the marriage relationship continues, but the joint filing requirement can be waived in three circumstances: if termination of conditional status and deportation would cause extreme hardship, if the marriage was entered into in good faith but has subsequently been terminated, or if the marriage was entered into in good faith but during the marriage the immigrant spouse was subject to abuse or mental cruelty.[139] Counsel representing a conditional resident spouse in divorce or annulment proceedings should consult with an immigration expert to determine whether factual allegations made in the family law matter may jeopardize his or her immigration status.[140]

Further Reading: Divorce Recognition

MÁIRE NÍ SHÚILLEABHÁIN, CROSS-BORDER DIVORCE LAW: BRUSSELS II BIS (2010).

Special Symposium, International Marriage and Divorce Regulation and Recognition: A Survey, 29 FAM. L.Q. 497 (1995).

Notes

1. See Chapter 4 for the jurisdictional rules governing the financial aspects of divorce litigation.
2. See Chapter 5 for jurisdiction in parentage and child custody matters, and Chapter 7 for jurisdictional rules in child-support cases.
3. 317 U.S. 287 (1942) (*Williams I*).
4. *See generally* RESTATEMENT (SECOND) OF CONFLICT OF LAWS §§ 70-72 (1971). Personal jurisdiction over the parties is generally not sufficient for this purpose. *See* Pennoyer v. Neff, 95 U.S. 714 (1877). On the issues discussed in this section, *see generally* 2 ROBERT C. CASAD & WILLIAM B. RICHMAN, JURISDICTION IN CIVIL ACTIONS § 9-2, at 259-65 (3d ed. 1998); 1 HOMER H. CLARK, JR., THE LAW OF DOMESTIC RELATIONS IN THE UNITED STATES § 13.2, at 703-32 (practitioner's ed., 2d ed. 1987). Jurisdiction to grant a judicial separation exists when the court could grant a decree dissolving the marriage or if the court has personal jurisdiction over both spouses. *See* RESTATEMENT (SECOND) OF CONFLICT OF LAWS § 75.
5. *See, e.g.*, Guedes v. Guedes, 845 N.Y.S.2d 416 (N.Y. App. Div. 2007); *but see* Midkiff v. Midkiff, 562 S.E.2d 177 (Ga. 2002) (domicile not sufficient to confer jurisdiction; actual residence required); Gutierrez v. Gutierrez, 921 A.2d 153 (Me. 2007) (same). On the definition of domicile, *see generally* CLARK, *supra* note 4, § 4.2, at 261-68; EUGENE F. SCOLES ET AL., CONFLICT OF LAWS 232-83 (4th ed. 2004). The American concept of domicile is much more fluid than the English approach; in the divorce context, it is similar to the concept of habitual residence used in Europe and the various Hague Conventions. *See* Friedrich Juenger, *Recognition of Foreign Divorces—British and American Perspectives*, 20 AM. J. COMP. L. 1, 31 (1972) ("Usually a person's habitual residence will be the same as his domicile in the American sense. Roughly speaking, one might say it equals domicile minus esoterics.") *See also* DAVID HODSON, A PRACTICAL GUIDE TO INTERNATIONAL FAMILY LAW 101-09 (2008) (addressing domicile and residence under English law).
6. *E.g.*, CAL. FAM. CODE § 2320 (2004) (requiring residence for six months); NEV. REV. STAT. § 125.020 (2004) (requiring residence for six weeks); N.Y. DOM. REL. LAW § 230 (1999) (requiring residence for two years in some circumstances). *See also* Vaile v. Eighth Judicial Dist. Court, 44 P.3d 506, 511-14 (Nev. 2002) (concluding that court did not have personal jurisdiction over either party or subject matter jurisdiction over their marital status).
7. Williams v. North Carolina, 325 U.S. 226 (1945) (*Williams II*).
8. *See* Sherrer v. Sherrer, 334 U.S. 343, 352 (1948); Cook v. Cook, 342 U.S. 126, 128 (1951). *See also* Vaile, 44 P.3d at 512-14 (concluding that decree entered without jurisdiction was voidable rather than void in the circumstances and concluding that spouse was estopped from

attacking the validity of the divorce). *See generally* RESTATEMENT (SECOND) OF CONFLICT OF LAWS § 73 (1971).

9. *See* Ankenbrandt v. Richards, 504 U.S. 689, 703 (1992) (upholding the "domestic relations exception" to federal jurisdiction). On federal court jurisdiction in family law matters, see Chapter 1.

10. SCOLES ET AL., *supra* note 5, § 4.30, at 266–67.

11. *Compare* Adoteye v. Adoteye, 527 S.E.2d 453, 456 (Va. Ct. App. 2000) (holding that Ghanaian wife working for the World Bank in U.S. on nonimmigrant visa had not established intention to become resident or domiciliary), *with* Alves v. Alves, 262 A.2d 111, 115–16 (D.C. 1970) (concluding that British husband working in the United States for the IMF had established domicile despite temporary visa). Rozsnyai v. Svacek, 723 N.W.2d 329 (Neb. 2006), held that a nonimmigrant alien must put forth evidence establishing an intention to make permanent home in the state. *See also* Emile F. Short, Annotation, *What Constitutes Residence or Domicile Within State by Citizen of Another Country for Purpose of Jurisdiction in Divorce*, 51 A.L.R.3d 223 (1973 & Supp. 2009).

12. Marriage of Dick, 18 Cal. Rptr. 2d 743, 746 (Cal. Ct. App. 1993). *See also* Babouder v. Abdennur, 566 A.2d 457, 461 (Conn. Super. Ct. 1989); Weber v. Weber, 929 So. 2d 1165, 1168 (Fla. Dist. Ct. App. 2006); Abou-Issa v. Abou-Issa, 189 S.E.2d 443, 445 (Ga. 1972); Kar v. Nanda, ____ N.W. 2d ____, 2011 WL 117258 (Mich. Ct. App. 2011); Wambugu v. Wambugu, 896 S.W.2d 756 (Mo. Ct. App. 1995); Polakova v. Polk, 669 N.E.2d 498 (Ohio Ct. App. 1995); Marriage of Pirouzkar, 626 P.2d 380, 383 (Or. Ct. App. 1981); Bustamante v. Bustamante, 645 P.2d 40, 42 (Utah 1982).

13. *E.g.*, Bourbon v. Bourbon, 687 N.Y.S.2d 426, 428 (N.Y. App. Div. 1999) (finding that husband was domiciled in France and also a resident of New York). Similarly, some state statutes authorize courts to enter a divorce decree based on the petition of a member of the armed services who has been stationed in the state for a minimum period of time. *See* HOMER H. CLARK, JR., THE LAW OF DOMESTIC RELATIONS IN THE UNITED STATES 426–28 (2d ed. 1988); MARK E. SULLIVAN, THE MILITARY DIVORCE HANDBOOK 404–07 (2d ed. 2011).

14. *E.g.*, Marriage of Kimura, 471 N.W.2d 869, 880 (Iowa 1991) (permitting divorce sought by permanent resident who was Japanese citizen from wife who remained in Japan and had no contacts with the state); Collins v. Collins, 844 N.E.2d 910, 913 (Ohio Ct. App. 2006) (allowing divorce sought by U.S. citizen husband from German citizen wife).

15. *See* Internal Revenue Serv., Publ'n 54: Tax Guide for U.S. Citizens and Resident Aliens Abroad (2010), http://www.irs.gov/pub/irs-pdf/p54.pdf.

16. *See* UNIFORMED AND OVERSEAS CITIZENS ABSENTEE VOTING ACT (UOCAVA), 42 U.S.C. §§ 1973ff to 1973ff-6 (2006).

17. *See* Perry v. Perry, 623 P.2d 513, 515 (Kan. Ct. App. 1981) ("Government employees, and particularly servicemen, may retain the residence from which they entered service no matter how long they are physically away, so long as there is no intent to change."). Although a service member may change his or her military home of record to a state without actually residing there, this may not be sufficient to confer divorce jurisdiction on the state courts. *See* Midkiff v. Midkiff, 562 S.E.2d 177 (Ga. 2002). On the jurisdictional questions involving members of the armed services, *see generally* SULLIVAN, *supra* note 13, at 397–410; George H. Fischer, Annotation, *Residence or Domicile, for Purpose of Divorce Action, of One in Armed Forces*, 21 A.L.R.2d 1163 (1952 & Supp.)

18. *E.g.*, Will of Brown, 505 N.Y.S.2d 334 (N.Y. Surr. Ct. 1986), discussed *infra* at note 87. For an argument in favor of recognition, see Hans W. Baade, *Marriage and Divorce in American Conflicts Law: Governmental-Interests Analysis and the Restatement (Second)*, 72 COLUM. L. REV. 329, 350 (1972).

19. *See* Forrest v. Forrest, 839 So. 2d 839, 841 (Fla. Dist. Ct. App. 2003); Conrad v. Conrad, 597 S.E.2d 369 (Ga. 2004); *cf.* Sherlock v. Sherlock, 545 S.E.2d 757, 762 (N.C. Ct. App. 2001). *See also* Caffyn v. Caffyn, 806 N.E.2d 415 (Mass. 2004) (allowing wife who had recently relocated from Italy to sue for divorce after brief period of residence on basis that irretrievable breakdown of marriage had occurred within the state).

20. Estin v. Estin, 334 U.S. 541, 548 (1948); Vanderbilt v. Vanderbilt, 354 U.S. 416, 418–19 (1957).

21. *E.g.*, Harris v. Harris, 922 N.E.2d 626, 634-35 (Ind. Ct. App. 2010); Marriage of Kimura, 471 N.W.2d 869, 875-76 (Iowa 1991).
22. *E.g.*, Akinci-Unal v. Unal, 832 N.E.2d 1, 3 (Mass. App. Ct. 2005) (holding that wife could pursue her claims for alimony and equitable distribution of assets in Massachusetts after husband had obtained divorce judgments in Turkey and Bahrain). Litigation of marital property and support issues is discussed in Chapter 4.
23. *E.g.*, Marriage of Brown, 587 N.E.2d 648, 653-54 (Ill. App. Ct. 1992) (finding that Illinois state courts have no subject matter jurisdiction to divide marital property under state law except in divorce proceedings); Villarroel v. Villarroel, 562 A.2d 1180, 1181 (Del. 1989) (concluding that Delaware state courts have no subject matter jurisdiction to make equitable distribution of marital property after California divorce decree). *See generally* 2 CLARK, *supra* note 4, § 17.4, at 241-52.
24. *See, e.g.*, Marriage of J.B. & H.B., 326 S.W.2d 654 (Tex. App. 2010); B.S. v. F.B., 883 N.Y.S.2d 458 (N.Y. Sup. Ct. 2009); O'Darling v. O'Darling, 188 P.3d 137 (Okla. 2008); Chambers v. Ormiston, 935 A.2d 956 (R.I. 2007); Rosengarten v. Downes, 802 A.2d 170 (Conn. App. Ct. 2002) (decided before passage of civil union law in Connecticut). Some courts in states that do not allow same-sex marriage have assumed jurisdiction over divorce claims for couples who obtained a same-sex marriage elsewhere. *See, e.g.*, Christiansen v. Christiansen, 253 P.3d 153 (Wyo. 2011); C.M. v. C.C., 867 N.Y.S.2d 884 (N.Y. Sup. Ct. 2008); Beth R. v. Donna M., 853 N.Y.S.2d 501 (N.Y. Sup. Ct. 2008).
25. An act respecting divorce and corollary relief (Divorce Act) § 3(1), R.S., 1985, c. 3 (2d Supp.) (Canada). *See* JULIEN D. PAYNE & MARILYN A. PAYNE, CANADIAN FAMILY LAW 176-78 (2d ed. 2006).
26. *E.g.*, Marriage of Tsarbopoulos, 104 P.3d 692, 697-98 (Wash. Ct. App. 2004).
27. *E.g.*, Farah v. Farah, 323 N.E.2d 361, 366 (Ill. App. Ct. 1975) (confirming personal jurisdiction over defendant in Nigeria who had previously maintained a matrimonial home in Illinois); *cf.* Perry v. Perry, 623 P.2d 513, 516 (Kan. Ct. App. 1981) (finding no personal jurisdiction over wife where parties had never established marital domicile in Kansas).
28. See the discussion of international service of process in Chapter 1.
29. *E.g.*, Collins v. Collins, 844 N.E.2d 910, 913 (Ohio Ct. App. 2006); Saysavanh v. Saysavanh, 145 P.3d 1166, 1169 (Utah Ct. App. 2006).
30. 747 N.Y.S.2d 704, 706-07 (N.Y. Sup. Ct. 2002).
31. 428 N.Y.S.2d 428, 431 (N.Y. Sup. Ct. 1980).
32. *See* RESTATEMENT (SECOND) OF CONFLICT OF LAWS § 285 (1971), *applied in* Sinha v. Sinha, 834 A.2d 600, 605-06 (Pa. Super. Ct. 2003) (concluding that Pennsylvania had dominant interest in parties' marital status).
33. CLARK, *supra* note 4, at 497; SCOLES ET AL., *supra* note 5, § 15.1, at 628-29.
34. *See* JEREMY D. MORLEY, INTERNATIONAL FAMILY LAW PRACTICE 113-25 (2009) (surveying choice of law rules in different countries).
35. *See id.*, at 104-13 (surveying grounds for divorce in different countries).
36. *See id.* at 89-100 (surveying divorce jurisdiction rules in different countries).
37. *See* Divorce Act § 3(1), *supra* note 25. *See generally* PAYNE & PAYNE, *supra* note 25, at 176-78 (2d ed. 2006). If the members of the couple are resident in different provinces and both file divorce petitions, the court in which the first action was filed generally assumes jurisdiction. *Id.*
38. Divorce Act § 8, *supra* note 25; *see* PAYNE & PAYNE, *supra* note 25, at 186-200.
39. *See* JORGE A. VARGAS, MEXICAN LAW FOR THE AMERICAN LAWYER 549-55 (2009).
40. *Id.*
41. Council Regulation (EC) (No. 2201/2003) Concerning Jurisdiction and the Recognition and Enforcement of Judgments in Matrimonial Matters and in Matters of Parental Responsibility (Brussels IIA). Although Denmark is a member of the EU, it has opted out of the Brussels IIA regime. Brussels IIA also does not apply in European jurisdictions are not part of the European Union, including Norway and Switzerland.
42. Brussels IIA, art. 3. *See generally* MÁIRE NÍ SHÚILLEABHÁIN, CROSS-BORDER DIVORCE LAW: BRUSSELS II *BIS* (2010).
43. Brussels IIA, art. 19. *See* SHÚILLEABHÁIN, *supra* note 42, at 188-96.

44. *See, e.g.*, Sinha v. Sinha, 834 A.2d at 606 (declining to defer to proceedings pending in India); Marriage of Kimura, 471 N.W.2d 869, 878–80 (Iowa 1991) (concluding that Japan was not a more convenient forum); Ismail v. Ismail, 702 S.W.2d 216, 223 (Tex. App. 1985) (concluding that Egypt was not a more convenient forum when wife could not sue there for divorce). *See generally* Robin Cheryl Miller, *Doctrine of Forum Non Conveniens: Assumption or Denial of Jurisdiction of Action Involving Matrimonial Dispute*, 55 A.L.R.5th 647 (1998 & Supp.).

45. *E.g., Sinha*, 834 A.2d at 604–05; *see also* Buckner v. Buckner, 622 P.2d 242, 244–45 (N.M. 1981); MacLeod v. MacLeod, 383 A.2d 39, 42 (Me. 1978).

46. *E.g.*, Maraj v. Maraj, 642 So. 2d 1103, 1004 (Fla. Dist. Ct. App. 1994); Apenyo v. Apenyo, ____ A.3d ____, 2011 WL 6015651 (Md. Ct. Spec. App. 2011).

47. *Kimura*, 471 N.W.2d at 878.

48. 330 U.S. 501 (1947). Under *Gulf Oil* there is a strong presumption that the plaintiff's choice of forum should be respected. *See generally* SCOLES ET AL., *supra* note 5, §§ 11.8–.12, at 492–502. *See also* Piper Aircraft Co. v. Reyno, 454 U.S. 235, 255–56 (1981) (distinguishing between resident and foreign plaintiffs and concluding that it may not be reasonable to assume that a U.S. forum is convenient when chosen by a foreign plaintiff). Since a divorce petitioner must be domiciled in the forum state, the *Piper Aircraft* rule is unlikely to apply in a divorce case, although it might be invoked in a proceeding on financial matters.

49. The court observed that although wife might not be permitted to bring a post-dissolution action for alimony and property division in Japan, she could bring such an action in Iowa and take advantage of "liberal rules" governing asset discovery and financial relief. *Kimura*, 471 N.W.2d at 880.

50. *E.g., In re* Ramadan, 891 A.2d 1186, 1191 (N.H. 2006), Vazifdar v. Vazifdar, 547 A.2d 249, 252 (N.H. 1988).

51. *See* Ismail v. Ismail, 702 S.W.2d 216, 223 (Tex. App. 1985). In MacLeod v. MacLeod, 383 A.2d 39 (Me. 1978), a wife sought to enforce a French divorce decree after she had moved to Virginia and her former husband had moved to Thailand. She began an action in Maine and had her former husband personally served within the state when he came for his parents' golden wedding anniversary. *Id.* at 40. The court denied his inconvenient forum motion, noting that the wife had no alternative forum within the United States. *Id.* at 43; *see also* Corning v. Corning, 563 A.2d 379, 380–81 (Me. 1989) (granting dismissal on the ground of forum non conveniens where a suitable alternate forum existed in Massachusetts). *See generally* RESTATEMENT (SECOND) OF CONFLICT OF LAWS § 84 (1971).

52. Jagger v. Superior Court, 158 Cal. Rptr. 163, 167–68 (Cal. Ct. App. 1979). The court concluded that a stay rather than dismissal was appropriate in the circumstances because the English courts had stayed Bianca's divorce proceedings there for so long as she continued to prosecute the action in California. *Id.* at 168. *See also* Marriage of Taschen, 36 Cal. Rptr. 3d 286 (Cal. Ct. App. 2005), *review denied* (2006).

53. 687 N.Y.S.2d 426, 428 (N.Y. App. Div. 1999) (*Bourbon I*). *See also* Mary F.B. v. David B., 447 N.Y.S.2d 375, 378 (N.Y. Fam. Ct. 1982) (allowing wife's action for support to proceed against husband located in New York despite pendency of husband's divorce action filed in France).

54. 751 N.Y.S.2d 302, 304 (N.Y. App. Div. 2002) (*Bourbon II*). The foreign divorce order must be a final judgment. *See* Cahen-Vorburger v. Vorburger, 725 N.Y.S.2d 343, 344 (N.Y. App. Div. 2001).

55. *See* PAYNE & PAYNE, *supra* note 25, at 178–79. For example, Canadian courts may conclude that the other forum is clearly more convenient and stay their own proceedings when the foreign jurisdiction is positioned to deal more comprehensively with the issues in the case. *See id.*

56. *See* HODSON, *supra* note 5, at 84–91; MORLEY, *supra* note 34, at 102–03.

57. *See* SHÚILLEABHÁIN, *supra* note 42, at 201–09.

58. *See generally* RESTATEMENT (SECOND) OF CONFLICT OF LAWS § 53 (1971). *E.g.*, Brown v. Brown, 387 A.2d 1051, 1055 (R.I. 1978) (upholding an injunction preventing husband from pursuing a suit for divorce in Maryland); Verdier v. Verdier, 22 Cal. Rptr. 93, 105 (Cal. Dist. Ct. App. 1962) (overruling an injunction on the basis that the domestic and foreign proceedings concerned separate issues). Injunctions were more commonly ordered on policy grounds to prevent migratory divorce in the time before no-fault divorce had been widely accepted; older cases

are collected in E. H. Schopler, Annotation, *Injunction Against Suit in Another State or Country for Divorce or Separation*, 54 A.L.R.2d 1240 (1957 & Supp. 2000, 2010). *See also* MORLEY, *supra* note 34, at 103–04.

59. See the discussion in Chapter 1; *see generally* SCOLES ET AL., *supra* note 5, § 24.9, at 1273–76. For the English practice on stays, *see* HODSON, *supra* note 5, at 61–100.

60. Arpels v. Arpels, 170 N.E.2d 670, 671 (N.Y. 1960).

61. *See* PAYNE & PAYNE, *supra* note 25, at 178.

62. *See Brown*, 387 A.2d at 1053–54.

63. *See Brown*, 387 A.2d at 1054; *cf.* Jewell v. Jewell, 751 A.2d 735, 738–39 (R.I. 2000) (granting injunction to defendant in divorce case when plaintiff initiated action in Rhode Island and then began new proceeding in Dominican Republic).

64. *See, e.g., Brown*, 387 A.2d at 1054–55. The injunction may not be permanent. *See* Scott v. Scott, 268 N.E.2d 458, 459 (Ill. App. Ct. 1971).

65. *E.g., In re* Sigmar, 270 S.W.3d 289, 295–96 (Tex. App. 2008); *see also* Chlupacek v. Reed, 169 S.E.2d 782 (Ga. 1969) (approving writ of ne exeat to prevent husband from returning to Austria). *Cf.* Fakiris v. Fakiris, 575 N.Y.S.2d 924 (N.Y. App. Div. 1991). *See generally* H.D. Warren, *Injunction Pendente Lite in Suit for Divorce or Separation*, 164 A.L.R. 321 (1946 & Supp.)

66. *E.g.*, Bansal v. Bansal, 748 So. 2d 335 (Fla. Dist. Ct. App. 1999). Courts in the United States may not issue the type of worldwide asset-freezing order known as a *Mareva* injunction in England. *See* HODSON, *supra* note 5, at 111–27; Jonathan I. Blackman, *Provisional Measures in Cross-Border Cases, in* INTERNATIONAL LITIGATION STRATEGIES AND PRACTICE 65 (Barton Legum ed., 2005).

67. *See, e.g.*, Cardenas v. Solis, 570 So. 2d 996, 997 (Fla. Dist. Ct. App. 1990); Marriage of Kosmond, 830 N.E.2d 596, 597 (Ill. App. Ct. 2005); *cf.* Nasser v. Nasser, 859 N.Y.S.2d 445, 445 (N.Y. App. Div. 2008).

68. *See* HODSON, *supra* note 5, at 111–24.

69. *See* REBECCA HENRY, THE CIVIL LAW MANUAL: PROTECTION ORDERS AND FAMILY LAW CASES 3–7 (3d ed. 2007). *See also* Felton v. Felton, 679 N.E.2d 672 (Ohio 1997) (discussing the need for protection orders during and after divorce proceedings).

70. *See* SULLIVAN, *supra* note 13, at 307–31.

71. *See* 18 U.S.C. § 2265, *discussed in* Catherine F. Klein, *Full Faith and Credit: Interstate Enforcement of Protection Orders under the Violence Against Women Act of 1994*, 29 FAM. L.Q. 253 (1995).

72. UNIF. INTERSTATE ENFORCEMENT OF DOMESTIC-VIOLENCE PROTECTION ORDERS ACT, 9 (IB) U.L.A. 159 (2005 & Supp. 2011).

73. For a comparative discussion of domestic violence laws in Australia, Canada, New Zealand and the United States, see PETER G. JAFFE ET AL., CHILD CUSTODY AND DOMESTIC VIOLENCE: A CALL FOR SAFETY AND ACCOUNTABILITY (2003).

74. *See* Shah v. Shah, 875 A.2d 931 (N.J. 2005) (citing state statutes); *see also* Hemenway v. Hemenway, 992 A.2d 575 (N.H. 2010).

75. 856 A.2d 5 (N.H. 2004). *Cf.* Caplan v. Donovan, 879 N.E.2d 117 (Mass. 2008).

76. *See generally* SARAH B. IGNATIUS & ELISABETH S. STICKNEY, IMMIGRATION LAW AND THE FAMILY §§ 4:34-:73 (Susan Compernolle updating ed., 2010).

77. Custody and child support determinations also follow a distinct set of jurisdictional and conflict-of-laws rules; these issues are taken up in Chapter 5 and Chapter 7.

78. *See* Mori v. Mori, 931 P.2d 854, 856 (Utah 1997) (finding that a Japanese divorce decree cannot be registered under Utah Foreign Judgment Act; plaintiff must file an action to have the judgment recognized on the basis of comity). For checklists of issues to consider in securing or opposing recognition of a foreign divorce, *see* MORLEY, *supra* note 34, at 168–73.

79. This was a substantial issue during the period when residents of states with highly restrictive laws traveled to places such as Mexico, Haiti, or the Dominican Republic to obtain a divorce.

80. *See* Hilton v. Guyot, 159 U.S. 113 (1895); RESTATEMENT (SECOND) OF CONFLICT OF LAWS § 98 (1971); RESTATEMENT (THIRD) OF FOREIGN RELATIONS LAW §§ 481–82 (1987). See also the discussion in Chapter 1.

81. *Hilton*, 159 U.S. at 167.
82. According to RESTATEMENT (THIRD) OF FOREIGN RELATIONS LAW § 484(2) (1987):

    Courts in the United States may, but need not, recognize a divorce, valid and effective under the law of the state where it was granted,

    (a) if that state was, at the time of the divorce, the state of domicile or habitual residence of one party to the marriage; or

    (b) if the divorce was granted by a court having jurisdiction over both parties, and if at least one party appeared in person and the other party had notice of and opportunity to participate in the proceeding.

83. *See, e.g.*, Rosenstiel v. Rosenstiel, 209 N.E.2d 709, 713 (N.Y. 1965) (upholding validity of Mexican divorce); Weber v. Weber, 265 N.W.2d 436, 441 (Neb. 1978) (refusing to extend comity to Dominican Republic divorce decree). Note that some states have statutes prohibiting recognition of a migratory divorce; *see, e.g.*, N.H. REV. STAT. ANN. § 459:1 (2007), construed in *In re* Ramadan, 891 A.2d 1186, 1190 (N.H. 2006).
84. Relatively recent examples include Jewell v. Jewell, 751 A.2d 735, 739 (R.I. 2000) (declining to recognize Dominican Republic divorce), and Kushnik v. Kushnik, 763 N.Y.S.2d 889, 893–94 (N.Y. Sup. Ct. 2003) (denying recognition for Mexican Internet divorce.) These issues remain important in a wide range of international divorce cases. *See generally* SCOLES ET AL., *supra* note 5, §§ 15.17–.25, at 648–62; R.F. Chase, Annotation, *Domestic Recognition of Divorce Decree Obtained in Foreign Country and Attacked for Lack of Domicile or Jurisdiction of Parties*, 13 A.L.R.3d 1419 (1967 & Supp. 2009).
85. *See supra* notes 20–23 and accompanying text.
86. SCOLES ET AL., *supra* note 5, at 651. *See also* MORLEY, *supra* note 34, at 167–98.
87. *See, e.g.*, Will of Brown, 505 N.Y.S.2d 334, 342 (N.Y. Surr. Ct. 1986) (giving effect to ex parte Korean divorce obtained by U.S. citizen who had lived in Korea for more than eight years). The court in *Will of Brown* determined that the divorce should be given effect based on petitioner's long-term residence in Korea even if he did not have a technical domicile there. *Id.; see also* Scott v. Scott, 331 P.2d 641, 643 (Cal. 1958); Gould v. Gould, 138 N.E. 490, 494–95 (N.Y. 1923). *See generally* RESTATEMENT (SECOND) OF CONFLICT OF LAWS §§ 71–72 (1971).
88. *E.g.*, Rosenbaum v. Rosenbaum, 210 A.2d 5, 7 (D.C. 1965) (sustaining Mexican bilateral divorce obtained by wife after she had relocated to the District of Columbia; Mexico was marital domicile and husband still lived there); *see also* Chaudry v. Chaudry, 388 A.2d 1000, 1005 (N.J. Super. Ct. App. Div. 1978) (sustaining Pakistani divorce obtained by husband who was resident of U.S.; wife resided in Pakistan).
89. *E.g.*, Basiouny v. Basiouny, 445 So. 2d 916 (Ala. Civ. App. 1984) (refusing recognition to ex parte Egyptian divorce); Matter of Ramadan, 891 A.2d 1186, 1190 (N.H. 2006) (refusing to extend comity to unilateral divorce by *talaq* in Lebanon); Farag v. Farag, 772 N.Y.S.2d 368, 371 (N.Y. App. Div. 2004) (declining to recognize ex parte Egyptian divorce); Atassi v. Atassi, 451 S.E.2d 371, 375 (N.C. Ct. App. 1995) (denying recognition to ex parte Syrian divorce); Tal v. Tal, 601 N.Y.S.2d 530, 533–34 (N.Y. Sup. Ct. 1993) (denying comity to ex parte religious divorce obtained in Israel); *see also* Aleem v. Aleem, 947 A.2d 489, 502 (Md. 2008) (denying comity to talaq divorce performed at Pakistan Embassy in Washington, D.C.).
90. *E.g.*, Marriage of Seewald, 22 P.3d 580, 584–85 (Colo. App. 2001) (declining to recognize Mexican divorce decree where record did not indicate that wife had notice and opportunity for hearing); Parker v. Parker, 21 So. 2d 141, 142 (Fla. 1945) (refusing comity to Cuban divorce obtained by husband where wife had no notice of proceeding).
91. *E.g.*, De Ganay v. De Ganay, 689 N.Y.S.2d 501, 502–03 (N.Y. App. Div. 1999) (enforcing French judgment based on personal service and appearance to request adjournment of proceedings).
92. *E.g.*, Bourbon v. Bourbon, 751 N.Y.S.2d 302, 303–04 (N.Y. App. Div. 2002) (giving effect to bilateral French divorce); Sherif v. Sherif, 352 N.Y.S.2d 781, 784 (N.Y. Fam. Ct. 1974) (giving effect to bilateral Egyptian divorce); Chaudry v. Chaudry, 388 A.2d 1000, 1005 (N.J. Super. Ct. App. Div. 1978) (giving effect to Pakistani talaq divorce decree obtained by husband domiciled in New Jersey that was later confirmed by court in Pakistan; wife lived in Pakistan

and participated in Pakistani court proceeding). Not all cases take this approach, however. *See, e.g.,* Cvitanovich-Dubie v. Dubie, 231 P.3d 983, 990-92 (Haw. Ct. App. 2010) (declining to recognize bilateral foreign divorce that was not based on domicile).

93. *See generally* CLARK, *supra* note 4, § 13.2, at 730-31; Chase, *supra* note 84. In some states, other individuals may also be estopped from challenging a divorce in this situation. *E.g., Cvitanovich-Dubie,* 231 P.3d at 992-97; *see* Newburgh v. Arrigo, 443 A.2d 1031, 1036 (N.J. 1982).

94. *See, e.g.,* Feinberg v. Feinberg, 351 N.E.2d 725 (N.Y. 1976); *cf.* Marriage of DeLeon, 804 S.W.2d 801 (Mo. Ct. App. 1991)

95. *But see* discussion *supra* at notes 20-23 and accompanying text.

96. *E.g.,* Asanov v. Hunt, 914 So. 2d 769, 772 (Miss. Ct. App. 2005).

97. *See* De Ganay v. De Ganay, 689 N.Y.S.2d 501 502-03 (N.Y. App. Div. 1999).

98. *See, e.g.,* Southern v. Southern, 258 S.E.2d 422, 424-25 (N.C. Ct. App. 1979) (refusing to give effect to support decree entered by English court against husband who did not have minimum contacts with England).

99. *E.g.,* Marriage of Seewald, 22 P.3d 580, 584 (Colo. App. 2001) (admitted documents insufficient to prove existence or validity of Mexican decree), Martens v. Martens; 31 N.E.2d 489, 489 (N.Y. 1940) (documents not admissible to prove foreign divorce because not properly authenticated); *see also* Meissner v. Meissner, 707 So. 2d 1040 (La. Ct. App. 1998) (admitting translated and authenticated Brazilian divorce documents); *but see* Yu v. Zhang, 885 N.E.2d 278 (Ohio Ct. App. 2008) (Chinese divorce records not translated because of expense; wife had burden to establish that Chinese court lacked subject matter jurisdiction to enter decree). As discussed in Chapter 1, U.S. embassies or consulates may be asked to authenticate a foreign divorce decree pursuant to 22 C.F.R. § 52 and the Hague Legalization Convention.

100. *E.g.,* Gotlib v. Ratsutsky, 635 N.E.2d 289, 290-91 (N.Y. 1994); Wolff v. Wolff, 389 A.2d 413, 419 (Md. Ct. Spec. App. 1978), *aff'd,* 401 A.2d 479 (Md. 1979).

101. *E.g.,* Kapigian v. Der Minassian, 99 N.E. 264, 266 (Mass. 1912) (holding that law of the spouses' domicile governs marital status, giving effect to dissolution of marriage under local custom in Turkey); Kaur v. Bharmota, 914 N.E.2d 1087, 1094 (Ohio Ct. App. 2009) (finding that marriage had been terminated by customary divorce in India). This is an important problem in immigration cases; *see also* Matter of Nwangwu, 16 I. & N. Dec. 61, 62-63 (BIA 1976) (interim decision) (considering customary dissolution of marriage in Nigeria).

102. 869 A.2d 124, 129 (Vt. 2005). The family court found that the parties had not separated at the time of the purported divorce, and continued to live together as husband and wife for almost 20 years. In declining to give effect to the decree, the court cited a requirement of Honduran law that a divorce could not be ordered if the parties had reconciled.

103. *E.g.,* Aleem v. Aleem, 947 A.2d 489, 502 (Md. 2008) (refusing to recognize talaq divorce performed at Pakistan Embassy in Washington, D.C.); Shikoh v. Murff, 257 F.2d 306, 309 (2d Cir. 1958) (upholding immigration ruling that divorce by talaq concluded in New York and registered with Pakistani consulate was not entitled to comity). *See generally* SCOLES ET AL., *supra* note 5, § 15.24, at 657-61; Note, *United States Recognition of Foreign, Nonjudicial Divorces,* 53 MINN. L. REV. 612, 627-31 (1969). *See also* Ann Laquer Estin, *Unofficial Family Law,* 94 IOWA L. REV. 449 (2009) (discussing interaction of religious and secular family law).

104. *E.g.,* Hansen v. Hansen, 8 N.Y.S.2d 655, 656 (N.Y. App. Div. 1938) (recognizing divorce granted by the King of Denmark where Denmark was "the situs of the marital domicile"); Leshinsky v. Leshinsky, 25 N.Y.S. 841, 842 (N.Y. Super. Ct. 1893) (recognizing rabbinic divorce valid under law of Russia); Kapigian v. Der Minassian, 99 N.E. 264, 265-66 (Mass. 1912) (recognizing dissolution of marriage under local custom in Turkey).

105. *E.g.,* Shapiro v. Shapiro, 442 N.Y.S.2d 928, 931 (N.Y. Sup. Ct. 1981) (recognizing and enforcing orders entered by Rabbinical Court in Israel after personal appearance by both parties, including order that husband "perform all the ritual acts of the 'get' ceremony in accordance with the directions of the Rabbinical court"). *Cf.* Tal v. Tal, 601 N.Y.S.2d 530, 533-34 (N.Y. Sup. Ct. 1993) (refusing to extend comity to divorce decree entered by Rabbinical Court in Israel when wife had no notice of proceeding, did not appear, and had not been a resident of Israel for the previous five years); T.T. v. K.A., 2008 WL 2468525 (N.Y. Sup. Ct. 2008) (unpublished) (comity not extended to Ghanaian customary divorce without notice, hearing, or basis for jurisdiction).

106. *E.g.*, Begay v. Miller, 222 P.2d 624, 628 (Ariz. 1950) (recognizing Navajo divorce); Rogers v. Cordingley, 4 N.W.2d 627, 629 (Minn. 1942) (allowing proof that members of Red Lake tribe were divorced by tribal custom).

107. For example, the talaq divorce in *Chaudry v. Chaudry* was later confirmed by a court in Pakistan, 388 A.2d 1000, 1004 (N.J. Super. Ct. App. Div. 1978), and the customary law divorce in *Kaur v. Bharmota* was partially documented by court records, 914 N.E.2d 1087, 1091 (Ohio Ct. App. 2009).

108. *See* MORLEY, *supra* note 34, at 187–89.

109. *See* cases cited *supra* note 89. This is a narrower rule than the one provided by the Hague Divorce Convention, which the United States has not ratified. *See infra* notes 126–28 and accompanying text.

110. *See* text accompanying note 81.

111. 947 A.2d 489, 500–01 (Md. 2008).

112. The court might have denied comity on other grounds, such as the fact that the parties were long-term residents of the United States, *see* cases cited *supra* note 89; or the fact that the talaq was carried out in the United States, *see* Shikoh v. Murff, 257 F.2d 306, 309 (2d Cir. 1958). The Maryland Court of Special Appeals declined to accept this type of public policy argument in a custody dispute in which the parties did not have connections to the United States at the time the foreign orders were entered. *See* Hosain v. Malik, 671 A.2d 988, 1003 (Md. Ct. Spec. App. 1996).

113. Matter of Ramadan, 891 A.2d 1186, 1191 (N.H. 2006).

114. *See* Juenger, *supra* note 5, at 24–29.

115. The problem is more difficult when it is faced by a spouse in a state with laws that deny the opportunity to litigate marital property and support issues after an ex parte divorce. Note that state courts have refused to allow one spouse's personal or religious objections to prevent the other from obtaining a divorce. *See, e.g.*, Waite v. Waite, 150 S.W.3d 797, 801–02 (Tex. App. 2004); Sharma v. Sharma, 667 P.2d 395, 396 (Kan. Ct. App. 1983).

116. *See* the discussion in Chapter 1.

117. *See generally* Juenger, *supra* note 5, at 29–30; SCOLES ET AL., *supra* note 5, § 15.26, at 662–63. *See also* Erwin N. Griswold, *Divorce Jurisdiction and Recognition of Divorce Decrees—A Comparative Study*, 65 HARV. L. REV. 193 (1951).

118. Family Law Act, 1986, c. 55, § 46 (validity of an overseas divorce shall be recognized if "at the relevant date either party to the marriage . . . was domiciled in that country"). *See generally* JOHN MURPHY, INTERNATIONAL DIMENSIONS IN FAMILY LAW 130–50 (2005) (analyzing the Family Law Act 1986 and the grounds on which recognition may be denied); HODSON, *supra* note 5, at 46–49 (discussing recognition of a foreign divorce obtained by means of proceedings).

119. Divorce Act, R.S.C., ch. 3, s. 22(1) (foreign divorce judgment will be recognized "if either former spouse was ordinarily resident in that country or subdivision for at least one year immediately preceding the commencement of proceedings for the divorce"). *See generally* MARVIN BAER ET AL., PRIVATE INTERNATIONAL LAW IN COMMON LAW CANADA 778–84 (1997) (analyzing the recognition of foreign divorce decrees in Canada and noting "time-honoured rule that a decree granted in the country where the parties are domiciled will be recognized as dissolving the marriage"); 2 JEAN-GABRIEL CASTEL & JANET WALKER, CANADIAN CONFLICT OF LAWS § 17.2 (6th ed. 2005) ("[I]f either spouse was ordinarily resident in the granting country for at least one year immediately preceding the institution of the proceeding, the decree will be recognized in Canada even if the foreign court took jurisdiction on a different ground.").

120. Family Law Act, 1975, s. 104(3) (foreign divorce judgment will be recognized when "the applicant or the respondent . . . was domiciled in the overseas jurisdiction at the relevant date"). *See generally* P.E. NYGH, CONFLICT OF LAWS IN AUSTRALIA 396–410 (6th ed. 1995) (describing the application of the Family Law Act 1975 to foreign divorce judgments); MICHAEL TILBURY ET AL., CONFLICT OF LAWS IN AUSTRALIA 659–93 (2002) (describing the Family Law Act 1975 and Australian common law in relation to the recognition of foreign divorce decrees).

121. Family Proceedings Act, 1980, s. 44 (stating that a foreign divorce judgment will be recognized in New Zealand where "[o]ne or both of the parties were domiciled in that country at the time of the decree, order, or enactment"). *See generally* 2 DICK WEBB ET AL., FAMILY LAW IN NEW

ZEALAND § 11.104, at 617 (13th ed. 2007) (describing the application of the Family Proceedings Act 1980). New Zealand also recognizes foreign divorce decrees when the order is recognized as valid in the country where at least one of the parties is domiciled. *Id.*

122. *See generally* RESTATEMENT (THIRD) OF FOREIGN RELATIONS LAW § 481, reporter's note 6; SCOLES ET AL., *supra* note 5, § 15.26, at 662-63.

123. *See* Bernard Audit, *Private International Law, in* INTRODUCTION TO FRENCH LAW 473-74 (George A. Bermann & Etienne Picard eds., 2008) (describing exequatur proceeding); PETER HERZOG & MARTHA WESER, CIVIL PROCEDURE IN FRANCE 598-600 (Hans Smit ed., 1967) (describing when exequatur is necessary and explaining the treatment of U.S. divorce judgments). On recent changes in the French law, see Alain Cornec & Julie Losson, *French Supreme Court Restates Rules on Jurisdiction, Recognition, and Enforcement of Foreign Decisions in Matrimonial Matters: A New Chance for Old Cases,* 44 FAM. L.Q. 83 (2010).

124. *See* Kurt Siehr, *Private International Law, in* INTRODUCTION TO GERMAN LAW 354 (Mathias Reimann & Joachim Zekoll eds., 2d ed. 2005) (foreign non-European divorce decrees must be submitted to the ministry of justice of the German state in which one of the spouses has habitual residence, unless both spouses were nationals of the foreign nation where the divorce decree was rendered).

125. *See generally* ENFORCEMENT OF FOREIGN JUDGMENTS (Dennis Campbell ed., 1997); ENFORCEMENT OF FOREIGN JUDGMENTS WORLDWIDE (Charles Platto & William G. Horton eds., 2d ed. 1993).

126. 978 U.N.T.S. 393, *reprinted in* 8 I.L.M. 31 (1969). The parties to the Divorce Convention include Australia, China (Hong Kong), Cyprus, Czech Republic, Denmark, Egypt, Estonia, Finland, Italy, Luxembourg, Moldova, Netherlands, Norway, Poland, Portugal, Slovakia, Sweden, Switzerland, and the United Kingdom. *See generally* Juenger, *supra* note 5.

127. Divorce Convention, arts. 7 & 10.

128. Divorce Convention, art. 1.

129. The EU member states are Austria, Belgium, Bulgaria, Cyprus, the Czech Republic, Denmark, Estonia, Finland, France, Germany, Greece, Hungary, Ireland, Italy, Latvia, Lithuania, Luxembourg, Malta, the Netherlands, Poland, Portugal, Romania, Slovakia, Slovenia, Spain, Sweden, and the United Kingdom. (Note that Norway and Switzerland are not EU members.)

130. 2003 O.J. (L 338), Council Regulation (EC) No. 2201/2003 of 27 Nov. 2003 concerning jurisdiction and the recognition and enforcement of judgments in matrimonial matters and the matters of parental responsibility (Brussels IIA).

131. *Id.* at 5. Article 3(1) states:
In matters relating to divorce, legal separation or marriage annulment, jurisdiction shall lie with the courts of the Member State

(a) in whose territory:

the spouses are habitually resident, or

the spouses were last habitually resident, insofar as one of them still resides there, or

the respondent is habitually resident, or

in the event of a joint application, either of the spouses is habitually resident, or

the applicant is habitually resident if he or she resided there for at least a year immediately before the application was made, or

the applicant is habitually resident if he or she resided there for at least six months immediately before the application was made and is either a national of the Member State in question or, in the case of the United Kingdom and Ireland, has his or her "domicile" there;

(b) of the nationality of both spouses or, in the case of the United Kingdom and Ireland, of the "domicile" of both spouses.

When no Member State has jurisdiction under Art. 3, a divorce petitioner may be able to invoke the "residual jurisdiction" recognized in Art. 7. *Id.*

132. *See id.*

133. Arts. 16 and 19. *See also* Cornec & Losson, *supra* note 123, at 89–93.

134. Council Regulation (EU) No. 1259/2010 of 29 December 2010 implementing enhanced cooperation in the area of the law applicable to divorce and legal separation.

135. *See, e.g.*, Marriage of Taschen, 36 Cal. Rptr. 286 (Cal. Ct. App. 2006) (considering spouse's immigration status in deciding motion to bifurcate proceedings and request for stay).

136. 8 U.S.C. § 1258 (2011); 8 C.F.R. pt. 248 (2011). *See also* IGNATIUS & STICKNEY, *supra* note 76, § 14:28–14:29.

137. 8 U.S.C. § 1101(a)(15)(U). *See* IGNATIUS & STICKNEY, *supra* note 76, § 4:73 and §§ 14.124–:127.

138. 8 U.S.C. § 1186a. *See generally* IGNATIUS & STICKNEY, *supra* note 76, §§ 5:1–5:79. The immigrant's children may also be admitted as conditional residents; *see id.* § 5:4.

139. 8 U.S.C. § 1186a(c)(4). *See, e.g.*, Cho v. Gonzales, 404 F.3d 96 (1st Cir. 2005) (granting hardship waiver). Relief may also be possible when the U.S.-citizen spouse has died; *see* IGNATIUS & STICKNEY, *supra* note 76, §§ 14:1–:3.

140. *See generally* IGNATIUS & STICKNEY, *supra* note 76, §§ 5.46–.52. *Cf.* Rodriguez v. INS, 204 F.3d 25, 26 (1st Cir. 2000) (affirming deportation order and noting prior annulment of marriage for fraud).

4

Financial Aspects of Marriage and Divorce

Couples embarking on international marriage or divorce often discover substantial diversity and uncertainty in the laws that shape the financial consequences of their relationship. Although they may attempt to enter into a premarital agreement to define their rights, the law governing marital agreements also varies significantly across jurisdictions. These differences generate conflict-of-laws problems in international divorce proceedings and lead to significant forum shopping.

International divorce cases are complex and difficult, particularly when substantial assets are at stake. Lawyers without international divorce experience should consider involving a colleague with more specialized experience from the outset, ideally before any litigation is filed. In addition, it will often be important to consult with or retain counsel in the other jurisdictions involved.[1] This chapter considers the background rules that govern marital property and support rights, the treatment of premarital and marital agreements, litigation of property and support rights in the context of divorce or separation, and recognition and enforcement of property and support orders.

Marital Property and Support Rights

States can be categorized as either common law or community property states. This distinction has important consequences for spouses' ownership and control of their property during marriage, and it may also generate different outcomes when a marriage ends by death or divorce.[2] Changes in state laws have substantially muted these differences over time, however, particularly with the enactment in common law property states of statutes providing for equitable distribution of marital property in the event of a divorce.[3] Most states in the United States also extend a variety of property rights to a surviving spouse after the death of the other.

In both common law and community property states, courts have jurisdiction to divide the parties' property at the time of a divorce or separation, including assets such as pensions, stock options, and other forms of deferred compensation. Many states define a category of separate property that is not subject to equitable division, typically including assets owned before the marriage and assets acquired by gift or inheritance during the marriage. Some states take a "hotchpot" approach, in which all of the parties' property is available for equitable division. Although "equitable" does not mean "equal," many courts begin with a roughly equal division of the parties' marital or community assets. Premarital agreements are widely accepted as a means of defining the property rights of spouses in the event of a divorce.[4]

State laws also define spousal support rights during marriage and after a separation or divorce.[5] Eligibility for spousal support, also referred to as alimony or maintenance, typically requires a showing of dependence or need. Support may be ordered for a limited term, for an indefinite period, or as a lump sum, also referred to as alimony in gross. It is most commonly awarded to fund a period of transition or rehabilitation after a marriage,[6] and support awards are most likely when there has been a long-term marriage and the couple has significantly divergent earning capacities. In some states, support payments are also used to compensate one spouse for contributions to the marriage or the other spouse's earnings or career. Spousal support orders are generally modifiable in the event of a substantial change in circumstances, and they usually terminate on the death of either party or the remarriage of the recipient spouse.[7]

In the context of divorce proceedings, state courts typically apply the law of the forum to property and support questions without regard to where the couple may have lived during their marriage or where their property was acquired.[8] For jurisdictional reasons, the forum state is usually the parties' last common residence or domicile.[9] Choice of law questions regarding matrimonial property may be important in other settings, however, particularly in inheritance and tax cases. For example, *Estate of Charania v. Shulman* considered English matrimonial property law in deciding the appropriate tax treatment of stock in an American corporation owned by a citizen of the United Kingdom who was domiciled in Belgium at the time of his death.[10] Under the English marital property regime in effect at the time of the couple's marriage in Uganda, the stock would

---

Foreign Property and Support Laws

These sources offer a useful introduction to foreign marital property and support laws:

Australia: GEOFF MONAHAN & LISA YOUNG, FAMILY LAW IN AUSTRALIA (6th ed. 2006).

Canada: JULIEN D. PAYNE & MARILYN A. PAYNE, CANADIAN FAMILY LAW (2d ed. 2006).

France: Helen Stalford, *Family Law, in* PRINCIPLES OF FRENCH LAW (John Bell et al., eds., 2d ed. 2008).

Germany: Dieter Martiny, *Family Law, in* INTRODUCTION TO GERMAN LAW (Joachim Zekoll & Mathias Reimann eds., 2d ed. 2005).

Mexico: JORGE A. VARGAS, MEXICAN LAW FOR THE AMERICAN LAWYER (2009).

United Kingdom: NIGEL LOWE & GILLIAN DOUGLAS, BROMLEY'S FAMILY LAW 980–1086 (10th ed. 2007).

See also 2 EUROPEAN FAMILY LAW IN ACTION: MAINTENANCE BETWEEN FORMER SPOUSES (Katharina Boele-Woelki et al., eds., 2003) (surveying spousal support laws in 22 European jurisdictions); 4 EUROPEAN FAMILY LAW IN ACTION: PROPERTY RELATIONS (Katharina Boele-Woelki et al., eds., 2093) (surveying marital property laws in 26 European jurisdictions); JEREMY D. MORLEY, INTERNATIONAL FAMILY LAW PRACTICE 125–46 (2009) (citing laws regarding division of assets in Australia, Canada, England and Wales, Finland, France, Germany, Greece, Ireland, Islamic countries, Israel, Japan, Netherlands, New Zealand, Singapore, South Korea, Sweden, Switzerland, and Thailand); JANET LEACH RICHARDS ET AL., PRACTICAL GLOBAL FAMILY LAW: UNITED STATES, CHINA AND ITALY (2009).

be characterized as the husband's separate property. Under the law of Belgium, where the couple had relocated before he purchased it, the stock would be community property. The court concluded that under English law the doctrine of immutability applied, so that the change in marital domicile did not automatically effect a change in the spouses' marital property regime.[11]

In looking around the world, wide variations occur in the financial entitlements that arise from a marriage. This is an important reason why international couples enter into agreements before they marry and engage in forum shopping at the time of divorce.[12] Attempts to harmonize the differences between the marital property and support rights of different jurisdictions have had only limited success. The 1978 Hague Convention on the Law Applicable to Matrimonial Regimes has been ratified in only a handful of countries and is not in effect in the United States.[13] The United States has signed the 2007 Hague Convention on the International Recovery of Child Support and Other Forms of Family Maintenance ("Maintenance Convention"),[14] which will mandate cross-border recognition of spousal support orders between participating countries when it comes into effect.[15] Within the European Union (EU), a number of countries have agreed to a regime of "enhanced cooperation" governing choice of law in divorce and separation matters.[16]

Marital Agreements

All states enforce premarital agreements governing property rights on death or divorce.[17] Most states also permit couples to contract around support rights in the event of divorce, and many allow postnuptial agreements concerning either property or support. Rules governing the validity of marital agreements are more stringent than those applied to commercial contracts, however, and the subjects of marital agreements may be limited as a matter of public policy.[18] Within these parameters, state courts have considered and enforced marital agreements entered into in other countries and legal traditions, including some aspects of agreements concluded under Muslim and Jewish law. Because the requirements for validity are different in each state, an important function of marital agreements is to designate the substantive law that the couple wishes to have govern their agreement and their financial relationship.

Enforceability

As with any other contract, a marital agreement is invalid if it was induced by fraud or duress, or if the parties lack capacity to contract.[19] Under the Statute of Frauds, marital agreements must be in writing and signed by the party against whom enforcement is sought. In addition, state laws treat individuals who are engaged or married as being in a confidential relationship, and they generally require that the individuals fully disclose their financial circumstances to each other at the time they enter into an agreement. Because of this confidential relationship, courts scrutinize the circumstances surrounding execution of a marital agreement to protect against the risk of overreaching or undue influence. This is sometimes described as a test of voluntariness. In an international context, when the parties to an agreement have different primary languages, courts also consider the problem of whether a prospective spouse adequately understood the language of the agreement.[20]

The Uniform Premarital Agreement Act (UPAA), which is in effect in some form in many states, requires that an agreement and any subsequent amendment or revocation must be in writing and signed by both parties.[21] Under § 6(a), an agreement is not enforceable if the party opposing enforcement proves that he or she did not execute the agreement voluntarily, or that the agreement was "unconscionable when it was executed" and the party either did not receive or waive the right to receive a fair and reasonable disclosure of the other party's property or financial obligations, or did not have an adequate knowledge of the other party's property or financial obligations.[22]

Independent legal advice for both individuals is an important factor in determining whether a marital agreement was freely entered into. California has particularly stringent requirements. Since 2001, marital property agreements entered into in California are enforceable only if the party against whom enforcement is sought had independent legal representation or was advised to seek counsel and expressly waived representation. The statute includes detailed requirements for waivers of counsel, including a provision that the court must find that an unrepresented party "was proficient in the language in which the explanation of the party's rights was conducted and in which the agreement was written."[23] The California statute also requires that a premarital agreement be presented, along with the advice to obtain independent representation, at least seven days before it is signed.[24]

California and several other states prohibit or give special scrutiny to premarital agreements that modify or eliminate spousal support. At the most permissive end of the spectrum, UPAA § 3(a)(4) allows parties to contract with respect to the modification or elimination of spousal support, and § 6(b) states that if such a provision "causes one party . . . to be eligible for support under a program of public assistance at the time of separation or marital dissolution, a court, notwithstanding the terms of the agreement, may require the other party to provide support to the extent necessary to avoid that eligibility." Several states decline to enforce any agreements concerning spousal support, and others have substituted a general test of unconscionability in place of the more specific provision in § 6(b).[25]

The law's heightened attention to waivers of spousal support is related to the public policy concern that changes in circumstances during a marriage may leave one party in a difficult financial position at the time of divorce, casting a new light on an agreement that may have seemed fair and reasonable at the outset. These concerns are greatest if one spouse would suffer significant economic losses or hardship due to the marriage. In some states, courts conduct a more substantive review of the agreement for unconscionability at the time of enforcement and consider these changes in circumstances.[26]

Foreign-Country Marital Agreements

Because of the diverse approaches to marital contracts in different legal systems, it can be difficult to predict whether and to what extent an agreement concluded in one country will be enforced in another. Several common law countries, including Australia,[27] Canada,[28] and New Zealand,[29] enforce marital agreements on terms generally similar to those in the United States. Although marital contracts contemplating divorce have been regarded as invalid and contrary to public policy in England and Wales,[30] the courts have given greater effect to premarital agreements in recent cases, particularly those involving foreign nationals. For example, *Radmacher v. Granatino* considered the prenuptial agreement of a French-citizen husband and his German-citizen wife, executed before a notary in Germany, which would be treated as valid and enforceable under either German or French law. Although the United Kingdom Supreme Court ruled that the case would be "governed exclusively by English law," it concluded that it was fair in the circumstances to hold the husband to the terms of the agreement.[31]

Marital agreements in the civil law tradition are concluded with different formalities, usually by a notary, who is a lawyer specially trained to prepare and authenticate documents such as wills, deeds, and certain types of contracts.[32] Statutes in many civil law countries define several different marital property systems, and they allow couples to choose among these systems in a marital agreement.[33] Courts in the United States recognize and enforce civil law marital property contracts, even when these agreements establish a regime very different from the background rules of the forum state.[34] Difficulties may arise, however, when the foreign procedures do not meet the standards of state law for disclosure or voluntariness.[35]

At the end of a long-term marriage, the court in *Van Kipnis v. Van Kipnis* enforced a marriage contract executed under French law while the parties were living in Paris, concluding that their choice of a separate property regime precluded equitable distribution under New York law.[36] Other New York cases have enforced a German prenuptial agreement providing for a separate property regime,[37] and a Mexican community property agreement entered into as part of a marriage ceremony in Acapulco.[38] Similarly, *Fernandez v. Fernandez* concluded that a separate property agreement concluded at the time of the spouses' marriage in Mexico should be given effect when the parties divorced in California many years later. In *Fernandez*, the court referred to Mexican law in determining the validity of the agreement.[39]

Choice of Law in Marital Contracts

Marital agreements entered into in one jurisdiction and presented for enforcement in another raise particular difficulties. Under traditional choice of law principles, the law of the place where a contract is executed governs its validity and interpretation, while the law of the place where the contract is to be performed governs matters of breach and enforcement.[40] Courts regularly apply this rule to marital agreements, particularly those involving property rights.[41] Under the *Restatement (Second) of Conflict of Laws* § 188, the law of the place having the most significant contacts with the parties and their dispute applies to their rights and duties under a contract.[42] If support rights are at issue, a court in the domicile or residence of the spouse seeking support has a particularly strong interest in addressing economic hardship that might result from a divorce.[43] In some circumstances, a court might conclude that the parties have abandoned their agreement or their initial implicit choice of law, particularly after a move from one legal system to another.[44] In international cases, the choice of law issue is sometimes discussed in terms of comity; and even under the traditional choice of law rule, a court is not likely to enforce an agreement that violates its strong public policy.[45]

If the parties include a choice of law term in a marital agreement, state courts generally enforce it, provided that the parties have some connection to the forum they select.[46]

UPAA § (a)(7) identifies choice of law as an appropriate subject for a premarital agreement. A choice of law provision may also be subject to public policy objections, however, particularly when there is a substantial difference between what the foreign law permits and what local law would require.[47] Thus, a premarital agreement entered into with no asset disclosure or independent legal advice, or one that includes a waiver of spousal support, might not be enforced in a jurisdiction that requires asset disclosure or legal advice or considers support waivers to be potentially unconscionable.[48] Similarly, a post-nuptial agreement valid in the place where it was executed might not be enforced in a state that prohibits postnuptial agreements.[49]

The variability of these rules makes it difficult to prepare a marital agreement likely to be fully effective in some future litigation in an undetermined time and place. Among other problems, the ordinary risks of ambiguity and omission are significantly increased when the agreement will move with a couple through different legal and financial systems.[50] To increase the likelihood of enforcement, counsel and the parties should pay careful attention to the various aspects of procedural and substantive fairness, including asset disclosure and independent counsel, as well as to choice of law language that clearly identifies the connections to the forum whose law they have selected and indicates their intention that this law should control even if they relocate.[51] Mirror agreements in different jurisdictions are another strategy, but this introduces significant additional complexity.[52] In the interest of protecting the parties' reasonable expectations and allowing for financial planning, courts should evaluate the general enforceability of a marital agreement under the law of the place where it was executed, and give effect to a clear and reasonable choice of law provision, reserving their public policy veto for cases of serious bargaining misconduct or significant unanticipated changes in the parties' circumstances.

Religious Marital Agreements

Courts apply the same general principles to marital agreements entered into in the Jewish or Muslim tradition. To the extent that these agreements provide for performance of a secular act, such as a financial payment, they can be enforced on the same terms as other marital agreements. Thus, a number of courts have enforced a husband's promise to pay a marriage gift, sometimes referred to as dower or *mahr*, even though the promise was made in an agreement that also has religious significance.[53] If an agreement requires performance of an act that the civil court regards as religious, however, a court in the United States will refuse to enforce the provision on First Amendment grounds. Courts have divided opinions on whether one spouse may be ordered to appear before a Jewish tribunal, or *bet din*, to carry out the process of concluding a divorce under Jewish law.[54] To address their concerns around religious divorce, couples sometimes agree to arbitrate their differences in a religious tribunal. As a result, courts have also enforced these agreements within the context of secular arbitration laws.[55]

Marital agreements from religious legal systems are tested under the same rules that courts apply to other marital agreements. For example, in *Marriage of Shaban*, a husband argued that an agreement executed at the time of the parties' marriage in Egypt established their intention to have their property rights governed by Islamic law rather than California community property law, and therefore that the wife should receive only payment of the *mahr* specified in the agreement, with a current value of about $30.00.

The court rejected this argument based on the Statute of Frauds, which requires that a "writing must state with reasonable certainty what the terms and conditions of the contract are. An agreement whose only substantive term in any language is that the marriage has been made in accordance with 'Islamic law' is hopelessly uncertain as to its terms and conditions."[56] In *Marriage of Obaidi and Qayoum*, the court held that under "neutral principles of contract law," an agreement to pay $20,000 in the event of a divorce was not enforceable when the groom could not speak, read, or write the language in which the agreement was written and had not known about it until shortly before he signed it.[57]

Immigration Support Agreements

Since 1996, federal law has required an individual who sponsors the immigration of a family member to file an Affidavit of Support with U.S. Citizenship and Immigration Services.[58] This document is commonly used in marriage cases when a U.S. citizen or lawful permanent resident seeks admission of a fiancé or spouse. Beyond its role as a matter of immigration law, the affidavit is a binding contract that may be enforced by the immigrant in state or federal court.[59] The affidavit requires the sponsor to support the immigrant at or above 125 percent of the federal poverty level unless the sponsor or immigrant dies, the immigrant becomes a U.S. citizen, the immigrant permanently departs the United States, or the immigrant is credited with 40 quarters of covered employment under the Social Security Act.[60] Divorce does not terminate the rights and obligations created by the affidavit, but an immigrant spouse who is capable of self-support at or above the guideline amount may not be able to enforce it.[61]

Separation Agreements

Spouses may enter into agreements to settle financial and other issues incident to their separation or divorce.[62] Courts in the United States favor the private settlement of marital disputes, and separation agreements are generally incorporated into the court's final separation or divorce judgment.[63] The process may be assisted through mediation or other forms of alternative dispute resolution. Agreements are subject to judicial review and may be set aside in cases of unfair bargaining or of unfair or unconscionable terms. The validity of a separation agreement entered into in another country is usually based on the law of the place where it was made. For example, the court in *Untersteiner v. Untersteiner* enforced the alimony and child-support provisions of an Austrian separation agreement against the former husband, who had relocated to the United States, noting that Austria had more significant contacts with the agreement and that Austrian law governed its validity and effect.[64]

Further Reading: Marital Agreements

Laura W. Morgan & Brett R. Turner, Attacking and Defending Marital Agreements (2001).

Jeremy D. Morley, International Family Law Practice 31–63 (2009).

Linda J. Radvin, Premarital Agreements: Drafting and Negotiation (2011).

Litigating Property and Support Rights

With divorce now widely available around the world on various no-fault grounds, forum shopping in divorce litigation centers on marital property and support rights. Despite broad similarities in the types of financial relief that may be available at dissolution of marriage, legal systems take different approaches to questions including what property interests are subject to division between spouses; what are appropriate purposes, amounts, and duration of spousal maintenance; whether marital fault may be considered in determining what financial relief will be awarded; and to what extent marital agreements may be enforced. In countries that apply the law of the forum to the grounds for divorce as well as ancillary financial matters, the question of jurisdiction takes on real strategic importance.

Under the prevailing jurisdictional rules in the United States, a court may enter an ex parte divorce decree based on the petitioner's domicile or residence within the forum state, and that decree will be entitled to full faith and credit in every state.[65] Court orders concerning marital property and support rights, however, are not entitled to full faith and credit unless the forum court had personal jurisdiction over the respondent.[66] For this reason, a state court generally will not decide financial matters unless it has personal jurisdiction over both spouses. Based on the same policies, courts in the United States give effect to many foreign ex parte divorce decrees as a matter of comity, but they do not recognize and enforce financial orders entered by a foreign court unless that court had full personal jurisdiction.[67]

Whenever a court has personal jurisdiction over both spouses, marital property and support issues should be litigated together with an action for divorce. Although these claims may not ordinarily be raised in subsequent litigation as a matter of collateral estoppel or res judicata,[68] these preclusion doctrines do not prevent either spouse from bringing a subsequent proceeding to address unresolved property and support issues after an ex parte divorce entered by a court with no personal jurisdiction over the respondent spouse has entered.[69] Under the law in some states, however, a spouse may be prevented from bringing a postdivorce action to determine his or her financial rights, either because state law holds that the right to spousal support or alimony is terminated by an out-of-state or foreign ex parte divorce or because state courts have concluded that they lack subject matter jurisdiction to entertain such claims apart from a divorce or separation proceeding.[70] In other states, and in the United Kingdom, statutes explicitly authorize courts to provide this type of relief.[71]

Obtaining Jurisdiction

In U.S. law, a state court with personal jurisdiction over the parties may adjudicate marital property issues, even with respect to property located outside the territory of the state.[72] Courts may also assert in rem jurisdiction to adjudicate marital interests in any real or personal property located within the forum state.[73] A decree allocating marital property is not subject to modification and is entitled to recognition in every state on the basis of full faith and credit.

Courts must also have personal jurisdiction and subject matter jurisdiction to adjudicate spousal support issues. Subject matter jurisdiction is conferred by state statutes including the Uniform Interstate Family Support Act (UIFSA), which also provides a choice of law rule.[74] Under UIFSA, a court that has entered a spousal support order retains continuing exclusive jurisdiction, so that no other state may modify the order.[75] Support orders may be registered and enforced in other states under UIFSA, which is also applicable to spousal support orders in international cases.[76]

Courts have several means of acquiring jurisdiction to enter financial orders in a divorce or separation action. By filing an action with a court, a petitioner submits to the court's personal jurisdiction.[77] The court may obtain personal jurisdiction over a respondent based on his or her residence or domicile within the state. For jurisdictional purposes, courts have construed residence and domicile generously in this context, extending their authority to individuals who maintain multiple residences and live only part-time within the state.[78] A court may also exercise personal jurisdiction based on a respondent's general appearance in a proceeding, and a respondent who files a responsive pleading without objecting to jurisdiction is typically deemed to have waived these defenses.[79] In addition, a state court may exercise personal jurisdiction over a respondent who is personally served with process within the forum state. The leading case on this type of "tag jurisdiction" is *Burnham v. Superior Court*, which upheld California's exercise of personal jurisdiction over a defendant in a child-support case based only on the fact that he had been served with process while he was present in the state.[80]

State courts may also exercise personal jurisdiction over nonresident defendants under the provisions of state long-arm statutes. Any assertion of long-arm jurisdiction must meet constitutional due process requirements, which mandate that a defendant have sufficient minimum contacts with the forum state. In the family law context, the leading authority is *Kulko v. Superior Court*, which involved a couple who had lived together in New York before their divorce and the wife's relocation to California.[81] In *Kulko*, the Supreme Court concluded that it would not be reasonable to allow the California courts to exercise personal jurisdiction over the husband, whose only contacts with the state were that he and his wife had been married there, and that he had allowed his children to go there to live with her after their divorce. Citing "basic considerations of fairness," the Court noted that the husband had "remained in the State of marital domicile, whereas it is appellee who has moved across the continent."[82] State courts addressing the question of minimum contacts after *Kulko* routinely find sufficient contacts for jurisdictional purposes where the couple lived together in the state in the relatively recent past, although visits to a state are generally not sufficient.[83]

Some state long-arm statutes extend the courts' jurisdiction to the full extent permitted by the Constitution, and accordingly reach any defendant who has minimum contacts with the state.[84] Other states have long-arm statutes with specific provisions for divorce and related proceedings. Such statutes may extend jurisdiction to any individual who maintained a matrimonial domicile in the state,[85] sometimes requiring that the parties lived together in the state at the time their marriage broke down, or for a minimum period of time, or that one of the parties continued to reside in the state until commencement of the litigation.[86] In some family law matters, courts have relied on long-arm provisions directed at contract and tort cases.[87] Owning property within a state is generally not a sufficient basis for the state courts to exercise long-arm jurisdiction in a divorce case, unless the action concerns allocation of that property.[88] For spousal support claims, the long-arm provision in UIFSA § 201, in effect in every state, extends jurisdiction to its full constitutional reach.[89]

For internationally mobile couples, it may be difficult to identify a forum in the United States that can take jurisdiction over the full range of financial issues in a divorce case.[90] For example, the couple in *Sherlock v. Sherlock* were married in North Carolina and lived in Egypt, Korea, the Philippines, India, Indonesia, Australia, and Thailand during their marriage; their only residence in the United States was a single six-month stay in Georgia. When the parties separated and wife filed an action in North Carolina for support and equitable distribution, the court concluded that their personal and financial ties to the state throughout their marriage were sufficient to support the exercise of personal jurisdiction.[91] In these unusual cases, courts are sometimes willing to push these rules to their limits in order to make a U.S. forum available to the petitioner.[92]

Military Divorces

Divorce cases involving members of the U.S. armed services raise additional complications, particularly when a spouse has been called to active duty.[93] In some cases, litigation will be subject to a stay under the Servicemembers Civil Relief Act.[94] Under the Uniformed Services Former Spouses' Protection Act, special requirements for jurisdiction and service of process apply to actions for equitable division of military retired pay.[95] The mechanics of dividing military pay can be extremely complex,[96] as is the process of obtaining transitional or long-term health care benefits for a nonmilitary spouse after divorce or separation.[97] Spousal and child-support orders may be enforced against a servicemember by garnishment or, if arrearages have accrued, by an involuntary allotment from the pay of an active duty servicemember.[98]

Divisible Divorce

Divorce jurisdiction in the United States is divisible, in the sense that the jurisdiction required to litigate marital status is different from what is required to litigate financial matters, and a court may enter a divorce decree on an ex parte basis even when it does not have jurisdiction over the ancillary issues.[99] After an ex parte divorce proceeding in a state or foreign country where the tribunal did not have personal jurisdiction over both spouses, most states allow either of the parties to bring a separate action for equitable division of marital property, for an award of spousal support, or for custody and child support.[100] These matters may also be raised in an ancillary proceeding following a bilateral divorce if jurisdiction was properly reserved at the time a bilateral divorce was entered.[101] Property rights that flow from the ongoing marriage end at the time of a valid divorce, however. For example, in *Marriage of Notash*, the former wife brought an action for division of community property in Texas several years after the couple was divorced in Iran. The court made a division of the property, but refused to approve damages for breach of fiduciary duty during the period after the divorce.[102]

In some states, the possibility that one spouse will obtain an ex parte divorce generates substantial complications that must be carefully navigated by practitioners. If the spouses have an opportunity to bring a subsequent action in a court with appropriate jurisdiction to resolve any outstanding property and support issues, divisible divorce is a reasonable and workable solution to the jurisdictional dilemmas of divorce.[103] In a small minority of states, which treat claims for spousal support or marital property division as automatically terminated by an out-of-state or foreign divorce judgment, an ex parte divorce may lead to harsh and unfair results.[104] For this reason, a husband or wife with a potential financial

> **Example: Divisible Divorce**
>
> Husband and Wife live together in Country X when their marriage ends. Wife returns to her original home in Country Y, where Husband has never lived and has few connections. Husband moves to the United States. If Wife obtains a divorce from a tribunal in Country Y, she may need to bring a separate action for spousal maintenance and equitable division of marital property in the state where Husband resides.

claim may be well advised not to follow this route, and a spouse who receives notice of an ex parte proceeding may need to act immediately to protect his or her financial rights.[105]

Courts in England and Wales have discretion to grant financial relief after a foreign divorce when either of the spouses is domiciled or resident in the country or when they had a matrimonial home there.[106] This authority is not limited to cases in which the foreign divorce court lacked jurisdiction over both parties, as would be the case in the United States. English courts have concluded, however, that litigants who have already obtained financial orders in foreign proceedings cannot use this procedure to get "another bite at the cherry."[107]

Divorce Jurisdiction in Other Countries

Foreign countries base jurisdiction for divorce on connecting factors including residence or domicile and, in some countries, the nationality of the parties to the marriage.[108] Thus, foreign citizens residing in the United States and U.S. citizens living in another country may find themselves defending divorce proceedings abroad. In Canada, the federal Divorce Act confers jurisdiction to grant a divorce on the court of a province where either spouse has been "ordinarily resident" for at least a year before commencing proceedings.[109] Marital property matters are governed by provincial or territorial law.[110] In Mexico, divorce jurisdiction is based on domicile.[111] Within the EU, divorce jurisdiction is defined by the Brussels IIA Regulation, also known as Brussels II *bis* or Brussels II Revised.[112] Under Brussels IIA, courts can exercise jurisdiction in divorce, legal separation, or marriage annulment proceedings based on the spouses' habitual residence, or based on the spouses' joint nationality or domicile.[113]

In contrast with the "divisible divorce" rule in the United States, many foreign countries do not distinguish between the jurisdiction required for a divorce or separation decree and the jurisdiction necessary to address the couple's property and support rights. From the perspective of courts in the United States, financial orders that

> **Overseas Americans**
>
> The U.S. State Department information circular on "Divorce Abroad" is available at http://www.travel.state.gov/law/family_issues/divorce/divorce_592.html.
>
> For divorce issues involving families of U.S. armed services members, see generally MARK E. SULLIVAN, THE MILITARY DIVORCE HANDBOOK (2d ed. 2011).
>
> Information on divorce issues involving U.S. Foreign Service families is available from the website of the State Department's Family Liaison Office at http://www.state.gov/m/dghr/flo/index.htm.

satisfied jurisdictional rules in the country where they were entered, but that were not based on facts that would give rise to personal jurisdiction over the respondent spouse, would not satisfy the due process requirements for recognition and enforcement in the United States.[114]

In situations where more than one country within the EU could assert divorce jurisdiction, Brussels IIA gives a strict priority to the first jurisdiction in which proceedings are filed, based on a lis pendens principle.[115] This rule prevents the problem of parallel and competing divorce litigation, but it has encouraged forum shopping and a race to the courthouse that is often criticized.[116] Although Brussels IIA does not apply to "property consequences of the marriage or any other ancillary measures,"[117] European courts with jurisdiction to enter a divorce routinely address financial matters in the same proceeding.[118] Because there are major differences between the property and support laws of the EU member countries, the jurisdictional race under Brussels IIA can have significant financial consequences. As a result, individual parties and their lawyers have an incentive to act strategically and to file immediately when problems develop in a marriage.

Within the EU, a group of countries have moved toward a system of "enhanced cooperation" that coordinates the choice of law in divorce and legal separation cases, giving priority to application of the law of the couple's habitual residence before separation.[119] This system should help reduce the jurisdictional race in participating countries, but a significant number of EU member countries, including the United Kingdom, have opted out of the enhanced cooperation regulation.

Managing Parallel Proceedings

International divorce cases present the possibility of concurrent jurisdiction and parallel litigation in courts of different countries. Judges and lawyers may seek to manage competing proceedings by means of stays or injunctions. Even when litigation is centered in one forum, courts in different jurisdictions may cooperate by entering provisional orders to secure assets pending resolution of the financial issues in the case. Cross-border judicial communication and cooperation may be particularly useful in these cases.

Inconvenient Forum

When divorce litigation is commenced in two different courts, each with a valid basis for jurisdiction, a party may seek a stay or dismissal of one proceeding on the basis that the other forum is more appropriate.[120] This happens in domestic as well as international divorce litigation, particularly when one forum has more favorable substantive law.[121] Outside the Brussels IIA regime in Europe, the second court has no obligation to defer to the first court to take jurisdiction, and the determination whether a particular forum is an inconvenient one lies within that court's discretion.[122]

Brussels IIA Regulation

Council Regulation (EC) No. 2201/2003 of 27 Nov. 2003 concerning jurisdiction and the recognition and enforcement of judgments in matrimonial matters and the matters of parental responsibility ("Brussels IIA").

Courts in the United States asked to decline jurisdiction in an international case on the grounds of inconvenient forum typically review a series of factors, often based on the list in the Supreme Court's opinion in *Gulf Oil Corp. v. Gilbert*.[123] If there is no alternative forum available, or no alternative forum in the United States, the court is unlikely to stay or dismiss the proceeding.[124] In divorce cases, one important factor is whether one forum would be able to exercise jurisdiction over all issues in a case while the other would have jurisdiction only to dissolve the marriage.[125] This factor is particularly important when one spouse's property or support rights could be lost due to a foreign ex parte divorce decree.

For example, *Marriage of Kimura* involved a husband who relocated from Japan to the United States and then sought a divorce in Iowa. His wife asked the court to decline jurisdiction, arguing that Japan had the most significant contacts with their marriage and that he would not be entitled to a divorce under Japanese law. Noting that its jurisdiction extended only to determining the parties' marital status, the court refused to decline jurisdiction.[126] Conversely, a California court declined jurisdiction when Bianca Jagger filed simultaneous divorce litigation in London and Los Angeles. Bianca and Mick had few marital contacts with the state and the court found that the balance of factors "weigh[ed] so heavily in favor of establishing inconvenience . . . as to compel trial court action to abate proceedings," noting also that "the probability, if it exists, that the California court may be more generous in its awards" could not be given any weight.[127]

If a court refuses initially to dismiss or stay its proceedings on inconvenient forum grounds, the issue may come up again after a final judgment is entered in the other forum. At this point, the question becomes one of comity and recognition for the foreign court's decree. For example, in *Bourbon v. Bourbon* the husband and wife were French citizens who had relocated to New York and lived there together for more than ten years. A week after the wife filed for a divorce in New York, the husband began proceedings in France. The husband moved for a dismissal or stay of the New York action and the New York courts refused, pointing out that the parties had extensive contacts with the state.[128] When the husband renewed his motions after the French court issued a divorce decree, the New York courts concluded that the French decree was entitled to recognition on the basis of comity.[129]

The inconvenient forum doctrine has long been used in other common law countries, including Canada[130] and the United Kingdom.[131] In a case that falls within the scope of the Brussels IIA Regulation in the EU, however, courts in the United Kingdom have no discretion to decline jurisdiction. For parallel litigation involving two courts subject to Brussels IIA, the first court seised with jurisdiction over the divorce matter is required to proceed, even if another forum would seem to be more appropriate.[132] Where there is a potential conflict between a divorce court in a country subject to Brussels IIA and one in a country, such as the United States, that is not subject to the regulation, the law is less clear.[133] Courts in the United Kingdom have concluded, however, that they have discretion to stay divorce proceedings in deference to litigation filed in a non-EU jurisdiction.[134]

Injunctions

Litigants anticipating complex divorce litigation in multiple jurisdictions may seek to obtain provisional orders to secure assets or an injunction to prevent the respondent from litigating in another forum. Some jurisdictions impose an automatic temporary restraining order on the parties at the time of a divorce action, and case law includes many decisions approving injunctive measures to prevent one spouse from transferring, encumbering, concealing, or disposing of financial assets during the pendency of divorce litigation.[135] Where there is a sufficient showing of potential harm, this relief may be available on an ex parte basis.[136]

Provisional orders sometimes extend to freezing assets held by banks or other third parties,[137] but courts in the United States may not issue the type of worldwide asset-freezing order known as a *Mareva* injunction in England.[138] To the extent that the assets in question are located in other countries, the court issuing an injunction may need to take into account the particular requirements of foreign law.[139] International cases may require cooperation between authorities in different countries. For example, *Cardenas v. Solis* approved a temporary injunction under Florida law, freezing half of the funds in defendant's bank accounts in the state, on the request of a Guatemalan family court.[140]

A litigant faced with parallel proceedings or the threat of parallel proceedings in another forum may attempt to secure an anti-suit injunction restraining the other party from filing or continuing to litigate in another forum.[141] Although courts may issue injunctions to protect their jurisdiction and prevent the confusion and complexity of multiple suits on the same issues, courts in the United States describe anti-suit injunctions as an extraordinary step, to be ordered only in unusual circumstances.[142] In *Arpels v. Arpels*, the New York Court of Appeals refused to approve an injunction against French divorce proceedings, writing that the injunctive power should be "rarely and sparingly employed, for its exercise represents a challenge, albeit an indirect one, to the dignity and authority of that tribunal. Accordingly, an injunction will be granted only if there is danger of fraud or gross wrong being perpetrated on the foreign court."[143] In *Jewell v. Jewell*, however, the Rhode Island Supreme Court upheld a restraining order and a subsequent contempt citation against a husband who filed for divorce in the state and then initiated another divorce action in the Dominican Republic.[144]

A court must have personal jurisdiction over the respondent to impose an anti-suit injunction.[145] The case law suggests that an injunction against maintaining a divorce suit in another jurisdiction is generally not available when the spouse who would be enjoined had a bona fide domicile in that jurisdiction that was established before the litigation began.[146] A respondent spouse may not be permanently enjoined from pursuing marital actions in other jurisdictions.[147] Injunctive relief is more appropriate to protect a spouse whose support or property rights would be extinguished by a foreign ex parte divorce,[148] or in circumstances where one party has filed multiple proceedings or refused to comply with the court's orders.[149]

Determining Choice of Law

Choice of law rules in the United States generally provide that the rights of a married couple in moveable property are governed by the law of their domicile at the time they acquired the property, while their rights in land are governed by the law of the place where the property is located.[150] This ruling generates substantial complexity for couples who have lived and acquired property in more than one place, particularly if they have

---

Further Reading: Litigating Property and Support Rights

DAVID HODSON, A PRACTICAL GUIDE TO INTERNATIONAL FAMILY LAW (2008).

BARON LEGUM, ED., INTERNATIONAL LITIGATION STRATEGIES AND PRACTICE (2005).

JEREMY D. MORLEY, INTERNATIONAL FAMILY LAW PRACTICE (2009).

---

moved between common law and community property jurisdictions.[151] For parties with significant assets, defining the legal regime that will apply to their marital property rights is an important purpose of a premarital or postmarital agreement.

In the context of divorce, the traditional choice of law rules have been criticized as "inconvenient and contrary to the interests of the parties and the divorcing state," which typically has the greatest concern with the spouses' financial circumstances after divorce.[152] Courts in many states apply their own law to all marital property and support issues in divorce, particularly if neither spouse requests application of another law.[153] In several community property states, this approach is mandated by statutes that provide for division of "quasi-community property," defined as all property acquired outside the state that would have been community property if the spouse who acquired it had been domiciled in the state at the time it was acquired.[154]

In spousal support cases, UIFSA § 303 provides that a responding tribunal applies its own procedural and substantive law in determining the duty of support and the amount of support payable. When a court acts to enforce a support order issued by another court, however, § 604(a) provides that the law of the issuing state or foreign country governs the nature, extent, amount, and duration of current payments as well as the computation and payment of arrearages and interest.[155]

A separation or settlement agreement entered into in another country is ordinarily interpreted and enforced under the law of the place of execution, unless the parties have agreed that another law should apply.[156] Similarly, a court interpreting or enforcing a foreign-country court order on the basis of comity will generally give the order the same effect it would have in the country where it was entered.[157]

Recognizing and Enforcing Marital Property Orders

State courts in the United States must extend full faith and credit to financial orders entered in other states, provided that the court had jurisdiction over the parties and that the other requirements of due process were met.[158] The same principles apply to international cases, in which recognition is based on comity. As the Restatements make clear, recognition and enforcement of a foreign decree are two distinct questions.[159] In most states, marital property and support orders may be enforced in a new civil action, based on the foreign court judgment, in a court where it is possible for the judgment creditor to obtain jurisdiction over the judgment debtor or the debtor's property.[160] The claim may be brought as an independent equitable action or raised as a counterclaim, cross-claim, or affirmative defense.[161] In support cases, an enforcement action often falls within the scope of UIFSA.[162] In property cases, a few states allow enforcement under the Uniform

Foreign Money-Judgments Recognition Act (UFMJRA).[163] In real property cases, other remedies may be available. Thus, when the wife in *Mackenzie v. Barthol* brought an ejectment action with respect to real property located in the state of Washington, the Washington court extended comity to a Canadian property division decree and granted her exclusive possession.[164] Although a court cannot enter a decree directly affecting title to real property in another state or country, it may establish and declare the interests of parties present before the court in such property.[165]

Extending Comity

State courts regularly recognize ex parte foreign divorce decrees if the petitioner was resident or domiciled in the foreign country where the divorce was ordered.[166] Because U.S. law requires that a court have personal jurisdiction over both spouses to enter orders concerning property or support matters, financial aspects of an ex parte foreign divorce are not given effect based on comity.[167] When a foreign court has exercised jurisdiction in factual circumstances that meet the requirements of U.S. law, however, the order should be recognized and enforced in state and federal courts.[168]

Building on the Supreme Court's approach to comity in *Hilton v. Guyot*,[169] *Restatement (Second) of Conflict of Laws* § 98 holds that a foreign judgment "rendered after a fair trial in contested proceedings will be recognized in the United States so far as the immediate parties and the underlying claim are concerned."[170] Most states in the United States have abandoned *Hilton's* requirement of reciprocity, which limited recognition based on comity to judgments from countries in which an American judgment would be accorded similar respect.[171] As with a judgment from another state, a foreign court judgment may be challenged on grounds such as the absence of personal or subject matter jurisdiction in the original forum, lack of reasonable notice, or fraud.[172] In the international context, where there is no requirement of full faith and credit, courts have discretion to deny comity when there is a strong public policy objection to the foreign judgment.[173]

To give effect to the property or support aspects of foreign-country divorce or separation decrees, a state court must be satisfied that the foreign court acquired personal jurisdiction over the respondent spouse. This is tested under the standards applied to cases in the United States.[174] In addition, the respondent spouse must have received adequate notice and an opportunity to be heard. When these conditions are met, even a foreign default judgment may be recognized on the basis of comity.[175]

Example: Recognition of Foreign Marital Property Order

Husband and Wife are living together in the United States when they separate. Husband returns to his original home in Country Z, where Wife has never lived and has few connections. After living in Country Z for a year, Husband commences divorce proceedings and obtains a divorce decree, an award of spousal maintenance, and division of marital assets. Unless there is a factual basis to support the court's exercise of personal jurisdiction over Wife, such as minimum contacts or personal service within Country Z, Husband will not be able to enforce the maintenance and property orders in the United States.

Although courts do not extend comity to foreign judgments that violate their strong public policy, courts do extend comity despite substantive differences between the property and support laws of the foreign country and the state where enforcement is sought. For example, in *Leitch v. Leitch* an Iowa court gave effect to a Canadian support judgment despite the possibility that the Canadian court had considered questions of marital fault in entering its order.[176] Similarly, in *Dart v. Dart* a Michigan court extended comity to an English divorce judgment, rejecting the argument that it violated local public policy and noting that the statutory factors governing property division under English law were "virtually identical" to its own standards.[177] In *Downs v. Yuen*, a New York court rejected an argument that a Hong Kong judgment for a lump sum of $10 million should not be recognized based on comity, where defendant had failed to establish his claim that the Hong Kong judicial system did not comport with due process.[178]

Uniform Foreign Money-Judgments Recognition Act

The UFMJRA and its successor, the Uniform Foreign-Country Money Judgments Recognition Act (UFCMJRA), codified common law comity principles to allow enforcement of foreign-country judgments in state courts on the same terms as judgments of other states.[179] By its terms, the UFMJRA does not apply to "judgments for support in matrimonial or family matters," which are subject to recognition based on comity or under UIFSA.[180] In some states, the UFMJRA has been applied to other types of money judgments in divorce cases, such as property division orders; and some states have enacted nonuniform versions of the statute extending to all types of matrimonial claims, including spousal support.[181] The more recent UFCMJRA has a broader exclusion for any "judgment for divorce, support, or maintenance, or other judgment rendered in connection with domestic relations."[182] Both versions of the act reaffirm that matrimonial judgments may be recognized based on comity or other legal principles.[183]

In the small group of jurisdictions in which the original UFMJRA may offer a basis for recognition of foreign divorce money judgments, Section 3 of the statute provides that the judgment "is enforceable in the same manner as the judgment of a sister state which is entitled to full faith and credit." Section 4 specifies a series of grounds for non-recognition of a foreign-country judgment, including lack of personal or subject matter jurisdiction in the issuing court or a finding that "the judgment was rendered under a system which does not provide impartial tribunals or procedures compatible with the requirements of due process of law."[184]

Foreign Recognition of Marital Property Judgments

When judgments from U.S. courts in business and tort cases are presented for recognition and enforcement in foreign courts, the courts may treat these judgments with substantial suspicion because of the different jurisdictional standards used in the United States and the different approach to matters such as contingent fee arrangements and punitive damage awards. There is no broad multilateral convention on recognition of judgments that would reconcile these differences.[185] There is also no multilateral treaty on recognition and enforcement of orders for division of marital property.[186]

Financial judgments in U.S. divorce cases may be recognized based on comity in common law jurisdictions including England, Canada, Australia, and New Zealand. For enforcement of these judgments, additional requirements apply, analogous to the U.S. rules that require personal jurisdiction over petitioner and respondent to adjudicate property rights.[187] In civil law countries, recognition and enforcement of financial judgments typically require an exequatur proceeding and may depend on proof that reciprocal treatment would be extended to comparable orders from that country.[188] Foreign financial judgments may be enforced in Mexico, if the foreign court had jurisdiction in accordance with Mexican principles of jurisdiction and other conditions are met, except that issues concerning title to real property in Mexico are within the exclusive jurisdiction of Mexican courts.[189]

Financial orders entered by a court in a divorce proceeding in the United States that was based on personal jurisdiction acquired through a minimum contacts approach or tag jurisdiction may prove difficult to enforce in a country that does not accept these grounds for jurisdiction. It should be possible to argue for foreign recognition of a U.S. order if the court exercised jurisdiction in factual circumstances that would provide an adequate basis for jurisdiction under the relevant foreign law. For example, many European countries view the residence within the jurisdiction of an individual in need of support as an appropriate basis for litigating family support obligations.

Enforcing and Modifying Spousal Support Orders

In the past, the process of recognizing and enforcing spousal support orders across state borders was complicated because these orders were subject to modification. In the interstate context, the rule developed that a claim for alimony arrearages that had been reduced to judgment was entitled to full faith and credit, but payments due under an alimony decree subject to prospective or retroactive modification could be enforced only on the basis of comity.[190] State courts routinely enforced foreign-country support orders based on comity, following the same principles.[191] In all interstate and most international cases, these questions are now controlled by UIFSA, which applies both to spousal support and child-support orders.[192]

Uniform Interstate Family Support Act (UIFSA)

UIFSA establishes a procedure through which spousal support orders entered in one state may be registered and enforced in another state. The same procedure is available for support orders entered in certain foreign countries. In an enforcement action, the law of the issuing state or foreign country governs the "nature, extent, amount, and duration of current payments" and other obligations of support and the payment of arrearages under the order.[193]

In cases that include orders for both child support and spousal support, a spousal support creditor may be eligible to use the services of the child-support recovery unit, established in each state under federal law. These services are available whenever there is an alimony or maintenance order in force for the custodial parent of a child for whom a child-support obligation is being enforced.[194] Support enforcement services for combined spousal and child-support orders are available in international as well as interstate

---

Foreign Reciprocating Countries

The U.S. government has designated these jurisdictions as reciprocating countries for the purpose of enforcing family support obligations as defined by 42 U.S.C. § 659(a):

Australia	Hungary	Norway	Switzerland
Czech Republic	Ireland	Poland	United Kingdom
El Salvador	Israel	Portugal	
Finland	Netherlands	Slovak Republic	

Canadian Provinces or Territories:

Alberta	New Brunswick	Newfoundland/Labrador	Saskatchewan
British Columbia	Northwest Territories	Nova Scotia	Yukon
Manitoba	Nunavut	Ontario	

International Resources from the U.S. Office of Child Support Enforcement (OCSE) are available at http://www.acf.hhs.gov/programs/cse/international/. State profiles with detailed information on child-support laws, including lists of the foreign countries with which each state has reciprocal support enforcement arrangements, are available through the OCSE Intergovernmental Referral Guide Public Map Page at https://extranet.acf.hhs.gov/irgps/stateMap.do.

---

cases.[195] Under the federal program, states also have the option to make enforcement services available for spousal support orders without a corresponding child-support order.[196]

Since the original version of UIFSA was adopted in 1992, the statute has provided a vehicle for enforcement of support orders entered in foreign countries. The most recent version, adopted in 2008, allows registration and enforcement of a foreign spousal support order if the order was entered by a court in a country that meets the definition of "foreign country" in UIFSA § 102(5).[197] This definition includes four categories: countries that have been declared to be "foreign reciprocating countries at the national level;[198] countries that have established reciprocal relationships with a particular state;[199] countries that have "enacted a law or established procedures for the issuance and enforcement of support orders which are substantially similar to the procedures under UIFSA";[200] and countries in which the Maintenance Convention is in force with respect to the United States.[201] The statute preserves the possibility that a support order from a foreign jurisdiction that is not a "foreign country" may be recognized and enforced on the basis of comity, and § 105(b) permits a court to "apply the procedural and substantive provisions" of UIFSA in such a case. Recognition of another country's support order on this basis is discretionary, however, while recognition and enforcement of "foreign support orders" from countries that fall within the statutory definition is mandatory.[202]

Foreign-country spousal support orders that meet the statutory definition in UIFSA § 102(5) may be registered for enforcement under UIFSA § 601. Once a support order issued in a foreign country is registered pursuant to the statute, § 603(b) provides that it "is enforceable in the same manner and is subject to the same procedures" as an order issued by a tribunal of this State." Under § 603(c), the state tribunal must "recognize and enforce, but may not modify, a registered order if the issuing tribunal had jurisdiction." The choice of law rule in § 604 stipulates that the law of the issuing tribunal governs most

> **Example: Enforcing Spousal Maintenance under UIFSA**
>
> Husband and Wife have lived together in Australia for ten years when their marriage ends and Husband relocates to the United States. After notice and an opportunity for a hearing, Wife obtains a divorce and financial orders from an Australian tribunal. Australia meets the definition of "foreign country" in UIFSA § 102(5), and the spousal maintenance order may be registered for enforcement under UIFSA in the United States.

questions, including the "nature, extent, amount, and duration of current payments" under a registered order, as well as the computation and payment of arrearages and interest. The responding tribunal applies its own procedures and remedies to enforce support and collect arrears; it also applies either its own statute of limitations or the statute of limitations of the issuing state, whichever is longer. UIFSA generally applies the same procedures to spousal and child support proceedings, but it draws a significant distinction between the jurisdiction required to modify spousal support and child-support orders.[203]

Modifying Spousal Support

Under UIFSA § 211(a), the court that enters a spousal support order maintains "exclusive, continuing jurisdiction" over the order throughout its existence. As a corollary to this principle, § 211(b) provides that a tribunal may not modify a spousal support order entered in another state. Any proceeding to modify or terminate spousal support must therefore be brought in the original forum, even if neither of the parties continues to live in that jurisdiction.[204] Mirroring this rule, § 603 provides that a state tribunal "shall recognize and enforce, but may not modify, a registered order if the issuing tribunal had jurisdiction." The Official Comments suggest that the drafters took this approach to minimize choice of law problems that would arise if spousal support orders were subject to modification in a second state.[205] When a request for modification of spousal support is made in a new forum, the tribunal may forward the request back to the tribunal with continuing exclusive jurisdiction.[206]

Within the United States, the rule of continuing, exclusive jurisdiction in spousal support cases may present an inconvenience if both spouses have left the original issuing state. Because UIFSA is in force in every state, however, the parties are assured a forum if they return for modification to the court in the issuing state. In international cases, the rule of continuing jurisdiction presented difficulties if the foreign tribunal that issued an initial spousal support order considered its jurisdiction to terminate after all parties had left.[207] In this circumstance, there was no forum with jurisdiction to modify within the parameters of UIFSA. For states that have not adopted UIFSA 2008, this problem will continue; but states with the more recent version of the statute have a solution. UIFSA § 211(b) now provides that "a tribunal of this state may not modify a spousal support order issued by a tribunal of another state or a foreign country having continuing exclusive jurisdiction over that order under the law of that state or foreign country." This language directs the state court to resolve the question of whether it may modify a foreign spousal support order with reference to the law of the issuing tribunal. In the case of a foreign spousal support order, the state court will need to consider the law of that country to determine whether it has jurisdiction to modify.[208]

Enforcing Support Orders Based on Comity

For cases in which enforcement under UIFSA is not available, a court may enforce a foreign maintenance order on the basis of comity. This approach was taken in *Kalia v. Kalia*, which enforced spousal and child support orders from a court in India.[209] UIFSA § 104 expressly preserves this possibility, and Section 105 states that a tribunal requested to enforce a support order on the basis of comity may apply UIFSA's procedural and substantive provisions.[210] Under a rule of comity, in circumstances in which arrearages of spousal support are subject to modification, it may be necessary to reduce the unpaid installments to judgment in the country where the support order was entered before seeking enforcement in a state court.[211] A foreign judgment that has been recognized in a state court on the basis of comity may also be enforced prospectively for future installments.[212]

Hague Family Maintenance Convention

The United States has signed and is expected to ratify the 2007 Hague Convention on the International Recovery of Child Support and Other Forms of Family Maintenance.[213] In the United States, the Convention will be implemented through the 2008 UIFSA amendments adding a new Article 7 to the statute. The Convention will have its most sweeping application in the area of child support, but it also applies to two types of spousal support cases. First, a claim for recognition and enforcement of a spousal support order from a Convention country may be raised in connection with a claim for child support under the Convention. In this situation, the system of administrative cooperation, established in Chapters II and III of the Convention, will be available to enforce the spousal support order. In the United States, this means that a spousal support order combined with a child-support order can be enforced through the Central Authority and the network of state Child Support Recovery Units.[214] Alternatively, if there is no related child-support matter, the Convention provides for the possibility of recognition and enforcement of spousal support orders by means of a direct request to the competent authority in the place where enforcement is sought under Article 37. Typically, this will involve a lawsuit filed by private counsel seeking to establish or modify a maintenance decision or to have the decision recognized and enforced.[215] In the United States, both of these alternatives are embraced within UIFSA.

Recognition and enforcement of spousal support decisions from other Contracting States is mandatory in many circumstances under the Convention. According to Article 19(1), the obligation of recognition and enforcement extends to all decisions "rendered by a judicial or administrative authority in respect of a maintenance obligation," including a "settlement or agreement concluded before or approved by such an authority." The decision "may include automatic adjustment by indexation and a requirement to pay arrears, retroactive maintenance or interest and a determination of costs or expenses." The same obligation extends to recognition and enforcement of private agreements known as "maintenance arrangements," as defined in Article 3(e) and Article 30.[216]

Article 20 of the Convention requires that a spousal maintenance decision made in one Contracting State must be recognized and enforced in other Contracting States if the respondent was habitually resident in the State of origin at the time proceedings were instituted, or if the respondent submitted to the tribunal's jurisdiction, or if (in a case that also involves child support) "the child for whom maintenance was ordered was habitually resident in the State of origin at the time proceedings were instituted, provided that the respondent has lived with the child in that State or has resided in that State and provided support for the child there."[217]

Recognition and enforcement of a spousal maintenance decision may be refused under Article 22 on grounds including a lack of notice,[218] fraud "in connection with a matter of procedure,"[219] certain circumstances involving multiple proceedings or inconsistent determinations,[220] and when recognition and enforcement would be "manifestly incompatible with the public policy ('*ordre public*') of the State addressed."[221]

Under Article 18, when a maintenance decision is made in a Contracting State where the creditor is habitually resident, proceedings to modify the decision generally cannot be brought by the debtor in any other Contracting State as long as the creditor remains habitually resident in the State where the decision was made.[222] This is largely consistent with the UIFSA approach, which places continuing exclusive jurisdiction to modify a spousal support order permanently with the court that entered the order, and provides that a state court may not modify a spousal support order issued by a tribunal of another country having continuing exclusive jurisdiction over the order under its own law.[223]

Under the Maintenance Convention, recognition and enforcement of spousal support orders are generally governed by the law of the State where recognition is requested, with additional requirements on matters such as notice, the documents that may be required from an applicant, grounds on which registration may be refused, and opportunity for challenge and appeal.[224] The Convention prohibits reconsideration of the findings of fact on which jurisdiction was premised[225] and prohibits any review of the merits of a decision.[226]

In the United States, these requirements have been incorporated into Article 7 of UIFSA 2008, which applies only to proceedings under the Convention. For the most part, Convention cases will follow the procedures set out in the other articles of UIFSA, but Article 7 controls to the extent that it is inconsistent with other provisions in the statute. Article 7 applies to proceedings initiated by the state authorities with responsibility for child-support enforcement[227] as well as to direct requests for modification or recognition and enforcement of a spousal support order or agreement.[228] Its terms implement the particular requirements of the Convention relating to registration and contest of registration of a Convention support order, and recognition and enforcement of a Convention support order.[229]

Foreign Recognition and Enforcement of Support Orders

The United States does not participate in the multilateral international treaties governing recognition and enforcement of family support orders that preceded the 2007 Hague

---

Hague Family Maintenance Convention

Hague Convention of 23 November 2007 on the International Recovery of Child Support and Other Forms of Family Maintenance, *reprinted in* 47 I.L.M. 257 (2008).

The full text and current information on the Maintenance Convention is available from the Hague Conference website at http://www.hcch.net (under "Conventions" and "39").

See also ALEGRÍA BORRÁS & JENNIFER DEGELING, EXPLANATORY REPORT, CONVENTION OF 23 NOVEMBER 2007 ON THE INTERNATIONAL RECOVERY OF CHILD SUPPORT AND OTHER FORMS OF FAMILY MAINTENANCE (2009).

Maintenance Convention, such as the 1956 New York Convention on the Recovery Abroad of Maintenance or the 1973 Hague Convention on the Recognition and Enforcement of Decisions Relating to Maintenance Obligations. Although U.S. spousal support orders are therefore not recognized under these treaties,[230] they may be recognized and enforced in other countries based on comity or an exequatur proceeding.[231]

The Maintenance Convention will facilitate the process of registering U.S. spousal maintenance orders for recognition and enforcement abroad. Under the Convention, all Contracting States agree to make available "effective measures" to enforce maintenance decisions, including spousal support decisions.[232] Unless there is an associated child-support matter, this process will take place through a direct request to competent authorities,[233] which will ordinarily require retaining counsel in the foreign jurisdiction to file an action with the appropriate tribunal.

Under the Maintenance Convention, enforcement takes place according to the law of the State addressed; but it must be prompt,[234] and at a minimum, enforcement measures must include the same range of methods available in domestic cases.[235] The competent court or authority in the state addressed is bound by the fact findings on which the court in the state of origin based its jurisdiction,[236] and it is not permitted to review the merits of the decision.[237] No bond or security may be required to guarantee payments of costs and expenses, and an applicant who received free legal assistance in the state of origin is entitled in proceedings for recognition or enforcement "to benefit, at least to the same extent, from free legal assistance as provided for by the law of the State addressed under the same circumstances."[238]

Using the Maintenance Convention

When it comes into effect in the United States, the Maintenance Convention will be a useful means of obtaining recognition and enforcement of spousal support orders made in the United States. An application under the Convention must be accompanied by the complete text of the decision; a document stating that it is enforceable in the state of origin; and if the respondent did not appear and was not represented in the proceedings, a document attesting either that the respondent had proper notice and an opportunity to be heard or that the respondent had proper notice of the decision and the opportunity to challenge or appeal it on fact and law.[239] In addition, if there is a request for collection of arrearages, the application must be accompanied by documents showing the amount of arrears and the date the amount was calculated, detailing the information necessary to calculate any automatic adjustment provided in the decision, or showing the extent to which the applicant received free legal assistance in the state of origin.[240] No legalization may be required, and any translation requirements will be indicated in the country profile information available on the Hague Conference website.[241]

The Maintenance Convention preserves, although it does not require, the opportunity to seek recognition and enforcement of a spousal support order by making a direct request to the competent authorities in another Convention country. Article 23(3) states: "That authority shall without delay declare the decision enforceable or register the decision for enforcement." A declaration or registration may be refused only if recognition would be manifestly incompatible with the public policy of the State addressed.[242] Recognition and enforcement may be refused, however, if the order was not based on one of the jurisdictional grounds enumerated in Article 20. For orders from the United

States, difficulties will be most likely with orders based on tag jurisdiction or a minimum-contacts approach, since neither of these bases for jurisdiction is included in Article 20. An order entered on one of these grounds may be entitled to recognition and enforcement on an alternative basis, however. For example, an order entered by a state court that concluded it had jurisdiction based on minimum contacts could be enforced in another Convention country on the basis that the spouse who was awarded support was habitually resident in the state at the time the proceedings were instituted.[243] Recognition and enforcement may also be refused under Article 22 on grounds such as a lack of notice or fraud in connection with a matter of procedure.[244]

In contrast to the practice in the United States, the Maintenance Convention permits a new jurisdiction to modify a spousal support decision, unless it was made in a Contracting State where the creditor was habitually resident at the time the support decision was rendered, and the creditor remains habitually resident in that State.[245] Some exceptions to this no-modification rule come into play if the parties agree in writing that another Contracting State may take jurisdiction, if the creditor submits to jurisdiction for this purpose (expressly or by waiver), if the competent authority in the State of origin cannot or will not exercise jurisdiction to modify, or if the decision from the State of origin "cannot be recognized or declared enforceable in the Contracting State where proceedings to modify the decision or make a new decision are contemplated."[246]

Notes

1. *See generally* JEREMY D. MORLEY, INTERNATIONAL FAMILY LAW PRACTICE 69–79 (2009).
2. *See generally* 2 HOMER H. CLARK, JR., THE LAW OF DOMESTIC RELATIONS IN THE UNITED STATES, § 16.1, at 175–83 (practitioner's ed., 2d ed. 1987); EUGENE F. SCOLES ET AL., CONFLICT OF LAWS, § 14, at 596–626 (4th ed. 2004); RESTATEMENT (SECOND) OF CONFLICT OF LAWS §§ 233–34, 257–59 (1971).
3. *See* 2 CLARK, *supra* note 2, § 16, at 175–219.
4. *See infra* notes 17–57 and accompanying text.
5. *See generally* 1 CLARK, *supra* note 2, § 7, at 423–97 (support rights during marriage); 2 CLARK, *supra* note 2, § 17, at 220–345 (support after divorce or separation).
6. *E.g.*, Martire v. Martire, 792 So. 2d 631 (Fla. Dist. Ct. App. 2001) (approving award of short-term rehabilitative alimony for wife who had come from Russia with 9-year-old son to marry husband who filed for divorce after less than a year of marriage).
7. *See generally* CLARK, *supra* note 2, § 17.6, at 272–93. On the treatment of marital agreements addressing support rights, *see infra* notes 25–26 and accompanying text.
8. *See* SCOLES ET AL., *supra* note 2, § 14.4, at 601 ("Most states apply a concept of marital property on dissolution during lifetime that allocates all assets acquired during the marriage in patterns similar to community property concepts, without regard to the location of the assets.") *See also* 2 CLARK, *supra* note 2, § 16.7, at 212–16. In several community property states, this result is accomplished by statutes that allow for the division of "quasi-community property." *See id.* at 215. Note, however, that many cases have applied conflict-of-laws analysis to reach a different result. These are discussed in the sources cited here.
9. State court orders concerning marital property and support rights are not entitled to full faith and credit unless the court has personal jurisdiction over the respondent spouse. *See infra* notes 65–92 and accompanying text.
10. Estate of Charania v. Shulman, 608 F.3d 67 (1st Cir. 2010). *See also* Nationwide Res. Corp. v. Massabni, 694 P.2d 290, 293–95 (Ariz. Ct. App. 1984) (applying law of Morocco as matrimonial domicile to determine whether property interest was separate or community property in dispute with creditor).

11. The court in *Charania* noted that the couple did not take advantage of a mechanism available under Belgian law to modify their matrimonial property regime.

    Other resources on matrimonial property and conflict of laws include Michael Davie, *Matrimonial Property in English and American Conflict of Laws*, 42 INT'L & COMP. L.Q. 855 (1993); Friedrich Juenger, *Marital Property and the Conflict of Laws: A Tale of Two Countries*, 81 COLUM. L. REV. 1061 (1981); J. Thomas Oldham, *Conflict of Laws and Marital Property Rights*, 39 BAYLOR L. REV. 1255 (1987); J. Thomas Oldham, *What if the Beckhams Move to L.A. and Divorce? Marital Property Rights of Mobile Spouses When They Divorce in the United States*, 42 FAM. L.Q. 263 (2008); Eugene Scoles, *Choice of Law in Family Property Transactions*, 209 RECUEIL DES COURS 17 (1988-II); Leslie K. Thiele, *The German Marital Property System: Conflict of Laws in a Dual-Nationality Marriage*, 12 CAL. W. INT'L L.J. 78 (1982).

12. *See* MORLEY, *supra* note 1, at 125–46 (surveying marital property and support laws in various countries).

13. March 14, 1978, Misc. 11 (1977), Cmnd. 6830, *reprinted in* 16 I.L.M. 14 (1977). The Convention, which is in effect between France, Luxembourg, and the Netherlands, allows spouses to designate, at the time of marriage, which country's law will govern their property relations. They must choose a country with which they have a connection such as nationality or habitual residence. If the spouses do not elect a matrimonial property regime, the law of the place where both spouses establish habitual residence immediately after their marriage will ordinarily control.

14. Convention on the International Recovery of Child Support and Other Forms of Family Maintenance, Nov. 23, 2007, 47 I.L.M. 257.

15. The United States does not plan to ratify the Protocol to the Maintenance Convention addressing choice of law issues. *See* Protocol of 23 November 2007 on the Law Applicable to Maintenance Obligations, http://www.hcch.net/index_en.php?act=conventions.text&cid =133. All member states of the European Union, except for Denmark and the United Kingdom, are bound by the Protocol. *See* Council Regulation (EC) No. 4/2009 (Dec. 18, 2009) on jurisdiction, applicable law, recognition, and enforcement of decisions and cooperation in matters relating to maintenance obligations.

16. *See infra* note 119 and accompanying text.

17. *See* UNIF. PREMARITAL AGREEMENT ACT (UPAA), 9C U.L.A. 39 (2001 & Supp. 2009); UNIF. PROBATE CODE § 2-204, 8 (pt. I) U.L.A. 104 (1998 & Supp. 2009). *See generally* 1 CLARK, *supra* note 2, § 1.9, at 41–63; SCOLES ET AL., *supra* note 2, § 14.15.

18. *E.g.*, Marriage of Littlefield, 940 P.2d 1362, 1371–72 (Wash. 1997) (declining to enforce provision regarding custody arrangements for any future child born into the marriage).

19. *See generally* LAURA W. MORGAN & BRETT R. TURNER, ATTACKING AND DEFENDING MARITAL AGREEMENTS (2001); LINDA J. RADVIN, PREMARITAL AGREEMENTS: DRAFTING AND NEGOTIATION (2011).

20. *See* Estate of Halmaghi, 457 N.W.2d 356, 359 (Mich. Ct. App. 1990) (finding that agreement entered into in Germany before a notary by a Romanian-speaking woman was invalid based on lack of fair disclosure of assets and effect of agreement on marital property rights); Marriage of Shirilla, 89 P.3d 1 (Mont. 2004) (holding that Russian wife with fiancé visa not enter in to prenuptial agreement voluntarily); Marriage of Obadi and Qayoum, 226 P.3d 78 (Wash. Ct. App. 2010) (declining to enforce agreement written in language groom could not speak, read, or write). This issue was also raised in Marriage of Bonds, 5 P.3d 815, 837–38 (Cal. 2000), which upheld the trial court's finding that a woman who had emigrated from Sweden several years earlier adequately understood a prenuptial agreement she signed. *But see infra* note 23 and accompanying text.

21. UPAA § 2. Many states have enacted the UPAA with substantial changes. *See, e.g.*, CAL. FAM. CODE § 1615(c) (2004) (altering § 6 of the UPAA); CAL. FAM. CODE § 1612(c) (2004) (altering § 3 of the UPAA).

22. Because the provisions of the UPAA were modified in many of the states that enacted it, reference to the specific terms of state law remains important.

23. CAL. FAM. CODE § 1615(c)(3) (2004). For a premarital agreement concerning spousal support, the law does not allow waivers of independent legal representation and provides that the agreement must not be unconscionable at the time of enforcement.

24. CAL. FAM. CODE § 1612(c) (2004). These requirements were added after the decisions in Marriage of Bonds, 5 P.3d 815 (Cal. 2000), and Marriage of Pendleton and Fireman, 5 P.3d 839 (Cal. 2000).

25. UPAA states that rejected § 3(a)(4) include California, Iowa, New Mexico, and South Dakota; states that modified or eliminated § 6(b) include California, Delaware, Illinois, Indiana, New Jersey, New Mexico, South Dakota, and Virginia. *See* 9C U.L.A. 43–45, 48–53 (2001 & Supp. 2009). *See generally* Susan Wolfson, *Premarital Waiver of Alimony*, 38 FAM. L.Q. 141 (2004).

26. *See, e.g.*, DeMatteo v. DeMatteo, 762 N.E.2d 797, 811–13 (Mass. 2002) (holding that conscionability is the appropriate standard of review at the time of enforcement); Rider v. Rider, 669 N.E.2d 160, 163–64 (Ind. 1996) (finding no unconscionability at the time of enforcement after evaluating the parties' respective assets and income); Gross v. Gross, 464 N.E.2d 500, 510 (Ohio 1984) (providing factors for a court to consider when determining conscionability at the time of divorce).

27. Family Law Amendment Act 2000 (Australia), *applied in* K. v. K. (Ancillary Relief: Pre-nuptial Agreement) [2003] 1 FLR 120.

28. Family Law Reform Act 1978 (Can.); *see generally* Hartshorne v. Hartshorne [2004] 1 SCR 550.

29. Property (Relationships) Act 1976 (N.Z.), and Property Relationships Amendment Act 2001.

30. *See* Radmacher v. Granatino [2010] UKSC 42; [2010] 3 FCR 583 (reviewing the evolution of case law); *see also* IAIN HARRIS & RACHEL SPICER, PRENUPTIAL AGREEMENTS: A PRACTICAL GUIDE (2008); DAVID HODSON, A PRACTICAL GUIDE TO INTERNATIONAL FAMILY LAW 209–21 (2008); MORLEY, *supra* note 1, at 49–63.

31. Radmacher v. Granatino [2010] UKSC 42; [2010] 3 FCR 583.

32. In addition to preparing a matrimonial property agreement, the notary may be charged with carrying out the division of assets when the marriage ends. *See generally* HENRY DYSON, FRENCH PROPERTY AND INHERITANCE LAW 205–08 (2003).

33. For example, the French Code Civil includes four standard matrimonial property regimes, including traditional community and separate property regimes, as well as a universal community property system and a hybrid regime in which property remains separate during marriage but the increase in value of the spouses' separate estates is divided when the marriage ends in death or divorce. *See id.*

34. SCOLES ET AL., *supra* note 2, § 14.15, cite a series of early examples.

35. *See, e.g.*, Estate of Halmaghi, 457 N.W.2d 356, 357 (Mich. Ct. App. 1990) (stating that an antenuptial agreement "must be entered into voluntarily by both parties with each understanding his or her rights and the extent of the waiver of such rights.")

36. Van Kipnis v. Van Kipnis, 900 N.E.2d 977, 978 (N.Y. 2008). The court did not consider whether the agreement complied with New York's statutory formalities, since it was executed before that law became effective. *Id.* at 980 n. 3.

37. Stawski v. Stawski, 843 N.Y.S.2d 544, 545 (N.Y. App. Div. 2007). A dissent in this case, concerned with the voluntariness of the wife's execution of the agreement, begins: "In December of 1974, an affianced young American women in the bloom of love, traveling with her German fiancé to his parents' home in Frankfurt, en route to a skiing vacation in Switzerland, experienced a sudden and unexpected detour to a lawyer's office in Frankfurt, where she was presented with a prenuptial agreement." *Id.* at 548 (Saxe, J., dissenting).

38. Stein-Sapir v. Stein-Sapir, 382 N.Y.S.2d 799, 800–01 (N.Y. App. Div. 1976). In this case, neither husband nor wife understood Spanish, but the court accepted evidence that they were required to select a matrimonial property regime and had the alternatives explained in English. *Id.* at 800.

39. Fernandez v. Fernandez, 15 Cal. Rptr. 374, 376 (Cal. Ct. App. 1961).

40. Auten v. Auten, 124 N.E.2d 99, 101 (N.Y. 1954).

41. *E.g.*, Nanini v. Nanini, 802 P.2d 438, 441 (Ariz. Ct. App. 1990); Norris v. Norris, 419 A.2d 982, 984 (D.C. 1980); DeLorean v. DeLorean, 511 A.2d 1257, 1261–62 (N.J. Super. Ct. Ch. Div. 1986); Marriage of Proctor, 125 P.3d 801 (Or. Ct. App. 2005). *See also* Black v. Powers, 628 S.E.2d 546 (Va. Ct. App. 2006) (applying Virgin Islands law to determine validity of marital agreement executed by Virginia couple immediately before their wedding in St. Croix). Courts take the same approach in international cases; *see Fernandez*, 15 Cal. Rptr. at 379; *Stein-Sapir*, 382

N.Y.S.2d at 800–01; Chaudry v. Chaudry, 388 A.2d 1000, 1005–06 (N.J. Super. Ct. App. Div. 1978) (concluding that Pakistani marital agreement barred claim for equitable distribution where parties married in Pakistan and wife continued to reside there). *See generally* MORLEY, *supra* note 1, at 40–49; Joan F. Kessler, *Can You Choose the Law to Govern Your Marital Agreement?* 8 J. AM. ACAD. MATRIMONIAL L. 107, 117–19 (1992); Julia Halloran McLaughlin, *Premarital Agreements and Choice of Law: "One, Two, Three, Baby, You and Me,"* 72 Mo. L. REV. 793 (2007).

42. *See* RESTATEMENT (SECOND) OF CONFLICT OF LAWS § 188 (1971). *E.g.,* Lewis v. Lewis, 748 P.2d 1362 (Haw. 1988). *See generally* 1 CLARK, *supra* note 2, § 1.9, at 47–48; SCOLES ET AL., *supra* note 2, §§ 14.15, 18.17–.18. In *Auten*, 124 N.E.2d at 102–03, the court concluded that English law should be applied to determine the impact and effect of a separation agreement executed in New York when England had "all the truly significant contacts." *See also* Kyle v. Kyle, 128 So. 2d 427 (Fla. Ct. App. 1961) (valid Canadian premarital agreement was not effective to relinquish wife's dower rights in Florida property).

43. *Lewis*, 748 P.2d at 1369–70 (distinguishing between support and property aspects of prenuptial agreement and remanding for consideration of unconscionability).

44. *E.g.,* Gustafson v. Jensen, 515 So. 2d 1298, 1301 (Fla. Dist. Ct. App. 1987) (Danish agreement abandoned when it was torn up after move to Florida); Brandt v. Brandt, 427 N.W.2d 126, 134 (Wis. Ct. App. 1988) (German postnuptial agreement abandoned by commingling of assets after move to Wisconsin); *see also* Scherer v. Scherer, 292 S.E.2d 662, 664 (Ga. 1982) (applying Georgia law to Michigan prenuptial with agreement of parties despite contractual choice of law provision).

　　Early cases often treated foreign marital property agreements as not applicable to property acquired after the parties immigrated to the United States. *E.g.,* Ross v. Ross, 253 N.Y.S. 871, 882 (N.Y. App. Div. 1931); Long v. Hess, 40 N.E. 335, 339 (Ill. 1895); *cf.* Kleb v. Kleb, 62 A. 396, 399–400 (N.J. Ch. 1905) (holding that parties intended Hessian marriage contract to apply to property acquired elsewhere).

45. *E.g., Gustafson*, 515 So. 2d at 1300 (stating that "principles of comity will not apply where the state in which the contract in dispute was entered into has little or no interest in the matter or controversy").

46. *See* RESTATEMENT (SECOND) OF CONFLICT OF LAWS § 187 (1971). Applying these principles, Mehtar v. Mehtar, 1997 WL 576540, at *1–2 (Conn. Super. Ct. 1997) (unpublished) concluded that a married couple's agreement, entered into in South Africa, "intended to give effect to their [Muslim] religious beliefs by opting out of the community property provisions of South African marital law" should be given effect as to the couple's property rights despite the lack of financial disclosures that would be required in Connecticut. *See also* Alamir v. Callen, 750 F. Supp. 2d 465 (S.D.N.Y. 2010) (discussing French premarital agreement with New York choice of law provision).

47. As stated in RESTATEMENT (SECOND) OF CONFLICT OF LAWS § 187(2)(b):

> The law of the state chosen by the parties to govern their contractual rights and duties will be applied, even if the particular issue is one which the parties could not have resolved by an explicit provision in their agreement directed to that issue, unless . . . application of the law of the chosen state would be contrary to a fundamental policy of a state which has a materially greater interest than the chosen state in the determination of the particular issue and which . . . would be the state of the applicable law in the absence of an effective choice of law by the parties.

48. *E.g.,* Estate of Davis, 184 S.W.3d 231, 238–39 (Tenn. Ct. App. 2004). *See also* Kyle v. Kyle, 128 So. 2d 427 (Fla. Ct. App. 1961).

49. *E.g.,* Brewsaugh v. Brewsaugh, 491 N.E.2d 748 (Ohio Com. Pl. 1985).

50. *E.g.,* Liedekerke v. Liedekerke, 635 A.2d 339, 343 (D.C. 1993) (concluding that Belgian premarital agreement was "at best ambiguous about the parties' intent with respect to separate property which becomes jointly titled").

51. See MORLEY, *supra* note 1, at 32–44; and Kessler, *supra* note 41, for drafting checklists.

52. *See Court Declines to Invalidate Hèrmes New York Prenuptial Agreement in Favor of French Version*, N.Y.L.J. Mar. 18, 2009 (order in Guerrand-Hermes v. Guerrand-Hermes).
53. *E.g.*, Odatalla v. Odatalla, 810 A.2d 93, 98 (N.J. Super. Ct. Ch. Div. 2002); Akileh v. Elchahal, 666 So. 2d 246, 249 (Fla. Dist. Ct. App. 1996); Aziz v. Aziz, 488 N.Y.S.2d 123, 124 (N.Y. Sup. Ct. 1985). *See also* Lashgari v. Lashgari, 496 A.2d 491 (Conn. 1985) (enforcing judgment on wife's counterclaim for *mahr* payment under Iranian marriage contract). In Canada, enforcement of a promise to pay *mahr* was denied in Kaddoura v. Hammoud, [1998] 168 D.L.R. 4th 503, 510-12 (Can.). *See generally* Ann Laquer Estin, *Embracing Tradition: Pluralism in American Family Law*, 63 MD. L. REV. 540, 572-77 (2004).

Several California cases declined to enforce this type of promise based on the public policy against enforcement of agreements that encourage divorce. *See* Marriage of Noghrey, 215 Cal. Rptr. 153, 154 (Cal. Ct. App. 1985) (husband promised to give his house to his wife in event of divorce and to pay $500,000 or one-half of his assets, whichever was greater); Marriage of Dajani, 251 Cal. Rptr. 871, 871 (Cal. Ct. App. 1988) (husband promised to pay 5,000 Jordanian *dinars*, worth about $1,700, in event of his death or divorce). In a later decision, the court retreated from *Dajani*, enforcing a payment designed "to ensure that, if [the] husband died or the marriage was dissolved, [the] wife would be no worse off than she would have been had she remained single." Marriage of Bellio, 129 Cal. Rptr. 2d 556, 560 (N.Y. Ct. App. 2003).
54. *Compare* Marriage of Goldman, 554 N.E.2d 1016, 1021-22 (Ill. App. Ct. 1990) (enforcing implied promises in Jewish *ketuba* to appear before a *bet din* to deliver or receive a *get*), *and* Minkin v. Minkin, 434 A.2d 665, 666, 668 (N.J. Super. Ct. Ch. Div. 1981) (same), *and* Stern v. Stern, 5 Fam. L. Rep. (BNA) 2810, 2811 (N.Y. Sup. Ct. Kings Cnty. 1979) (same), *with* Victor v. Victor, 866 P.2d 899, 902 (Ariz. Ct. App. 1993) (concluding that granting such an order would violate the First Amendment), *and* Aflalo v. Aflalo, 685 A.2d 523, 531 (N.J. Super. Ct. Ch. Div. 1996) (same). *See also* Mayer-Kolker v. Kolker, 819 A.2d 17, 22 (N.J. Super. Ct. App. Div. 2003) (remanding for further evidence on terms of the agreement and requirements of Jewish law). *See generally* Estin, *supra* note 53, at 578-82; Andrea G. Nadel, Annotation, *Enforceability of Agreement Requiring Spouse's Co-operation in Obtaining Religious Bill of Divorce*, 29 A.L.R. 746, 747 (1984).
55. *See* Avitzur v. Avitzur, 446 N.E.2d 136, 138 (N.Y. 1983) (concluding that agreement to arbitrate marital disputes before bet din could be enforced based "solely upon the application of neutral principles of contract law, without reference to any religious principle"); Jabri v. Qaddura, 108 S.W.3d 404, 413 (Tex. App. 2003) (enforcing agreement to arbitrate marital disputes in Texas Islamic court). Arbitration in a religious tribunal must conform to state arbitration laws; *see generally* Estin, *supra* note 53, at 582-85.
56. Marriage of Shaban, 105 Cal. Rptr. 2d 863, 865 (Cal. Dist. Ct. App.), *reh'g denied*, (2001). *See* Farag v. Farag, 772 N.Y.S.2d 368, 371-72 (N.Y. App. Div. 2004), which rejected a similar argument both because there was no proof that the agreement "had been duly executed pursuant to" the New York statutes, and because the agreement included the husband's promise to make a dowry payment but did not include a waiver of equitable distribution or support rights in the event of divorce. *See also* Atassi v. Atassi, 451 S.E.2d 371, 373-74, 376 (N.C. Ct. App. 1995), *reh'g denied*, 456 S.E.2d 310 (N.C. 1995) (Syrian marriage contract does not meet requirements of state premarital agreement act; genuine issues of material fact regarding enforceability of agreement signed after marriage in North Carolina).
57. 226 P.3d 787 (Wash. Ct. App. 2010). *See also* Ahmed v. Ahmed, 261 S.W.3d 190 (Tex. App. 2008) (holding that *mahr* agreement signed after parties' civil wedding ceremony was not a valid postmarital agreement under Texas law); Zawahiri v. Alwattar, 2008 WL 2698679, at *6 (Ohio Ct. App. 2008) (refusing enforcement of agreement that husband was coerced into signing) (unpublished).
58. 8 U.S.C. § 1183a (2010).
59. *See id.* § 1183a(a)(1)(b), (e)(1). *E.g.*, Younis v. Farooqui, 597 F. Supp. 2d 552 (D. Md. 2009); Shumye v. Felleke, 555 F. Supp. 2d 1020 (N.D. Cal. 2008). *Cf.* Schwartz v. Schwartz, 409 B.R. 240 (B.A.P. 1st Cir. 2008).
60. *See* 8 U.S.C. § 1183a(a)(2) (2010).

61. *E.g.,* Barnett v. Barnett, 238 P.3d 594 (Alaska 2010); Marriage of Sandhu, 207 P.3d 1067, Kan. Ct. App. 2009); Naik v. Naik, 944 A.2d 713 (N.J. Super. Ct. App. Div. 2008). Iannuzzelli v. Lovett, 981 So. 2d 557 (Fla. Dist. Ct. App. 2008), suggests that a spouse who is currently self-supporting at the required level may have the right to seek enforcement in the future if his or her circumstances change.

62. *See generally* CLARK, *supra* note 2, § 19.

63. *See generally* MORGAN & TURNER, *supra* note 19.

64. 650 P.2d 256, 258-59 (Wash. Ct. App. 1982). *See generally* 2 CLARK, *supra* note 2, § 19.3, at 420-21; SCOLES ET AL., *supra* note 2, §§ 18.17-.18, at 992-95; *see also* RESTATEMENT (SECOND) OF CONFLICT OF LAWS § 188 (1971) ("The rights and duties of the parties with respect to an issue in contract are determined by the local law of the state which, with respect to that issue, has the most significant relationship to the transaction and the parties.").

65. See the discussion of divorce jurisdiction in chapter 3.

66. *See* Estin v. Estin, 334 U.S. 541, 548-49 (1948); Vanderbilt v. Vanderbilt, 354 U.S. 416, 418-19 (1957); *see generally* RESTATEMENT (SECOND) OF CONFLICT OF LAWS § 77 (1971). For an international illustration of the *Estin* problem, see Herczog v. Herczog, 9 Cal. Rptr. 5, 9 (Cal. Dist. Ct. App. 1960) (husband's ex parte Nevada divorce did not terminate wife's rights under prior English separate maintenance decree). On the requirements of personal jurisdiction, *see also, e.g.,* Von Schack v. Von Schack, 893 A.2d 1004, 1007 (Me. 2006); Miller v. Miller, 861 N.E.2d 393, 400 (Mass. 2007); *see generally* 2 ROBERT C. CASAD & WILLIAM B. RICHMAN, JURISDICTION IN CIVIL ACTIONS § 9-2, at 5265-83 (3d ed. 1998).

67. *See, e.g.,* Pawley v. Pawley, 46 So. 2d 464, 475 (Fla. 1950) (recognizing ex parte Cuban divorce based on comity and holding that decree did not preclude respondent's subsequent action for alimony in Florida); Southern v. Southern, 258 S.E.2d 422, 425 (N.C. Ct. App. 1979) (declining to enforce English judgment for alimony and child support where court lacked basis to exercise personal jurisdiction over obligor).

68. *See, e.g.,* Akinci-Unal v. Unal, 832 N.E.2d 1, 6-7 (Mass. App. Ct. 2005); Bourbon v. Bourbon, 751 N.Y.S.2d 302, 304 (N.Y. App. Div. 2002) (*Bourbon II*). *See generally* 2 CLARK, *supra* note 2, § 17.4.

69. *See, e.g., Akinci-Unal,* 832 N.E.2d at 7. *See also infra* notes 99-107 and accompanying text.

70. *E.g.,* Villarroel v. Villarroel, 562 A.2d 1180, 1183 (Del. 1989); Marriage of Brown, 587 N.E.2d 648, 653 (Ill. App. Ct. 1992). *See also* Weber v. Superior Court of L.A. Cnty., 348 P.2d 572, 573 (Cal. 1960) (rejecting both arguments). The court in *Villarroel* notes that in Delaware the courts have statutory authority to hear postdivorce property division proceedings but not support claims. *Villarroel,* 562 A.2d at 1183. *See generally* CLARK, *supra* note 2, § 17.4; *see also infra* note 104.

71. *E.g.,* N.J. STAT. ANN. § 2A:34-23 (2010), applied in Pierrakos v. Pierrakos, 372 A.2d 1331, 1333 (N.J. Super. Ct. App. Div. 1977); *but see* Chaudry v. Chaudry, 388 A.2d 1000, 1006 (N.J. Super. Ct. App. Div. 1978) (declining to award separate maintenance to Pakistani wife in action brought following Pakistani divorce, on ground that there was not an adequate nexus between the marriage and the state). For the approach in the United Kingdom, *see infra* notes 106-107 and accompanying text.

72. *See* CLARK, *supra* note 2, § 16.1, at 176.

73. *E.g.,* Abernathy v. Abernathy, 482 S.E.2d 265, 268-69 (Ga. 1997); Searles v. Searles, 420 N.W.2d 581, 584 (Minn. 1988); McCasland v. McCasland, 497 N.E.2d 696, 697 (N.Y. 1986); Weller v. Weller, 988 P.2d 921, 926-27 (Or. Ct. App. 1999).

74. UNIF. INTERSTATE FAMILY SUPPORT ACT (UIFSA) (amended 2008), 9 (1B) U.L.A. 72 (Supp. 2011).

75. UIFSA § 211. *See infra* notes 204-08 and accompanying text.

76. UIFSA § 105 extends the coverage of the statute to "an obligee, obligor, or child residing in a foreign country." "Foreign country" is a term of art under UIFSA, and not all foreign nations meet this definition. *See infra* notes 197-202 and accompanying text.

77. *E.g.,* Laskosky v. Laskosky, 504 So. 2d 726, 730, 731 (Miss. 1987); Asanov v. Hunt, 914 So. 2d 769, 772 (Miss. Ct. App. 2005).

78. *E.g.,* Bourbon v. Bourbon, 687 N.Y.S.2d 426, 428 (N.Y. App. Div. 1999) (*Bourbon I*); Roa v. Roa, 970 S.W.2d 163, 164 (Tex. App. 1998).

79. Under the uniform statutes governing child custody and child support proceedings, however, bringing or responding to such a claim in another state does not constitute a general appearance.
80. 495 U.S. 604 (1990). *See generally* 2 CLARK, *supra* note 2, § 13.4. International divorce cases upholding tag jurisdiction include Vazifdar v. Vazifdar, 547 A.2d 249, 252 (N.H. 1988), and MacLeod v. MacLeod, 383 A.2d 39, 43 (Me. 1978).
81. 436 U.S. 84, 85 (1978).
82. *Kulko*, 436 U.S. at 97.
83. *E.g.*, Ali v. Ali, 652 A.2d 253, 260-61 (N.J. Super. Ct. Ch. Div. 1994); Akinci-Unal v. Unal, 832 N.E.2d 1, 4-5 (Mass. App. Ct. 2005); Cooke v. Cooke, 594 S.E.2d 370, 371-72 (Ga. 2004); Farah v. Farah, 323 N.E.2d 361, 365 (Ill. App. Ct. 1975); Venizelos v. Venizelos, 293 N.Y.S.2d 20, 21 (N.Y. App. Div. 1968).
84. *E.g.*, CAL. CIV. PROC. CODE § 410.10 (2010) ("A court of this state may exercise jurisdiction on any basis not inconsistent with the Constitution of this state or of the United States.").
85. *E.g.*, ME. REV. STAT. ANN. tit. 14, § 704-A(2)(G) (2009) ("Maintaining a domicile in this State while subject to a marital or family relationship out of which arises a claim for divorce, alimony, separate maintenance, property settlement, child support or child custody; or the commission in this State of any act giving rise to such a claim."); N.Y. C.P.L.R. § 302(b) (2010) (court may exercise personal jurisdiction over nonresident defendant if the state "was the matrimonial domicile of the parties before their separation, or the defendant abandoned the plaintiff in this state, or the claim for support, alimony, maintenance, distributive awards or special relief in matrimonial actions accrued under the laws of this state or under an agreement executed in this state").
86. *E.g.*, Horlander v. Horlander, 579 N.E.2d 91, 93-94 (Ind. Ct. App. 1991) (state rule extends jurisdiction to any person who lived in marital relationship in the state and has left behind a spouse who continues to reside in the state). *See also, e.g.*, WIS. STAT. ANN. § 801.05(11) (2010) (long-arm jurisdiction available if respondent "resided in this state in a marital relationship with the petitioner for not less than 6 consecutive months within the 6 years next preceding the commencement of the action"); N.C. GEN. STAT. ANN. § 1-75.4(12) (2009) (long-arm jurisdiction in action arising "out of the marital relationship within this State, notwithstanding subsequent departure from this State, if the other party to the marital relationship continues to reside in this State").
87. *See* 1 CLARK, *supra* note 2, § 13.4.
88. *See* Forrest v. Forrest, 839 So. 2d 839, 841 (Fla. Dist. Ct. App. 2003) (home and bank account in Florida not sufficient to allow long-arm jurisdiction over husband living in Singapore); *cf.* Marshall v. Marshall, 988 So. 2d 644 (Fla. Dist. Ct. App. 2008) (husband's ownership of real property in state gave court jurisdiction over wife's claim for partition of property).
89. If there is no factual basis for long-arm jurisdiction, UIFSA provides a route through which a petitioner can commence a proceeding in one state for establishment of a spousal support and have the proceeding transmitted to another state where it is possible to obtain jurisdiction over the respondent. This involves filing a petition under § 304, which the "initiating tribunal" then forwards to a "responding tribunal" in a state where jurisdiction can be obtained. The duties and powers of the responding tribunal are described in § 305.
90. *E.g.*, Perry v. Perry, 623 P.2d 513, 515-16 (Kan. Ct. App. 1981) (husband in military service obtained divorce in state from which he entered service; court has no personal jurisdiction over wife who never lived in a marital relationship in the state).
91. 545 S.E.2d 757, 762 (N.C. Ct. App. 2001). The court noted that this was an unusual result, which might not be proper in the "ordinary divorce case." *Cf.* Forrest v. Forrest, 839 So. 2d 839, 841 (Fla. Dist. Ct. App. 2003) (opening bank account and purchasing home during one-week visit not sufficient to establish matrimonial domicile in state).
92. *See, e.g.*, *Ex parte* Brislawn, 443 So. 2d 32, 34 (Ala. 1983); Crommelin-Monnier v. Monnier, 638 So. 2d 912, 915-16 (Ala. Civ. App. 1994); Goodenbour v. Goodenbour, 64 S.W.3d 69, 76-81 (Tex. App. 2001); *but see* Harris v. Harris, 922 N.E.2d 626, 635-38 (Ind. Ct. App. 2010) (concluding that court had no personal jurisdiction over husband who was stationed in Germany). *See also* Brett R. Turner, *Pursuing the Divisible Divorce: Recent Case Law on State Court Jurisdiction in Divorce Cases*, 12 DIVORCE LITIG. 125 (July 2000). Courts in several cases have cited the

lack of an alternative U.S. forum as grounds for denying a motion to dismiss on grounds of inconvenient forum. *See* Horlander v. Horlander, 579 N.E.2d 91, 94 (Ind. Ct. App. 1991); MacLeod v. MacLeod, 383 A.2d 39, 42 (Me. 1978).

93. These issues are also noted in chapter 1 and other points in this book; *see generally* MARK E. SULLIVAN, THE MILITARY DIVORCE HANDBOOK: A PRACTICAL GUIDE TO REPRESENTING MILITARY PERSONNEL AND THEIR FAMILIES (2d ed. 2011).

94. 50 U.S.C. App. §§ 501–596. *See, e.g.,* Smith v. Smith, 149 S.E.2d 468 (Ga. 1966); *see generally* SULLIVAN, *supra* note 93, at 55–89.

95. 10 U.S.C. § 1408 (2010). Under § 1408(c)(4), there must be jurisdiction based on the servicemember's residence, domicile, or consent; some courts have read this to require that the servicemember consent to distribution of his or her pension, and not merely to other aspects of the divorce proceeding. *See* Wagner v. Wagner, 768 A.2d 1112 (Pa. 2001). *See generally* Ann K. Wooster, *Construction and Application of Federal Uniformed Services Former Spouse Protection Act in State Court Divorce Proceedings*, 2003 A.L.R.5th 7 (2003).

96. SULLIVAN, *supra* note 93, at 473–681.

97. SULLIVAN, *supra* note 93, at 261–78; William J. Camp, *Health Care Options for Former Military Spouses: Tricare and the Continued Health Care Benefit Program*, 43 FAM. L.Q. 227 (2009).

98. SULLIVAN, *supra* note 93, at 289–98.

99. *See* Estin v. Estin, 334 U.S. 541, 549 (1948) ("The result in this situation is to make the divorce divisible—to give effect to the Nevada decree insofar as it affects marital status and to make it ineffective on the issue of alimony").

100. *E.g.,* Hudson v. Hudson, 344 P.2d 295, 300–01 (Cal. 1959); Pawley v. Pawley, 46 So. 2d 464 (Fla. 1950), Altman v. Altman, 386 A.2d 766, 769–70, 772 (Md. 1978); Nikrooz v. Nikrooz, 561 N.Y.S.2d 301 (N.Y. App. Div. 1990).

101. This issue involves complex questions of collateral estoppel, res judicata, and full faith and credit, and is often affected by statutes in the state addressed. *Compare* O'Connell v. Corcoran, 802 N.E.2d 1071, 1074 (N.Y. 2003) (bilateral Vermont divorce decree precluded wife's subsequent action for equitable distribution), *with* Braunstein v. Braunstein, 497 N.Y.S.2d 58 (N.Y. App. Div. 1985) (allowing equitable distribution claim following bilateral Swedish divorce). *See generally* 2 CLARK, *supra* note 2, § 17.4.

102. Marriage of Notash, 118 S.W.3d 868, 871, 873–74 (Tex. App. 2003) (court held "no fiduciary duty existed after the Iranian divorce"); *but see* Sidebotham v. Robison, 216 F.2d 816, 824–25 (9th Cir. 1955) (fiduciary relationship as to community property did not terminate with ex parte divorce).

103. Statutes that expressly confer jurisdiction for postdivorce support or property claims include GA. CODE ANN. § 19-6-17 (2010); MD. CODE ANN., FAM. LAW §§ 8-212, 11-105 (2010); MASS. GEN. LAWS ANN. ch. 208, § 34 (2010); N.J. STAT. ANN. § 2A-34-24.1 (2010); N.Y. DOM. REL. LAW § 236(B) (2010).

104. *Compare, e.g., Hudson*, 344 P.2d at 300 (holding that wife's support claim survived husband's ex parte divorce), *with* Loeb v. Loeb, 114 A.2d 518, 526 (Vt. 1955) (holding that statute did not permit entry of support order following out-of-state ex parte divorce). *See generally Altman*, 386 A.2d at 771–72 (collecting cases). *See also supra* notes 68–71 and accompanying text. Since *Altman* was decided in 1978, several states have enacted statutes to allow claims for spousal support after an ex parte foreign divorce, including Georgia and Massachusetts. See statutes cited *supra* note 103. The case law in Oregon requires that an action for divorce must be already pending in Oregon at the time an ex parte divorce is entered somewhere else in order for the courts to have subject matter jurisdiction over unresolved financial claims. *See* Marriage of Anderson, 793 P.2d 1378, 1380–81 (Or. Ct. App. 1990). Illinois courts may award spousal support following an ex parte divorce, but have concluded that they have no subject matter jurisdiction to divide marital property in this situation. *Compare* Schwarz v. Schwarz, 188 N.E.2d 673, 677 (1963), *with* Marriage of Brown, 587 N.E.2d 648 (Ill. Ct. App. 1992).

105. *See, e.g.,* Weller v. Weller, 988 P.2d 921, 926 (Or. Ct. App. 1999).

If the parties are able to come to an agreement on some but not all issues in their divorce, it may be possible to enter a separation agreement that includes a choice of law term and preserves certain issues to be resolved later by a court in the United States. *See, e.g.,* Torres

v. McClain, 535 S.E.2d 623, 626-27 (N.C. Ct. App. 2000) (enforcing separation agreement concerning division of U.S. military pension following bilateral Japanese divorce).

106. Part III of the Matrimonial and Family Proceedings Act 1984. *See generally* Hodson, *supra* note 30, at 191-207.

107. *See id.*

108. Both France and Germany assume divorce jurisdiction based on the nationality of either spouse. *See* Bernard Audit, *Private International Law, in* Introduction to French Law 453, 460 (George A. Bermann & Etienne Picard eds., 2008); Kurt Siehr, *Private International Law, in* Introduction to German Law 337, 353 (Mathias Reimann & Joachim Zekoll eds., 2d ed. 2005). *See also* Morley, *supra* note 1, at 89-100 (surveying divorce jurisdiction rules in other countries).

109. An act respecting divorce and corollary relief (Divorce Act) § 3(1), R.S., 1985, c. 3 (2d Supp.) (Can.). *See* Julien D. Payne & Marilyn A. Payne, Canadian Family Law 176-78 (2d ed. 2006). If the members of the couple are resident in different provinces and both file divorce petitions, the court in which the first action was filed generally assumes jurisdiction. *Id.*

110. *See id.* at 444-46.

111. *See* Jorge A. Vargas, Mexican Law for the American Lawyer 549-55 (2009).

112. Council Regulation (EC) No. 2201/2003 Concerning Jurisdiction and the Recognition and Enforcement of Judgments in Matrimonial Matters and in Matters of Parental Responsibility (Brussels IIA). Although Denmark is a member of the EU, it has opted out of the Brussels IIA regime. Brussels IIA also does not apply in European jurisdictions that are not part of the European Union, including Norway and Switzerland.

113. Brussels IIA, *supra* note 112, art. 3. Under article 3, a court may take jurisdiction in the country where both spouses are habitually resident, or where the respondent is habitually resident, and both of these grounds are consistent with the U.S. approach to bilateral divorce jurisdiction. Article 3 also allows jurisdiction in the country where the applicant is habitually resident if he or she has either lived there for at least a year before filing or has lived there for at least six months and has the nationality of or is domiciled in that country. Unless the respondent consented to jurisdiction, a divorce obtained in these circumstances would likely be treated as an ex parte divorce by a court in the United States if it were later asked to recognize and enforce the European court's orders.

114. *See supra* note 67 and *infra* notes 166-78 and accompanying text.

115. Brussels IIA, *supra* note 112, art. 19. *See* Máire Ní Shúilleabháin, Cross-Border Divorce Law: Brussels II *bis* 188-96 (2010).

116. *E.g.,* Hodson, *supra* note 30 at 70-73; Shúilleabháin, *supra* note 115, at 149-52.

117. Brussels IIA, *supra* note 112, recital (8).

118. See Shúilleabháin, *supra* note 115, at 165-75.

119. Council Regulation (EU) No. 1259/2010 of 29 December 2010 implementing enhanced cooperation in the area of the law applicable to divorce and legal separation. *See generally* Michael Wells-Greco, *Evolving EU Private International Law: An Overview of the Commission's Proposal on the Law Applicable to Divorce and Legal Separation,* International Family Law, Nov. 2010, at 333-34. There are 14 participating EU member states: Austria, Belgium, Bulgaria, France, Germany, Hungary, Italy, Latvia, Luxembourg, Malta, Portugal, Romania, Slovenia, and Spain.

120. *See, e.g.,* Sinha v. Sinha, 834 A.2d 600, 606 (Pa. Super. Ct. 2003) (declining to defer to proceedings pending in India); Marriage of Kimura, 471 N.W.2d 869, 878-80 (Iowa 1991) (concluding that Japan was not a more convenient forum); Ismail v. Ismail, 702 S.W.2d 216, 223 (Tex. App. 1985) (concluding that Egypt was not a more convenient forum when wife could not sue there for divorce). *See generally* Robin Cheryl Miller, *Doctrine of Forum Non Conveniens: Assumption or Denial of Jurisdiction of Action Involving Matrimonial Dispute,* 55 A.L.R.5th 647 (1998 & Supp.).

121. *E.g., Sinha,* 834 A.2d at 604-05; *see also* Buckner v. Buckner, 622 P.2d 242, 244-45 (N.M. 1981); MacLeod v. MacLeod, 383 A.2d 39, 42 (Me. 1978).

122. *E.g.,* Maraj v. Maraj, 642 So. 2d 1103, 1004 (Fla. Dist. Ct. App. 1994).

123. 330 U.S. 501 (1947). Under *Gulf Oil* there is a strong presumption that the plaintiff's choice of forum should be respected. *See generally* SCOLES ET AL., *supra* note 2, §§ 11.8–.12, at 492–502. *See also* Piper Aircraft Co. v. Reyno, 454 U.S. 235, 255–56 (1981) (distinguishing between resident and foreign plaintiffs and concluding that it may not be reasonable to assume that a U.S. forum is convenient when chosen by a foreign plaintiff).

124. *See* Dorati v. Dorati, 342 A.2d 18 (D.C. 1975); Ismail v. Ismail, 702 S.W.2d 216, 223 (Tex. App. 1985). In MacLeod v. MacLeod, 383 A.2d 39 (Me. 1978), a wife sought to enforce a French divorce decree after she had moved to Virginia and her former husband had moved to Thailand. She began an action in Maine and had her former husband personally served within the state when he came for his parents' golden wedding anniversary. *Id.* at 40. The court denied his inconvenient forum motion, noting that the wife had no alternative forum within the United States. *Id.* at 43; *cf.* Corning v. Corning, 563 A.2d 379, 380–81 (Me. 1989) (granting dismissal on the ground of forum non conveniens where a suitable alternate forum existed in Massachusetts). *See generally* RESTATEMENT (SECOND) OF CONFLICT OF LAWS § 84 (1971).

125. *E.g., In re* Ramadan, 891 A.2d 1186, 1191 (N.H. 2006), Vazifdar v. Vazifdar, 547 A.2d 249, 252 (N.H. 1988).

126. The court observed that although wife might not be permitted to bring a post-dissolution action for alimony and property division in Japan, she could bring such an action in Iowa and take advantage of "liberal rules" governing asset discovery and financial relief. Marriage of Kimura, 471 N.W.2d 869, 880 (Iowa 1991).

127. Jagger v. Superior Court, 158 Cal. Rptr. 163, 167–68 (Cal. Ct. App. 1979). The court concluded that a stay rather than dismissal was appropriate in the circumstances, because the English courts had stayed Bianca's divorce proceedings there for so long as she continued to prosecute the action in California. *Id.* at 168. *See also* Marriage of Taschen, 36 Cal. Rptr. 3d 286 (Cal. Ct. App. 2005), *review denied* (2006).

128. 687 N.Y.S.2d 426, 428 (N.Y. App. Div. 1999) (*Bourbon I*). *See also* Mary F.B. v. David B., 447 N.Y.S.2d 375, 378 (N.Y. Fam. Ct. 1982) (allowing wife's action for support to proceed against husband located in New York despite pendency of husband's divorce action filed in France).

129. Bourbon v. Bourbon, 751 N.Y.S.2d 302, 304 (N.Y. App. Div. 2002) (*Bourbon II*). The foreign divorce order must be a final judgment. *See* Cahen-Vorburger v. Vorburger, 725 N.Y.S.2d 343, 344 (N.Y. App. Div. 2001).

130. *See* PAYNE & PAYNE, *supra* note 109, at 178–79.

131. *See* HODSON, *supra* note 30, at 84–91; MORLEY, *supra* note 1, at 102–03.

132. Brussels IIA, *supra* note 112, art. 19.

133. *See* SHÚILLEABHÁIN, *supra* note 115, at 201–09.

134. *See* JKN v. JCN [2010] EWHC 843 (Fam).

135. *E.g., In re* Sigmar, 270 S.W.3d 289, 295–96 (Tex. App. 2008); *see also* Chlupacek v. Reed, 169 S.E.2d 782 (Ga. 1969) (approving writ of ne exeat to prevent husband from returning to Austria). *Cf.* Fakiris v. Fakiris, 575 N.Y.S.2d 924 (N.Y. App. Div. 1991). *See generally* H.D. Warren, *Injunction Pendente Lite in Suit for Divorce or Separation*, 164 A.L.R. 321 (1946 & Supp.)

136. *E.g.,* Bansal v. Bansal, 748 So. 2d 335 (Fla. Dist. Ct. App. 1999).

137. *E.g.,* Marriage of Kosmond, 830 N.E.2d 596, 597 (Ill. App. Ct. 2005); *but see* Am. Univ. of the Caribbean v. Tien, 26 So. 3d 56 (Fla. Dist. Ct. App. 2010) (vacating injunction directed at husband's corporations).

138. *See* HODSON, *supra* note 30, at 111–27; MORLEY, *supra* note 1, at 151–53; Jonathan I. Blackman, *Provisional Measures in Cross-Border Cases, in* INTERNATIONAL LITIGATION STRATEGIES AND PRACTICE 65 (Barton Legum ed., 2005).

139. *Kosmond,* 830 N.E.2d at 601–02.

140. 570 So. 2d 996, 997 (Fla. Dist. Ct. App. 1990); *cf.* Nasser v. Nasser, 859 N.Y.S.2d 445, 445 (N.Y. App. Div. 2008).

141. *See generally* RESTATEMENT (SECOND) OF CONFLICT OF LAWS § 53 (1971). *E.g.,* Brown v. Brown, 387 A.2d 1051, 1055 (R.I. 1978) (upholding an injunction preventing husband from pursuing a suit for divorce in Maryland); Verdier v. Verdier, 22 Cal. Rptr. 93, 105 (Cal. Dist. Ct. App. 1962) (overruling an injunction on the basis the domestic and foreign proceedings concerned separate

issues). Injunctions were more commonly ordered to prevent migratory divorce in the time before no-fault divorce had been widely accepted; older cases are collected in E. H. Schopler, Annotation, *Injunction Against Suit in Another State or Country for Divorce or Separation*, 54 A.L.R.2d 1240 (1957 & Supp. 2000, 2010). *See also* MORLEY, *supra* note 1, at 103–04.

142. See the discussion in chapter 1; *see generally* SCOLES ET AL., *supra* note 2, § 24.9, at 1273–76. For the English practice on stays, see HODSON, *supra* note 30, at 61–100.

143. Arpels v. Arpels, 170 N.E.2d 670, 671 (N.Y. 1960).

144. Jewell v. Jewell, 751 A.2d 735 (R.I. 2000).

145. *See Brown*, 387 A.2d at 1053–54.

146. *See Brown*, 387 A.2d at 1054; *cf. Jewell*, 751 A.2d at 738–39.

147. *See* Scott v. Scott, 268 N.E.2d 458, 459 (Ill. App. Ct. 1971).

148. *See supra* notes 104–05 and accompanying text.

149. *See, e.g., Brown*, 387 A.2d at 1054–55.

150. *See generally* 2 CLARK, *supra* note 2, § 16.7; SCOLES ET AL., *supra* note 2, § 14. *See also* RESTATEMENT (SECOND) OF CONFLICT OF LAWS §§ 233–34, and 257–59 (1971).

151. These rules are important in a variety of legal contexts beyond the scope of this volume, including inheritance and tax matters and creditors' rights. *See, e.g.*, Nationwide Res. Corp. v. Massabni, 694 P.2d 290, 293–95 (Ariz. Ct. App. 1984) (applying law of Morocco as matrimonial domicile to determine whether property interest was separate or community property in dispute with creditor).

152. 2 CLARK, *supra* note 2, § 16.7.

153. *See generally* SCOLES ET AL., *supra* note 2, § 14.4 (advocating a single reference to the law of the parties' domicile at the time of divorce).

154. *See, e.g.*, Ismail v. Ismail, 702 S.W.2d 216, 221 (Tex. App. 1985), *reh'g denied*, (1985) (applying quasi-community property statute to property of Egyptian couple where wife had settled in Texas and husband had significant contacts with the state).

155. UIFSA, 9 U.L.A. (1B) 235 § 604(a) (1999 & Supp. 2009). The responding tribunal applies its own procedures and remedies "to enforce current support and collect arrears and interest," *see id.* § 604(c), and either the statute of limitations of the enforcing state or the issuing state or foreign country applies, whichever is longer; *see id.* § 604(b).

156. *See supra* note 64 and accompanying text.

157. *See* RESTATEMENT (SECOND) OF CONFLICT OF LAWS § 98, cmt. g (1988 Revision). One unusual example is *Cardy v. Cardy*, where the court gave res judicata effect to a "transaction" entered into by parties under Quebec Civil Code in connection with Canadian parliamentary divorce. 258 N.Y.S.2d 955, 958, 960 (N.Y. App. Div. 1965).

158. *Cf.* Estin v. Estin, 334 U.S. 541 (1948); Vanderbilt v. Vanderbilt, 354 U.S. 416 (1957).

159. *See* RESTATEMENT (THIRD) OF FOREIGN RELATIONS LAW § 481 cmt. b (1987).

160. *E.g.*, Wolff v. Wolff, 389 A.2d 413, 419–22 (Md. Ct. Spec. App. 1978), *aff'd*, 401 A.2d 479 (Md. 1979). Courts in some states have concluded that they have no equitable or statutory authority to enforce marital property or support orders from foreign nations; *see, e.g.*, Nardi v. Segal, 234 N.E.2d 805, 808 (Ill. App. Ct. 1967). This approach was criticized by the Maryland courts in *Wolff*, 389 A.2d at 421. When there is a separation or settlement agreement that has not been merged or incorporated in to a court decree, it may be enforced with an action on the contract. *See, e.g.*, Torres v. McClain, 535 S.E.2d 623, 626 (N.C. Ct. App. 2000).

161. *See* RESTATEMENT (THIRD) OF FOREIGN RELATIONS LAW § 481 cmt. g (1987). The Comment notes:

No procedures exist in the United States for registration of foreign country judgments, or for their validation by exequatur, (i.e. endorsement by order of a court authorizing execution). Therefore, enforcement of a debt arising out of a foreign judgment must be initiated by a civil action, and the judgment creditor must establish a basis for the exercise of jurisdiction by the enforcing court over the judgment debtor or his property.

162. *See infra* notes 192–208 and accompanying text.

163. *See infra* notes 179–84 and accompanying text.

164. Mackenzie v. Barthol, 173 P.3d 980, 983 (Wash. Ct. App. 2007).

165. *See* Marriage of Kowalewski, 182 P.3d 959, 963 (Wash. 2008) (approving orders concerning interests in property located in Poland); Marriage of Ben-Yehoshua, 154 Cal. Rptr. 80, 87 (Cal. Ct. App. 1979) (same; property in Israel).
166. See the discussion in chapter 3.
167. *See* cases noted *supra* note 67.
168. *See generally* SCOLES ET AL., *supra* note 2, § 24.42.
169. 159 U.S. 113 (1895). The *Hilton* formulation provided:

> When [a] foreign judgment appears to have been rendered by a competent court, having jurisdiction of the cause and of the parties, and upon due allegations and proofs, and opportunity to defend against them, and its proceedings are according to the course of a civilized jurisprudence, and are stated in a clear and formal record, the judgment is prima facie evidence, at least, of the truth of the matter adjudged; and it should be held conclusive upon the merits tried in the foreign court, unless some special ground is shown for impeaching the judgment, as by showing that it was affected by fraud or prejudice, or that by the principles of international law, and by the comity of our own country, it should not be given full credit and effect.

> *Id.* at 159–60.

170. RESTATEMENT (SECOND) OF CONFLICT OF LAWS § 98 (1971, 1988 Revision). *See also* RESTATEMENT (THIRD) OF FOREIGN RELATIONS LAW §§ 481–82 (1987).
171. RESTATEMENT (SECOND) OF CONFLICT OF LAWS § 98 cmt. e (1971); *e.g.*, Nicol v. Tanner, 256 N.W.2d 796, 801 (Minn. 1976) (rejecting reciprocity requirement). Laws in some states impose a reciprocity rule, however; *see, e.g.*, MASS. GEN. LAWS ANN. ch. 235, § 23A(7) (2010). Under this approach, a party will be permitted to raise substantive defenses to enforcement of the foreign judgments if courts in that country would allow this type of reconsideration. *See, e.g.*, Desjardins Ducharme v. Hunnewell, 585 N.E.2d 321 (Mass. 1992).
172. RESTATEMENT (THIRD) OF FOREIGN RELATIONS LAW § 482 (1987); RESTATEMENT (SECOND) OF CONFLICT OF LAWS §§ 98 cmt. g, 115–16 (1971, 1988 Revision). *E.g.*, Southern v. Southern, 258 S.E.2d 422, 425 (N.C. Ct. App. 1979) (denying enforcement of English support order for lack of personal jurisdiction); Feinberg v. Feinberg, 351 N.E.2d 725, 727–28 (N.Y. 1976) (considering challenge to Dominican Republic divorce decree based on fraud).
173. RESTATEMENT (THIRD) OF FOREIGN RELATIONS LAW § 482(2)(d) (1987); *cf.* RESTATEMENT (SECOND) OF CONFLICT OF LAWS § 117 cmt. c (1971) ("enforcement will usually be accorded the judgment except in situations where the original claim is repugnant to fundamental notions of what is decent and just in the State where enforcement is sought").
174. *See supra* notes 77–92 and accompanying text; *see also* RESTATEMENT (THIRD) OF FOREIGN RELATIONS LAW §§ 421, 482(1)(b), 486(1) (1987).
175. *E.g.*, *Nicol*, 256 N.W.2d at 802 ("[T]he default status of the judgment, if reasonable notice and opportunity to be heard were afforded, and other requirements of basic fairness were met, should not affect the force of the judgment."); *see also* De Ganay v. De Ganay, 689 N.Y.S.2d 501, 502–03 (N.Y. App. Div. 1999) (extending comity to French judgments; wife had dual residency in France and New York, was personally served and made a "calculated determination not to appear"). *See* RESTATEMENT (SECOND) OF CONFLICT OF LAWS § 98 cmt. d (1971).
176. 382 N.W.2d 448, 450 (Iowa 1986).
177. 568 N.W.2d 353, 356–57 (Mich. Ct. App. 1997).
178. 748 N.Y.S.2d 131, 132 (N.Y. App. Div. 2002).
179. UNIF. FOREIGN MONEY JUDGMENT RECOGNITION ACT (UFMJRA), 13 (pt. II) U.L.A. 39 (2002); UNIF. FOREIGN-COUNTRY MONEY JUDGMENTS RECOGNITION ACT (UFCMJRA), 13 (pt. II) U.L.A. 7 (Supp. 2009). *See generally* the discussion in chapter 1.
180. UFMJRA § 1(2). *See* Wolff v. Wolff, 389 A.2d 413, 422 (Md. Ct. Spec. App. 1978) (holding that alimony provisions of English decree were not enforceable under the UFMJRA, but could be enforced in an independent equitable action on basis of comity). The UFMJRA exclusion of support obligations has been interpreted to include an amount awarded for attorneys' fees in English divorce proceedings. *See* Marriage of Lyustiger, 99 Cal. Rptr. 3d 922 (Cal. Ct. App. 2009). UIFSA is discussed *infra* at notes 192–208 and accompanying text.

181. Florida, Iowa, Michigan, and Minnesota deleted this exclusion of support judgments when they enacted the original UFMJRA but three of these states subsequently enacted the UFCMJRA.

182. UFCMJRA § 3(b)(3).

183. *See* UFMJRA § 7; UFCMJRA §§ 11, 3 cmt. 4.

184. UFMJRA, *supra* note 114 § 4(a)(1). In addition, a foreign judgment need not be recognized on grounds such as lack of notice, fraud, public policy, conflict with another judgment or, in cases of tag jurisdiction, if the foreign court was a "seriously inconvenient forum." *Id. See, e.g.*, Isack v. Isack, 733 N.W.2d 85, 89 (Mich. Ct. App. 2007) (declining to recognize Canadian divorce judgment based on wife's lack of notice).

185. The 1971 Hague Convention on the Recognition and Enforcement of Foreign Judgments in Civil and Commercial Matters entered into force in 1979, but it has gained only a handful of ratifications and accessions. Negotiations were carried out from 1992 through 2001 in an attempt to conclude a multilateral jurisdiction and judgments convention, but the effort eventually collapsed. *See* GARY B. BORN & PETER B. RUTLEDGE, INTERNATIONAL CIVIL LITIGATION IN UNITED STATES COURTS 101-02, 1017-18 (2007); Linda Silberman, *Comparative Jurisdiction in the International Context: Will the Proposed Hague Judgments Convention Be Stalled?*, 52 DEPAUL L. REV. 319 (2002).

186. The 1978 Hague Convention on the Law Applicable to Matrimonial Property Regimes addresses choice of law questions, and not recognition and enforcement of judgments. Within the EU, the Brussels IIA Regulation addresses recognition and enforcement of divorce judgments, but it does not apply to ancillary matters. *See supra* note 117 and accompanying text.

187. For the United Kingdom, see HODSON, *supra* note 30, at 1242-46. *See also* Ackerman v. Ackerman, 676 F.2d 898, 905 (2d Cir. 1982) (enforcing English judgment for breach of separation agreement entered into in New York divorce proceedings). For Australia, see MARTIN DAVIES ET AL., NYGH'S CONFLICT OF LAWS IN AUSTRALIA 567-69 (8th ed. 2010). For New Zealand, see 2 DICK WEBB ET AL., FAMILY LAW IN NEW ZEALAND § 11.93 (13th ed. 2007).

188. *See* sources cited in chapter 3.

189. STEPHEN ZAMORA ET AL., MEXICAN LAW 694-99 (2004).

190. *See* Barber v. Barber, 323 U.S. 77, 86 (1944); Worthley v. Worthley, 283 P.2d 19, 22, 25 (Cal. 1955). If necessary, the creditor might have the unpaid arrearages reduced to judgment by the court that entered the decree in order to have a judgment entitled to full faith and credit in other states. *See also* Mandel-Mantello v. Treves, 434 N.Y.S.2d 29 (N.Y. App. Div. 1980) (holding that foreign matrimonial awards may be recognized if they are final and not subject to modification).

191. *See infra* notes 209-12 and accompanying text.

192. Throughout this chapter, analysis of UIFSA is based on the 2008 amended version of the statute. UIFSA § 102(23) defines "support order" broadly to include

[A] judgment, decree, order, or directive, whether temporary, final, or subject to modification, issued by a tribunal for the benefit of a child, a spouse, or a former spouse, which provides for monetary support, health care, arrearages, or reimbursement and may include related costs and fees, interest, income withholding, attorneys' fees, and other relief.

For the definition of "foreign country," *see infra* notes 197-201 and accompanying text.

193. *Id.* § 604(a)(1)-(3).

194. 42 U.S.C. § 654(4)(B) (2010). This program is discussed in chapter 7.

195. *E.g.*, Office of Child Support Enforcement v. Gauvey, 241 S.W.3d 771, 773 (Ark. Ct. App. 2006) (approving enforcement of German spousal and child support orders by state OCSE).

196. *See* 42 U.S.C. § 654 (32)(B) (2010).

197. UIFSA § 105 provides that the statute applies to "a support proceeding involving: (1) a foreign support order; (2) a foreign tribunal; or (3) an obligee, obligor, or child residing in a foreign country." *Id.* § 105. Note that the definitions of "foreign support order" in UIFSA § 102(6) and of "foreign tribunal" in § 102(7) incorporate the definition of "foreign country" in § 102(5).

198. UIFSA § 102(5)(A). These jurisdictions are designated under 42 U.S.C. § 659(a).

199. UIFSA § 102(5)(B). *E.g.*, Willmer v. Willmer, 51 Cal. Rptr. 3d 10, 13-14 (Cal. Dist. Ct. App. 2006) (enforcing German child and spousal support based on reciprocal relationship between Germany and California). The list of these countries is different for each state; current information is available through the OCSE Intergovernmental Referral Guide Public Map Page at https://extranet.acf.hhs.gov/irgps/stateMap.do.

200. UIFSA § 102(5)(C). It is less clear which countries meet this test, which brings forward language used in the original 1993 version of UIFSA. The touchstone of this inquiry is reciprocity; *see, e.g.*, Foreman v. Foreman, 550 S.E.2d 792, 794-95 (N.C. Ct. App. 2001), in which the court approved registration and enforcement of an English spousal support order after concluding that various statutory instruments in England had established a procedure that would allow enforcement of North Carolina maintenance orders. *Cf.* Haker-Volkening v. Haker, 547 S.E.2d 127, 131 (N.C. Ct. App. 2001) (record failed to establish that Switzerland had enacted procedures substantially similar to those under UIFSA).

201. UIFSA § 102(5)(D). This looks forward to the time when the Convention takes effect. Information on the status of ratifications and accessions to the Convention will be available on the Hague Conference website. Note that the definition of "foreign country" incorporates an implicit reciprocity requirement, since any non-U.S. jurisdiction that does not recognize and enforce U.S. support orders will not qualify as a "foreign country" under UIFSA.

202. *See, e.g.*, Kalia v. Kalia, 783 N.E.2d 623, 632-34 (Ohio Ct. App. 2002) (holding that India was not a "state" for purposes of UIFSA and enforcing spousal and child support orders based on comity).

203. Chapter 7 addresses UIFSA's mechanisms for registering, contesting, and enforcing support orders, including the defenses that may be raised in these cases.

204. *E.g.*, Hook v. Hook, 611 S.E.2d 869, 872 (N.C. Ct. App. 2005); Marriage of Rassier, 118 Cal. Rptr. 2d 113, 115-16 (Cal. Ct. App. 2002). Several sections of UIFSA were renumbered after these cases; the current § 211 was § 205(f) in the 1996 version of UIFSA. *See generally* Brett R. Turner, *Interstate Modification of Spousal Support Under UIFSA*, 17 Divorce Litig. 125 (Aug. 2005). *See also* the Comment to UIFSA § 205, which suggests that the parties may be able to shift jurisdiction by consent.

205. *See generally* John J. Sampson, *Uniform Interstate Family Support Act (1996) (With More Unofficial Annotations)*, 32 Fam. L.Q. 385, 437 (1998). Sampson notes, however, that "the avoidance of interstate modification of alimony decrees reflects, at least in part, a disinterest in the topic of the original UIFSA Drafting Committee," which was focused "almost entirely on child support." *Id.* at 436 n. 94.

206. *E.g.*, Underwood v. Colley, 137 P.3d 365, 372-73 (Haw. Ct. App. 2006) (holding that court had no subject matter jurisdiction to modify order but that it could serve as initiating state to forward the request to New Mexico).

207. In the child support context, UIFSA § 616 permits registration and modification of a foreign-country child-support order. See chapter 7.

208. As explained in the Comment to § 211, "if a foreign spousal-support order were subject to modification in another country by the law of the issuing tribunal, this section would permit modification in a tribunal of this state."

209. 783 N.E.2d 623, 631 (Ohio Ct. App. 2002). In a few states, nonuniform versions of the UFMJRA have extended its provisions to support orders. *See, e.g.*, Fla. Stat. Ann. § 55.602(2) (2010); Iowa Code § 626B.1(2) (2010); Mich. Comp. Laws § 691.1151(1)(b) (2010); *see also supra* note 181 and accompanying text.

210. This language in UIFSA § 105 was added in 2008. *Kalia*, which did not allow registration of the Indian order under UIFSA, was decided under an earlier version of the statute.

211. *See* Zarembka v. Zarembka, 438 N.Y.S.2d 420 (N.Y. App. Div. 1981) (allowing recovery of monthly payments due under separation agreement incorporated into parties' Swiss divorce decree up to the date action was commenced); Mandel-Mantello v. Treves, 434 N.Y.S.2d 29 (N.Y. App. Div. 1980) (foreign matrimonial awards may be enforced in New York if they are final and incapable of being modified by the rendering country). Enforcement of a foreign support order through contempt sanctions may not be permitted; *see* Cooperman v. Cooperman, 309 N.Y.S.2d 683 (N.Y. Sup. Ct. 1970).

212. *E.g.*, Smith v. Smith, 543 So. 2d 1305 (Fla. Dist. Ct. App. 1989) (allowing domestication and prospective enforcement of alimentary allowance provisions of Canadian divorce decree).
213. Convention on the International Recovery of Child Support and Other Forms of Family Maintenance, art. 37(1), Nov. 23, 2007, 47 I.L.M. 257.
214. This is the current practice under federal child-support enforcement guidelines. *See supra* note 195 and accompanying text.
215. Contracting states are not obligated to allow direct applications for recognition and enforcement if no such procedure is available under their internal law. Art. 37(1) provides that "The Convention shall not exclude the possibility of recourse *to such procedures as may be available under the internal law of a Contracting State*" for a direct application to establish or to recognize and enforce of spousal support (emphasis supplied).
216. *See* art. 19(4). Under article 3(e):

    [M]aintenance arrangement" means an agreement in writing relating to the payment of maintenance which—

    i) has been formally drawn up or registered as an authentic instrument by a competent authority; or

    ii) has been authenticated by, or concluded, registered or filed with a competent authority, and may be the subject of review and modification by a competent authority.

217. Article 20 provides several additional bases for recognition and enforcement of spousal maintenance orders that are optional, in the sense that Contracting States may make a reservation declining to recognize and enforce decrees based on these jurisdictional grounds. These are that "the creditor was habitually resident in the State of origin at the time proceedings were instituted," art. 20(1)(c); that "there has been agreement to the jurisdiction in writing by the parties," art. 20(1)(e); and that "the decision was made by an authority exercising jurisdiction on a matter of personal status or parental responsibility," art. 20(1)(f). Under article 20(3), however, a Contracting State that makes this reservation must nevertheless recognize and enforce a maintenance decision "if its law would in similar factual circumstances" have conferred jurisdiction to make the decision. The United States intends to make this reservation, since jurisdiction on these other grounds would be inconsistent with our norms of due process. *See* S. Doc. No. 110-21, at xv (2008).
218. Art. 22(e).
219. Art. 22(b).
220. Art. 22(c)-(d).
221. Art. 22(a).
222. Art. 18(2) includes a series of exceptions to this rule that include an agreement in writing between the parties to the jurisdiction of another Contracting State (except in disputes relating to maintenance obligations in respect of children); where a creditor submits to the jurisdiction of another Contracting State; "where the competent authority in the State of origin cannot, or refuses to, exercise jurisdiction to modify the decision" or "make a new decision, or where the decision made in the State of origin cannot be recognised or declared enforceable in the Contracting State where proceedings to modify the decision or make a new decision are contemplated." Recognition and enforcement of a decision may be refused if it violates the limits on modification under article 18; *see* art. 22(f).
223. UIFSA § 211. *See supra* note 208 and accompanying text.
224. *See* art. 23(1): "Subject to the provisions of the Convention, the procedures for recognition and enforcement shall be governed by the law of the State addressed." Art. 32(1) provides that "Subject to the provisions of this Chapter, enforcement shall take place in accordance with the law of the State addressed."
225. Art. 27.
226. Art. 28. The physical presence of the applicant may not be required in a proceeding for recognition and enforcement, *see* art. 29, and the State addressed must provide at least the same range of enforcement methods for cases under the Convention as are available in domestic cases, *see* art. 33. One advantage of proceeding under the Convention is that no

legalization or similar formality may be required in these cases. *See* art. 41. A Contracting State may require that any application and related documents be translated into one of its official languages. *See* art. 44.

227. UIFSA §§ 703–704.
228. UIFSA § 705.
229. UIFSA §§ 706–713.
230. Bilateral agreements between foreign countries and the state or federal government often include enforcement of spousal support orders tied to child-support cases. *See, e.g.,* Office of Child Support Enforcement v. Gauvey, 241 S.W.3d 771, 773 (Ark. Ct. App. 2006) (enforcing combined spousal and child support order under reciprocal agreement with Germany).
231. See the discussion of English law in *Foreman v. Foreman,* 550 S.E.2d 792, 794–95 (N.C. Ct. App. 2001), and HODSON, *supra* note 30, at 142–47. *See also* SCOLES ET AL., *supra* note 2, § 15.37.
232. Art. 34(1); *see also* art. 1(c) (Convention applies to spousal support with the exception of provisions on administrative cooperation and enforcement).
233. *See* arts. 19(5), 37.
234. Art. 32(1)–(2).
235. Art. 33.
236. Art. 27.
237. Art. 28.
238. Arts. 14(5) and 17(b), made applicable in direct request cases by art. 37(2).
239. Art. 25(1)(a)–(c).
240. Art. 25(1)(d)–(f).
241. Arts. 41, 44.
242. Arts. 23(4) and 22(a). At this stage neither the applicant nor the respondent is entitled to make any submissions. The respondent must be promptly notified of the declaration or registration, or the refusal to register, and "may bring a challenge or appeal on fact and on a point of law" on one of a number of specified grounds within 30 days of notification, or 60 days if the contesting party is not resident in the state in which the declaration or registration was made or refused. *See* art. 23.
243. Art. 20(1)(c). Art. 20(3) incorporates the principle that Contracting states will recognize and enforce a decision "if its law would in similar factual circumstances confer or would have conferred jurisdiction on its authorities to make such a decision." *Id.* at art. 20(3).
244. *See supra* notes 218–22.
245. Art. 18(1).
246. Art. 18(2).

5

Parental Responsibility

Although all nations affirm the general principle that legal decisions affecting parent-child relationships must be based on the best interests of the child, this standard is differently understood in different legal systems. In the United States, parental rights and responsibilities are primarily defined by state laws coordinated within the framework of the Uniform Child Custody Jurisdiction and Enforcement Act (UCCJEA).[1] Cases involving the establishment of termination of parental rights are also subject to important requirements of federal statutes and constitutional law. International human rights laws recognize the fundamental importance of parent-child relations. The Convention on the Rights of the Child affirms the child's right "to maintain personal relations and direct contact with both parents on a regular basis, except if it is contrary to the child's best interests."[2]

This chapter addresses the law on establishing parent-child relationships, terminating parent-child relationships, and determining custody and access rights. It also outlines the procedures involved in litigating parental responsibility and obtaining recognition and enforcement of custody and access orders. The special problems of international child abduction are discussed in Chapter 6, and parents' financial responsibilities for children are considered in Chapter 7.

Establishing Parent-Child Relationships

From the child's perspective, establishment of legal parentage confers important rights. This is recognized in international human rights law, which protects the child's right to a name, to acquire a nationality, and "as far as possible, the right to know and be cared for by his or her parents."[3] Over the past generation, the dramatic increase in nonmarital births, the development of genetic tests of parentage and assisted reproductive technologies, and the growing acceptance of same-sex unions have complicated the question of determining parentage.

Legitimacy

Under the common law, a child born to a married woman was deemed legitimate, and this status determined the rights and responsibilities of both parents and child. Illegitimate

children suffered enormous legal discrimination, which could sometimes be reme-
died by a process of legitimation or acknowledgment.[4] Many jurisdictions, within and
beyond the United States, have enacted statutes that seek to eliminate all legal distinctions between legitimate and illegitimate children. In the United States, most classifications based on legitimacy of birth are now unconstitutional on grounds of due process
and equal protection.[5] The International Covenant on Civil and Political Rights (ICARA)
and the Convention on the Rights of the Child (CRC) also prohibit discrimination on the
basis of "birth or other status."[6] Nonmarital children may still be subject to some forms
of disadvantage, however, particularly when their paternity has not been formally established.[7] Although parentage laws have undergone similar changes around the world, this
remains a complicated subject in many countries.[8]

Legitimacy of birth remains relevant to the immigration and citizenship rights of
nonmarital children born outside the United States. Federal immigration law defines the
term "child" to include six separate categories of children.[9] Under the current statute, a
person born out of wedlock is treated as the child of his or her father if the person was
legitimated before the age of 18 while in the legal custody of the legitimating parent, or if
the father "has or had a bona fide parent-child relationship with the person."[10] Individuals who meet this definition may be able to acquire legal immigration status from a father
who is a permanent resident or U.S. citizen.[11]

Federal statutes define "child" more narrowly for citizenship purposes, with additional requirements for nonmarital children.[12] Children born outside of the United States
with married parents may acquire U.S. citizenship at birth according to rules that generally require that their U.S. citizen parent must have lived for some period of time in the
United States.[13] Children born outside the United States with unmarried parents are also
subject to 8 U.S.C. § 1409, which imposes additional requirements before the nonmarital
child of a U.S. citizen father can inherit his or her father's citizenship, including a legitimation or a sworn acknowledgement or adjudication of paternity before the child turns
18.[14] The same statute makes it easier for the nonmarital child of a U.S. citizen mother to
inherit his or her mother's citizenship.[15]

Traditional conflict-of-laws principles seek to uphold legitimacy, and the cases
sometimes state that this status is favored in the law. Under *Restatement (Second) of Conflict of Law* § 187, a child is held to be legitimate if he or she would be treated as legitimate
under either the law of the place where the child and parent were domiciled from the
time of the child's birth, or under the law of the father's domicile or the child's domicile
where that state has a significant connection to the particular question in dispute.[16] Similar principles are applied in federal immigration cases.[17] In disputes over legal parentage,
which is now a more important legal problem than the question of legitimacy, courts
have borrowed these older choice-of-law principles.[18]

Determining Parentage

The law of legitimacy placed marriage at the center of the inquiry, and the traditional
presumption of legitimacy based on a man's marriage to the child's birth mother has
been succeeded by a presumption of parentage based on marriage to the child's birth
mother. At the same time, contemporary statutes provide other presumptions of parentage, and more recent laws focus particular attention on genetic evidence of parentage. To

try to assure that all children benefit from legally established parent-child relationships, procedures for paternity establishment have been simplified and made more routine. In the United States, these procedures follow similar patterns in each state, based on the requirements of the federal child-support enforcement program.

Parentage Statutes

The Uniform Interstate Family Support Act (UIFSA) provides a framework for adjudicating parentage issues that is available in every state.[19] When custody matters are also in dispute, parentage may be adjudicated under the UCCJEA.[20] In addition, many states have enacted statutes based on the Uniform Parentage Act (UPA),[21] using either the original 1973 version or the 2000 or 2002 revision.[22]

All versions of the UPA provide that the parent and child relationship does not depend on the marital status of the parents.[23] A parent-child relationship may be established between a mother and child by proof that she gave birth to the child, by adjudication of her maternity, or by her adoption of the child. A father-child relationship is established based on an unrebutted presumption of paternity, an effective acknowledgment of paternity, an adjudication of paternity, or by his adoption of the child.[24] Presumptions of paternity arise from a marriage between a man and the mother of a child, even if the marriage was invalid, or on the basis of a parent living in a household with the child and holding the child out as his or her own.[25] State statutes provide a process for voluntary acknowledgment of paternity, often accomplished at the hospital at the time of child's birth. The new UPA also addresses the parentage of children born by means of assisted reproduction, including surrogacy arrangements.[26]

In those states that recognize same-sex marriage or an equivalent status, presumptions of parentage under state law also apply to same-sex couples.[27] The California courts have concluded that parentage statutes must be applied on a gender-neutral basis, which has made it possible for a woman to have the benefit (or burden) of a presumption of maternity based on living with a child and holding the child out as her own.[29] In California, this presumption has been applied in a range of different types of cases. For example, *In re Salvador M.* extended a presumption of maternity to a woman who had raised her younger half-brother after their mother died in an accident.[30]

Jurisdiction, Procedure, and Choice of Law

Personal jurisdiction is required before an adult may be adjudicated to be the parent of a child.[31] This is facilitated by UIFSA § 201, which extends personal jurisdiction to the full extent permitted by the U.S. Constitution. Among the specific grounds detailed in § 201, a state court may exercise personal jurisdiction over a nonresident individual who resided with the child in the state, who resided in the state and provided prenatal expenses or support for the child, or who engaged in sexual intercourse in the state that might have led to the child's conception.[32] Residents of foreign countries who come within the scope of § 201 may be subject to suit in the United States to establish parentage within this framework.[33]

UIFSA is expressly applicable to international cases and may be used by state child-support authorities to bring an action to establish paternity in the United States at the request of an authority in a foreign country.[34] Foreign residents may also bring a parentage action directly in state courts. For example, *Nissen v. Cortez Moreno* allowed a mother living with her child in Guatemala to bring a paternity suit against the child's alleged father in Florida, where he resided.[35] A foreign court's parentage order is generally given effect on the basis of comity when the court had a basis for exercising personal and subject matter jurisdiction, and the respondent had adequate notice and opportunity for a fair hearing.[36]

In international cases, federal courts may provide assistance under 28 U.S.C. § 1782 in obtaining evidence such as blood or DNA samples that may be needed for parentage proceedings pending in a foreign court.[37] Although the statute is discretionary, the courts routinely grant these requests. For proceedings pending in the United States, similar assistance may be requested from foreign authorities by means of letters rogatory or a Letter of Request under the Hague Convention on the Taking of Evidence in Civil or Commercial Matters.[38]

Courts hearing parentage disputes approach choice of law questions based on the rules traditionally applied to questions of legitimacy.[39] In this context, *Restatement (Second) of Conflict of Laws* § 287 directs a court to look to the local law of the state that, "with respect to the particular issue, has the most significant relationship to the child and the parent."[40] In an interstate proceeding, UIFSA § 303 directs a responding tribunal to apply the laws generally applicable to similar proceedings in the state, which allows that tribunal to apply the law it is most familiar with. The UCCJEA does not include a choice of law provision.

Within the United States, a court order establishing parentage in one state must be recognized in every other state pursuant to the Full Faith and Credit Clause of the Constitution. Because there is no public policy exception to this obligation, states must recognize the parental rights of same-sex partners reflected in a court order from another state, even if those rights would not be recognized under state law.[41] Full faith and credit does not extend to foreign country adoption or parentage orders, but these may be recognized based on comity. Comity will also determine whether a state court gives effect to a parent-child relationship created by operation of law in another state or country. For this reason, same-sex partners with parental rights that flow from their marriage or civil union will be on stronger ground if they obtain a court judgment recognizing their parental rights. For example, in a case involving a same-sex couple who had been married in the Netherlands and later gave birth to a child in New York, a New York court granted their request for a second-parent adoption to assure that their joint parental rights would be respected in other states.[42]

Nonmarital Parents and Rights of Custody

Traditionally, the mother of a nonmarital child was said to have a prima facie or primary right to the child's custody, sometimes expressed as a presumption in her favor absent evidence showing her to be unfit.[43] This tradition survives in the United States to the extent that an unmarried mother has legally protected parental rights from the time of the child's birth, while an unmarried biological father does not generally obtain full parental rights until his paternity is established.[44] As a constitutional matter, a biological parent who has developed a significant parental relationship with a nonmarital child acquires some important rights even when parentage has not been formally determined. These include the right to notice and a hearing on his or her fitness before parental rights may be terminated.[45]

State parentage laws generally recognize a presumed father's standing to bring an action to determine the existence of a parent-child relationship.[46] In addition, different categories of presumed fathers are entitled to notice and an opportunity for a hearing before their parental rights can be terminated. An unmarried father without the benefit of a statutory presumption may protect his potential parental rights by commencing a proceeding to adjudicate his paternity or registering with the state paternity or putative fathers registry.[47]

When courts adjudicate custody and access rights with respect to nonmarital children, they handle these cases as they would the same types of disputes in marital families.[48] In every state, the primary concern is to protect the child's best interests, and courts today generally place unmarried fathers and mothers on the same footing in making this determination. For jurisdictional purposes, custody and visitation issues concerning nonmarital children are subject to the UCCJEA, whether these issues arise in a parentage action or a separate proceeding.[49]

To bring a return proceeding under the Hague Abduction Convention, a parent must have "rights of custody" under the law of the child's habitual residence.[50] For children with a habitual residence in the United States, this issue is determined by the law of the state where the child resides. Typically, a nonmarital father whose parentage has not been legally established will not have custody rights. This issue was addressed in *In re Vernor*, in which an unmarried father brought an action under the Abduction Convention after the unmarried mother relocated to Australia with the parties' child. In response to a request from the Australian Family Court for a determination whether the child's removal was in breach of the father's rights of custody under Texas law, the Texas court held that the mother "alone had rights of custody to the child and she was the only person empowered to determine the child's primary residence. Because the parties never

The U.S. State Department information circular with Important Information for U.S. Citizens Considering the Use of Assisted Reproductive Technology (ART) Abroad is available at http://travel.state.gov/law/citizenship/citizenship_5177.html#.

married, [the father] had to legally establish his paternity to be named a parent with custodial rights."[51]

Assisted Reproduction and International Surrogacy

Many individuals and couples from other countries seeking assisted reproduction come to California and other states with laws that are particularly favorable for surrogacy. U.S. citizens also travel abroad to have children with the assistance of a foreign surrogate. International surrogacy cases generate substantial legal difficulties, however, particularly for intending parents from countries that prohibit surrogacy.[52] The Hague Intercountry Adoption Convention does not apply to cases of international surrogacy, but the Hague Conference has begun to explore the possibilities for international cooperation in addressing some of these difficulties.[53]

Laws on assisted reproduction and surrogacy vary significantly within the United States. Interstate surrogacy is widely practiced, facilitated by the requirement that every state must give full faith and credit to parentage orders, judgments declaring parental rights, or adoption decrees entered in other states.[54] Parentage laws in some states permit the intending parents to be listed on the birth certificate of a child born to a gestational surrogate, particularly when one or both parents have a genetic relationship to the child.[55] California allows a pre-birth declaration of parentage in surrogacy cases. In some situations, an adoption decree may be necessary to confirm parental rights in the intended parents after a surrogate birth,[56] and in interstate cases an adoption must comply with the Interstate Compact on the Placement of Children.

Internationally, the citizenship and immigration status of children born from surrogacy arrangements can be quite problematic. To acquire U.S. citizenship at birth, children born aboard to a foreign surrogate must be genetically related to a U.S. citizen parent; if they are not, they may not be able to enter the United States. For children born to surrogates in countries that do not confer birthright citizenship, there is also a risk that the child will be stateless.[57] Intending parents may face difficulties in obtaining recognition of foreign birth certificates or parentage judgments when they return home with their child, particularly in those countries that prohibit surrogacy. Even when legal recognition is possible in the intending parents' home country, authorities in the child's country of birth may have difficulty in providing parentage orders in the form required.[58]

Terminating Parent-Child Relationships

The parent-child relationship is constitutionally protected in the United States, and parental rights cannot ordinarily be terminated without notice and an opportunity for a hearing,[59] as well as proof by clear and convincing evidence of grounds such as parental unfitness or abandonment.[60] Involuntary termination of parental rights follows a process of intervention in the family by state child welfare authorities. In these cases, the initial goal is usually to reunify the family; but if the state's reasonable efforts to preserve the family do not succeed, there is a shift toward termination.[61] Jurisdiction for these purposes depends on the child's residence in the state, without regard to nationality or the parents' place of residence, and some child welfare cases raise complex international issues.[62] International human rights law also protects the parent-child relationship. A number of provisions in the CRC emphasize that a child has the right, as far as possible, "to know and be cared for by his or her parents"[63] and that a child "shall not be separated from his or her parents against their will, except when competent authorities subject to judicial review determine, in accordance with applicable law and procedures, that such separation is necessary for the best interests of the child. [64]

Determining Jurisdiction

Courts in the United States take jurisdiction in child welfare cases under the UCCJEA, which applies to any proceeding in which legal custody, physical custody, or visitation with respect to a child is an issue.[65] The statute accords a jurisdictional priority to the child's "home state," defined as the state "in which a child lived with a parent or a person acting as a parent for at least six consecutive months immediately before commencement of a child-custody proceeding."[66] Under § 105(a), the child's home state may be a foreign country. When a child has been living in a state for at least six months, a court may take jurisdiction based on the child's residence, without regard to the nationality or immigration status of the child or his or her parents.[67] If no court in the United States or a foreign country can assert "home state" jurisdiction, or if a court in the home state has declined to exercise jurisdiction, a court in another state may assume jurisdiction provided that two additional requirements are met. The child and at least one parent (or "person acting as a parent") must have a significant connection to the state other than mere physical presence, and there must be substantial evidence available in the state concerning "the child's care, protection, training, and personal relationships."[68] For these purposes, a "person acting as a parent" must have physical custody of the child and legal custody, or a claim to legal custody, under state law.[69]

Examples: UCCJEA Jurisdiction in Child Welfare Proceedings

- Two parents and their child are foreign citizens living in State A when local authorities commence child welfare proceedings concerning the child:
  1. If the child has lived in State A for at least six months with at least one parent, State A is the child's "home state" and a court in State A may assume jurisdiction under UCCJEA § 201(a)(1).
  2. If the child has lived in State A for less than six months, and previously lived in another state or foreign country for six months or more, the other state or country is regarded as the child's home state under the UCCJEA and the courts in State A may assume only temporary emergency jurisdiction under UCCJEA § 204.

- A child has been living in State A for more than six months without a parent or person acting as a parent. The child has no home state under the UCCJEA. A court in State A may take jurisdiction under one of the alternative grounds in UCCJEA § 201(a).

Even when a child's home state is in another state or foreign country, a state court may exercise temporary emergency jurisdiction under UCCJEA § 204 if the child is present in the state and "the child has been abandoned or it is necessary in an emergency to protect the child because the child, or a sibling or parent of the child, is subjected to or threatened with mistreatment or abuse."[70] Thus, if a parent dies or disappears or abuses a child shortly after arriving in a state with a child, the state court will be permitted to exercise temporary emergency jurisdiction, at least until the child's other parent is located and arrangements for the child's safe transfer can be made. The same basis for jurisdiction could be applied to an unaccompanied, undocumented immigrant minor found in the United States.[71] If the court hearing an emergency matter is informed of a custody proceeding or determination in another state or foreign country, the UCCJEA provides that the court "shall immediately communicate" with the other court.[72] A child-custody determination made on this emergency basis may become a final determination, and the state in which it is made may become the child's home state, if no proceeding is commenced in a state or foreign country with a basis for jurisdiction consistent with the grounds under the UCCJEA.[73]

The UCCJEA does not require courts to have personal jurisdiction over parents in order to adjudicate custody rights or terminate parental rights.[74] Many state courts have concluded that these cases fall within the status exception to the personal jurisdiction rule, concluding that constitutional due process norms are adequately addressed when nonresident parents are given notice and an opportunity for a hearing.[75] State statutes may provide expressly for jurisdiction over nonresident parents in juvenile cases,[76] and in some circumstances personal jurisdiction might be asserted under a long-arm statute applying a "minimum contacts" theory of personal jurisdiction. Not every case is appropriate for this approach, however. In *In re John Doe*, the Hawaii Supreme Court concluded that it was unreasonable and unfair on the facts of that case to terminate the parental rights of a mother who was living in the Philippines and whose only contact with the state of Hawaii was to acquiesce in the father's request to bring the child to the state for a brief visit.[77]

These jurisdictional standards are substantially consistent with the 1996 Hague Child Protection Convention, which applies to public sector child welfare proceedings as well as private litigation of custody and access rights.[78] Article 5 allocates primary responsibility in matters concerning children to the authorities of the child's place of habitual residence. Article 6 allows authorities to exercise jurisdiction based on the child's physical presence in cases involving refugee children, children who are internationally displaced because of disturbances in their country, and children whose habitual residence cannot be identified. In urgent situations, Article 11 allows the authorities of a country where the child is present to order temporary measures to protect a child.

Providing Notice and Opportunity for a Hearing

As a constitutional matter, parents are entitled to notice and an opportunity for a hearing, and proof of unfitness by clear and convincing evidence, before their parental rights may be terminated.[79] These rights apply regardless of the parents' citizenship or immigration status, but protecting these rights can be difficult in cross-border cases. If a parent's whereabouts are unknown, due process requires that authorities make reasonable

Assistance with International social work services, including assistance in locating family members in another country, is available from International Social Service (ISS), which has branches or affiliates in 140 countries. Contact the U.S. branch of ISS at 200 E. Lexington Street, Suite 1700, Baltimore, MD 21202—phone: 443-451-1200; fax: 333-451-1220; e-mail: iss-usa@iss-usa.org; website: http://www.iss-usa.org.

efforts to locate the parent.[80] Assistance may be available from the appropriate consulate, or from the U.S. branch of International Social Service (ISS). Once a parent is located abroad, it may be necessary to use the Hague Service Convention or letters rogatory to serve notice of the proceedings.[81]

Under the Vienna Convention on Consular Relations (VCCR),[82] local authorities must notify the appropriate consulate whenever a guardian or trustee is appointed for a minor or incapacitated person who is a foreign citizen,[83] and they must inform a foreign citizen who is arrested, imprisoned, or detained of his or her right to consular notice and access.[84] Consular officials may provide assistance to the authorities or to parents who are foreign nationals in resolving child welfare matters. Under the VCCR, consular officials of the United States have the same rights to notice and communication with U.S. nationals who may be caught up in foreign child protection, guardianship, or criminal proceedings.[85]

State courts have concluded that failure to give notice under the VCCR does not deprive the court of jurisdiction in child protection cases,[86] but they have also urged agency caseworkers to comply with consular notice requirements, noting that these procedures help to protect the child's best interests.[87] Some states have incorporated consular notice requirements into their agency practice, often by entering into a Memorandum of Understanding with a foreign consulate to spell out notice procedures.[88]

The opportunity for a hearing in a parental rights termination case has significant constitutional weight, but differences in language and legal culture and the obstacles posed by immigration law regularly complicate the process in international cases.[89] It may be possible for a parent to obtain a temporary humanitarian or "significant public benefit" immigration parole to enter the country for child welfare or custody proceedings.[90] For a parent who cannot attend, arrangements may be made for a telephone conference call or videoconferencing.[91]

Resources: Consular Notice

The U.S. State Department information circular on Consular Notice and Access is available at http://travel.state.gov/law/consular/consular_753.html.

Practical information for state and local authorities in the United States, including sample consular notification forms, is available on the same page. See also U.S. Department of State, *Consular Notification and Access* (3d ed. 2010), available at http://travel.state.gov/pdf/cna/CNA_Manual_3d_Edition.pdf.

> **Immigration Remedies for Children**
>
> Judges and advocates exploring immigration remedies for children may obtain information and assistance from the Immigrant Legal Resource Center (IRLC), 1663 Mission Street, Suite 602, San Francisco CA 94103—phone: (415) 255-9499; fax: (415) 255-9792; website: http://www.ilrc .org. The IRLC *Immigration Benchbook for Juvenile and Family Court Judges* is available on the website. Lawyers with questions regarding Special Immigrant Juvenile Status (SIJS) may contact the ILRC attorney of the day by phone at (415) 255-9499 (ext. 6263) or by e-mail at aod@ ilrc.org.

Immigration Issues in Terminating Parental Rights

Appellate courts in the United States agree that a parent's rights may not be terminated based on the parent's undocumented status.[92] Courts have also refused to rule that children have been abandoned based solely on the fact that their parent has been deported,[93] left the country to obtain a visa,[94] or failed to come forward when the child was taken into state custody.[95] A parent's immigration status may contribute to circumstances that present an imminent danger of abuse or neglect for a child, however.[96] Evidence that a parent placed his or her child informally for temporary care with relatives or friends or through an agency is also not sufficient proof that the child was abandoned.[97] In these cases, courts focus attention on parents' efforts to arrange appropriate care for their children, to maintain regular contact, and to provide financial support as far as they are able.[98] Courts have also emphasized that the perceived advantages of living in the United States cannot be a basis for termination of parental rights.[99]

In child welfare cases involving a parent who does not reside in the United States, the most appropriate course of action may be to arrange for children to return to the care of that parent.[100] If return is not appropriate, a child who is not a U.S. citizen or lawful permanent resident may be able to obtain lawful permanent residence (LPR) status as a "special immigrant juvenile." Eligibility requires a state court determination, before the child reaches age 21, that "reunification with one or both immigrant's parents is not viable due to abuse, neglect, abandonment or a similar basis found under State law,"[101] and also that it would not be in the child's best interest to be returned to the child's or parent's previous country of nationality or the country of last habitual residence.[102] This relief is available even if the child is out of immigration status or entered the country illegally.[103]

Custody and Access Rights

Every jurisdiction in the United States allocates custodial rights and responsibilities between a child's parents based on the child's welfare or best interests, and no presumptions are made based on the gender of the parent or child.[104] Many states encour-

> **Further Reading: Terminating Parental Rights**
>
> Ann Laquer Estin, *Global Child Welfare: The Challenges for Family Law*, 63 Okla. L. Rev. 691 (2011).

age shared parenting, including both joint decision making, or legal custody, and joint caretaking, or physical custody. Contemporary statutes often refer to parenting plans or parental responsibilities rather than conceptualizing these as rights of custody or visitation. Whenever possible, parents are encouraged to work together, and many cases are concluded with detailed agreements allocating parental rights and responsibilities.[105] Whether or not parents share decision-making authority, state laws seek to protect the child's right to maintain a relationship with both parents as well as the parent's right to continuing access to his or her child. These rights may be described in terms of access, parental contact, or parenting time.

In contested cases, the statutes and case law direct courts to consider factors such as the child's interactions and relationships with parents and other family members, the child's adjustment to home, school, and community, and the wishes of the child and the child's parents.[106] The law may specify that a court may not consider "conduct of a proposed custodian that does not affect his relationship to the child," so that custody may not be denied as a form of punishment for marital misconduct.[107] A few states have experimented with presumptions that custody should be awarded to the child's primary caretaker, presumptions of joint custody, or an approach that would allocate to each parent the same percentage of a child's time after divorce as that parent spent with the child before the dissolution of the family.[108] In a few states, statutes permit older children to decide the parent with which they wish to live, subject to the court's approval.[109] To protect the best interests of the child, custody orders are always subject to modification upon a showing of a significant change in circumstances.[110]

Language, Religion, Culture, and Citizenship

If one adult is designated as the child's sole legal custodian, that individual ordinarily has authority to decide major questions concerning the child's education, health care, or religious upbringing. In cases of joint parental responsibility, these decisions are shared. Some court orders or parenting agreements allocate different aspects of decision-making authority between the joint custodians. For example, in *Martinez v. Kurt*, a court enforced provisions of an agreement that allowed one parent to relocate with the children to Turkey but required that the children would attend a full-time English-speaking school.[111] Although there are exceptions, courts are generally reluctant to address questions of religious affiliation or practice in custody disputes. This is particularly true when one party asks the court to enter an order compelling some type of religious observance.[112] In the United States, custody awards may not be based on the parties' race or religion,[113] but courts sometimes refer to cultural factors in determining the child's best interests.[114]

Case law suggests that a court deciding a custody dispute may consider a parent's immigration status as one factor in determining a child's best interests, but immigration status should not be permitted to trump other factors, such as the strength and quality of the parents' relationships with a child.[115] Many foreign-born residents of the United States live in "mixed-status" families, and within these families differences in immigration status may create or exacerbate power differentials in ways that are harmful to a dependent spouse or children.[116] Basic parental rights are protected by the Constitution regardless of immigration status. In some practical circumstances, however, as when a parent will have difficulty obtaining a visa to live with or visit with children in the United States, immigration status may be a significant consideration.[117]

Beyond allocating decision-making authority, an award of custodial or joint custodial authority may have additional consequences. Rights to seek the return of a child under the Hague Abduction Convention depend upon having a "right of custody" under the law of the child's habitual residence.[118] For citizenship purposes, a child under the age of 18 who was born outside the United States may gain access to U.S. citizenship if the child resides in the United States in the legal and physical custody of a parent who is a U.S. citizen.[119] This would provide a path to derivative citizenship for a child whose custodial parent is naturalized.[120]

Parents and Nonparents

Individuals other than parents may have standing to file an action for custody in some circumstances, particularly when the child has been in their custody.[121] Statutes in many states allow grandparents to seek visitation with a child.[122] Stepparents, foster parents, and individuals who have attempted unsuccessfully to adopt a child may also seek custody or visitation rights. In some states, a parent's former spouse or cohabitant may have standing as the child's de facto or psychological parent.[123]

The legal test applied in custody disputes between parents and nonparents usually differs from the best interests standard applied to disputes between a child's legal parents. The traditional presumption in favor of the legal or "natural" parent could be rebutted only by proof of the parent's unfitness. The principle of deference to a child's parents has constitutional force, recognized in the Supreme Court's decision in *Troxel v. Granville*;[124] but the law permits an award of custody to someone other than a legal parent when there are compelling circumstances, particularly if it is shown that parental custody would be detrimental to the child.

Custody and Visitation in Military Families

When a parent is in military service, custody and visitation cases raise additional procedural and substantive issues. These begin with the Servicemembers Civil Relief Act (SCRA), which allows a servicemember to request a stay of custody proceedings when current military requirements materially affect the servicemember's ability to appear.[125] The complexities of military divorces are illustrated by *Harris v. Harris*, which applied the SCRA to a custody proceeding brought after a wife separated from her husband and relocated to Indiana. The husband, who was stationed in Germany, declined to accept voluntary service. Although the decision concluded that the Indiana courts had jurisdiction to dissolve the parties' marriage, it reversed the lower court's financial orders based on the absence of personal jurisdiction over the husband and held that the lower court erred by failing to comply with the SCRA.[126]

A significant group of states have enacted legislation to address the rights of a parent called to active duty in the armed forces.[127] These laws may provide for expedited

Resources: Military Family Issues

MARK E. SULLIVAN, THE MILITARY DIVORCE HANDBOOK: A PRACTICAL GUIDE TO REPRESENTING MILITARY PERSONNEL AND THEIR FAMILIES (2d ed. 2011)

hearings, delegation of visitation rights to another family member, and an approach to remodification of custody and visitation after the deployment ends. In the absence of such a statute, state courts decide these issues within the framework of their existing custody and visitation laws.[128]

Children living overseas as military dependents with a parent on active duty may be the subject of child protection or custody proceedings governed by the law of the country where the family is stationed.[129] Alternatively, a court in the state where the family is domiciled in the United States may be able to assert jurisdiction over these issues under state laws, if this can be accomplished within the parameters of the UCCJEA.[130]

Custody and Access Rights in Other Countries

There is broad agreement around the world that a child has the right to an ongoing relationship with both of his or her parents and that parental responsibilities should be allocated on the basis of the child's best interests.[131] Courts in different places may have quite different understandings of this standard, however, shaped by a variety of cultural and legal factors. Some systems include important concepts that are foreign to the common law tradition, such as *patria potestad* in the Latin American countries.[132] Some countries, particularly those with systems of customary or religious law, extend different rights to mothers and fathers.[133]

The question of whether the applicant possesses "rights of custody" under the law of the child's place of habitual residence is an important aspect of any case seeking return of a child under the Hague Abduction Convention. As a result, many cases decided under the Convention consider questions of comparative custody law.[134] For Convention purposes, however, "rights of custody" has an autonomous definition that is ultimately governed by the treaty itself. As noted by the U.S. Supreme Court in *Abbott v. Abbott*, "This Court consults Chilean law to determine the content of Mr. Abbott's right, while following the Convention's text and structure to decide whether the right at issue is a 'righ[t] of custody.'"[135]

International Access and Relocation

Shared parenting is particularly difficult in families that stretch across state or national borders, and large geographic distances raise the stakes substantially in custody

---

Resources: Comparative Custody Law

For useful introductions to foreign custody laws, see D. Marianne Blair & Merle H. Weiner, *Symposium on Comparative Custody Law*, 39 Fam. L.Q. 247–571 (2005) (including Argentina, Australia, Brazil, China, England and Wales, France, Germany, Greece, India, Iran, Ireland, Japan, Mexico, Nigeria, Russia, South Africa, and Sweden).

For the law of parental responsibility in Canada, see Julien D. Payne & Marilyn A. Payne, Canadian Family Law 373–410 (2d ed. 2006).

Parental responsibility laws of 23 European countries are surveyed in 3 European Family Law in Action: Parental Responsibilities (Katharina Boele-Woelki et al., eds. 2005).

See also the information available on the U.S. State Department web page at http://www.travel.state.gov (under "Child Abduction" and "Country Information").

disputes. Maintaining parent-child relationships over significant distances can be complicated and expensive. Courts have authority to enter orders for contact visits in another country,[136] and they may enter orders allocating the costs of international travel between the parents or requiring that a parent post bond to assure that the child is returned at the appointed time.[137] If the parties do not agree, a court may grant a parent explicit permission to travel to another country with a child. Conversely, the courts may enter orders that forbid either parent from removing a child from the jurisdiction; this is sometimes referred to as a ne exeat order. In some countries, the ne exeat rule takes effect by operation of law. When court permission is required, courts have been more likely to approve foreign travel or visitation when the other country involved is also a party to the Hague Abduction Convention.[138] If there is a concern regarding the possibility that the child will be wrongfully retained in another country, it may be possible to secure a mirror order from authorities in that country reflecting the terms of the parents' custody and access rights.

Relocation issues may come up either at the time of an initial custody determination, or on a motion to modify the prior orders to permit a parent to (or prevent a parent from) changing the child's place of residence to another country.[139] Many states have established criteria that apply to relocation cases, and these standards generally apply to both interstate and international situations.[140] In *Marriage of Condon*, the court described three additional considerations for international relocation cases: "cultural conditions and practices," geographic distance (and related problems concerning the expense of long-distance visits), and jurisdictional problems.[141] The California courts in *Condon* approved a mother's relocation with the children to Australia subject to certain conditions, but the appellate court concluded that the order did not sufficiently consider how to guarantee enforcement of the order in Australia and assure that the California court could retain jurisdiction.[142] Similar cases in other states have affirmed orders allowing custodial parents to relocate with children to Bosnia, Indonesia, Israel, Japan, and Thailand.[143] In many of these cases, the relocating parent was returning to her original home with her children, who also had strong ties to that place.[144] Courts are most likely to deny relocation requests when the parent seeking to move has previously attempted to thwart the child's relationship with the other parent.[145] A number of cases consider practical measures to support ongoing contact between children and their noncustodial parent after an international relocation, such as the allocation of travel costs.[146]

International Travel with Children

For U.S. citizens, passports are required for most travel outside the United States.[147] To obtain a U.S. passport for a minor, the child must appear in person, and both of the child's parents or guardians must give their consent.[148] A parent with sole legal authority to apply for the child may provide alternative documentation, such as a custody order or a death certificate for the other parent. For children with dual nationality, however, one parent may be able to obtain a passport from the other country without obtaining the other parent's consent.[149]

When a minor child travels abroad without both of his or her parents, the child should be accompanied by parental consent documents authorizing the child's travel. A birth certificate or adoption decree proving the parent's relationship to the child may also be important when the child has a different surname. For a child traveling with one

Relocation Principles

The Washington Declaration on International Family Relocation, a set of principles prepared by an international group of judges and family law experts, proposes that relocation cases should be decided on the basis of the child's best interests with no presumption for or against relocation. The Declaration suggests that in deciding whether to grant or deny a relocation request, judges should consider these factors:

- the right of the child separated from one parent to maintain personal relations and direct contact with both parents on a regular basis in a manner consistent with the child's development, except if the contact is contrary to the child's best interest;
- the views of the child, having regard to the child's age and maturity;
- the parties' proposals for the practical arrangements for relocation, including accommodation, schooling, and employment;
- where relevant to the determination of the outcome, the reasons for seeking or opposing the relocation;
- any history of family violence or abuse, whether physical or psychological;
- the history of the family and particularly the continuity and quality of past and current care and contact arrangements;
- preexisting custody and access determinations;
- the impact of grant or refusal on the child, in the context of his or her extended family, education and social life, and on the parties;
- the nature of the interparental relationship and the commitment of the applicant to support and facilitate the relationship between the child and the respondent after the relocation;
- whether the parties' proposals for contact after relocation are realistic, having particular regard to the cost to the family and the burden to the child;
- the enforceability of contact provisions ordered as a condition of relocation in the State of destination;
- issues of mobility for family members; and
- any other circumstances deemed to be relevant by the judge.[150]

parent or guardian, this could be a notarized affidavit from the absent parent consenting to the trip, or proof (such as a certified copy of a court order) that the person traveling with the child has sole legal custody and authorization to travel outside the country. This documentation may be required by airlines, buses, or cruise ships before the child is allowed to leave the United States, and it may be necessary in obtaining a visa to enter or leave another country.[151]

Litigating Parental Responsibilities

Forum shopping has been a chronic problem in custody litigation, both within the United States and in a global context. Courts in different places may take different approaches

Children's Passport Issuance Alert Program

In cases involving a risk of parental child abduction, a parent may register with the State Department's Child Passport Issuance Alert Program (CPIAP) to receive notice before a U.S. passport is issued for his or her child. The State Department information circular on Passport Issuance and Denial to Minors Involved in Custody Disputes is available at http://www.travel.state.gov/passport/ppi/family/family_866.html.

to the question of the child's best interests, and the general rule is that orders assigning parental responsibility and providing for the child's access to each parent are subject to modification as the child's circumstances change. Because custody orders remain modifiable, they are often not extended comity or full faith and credit in other jurisdictions.[152] These factors encourage forum shopping by parents who may be unhappy with a particular court's order and anticipate a more favorable outcome in another jurisdiction. For this reason, conflict-of-laws questions have become extraordinarily important in child-custody matters.

The principal international instrument on this subject is the 1996 Hague Convention on Jurisdiction, Applicable Law, Recognition, Enforcement and Co-operation in Respect of Parental Responsibility and Measures for the Protection of Children (Child Protection Convention), which the United States has signed and intends to ratify. Implementation of the Child Protection Convention in the United States will be carried out largely through new provisions in the UCCJEA. There are some important differences between the two regimes; the information outlined here is based on the current version of the UCCJEA, without regard to the proposed amendments or the Child Protection Convention.[153]

Working with the Uniform Child Custody Jurisdiction and Enforcement Act (UCCJEA)

Although traditional doctrine placed jurisdiction over custody proceedings in the state where the child was domiciled, more contemporary case law recognized a variety of appropriate bases for jurisdiction.[154] With this shift came the possibility that several states would have concurrent jurisdiction over custody matters, and a new set of conflict-of-laws problems. In the United States, these issues were addressed by uniform legislation developed in 1968[155] and the federal Parental Kidnapping Prevention Act (PKPA) in 1980.[156] The 1997 UCCJEA, which is in effect in almost every state,[157] recognizes multiple grounds for jurisdiction but extends a clear jurisdictional priority to the child's "home state" and provides a relatively precise definition of this term. In addition, the UCCJEA provides for "exclusive continuing jurisdiction" in a court that has taken jurisdiction under the statute to limit the potential for subsequent jurisdictional conflict between states.

The UCCJEA extends to the international context and generally requires state courts to treat foreign countries as if they were sister states.[158] It applies to a wide range of proceedings in which custody and visitation issues arise, including divorce, separation, neglect, abuse, dependency, guardianship, paternity, termination of parental rights, and protection from domestic violence.[159] It applies in states that still use the terminology of "custody and visitation" as well as states that have adopted new language to describe parental rights and responsibilities. In the international context, the term includes proceedings of another country relating to institutions that are analogous to custody.[160]

Because custody litigation was traditionally understood to concern a status, there was no requirement of personal jurisdiction over the child's parents. The personal jurisdiction question has been debated in the United States since the Supreme Court held in *May v. Anderson* that a custody decree entered in Wisconsin, where the children were domiciled, was not entitled to full faith and credit in another state because the court in Wisconsin had not acted with personal jurisdiction over both parents.[161] The Court's subsequent rulings have not clarified whether it considers personal jurisdiction to be necessary as a matter of due process in custody litigation,[162] and many state courts have concluded that it is not required.[163] The federal PKPA defines circumstances in which state courts must respect custody orders entered in other states and makes no reference to personal jurisdiction. UCCJEA § 201(c) states explicitly: "Physical presence of, or personal jurisdiction over, a party or a child is not necessary or sufficient to make a child-custody determination." Both the PKPA and the UCCJEA require that a responding parent or parents have notice and an opportunity for a hearing in a custody proceeding,[164] however, and this is also necessary as a matter of constitutional due process.[165]

Determining the Child's Home State

Jurisdictional priority under the UCCJEA is accorded to the child's home state, defined in § 102(7) as "the State in which a child lived with a parent or a person acting as a parent for at least six consecutive months immediately before the commencement of a child-custody proceeding."[166] For a child less than six months old, home state means "the State in which the child lived from birth with any of the persons mentioned." Under this definition, "A period of temporary absence of any of the mentioned persons is part of the period." The definition is intended to be the same in substance as the definition used under the prior uniform statute, and state courts draw on their prior experience in applying this concept. With UCCJEA § 105, however, it has been made clear that a child's "home state" may be a foreign country.[167] The child's home state often is also the child's habitual residence under the Hague Children's Conventions, but the UCCJEA test is intended to draw a bright line. In most cases it is easy to determine where the child has resided for the past six months. In some, the inquiry is more complex, particularly when a family moves often or lives in multiple homes.[168]

Many international disputes force courts to determine whether a parent's trip abroad with a child has established a new home state, or whether the trip should be treated as a "period of temporary absence" under the UCCJEA. The same question may arise when a parent and child have come to the United States from another country. The UCCJEA does not define "period of temporary absence," and courts have disagreed on how the term should be construed.[169] *In re Calderon-Garza*, a paternity case that straddled the border between Texas and Mexico, concluded that Texas was the home state of a child when the child's mother came to El Paso to live with her parents shortly before the child was born and remained there for two months before returning to her home in Guadalajara,

Examples: Defining the Home State

- Children have lived for several years with their parents in Country X when the parents sell their home and relocate the family with their possessions to State A in the United States. After six months, State A will be the home state of the children for purposes of the UCCJEA.
- Children have lived for several years with their parents in Country X when the family moves to State A for a one-year academic exchange. Because the time spent in State A may be characterized as a period of temporary absence from Country X, Country X remains the home state of the children for purposes of the UCCJEA.
- Children move with their parents from State A to Country X, where they live for three months, and then to Country Y, where they live for four months. At this point, the children have no home state for purposes of the UCCJEA.

Mexico. In that case, the court held that Texas was where the child had "lived from birth with a parent" and rejected the mother's argument that she did not "live" in El Paso because her visit was intended as a temporary absence from Mexico.[170] In *Karam v. Karam*, the court rejected a father's argument that a family's stay of more than two years in Florida constituted a temporary absence from their usual home in France.[171] Similarly, state courts have held that time a child spends living abroad with a parent on active duty in the U.S. military is not a "period of temporary absence" from the United States.[172] Other courts have treated relatively long periods of residence outside the country as temporary absences, however, particularly when a parent and child have returned to their original residence before custody proceedings begin.[173]

The definition of home state is particularly important in cases involving children who may have been wrongfully removed from or retained in a country that is not their habitual residence.[174] State courts should be alert to the possibility that one parent has misrepresented a trip with a child to the United States as temporary in order to prevent the left-behind parent from starting custody proceedings until after six months have elapsed. Depending on the facts, a state court applying the UCCJEA might determine that the time was a period of temporary absence that has not shifted the child's home state, or the court might decline to exercise jurisdiction under the inconvenient forum provisions in § 207 or by reason of the petitioner's conduct under § 208.

Establishing Initial Jurisdiction

Under UCCJEA § 201(a)(1), a state court has jurisdiction to make an initial child-custody determination if the state was the child's home state on the date the proceeding was begun, or if the state was the child's home state within the six months before the proceeding began and a parent or person acting as a parent continued to live in this State.[175] If the courts of some state or foreign country meet the "home state jurisdiction" test of § 201(a)(1), no other state court may take jurisdiction unless the court of the home state declines to exercise jurisdiction on one of the two grounds described below.[176] Because this question is decided based on the date the proceeding began, time spent living in a place after filing of a petition is not considered.[177]

In many cases, on the breakup of a family that has been living abroad, one parent will return to the United States with the children, before any child-custody proceedings have been commenced, while the other parent continues to live abroad. This may raise issues under the Hague Abduction Convention (discussed in Chapter 6). For purposes of custody jurisdiction, the country where the family was living will typically be considered the children's home state, and the new state will not be able to take jurisdiction under § 201(a)(1) until the children have lived there for six months.[178] The court in the new state can assume jurisdiction if the court in the foreign country declines it as an inconvenient forum,[179] or it can take temporary emergency jurisdiction if the requirements of § 204 are met.

If there is no other place where a court could take home state jurisdiction consistently with the standards of § 201(a)(1), a state court may take jurisdiction on the alternative ground in § 201(a)(2). Jurisdiction is available if two additional tests are met. First, the child and the child's parents, or the child "and at least one parent or a person acting as a parent," must have "a significant connection with this State other than mere physical

Examples: Home State Jurisdiction

- Parents live together for several years with their children in Country X when their relationship ends. One parent brings the children to State A in the United States and begins proceedings for an initial custody determination.
    1. If the children have lived with their parent in State A for less than six months when the parent commences proceedings there, and the other parent continues to live in Country X, the court in State A cannot exercise initial custody jurisdiction unless the court in Country X declines to hear the case.
    2. If the children and their parent have lived in State A for more than six months when the parent commences proceedings there, the court in State A will have home state jurisdiction under UCCJEA § 201(a)(1).

- Parents and their children live together for several years in State A when one parent relocates with the children to Country X. If the left-behind parent continues to live in State A, the courts in State A will continue to have jurisdiction for six months to enter an initial custody determination under UCCJEA § 201(a)(1). Once the children have lived in Country X for six months, however, State A will no longer have home state jurisdiction.

- Parents and their children have lived together for nine months in State A when one parent takes the children on a trip to Country X for the summer to visit their grandparents. At the end of the summer, the parent refuses to return to State A with the children. The summer visit could be treated as a period of temporary absence from State A, so that State A's home state jurisdiction would continue for another six months.

presence." Second, there must be "substantial evidence . . . available in this State concerning the child's care, protection, training, and personal relationships."[180] In applying this test, courts consider such connections as the presence of other family members and time the child has spent living in the state.[181] Courts have reached different conclusions on whether visits to a state were sufficient to establish a "significant connection."[182] The deeper the child's connections, however, the more likely it is that a court will be able to conclude that substantial evidence is available in the state.

Although the Uniform Child Custody Jurisdiction Act (UCCJA) permitted a state to take jurisdiction based on a significant connection and substantial evidence even if another state might qualify as the home state, this is no longer true under the UCCJEA.[183] Thus, in *Calderon-Garza*, the priority for home state jurisdiction in Texas prevailed over what appeared to be stronger connections with Mexico.[184] When there is no state with home state jurisdiction, and the parties have filed competing proceedings in different states based on significant connection jurisdiction, § 206 encourages communication between the courts involved and gives priority to the first action filed unless that court declines jurisdiction.

Example: Significant Connection Jurisdiction

Children relocate with their parents from State A to Country X, where they live for three months, and then to Country Y, where they live for four months. One parent returns to State A with the children and commences custody proceedings. Because no state or foreign country could exercise home state jurisdiction within the meaning of UCCJEA § 201(a)(1), a court in State A may assume jurisdiction if there is a significant connection between the children and their parent and State A as well as substantial evidence in State A concerning the children's care, protection, training, and personal relationships.

If there is no court that could exercise jurisdiction under either § 201(a)(1) or § 201(a)(2), or if those courts have declined to exercise jurisdiction, a state court may assume jurisdiction under the default provision in § 201(a)(3). Because this is a question of subject matter jurisdiction, it cannot be based solely on the consent of the parties.[185] Additionally, a state court may take jurisdiction under § 201(a)(4) if no court of any other state or country would have jurisdiction under the prior tests.[186] The priority of home state jurisdiction under the UCCJEA is emphasized by § 201(b), which states that the framework established in § 201(a) "is the exclusive jurisdictional basis for making a child-custody determination by a court of this State."

Except in emergency situations, a state court is not permitted to take initial jurisdiction based on § 201 if a court in another state or country has already begun to exercise jurisdiction to make a child-custody determination consistently with the provisions of the UCCJEA.[187] To reinforce this rule, the UCCJEA requires that the parties must submit and the court must consider information concerning any other proceeding concerning the custody of or visitation with the child, including proceedings relating to domestic violence, protective orders, termination of parental rights, or adoption.[188]

Invoking Temporary Emergency Jurisdiction

UCCJEA § 204 allows a state court to exercise temporary emergency jurisdiction if a child is present in the state and has been abandoned or "it is necessary in an emergency to protect the child because the child, or a sibling or parent of the child, is subjected to or threatened with mistreatment or abuse." Any order the court enters is temporary in the sense that it continues only until the court that would otherwise have jurisdiction has an opportunity to act.[189] Emergency jurisdiction may be invoked whether or not there has been a previous child-custody determination. Under § 204(d), the court asked to make an emergency order—and any court informed of emergency proceedings in another forum—must immediately communicate with each other "to resolve the emergency, protect the safety of the parties and the child, and determine a period for the duration of the temporary order."

Courts may be called on to enter temporary orders under § 204 in the context of disputes under the Hague Abduction Convention.[190] Emergency jurisdiction is especially important in circumstances of family violence. For example, when child protective services intervene in cases of abuse or neglect, courts have asserted jurisdiction so long as the reasons for the intervention exist. *In re Nada R.* involved two children, placed in

---

Examples: Temporary Emergency Jurisdiction

- Parents from Country X are traveling for several months in State A with their children when they are arrested for serious child abuse and the children are taken into state custody. A court in State A may exercise temporary emergency jurisdiction under UCCJEA § 204.
- Parents and their children live together in Country X, when one parent flees with the children to State A to escape domestic violence. Immediately after arriving in State A, that parent brings an action to obtain a civil protection order. The court in State A may make a temporary child-custody determination as part of this proceeding.

their father's custody following a divorce in Saudi Arabia, who were removed from his custody several years later based on events that occurred while they were vacationing in the United States. The court adjudicated the children to be dependent, finding by clear and convincing evidence that returning the children to their father would place them at substantial risk of harm, and concluded that the determination should be treated as temporary until it was possible to decide whether the Saudi decree was enforceable under the UCCJEA.[191]

Emergency jurisdiction under § 204 may also be invoked in the context of proceedings for civil protection orders in spousal or partner abuse cases. For the custody aspects of a protection order to be enforceable in other states, the order should be made in compliance with the UCCJEA and the PKPA.[192] For example, a New York court exercised temporary emergency jurisdiction in *Hector G. v. Josefina P.* when it stayed the father's action to enforce a custody decree from the Dominican Republic "until the underlying issues of domestic violence and the safety of the children could be resolved or a determination could be made that it was appropriate for this court to assume full jurisdiction of the matter."[193]

Grounds to Decline Jurisdiction

UCCJEA § 206 requires a court to decline to exercise jurisdiction, except in emergency circumstances, if a court in another state or country is already exercising jurisdiction on grounds consistent with the UCCJEA.[194] In addition, the statute provides two grounds on which a state court may decline to exercise its jurisdiction. The court may conclude that it is an inconvenient forum and another court is more appropriate under § 207, and it must decline to act if "a person seeking to invoke its jurisdiction has engaged in unjustifiable conduct" under § 208.[195]

UCCJEA § 207 allows the question of inconvenient forum to be raised at any time on the motion of a party, the court's own motion, or the request of another court.[196] A court may determine that it is an inconvenient forum only if it also concludes that another court is a more appropriate forum; and if it makes this determination, "it shall stay the proceedings upon condition that a child-custody proceeding be promptly commenced

When Is a Forum Inconvenient?

UCCJEA § 207 directs courts to consider these factors in deciding inconvenient forum motions:

- whether domestic violence has occurred and is likely to continue in the future and which state could best protect the parties and the child;
- the length of time the child has resided outside the state;
- the distance between the court deciding the motion and the court that would assume jurisdiction;
- the relative financial circumstances of the parties;
- any agreement of the parties as to which court should assume jurisdiction;
- the nature and location of the evidence required to resolve the pending litigation, including testimony of the child;
- the ability of each court to decide the issue expeditiously and the procedures necessary to present evidence; and
- the familiarity of each court with the facts and issues in the pending litigation.

in another designated state."[197] It is important to note that even if a court with home state jurisdiction under § 201(a)(1) or continuing exclusive jurisdiction under § 202 determines that it should defer to another court under § 207, that other court will be able to assume jurisdiction only if the subject matter jurisdiction requirements of § 201(a) are satisfied.[198]

Although the decision whether to decline jurisdiction under § 207 is discretionary,[199] the court must decline jurisdiction under § 208(a) if it "has jurisdiction under this Act because a person seeking to invoke its jurisdiction has engaged in unjustifiable conduct."[200] There is a narrow set of exceptions to this rule.[201] The statute does not define "unjustifiable conduct," but the Comment to this section makes it clear that it is directed to conduct such as removing, secreting, retaining, or restraining a child in order to create jurisdiction.[202] The Comment states: "Domestic violence victims should not be charged with unjustifiable conduct for conduct that occurred in the process of fleeing domestic violence, even if their conduct is technically illegal." Instead, the court must inquire into "whether the flight was justified under the circumstances of the case."[203]

Effect of a Pending Hague Abduction Petition

If judicial authorities are notified that a child has been wrongfully removed to or retained in the state, Article 16 of the Child Abduction Convention provides that they "shall not decide on the merits of rights of custody until it has been determined that the child is not to be returned under this Convention or unless an application under this Convention is not lodged within a reasonable time following receipt of notice." Accordingly, a state court in this situation should suspend custody proceedings until the Hague Convention issues are resolved.[204] Moreover, custody orders entered by a state court before return proceedings are commenced under the Convention are not relevant to determining whether a child must be returned.[205] If the return petition is denied, custody proceedings may resume, and Article 19 of the Convention provides specifically that "[a] decision under this Convention concerning the return of the child shall not be taken to be a determination on the merits of any custody issue."[206] If a return order is entered under the Convention, state courts are obligated to enforce that order under the UCCJEA as if it were a child-custody determination.[207] A Hague return order implies that any further custody litigation will be carried out in the country to which the child is returned.[208]

Examples: Declining Jurisdiction

- Parents and their children live together for many years in Country X when the parents' relationship ends. One parent brings the children to State A in the United States, and begins initial custody proceedings in State A six months later. Although the court in State A has home state jurisdiction, it may decline to its jurisdiction under UCCJEA § 207 on the basis that the court in Country X is a more appropriate forum.

- Parents and their children live in Country X when one parent disappears with the children. A year later, the parent who remained in Country X is able to trace the children to State A. When the parent in State A brings proceedings there to obtain custody, the court should ordinarily decline to exercise jurisdiction based on the parent's unjustifiable conduct as provided in UCCJEA § 208.

> **Example: Intersecting Custody and Hague Abduction Proceedings**
>
> Parents and their children live together in Country X when the parents' relationship ends. One parent brings the children to State A in the United States and begins custody proceedings in State A six months later. While custody proceedings are pending in state court, the parent in Country X commences a separate return proceeding under the Abduction Convention. The court in State A must stay its custody proceedings, and if a return order is entered under the Convention the state court must enforce that order.

Exclusive, Continuing Jurisdiction

One innovation of the UCCJEA was the concept of continuing jurisdiction in § 202. Once a state court has made a child-custody determination that is consistent with the UCCJEA's jurisdictional requirements, that court has exclusive, continuing jurisdiction over the matter until one of two events occurs. A court may determine that its own continuing jurisdiction should end under § 202(a)(1) because "neither the child, nor the child and one parent, nor the child and a person acting as a parent have a significant connection with this State and . . . substantial evidence is no longer available in this State concerning the child's care, protection, training, and personal relationships."[209] The statute reserves this determination to the court with continuing jurisdiction.[210] Alternatively, continuing jurisdiction also comes to an end under § 202(a)(2) if "the child, the child's parents, and any person acting as a parent do not presently reside in this State."[211] A court with continuing jurisdiction may also determine that another court is a more appropriate forum under § 207 to hear new proceedings in a case.

Section 203, defining jurisdiction to modify a custody determination, is the mirror image of § 202. In requiring deference to a court that has made a previous child-custody determination, this section of the UCCJEA is applicable, by virtue of § 105(a), whether that other court is in another state or a foreign country.[212] The statute provides that a state court may not modify a child-custody determination made by a court of another state (or country) unless the new court has jurisdiction to make an initial determination under the rules in § 201(a)(1) or (2), and one of two conditions is met. Under § 203(1), the new state court may modify the prior determination if the original forum determines that it no longer has exclusive, continuing jurisdiction or concludes that the court in the new state would be a more convenient forum. Alternatively, under § 203(2), the new state court may modify the prior determination if it determines that "the child, the child's parents, and any person acting as a parent do not presently reside" in the state or country of the original forum.[213] In *Atchison v. Atchison*, a Michigan court applying the UCCJEA refused to modify a child-custody determination originally made in Ontario, even though the child had lived with her father in Michigan for two years, when the mother continued to reside in Ontario.[214] Conversely, in *Bjornson v. Bjornson*, the New York court concluded that it retained exclusive, continuing jurisdiction to modify its order two years after the mother moved with the child to Norway.[215] The question of a father's continued residence in California was contested in *Marriage of Nurie*, when he had spent substantial periods of time in Pakistan attempting to see his son and resisting his former wife's motions to modify a California custody determination.[216]

The court in *Hector G. v. Josefina P.* carefully followed the requirements of § 203, ultimately concluding that it had jurisdiction to modify a prior Dominican Republic decree. First, the court considered its jurisdiction under § 201(a)(1) and (2) and found that while New York did not qualify as the children's home state at the time the action was commenced, jurisdiction was appropriate under § 201(a)(2) because the Dominican court had declined to retain jurisdiction, the children and their mother had significant connections with New York, and substantial evidence was available in New York.[217] After resolving these threshold questions, the court considered whether the other requirements in § 203 could be satisfied. Because the court of the Dominican Republic had determined that the New York court should take jurisdiction, this test was easily met, and the court asserted jurisdiction to modify.[218]

Once a court assumes jurisdiction to modify under § 203, it acquires exclusive, continuing jurisdiction under § 202. This was important in *Michael McC. v. Manuela A.*, when a New York court took jurisdiction to modify an Italian custody order after all of the parties had relocated to New York. When the mother subsequently took the child back to Italy and filed a new proceeding there, the New York court concluded that the Italian court was no longer exercising jurisdiction in substantial conformity with the UCCJEA and that the mother's departure had not deprived the court of jurisdiction to modify.[219]

In international cases, the rules in § 202 and § 203 may cause some difficulty to the extent that they are different from the rules on modification that prevail in other countries. For example, the Hague Child Protection Convention takes a different approach to modification jurisdiction, providing in Article 5(2) that, except in the event of a wrongful removal or retention, "a change of the child's habitual residence to another Contracting State, the authorities of the State of the new habitual residence have jurisdiction."[220] If other countries follow this approach in custody cases involving the United States, there will be two types of conflicts. A child-custody determination made by a state court in the United States that is not subject to modification in another state under the UCCJEA rule of exclusive, continuing jurisdiction might be modified in another country if the child acquires a new habitual residence in that country.[221] This would create difficulties if a party subsequently sought to enforce that foreign modification order in the United States. The rules in UCCJEA Article 3 on registration and enforcement of custody orders, discussed below, provide a defense to registration and enforcement for any order entered by a court that "did not have jurisdiction under Article 2."[222] Based on this language, a foreign order that modifies a state court child-custody determination when the origi-

---

Example: Exclusive, Continuing Jurisdiction

Parents and their children have been living in Country X for several years when a court in Country X enters an order determining parental responsibilities and allowing one parent to relocate to State A with the children. After that parent and the children have lived for several years in State A, the parent in State A seeks a modification of the orders entered in Country X. If the other parent continues to reside in Country X, the court there will be deemed to have exclusive continuing jurisdiction under UCCJEA § 202, and the court in State A is not permitted to modify the orders under § 203. If the other parent no longer resides in Country X, the court in State A may assume jurisdiction to modify under § 203(2).

nal court in the United States still retains exclusive, continuing jurisdiction under the UCCJEA would appear not to be enforceable in the United States.

A second type of problem arises when a child-custody determination is made in a foreign country before the child relocates to the United States. The foreign determination is not modifiable under the UCCJEA as long as a parent continues to reside in the original forum country, even if the courts of that country see their jurisdiction as ending when the child establishes a new habitual residence in the United States. In this situation, the problem is whether any court has jurisdiction to modify the prior decree. The problem might be resolved by requesting a ruling from the original court confirming that it no longer has jurisdiction in the matter and finding that the court in the new habitual residence is a more appropriate forum.

Parties to a child-custody proceeding cannot confer jurisdiction by consent on a court that would not otherwise have a basis for jurisdiction under the UCCJEA.[223] An agreement as to which court should assume jurisdiction is one of the factors to be considered in deciding whether a court is an inconvenient forum under § 207, provided that the parties have selected a court that has a basis for exercising jurisdiction under § 203. In relocation cases in which the child and a parent will leave the state, parties often agree as part of a settlement that jurisdiction will remain with a particular court. These stipulations may be given effect in domestic cases, provided that the initial court retains a sufficient connection to the child to continue exercising jurisdiction under § 202.[224] In international cases, however, this type of stipulation will be more difficult to enforce.[225]

Notice and Procedure in International Cases

Before a child-custody determination is made under the UCCJEA, § 205 requires that notice must be provided to any parent whose parental rights have not previously been terminated, any person having physical custody of the child, and all persons entitled to notice under other state laws.[226] If notice has not been given, as might be the case when courts are authorized to enter ex parte temporary custody orders, the order will not be enforceable in other states under the UCCJEA. When notice is required to a person outside the state, § 108(a) states that it "may be given in a manner prescribed by the law of this State for service of process or by the law of the State in which the service is made." In international cases, service must comply with the requirements of any foreign country in which service is made, which often will be based on the Hague Service Convention.[227] Notice is not required for the court to exercise jurisdiction with respect to a person who submits to the jurisdiction of the court.[228]

A number of provisions in the UCCJEA are designed to help assure that all parties will be present before the court that makes a child-custody determination. Section 109(a) provides a limited immunity to individuals who are not otherwise subject to personal jurisdiction in a state who come to that state to participate in child-custody proceedings: A party "is not subject to personal jurisdiction in this State for another proceeding or purpose solely by reason of having participated, or having been physically present for the purpose of participating, in the proceeding." In light of the requirement of personal jurisdiction in cases involving child support or spousal support and marital property, and the expansive approach to "tag" jurisdiction in the United States, this immunity allows an individual to participate in custody litigation (which does not require personal

---

Immigration Parole

A parent who is unable to obtain a visa to enter the United States for a child-custody hearing may request a temporary parole into the United States from U.S. Citizenship and Immigration Services (USCIS), based on humanitarian or significant public benefit grounds under 8 U.S.C. § 1182(d)(5). Information is available on the USCIS website at http://www.uscis.gov (under "Humanitarian" and "Humanitarian Parole").

---

jurisdiction under the UCCJEA) without being forced to waive objections to the exercise of personal jurisdiction in these other contexts.[229]

A court has authority under § 210 to order a party who is in the state to appear "in person with or without the child." In addition, the court may order any person who is in the State and who has physical custody or control of the child to appear in person with the child. If a party "whose presence is desired by the court is outside th[e] State," the court may issue a notice directing the party to appear "and informing the party that failure to appear may result in a decision adverse to the party."[230] In addition, under § 210(d) the court may require another party to pay reasonable and necessary travel and other expenses for a party outside the state who desires or is directed to appear personally before the court.

Other provisions of the UCCJEA address matters such as communication and cooperation between courts and taking testimony in another state, which are particularly important in international cases.[231] Judicial communication is required in a number of circumstances under the UCCJEA, including situations involving emergency jurisdiction and simultaneous proceedings, and is likely also to be helpful in cases involving the modification difficulties described above. In international cases, however, practitioners will generally need to look beyond the UCCJEA to the general procedures for international judicial assistance.[232]

Child's Right to Be Heard

Every state in the United States has procedures that permit a court to interview children in custody cases or to appoint a guardian ad litem or other representative for the child. In some states, children of a certain age have a statutory right to choose which parent will be their custodian.[233] These procedures are not mandatory, but they are particularly important in international cases. Article 12 of the United Nations Convention on the Rights of the Child (CRC) recognizes that a child "who is capable of forming his or her own views" has "the right to express those views freely in all matters affecting the child." This includes specifically "the opportunity to be heard in any judicial and administrative proceedings affecting the child," either directly or through a representative. Article 12 recognizes that the child should be heard "in a manner consistent with the procedural rules of national law." The provision also states that the child's views should be "given due weight in accordance with the age and maturity of the child." This standard has been incorporated into private international law conventions and other human rights instruments. A custody order entered in the United States, which has not ratified the CRC, will be more readily enforceable in the rest of the world if it conforms to this norm.

Preventing Child Abduction

Measures to prevent child abduction are an important consideration in international custody cases.[234] A court with jurisdiction over custody can reduce the risk that a parent or custodian will interfere with another party's custody or access rights, by issuing orders designed to prevent a wrongful removal of the child.[235] A ne exeat provision is often sufficient to create a right of custody within the scope of the Hague Abduction Convention.[236] The custody decree should be carefully drafted to maximize the likelihood that it will be respected and enforced across borders. This is particularly important in circumstances of joint or shared custody rights, when the order must be sufficiently detailed so that a court or law enforcement officer will be able to determine when the order is being violated.

The Uniform Child Abduction Prevention Act (UCAPA)[237] provides a framework for approaching these cases with provisions that may be useful for courts even in states that have not enacted the statute. For example, § 7(a) enumerates factors for courts to consider in determining whether there is a credible risk of abduction, based on research into these cases.[238] Some of the factors are specific to international cases. For example, § 7(a) directs courts to consider whether a party is likely to take the child to a country that does not participate in the Abduction Convention, or one that has not complied with the Convention or lacks mechanisms to enforce return orders under the Convention.[239] If the court finds a credible risk of abduction, § 8(b) directs the court to enter an abduction prevention order including measures and conditions "reasonably calculated to prevent abduction of the child, giving due consideration to the custody and visitation rights of the parties."[240] Several provisions of UCAPA acknowledge the special problems presented by family violence.[241] UCAPA also authorizes measures to prevent the imminent abduction of a child, including a warrant to take physical custody of the child.[242]

Although courts are likely to approve foreign travel or visitation more readily when the country in question has a relationship with the United States under the Hague Abduction Convention, courts have refused to "adopt a bright-line rule prohibiting out-of-country visitation by a parent whose country has not adopted the Hague Convention or executed an extradition treaty with the United States," approaching the determination as part of

---

Drafting to Secure Cross-Border Recognition

A carefully drafted parental responsibility order is more likely to be recognized and enforced in other jurisdictions. Under UCAPA § 8(a), orders for preventive measures must include

- the basis for the court's jurisdiction;
- the manner in which notice and opportunity to be heard were provided;
- a detailed description of each party's custody and visitation rights and the child's residential arrangements;
- a provision stating that a violation of the order may subject the party in violation to civil and criminal penalties; and
- an identification of the child's country of habitual residence at the time the order was issued.

Including these items "makes it apparent on the face of the order that due process was met." In addition, the order may be more widely enforceable if it reflects how the court considered the views of the child concerned.

the larger inquiry into the child's best interests.[243] Courts sometimes require supervised visitation or impose a complete bar on international travel,[244] and lesser restrictions are common, including requirements that bond be posted or that passports be held by the court or a third party.[245] The proof often includes expert testimony on international child abduction,[246] and courts also rely on country information from the State Department and other sources when it is properly entered into evidence or an appropriate subject of judicial notice.[247]

Litigating Custody in Other Countries

Foreign countries often assert jurisdiction in matters concerning children based on factors such as presence or habitual residence, which correspond readily with the bases for jurisdiction used in the United States.[248] Foreign courts may also exercise custody jurisdiction based on factors such as the child's religion, nationality, or domicile.[249] Although custody orders on these grounds may be fully valid in these countries, they may not be recognized in the United States. For example, *Bellew v. Larese* considered an Italian custody order concerning a child who had both Italian and U.S. citizenship.[250] The family had lived for several years in the United States when the mother returned to Italy for a summer visit and filed an action there for divorce and custody. The Italian tribunal based its jurisdiction over the divorce on the wife's Italian citizenship and the fact that the couple had been married in Italy, and made no findings regarding the basis for its jurisdiction over custody. Whatever the strength of the connecting factors between the child and Italy, the court in the United States declined to enforce the order.[251]

In the European Union (EU), the jurisdictional rules of the Brussels IIA Regulation, also known as Brussels II Revised or Brussels II *bis*, apply to litigation of parental responsibility issues whether or not these issues arise in the context of divorce, separation, or annulment proceedings.[252] In proceedings that are subject to Brussels IIA,[253] courts generally have jurisdiction in the country where the child is habitually resident.[254] When separate proceedings concerning a child are initiated in different member states, there is a mandatory lis pendens stay in favor of the first court seised with jurisdiction, subject to the possibility that jurisdiction may be transferred from that court if it concludes that authorities in a different jurisdiction would be better placed to hear the case or specific issues in the case. These aspects of the Brussels IIA Regulation apply only to conflicts in

---

Resources: Preventing Abduction

For assistance with measures to prevent parental child abductions, contact the National Center for Missing and Exploited Children (NCMEC), Charles B. Wang International Children's Building, 699 Prince Street, Alexandria, VA 22314-3175—24-hour hotline: (800) 843-5678; phone: (703) 224-2150; fax: (703) 224-2122; website: http://www.missingkids.com.

The U.S. State Department information circular on "Guarding against International Parental Child Abduction" is available at http://www.travel.state.gov/abduction/prevention/prevention_560.html.

See also FAMILY ABDUCTION: PREVENTION AND RESPONSE (Patricia M. Hoff ed., 6th ed. 2009), available from NCMEC at www.missingkids.com.

Further Reading: Litigating Parental Responsibilities

DAVID HODSON, A PRACTICAL GUIDE TO INTERNATIONAL FAMILY LAW (2008).

JEREMY D. MORLEY, INTERNATIONAL FAMILY LAW PRACTICE (2009).

jurisdiction between member countries. The mandatory lis pendens would therefore not apply to parental responsibility proceedings filed in a Brussels IIA member country after custody litigation had already begun in a nonmember country, such as the United States.

The Hague Child Protection Convention defines bases for jurisdiction in matters concerning children and mandates that contracting states recognize and enforce orders entered on these jurisdictional grounds.[255] In most cases, the Convention places jurisdiction in the child's country of habitual residence, but it allows for a transfer of jurisdiction in some circumstances. The Convention does not prohibit contracting states from exercising jurisdiction on other bases, but orders based on different jurisdictional grounds would not be entitled to respect in other contracting states.

With habitual residence as the common jurisdictional basis of the Brussels IIA Regulation and the various Hague Children's Conventions, international custody litigation is increasingly channeled in this direction. The framework of Brussels IIA and the Hague Conventions suggest that authorities will usually apply the law of the child's habitual residence to determine questions of parental responsibility.[256] Moreover, these regimes require recognition and enforcement of foreign parental responsibility orders even if the substance of the child-custody law that was applied is different from the applicable law in the country where recognition is sought.[257]

Recognizing and Enforcing Parental Responsibility Orders

State courts employ a range of methods for enforcing their own custody and visitation orders, including contempt citations and the writ of habeas corpus. Under the federal PKPA, state courts must also enforce custody or visitation determinations made by other states that are consistent with the standards of the PKPA.[258] The PKPA does not extend to foreign custody or visitation orders, but many courts in the United States have enforced these orders based on comity, particularly when an individual who has violated the order seeks to have it modified. With the widespread enactment of the UCCJEA, Article 3 provides a set of remedies for enforcing custody and visitation orders that apply both to interstate and international cases.

Remedies for Violation of Custody Orders

Civil or remedial contempt sanctions are available to compel compliance with custody orders. Courts may also use criminal contempt sanctions to punish violations of their orders. A contempt proceeding may be a separate collateral action;[259] the court must have personal jurisdiction over the alleged contemnor to enter judgment.[260] If an order for which contempt sanctions are sought was issued by a different court, that order must first be recognized by the enforcing court.[261] Once a foreign custody judgment is recognized by a state court, any continuing violations of the judgment may be the basis for a contempt finding.[262]

Courts may hold a custodial parent in contempt for refusing to allow the other parent to have court-ordered access to the child.[263] In cases of child abduction, courts may order incarceration based on a finding of contempt to pressure a party to return a child who has been hidden or removed from the jurisdiction.[264] In addition to the parent, contempt sanctions may be directed at third parties such as family members for aiding the contemnor in violating the court's orders.[265] A party may defend a civil contempt charge by demonstrating that the violation was not willful or that he or she is unable to comply with the order.[266]

Beyond contempt sanctions, an individual's obstruction or interference with a parent's custody rights may be the basis for tort liability or criminal prosecution, whether or not those custody rights have been reduced to a court judgment.[267] Here as well, parents and third parties may be held liable, and the fact that the abductor also has custodial rights may not be a defense.[268] In addition to state laws, child abduction across international borders may be a violation of the federal International Parental Kidnapping Crime Act (IPKCA) or the Hague Convention on the Civil Aspects of International Child Abduction.[269]

Extending Comity

Courts apply the doctrine of comity in child-custody cases, particularly in circumstances where one parent has acted in defiance of a foreign-country custody decree,[270] considering the child's best interests as one aspect of the comity decision.[271] In *Oehl v. Oehl*, the court set out a three-part inquiry to determine when comity should be granted to a child-custody order of a foreign nation, focusing on the foreign court's jurisdiction, whether "the procedural and substantive law applied by the foreign court [was] reasonably comparable" to the law of the state where comity was sought, and whether the foreign court order was "based upon a determination of the best interests of the child."[272] According to the *Restatement (Third) of Foreign Relations Law* § 485, a court in the United States will recognize a foreign custody order, valid and effective in the state where it was issued, if the foreign court had jurisdiction on one of several specified grounds and notice of the proceeding was given to each parent and to any other person who had physical custody of the child.[273] Under the 1968 UCCJA and the 1997 UCCJEA, the comity approach has been replaced with a more precisely focused set of criteria for recognition and enforcement of foreign custody decrees.

In the United States, under the UCCJEA, the primary connecting factor used as a basis for custody jurisdiction is the child's residence or "home state." This is comparable to international instruments that look to the child's habitual residence. The child's nationality or citizenship is not relevant. Although parents have sometimes sought injunctive relief in state and federal courts on constitutional grounds to block orders sending a child with U.S. citizenship to live with a parent abroad, these have not been successful.[274]

Under § 23 of the original UCCJA, state courts recognized that a child's "home state" might be a foreign country,[275] and that a foreign custody determination made in the child's home should not be modified so long as the original court continued to have a basis for exercising jurisdiction.[276] Many decisions deferred to foreign proceedings or enforced foreign custody orders on this basis.[277] Several states did not include § 23 in their versions of the act, however,[278] and courts in states with § 23 often treated it as a discretionary rule broadly analogous to the doctrine of comity.[279] With the development of the UCCJEA, international cases have been fully integrated into the statute.[280]

Applying the UCCJEA to Foreign Custody and Access Orders

UCCJEA § 105(a) provides that "a court of this State shall treat a foreign country as if it were a State of the United States" in making its jurisdictional determination.[281] In addition, § 105(b) requires that "a child-custody determination made in a foreign country under factual circumstances in substantial conformity with the jurisdictional standards of this [act]" must be recognized and enforced under the act. The UCCJEA defines "child-custody determination" broadly to include "a judgment, decree, or other order of a court providing for the legal custody, physical custody, or visitation with respect to a child," regardless of the local terminology used for these concepts.[282] In addition, § 302 provides for enforcement of a return order under the Abduction Convention "as if it were a child-custody determination."[283]

There are two exceptions to the obligation to enforce foreign custody orders under the UCCJEA. A respondent may establish that the foreign order was not made in conformity with the statute, either because the foreign court did not have jurisdiction under the standards of the UCCJEA[284] or because there was not adequate notice and opportunity for a hearing.[285] In addition, a court need not enforce a foreign child-custody determination under § 105(c) "if the child custody law of a foreign country violates fundamental principles of human rights." The Comment to this section emphasizes that "the court's scrutiny should be on the child custody law of the foreign country and not on other aspects of the other legal system," and it notes that: "While the provision is a traditional one in international agreements, it is invoked only in the most egregious cases."[286] This language suggests that courts should grant greater deference to foreign court orders than what was typical under a comity regime or the UCCJA, which permitted an independent consideration of the child's best interests.[287]

Some state courts legislatures and courts have incorporated an explicit best interests requirement into the analysis of foreign custody orders under UCCJEA § 105.[288] Under these authorities, a court need not enforce a foreign custody order if the law that was applied does not require consideration of the child's best interests. This position has clear support in international human rights law, since the CRC provides that the best interests of the child "shall be a primary consideration" in all actions concerning children.[289] From the perspective of the UCCJEA and international comity, the more difficult problem is whether a court asked to enforce a foreign custody order may invoke § 105(c) as the basis for making an independent determination of the child's best interests. A Florida court refused to do this in *Dyce v. Christie*, writing: "We do not think that public policy considerations require a Florida court to reevaluate the merits of every foreign custody decree to determine whether a child's best interest has been served by the foreign decree. Indeed, the very purpose of the [UCCJEA] is to avoid jurisdictional conflicts and relitigation of custody decisions of other states."[290] In contrast, the court in *J.A. v. A.T.* reevaluated the evidence behind a Greek custody order under New Jersey law, when references the child's best interests in § 105(c), and concluded that it should not be enforced.[291]

Child Custody and Human Rights

The U.N. Convention on the Rights of the Child (CRC) and the Convention on the Elimination of All Forms of Discrimination against Women (CEDAW) include provisions directly relevant to child-custody determinations.

- Courts and agencies must treat the best interests of the child as a primary consideration in all actions concerning children—CRC article 3(1).
- A child has the right to maintain personal relations and direct contact with both parents on a regular basis, except if it is contrary to the child's best interests—CRC articles 9(3) and 10(2).
- A child who is capable of forming his or her own views must be afforded the opportunity to be heard, either directly or through a representative, in any judicial proceeding affecting the child—CRC article 12(1).
- Children should be protected from all forms of physical or mental abuse, neglect, or exploitation including sexual abuse—CRC article 19.
- Women and men have common responsibility for the upbringing of their children, and equal rights and responsibilities as parents, irrespective of their marital status—CEDAW articles 5(b) and 16(1)(d).

Registering a Foreign Child-Custody Determination

Registration of a child-custody determination from another state or foreign country under UCCJEA § 305 begins with a party sending a letter or other document requesting registration to the appropriate court, together with copies of the determination sought to be registered, and a sworn statement that the order has not been modified. Ordinarily, the applicant must also provide his or her name and address and the same information for any parent or person acting as a parent who was awarded custody or visitation in the order presented for registration.[292] On receipt of these documents, the registering court must notify the other party named in the registration request, and that person has a period of 20 days to request a hearing to contest the validity of the registered order. If no timely request is made, the registration is confirmed as a matter of law. If there is a hearing, the statute directs the court to confirm the order unless the person contesting registration establishes one of three defenses: that the court issuing the child-custody determination did not have jurisdiction under the standards of the UCCJEA; that the determination sought to be registered has been vacated, stayed, or modified by a court having jurisdiction to do so;[293] or that the person contesting registration was entitled to notice and did not receive notice in accordance with the standards of UCCJEA § 108.[294]

A custody determination may be registered without any accompanying request for enforcement. This procedure allows state courts to enter what are essentially mirror orders, which are particularly important in international cases. Advance registration helps ensure that a foreign child-custody order will be respected when a child is brought into the state for visitation. Similarly, parents might seek to register a foreign order in a state before one parent is permitted to relocate there with the child.[295]

Following registration, the court must recognize and enforce the registered order and is generally barred from modifying it. The state court may grant any type of relief or remedy normally available under state law, or it may use the additional remedies specified in the UCCJEA.[296] These include a procedure for expedited enforcement of a child-custody determination, and the possibility of an ex parte warrant under § 311 to take physical custody of a child who is "imminently likely to suffer serious physical harm or be removed from this State."

Obtaining Expedited Enforcement

The UCCJEA's summary enforcement procedure in § 308, based on the traditional habeas corpus remedy, is initiated when a party seeking enforcement of a child-custody determination files a petition including certain basic information and an indication of the date and place of registration if the order has been registered and confirmed.[297] Once this filing is made, "the court shall issue an order directing the respondent to appear in person with or without the child at a hearing and may enter any order necessary to ensure the safety of the parties and the child." The objective here is to provide speedy relief: "The hearing must be held on the next judicial day after service of the order unless that date is impossible."[298]

At the hearing, "upon a finding that a petitioner is entitled to immediate physical custody of the child, the court shall order that the petitioner may take immediate physical custody," unless the respondent establishes either that the order has not been registered and one of the defenses to registration applies or that the order has been vacated, stayed, or modified by a court having jurisdiction to do so.[299] Beyond these defenses, if the child would be endangered by enforcement of the order, the respondent may ask the court to assume temporary emergency jurisdiction to enter a different order.[300] When there is a previous child-custody determination entitled to enforcement, an emergency order will continue only for the time needed to obtain a new order from the court that has appropriate jurisdiction to modify.

Obtaining an Emergency Warrant

A petitioner who believes that a child "is immediately likely to suffer serious physical harm or be removed from this state" may file a verified application for a warrant to take physical custody of the child together with the petition for expedited enforcement of a child-custody determination.[301] The court must hear testimony from the petitioner or other witness; testimony may be in person or by telephone or other means permitted by the court.[302] If the court finds that a serious risk exists, the court may temporarily waive the notice requirements of § 308 and issue a warrant.[303] The warrant must "(1) recite the facts upon which a conclusion of imminent serious physical harm or removal from the jurisdiction is based; (2) direct law enforcement officers to take physical custody of the child immediately; and (3) provide for the placement of the child pending final relief."[304] If the court finds, based on the testimony, that a less intrusive remedy is not effective, the warrant may authorize law enforcement officers to enter private property to take physical custody of the child or, "[i]f required by exigent circumstances of the case," to make a forcible entry at any hour.[305] Immediately after the child is taken into physical custody, the respondent must be served with the petition, warrant, and order.[306] The court must hear the petition on the next judicial day after the warrant is executed, unless that date is impossible.[307] These extraordinary remedies are most likely to be invoked in international child abduction cases where there is a risk of further abduction.

> **Hague Enforcement**
>
> Although return proceedings under the Hague Abduction Convention may take place before any court has entered a child-custody determination, UCCJEA § 302 authorizes state courts to "enforce an order for the return of the child made under the Hague Convention on the Civil Aspects of International Child Abduction as if it were a child-custody determination."

Assistance of Public Authorities

Prosecutors or other public officials have a role in cases arising under the UCCJEA or the Abduction Convention when there is an existing child-custody determination, a request for assistance from a court in a pending proceeding, and a reasonable belief that a criminal statute has been violated or that the child has been wrongfully removed or retained in violation of the Abduction Convention. In these circumstances, UCCJEA § 315 states that a public official may take "any lawful action," including initiating a proceeding under the UCCJEA, "to locate a child, obtain the return of a child, or enforce a child-custody determination." In taking this action, the official "acts on behalf of the court and may not represent any party." The statute does not mandate that public authorities must become involved in all cases that may be referred to them, and the Comment to this section suggests that authorities will eventually develop guidelines to determine which cases will receive priority. In addition to this authority, prosecutors may have access to remedies under the criminal law for child abduction or interference with custodial rights.[308]

Enforcing Access Rights

Orders for access or visitation fall within the broad definition of "child-custody determination" included in UCCJEA § 102(3), and the statute allows a court to enforce "a visitation schedule made by a court of another State" or a foreign country.[309] The order may be registered and confirmed under § 305 and enforced under § 306 using any remedy available under state law. The primary method of enforcing visitation in state courts is an action for contempt of court.[310] Courts sometimes condition the payment of child support on the custodial parent's cooperation in allowing visitation, but states are divided on this question and many view this approach as harmful to the child's interests.[311] In rare and extreme cases, after repeated violations of visitation provisions by a custodial parent, a court may change custody to the other parent.[312] In cases that present a particular abduction risk, visitation may be ordered with safeguards, such as supervision or posting of a bond.[313]

Under the UCCJEA, the enforcing court typically does not have jurisdiction to modify an access order. In this situation, if the visitation provisions of an order do not include a specific visitation schedule, § 304 authorizes the enforcing court to issue a temporary order with a specific schedule. This temporary order remains in effect for a period that will allow the petitioner to obtain a more specific visitation order from the court with jurisdiction to modify. A temporary order under § 304 may be of limited use, however, when the parties live in different countries. For example, in *Marriage of Paillier*, a father in France sought to enforce his visitation rights after the mother moved unilaterally to California with the child in violation of a French decree. The California court was obli-

Assistance in arranging access in international situations may be available from the
Office of Children's Issues, Bureau of Consular Affairs, U.S. Department of State, 2201 C
Street, NW; Washington, DC 20520—phone: (888) 407-4747 (from U.S. and Canada);
(202) 501-4444 (from outside the U.S. and Canada); e-mail: abductionUSCA@state.gov;
website: http://www.travel.state.gov.

gated under § 303 to enforce the French decree, including the father's access rights. In applying § 304(a), however, the court concluded that it could not enforce the visitation provisions of the French decree as issued, which anticipated that both father and child would be located in France. At the same time, because of the UCCJEA's limits on modification of custody orders, the California court could not attempt to enforce the French decree by ordering that custody be transferred to the father if the mother refused to return the child to France.[314]

As a step toward more effective implementation of the Abduction Convention and the Child Protection Convention, the Hague Conference on Private International Law has prepared *Transfrontier Contact Concerning Children: General Principles and Guide to Good Practice*. The principles affirm the importance for children of regular contact with both parents and encourage "simple, inexpensive, and swift" procedures for recognition and enforcement of decisions concerning contact. Contact or visitation orders are not readily enforceable through the Abduction Convention, and this is one reason the Hague Conference has urged participating states to join the Child Protection Convention.

Hague Child Protection Convention

International recognition and enforcement of custody and access orders is greatly facilitated by the 1996 Hague Convention on Jurisdiction, Applicable Law, Recognition, Enforcement and Co-operation in Respect of Parental Responsibility and Measures for the Protection of Children.[315] The United States plans to ratify the Child Protection Convention, relying primarily on amendments to the UCCJEA to implement the treaty. Like the UCCJEA, the Convention applies to various types of proceedings, described collectively as "measures directed to the protection of the person or property of the child." The Convention establishes principles for jurisdiction, choice of law, and recognition and enforcement of judgments, and it establishes a system of cooperation through Central Authorities in member states to facilitate communication and assistance in cross-border cases. It has been ratified in many European nations as well as Australia, Ecuador, Morocco, and Uruguay.[316]

Resources: International Child Access Disputes

Hague Conference on Private International Law, TRANSFRONTIER CONTACT CONCERNING CHILDREN: GENERAL PRINCIPLES AND GUIDE TO GOOD PRACTICE (2008), available in English, French, Spanish, and Arabic at http://www.hcch.net/index_en.php?act=publications.details&pid=4582.

Scope of the Child Protection Convention

When and where it is in force, the Hague Child Protection Convention applies to children from birth to age 18, and to proceedings concerning:

- the attribution, exercise, termination, restriction or delegation of parental responsibility;
- rights of custody, including rights relating to the care of the person of the child and, in particular, the right to determine the child's place of residence;
- rights of access including the right to take a child for a limited period of time to a place other than the child's habitual residence;
- guardianship, curatorship, and analogous institutions;
- the designation and functions of any person or body having charge of the child's person or property, representing or assisting the child;
- the placement of the child in a foster family or in institutional care, or provision of care by *kafala* or an analogous institution; and
- the supervision by a public authority of the care of a child by any person having charge of the child.

In addition, contracting states may choose whether to apply the Convention to the administration, conservation, or disposal of the child's property.[317]

The Child Protection Convention provides generally in Article 5 that the authorities of the child's place of habitual residence have jurisdiction to take measures directed to the protection of the child's person or property. In this respect, it is consistent with the priority that the UCCJEA gives to home state jurisdiction. If there is a change in the child's habitual residence, however, Article 5 provides that the authorities of the new habitual residence acquire jurisdiction. Because this approach is inconsistent with the UCCJEA, which provides for exclusive, continuing jurisdiction in the previous forum, amendments to the UCCJEA rule for international cases will be necessary to implement the Convention in the United States.[318]

In case of a wrongful removal or retention of the child from the child's habitual residence, the change in jurisdiction contemplated by Article 5 does not occur immediately. In this situation, Article 7 provides that the authorities of the state in which the child was habitually resident immediately before the removal or retention keep their jurisdiction until one of two events occurs. Jurisdiction shifts to the child's new habitual residence under Article 7(a) if all parties having rights of custody have acquiesced in the child's removal or retention. Alternatively, jurisdiction shifts to the child's new habitual residence under Article 7(b) if the child resides in the new state for at least one year after the left-behind party "has or should have had knowledge of the whereabouts of the child," no request for return lodged within that period is still pending, and the child is settled in his or her new environment. These three requirements are intended to assure that there will be an opportunity to use the remedy for a wrongful removal or retention provided by the Abduction Convention.

Like the UCCJEA, the Child Protection Convention allows authorities in one state to defer to the authorities of another jurisdiction that "would be better placed in the particular case to assess the best interests of the child."[319] The Convention also permits authorities to take limited jurisdiction in cases of urgency or to take temporary or provisional measures in some circumstances. Authorities exercising jurisdiction under the Convention generally apply their own law.

Under Article 23, measures for the protection of children taken by the authorities of a Contracting State must be recognized by operation of law in other participating nations. Recognition can be refused if the measure was taken by an authority that did not have jurisdiction consistent with the terms of the Convention under Article 23(2)(a); if the child was not "provided the opportunity to be heard, in violation of fundamental principles of procedure of the requested State" under Article 23(2)(b); if a party claims that the measure "infringes his or her parental responsibility" and that he or she was not given an opportunity to be heard under Article 23(2)(c); and if "such recognition is manifestly contrary to public policy of the requested State, taking into account the best interests of the child," under Article 23(2)(d).[320] An authority requested to enforce a measure is bound by the original findings of fact and may not review the merits of the determination. Measures must be enforced as if they had been taken by the authorities in the requested state, and enforcement "takes place in accordance with the law of the requested State to the extent provided by such law, taking into consideration the best interests of the child."[321]

The Child Protection Convention also provides a mechanism for advance recognition to be certain that a measure of protection ordered in one Convention country will be recognized and enforced in another. The procedure for registering and declaring the enforceability of protection measures must be simple and rapid, and it can be refused only on the basis of the grounds in Article 23(2). This is potentially useful for circumstances in which a parent seeks to travel with a child to another country or is granted permission to relocate with a child, and the parent left behind seeks assurance that the custody or access orders will be respected in the other country. It also provides a basis on which "mirror orders" can be entered when a court orders a child's return to another country under the Abduction Convention.[322]

Obtaining Recognition and Enforcement Abroad of U.S. Custody and Access Orders

Because custody orders are subject to modification to protect the child's best interests, these orders have traditionally not been accorded automatic recognition or enforcement across state or international borders. For the United States, the primary benefit to be achieved from joining the Child Protection Convention would be the mechanism it provides for recognition and enforcement of U.S. custody and access orders in a substantial group of foreign nations, including most of the EU member countries.[323] Until that time, and in cases involving countries that have not yet joined the Child Protection Convention, the effect given to U.S. custody or visitation orders is difficult to determine and highly variable from one country to the next.

Hague Child Protection Convention

Hague Convention of 19 October 1996 on Jurisdiction, Applicable Law, Recognition, Enforcement and Co-operation in Respect of Parental Responsibility and Measures for the Protection of Children, *reprinted at* 35 I.L.M. 1391 (1996).

The full text and current information for two Divorce Convention is available from the Hague Conference website at http://www.hcch.net (under "Conventions" and "34"). See also Paul Lagarde, *Explanatory Report, Convention on Jurisdiction, Applicable Law, Recognition, Enforcement and Co-operation in Respect of Parental Responsibility and Measures for the Protection of Children*, 2 ACTES ET DOCUMENTS DE LA DIX-HUITIÈME SESSION 534 (1980).

Consular Agreements on Parental Access to Children

The U.S. State Department has entered into memoranda of understanding with several countries that are not Contracting States to the Hague Abduction Convention:

Egypt: *Memorandum of Understanding between the United States and Egypt Concerning Parental Access to Children* (2003), http://www.state.gov/s/l/2003/44396.htm.

Lebanon: *Memorandum of Understanding on Consular Cooperation in Cases Concerning Parental Access to Children* (2004), http://www.state.gov/s/l/2005/87381.htm.

Jordan: *Memorandum of Understanding on Consular Cooperation in Cases Concerning Parental Access to Children* (2006), http://www.state.gov/documents/organization/101710.pdf.

In England and Wales, a foreign-country custody or access order may be registered for recognition and enforcement.[324] The foreign order is not treated as binding, because of the principle that the welfare of a child must always be the court's paramount consideration. The foreign order is taken into consideration and may be accorded significant weight as a matter of comity.[325] Similarly, foreign-country custody determinations are not automatically enforced in Canada, but are weighed by a judge considering the child's best interests.[326] Australia and New Zealand have registration schemes in place to aid in enforcement of foreign parenting orders.[327] In Germany, recognition of these judgments is based on the German Act on Voluntary Jurisdiction.[328] Mexico enforces decisions of courts in other countries on parental authority and visitation that conform to prevailing Mexican law.[329] Some countries require an exequatur proceeding, or proof of reciprocity.[330] Within the European Community, issues of jurisdiction and cross-border enforcement of custody and visitation orders are governed by the Brussels IIA Regulation, but this does not extend to recognition of orders from non-EC countries.[331]

A parent may seek assistance with securing "the effective exercise of access rights" in another country under Article 21 of the Abduction Convention by applying to the U.S. Central Authority. In addition to the network of countries covered by the Convention, the State Department may be able to assist parents in arranging for access to a child in other countries. The United States has entered into consular agreements with Egypt, Lebanon, and Jordan for this purpose, and State Department consular officers may be able to aid U.S. citizens in other countries as well.

Further Reading: Recognizing and Enforcing Parental Responsibility Orders

David Hodson, A Practical Guide to International Family Law (2008).

Jeremy D. Morley, International Family Law Practice (2009).

Hague Child Protection Convention Contracting States (as of November 15, 2011)

Albania	Estonia	Morocco
Armenia	Finland	Netherlands
Australia	France	Poland
Austria	Germany	Portugal
Bulgaria	Hungary	Romania
Croatia	Ireland	Slovakia
Cyprus	Latvia	Slovenia
Czech Republic	Lithuania	Spain
Denmark	Luxembourg	Switzerland
Dominican Republic	Malta	Ukraine
Ecuador	Monaco	Uruguay

Notes

1. Unif. Child Custody Jurisdiction and Enforcement Act (UCCJEA), 9 (1A) U.L.A. 649 (1999).
2. *See* International Covenant on Civil and Political Rights (ICCPR), art. 9, 993 U.N.T.S. 171, 1966 U.N.J.Y.B. 193, 1977 U.K.T.S. 6, Cmnd. 6702, *reprinted in* 6 I.L.M. 368 (1967); Convention on the Rights of the Child (CRC), art. 7, G.A. Res. 44/25 (Annex), U.N. GAOR, 44th Sess., Supp. No. 49, at 166, U.N. Doc. A/RES/44/49 (1990) *reprinted in* 30 I.L.M. 1448 (1989).
3. CRC, *supra* note 2, at art. 24.
4. *See* Homer H. Clark, Jr., The Law of Domestic Relations in the United States § 4.1 (2d Student ed. 1988); Eugene F. Scoles et al., Conflict of Laws § 16.1-.3 (4th ed. 2004). *See also* Restatement (Second) of Conflict of Laws §§ 287-88 (1971).
5. Clark, *supra* note 4, § 4.2.
6. *See* ICCPR, *supra* note 2, at art. 2; CRC, *supra* note 2, at art. 2. The European Court of Human Rights has also rejected laws that differentiate between marital and nonmarital children. *E.g.*, Marckx v. Belgium, 2 Eur. H.R. Rep. 330 (1979); Mazurek v. France, [2000] Eur. Ct. H.R. 48.
7. These questions are extremely rare in domestic law since the Supreme Court's decisions in *Trimble v. Gordon*, 430 U.S. 762, 762 (1977), and *Lalli v. Lalli*, 439 U.S. 259, 261 (1978). While states may not deny inheritance rights to illegitimate children, *Lalli* sustained an intestate succession statute that required a determination of paternity during the father's lifetime. *Lalli*, 439 U.S. at 275-76.
8. *See* Catherine LaBrusse-Riou, *Family Law*, in Introduction to French Law 263, 281-84 (George A. Bermann & Etienne Picard eds., 2008); Nigel Lowe & Gillian Douglas, Bromley's Family Law 305-49 (10th ed. 2007) (United Kingdom); Dieter Martiny, *Family Law*, in Introduction to German Law 251, 260-62 (Mathias Reimann & Joachim Zekoll eds., 2d ed. 2005); Julien D. Payne & Marilyn A. Payne, Canadian Family Law 49-50 & 283-93 (2d ed. 2006); Stephen Zamora et al. Mexican Law 474-82 (2004).
9. 8 U.S.C. § 1101(b)(1) (2010). For immigration purposes, the term "child" means an unmarried person under age 21 who falls into one of these six categories. *See generally* Sarah Ignatius & Elisabeth Stickney, Immigration Law and the Family § 6:2 (Susan Compernolle updating ed., 2010); David Thronson, *Custody and Contradictions: Exploring Immigration Law as Federal Family Law in the Context of Child Custody*, 59 Hastings L.J. 453, 483 (2008).
10. 8 U.S.C. § 1101(b)(1)(D) (2010). A person born out of wedlock is the child of his or her natural mother for immigration purposes under § 1101(b)(1)(D). *See also* Fiallo v. Bell, 430 U.S. 787,

799–800 (1977) (sustaining classifications based on gender and legitimacy in earlier version of statute).

11. *See* IGNATIUS & STICKNEY, *supra* note 9, § 6:1.

12. These requirements vary depending on the person's date of birth. *See generally* IGNATIUS & STICKNEY, *supra* note 9, § 15:16–:26.

13. 8 U.S.C. § 1401(c)–(e), (g)–(h). *See* IGNATIUS & STICKNEY, *supra* note 9, §§ 15:6–:15. All children born within the United States acquire U.S. citizenship at birth under 8 U.S.C. § 1401(a).

14. 8 U.S.C. § 1409(a) (2010). There are additional requirements, including that "a blood relationship between the person and the father is established by clear and convincing evidence," and that "the father (unless deceased) has agreed in writing to provide financial support for the person until the person reaches the age of 18 years." *Id.* § 1409(a)(1), (3).

15. *Compare* 8 U.S.C. § 1409(c), *with* § 1401(g). Constitutional challenges to the differing requirements for mothers and fathers have not succeeded. *See* Nguyen v. INS., 533 U.S. 53, 53–54 (2001); Miller v. Albright, 523 U.S. 420, 421 (1998).

16. *See* RESTATEMENT (SECOND) OF CONFLICT OF LAWS § 287; *e.g.*, Estate of Janussek, 666 N.E.2d 774, 776 (Ill. App. Ct. 1996); Pilgrim v. Griffin, 237 S.W.2d 448 (Tex. Civ. App. 1950); Lund's Estate, 159 P.2d 643, 656 (Cal. 1945). *See generally* SCOLES ET AL., *supra* note 4, § 16.1.

17. For cases in the immigration context, see IGNATIUS & STICKNEY, *supra* note 9, § 6:26. *See also* Solis-Espinoza v. Gonzales, 401 F.3d 1090, 1094 (9th Cir. 2005) (treating child as legitimate son of father and U.S. citizen stepmother under California statute).

18. *See infra* notes 39–40 and accompanying text.

19. 9 U.L.A. (pt. 1B) 185 (2005). UIFSA is discussed in Chapter 7.

20. *See infra* notes 154–233 and accompanying text. 9 U.L.A. (pt. 1A) 662 (1999). *Cf.* Nissen v. Cortez Moreno, 10 So. 3d 1110 (Fla. Dist Ct. App. 2009) (UCCJEA applies only when custody is in issue).

21. UNIF. PARENTAGE ACT (UPA) § 1, 9B U.L.A. 387 (2001 & Supp. 2011 (as amended 2002)).

22. As of this writing, the new version of the UPA has been enacted in Alabama, Delaware, New Mexico, North Dakota, Oklahoma, Texas, Utah, Washington, and Wyoming.

23. UPA § 202 (2002); UPA § 2 (1973).

24. UPA § 201 (2002); UPA §§ 3–4 (1973).

25. The parentage acts apply to determination of parentage, but do not "create, enlarge, or diminish parental rights or duties" under state law. UPA § 103 (2002). As a choice of law matter, the UPA provides that a court "shall apply the law of this State to adjudicate the parent-child relationship," and that applicable law does not depend on the child's place of birth or past or present residence. *Id.*

26. *See* UPA art. 7 (child of assisted reproduction) and art. 8 (gestational agreement) (2002).

27. *See* UPA § 106 (2002) (provisions relating to determination of paternity also apply to maternity).

28. *See* U.S. Dep't of State, Applying for a Consular Report of Birth Abroad (CRBA), http://travel .state.gov/travel/living/living_5497.html. *See also* 7 U.S. DEP'T OF STATE, FOREIGN AFFAIRS MANUAL (FAM) § 1130, Acquisition of U.S. Citizenship by Birth Abroad to U.S. Citizen Parent (2005), http://www.state.gov/m/a/dir/regs/fam/.

29. *See* Elisa B. v. Superior Court, 117 P.3d 660 (Cal. 2005) (former lesbian partner was presumed parent and obligated to pay support for children conceived during parties' relationship); Amy G. v. M.W., 47 Cal. Rptr. 3d 297 (Cal. Ct. App. 2006) (considering parentage of nonmarital child raised by biological father and his wife).

30. 4 Cal. Rptr. 3d 705 (Cal. Ct. App. 2003). *See also In re* Karen C., 124 Cal. Rptr. 2d 677 (Cal. Ct. App. 2002) (birth mother gave birth under a different woman's name; birth parents left the country and child raised by woman whose name was on birth certificate).

31. *See generally* 2 ROBERT C. CASAD & WILLIAM B. RICHMAN, JURISDICTION IN CIVIL ACTIONS § 9-2[6], at 299–303 (3d ed. 1998). On the jurisdiction required for termination of parental rights, see *infra* notes 65–77 and accompanying text.

32. Other grounds include consent, personal service within the forum state, or an assertion of parentage in the putative father registry of the state. *See also* UPA § 604 (2002); UPA § 8(b) (1973).

33. *See, e.g., In re* Gonzalez, 993 S.W.2d 147 (Tex. Ct. App. 1999) (exercising jurisdiction over resident of Mexico based on personal service within the state and significant contacts including conception of the child within the state); Matter of Constance P., 813 N.Y.S.2d 463 (N.Y. App. Div. 2006) (jurisdiction based on conception of child within the state).

34. *See, e.g.,* H.M. v. E.T., 930 N.E.2d 206 (N.Y. 2010).

35. 10 So. 3d 1110, 1112 (Fla. Dist. Ct. App. 2009); *see also* de Moya v. de Pena, 148 So. 2d 735, 736–37 (Fla. Dist. Ct. App. 1963); State v. Carmena, 189 N.W.2d 191, 194 (Minn. 1971); Urbancig v. Pipitone, 259 N.Y.S.2d 625 (N.Y. App. Div. 1965). A much older, minority approach did not allow a nonresident to bring a paternity action; *see generally* Yuin v. Hilton, 134 N.E.2d 719 (Ohio 1956) (discussing older authorities and allowing action to proceed).

36. *E.g.,* North Carolina *ex rel.* Desselberg v. Peele, 523 S.E.2d 125, 129 (N.C. Ct. App. 1999) (recognizing and enforcing German paternity and support order based on comity); *see also* Nicol v. Tanner, 256 N.W.2d 796, 801–02 (Minn. 1976).

37. *E.g., In re* Letter of Request from Amtsgericht Ingolstadt, 82 F.3d 590, 592 (4th Cir. 1996); *In re* Letter Rogatory from the Nedenes Dist. Court, Nor., 216 F.R.D. 277, 278 (S.D. Nor., N.Y. 2003).

38. The Hague Evidence Convention is discussed in Chapter 1.

39. *E.g.,* Hermanson v. Hermanson, 887 P.2d 1241, 1244–45 (Nev. 1994); Marriage of Adams, 551 N.E.2d 635, 639 (Ill. 1990).

40. *See Hermanson,* 887 P.2d at 1244 (holding that trial court erred in applying law of California to paternity issue when parties had not lived in that state for previous ten years).

41. *See* Finstuen v. Crutcher, 496 F.3d 1139, 1154–55 (10th Cir. 2007); *cf.* Miller-Jenkins v. Miller-Jenkins, 637 S.E.2d 330, 337 (Va. Ct. App. 2006) (applying federal Parental Kidnapping Prevention Act (PKPA) to require recognition and enforcement of Vermont custody order following dissolution of civil union).

42. Adoption of Sebastian, 879 N.Y.S.2d 677, 678 (N.Y. Surr. Ct. 2009). One spouse was the genetic mother and the other the gestational mother of the child. The court granted the adoption although the couple's marriage and shared parenthood were recognized under New York law. *Id.* at 682.

43. *See generally* CLARK, *supra* note 4, § 4.5; B. Finberg, Annotation, *Right of Mother to Custody of Illegitimate Child,* 98 A.L.R.2d 417 (1964 & Supp.).

44. *E.g.,* Taylor v. Commonwealth, 537 S.E.2d 592 (Va. 2000) (father with only a biological relationship to child guilty of child abduction when he took child from mother). *Cf.* Ollivierra v. Fateh, 815 N.Y.S.2d 721, 722 (N.Y. App. Div. 2006) (noting that father was not married to child's mother and that "[a]t the time the mother left the country, the father had not filed a petition for custody and there were no orders adjudicating him the legal father, awarding him custody or visitation, or prohibiting the mother from leaving New York with the child").

45. A significant body of Supreme Court decisions addresses the constitutional parental rights of nonmarital fathers. *See* Lehr v. Robertson, 463 U.S. 248 (1983); Caban v. Mohammed, 441 U.S. 380 (1979); Stanley v. Illinois, 405 U.S. 645 (1972). *See also* Michael H. v. Gerald D., 491 U.S. 110 (1989). *See generally* CLARK, *supra* note 4, § 20.2.

46. UPA § 602 (2002); UPA § 6 (1973).

47. *See generally* UPA art. 4 (2002); UPA § 4(a)(5) (1973). This filing should be made promptly; in some circumstances, a nonmarital father may lose the opportunity to establish paternity if he fails to file within 30 days of the child's birth. *See, e.g.,* Heidbreder v. Carton, 645 N.W.2d 355 (Minn. 2002) (putative father who does not file with the registry within 30 days is not entitled to notice and opportunity to prevent proposed adoption).

48. *E.g.,* Bazemore v. Davis, 394 A.2d 1377 (D.C. 1978) (best interests are sole consideration in custody dispute between unmarried biological parents); Rosero v. Blake, 581 S.E.2d 41 (N.C. 2003), *cert. denied,* 540 U.S. 1177 (2004) (rights of unmarried fathers and mothers are equal after formal acknowledgment of paternity); *In re* Byrd, 421 N.E.2d 1284, 1287 (Ohio 1981) (father who participated in raising nonmarital child has "equality of standing with the mother with respect to the custody of the child"). Not all courts go this far; *see, e.g.,* Rainer v. Feldman,

568 So. 2d 1226 (Ala. 1990) (paternity acknowledgment does not override presumption of custody in favor of mother).

49. *See infra* notes 154–233 and accompanying text. *E.g.*, Khan v. Saminni, 842 N.E.2d 453 (Mass. 2006).

50. See Chapter 6 for coverage of the Hague Abduction Convention.

51. *In re* Vernor, 94 S.W.3d 201, 209 (Tex. App. 2002).

52. Surrogacy is banned or tightly regulated in Italy, Germany, France, Switzerland, Greece, Spain, Norway, New Zealand, and several Australian states. *See* Hague Conference on Private International Law, *Private International Law Issues Surrounding the Status of Children, Including Issues Arising from International Surrogacy Arrangements, General Affairs and Policy*, Prel. Doc. 11 of March 2011, p. 7, http://www.hcch.net/upload/wop/genaff2011pd11e .pdf.

53. *See id.*

54. 28 U.S.C. § 1738; *see* Prashad v. Copeland, 685 S.E.2d 199 (Va. Ct. App. 2009). An order may also be subject to recognition under the UCCJEA; *see id. See also* Berwick v. Wagner, 336 S.W.3d 805 (Tex. Ct. App. 2011). There is no public policy exception to the requirement of full faith and credit, and therefore even states that prohibit enforcement of surrogacy contracts must give effect to judgments based on surrogacy arrangements in other states. *See* Adoption of Doe, 793 N.Y.S.2d 878 (N.Y. Surr. Ct. 2005).

55. *See, e.g., In re* T.J.S., 16 A.3d 386 (N.J. Super. Ct. 2011) (applying N.J. Parentage Act)

56. Adoption may not be necessary, however; *see, e.g.,* Raftopol v. Ramey, 12 A.3d 783 (Conn. 2011) (applying CONN. GEN. STAT. § 7-48a).

57. All children born in the United States are U.S. citizens. *See* 8 U.S.C. § 1401(a).

58. *E.g., In re* I.L.P., 965 A.2d 251 (Pa. Super. Ct. 2009) (ordering lower court to clarify birth certificates to assist genetic father in obtaining Taiwanese citizenship for children born to surrogate).

59. Stanley v. Illinois, 405 U.S. 645 (1972).

60. Santosky v. Kramer, 455 U.S. 745 (1982) (applying the Due Process Clause of the Fourteenth Amendment).

61. Federal legislation under Title IV-B and IV-E of the Social Security Act defines the framework for state child welfare laws. *See generally* Ann Laquer Estin, *Sharing Governance: Family Law in Congress and the States*, 18 CORNELL J.L. & PUB. POL'Y 267, 286–90 (2009).

62. *See generally* Ann Laquer Estin, *Global Child Welfare: The Challenges for Family Law*, 63 U. OKLA. L. REV. 691 (2011).

63. CRC, *supra* note 2, at art. 7(1).

64. CRC, *supra* note 2, at art. 9(1). *See also id.* at art. 19.

65. UCCJEA § 102(4). In addition to cases of divorce or separation, this includes proceedings for neglect, abuse, dependency, guardianship, paternity, termination of parental rights, and protection from domestic violence.

66. UCCJEA § 102(7). For a child less than six months of age, the home state is the state "in which the child lived from birth with any of the persons mentioned." The definition also provides that "a period of temporary absence" from the state of any of the persons mentioned is counted as part of the jurisdictional period. The phrase "person acting as a parent" is defined in § 102(13).

67. *See, e.g.,* Welfare of Children of D.M.T.-R., 802 N.W.2d 759 2011 WL 2519221 (Minn. Ct. App. 2011). *Cf. In re* Angelica L., 767 N.W.2d 74, 89 (Neb. 2009); Arteaga v. Tex. Dep't of Protective and Regulatory Servs., 924 S.W.2d 756, 760 (Tex. Ct. App. 1996); *In re* Stephanie M., 867 P.2d 706, 713–17 (Cal. 1994).

68. UCCJEA § 201(a)(2).

69. UCCJEA § 102(13). *See infra* note 166.

70. UCCJEA § 204(a). If there is no previous child-custody determination entitled to enforcement under the UCCJEA, a determination made under this section can become a final determination, "if it so provides and this State becomes the home State of the child."

71. *E.g., In re* Jorge G., 78 Cal. Rptr. 3d 552, 558 (Cal. Ct. App. 2008).

72. UCCJEA § 204(d). *See, e.g., In re* Nada R., 108 Cal. Rptr. 2d 493 (Cal. Ct. App. 2001).

73. UCCJEA § 204(d).

74. *See In re* Claudia S., 31 Cal. Rptr. 3d 697 (Cal. Ct. App 2005).

75. *E.g.*, Utah *ex rel.* W.A. (D.A. v. Utah), 63 P.3d 607, 613–17 (Utah 2002) (citing cases); *see also Claudia S.*, 31 Cal. Rptr. 3d at 703–04; J.D. v. Tuscaloosa Dep't of Human Res., 923 So. 2d 303 (Ala. Civ. App. 2005); *In re R.W.* and N.W. ___ A 3.d ___ 2011 WL 5600636 (Vt. 2011); Velasco v. Ayala, 312 S.W.3d 783, 798 (Tex. Ct. App. 2009); Tammie J.C. v. Robert T.R., 663 N.W.2d 734, 741 (Wis. 2003) (pt. III).

76. *E.g.*, UTAH CODE ANN. § 78-3a-110(13) (*cited in Utah ex rel. W.A.*, 63 P.3d at 611–13); WIS. STAT. § 822.12 (*cited in Tammie J.C.*, 663 N.W.2d at 744–45).

77. *In re* John Doe, 926 P.2d 1290, 1300 (Haw. 1996). *Doe* was decided before adoption of the UCCJEA, under a statute that allowed the courts to take jurisdiction in child protection proceedings concerning any child "found within the State." Note that UCCJEA § 207 authorizes a court to decline to exercise jurisdiction. Cf. *In re R.W., supra* note 75.

78. *See infra* notes 315–22 and accompanying text.

79. *See supra* notes 59 and 60 and accompanying text.

80. *See, e.g., In re Claudia S.*, 31 Cal. Rptr. 3d at 704. *In re R.W. supra* note 75.

81. *E.g.*, Velasco v. Ayala, 312 S.W.3d 783, 798 (Tex. Ct. App. 2009) (mandating service, waiver of service, or personal appearance). *See generally* Chapter 1.

82. Done at Vienna 24 April 1963, entered in force 19 Mar. 1967. UNTS v. 596 p. 261, ratified by the United States on 24 November 1969, 21 U.S.T. 77, T.I.A.S. No. 6820 (1970).

83. VCCR, *supra* note 82, at art. 37.

84. VCCR, *supra* note 82, at art. 36(1). The implementation of these rights in the United States was addressed in the criminal law context in *Medellín v. Texas*, 552 U.S. 491 (2008).

85. *See generally* 7 U.S. Dep't of State Foreign Affairs Manual (FAM) § 000, Consular Protection of U.S. Nationals Abroad (2005); *see also* LUKE T. LEE & JOHN QUIGLEY, CONSULAR LAW AND PRACTICE (2008).

86. *See, e.g., In re* Angelica L., 767 N.W.2d 74 (Neb. 2009); Arteaga v. Tex. Dep't of Protective & Regulatory Servs., 924 S.W.2d 756 (Tex. Ct. App. 1996); *In re* Stephanie M, 867 P.2d 706, 712–13 (Cal. 1994).

87. *Arteaga*, 924 S.W.2d at 756 n. 6; E.R. v. Marion Cnty. Office of Family & Children, 729 N.E.2d 1052, 1058 n. 11 (Ind. Ct. App. 2000). *See also Angelica L.*, 767 N.W.2d at 91 (Gerrard, J., concurring); *In re R.W. supra* note 75.

88. *E.g.*, NEB. REV. STAT. § 43-3804(2) (discussed in *Angelica L.*, 767 N.W.2d at 90–91). *See generally* Estin, *supra* note 61.

89. *See, e.g., In re* Angelica L., 767 N.W.2d 74 (Neb. 2009); *In re* Mainor T., 674 N.W.2d 442 (Neb. 2004).

90. *See* 8 U.S.C. § 1182(d)(5), 8 C.F.R. § 212.5.

91. *E.g.*, Termination of Parental Rights to Adrianna A.E., 745 N.W.2d 701 (Wis. Ct. App. 2007) (webcam); *In re* M.G.F., 476 S.E.2d 100 (Ga. Ct. App. 1996) (conference call). *See also* New Mexico *ex rel.* Steven, 992 P.2d 317 (N.M. Ct. App. 1999); *In re R.W. supra* note 75.

92. *See* Marina P. v. Ariz. Dep't of Econ. Sec., 152 P.3d 1209 (Ariz. Ct. App. 2007); *In re* M.M., 587 S.E.2d 825 (Ga. Ct. App. 2003).

93. *E.g., In re Angelica L.*, 767 N.W.2d at 74; *In re* B & J, 756 N.W.2d 234, 239 n. 3 (Mich. Ct. App. 2008).

94. *See* J.B. v. DeKalb Cnty. Dep't of Human Res., 12 So. 3d 100 (Ala. Civ. App. 2008).

95. *Marina P.*, 152 P.3d at 1214–15. *See also In re* V.S., 548 S.E.2d 490 (Ga. Ct. App. 2001) (reversing termination of parental rights).

96. *Marina P.*, 152 P.3d at 1216 n. 9; *see also In re* Aaron D., 691 N.W.2d 164 (Neb. 2005).

97. *E.g.*, Adoption of A.M.H., 215 S.W.3d 793 (Tenn. 2007); Matter of Sanjivini K., 391 N.E.2d 1316 (N.Y. 1979).

98. *E.g., Angelica L.*, 767 N.W.2d at 94–96; *J.B.*, 12 So. 3d at 113–14; *In re* Mainor T., 674 N.W.2d 442, 462–63 (Neb. 2004).

99. *E.g., Angelica L.*, 767 N.W.2d at 93–94; *Adoption of A.M.H.*, 215 S.W.3d at 813.

100. *In re* B & J, 756 N.W.2d 234, 241–42 (Mich. Ct. App. 2008).

101. *See* 8 U.S.C. § 1101(a)(27)(J); 8 C.F.R. § 204.11(2009).

102. 8 U.S.C. § 1101(a)(27)(J)(ii) (2011). *See, e.g., In re* T.J., 59 So. 3d 1187 (Fla. Ct. App. 2011); *In re* Luis G., 764 N.W.2d 648 (Neb. Ct. App. 2009); *In re* Emma M., 902 N.Y.S.2d 651 (N.Y. App. Div. 2010). The Department of Homeland Security must consent to the grant of special immigrant juvenile status. *See* 8 U.S.C. § 1101(a)(27)(J)(iii). *See generally* IGNATIUS & STICKNEY, *supra* note 9, §§ 14:84–:87 (2010 update). Although relief under the statute may be available as long as the petition is filed before the child reaches age 21, juvenile court jurisdiction in many states ends when a child reaches age 18. *See id.* § 14:84; *see, e.g.,* Trudy-Ann W. v. Joan W., 901 N.Y.S.2d 296 (N.Y. App. Div. 2010).

103. Undocumented immigrant children apprehended by U.S. immigration authorities at the border are usually returned immediately to their country of origin. Children detained or apprehended within the United States are placed in the custody of the U.S. Department of Health and Human Services (HHS), and these children may petition for special immigrant juvenile status with the consent of HHS. *See* 8 U.S.C. § 1101(a)(27)(J)(iii)(I). The current HHS procedure is set out in this program instruction: http://www.acf.hhs.gov/programs/orr/whatsnew/Special_Immigrant_Juvenile_Status-Interim_Specific_Consent_Program_Instructions.pdf. According to these instructions, juveniles in HHS custody do not need "specific consent" from HHS unless they ask the state juvenile court to determine or alter their custody status.

104. *See generally* CLARK, *supra* note 4, § 19.4.

105. *E.g.,* Martinez v. Kurt, 9 So. 3d 54 (Fla. Dist. Ct. App. 2009) (enforcing agreement providing that mother could relocate with children to Turkey and requiring that she enroll children in a full-time English-language private school as agreed).

106. UNIF. MARRIAGE AND DIVORCE ACT (UMDA) § 402 (amended 1973), 9A U.L.A. (pt. 2) 282 (1998) (now Model Marriage and Divorce Act).

107. *Id.*

108. The ALI Principles of the Law of Family Dissolution refer to this as an approximation standard. *See* Principles of the Law of Family Dissolution § 2.08 (A.L.I. 2002) (Reporter's Notes, cmt. b).

109. *E.g.,* GA. CODE ANN. § 19-9-3(a)(5) (2010) (age 14); W. VA. CODE § 48-9-206(a)(2) (2010) (age 14).

110. *Cf.* Dixson v. Cantrell, 564 So. 2d 1138 (Fla. Dist. Ct. App. 1990) (refusing to modify custody determination made in the Netherlands where there was no showing of changed circumstances).

111. Martinez v. Kurt, 9 So. 3d 54, 56 (Fla. Dist. Ct. App. 2009).

112. *E.g.,* Sagar v. Sagar, 781 N.E.2d 54 (Mass. App. Ct.), *rev. denied,* 786 N.E.2d 395 (Mass.), *cert. denied,* 540 U.S. 874 (2003) (denying Hindu father's request for permission to perform Chudakarana ritual unless both parents agreed in writing or child was of age to make decision herself). *See generally* George L. Blum, Annotation, *Religion as Factor in Child Custody Cases,* 124 A.L.R.5th 203 (2004 & Supp. 2009).

113. Palmore v. Sidodi, 466 U.S. 429 (1984). *But see* Marriage of Gambla, 853 N.E.2d 847, 868–71 (Ill. App. Ct. 2006) (affirming custody award to black parent of interracial couple based in part on her ability to help child "learn to exist as a biracial individual in a society that is sometimes hostile toward people of different races").

114. *Compare* Carle v. Carle, 503 P.2d 1050 (Alaska 1972) (custody decision improperly preferred urban over rural subsistence lifestyle), *with* Jones v. Jones, 542 N.W.2d 119 (S.D. 1996) (court may consider which parent is more prepared to expose child to their Native American heritage). *See* Heneggeler v. Hanson, 510 S.E.2d 722 (S.C. Ct. App. 1999) (court may consider parent's greater sensitivity to national origin of internationally adopted children). *Cf.* Marriage of Kleist, 538 N.W.2d 273 (Iowa 1995). *See also* In Adoption of A.M.H., 215 S.W.3d 793 (Tenn. 2007) (holding, in a dispute between the foster parents and birth parents of a Chinese child, that "general conditions in China" were irrelevant to the determination of whether a child would suffer "substantial harm" if returned to her natural parents.

115. *E.g.,* Rico v. Rodriguez, 120 P.3d 812 (Nev. 2005); *see* Kerry Abrams, *Immigration Status and the Best Interests of the Child Standard,* 14 VA. J. SOC. POL'Y & L. 87, 96 (2006). Questions of

immigration and citizenship are particularly difficult in child protection cases involving unaccompanied minors and children whose parents are subject to deportation. *See, e.g., In re* Stephanie M., 867 P.2d 706 (Cal.), *cert. denied,* 513 U.S. 908, *and cert. denied,* 513 U.S. 937 (1994); *In re* Angelica L., 767 N.W.2d 74 (Neb. 2009).

116. One parent may not be permitted to work, or may be dependent on the other to sponsor his or her immigration. *E.g.,* Stonham v. Widiastuti, 79 P.3d 1188 (Wyo. 2003).

117. Abrams, *supra* note 115, provides a helpful analysis of this dilemma, with a recommendation that courts adopt a presumption that immigration status is not relevant to a child-custody determination, subject to specific exceptions in carefully defined circumstances. *See also* Thronson, *supra* note 9.

118. *See, e.g.,* Ish-Shalom v. Whittmann, 797 N.Y.S.2d 111 (N.Y. App. Div. 2005) (awarding joint custody to preserve parent's right to seek the child's return under the Abduction Convention); *see also supra* notes 50-51 and accompanying text. Something less than full joint custody may be sufficient, particularly if it includes a right to determine the child's place of residence within the meaning of the Convention. *See* Abbott v. Abbott, 560 U.S. ___, 130 S. Ct. 1983 (2010); *see generally* Chapter 6.

119. *See* 8 U.S.C. § 1431 (2009).

120. *E.g.,* Pina v. Mukasey, 542 F.3d 5 (1st Cir. 2008). Minasyan v. Gonzales, 401 F.3d 1069 (9th Cir. 2005). This is a particularly complicated inquiry for children who reached age 18 before the current version of the statute came into effect in February 2001. *See, e.g.,* Bustamante-Barrera v. Gonzales, 447 F.3d 388 (5th Cir. 2006), *cert. denied,* 549 U.S. 1205 (2007) (decided under predecessor statute); Bagot v. Ashcroft, 398 F.3d 252 (3d Cir. 2005); Nehme v. I.N.S., 252 F.3d 415 (5th Cir. 2001). *See generally* Thronson, *supra* note 9, at 500-06.

Similarly, an unmarried father who seeks to sponsor his child's immigration as a legitimated child under 8 U.S.C. § 1101(b)(1)(C) must have legal custody at the time of the legitimation.

121. UMDA § 401(d)(2).

122. Although every state had a grandparent visitation statute on the books, many of these were subject to constitutional question after the decision in *Troxel v. Granville,* 530 U.S. 57 (2000).

123. *E.g.,* T.B. v. L.R.M., 786 A.2d 913 (Pa. 2001).

124. 530 U.S. 57 (2000).

125. *E.g.,* Carmichael v. Rollins, 783 N.W.2d 763 (Neb. 2010). *See generally* MARK E. SULLIVAN, THE MILITARY DIVORCE HANDBOOK (2d ed. 2011); Sara Estrin, *The Servicemembers Civil Relief Act: Why and How This Act Applies to Child Custody Proceedings,* 27 LAW & INEQ. 211 (2009); Kristen M.H. Coyne et al., *The SCRA and Family Law: More Than Just Stays and Delays,* 43 FAM. L.Q. 315 (2009); Natasha Gonzalez, *SCRA in Child Custody Cases: Shield or Sword?* MATRIMONIAL STRATEGIST, Jan. 2007, at 1.

126. Harris v. Harris, 922 N.E.2d 626 (Ind. Ct. App. 2010).

127. Lt. Col. Jeffrey P. Sexton & Jonathan Brent, *Child Custody and Deployments: The States Step in to Fill the SCRA Gap,* ARMY LAW., Dec. 2008, at 9. In 2009, the Uniform Law Commission established a committee to draft a uniform act addressing custody orders involving military families.

128. *E.g.,* Marriage of Sullivan, 795 N.E.2d 392 (Ill. App. Ct. 2003) (allowing award of visitation to parent's family members when special circumstances are shown); *In re* Marriage of Grantham, 698 N.W.2d 140 (Iowa 2005) (modifying custody to mother when children's father was called to active duty with National Guard); Fischer v. Fischer, 157 P.3d 682 (Mont. 2007) (holding that trial court lacked authority to grant temporary guardianship of child to friend named by custodial father); Carmichael v. Rollins, 783 N.W.2d 763 (Neb. 2010); Faucett v. Vasquez, 984 A.2d 460 (N.J. Super. Ct. App. Div. 2009) (holding that deployment of primary residential parent for one year or more states a prima facie case for hearing on modification of custody). *See generally* Jay M. Zitter, Annotation, *Effect of Parent's Military Service upon Child Custody,* 21 A.L.R.6th 577 (2007).

129. *E.g.,* L.H. v. Youth Welfare Office of Wiesbaden, Germany, 568 N.Y.S.2d 852 (N.Y. Fam. Ct. 1991) (child protection proceedings commenced in Germany); Vause v. Vause, 409 N.W.2d 412 (Wis. Ct. App. 1987) (divorce and custody decree entered in Germany). The SCRA has no application to custody proceedings in a foreign country. *See id.* at 415-16.

130. *E.g.*, Catlin v. Catlin, 494 N.W.2d 581 (N.D. 1992). *See also* Lemley v. Miller, 932 S.W.2d 284, 285 (Tex. App. 1996).

131. CRC, *supra* note 2, at art. 3(1) and art. 18(1). *See generally* D. Marianne Blair & Merle H. Weiner, *Resolving Parental Custody Disputes: A Comparative Exploration*, 39 FAM. L.Q. 247, 252 (2005).

132. *See* Patricia Begné, *Parental Authority and Child Custody in Mexico*, 39 FAM. L.Q. 527 (2005); Cecilia P. Grosman & Ida Ariana Scherman, *Argentina: Criteria for Child Custody Decision-Making upon Separation and Divorce*, 39 FAM. L.Q. 543 (2005).

133. *See* Blair & Weiner, *supra* note 131, at 260–61.

134. *E.g.*, Abbott v. Abbott, 560 U.S., 130 S. Ct. 1983 (2010); Whallon v. Lynn, 230 F.3d 450 (1st Cir. 2000) (Mexico); Furnes v. Reeves, 362 F.3d 702, 712–16 (11th Cir. 2004) (Norway).

135. *Abbott*, 560 U.S. at ____, 130 S. Ct. at 1990. Some basic information on acquisition and exercise of rights of custody in different countries is available in the Country Profiles posted on the website of the Hague Conference, at http://www.hcch.net (under "Child Abduction Section" and then "Country Profiles—Responses").

136. *E.g.*, Schiff v. Schiff, 611 N.W.2d 191 (N.D. 2000). The Hague Conference's Transfrontier Contact Concerning Children: General Principles and Guide to Good Practice is available from the Hague Conference website at http://www.hcch.net (under "Publications" and then "Guides to Good Practice").

137. On enforcement of access rights in international case, *see infra* notes 309–14 and accompanying text.

138. *See infra* notes 243–47 and accompanying text.

139. Cases are collected in Jay M. Zitter, Annotation, *Custodial Parent's Relocation as Grounds for Change of Custody*, 70 A.L.R.5th 377 (1999 & Supp.), and M. David LeBrun, Annotation, *Propriety of Awarding Custody of Child to Parent Residing or Intending to Reside in Foreign Country*, 20 A.L.R.4th 677 (1983 & Supp.). For useful practical advice, see JEREMY D. MORLEY, INTERNATIONAL FAMILY LAW PRACTICE 257–82 (2009).

140. *See generally* Lawrence Katz, *When the Question Involves an International Move, the Answer May Lie in Retaining U.S. Jurisdiction*, 28 FAM. ADVOC. 40, 40 (Spring 2006); Carroll J. Miller, Annotation, *Court-Authorized Permanent or Temporary Removal of Child by Parent to Foreign Country*, 30 A.L.R.4th 548 (1984 & Supp. 2009).

141. Marriage of Condon, 73 Cal. Rptr. 2d 33, 42–43 (Cal. Ct. App. 1998).

142. *Id.* at 48–53. *See also* MORLEY, *supra* note 139, at 272–74.

143. Marriage of Abargil, 131 Cal. Rptr. 2d 429 (Cal. Ct. App. 2003) (Israel); MacKinnon v. MacKinnon, 922 A.2d 1252 (N.J. 2007), *stay denied*, 551 U.S. 1177 (2007) (Japan); Hissam v. Mancini, 916 N.Y.S.2d 248 (N.Y. App. Div. 2011) (Thailand); Osmanagic v. Osmanagic, 872 A.2d 897 (Vt. 2005) (Bosnia); Stonham v. Widiastuti, 79 P.3d 1188 (Wyo. 2003) (Indonesia). *Cf.* Marriage of Nodot, 401 N.E.2d 1189 (Ill. Ct. App. 1980) (denying relocation and changing custody to father where mother planned series of international moves); Fuehrer v. Fuehrer, 906 A.2d 1198 (Pa. Super. Ct. 2006) (reversing order allowing relocation to the Netherlands to allow custodial parent to pursue new romantic interest).

144. *See* MORLEY, *supra* note 139, at 269–72. In Hissam v. Mancini, 916 N.Y.S.2d 248 (N.Y. App. Div. 2011), a custodial father was permitted to relocate to Thailand after his current spouse was "offered a transfer by the French corporation for which she worked, with lucrative pay and benefits."

145. *E.g.*, Helen H. v. Christopher T., 850 N.Y.S.2d 99 (N.Y. App. Div. 2008); Fatemi v. Fatemi, 537 A.2d 840 (Pa. Super. Ct. 1988). *See also* Daghir v. Daghir, 439 N.E.2d 324 (N.Y. 1982), *aff'g* 441 N.Y.S.2d 494 (App. Div. 1981).

146. *E.g.*, Lazarevic v. Fogelquist, 668 N.Y.S.2d 320 (N.Y. Sup. Ct. 1997) (allowing relocation to Saudi Arabia under specified conditions); Vogel v. Vogel, 637 N.W.2d 611 (Neb. 2002). *See also* Lucy S. McGough, *Starting Over: The Heuristics of Family Relocation Decision Making*, 77 ST. JOHN'S L. REV. 291 (2003).

147. *See* 8 U.S.C. § 1185(b); 22 C.F.R. § 53.2.

148. *See* 22 C.F.R. § 51.28. Detailed information is available on the U.S. State Department website at http://www.travel.state.gov (under "Passports"). Divorced parents were ordered to cooperate

in obtaining a passport for their child in *Muscarella v. Muscarella*, 2011 WL 861153 (Ohio Ct. App. 2011).

149. The U.S. State Department information circular on dual nationality is available at http://www .travel.state.gov/travel/cis_pa_tw/cis/cis_1753.html.

150. Int'l Judicial Conference on Cross-Border Family Relocation, Washington Declaration on International Family Relocation, Mar. 25, 2010, http://www.hcch.net/upload/decl _washington2010e.pdf. The principles also advocate greater use of mediation to encourage voluntary settlement of relocation disputes and the use of direct judicial communications between judges in the affected jurisdictions to help "establish, recognise and enforce, replicate and modify, where necessary, relocation orders."

151. *See* Julia Alanen, *Child Travel Abroad: Legal Requirements for Proving Parentage and Documenting Consent*, 37 FAM. L. REP. 1216 (2011).

152. *See* Ford v. Ford, 371 U.S. 187 (1962); Kovacs v. Brewer, 356 U.S. 604 (1958).

153. *See generally* Linda Silberman, *The 1996 Hague Convention on the Protection of Children: Should the United States Join?* 34 FAM. L.Q. 239 (2000).

154. *See generally* RESTATEMENT (SECOND) OF CONFLICT OF LAWS § 79 (1971); CASAD & RICHMAN, *supra* note 31, § 9-2[5], at 283–99; CLARK, *supra* note 4, § 12.5; SCOLES ET AL., *supra* note 4, § 15.39.

155. For a survey of this history in the context of the UCCJEA, see *Uniform Child-Custody Jurisdiction and Enforcement Act (with Prefatory Note and Comments by Robert G. Spector)*, 32 FAM. L.Q. 303, 305–13 (1998).

156. 28 U.S.C. § 1738A (2009).

157. UCCJEA, 9 (1A) U.L.A. 649 (1999). As of November 15, 2011, all states except Massachusetts had enacted the UCCJEA in some form. The law in Massachusetts was based on the previous uniform statute, *see* MASS. GEN. LAWS ch. 209B.

158. UCCJEA § 105.

159. UCCJEA § 102(4). On the application of the UCCJEA to custody issues in a domestic violence proceeding, see *Marriage of Fernandez-Abin*, 120 Cal. Rptr. 3d 227 (Cal. Ct. App. 2011).

The UCCJEA does not apply to adoption, in order to avoid conflict with the 1994 Uniform Adoption Act, or to proceedings involving juvenile delinquency or contractual emancipation. The Uniform Adoption Act has not been widely enacted, however. The District of Columbia has added adoption to the list of proceedings covered by the UCCJEA. D.C. CODE § 16-4601.01(4) (2010). Alabama specifically excludes adoption from its version of the UCCJEA, ALA. CODE § 30-3B-102(4). New Mexico adds it in the following manner: "termination of parental rights *whether filed alone or with an adoption proceeding*," N.M. STAT. ANN. § 40-10A-102(4) (emphasis added).

160. *See* Comment to UCCJEA § 105; *e.g.*, Marriage of Paillier, 50 Cal. Rptr. 3d 459, 462 (Cal. Ct. App. 2006) (French order placing child's habitual residence with mother constitutes a child-custody determination within the UCCJEA).

161. 345 U.S. 528 (1953). *See* CLARK, *supra* note 4, § 12.5. As noted above, the Court held in earlier decisions that custody orders were not subject to full faith and credit since they were subject to modification.

162. *Compare* Kulko v. Superior Court, 436 U.S. 84, 97 (1978) (citing *May* with approval), *with* Shaffer v. Heitner, 433 U.S. 186, 208 n. 30 (1977) (noting that personal jurisdiction is not required to litigate status questions). *See also* Karen W. v. Roger S., 793 N.Y.S.2d 693 (N.Y. Fam. Ct. 2004) (considering due process objections of German father who was served personally while in New York).

163. *E.g.*, Termination of Parental Rights to Thomas J.R., 663 N.W.2d 734 (Wis. 2003) ("we agree with the majority of the courts . . . that traditional personal jurisdiction is not required in child custody proceedings"). *See also supra* notes 74–77 and accompanying text.

164. UCCJEA § 205; PKPA § 1738A(e) (2009).

165. *E.g.*, Stanley v. Illinois, 405 U.S. 645 (1972) (failure to provide father with notice and hearing in dependency and neglect action violated his due process and equal protection rights); Armstrong v. Manzo, 380 U.S. 545 (1965) (failure to notify father of adoption proceeding was

violation of his due process rights). UCCJEA § 109 protects a party who is physically present in a state to participate in a child-custody proceeding from service of process with respect to another proceeding while in the state. *See infra* note 229 and accompanying text.

166. The term "person acting as a parent" is defined in § 102(13):

"Person acting as a parent" means a person, other than a parent, who:

(A) has physical custody of the child or has had physical custody for a period of six consecutive months, including any temporary absence, within one year immediately before the commencement of a child-custody proceeding; and

(B) has been awarded legal custody by a court or claims a right to legal custody under the law of this State.

167. *See* Marriage of Medill, 40 P.3d 1087, 1095 (Or. Ct. App. 2002).

168. *E.g.*, Shao v. Ma, 861 N.E.2d 788 (Mass. App. Ct. 2007) (parents have homes in Massachusetts and Beijing, daughter attends school in Beijing); Koons v. Koons, 615 N.Y.S.2d 563, 566–67 (N.Y. Sup. Ct. 1994) (parents have homes in New York and Rome). *See also* Marriage of Akula, 935 N.E.2d 1070 (Ill. App. Ct. 2010), on the distinction between residence under the UCCJEA and the law of domicile in an international case.

169. *See, e.g.*, Karam v. Karam, 6 So. 3d 87, 90–91 (Fla. Dist. Ct. App. 2009). Courts in the United States have developed different tests for determining what constitutes a temporary absence. *E.g.*, Chick v. Chick, 596 S.E.2d 303, 308 (N.C. Ct. App. 2004). *See also* Spector, *supra* note 155, at 319 n. 32.

170. 81 S.W.3d 899, 903–04 (Tex. App. 2002). The father, who lived in New York, filed a paternity action in Texas the day after the mother left the state. The court concluded that the two months the child spent in El Paso could not be a "period of temporary absence" because the child was not previously present in Mexico.

171. 6 So. 3d at 90–91.

172. *E.g.*, Carter v. Carter, 758 N.W.2d 1 (Neb. 2008) (more than two years in Japan was not a period of temporary absence). Courts reached similar conclusions under the UCCJA. *See* Lemley v. Miller, 932 S.W.2d 284 (Tex. App. 1996) (period of 11 months in Germany while parent was in active military service); L.H. v. Youth Welfare Office of Wiesbaden, Germany, 568 N.Y.S.2d 852 (N.Y. Fam. Ct. 1991) (Germany was home state of child of U.S. military servicemember).

173. *See, e.g.*, Sarpel v. Eflani, 65 So. 3d 1080 (Fla. Ct. App. 2011) (concluding that family's trip to Turkey was a period of temporary absence); Ogawa v. Ogawa, 221 P.3d 699 (Nev. 2009) (eight months in Japan that began as three-month month summer vacation); Arnold v. Harari, 772 N.Y.S.2d 727 (N.Y. App. Div. 2004) (one-year stay in Israel); Marriage of Donboli, No. 53861-6-I, 2005 WL 1772328 (Wash. Ct. App. July 18, 2005) (stay in Iran was temporary absence when father had prevented mother and child from leaving country). *See also* Maqsudi v. Karimova Maqsudi, 830 A.2d 929 (N.J. Super. Ct. Ch. Div. 2002) (two-year stay in Uzbekistan; decided under UCCJA).

174. *E.g.*, Krymko v. Krymko, 822 N.Y.S.2d 570 (N.Y. App. Div. 2006); *see also* Insanally v. Insanally, 644 N.Y.S.2d 192 (N.Y. App. Div. 1996) (decided under UCCJA).

175. *See, e.g.*, Sarpel v. Eflani, 65 So. 3d 1080 (Fla. Ct. App. 2011). On the potential conflict between § 102(7), defining home state as the state in which the child lived with a parent "immediately before" commencement of the proceeding, and § 201(a)(1), which refers to the home state "on the date of the commencement" of the proceeding, *see also In re Calderon-Garza*, 81 S.W.3d 899, 902–03 (Tex. App. 2002).

176. Home state jurisdiction under § 201(a)(1) was sustained in *Calderon-Garza*, 81 S.W.3d at 903–04, and in *Karen W. v. Roger S.*, 793 N.Y.S.2d 693, 694–95 (N.Y. Fam. Ct. 2004). In some older cases, decided under the UCCJA, state courts gave priority to the courts of the home state even if that was a foreign country. *E.g.*, Plas v. Superior Court, 202 Cal. Rptr. 490 (Cal. Ct. App. 1984); Dincer v. Dincer, 701 A.2d 210 (Pa. 1997); *cf.* Horlander v. Horlander, 579 N.E.2d 91 (Ind. Ct. App. 1991) (Indiana, not France, was child's home state).

177. *See* Marriage of Sareen, 62 Cal. Rptr. 3d 687 (Cal. Ct. App. 2007), *cert. denied*, 128 S. Ct. 1670 (2008).
178. *E.g.*, Ruffier v. Ruffier, 190 S.W.3d 884 (Tex. App. 2006); *In re* McCoy, 52 S.W.3d 297 (Tex. App. 2001), *but see* cases cited *supra* note 173. This makes a substantial break with the UCCJA, which allowed state courts in the United States to take jurisdiction before six months had passed based on a significant connection between the child and the state. *E.g.*, Custody of Rose, 666 N.E.2d 1228 (Ill. App. Ct. 1996) (four months in Illinois); Marriage of Horiba, 950 P.2d 340 (Or. Ct. App. 1997) (less than a month in Oregon). Other state courts concluded that jurisdiction was not appropriate in this situation. *See, e.g., Plas*, 202 Cal. Rptr. at 490 (finding abuse of discretion when trial court took jurisdiction in case filed four months after mother brought child to the state for a holiday visit); *Dincer*, 701 A.2d at 210 (holding that state court did not have jurisdiction in action filed two weeks after mother and children arrived in the state).
179. In *McCoy*, after the mother and children moved from Qatar to Arkansas, a court in Qatar granted a divorce but deferred to Texas as a more convenient forum to decide the custody issue. By the time the father filed in Texas, Arkansas was the children's home state, and the Texas courts concluded that they had no basis to exercise jurisdiction under § 201(a). *See also* Hirani v. Superior Court, 2008 WL 4216323 (Cal. Ct. App. 2008) (deferring to Japan as more convenient forum; family had lived in California for more than two years).
180. *E.g.*, Hindle v. Fuith, 33 So. 3d 782 (Fla. Ct. App. 2010) (finding that child had no home state; mother and child had relocated several times in the six months before commencement of custody proceeding). In *Marriage of Sareen*, a California court approved jurisdiction on this basis although mother and child had lived in India more than a year and had arrived in California less than three months before the proceeding was commenced. The court concluded that India was not the child's home state for purposes of § 201(a) because the child's father had instituted custody proceedings there immediately after moving his wife and child from New York to India. On the facts of the case, the court concluded that there was a strong enough connection between California and the child to support jurisdiction under § 201(a)(2): "[W]e are persuaded a parent may not take a child to a jurisdiction, file a premature custody petition, and then use the time the child remains in that jurisdiction pending resolution of the petition to meet the six-month UCCJEA home state period." 62 Cal. Rptr. 3d at 694.
181. These questions are litigated more often in the context of continuing jurisdiction under UCCJEA § 202. *E.g.*, Hector G. v. Josefina P., 771 N.Y.S.2d 316 (N.Y. Sup. Ct. 2003). *See infra* notes 209–18 and accompanying text.
182. *Compare* Marriage of Medill, 40 P.3d 1087 (Or. Ct. App. 2002) (children's visit to father in Oregon did not create a significant connection to the state), *with* EB v. EFB, 793 N.Y.S.2d 863 (N.Y. Sup. Ct. 2005) (visits back to New York after relocation to Norway sufficient to maintain significant connection to the state).
183. *See* cases cited *supra* note 178.
184. *See supra* note 170 and accompanying text.
185. *See* the Comment to UCCJEA § 201. For the same principle under the UCCJA, see *Marriage of Arnold & Cully*, 271 Cal. Rptr. 624 (Cal. Ct. App. 1990); and *Marriage of Ben-Yehoshua*, 154 Cal. Rptr. 80 (Cal. Ct. App. 1979).
186. Amin v. Bakhaty, 812 So. 2d 12, 28 (La. Ct. App. 2001) illustrates the use of residual jurisdiction under the UCCJA when a mother filed a custody proceeding one month after she and the child arrived in the state from Egypt. As noted above, there is no requirement of physical presence or personal jurisdiction over the child or any party. UCCJEA § 201(c).
187. *See* UCCJEA § 206(a):

> a court of this State may not exercise its jurisdiction . . . if, at the time of the commencement of the proceeding, a proceeding concerning the custody of the child has been commenced in a court of another State having jurisdiction substantially in conformity with this [Act], unless the proceeding has been terminated or is stayed by the court of the other State because a court of this State is a more convenient forum under Section 207.

> *Cf.* Karam v. Karam, 6 So. 3d 87, 90–91 (Fla. Dist. Ct. App. 2009).

188. *See* UCCJEA § 206(b), § 209. The court did not address this requirement in J.A. v. A.T., 960 A.2d 795 (N.J. Super. Ct. App. Div. 2008), which affirmed a custody order entered by a court that took jurisdiction under UCCJEA § 201 (a) although a Greek court had exercised jurisdiction more than two years before the father filed in New Jersey. Applying a nonuniform version of UCCJEA § 105(c), the court concluded that it was not required to respect the prior Greek decree, writing that the findings on which the Greek court based its decision "fall woefully short of the factors our Legislature has mandated that New Jersey courts consider in making custody determinations." *Id.* at 804. *See also* Stock v. Stock, 677 So. 2d 1341, 1345–47 (Fla. Dist. Ct. App. 1996) (applying simultaneous proceedings provision of UCCJA).

189. Cases concluding that there was no emergency warranting an order under UCCJEA § 204 include Marriage of Paillier, 50 Cal. Rptr. 3d 459 (Cal. Ct. App. 2006), and *In re* A.C., 30 Cal. Rptr. 3d 431 (Cal. Ct. App. 2005). UCCJA § 3(a)(3) provided for emergency jurisdiction, but without the strict limits imposed by UCCJEA § 204. *See, e.g.,* Tataragasi v. Tataragasi, 477 S.E.2d 239, 246 (N.C. Ct. App. 1996), *rev. denied,* 485 S.E.2d 309 (N.C. 1997) (approving custody order based on emergency jurisdiction); *but see* Garza v. Harney, 726 S.W.2d 198, 203 (Tex. App. 1987) (emergency authority "does not encompass jurisdiction to make a permanent custody determination or to modify the custody decree of a court with continuing jurisdiction" (citation omitted)).

190. *E.g.,* Marriage of Witherspoon, 66 Cal. Rptr. 3d 586 (Cal. Ct. App. 2007) (considering involvement of social services agencies in Germany and California in context of Hague abduction case).

191. 108 Cal. Rptr. 2d 493 (Cal. Ct. App. 2001).

192. The relationship between the UCCJEA, the PKPA, and the Violence Against Women Act in this context are discussed in the Comment to § 204.

193. 771 N.Y.S.2d 316, 325 (N.Y. Sup. Ct. 2003). As directed by the statute, the New York court communicated with its counterpart in the Dominican Republic, which declined to exercise jurisdiction since it appeared that both parents and the children were living in New York. *Id.* at 325–26. *See also* Marriage of Fernandez-Abin, 120 Cal. Rptr. 3d 227 (Cal. Ct. App. 2011).

194. *E.g., In re* Marriage of Sareen, 62 Cal. Rptr. 3d 687 (Cal. Ct. App. 2007), *cert. denied,* 128 S. Ct. 1670 (2008); Karam v. Karam, 6 So. 3d 87, 90–91 (Fla. Dist. Ct. App. 2009); London v. London, 32 So. 3d 107 (Fla. Dist. Ct. App. 2009). If the foreign court is exercising jurisdiction on some other basis, such as the nationality of the parties, the state court is not required to defer under § 206, but it may decline to exercise jurisdiction under § 207 or § 208.

195. Both of these issues were raised in *Hector G.* in circumstances of domestic violence, *see* 771 N.Y.S.2d at 330–32. Comparable defenses under the UCCJA were litigated in *Horlander v. Horlander,* 579 N.E.2d 91, 97–98 (Ind. Ct. App. 1991) (inconvenient forum); Ali v. Ali, 652 A.2d 253, 261 (N.J. Super. Ct. Ch. Div. 1994) (inconvenient forum); Klien v. Klien, 533 N.Y.S.2d 211, 214 (N.Y. Sup. Ct. 1988) (inconvenient forum); Lotte U. v. Leo U., 491 N.Y.S.2d 581 (N.Y. Fam. Ct. 1985) (improper conduct); Marriage of Horiba, 950 P.2d 340, 344–46 (Or. Ct. App. 1997) (inconvenient forum); Marriage of Ieronimakis, 831 P.2d 172, 179 (Wash. Ct. App. 1992) (inconvenient forum and petitioner's misconduct). *See also* Ivaldi v. Ivaldi, 685 A.2d 1319, 1326–28 (N.J. 1996) (remanding for determination of inconvenient forum issue).

196. The court must allow the parties to submit information and consider "all relevant factors" under § 207(b). *See, e.g.,* Marriage of Nurie, 98 Cal. Rptr. 3d 200, 230–31 (Cal. Ct. App. 2009). For a complex illustration of this problem, decided under the UCCJA, see *Miller v. Miller,* 965 A.2d 524 (Vt. 2008). See also Apenyo v. Apenyo, ___ A.3d ___, 2011 WL 6015651 (Md. Ct. Spec. App. 2011).

197. § 207(c). The court "may impose any other condition the court considers just and proper," *see id.,* and it may decline to exercise jurisdiction over child custody while retaining jurisdiction over divorce or another related proceeding, *see* § 207(d).

198. This is made clear in the modification situation in § 203; *see also In re* McCoy, 52 S.W.3d 297 (Tex. App. 2001).

199. The decision whether to decline jurisdiction might be reviewed by an appellate court, however. *E.g., Horlander,* 579 N.E.2d at 98 (trial court abused discretion in declining to hear case on basis of inconvenient forum).

200. Note that in *Nurie*, 98 Cal. Rptr. 3d at 228–30, the court refused to apply § 208 as a basis to decline continuing jurisdiction where there had been no misconduct before the court's initial assumption of jurisdiction. *See also Miller*, 965 A.2d at 532–34 (deferring jurisdiction to Canadian court based on child's best interests despite mother's misconduct in violating prior orders).

201. A court need not decline jurisdiction under § 208(a) if:

(1) the parents and all persons acting as parents have acquiesced in the exercise of jurisdiction;

(2) a court of the State otherwise having jurisdiction under Sections 201 through 203 determines that this State is a more appropriate forum under Section 207; or

(3) no court of any other State would have jurisdiction under the criteria specified in Sections 201 through 203.

In addition, there is no obligation to decline jurisdiction based on unjustifiable conduct in temporary emergency jurisdiction cases under § 204.

202. In *In re Lewin*, 149 S.W.3d 727 (Tex. App. 2004), after a trial court modified custody in favor of the father despite his repeated violations of court orders over several years, including a Canadian court order under the Hague Abduction Convention, the appellate court vacated the trial court's order, pointing out that the provisions of § 208 are mandatory and holding that the father's conduct had deprived the court of subject matter jurisdiction.

203. This issue divided the Vermont Supreme Court in *Miller* when it was asked to determine whether the Vermont courts should defer to a Canadian court that had assumed jurisdiction after the child's mother hid the child in Canada in violation of prior court orders. 965 A.2d at 524. *See also* Hector G. v. Josefina P., 771 N.Y.S.2d 316 (N.Y. Sup. Ct. 2003).

204. *See, e.g.*, Yang v. Tsui, 416 F.3d 199, 203 (3d Cir. 2005).

205. *See* art. 17 ("The sole fact that a decision relating to custody has been given in or is entitled to recognition in the requested State shall not be a ground for refusing to return a child under this Convention, but the judicial or administrative authorities of the requested State may take account of the reasons for the decision in applying this Convention.").

206. *See also* International Child Abduction Remedies Act (ICARA), 42 U.S.C. § 11601(b)(4) (2010).

207. *See Lewin*, 149 S.W.3d at 727 (granting mandamus where trial court failed to enforce Canadian return order under Abduction Convention).

208. *E.g.*, Tyszka v. Tyszka, 503 N.W.2d 726 (Mich. Ct. App. 1993). *See* ELISA PÉREZ-VERA, EXPLANATORY REPORT, CONVENTION ON THE CIVIL ASPECTS OF INTERNATIONAL CHILD ABDUCTION, HAGUE CONFERENCE ON PRIVATE INTERNATIONAL LAW, III ACTES ET DOCUMENTS DE LA QUARTORZIÈME SESSION 426, 429–30 (1980) (convention "rests implicitly on the principle that any debate on the merits of the question, *i.e.* of custody rights, should take place before the competent authorities in the State where the child had its habitual residence prior to its removal"). Note, however, that the Abduction Convention does not specify that the child must be returned to the original country of habitual residence, because of the possibility that the applicant may no longer live there. *See id.* at 459.

209. *E.g.*, Marriage of Medill, 40 P.3d 1087 (Or. Ct. App. 2002) (holding that children did not have sufficient connections with Oregon to sustain jurisdiction).

210. For a discussion of different approaches to the question whether a child who has left a state retains sufficient connections to sustain continuing jurisdiction, see *Harrison v. White*, 760 N.W.2d 691, 696–98 (Mich. Ct. App. 2008).

211. *See, e.g.*, *In re* Marriage of Nurie, 98 Cal. Rptr. 3d 200, 218–22 (Cal. Ct. App. 2009) (California did not lose exclusive, continuing jurisdiction where neither the court in Pakistan nor California had determined that all parties had ceased living in California.); *Lewin*, 149 S.W.3d at 736–38 (Section 202(a)(2) was satisfied when a Canadian court determined that the parties no longer resided in Texas). Exclusive jurisdiction is not reestablished if the noncustodial parent returns to the state after jurisdiction has been relinquished to another state. *See* § 202 cmt. Under

§ 202(b), a court that has lost exclusive continuing jurisdiction may modify its prior decree if it has jurisdiction to make an initial determination under § 201.

212. *E.g., Medill*, 40 P.3d at 1095-96.

213. *E.g.*, Guzman v. Sartin, 31 So. 3d 426 (La. Ct. App. 2009) (allowing modification of Venezuelan decree where all parties had left the country).

214. 664 N.W.2d 249 (Mich. Ct. App. 2003). *See also, e.g.*, J.T. v. A.C., 892 So. 2d 928 (Ala. Civ. App. 2004); Marriage of Fernandez-Abin, 120 Cal. Rptr. 3d 227 (Cal. Ct. App. 2011); Razo v. Vargas ___ S.W. 3d ___, 2011 WL 5428956 (Tex. App. 2011). The court in *Susan L. v. Steven L.*, 729 N.W.2d 35 (Neb. 2007), rejected constitutional challenges to international application of the UCCJEA.

215. 799 N.Y.S.2d 250 (N.Y. App. Div. 2005).

216. *Nurie*, 98 Cal. Rptr. 3d at 216-22. *See also* Marriage of Akula, 935 N.E.2d 1070 (Ill. App. Ct. 2010).

217. 771 N.Y.S.2d 316, 326-30 (N.Y. Sup. Ct. 2003). The court also noted that, to the extent that information was located in the Dominican Republic, it could make use of the UCCJEA procedures for taking evidence in another state or foreign country. *Id.* at 328-29. By contrast, in *Susan L.*, 729 N.W.2d at 40, the Nebraska court did not have jurisdiction for modification where the court in British Columbia rejected Susan's requests that it cede jurisdiction to Nebraska as a more appropriate forum, and Steven continued to live in Canada.

218. There was confusion in the facts of *Hector G. v. Josefina P.* as to whether the father was also living in New York. 771 N.Y.S.2d 316. If it had been clear that he was no longer living in the Dominican Republic, the question of modification jurisdiction would have been more easily resolved under § 203(2).

219. 848 N.Y.S.2d 147 (N.Y. App. Div. 2007). Both the mother and father had petitioned for modification in New York, the mother asking that father's visitation rights be suspended and father asking for sole custody. In returning to Italy, the mother violated a New York court order not to take the child out of the state.

220. In a case of wrongful removal or retention, Article 7 of the Child Protection Convention provides that the authorities of the child's habitual residence retain jurisdiction for one year, and Article 23 requires that participating states generally recognize and enforce the custody or access orders entered by the authorities of the habitual residence.

221. The facts of *Bjornson v. Bjornson*, 799 N.Y.S.2d 250 (N.Y. App. Div. 2005), illustrate the kind of circumstances when this could occur. When the parents divorced in 2002, the mother was awarded physical custody, and the parents agreed that she could live with the child in Norway for two years to further her education. *Id.* at 251. At the end of the period, mother decided to remain there permanently. Although the New York court determined that it had exclusive continuing jurisdiction, *id.* at 251-52, a Norwegian court might well have taken jurisdiction based on the child's two years of residence.

222. *See* UCCJEA §§ 305(d)(1), 308(d)(1)(A), 310(a)(1)(A).

223. *See* the Comments to UCCJEA § 201, *supra* note 155, at 339 n. 79. *E.g.*, Seligman-Hargis v. Hargis, 186 S.W.3d 582 (Tex. App. 2006).

224. *See* Peregoy v. Peregoy, 817 A.2d 381, 390-92 (N.J. Super. Ct. App. Div. 2002) (holding that stipulation is only one factor to be considered in determining whether to exercise jurisdiction).

225. The emerging international norm is that custody jurisdiction shifts along with the child's habitual residence. *See infra* text accompanying note 318.

226. "Person" is defined in UCCJEA § 102(12) to include an individual as well as various types of legal entities, including a government or a governmental subdivision, agency, or instrumentality.

227. *See* Chapter 1.

228. UCCJEA § 108(c).

229. Note that this immunity is limited and does not prevent a court from exercising jurisdiction over that individual on a basis other than physical presence, or extend to civil litigation based on acts unrelated to the enforcement action. *See* UCCJEA § 109(b), (c). This may be the result under state law even without reference to these statutes. *See also* Golodner v. Women's Ctr. of Se. Conn., 917 A.2d 959 (Conn. 2007).

230. UCCJEA § 210(b).
231. UCCJEA § 110 (Communication Between Courts); § 111(Taking Testimony in Another State); § 112 (Cooperation Between Courts; Preservation of Records). The court considered a number of these provisions in *Hector G. v. Josefina P.*, describing its communications with the foreign court and noting that the statute authorizes taking evidence in another state or foreign country. 771 N.Y.S.2d 316, 327-29 (N.Y. Sup. Ct. 2003). Other cases referring to international communication between courts include Marriage of Paillier, 50 Cal. Rptr. 3d 459, 462-63 (Cal. Ct. App. 2006); London v. London, 32 So. 3d 107 (Fla. Dist. Ct. App. 2009); Stock v. Stock, 677 So. 2d 1341, 1345-46 (Fla. Dist. Ct. App. 1996) (applying UCCJA); Ivaldi v. Ivaldi, 685 A.2d 1319, 1327 (N.J. 1996).
232. *See* Chapter 1 for coverage of international judicial assistance.
233. *See* CLARK, *supra* note 4, § 19.4.
234. Chapter 6 addresses the broader subject of child abduction and the return remedy available under the Abduction Convention. *See also* Janet R. Johnston & Linda K. Girdner, *Early Identification of Parents at Risk for Custody Violations and Prevention of Child Abduction*, 36 FAM. & CONCILIATION CTS. REV. 392 (1998); Rebecca L. Hegar & Geoffrey L. Greif, *Parental Abduction of Children from Interracial and Cross-Cultural Marriages*, 25 J. COMP. FAM. STUD. 135 (1994). For practical, nonjudicial steps to help prevent international abduction, *see* MORLEY, *supra* note 139, at 372-73.
235. This is based on the writ of ne exeat; *see In re* B.C., 981 P.2d 145 (Colo. 1999) (holding that court retains general authority to issue writs including writ of ne exeat).
236. *See* Abbott v. Abbott, 560 U.S. ___; 130 S. Ct. 1983 (2010). *E.g.*, White v. White, 898 N.Y.S.2d 8 (N.Y. App. Div. 2010) (noting that custody order would fall within scope of the Abduction Convention).
237. 9(1A) U.L.A. 41 (Supp. 2010). *See generally Uniform Child Abduction Prevention Act (Statutory Text, Comments, and Unofficial Annotations by Linda D. Elrod, Reporter)*, 41 FAM. L.Q. 23 (2007); Patricia M. Hoff, *"UU" UCAPA: Understanding and Using UCAPA to Prevent Child Abduction*, 41 FAM. L.Q. 1 (2007). As of September 15, 2011, UCAPA had been enacted in some form in the District of Columbia and 11 states: Alabama, Colorado, Florida, Kansas, Louisiana, Mississippi, Nebraska, Nevada, South Dakota, Tennessee, and Utah. The prefatory note to UCAPA lists several other states with abduction prevention statutes, including Arkansas, California, Oregon, and Texas.
238. UCAPA § 7(a) directs courts, in determining "whether there is a credible risk of abduction of a child," to consider evidence of specific factors, including whether the petitioner or respondent has recently engaged in various activities that may indicate a planned abduction; lacks strong familial, financial, emotional, or cultural ties to the United States (or has strong ties to another country); is likely to take the child to a country that is not a party to the Hague Abduction Convention; or is undergoing a change in immigration or citizenship status that would adversely affect the respondent's ability to remain in the United States legally.
239. *E.g., In re* Sigmar, 270 S.W.3d 289 (Tex. Ct. App. 2008) (finding that evidence was sufficient to support visitation restrictions under UCAPA).
240. The court must also consider "the age of the child, the potential harm to the child from an abduction, the legal and practical difficulties of returning the child to the jurisdiction if abducted, and the reasons for the potential abduction, including evidence of domestic violence, stalking, or child abuse or neglect." *See* Mohsen v. Mohsen, 5 So. 3d 218 (La. Ct. App. 2008) (holding that trial court should have considered all of the factors in UCAPA, and not solely the fact that Nicaragua did not participate in the Abduction Convention).
241. *See, e.g.*, UCAPA § 7(b) (directing courts to consider "any evidence that the respondent believed in good faith that the respondent's conduct was necessary to avoid imminent harm to the child or respondent"). *See* Merle Weiner & Darren Mitchell, *The Uniform Child Abduction Prevention Act: Understanding the Basics*, SYNERGY (National Council of Juvenile and Family Court Judges), Summer 2009, at 2-5.
242. UCAPA §§ 8(e), 9; *see also* UCCJEA § 311.
243. Matter of Rix 20 A.3d 326 (N.H. 2011) allowing father to take child to India for vacation); Mackinnon v. Mackinnon, 922 A.2d 1252, 1258-62 (N.J. 2007) (allowing mother to relocate

with children to Japan); Abouzahr v. Matera-Abouzahr, 824 A.2d 268, 281 (N.J. Super. App. Div. 2003) (refusing to restrict visitation to Lebanon, but requiring father to provide mother with four weeks' advance notice of any travel to the Middle East with children); Long v. Ardestani, 624 N.W.2d 405 (Wis. Ct. App. 2001) (refusing to prohibit father's travel to Iran with children; burden of proof lies with party seeking restriction). *See also Mohsen,* 5 So. 3d at 224; Al-Zouhayli v. Al-Zouhayli, 486 N.W.2d 10 (Minn. Ct. App. 1992); Bergstrom v. Bergstrom, 320 N.W.2d 119 (N.D. 1982). *See also* Marriage of Katare, 105 P.3d 44 (Wash. Ct. App. 2004) (court must make findings of fact to support restrictions it imposes).

244. *See* Ahmad v. Naviwala, 762 N.Y.S.2d 125 (N.Y. App. Div. 2003) (ordering change of custody and visitation restrictions after father retained children in Saudi Arabia); *see also* Lee v. Lee, 49 So. 3d 211 (Ala. Civ. App. 2010) (same); Shady v. Shady, 858 N.E.2d 128 (Ind. Ct. App. 2007) (ordering supervised visitation); Abu-Dalbouh v. Abu-Dalbouh, 547 N.W.2d 700 (Minn. Ct. App. 1996) (same); *cf.* Sohrabi v. Sohrabi, 568 So. 2d 940 (Fla. Dist. Ct. App. 1990) (refusing to order supervised visitation). The possibilities listed in UCAPA § 8(c) include a prohibition on removing the child from the United States without written permission of the other parent or the court's approval; a requirement that a party traveling with the child outside a designated geographical area provide the other party with a travel itinerary, copies of travel documents, and a list of physical addresses and telephone numbers where the child can be reached at specified times; or a requirement that a party obtain a mirror order from the relevant foreign country with terms identical to the order issued in the United States.

245. *E.g., Long,* 624 N.W.2d at 411 (allowing travel but requiring parent to post performance bond); Marriage of Saheb and Khazal, 880 N.E.2d 537 (Ill. Ct. App. 2007) (same). *See* UCAPA § 8(d). These restrictions may be agreed to in a mediation or settlement agreement; *see, e.g.,* Sullivan v. Sullivan, 764 N.W.2d 895, 897 (S.D. 2009). For advice on representing parents who seek or oppose foreign travel restrictions, see MORLEY, *supra* note 139, at 373–89.

246. *E.g., Shady,* 858 N.E.2d at 133–35, 138–39; *Abouzahr,* 824 A.2d at 275–76; *Ahmad,* 762 N.Y.S.2d at 125; *Al-Zouhayli,* 486 N.W.2d at 11. *See also* Marriage of Jawad & Whalen, 759 N.E.2d 1002 (Ill. Ct. App. 2001) (requiring *Frye* hearing for expert testimony regarding child abduction).

247. *See In re* Sigmar, 270 S.W.3d 289 (Tex. Ct. App. 2008). *Cf.* Waliagha v. Kaiser, 989 So. 2d 660 (Fla. Ct. App. 2008).

248. For the law governing custody jurisdiction in Canada, see 2 JEAN-GABRIEL CASTEL & JANET WALKER, CANADIAN CONFLICT OF LAWS § 18.1 (6th ed. 2005); STEPHEN G.A. PITEL & NICHOLAS S. RAFFERTY, CONFLICT OF LAWS 444–47 (2010). For England and Wales, see NIGEL LOWE ET AL., INTERNATIONAL MOVEMENT OF CHILDREN: LAW PRACTICE AND PROCEDURE 41–78 (2004). For Australia, see MICHAEL TILBURY ET AL., CONFLICT OF LAWS IN AUSTRALIA 700–10 (2002), and NYGH'S CONFLICT OF LAWS IN AUSTRALIA 583–90 (Martin Davies et al. eds., 8th ed. 2010).

249. Jurisdiction over matters of personal status, including child custody, is based on religion in many countries in the Middle East. *See, e.g.,* Charara v. Yatim, 937 N.E.2d 490 (Mass. Ct. App. 2010) (Lebanon).

250. 706 S.E.2d 78 (Ga. 2011).

251. Enforcement of a foreign court's custody order in the United States requires that the court was exercising jurisdiction in substantial conformity with the UCCJEA; *see infra* note 284 and accompanying text.

252. Council Regulation (EC) No. 2201/2003 Concerning Jurisdiction and the Recognition and Enforcement of Judgments in Matrimonial Matters and the Matters of Parental Responsibility (Brussels IIA), Preamble (5) & art. 1.

253. Brussels IIA does not apply in European jurisdictions that are not part of the European Union, including Norway and Switzerland. In addition, although Denmark is a member of the EU, it has opted out of the Brussels IIA regime.

254. Brussels IIA, *supra* note 252, at art. 8. *See generally* NIGEL LOWE ET AL., THE NEW BRUSSELS II REGULATION: A SUPPLEMENT TO INTERNATIONAL MOVEMENT OF CHILDREN 15–24 (2005).

255. Convention on Jurisdiction, Applicable Law, Recognition, Enforcement and Co-operation in Respect of Parental Responsibility and Measures for the Protection of Children art. 3, Oct. 19, 1996, 35 I.L.M. 1391. *See generally infra* notes 315–22 and accompanying text.

256. *See* Child Protection Convention, *supra* note 255, at art. 15. On the substantive law governing parental responsibility in different jurisdictions, see *supra* notes 131–35 and accompanying text.
257. *See infra* notes 320–21 and accompanying text.
258. 28 U.S.C. § 1738A (2010).
259. The procedural and substantive standards for civil and criminal contempt proceedings are different, regulated by the provisions of state law. *See generally* CLARK, *supra* note 4, § 19.10.
260. Goldstein v. Goldstein, 494 S.E.2d 745 (Ga. Ct. App. 1997),
261. *See* Marriage of Alush, 527 N.E.2d 66, 69 (Ill. App. Ct. 1988).
262. *Id.* at 69–70.
263. The most famous illustration is *Morgan v. Foretich*, 521 A.2d 248 (D.C. 1987) (*Morgan I*); 528 A.2d 425 (D.C. 1987) (*Morgan II*); 546 A.2d 407 (D.C. 1988), *cert. denied*, 488 U.S. 1007 (1989) (*Morgan III*); 564 A.2d 1 (D.C. 1989) (*Morgan IV*). Elizabeth Morgan spent more than two years in jail and was released while litigation was ongoing when Congress passed legislation to change the contempt law of the District of Columbia retroactively and temporarily to obtain her release.
264. *E.g.*, Amro v. Dist. Court, 429 N.W.2d 135 (Iowa 1988) (affirming remedial contempt order to compel father to return child from Jordan); Anyanwu v. Anyanwu, 771 A.2d 672 (N.J. Super. Ct. App. Div. 2001) (affirming contempt sanction where father refused to return child from Nigeria); Harcar v. Harcar, 982 A.2d 1230 (Pa. Super. Ct. 2009) (holding that it was error for trial court to refuse to impose sanction for contempt when mother refused to return child from Turkey). As described in *Morgan IV*:

> Incarceration upon a finding of civil contempt is a remedial measure designed to enforce compliance with a court order. A contemnor may purge herself of contempt and obtain release from jail at any time by complying with that order. This control over one's imprisonment distinguishes a civil contempt proceeding from a criminal proceeding and, accordingly, justifies the state's power to incarcerate without affording the usual safeguards of indictment and jury. Once it becomes clear, however, that incarceration will not coerce compliance, the rationale for the imprisonment ceases—its character changes from remedial to punitive—and due process requires the contemnor's release.

564 A.2d at 4 (citations omitted).
265. *E.g.*, Dennison v. Mobley, 515 S.W.2d 215 (Ark. 1974); Hendershot v. Handlan, 248 S.E.2d 273 (W. Va. 1978).
266. Courts rejected these defenses in *Amro* and *Anyanwu* when defendants claimed that the law in the country where the children had been taken prevented their being able to return the children to the United States as ordered; in each case, the courts concluded that the defendants had not done everything within their power to obtain the children's return. *Amro*, 429 N.W.2d at 140–41; *Anyanwu*, 771 A.2d 672.
267. On civil tort liability, see generally William B. Johnson, Annotation, *Liability of Legal or Natural Parent, or One Who Aids and Abets, for Damages Resulting from Abduction of Own Child*, 49 A.L.R.4th 7 (1986 & Supp. 2009). On criminal responsibility, see generally William B. Johnson, Annotation, *Kidnapping or Related Offense by Taking or Removing of Child By or Under Authority of Parent or One in Loco Parentis*, 20 A.L.R.4th 823 (1983 & Supp. 2009).
268. *E.g.*, State v. Vakilzaden, 742 A.2d 767 (Conn. 1999) (child's uncle properly charged with custodial interference for assisting father in abducting child).
269. *See* Chapter 6 for discussion of the IPKCA and the Abduction Convention.
270. *E.g.*, Adamsen v. Adamsen, 195 A.2d 418 (Conn. 1963) (enforcing Norwegian judgment in habeas proceeding); Willson v. Willson, 55 So. 2d 905 (Fla. 1951), *reh'g denied* (1952) (Canadian judgment); Lang v. Lang, 193 N.Y.S.2d 763 (N.Y. App. Div. 1959) (Swiss judgment). *But see* Pelaez v. Pelaez, 210 N.Y.S.2d 440, 441 (N.Y. App. Div. 1961) (denying comity to Cuban decree "in view of the financial and international situation affecting American citizens presently residing in Cuba or who previously resided there").
271. *E.g.*, Levicky v. Levicky, 140 A.2d 534 (N.J. Super. Ct. Ch. Div. 1958).

272. 272 S.E.2d 41, 443–44 (Va. 1980).

273. The specified grounds for jurisdiction are:

(a) the issuing state was the habitual residence of the child;

(b) the child and at least one party to the custody proceeding had a significant connection with that state; or

(c) the child was present in that state and emergency conditions required a custody order for protection of the child.

§ 485(1) (1987).

274. *E.g.*, Schleiffer v. Meyers, 644 F.2d 656 (7th Cir.), *cert. denied*, 454 U.S. 823 (1981); Bergstrom v. Bergstrom, 623 F.2d 517 (8th Cir. 1980). *See generally* RESTATEMENT (THIRD) OF FOREIGN RELATIONS LAW § 485, Reporter's Note 6 (1987).

275. *See generally* Ivaldi v. Ivaldi, 685 A.2d 1319, 1323–25 (N.J. 1996) (citing cases). Cases in which state courts declined to exercise jurisdiction under the UCCJA on the basis that the child's home was in a foreign country include *Dincer v. Dincer*, 701 A.2d 210 (Pa. 1997) (Belgium), *Marriage of Ieronimakis*, 831 P.2d 172, 176–79 (Wash. Ct. App. 1992) (Greece), and *Suarez Ortega v. Pujals de Suarez*, 465 So. 2d 607, 609 (Fla. Dist. Ct. App. 1985) (Mexico). *Cf. Ivaldi*, 685 A.2d at 1326 (finding that Morocco was not child's home state). A minority of courts reached the opposite conclusion; *see infra* notes 278–79.

276. *See, e.g.*, Hovav v. Hovav, 458 A.2d 972, 976 (Pa. Super. Ct. 1983) (declining jurisdiction in light of existing Israeli decree). *See also* RESTATEMENT (THIRD) OF FOREIGN RELATIONS LAW § 485.

277. Miller v. Superior Court, 587 P.2d 723 (Cal. 1978) (enforcing Australian order); Marriage of Malak, 227 Cal. Rptr. 841 (Cal. Ct. App. 1986) (Lebanese decree); Woodhouse v. Dist. Court, 587 P.2d 1199 (Colo. 1978) (English order); Bliss v. Bliss, 733 A.2d 954, 958–60 (D.C. 1999) (Russian order); Custody of a Minor (No. 3), 468 N.E.2d 251, 256 (Mass. 1984) (Australian decree); Klont v. Klont, 342 N.W.2d 549, 550–51 (Mich. Ct. App. 1983) (German temporary custody order). *Cf.* Al-Fassi v. Al-Fassi, 433 So. 2d 664, 667–68 (Fla. Dist. Ct. App. 1983) (declining to enforce Bahamian decree that "contravene[d] the jurisdictional standards of the UCCJA [and defeated] the purposes and policies of the Act"); *Ivaldi*, 685 A.2d at 1326–28.

278. *See, e.g.*, State *ex rel.* Rashid v. Drumm, 824 S.W.2d 497, 503 (Mo. Ct. App. 1992); Schroeder v. Vigil-Escalera Perez, 664 N.E.2d 627, 636–37 (Ohio Ct. Com. Pl. 1995). This group included Indiana, Missouri, New Mexico, and Ohio. *See* Robert G. Spector, *International Child Custody Jurisdiction and the Uniform Child Custody Jurisdiction and Enforcement Act*, 33 N.Y.U. J. INT'L L. & POL. 251, 259–60 (2000).

279. *E.g.*, Massey v. Massey, 452 N.Y.S.2d 101 (App. Div. 1982) (declining to treat Quebec as a state for purposes of UCCJA); Klien v. Klien, 533 N.Y.S.2d 211, 214 (N.Y. Sup. Ct. 1988) (Israel); Lotte U. v. Leo U., 491 N.Y.S.2d 581, 582–83 (N.Y. Fam. Ct. 1985) (Switzerland); *In re* Marriage of Horiba, 950 P.2d 340, 344–46 (Or. Ct. App. 1997) (Japan).

Some cases raised public policy concerns, particularly when application of § 23 would mean deferring to tribunals that apply religious law. *See, e.g.*, Amin v. Bakhaty, 798 So. 2d 75, 84–85 (La. 2001) (declining to defer to jurisdiction of "foreign Islamic state" after finding that country would not decide custody based on the best interests of the child); Ali v. Ali, 652 A.2d 253, 258–60 (N.J. Super. Ct. Ch. Div. 1994) (declining to enforce custody order of court in Gaza that was not based on best interests inquiry); Tataragasi v. Tataragasi, 477 S.E.2d 239, 246 (N.C. Ct. App. 1996) (declining to defer to Turkish court order that did not address best interests). *Cf.* Tazziz v. Tazziz, 533 N.E.2d 202 (Mass. App. Ct. 1988) (remanding case for consideration of law applied in custody proceeding in Sharia court in Israel). *See also* McDaniel v. McDaniel, 693 N.Y.S.2d 778, 779–80 (N.Y. App. Div. 1999) ("Moreover, although principles of international comity are important under the UCCJA, New York should defer only to those foreign nations whose 'legal institutions [are] similar in nature' to our own . . ., and whose regard for the rule of law and due process parallels that of American courts.").

Courts have recognized that religious and cultural factors are a legitimate part of a best interests analysis, however, and have been willing to enforce custody orders entered by religious tribunals in countries where those authorities have jurisdiction over custody matters, provided that the proceeding otherwise conforms to the standards for jurisdiction and notice. Cases decided under the UCCJA include *Malak*, 227 Cal. Rptr. at 845-48; Hosain v. Malik, 671 A.2d 988 (Md. Ct. Spec. App. 1996); Zwerling v. Zwerling, 636 N.Y.S.2d 595 (N.Y. Sup. Ct. 1995).

280. *See generally* Spector, *supra* note 278.
281. On the general application of the UCCJEA, *see supra* notes 154-225 and accompanying text.
282. UCCJEA § 102(3) & cmt.; *see also supra* notes 159-60 and accompanying text.
283. *E.g., In re* Lewin, 149 S.W.3d 727, 736 (Tex. App. 2004).
284. *E.g., In re* Marriage of Nurie, 98 Cal. Rptr. 3d 200, 224-26 (Cal. Ct. App. 2009); Bellew v. Larese, 706 S.E.2d 78 (Ga. 2011). In *Tostado v. Tostado*, 151 P.3d 1060 (Wash. Ct. App. 2007), the court held that a Mexican custody ruling must be enforced under UCCJEA § 105, but did not analyze whether the Mexican court exercised jurisdiction consistently with the provisions of the UCCJEA. Based on facts in the opinion indicating that the family was living in Washington state at the time the custody proceedings took place in Mexico, it appears that the court should not have enforced that order.
285. Many cases under the UCCJA declined to enforce foreign custody judgments entered without sufficient notice and opportunity for a hearing. *See, e.g.*, Al-Fassi v. Al-Fassi, 433 So. 2d 664, 666 (Fla. Dist. Ct. App. 1983); Farrell v. Farrell, 351 N.W.2d 219, 223 (Mich. Ct. App. 1984); Maqsudi v. Karimova Maqsudi, 830 A.2d 929, 934-35, 939-40 (N.J. Super. Ct. Ch. Div. 2002); Ali v. Ali, 652 A.2d 253, 257-58 (N.J. Super. Ct. Ch. Div. 1994); Koester v. Montgomery, 886 S.W.2d 432, 434-35 (Tex. App. 1994); Marriage of Zadorozny, 853 P.2d 960, 964 (Wash. Ct. App. 1993). *See also* Bliss v. Bliss, 733 A.2d 954, 958-60 (D.C. 1999) (enforcing foreign decree where party had opportunity for hearing); Laskosky v. Laskosky, 504 So. 2d 726, 730-31 (Miss. 1987) (same). In Custody of R., 947 P.2d 745, 751 (Wash. Ct. App. 1997), the court held that a party opposing enforcement of a foreign court order "must be given an opportunity to show the foreign judgment would not be entitled to cognition in the foreign state itself." In that case, the question was whether the order of a Sharia court in the Philippines was valid under Philippines law. Under the UCCJEA, *see* Marriage of Donboli, 2005 WL 1772328 (Wash. Ct. App. 2005) (declining to enforce Iranian custody order).
286. The Comment references the similar language in § 20 of the Hague Abduction Convention. In his additional comments to the act, Robert Spector, who served as the UCCJEA Reporter, points out that a respondent must establish the Article 20 defense by clear and convincing evidence, and he states that "[t]he same burden should be applicable to a person invoking this section of the UCCJEA." Spector, *supra* note 155, at 325 n. 48. *See also* D. Marianne Blair, *International Application of the UCCJEA: Scrutinizing the Escape Clause*, 38 FAM. L.Q. 547 (2004).
287. *See Tostado*, 151 P.3d at 1064-65; *cf.* Charara v. Yatim, 937 N.E.2d 490 (Mass. App. Ct. 2010) (decided under UCCJA); *Custody of R.*, 947 P.2d at 752-53 (same).
288. *See, e.g.*, N.J. STAT. ANN. § 2A:34-57(c) (2010) (adding "or does not base custody decisions on evaluation of the best interests of the child" to § 105(c)). *See generally* MORLEY, *supra* note 139, at 246-48.
289. CRC, *supra* note 2, at art. 3.
290. 17 So. 3d 892 (Fla. Dist. Ct. App. 2009).
291. 960 A.2d 795 (N.J. Super. Ct. App. Div. 2008), discussed *supra* at note 188. *See also* Marriage of Donboli, 2005 WL 1772328 (Wash. Ct. App. 2005) (unpublished) (reading best interests requirement into the UCCJEA). For an elaboration of arguments that might be made in these cases, see MORLEY, *supra* note 139, at 248-56.
292. *See e.g.*, Razo v. Vargas, ___ S.W. 3d ___, 2011 WL 5428956 (Tex. App. 2011). Section 209(e) allows for sealing of identifying information "[i]f a party alleges in an affidavit or a pleading under oath that the health, safety, or liberty of a party or child would be jeopardized by disclosure of identifying information."
293. *See, e.g.*, Morrison v. Morrison, 704 S.E.2d 617 (Va. Ct. App. 2011) (upholding court's refusal to register and enforce custody decree that was modified after mother took child to another country without authorization).
294. Cases that illustrate notice problems with foreign country decrees are cited *supra* at note 285. In Razo, a Texas court dismissed a mother's petition to modify a registered Mexican custody

judgement on jurisdictional grounds, but held that she was entitled to an evidentiary hearing on her claim that the judgement had been entered without notice and an opportunity for a hearing.

295. See the Comment to UCCJEA § 305, which also notes that an advance registration procedure is required by Article 26 of the Hague Child Protection Convention. *See infra* note 322 and accompanying text.

296. *See* UCCJEA §§ 303, 306. Note that under UCCJEA § 313, a state must accord full faith and credit to an enforcement order issued in another state that is consistent with the UCCJEA.

297. UCCJEA § 308(b).

298. If that date is impossible, "the court shall hold the hearing on the first judicial day possible. The court may extend the date of hearing at the request of the petitioner." UCCJEA § 308(c). Service is made by any method available under state law. UCCJEA § 309.

299. UCCJEA § 310(a).

300. This is discussed above; the basis for temporary jurisdiction is that "it is necessary in an emergency to protect the child because the child, or a sibling or parent of the child, is subjected to or threatened with mistreatment or abuse." UCCJEA § 204.

301. *See* UCCJEA § 311(a).

302. UCCJEA § 311(b); *see also* § 311 cmt.

303. UCCJEA § 311 cmt.

304. UCCJEA § 311(c). Under § 311(f): "The court may impose conditions upon placement of a child to ensure the appearance of the child and the child's custodian." The Comment suggests that placement with the petitioner "may not be indicated if there is a likelihood that the petitioner also will flee the jurisdiction."

305. UCCJEA § 311(e).

306. UCCJEA § 311(d).

307. UCCJEA § 311(b).

308. Criminal and Tort law remedies for child abduction are discussed in Chapter 6.

309. *See* UCCJEA §§ 304(a)(1), 105(b).

310. *See* CLARK, *supra* note 4, § 19.10; *see also supra* notes 259–266.

311. *See* CLARK, *supra* note 4, § 19.10; *see, e.g.*, Marriage of Condon, 73 Cal. Rptr. 2d 33, 43 (Cal. Ct. App. 1998). *See generally* Marguerite C. Walter, Note, *Toward the Recognition and Enforcement of Decisions Concerning Transnational Parent-Child Contact*, 79 N.Y.U. L. REV. 2381 (2004).

312. Debra E. Wax, Annotation, *Interference by Custodian of Child with Noncustodial Parent's Visitation Rights as Ground for Change of Custody*, 28 A.L.R.4th 9 (1984).

313. These safeguards are discussed generally in Chapter 6. *See, e.g.*, Farrell v. Farrell, 351 N.W.2d 219, 221 (Mich. Ct. App. 1984) (order "granted defendant the right to see his children in Michigan provided he surrender his passport and satisfy a bonding requirement").

314. Marriage of Paillier, 50 Cal. Rptr. 3d 459 (Cal. Ct. App. 2006).

315. Child Protection Convention, *supra* note 255, at art. 3.

316. As of November 15, 2011, there were 33 contracting states for the Child Protection Convention, including most of the EU member countries. For current information, see the Hague Conference web page at http://www.hcch.net under "Conventions" and number 34.

317. Child Protection Convention, *supra* note 255, at art. 55. The Convention does not apply to (a) the establishment or contesting of a parent-child relationship; (b) decisions on adoption, measures preparatory to adoption, or the annulment or revocation of adoption; (c) the name or forenames of the child; (d) emancipation; (e) maintenance obligations; (f) trusts or succession; (g) social security; (h) public measures of a general nature in matters of education or health; (i) measures taken as a result of penal offences committed by children; and (j) decisions on the right of asylum and on immigration. *See id.* at art. 4.

318. Continuing jurisdiction is discussed at notes 209–25 and accompanying text.

319. Child Protection Convention, *supra* note 255, at art. 8.

320. There are two other exceptions in Article 23: if the measure is incompatible with a later measure taken in a noncontracting State that was the child's habitual residence, and in cases involving foster care, institutional care, or *kafala* where additional procedures set out in Article 33 were not followed.

321. Child Protection Convention, *supra* note 255, at art. 28.
322. Child Protection Convention, *supra* note 255, at arts. 24-28.
323. *See supra* note 316.
324. *See* Child Abduction and Custody Act, 1985, c. 60, § 16 (Eng); *see also* Walter, *supra* note 311, at 2391 n.41.
325. *See* N. V. Lowe, *The Allocation of Parental Rights and Responsibilities—The Position in England and Wales*, 39 FAM. L.Q. 267, 292-94 (2005). *See also* DAVID HODSON, A PRACTICAL GUIDE TO INTERNATIONAL FAMILY LAW 245 (2008) ("Until an English court has been called upon to determine any question relating to a child's welfare, any foreign children orders should in practice be assumed to be effective.").
326. *See generally* CASTEL & WALKER, *supra* note 248, § 18.2; PITEL & RAFFERTY, *supra* note 248, at 444-47; ANN WILTON & JUDY S. MIYAUCHI, ENFORCEMENT OF FAMILY ORDERS AND AGREEMENTS: LAW AND PRACTICE 2 § 9 (2005).
327. In Australia, the Family Law Act 1975 (as amended) provides for registration of overseas orders dealing with children in §§ 70G-70L. *See* MICHAEL TILBURY ET AL., CONFLICT OF LAWS IN AUSTRALIA 716-24 (2002); *see also* Marriage of Condon, 73 Cal. Rptr. 2d 33, 50 (Cal. Ct. App. 1998) (discussing prior statute).

    In New Zealand, the Care of Children Act 2004 provides for registration and enforcement of foreign parenting orders; § 83 effectively creates a presumption that the foreign order is in accord with the child's best interests, and the New Zealand High Court has held that a court should not modify a foreign parenting order absent a "major new circumstance" or a "substantial matter of concern." 1 DICK WEBB ET AL., FAMILY LAW IN NEW ZEALAND § 6.141, at 635 (13th ed. 2007).
328. *See* Nina Dethloff, *Parental Rights and Responsibilities in Germany*, 39 FAM. L.Q. 315, 334-35 (2005). *See also* Kurt Sier, *Private International Law, in* INTRODUCTION TO GERMAN LAW 358 (Mathias Reimann & Joachim Zekoll eds., 2d ed. 2005).
329. Begné, *supra* note 132, at 540-41. *See also* ZAMORA ET AL. , *supra* note 8, at 695-99.
330. *See* Walter, *supra* note 311, at 2389-92. *See generally* ENFORCEMENT OF FOREIGN JUDGMENTS (Dennis Campbell ed., 1997 & Supp. 2009), and ENFORCEMENT OF FOREIGN JUDGMENTS WORLDWIDE (Charles Platto & William G. Horton eds., 2d ed. 1993).
331. *See supra* notes 252-54 and accompanying text. Brussels IIA applies only to persons who are either nationals of or habitually resident (or domiciled) in a member state of the European Community. *See generally* LOWE ET AL., *supra* note 248.

6
International Child Abduction

For the hundreds of families in the United States that experience international child abduction each year, the 1983 Hague Convention on the Civil Aspects of International Child Abduction is the primary legal and diplomatic tool available to assist in resolving these disputes.[1] Implemented in the United States with the International Child Abduction Remedies Act (ICARA),[2] the Abduction Convention requires the prompt return of a child who has been wrongfully removed to or retained in a country that is not the child's habitual residence.[3] Under Article 4, the Convention applies "to any child who was habitually resident in a Contracting State immediately before any breach of custody or access rights." It ceases to apply when a child reaches age 16.

The Office of Children's Issues (OCI) in the U.S. State Department provides information and assistance in both incoming and outgoing abduction cases. Services are more extensive for cases involving countries that participate in the Abduction Convention, but OCI also provides assistance for cases involving countries where the Convention is not in force with respect to the United States. Beyond the Abduction Convention remedies, there is the possibility of federal criminal prosecution under the International Parental Kidnapping Crime Act (IPKCA).[4] Parental child abduction may also give rise to liability under state criminal and tort laws.[5]

In the United States, requests for return under the Abduction Convention may be filed in state or federal court. Courts interpret and apply the Convention using its text and ICARA, as well as case law decisions from the United States and other countries. As noted by the U.S. Supreme Court in *Abbott v. Abbott*, a "uniform, text-based approach ensures international consistency in interpreting the Convention."[6] Courts also consider

---

Hague Abduction Convention

Hague Convention of on the Civil Aspects of International Child Abduction, October 25, 1980, T.I.A.S. No. 11,670, *reprinted at* 19 I.L.M.1501.

See also Elisa Pérez-Vera, *Explanatory Report, Convention on the Civil Aspects of International Child Abduction, Hague Conference on Private International Law*, 3 ACTES ET DOCUMENTS DE LA QUATORZIÈME SESSION 426 (1980).

The full text and current information on the Abduction Convention is available on the Hague Conference website at http://www.hcch.net (under "Specialized sections" and "Child Abduction Section").

Assistance in international child abduction cases is available from these organizations:

U.S. State Department, Bureau of Consular Affairs, Office of Children's Issues (OCI), SA-29, 2201 C Street, NW, Washington, DC 20520—phone: (888) 407-4747 (from U.S. and Canada), (202) 501-4444 (from outside the U.S. and Canada); fax: (202) 736-9132; e-mail: AbductionUSCA@state.gov; website: http://www.travel.state.gov (under "Children and Family").

National Center for Missing and Exploited Children (NCMEC), Charles B. Wang International Children's Building, 699 Prince Street, Alexandria, VA 22314-3175—phone: (703) 224-2150, (800) 843-5678 (24-hour hotline); fax: (703) 224-2122; website: http://www.missingkids.com.

International Center for Missing and Exploited Children (ICMEC), 1700 Diagonal Road, Alexandria, VA 22314—phone: (703) 837-6313; fax: (703) 549-4504; website: http://www.icmec.org.

---

the Explanatory Report that was prepared for the Hague Conference at the time the Convention was negotiated[7] as well as the views of the U.S. State Department, incorporated in a Legal Analysis of the Convention that was provided to Congress before it enacted ICARA.[8]

Working with the U.S. Central Authority

The OCI has a staff of case officers to assist parents or other left-behind parties after a parental child abduction and maintains an excellent website with general and country-specific information. Each U.S. embassy also has an employee designated to serve as the point of contact for matters relating to international parental child abduction. These services are available both with respect to foreign countries that participate in the Abduction Convention and those that do not.[9]

Seeking Assistance after a Wrongful Removal or Retention

After a parental abduction, the left-behind parent in the United States should file a missing person's report with local law enforcement authorities and request that the child's name be entered into the National Crime Information Center (NCIC) database.[10] In some parental abduction cases, the first problem is to locate the abducted child. Local law enforcement and the Federal Bureau of Investigation (FBI) have investigation techniques to help locate a taking parent and missing children. Advice and assistance is also available from the National Center for Missing and Exploited Children (NCMEC) and the International Center for Missing and Exploited Children (ICMEC).

Emergencies: Call OCI's 24-hour telephone line for emergency assistance if a child is in the process of being abducted internationally by a family member: (202) 736-9090 (Monday through Friday, 9 AM to 5 PM EST) and (888) 407-4747 (evenings, holidays, and weekends).

The Office of Children's Issues website includes country-specific information circulars on custody and parental child abduction issues for more than 50 different countries at http://www .travel.state.gov/abduction/country/country_3781.html.

If local authorities issue an arrest warrant for a taking parent, they can request a search for the child in another country through the International Police Organization (INTERPOL). If the child is a U.S. citizen, and the left-behind parent has an address in a foreign country where the child might be located, OCI can request that the appropriate U.S. embassy or consulate conduct a "welfare and whereabouts" visit with the child; but this requires the permission of the taking parent.[11] If a child who was habitually resident in the United States is removed to or retained in another Convention country, the United States may request assistance in locating the child from the Central Authority of that country. The Central Authority's obligations to provide this type of assistance apply to applications from individuals with either custody or access rights.[12]

In all parental child abduction cases, a left-behind parent may retain private counsel and pursue whatever remedies may be available through the civil justice system in the country where the child has been retained. Although U.S. custody orders are not automatically enforced by foreign courts, it may be possible to obtain recognition and enforcement through a court proceeding. The United States has begun to pursue ratification of the 1996 Hague Child Protection Convention, which would significantly improve the process of obtaining recognition and enforcement abroad for U.S. custody orders.[13] It is important to follow the legal procedures available in the country where the child is located, rather than resorting to "self-help" measures to seize and return a child to the United States. Attempts at re-abduction are traumatic and dangerous for the child and are likely to result in civil and criminal sanctions.[14]

Outgoing Hague Abduction and Access Cases

To facilitate cooperation among participating states, to prevent removal of children from their place of habitual residence, and to obtain prompt return after a removal or retention occurs, the Abduction Convention requires each Contracting State to designate a Central Authority. The OCI serves in this role in the United States.[15] For cases in which a child who was habitually resident in the United States has been wrongfully removed to or retained in another Hague country, this is the place to begin the effort to locate the child and have the child returned.

Finding Counsel Abroad

Members of the International Academy of Matrimonial Lawyers (IAML) are experienced, English-speaking international family lawyers working in more than 40 different countries. A searchable membership directory is available on the IAML website at http://www.iaml .org (under "Members").

The U.S. State Department information circular on Retaining a Foreign Attorney is available at http://www.travel.state.gov/law/retain/retain_714.html.

Central Authority Functions

Article 7 of the Abduction Convention provides that Central Authorities must, directly or through intermediaries, take all appropriate measures—

- to discover the whereabouts of a child who has been wrongfully removed or retained;
- to prevent further harm to the child or prejudice to interested parties by taking or causing to be taken provisional measures;
- to secure the voluntary return of the child or to bring about an amicable resolution of the issues;
- to exchange, where desirable, information relating to the social background of the child;
- to provide information of a general character as to the law of their State in connection with the application of the Convention;
- to initiate or facilitate the institution of judicial or administrative proceedings with a view to obtaining the return of the child and, in a proper case, to make arrangements for organizing or securing the effective exercise of rights of access;
- where the circumstances so require, to provide or facilitate the provision of legal aid and advice, including the participation of legal counsel and advisers;
- to provide such administrative arrangements as may be necessary and appropriate to secure the safe return of the child;
- to keep each other informed with respect to the operation of this Convention and, as far as possible, to eliminate any obstacles to its application.

Under Article 26, administrative services of the Central Authority must be provided without charge. Contracting States may declare by way of a reservation that applicants will be required to cover the costs of legal counsel and court proceedings. If a return order or an order concerning rights of access is entered under the Convention, Article 26 provides that the respondent may be ordered to pay the applicant's expenses "including travel expenses, any costs incurred of payments made for locating the child, the costs of legal representation of the applicant, and those of returning the child."

If a child has been abducted to a country that is a party to the Abduction Convention, the left-behind parent may file an application for assistance with OCI or directly with the Central Authority in the country where the child has been retained. This should be done as soon as possible, since the case for return order under the Convention is much stronger if legal proceedings are begun within one year of the date of wrongful removal or retention. Application forms (in Spanish and English) with instructions and detailed information about the Convention are available on the OCI website. OCI can also assist in referring the case for mediation, but parties should be certain that mediation does not overly delay or preclude the possibility of return proceedings under the Convention.[16]

Abductions to Non-Hague Countries

In the United States, OCI also provides assistance to left-behind parents or other parties when a child has been wrongfully removed to or retained in a country that is not a partner country under the Abduction Convention. Although the Convention is not available as a tool to seek the child's return from these countries, case officers at OCI may be able to obtain return or access to the child by working through consular or diplomatic channels.[17] Building on the norm of consular cooperation, the United States has signed nonbinding memoranda of understanding with Egypt, Lebanon, and Jordan to help facilitate and improve cooperation in cases concerning parental access to children.[18]

Beyond consular cooperation, U.S. authorities have access to several additional tools in non-Hague abduction cases, including passport sanctions, immigration sanctions, and criminal prosecution under state or federal law.[19] Working with private counsel in the United States and abroad, left-behind parents may seek to obtain and enforce custody orders through the civil justice system in the country where the child has been retained.[20] In many states, there are also tort law remedies for tortious interference with custody or visitation rights.[21]

Incoming Abduction and Access Cases

As the U.S. Central Authority under the Abduction Convention, OCI handles cases involving abductions of children to the United States from its partner countries under the Convention. Central Authority services include accepting applications from foreign Central Authorities, assisting with locating children within the United States, attempting to achieve voluntary return, and assisting left-behind parents with finding counsel to represent them in return or access proceedings under the Convention. The OCI website includes information for left-behind parents interested in pursuing remedies under the Abduction Convention in the United States, including answers to frequently asked questions and a checklist for incoming applications for assistance.

The U.S. Central Authority does not initiate legal proceedings, and applicants in incoming Hague abduction and access cases are generally required to cover the costs of legal counsel and court proceedings.[22] OCI makes available a referral network of lawyers to take incoming abduction cases, often on a pro bono or reduced-fee basis. In California, public prosecutors may handle incoming Hague Convention matters.[23] Through OCI, lawyers handling Hague return applications in the United States have access to resources including experienced lawyer mentors and a free language line translation service to facilitate telephone communications. In addition, a litigation manual developed to assist lawyers bringing Hague return actions is available at the NCMEC website.

OCI also accepts requests for assistance from foreign embassies or left-behind parents when children have been removed to or retained in the United States from a country that does not have a partner relationship with the United States under the Abduction Convention. Although the services are more limited, it may be possible to help locate children in the United States, to refer the parties to legal counsel or mediation services, or to facilitate a parent's access to the child. An applicant with a custody order from another country may be able to obtain return of the child through proceedings in state courts for recognition and enforcement of the foreign custody order under the Uniform Child Custody Jurisdiction and Enforcement Act (UCCJEA).[24]

Finding Counsel in the United States

The U.S. State Department information circular, Hague Abduction Convention—Legal Representation Options and Procedures in the United States, is available at http://www.travel.state.gov/abduction/incoming/legalaid/legalaid_5394.html.

Members of the International Academy of Matrimonial Lawyers (IAML) are available in many U.S. states to handle international family law matters including Hague Abduction cases. The IAML's searchable membership directory is available on its website at http://www.iaml.org (under "Members").

Federal courts in the United States do not hear cases claiming that a child was wrong-fully removed to the United States from a non-Hague country.[25] In *Taveras v. Taveras*, a left-behind parent in the Dominican Republic filed an action in federal court seeking return of two children under the Convention and also seeking recovery under the Alien Tort Statute, 28 U.S.C. § 1350 (ATS). At the time the children were retained in the United States, the Convention was not yet in effect in the Dominican Republic; and at the time the claim was filed, the United States had not yet accepted the Dominican Republic's accession. The court dismissed both claims, concluding that it had no subject matter jurisdiction under either the Convention or the ATS.[26]

Litigating Hague Abduction Cases

In the United States, ICARA provides for concurrent jurisdiction in state and federal court for actions arising under the Abduction Convention.[27] A petitioner must file in a state or federal court of appropriate jurisdiction "in the place where the child is located at the time the petition is filed." This rule may be the source of significant delay in some incoming cases, when the left-behind party does not know where the child has been taken.[28] To come within the scope of ICARA, a return proceeding must allege that the child was habitually resident in a country that has ratified or acceded to the Abduction Convention, and also that the child was removed to or retained in the United States after the date when the Convention came into force between that country and the United States.[29]

Countries such as the United States that were members of the Hague Conference on Private International Law at the time the Abduction Convention was approved in 1980 have the right to ratify the Convention, and it comes into force between these countries automatically at the time of ratification. Other countries may accede to the Convention, but these accessions take effect only with respect to those Contracting States that declare their acceptance of the accession. As a result, although more than 85 nations have rati-fied or acceded to the Convention, the United States has treaty relations with a somewhat smaller number.[30]

In an action seeking return of a child, ICARA assigns burdens of proof. A petitioner must first establish, by a preponderance of the evidence, "that the child has been wrong-fully removed or retained within the meaning of the Convention." If the petitioner makes this prima facie showing, the burden shifts to the respondent to establish one of the Con-vention's exceptions to return.[31] Under ICARA, the exceptions in Article 13(b) and Article 20 of the Convention must be established by clear and convincing evidence, while the other exceptions may be established by a preponderance of the evidence.[32]

For a petitioner, it is extremely important to file proceedings within a year of the child's wrongful removal or retention if possible. Under Article 12, the authorities must "order return of the child forthwith" if, when proceedings are commenced, a period of less than one year has elapsed from the date of the wrongful removal or retention. In proceedings commenced a year or more after the child's removal or retention, Article 12 provides that the authorities "shall also order the return of the child unless it is dem-onstrated that the child is now settled in its new environment." The court's discretion available under this provision to order a return despite the passage of time is reinforced

---

Resources for Interpreting the Abduction Convention

To achieve international consistency in interpretation and application of the Abduction Convention, courts working with the Convention consider its text and history as well as decisions from other Contracting States.

Many case decisions from around the world are collected in the International Child Abduction Database (INCADAT) (http://www.incadat.com), a searchable database with summaries of decisions, links to full opinions, case law analysis organized by topic, and additional materials such as the Hague Conference Guides to Good Practice and Judges' Newsletters.

- The Explanatory Report for the Abduction Convention and statistical and other materials prepared by the Hague Conference for periodic reviews of the Convention are available on the Hague conference website (http://www.hcch.net under "Child Abduction Section").
- Country Profiles with detailed information on child custody laws and the implementation of the Abduction Convention for more than 45 Contracting States have been posted on the Hague Conference website (http://www.hcch.net under "Child Abduction Section").
- In the United States, courts applying the Convention through the ICARA also refer to the Legal Analysis prepared for Congress by the State Department before it considered the implementing legislation (51 Fed. Reg. 10494 (1986), *available at* http://travel.state .gov/pdf/Legal_Analysis_of_the_Convention.pdf.

---

by Article 18, which states that the Convention's provisions on return "do not limit the power of a judicial or administrative authority to order the return of the child at any time."

Terms used in the Abduction Convention have an autonomous meaning, in the sense that they should be understood as standing apart from similar terminology that might be used in the domestic law of a country where the Convention will be enforced. In *Abbott v. Abbott*, the U.S. Supreme Court endorsed this approach, noting that a "uniform, text-based approach ensures international consistency in interpreting the Convention."[33] *Abbott* directs courts to consider the Convention text and purposes as well as the decisions from other Contracting States[34] and the Explanatory Report that was prepared for the Hague Conference at the time the Convention was negotiated.[35] Courts also consider the views of the State Department,[36] incorporated in a Legal Analysis of the Convention that was provided to Congress before it enacted the statute.[37]

Establishing a Wrongful Removal or Retention

Article 3 of the Abduction Convention articulates two conditions that must be met before a removal or retention of a child is considered wrongful. The first is that the removal must be "in breach of rights of custody attributed to a person, institution or any other body, either jointly or alone, under the law of the state in which the child was habitually resident immediately before the removal or retention." This is referred to in the Explanatory Report as the "juridical element," and the terms "rights of custody" and "habitual residence" have been the focus of extensive analysis in the application of the Convention. The second requirement is that "at the time of the removal or retention those rights were actually exercised, either jointly or alone, or would have been so exercised but for the removal or retention." This has been characterized as the "factual element" and is intended to be relatively easy to demonstrate at this stage of the proceeding.[38]

> **Proving the Prima Facie Case**
>
> To establish a wrongful removal or retention under Article 3 of the Abduction Convention, an applicant must establish
>
> - that the child was habitually resident in a country that has joined the Abduction Convention;
> - that the child was removed to or retained in another country in which the Convention is in force with respect to the child's country of habitual residence;
> - that the applicant had rights of custody under the law of the child's habitual residence at the time of removal or retention; and
> - that the applicant actually exercised those rights of custody at the time or removal or retention (or would have exercised those rights but for the removal or retention).
>
> Sample pleadings and orders are available on the NCMEC website at http://www.missingkids .com (under "Resources for Attorneys," "International Abductions," "Bringing Hague Return Proceedings in the U.S." and "Sample Pleadings").[39]

A court may request under Article 15 that the applicant for a return order "obtain from the authorities of the State of the habitual residence of the child a decision or other determination that the removal or retention was wrongful within the meaning of Article 3 of the Convention."[40] In some cases, a left-behind parent requests a determination from a court in the country of habitual residence that the child was wrongfully removed, without waiting for an Article 15 request from the court considering the Hague return application. Although the court deciding the return matter may consider such a determination, it is not obligated to follow it.[41]

Habitual Residence

As with other Hague conventions that use this term, the Abduction Convention and its Explanatory Report do not define "habitual residence." The Hague Conference regards habitual residence "as a question of pure fact, differing in that respect from domicile."[42] Although it was not intended to be the subject of complex legal rules, the question of habitual residence is of central importance in return cases, and it has generated a significant body of case law and discussion in the secondary literature.[43] In construing this term, courts rely on decisions in other jurisdictions interpreting the Abduction Convention as well as on the negotiating history and ongoing implementation efforts of the Hague Conference.[44]

Habitual residence is relatively easy to determine when a child has been settled in a country with his or her parents for a significant period of time, regardless of factors such as nationality or whether residence in a given place was intended to be permanent.[45] In *Friedrich v. Friedrich*, the Sixth Circuit Court of Appeals held that the inquiry into must "focus on the child, not the parents, and examine past experience, not future intentions."[46] In *Feder v. Evans-Feder*, the Third Circuit court wrote that "a child's habitual residence is the place where he or she has been physically present for an amount of time sufficient for acclimatization and which has a 'degree of settled purpose' from the child's perspective."[47] This focus on the child's circumstances is consistent with the Convention's goal of "protecting the right of children to have the stability which is so vital to them respected."[48]

The case law suggests a number of factors to consider in determining when a child is settled or acclimatized. It does not suggest how long this process will take, but courts are often skeptical of claims that it can be accomplished in several weeks.[49] Conversely, the conclusion that a child had not acclimatized after a year or more requires relatively unusual circumstances.[50] This is especially true in light of the Convention's use of one year as the limit for seeking a mandatory return order under Article 12, and the use of a one-year time period for establishment of a new habitual residence under Article 7 of the Child Protection Convention.[51] In the United States, custody jurisdiction laws treat six months of residence as sufficient for a court to take jurisdiction as the child's "home state,"[52] suggesting the view that this is typically a sufficient period for the child to become settled in a new place. The case law suggests that every child must have a single habitual residence: Courts resist the conclusion that a child has no habitual residence, except for very young infants in unusual circumstances,[53] and have held that a child cannot have multiple or concurrent habitual residences.[54]

The more difficult cases involve family relocation across international borders, particularly when the parents' intentions are unclear, changing, or in conflict. Substantial case law suggests that an established habitual residence may be lost or abandoned when a family relocates for a parent's employment or other purposes. In this circumstance, the child may obtain a new habitual residence relatively quickly, particularly when there is evidence of the parents' mutual intention to abandon the prior residence.[55] This can be distinguished from the situation in which the family or child retain their ties in one place and travel to another country for a fixed period of time or simply to explore the possibilities for a move.[56] In drawing this distinction, courts consider factors such as the sale of homes and belongings, the length of time spent living away from the original residence, and the child's acclimatization to the new environment.[57] When possible, courts also refer to the parents' shared intentions regarding a move, even if one parent has doubts about the move or the marriage, or later comes to regret the decision to relocate.[58]

The federal appellate courts have articulated a variety of tests for determining habitual residence when the parents had different intentions regarding an international move. In *Mozes v. Mozes*, the Ninth Circuit Court of Appeals focused on whether the parents had a "settled mutual intent" to abandon their residence in Israel when a father agreed to his wife and children spending 15 months living in California. Without evidence of such an intention, the court was unwilling to conclude that the residence in Israel had been abandoned.[59] Although a number of other circuit courts have followed this approach,[60] it seems to contradict the Convention's purposes when applied to relatively long-term periods of residence in another country. For example, in *Ruiz v. Tenorio* the court concluded that children who had been living with their parents in Mexico for almost three years were still habitual residents of the United States because the move to Mexico was "conditional."[61]

Courts in other circuits have been critical of the *Mozes* approach, emphasizing the child's lived experience rather than the parents' intentions.[62] Parental intent may be a more important factor in cases involving a very young child, who is unlikely to "form meaningful connections with the people and places he encounters each day."[63] Courts also agree that even a settled intention is not sufficient to shift a child's habitual residence unless there is "an actual 'change in geography'" and there is sufficient time for acclimatization.[64] For the same reason, a stipulation between the parents as to the child's

Caution: Counsel and courts should research and evaluate the case law on habitual residence especially carefully, given its central importance in Hague abduction cases and the emerging split among the federal circuit courts of appeal.

habitual residence may not be effective under the Convention if it does not correspond with the child's experience.[65]

The habitual residence inquiry is also complicated when children travel between parents' homes in different countries, particularly when a child spends significant periods in each place. In these alternating custody circumstances, courts have concluded that the child's habitual residence shifts when the child changes from one location to another. For example, in *Whiting v. Krassner*, the court concluded that a young child's habitual residence was in Canada, pointing to the parents' agreement that the mother and child could relocate there for two years as evidence of their shared intent "that she would remain in Canada for at least two years."[66]

Due to the importance under Article 12 of commencing proceedings before a year has passed, the habitual residence inquiry is sometimes complicated by a timing problem. Under Article 3 and ICARA, the habitual residence inquiry looks to the period of time "immediately before the removal or retention." For purposes of the exception to return under Article 12, a court must consider whether the return proceeding was commenced a year or more after the date of wrongful removal or retention. To come within the one-year time frame, an applicant may need to establish that the initial removal to, or retention in, another country was not wrongful, but that it became wrongful at a specific point in time. The case law generally suggests that a wrongful retention begins when one party informs the other that the child will not be returning as previously planned or agreed,[67] but the case law also indicates that a claim may not be brought for an anticipatory retention.[68] To the extent that an initial removal or retention was not wrongful, there is also the possibility the child's habitual residence will have shifted by the date when it is claimed to have become wrongful. This was the outcome in *Stern v. Stern*, where the parents agreed to allow the mother to relocate from Israel to the United States with their two-year-old son when she began a PhD program. In return proceedings brought by the father after the mother completed her degree four years later, the courts concluded that the child was no longer habitually resident in Israel.[69]

Rights of Custody

Article 3 of the Abduction Convention defines a wrongful removal or retention as one that is in breach of rights of custody "attributed to a person, an institution or any other body, either jointly or alone," under the law of the child's habitual residence. Article 3 also states that these rights "may arise in particular by operation of law or by reason of a judicial or administrative decision, or by reason of an agreement having legal effect under the law of that State." This definition is expanded in Article 5a with the further provision that, for purposes of the Convention, "rights of custody' shall include rights relating to the care of the person of the child and, in particular, the right to determine the child's place of residence." Rights of custody under the Convention should be distinguished from "rights of access," which are not enforceable by the remedy of return under Article 12. As defined in Article 5b, rights of access include "the right to take a child for a limited period of time to a place other than the child's habitual residence."

Because the Convention requires that rights of custody must be determined with reference to the law of the child's habitual residence, this inquiry requires an analysis of foreign law. For example, in *Whallon v. Lynn*, the court considered the doctrine of *patria potestad* under Mexican law to determine whether an unmarried father had rights of custody protected by the Convention.[70] In *Furnes v. Reeves*, the court considered a divorced parent's rights under several provisions of the Norwegian Children Act.[71] The Convention's reference to the law of the child's habitual residence includes not only the internal law of that country but also its conflict-of-law rules, which means that the inquiry may point toward the internal law of another country.[72] To determine whether an applicant has rights of custody under the law of the child's habitual residence, a court may take judicial notice of the law of that country under Article 14 of the Abduction Convention or may request under Article 15 that the applicant "obtain, if possible, from the authorities of the child's State of habitual residence a decision or other determination that the removal or retention was wrongful within the meaning of Article 3."[73]

Rights of custody are relatively easily established by operation of law when the child's parents are married and have not separated or divorced. An unwed mother also generally holds rights of custody by operation of law. In many countries, an unmarried father is required to register or adjudicate paternity before he acquires rights of custody, and the failure to take this step may prevent him from establishing a case for return under the Convention.[74] This is a question of state law in the United States.[75] In the event of family separation, existing custody rights continue until there is a judicial or administrative decision or a legally effective agreement between the parties.[76] Because an agreement must have legal effect under the law of the habitual residence to fall within the scope of Article 3, informal custody arrangements made between the parties are not enforceable under the Convention.[77] As Article 3 makes clear, rights of custody may be held by individuals other than parents[78] or by an institution or agency.[79]

In determining whether a party has rights of custody, Article 3 looks to the law of the place where the child was habitually resident immediately before the removal or retention, and it specifies that those rights actually must have been exercised at the time of the removal or retention. If a child is taken from the habitual residence before custody rights are established, the removal is not wrongful. If the left-behind party obtains a decision conferring rights of custody after the child has departed, known as a "chasing order," he or she may argue that there has been a wrongful retention beginning on the date when

---

Foreign Custody Laws

Country Profiles with information on custody laws for more than 45 countries that participate in the Abduction Convention are posted on the Hague Conference website at http://www.hcch .net under "Child Abduction Section" and "Country Profiles."

See also D. Marianne Blair & Merle H. Weiner, *Symposium on Comparative Custody Law*, 39 Fam. L.Q. 247–571 (2005), which includes information on custody laws in Argentina, Australia, Brazil, China, England and Wales, France, Germany, Greece, India, Iran, Ireland, Japan, Mexico, Nigeria, Russia, South Africa, and Sweden.

the decision was entered. In this situation, the analysis of custody rights may become entangled with questions of habitual residence and recognition of judgments.[80]

Because the return remedy of the Convention is available to protect rights of custody but not rights of access, the dividing line between these two categories is also important. One disputed question has been whether a party who holds access or visitation rights in combination with a ne exeat order, providing that the child may not be removed from the jurisdiction without that party's consent or a court order, has a right of custody within the meaning of the Convention. The Supreme Court addressed this issue in *Abbott v. Abbott*, which considered an order entered by a court in Chile granting daily care and control to the child's mother and visitation to his father. In addition, under Chilean law, when a parent has visitation rights his or her authorization is required before the child may be taken out of the country.[81] The Supreme Court concluded that this amounted to a joint right to decide the child's country of residence under Chilean law, and that the father's veto power was a joint right of custody within the scope of Article 5 of the Convention.[82] In reaching this conclusion, the Court gave "considerable weight" to the decisions of courts in other contracting states, noting that ICARA directs the courts to work toward a uniform international interpretation of the Convention.[83]

Actual Exercise

As noted, a petitioner bringing an action under the Abduction Convention must establish not only that he or she had rights of custody but also that "at the time of the removal or retention those rights were actually exercised, either jointly or alone, or would have been so exercised but for the removal or retention." According to the Explanatory Report, this "requires that the applicant provide only some preliminary evidence that he actually took physical care of the child, a fact which normally will be relatively easy to demonstrate."[84] In the United States, *Friedrich v. Friedrich* established that courts should "liberally find 'exercise' whenever a parent with de jure custody rights keeps, or seeks to keep, any sort of regular contact with his child,"[85] and further held that a person with valid custody rights under the law of the habitual residence, "cannot fail to 'exercise' those custody rights under the Hague Convention short of acts that constitute clear and unequivocal abandonment of the child."[86]

Establishing an Exception to Return

Once a petitioner establishes a prima facie case, the Abduction Convention provides a respondent with several potential arguments against return in Articles 12, 13, and 20. Under ICARA, two of these must be established by clear and convincing evidence, while the others may be established by a preponderance of the evidence. The heightened burden of proof is consistent with the views of the Hague Conference members in negotiating the Convention, as described in the Explanatory Report, that the exceptions to the obligation of return must be "interpreted in a restrictive fashion" in order to prevent "the collapse of the whole structure of the convention by depriving it of the spirit of mutual confidence which is its inspiration."[87] Although these are sometimes described as affirmative defenses, they are properly understood as exceptions to the court's obligation to order return. The court maintains discretion under the Convention to order return even when the basis for one of these exceptions has been established.[88]

Exceptions to the Return Obligation

A court may refuse return of a child who has been wrongfully removed or retained under the Abduction Convention based on one of five grounds:

1. More than a year has passed since the wrongful removal or retention, and the child is now settled in its new environment (Art. 12);
2. The person seeking return was not actually exercising custody rights at the time of the removal or retention, or consented to or subsequently acquiesced in the removal or retention (Art. 13a);
3. There is a grave risk that return would expose the child to physical or psychological harm or otherwise place the child in an intolerable situation (Art. 13b);
4. The child objects to being returned and has reached an age and degree of maturity at which it is appropriate to take account of the child's views (Art 13); or
5. Return would not be permitted by fundamental principles of the requested state relating to human rights and fundamental freedoms (Art. 20).

Article 12: More than One Year/Child Settled in New Environment

If the return proceeding was commenced a year or more after the date of wrongful removal or retention, Article 12 provides that the authorities "shall order return of the child, unless it is demonstrated that the child is now settled in its new environment." Although the drafters did not want an inflexible time limit on the Convention remedies, they believed that a child's best interests would change as he or she became settled in a new place.[89]

A child's removal to or retention in another country may be by agreement of the parents at the outset, but it becomes wrongful when the taking parent indicates that the child will not be returned to the prior residence as previously agreed. Courts in the United States hold that a wrongful removal or retention begins when the left-behind parent knew or should have known that the child would not be returned. These issues sometimes have a complicated intersection with the determination of habitual residence[90] and the defense based on consent or acquiescence.[91]

Case law suggests a number of factors to be considered in determining whether a child is "well settled," including the child's age, the stability of the child's residence, whether the child has friends and relatives in the new community, and whether the child has educational or religious ties in the new community, including attending school or day care or church.[92] Under these tests, very young children are less likely to become settled in a community in this sense, particularly when there were also strong family or community ties in the habitual residence.[93] Some courts have seen factors such as the parent's employment or immigration status as significant.[94] The amount of time spent in the new location is also a consideration.

The most problematic circumstance in which proceedings may be commenced more than a year after a wrongful removal or retention arises when the taking party has hidden the child so that the left-behind parent does not know where to file. While the services of the Central Authorities can be useful in locating an abducted child, they are not always immediately successful. One dramatic illustration is *Lops v. Lops*, in which locating the children took two and a half years and was accomplished only with the assistance of local law enforcement authorities and telephone wiretaps. In *Lops*, the courts concluded that the children were not well settled within the meaning of Article 12, largely because of the extensive measures the children's father and grandmother were taking to conceal the children.[95]

Some courts have considered whether "equitable tolling" of the one-year rule is appropriate in these difficult cases. There is no provision in the Convention or ICARA on this question, but several appellate courts in the United States have concluded that equitable principles may be applied to toll the one-year filing period when circumstances suggest that the abducting parent took steps to conceal the whereabouts of the child from the parent seeking return, and such concealment delayed the filing of the petition for return.[96] In *Furnes v. Reeves*, the left-behind parent presented evidence of his efforts over more than a year to locate his daughter in Norway and the United States, and the court concluded that "the one-year period of limitations began from the date that Plaintiff Furnes confirmed Jessica's location in the United States."[97] The goal of the tolling rule is to avoid rewarding an abductor for concealing the child's whereabouts and making it necessary to conduct a long search.[98] Not all courts have embraced this approach, however, in light of the contrasting policy interest in not uprooting a settled child.[99] Whether or not a court accepts the tolling theory, however, it may order the child's return in a proceeding filed after more than a year, based either on the conclusion that the child is not well settled or as a discretionary matter under Article 18.[100]

Article 13a: Rights Not Exercised, Consent or Acquiescence

A court may deny a return order under Article 13a if the party opposing return establishes that "the person, institution or other body having care of the person of the child was not actually exercising the custody rights at the time of the removal or retention, or had consented to or subsequently acquiesced in the removal or retention." The Convention does not define "actual exercise," but the Explanatory Report emphasizes that this is an inquiry focused on the care of the child, which is to be determined by the judge according to the particular circumstances in each case. The Report also notes that "custody is exercised effectively when the custodian is concerned with the care of the child's person, even if, for perfectly valid reasons (illness, education, etc.) in a particular case, the child and its guardian do not live together."[101] Although framed here as an exception to the return obligation, this inquiry is similar to the actual exercise element of the prima facie case discussed above.

Consent and acquiescence are related concepts that refer to different points in time. In *Baxter v. Baxter*, the court wrote that "The consent defense involves the petitioner's conduct prior to the contested removal or retention, while acquiescence addresses whether the petitioner subsequently agreed to or accepted the removal or retention."[102] Both defenses turn on the intent of the parent who is claimed to have agreed to the child's relocation. Consent was established in *Gonzalez-Caballero v. Mena*, when the evidence established that a parent had initially agreed to allow the child to live in the United States and later came to regret that decision.[103] A mother's consent defense was rejected in *Friedrich v. Friedrich*, in which the court commented that "the deliberately secretive nature of her actions is extremely strong evidence that Mr. Friedrich would not have consented" to the child's removal.[104] In addition, the court expressed its view "that acquiescence under the Convention requires either: an act or statement with the requisite formality, such as testimony in a judicial proceeding; a convincing written renunciation of rights; or a consistent attitude of acquiescence over a significant period of time."[105] A parent's agreement to allow the court of another country to make a final custody determination would also be likely to meet this standard.[106]

Article 13b: Grave Risk of Harm or Intolerable Situation

The most complex and controversial of the exceptions to return is available under Article 13b when the party opposing return establishes that "there is a grave risk that his or her return would expose the child to physical or psychological harm or otherwise place the child in an intolerable situation." According to the Explanatory Report: "Each of the terms used in this provision is the result of a fragile compromise reached during the deliberations" on the Convention. The Report accordingly does not offer further elaboration on what may or may not have been intended by this language.[107] As implemented in the United States, there is a high threshold for this defense, since ICARA requires that a party opposing return on this basis establish the defense by clear and convincing evidence.

The State Department's Legal Analysis, published before the United States acted to ratify the Convention, indicates that Article 13b "was not intended to be used by defendants as a vehicle to litigate (or relitigate) the child's best interests." In addition, it states that "The person opposing return must show that the risk to the child is grave, not merely serious." These general statements are followed by several examples:

> A review of deliberations on the Conventions reveals that "intolerable situation" was not intended to encompass return to a home where money is in short supply, or where educational or other opportunities are more limited than in the requested State. An example of an "intolerable situation" is one in which a custodial parent sexually abuses a child. If the other parent removes or retains the child to safeguard it against further victimization, and the abusive parent then petitions for the child's return under the Convention, the court may deny the petition. Such action would protect the child from being returned to an "intolerable situation" and subjected to a grave risk of psychological harm.[108]

Following this guidance, the court in *Cuellar v. Joyce* rejected the argument that a mother's living conditions in Panama, where her home had no indoor plumbing and "no climate control, no refrigeration, and very little furniture," created a grave risk of harm to her child.[109]

Further emphasizing the distinction between the grave risk of harm defense and considerations relevant to a best interests determination, the court in *Friedrich v. Friedrich* held that the harm that might result from uprooting a child who had settled into a new environment was not sufficient to meet the test of Article 13b. In a frequently quoted passage, the court wrote:

> If we are to take the international obligations of American courts with any degree of seriousness, the exception to the Hague Convention for grave harm to the child requires far more than the evidence that Mrs. Friedrich provides. Mrs. Friedrich alleges nothing more than *adjustment* problems that would attend the relocation of most children. There is no allegation that Mr. Friedrich has ever abused Thomas. The district court found that the home that Mr. Friedrich has prepared for Thomas in Germany appears adequate

to the needs of any young child. The father does not work long hours, and the child's German grandmother is ready to care for the child when the father cannot. There is nothing in the record to indicate that life in Germany would result in any permanent harm or unhappiness.

Furthermore, even *if* the home of Mr. Friedrich were a grim place to raise a child in comparison to the pretty, peaceful streets of Ironton, Ohio, that fact would be irrelevant to a federal court's obligation under the Convention. We are not to debate the relevant virtues of Batman and *Max und Moritz*, Wheaties and *Milchreis*. The exception for grave harm to the child is not license for a court in the abducted-to country to speculate on where the child would be happiest. That decision is a custody matter, and reserved to the court in the country of habitual residence.[110]

In dicta, the court in *Friedrich* went on to suggest that a grave risk of harm "can exist in only two circumstances." One is independent of the custody dispute, when the child would be returned to "a zone of war, famine, or disease."[111] The other situation described by the court involves "cases of serious abuse or neglect, or extraordinary emotional dependence, when the court in the country of habitual residence, for whatever reason, may be incapable or unwilling to give the child adequate protection." These dicta go beyond the text and history of the Convention and implementing legislation, which do not limit the factual circumstances in which a grave risk to the child can be established and do not suggest that proof of a grave risk to the child can be rebutted by evidence that a court in the habitual residence could take measures to protect the child.[112] They draw support, however, from the discretion conferred generally by Article 13 and Article 18 to order return of a child even when not required by the Convention.[113]

In drawing a firm line excluding general "best interests" factors from the court's consideration under Article 13b, the *Friedrich* court interpreted the Convention consistently with the stance taken by its drafters and the views of most participating countries, expressed in the Special Commission meetings that have reviewed implementation of the Convention. This has been a subject of ongoing debate, however, and some foreign courts have refused to return abducted children based on best interests arguments. These rulings often point to the requirement under Article 3 of the 1989 United Nations Convention on the Rights of the Child (CRC) that "[i]n all actions concerning children ... the best interests of the child shall be a primary consideration."[114] The issue was placed in sharp relief with the 2010 ruling of the European Court of Human Rights in *Neulinger & Shuruk v. Switzerland*, which seemed to hold that the European Convention on Human Rights mandates an individualized best interests analysis as part of the grave risk determination under Article 13b.[115] Subsequent developments indicate that this may have been too broad a reading of the *Neulinger* judgment, but the case law that has followed counsels against an overly narrow interpretation of the 13b exception.[116]

The tension between enforcing the return obligation under the Abduction Convention and protecting a child's best interests was not fully anticipated, both because it preceded the CRC and because the drafters of the Convention understood child abduction as principally a problem of children being taken from their primary caregivers by a parent seeking to obtain the advantage of a different and more sympathetic forum. In fact, the more common circumstance has been a primary caregiving parent who relocates with the child. In this circumstance, an order returning the child to the habitual residence or the other parent may require a de facto change in custody, depending on whether the caregiving parent is able to return with the child.[117] In these cases, courts in the United States have uniformly concluded that the prospect of separating a child from his or her primary carer is not enough to establish a grave risk of psychological harm.[118]

Courts in the United States and elsewhere have struggled to establish the appropriate reach of Article 13b in family violence cases.[119] One difficulty has been the perception of some courts in early cases that violence is a concern only when it is directed at the child.[120] More recent rulings from appellate courts have rejected this view. In *Van de Sande v. Van de Sande*, the Seventh Circuit Court of Appeals reversed a lower court's summary return order on the basis that the court had not adequately evaluated the risks of violence. As the court noted, "given [the father's] propensity for violence and the grotesque disregard for the children's welfare that he displayed by beating his wife severely and repeatedly in their presence . . . it would be irresponsible to think the risk to the children less than grave."[121]

The family violence cases have been made more difficult by the *Friedrich* dicta, which have been widely repeated, suggesting that return should be ordered, even when there is clear and convincing proof of a grave risk of harm, based on undertakings designed to protect the child. For example, in *Blondin v. Dubois*, after the trial court concluded that the mother had established a grave risk of harm to the children, the Second Circuit Court of Appeals remanded the case, holding that the Convention "requires a more complete analysis of the full panoply of arrangements that might allow the children to be returned . . . in order to allow the courts of that nation an opportunity to adjudicate custody."[122] As the courts have gained greater experience with the Convention, however, they have begun to take a more cautious approach to the use of undertakings in family violence cases. In *Walsh v. Walsh*, the First Circuit concluded that the lower court had "raised the article 13(b) bar higher than the Convention requires" when it required a showing of a "truly extraordinary threat" to the children's health and safety.[123] Accepting the proposition that "a potential grave risk of harm can, at times, be mitigated sufficiently by the acceptance of undertakings and sufficient guarantees of performance of those undertakings," the appellate court ruled that the lower court had "underestimated the risks to the children and overestimated the strength of the undertakings in this case."[124]

In contrast to decisions such as *Van de Sande* and *Walsh*, the courts concluded in *Charalambous v. Charalambous* that a mother had not offered clear and convincing evidence of a grave risk of harm to the children based on her testimony of an incident in which the husband had "braced [the wife] against a wall during an argument and held his hand next to her face."[125] The mother's "subjective perception of a threat" was not "corroborated by other evidence in the record," and the court ruled that even if she refused to return to Cyprus with the children, "the alternative of allowing these children to remain wrongfully retained in this country is equally likely to traumatize the children."

Hague Domestic Violence Project

Resources and information for mothers, lawyers, judges, and advocates in Hague Abduction cases involving domestic violence is available from the Hague Domestic Violence Project at http://www.haguedv.org.

There is relatively little case law applying the "intolerable situation" aspect of Article 13b, which was apparently intended to provide flexibility for a narrow range of unusual cases in which return should be discretionary.[126] The history indicates that it was not intended "to encompass return to a home where money is in short supply, or where educational or other opportunities are more limited than in the requested State."[127] This is another circumstance in which undertakings are sometimes devised to minimize the risk of harm to the child.

Article 13: Child's Objections to Return

Also under Article 13, the authorities in the requested state may refuse to order a child's return if it is found "that the child objects to being returned and has attained an age and degree of maturity at which it is appropriate to take account of its views." By definition, this provision applies only to children younger than 16, since under Article 4 the Convention ceases to apply when a child reaches age 16. Application of this exception is left to the discretion of the competent authorities, but the Explanatory Report cautions that "this provision could prove quite dangerous if it were applied by means of the direct questioning of young people who may admittedly have a clear grasp of the situation but who may also suffer from serious psychological harm if they think they are being forced to choose between two parents."[128] The child's opportunity to be heard is an important right, however, recognized by Article 12 of the CRC.[129]

Under ICARA, this exception to return must be established by a preponderance of the evidence,[130] and much of the decisional law addresses the question of when a child is sufficiently mature to have his or her views considered. Although some courts have relied on the wishes of children as young as 8 or 9, the provision is more frequently applied to young teenagers.[131] Courts have differed on whether to allow expert testimony as to the child's maturity in this context.[132] The exception is more difficult to apply in situations where a child's views may have been overly influenced by a parent, or when a case involves multiple siblings with different ages and maturity levels.[133] As with the other exceptions, the determination whether to refuse return based on the child's objections is within the court's discretion.[134]

Article 20: Public Policy: Human Rights and Fundamental Freedoms

Article 20 includes a final exception, stating that return of a child "may be refused if this would not be permitted by the fundamental principles of the requested State relating to the protection of human rights and fundamental freedoms." The Explanatory Report describes this as another careful compromise, formulated to reduce the possibility that states might refuse to return a child under the Convention based on their own internal law or public policy. It was intended to establish a higher threshold than the traditional public policy exception of other conventions. This is reinforced by the ICARA, which requires proof of this defense by clear and convincing evidence. Because there are potentially broad implications of a ruling that a foreign legal system violates human rights, the Explanatory Report suggests that courts will be exceptionally cautious in upholding this defense.[135] This suggestion is reinforced by the fact that there is very little case law in the United States or elsewhere applying the Article 20 defense.[136]

Equitable Arguments: Unclean Hands and Fugitive Disentitlement

A number of cases have considered whether courts may exercise their inherent powers to refuse to hear claims under the Abduction Convention brought by petitioners who have engaged in unconscionable conduct, such as failure to obey court orders in the United States or flight to avoid a criminal conviction. In *Karpenko v. Leendertz*, the court rejected the argument that a petitioner's claim should be dismissed because she had prevented the child's father from having any access to the child, in clear violation of the initial custody order.[137] The court majority wrote:

> [A]pplication of the unclean hands doctrine would undermine the Hague Convention's goal of protecting the well-being of the child, of restoring the status quo before the child's abduction, and of ensuring "that rights of custody and of access under the law of one Contracting State are effectively respected in other Contracting States."[138]

A strong dissent argued that Hague litigation is not immune from traditional equitable doctrines and that the case involved exceptional circumstances warranting application of the unclean hands rule.[139]

Although there is early case law applying the fugitive disentitlement doctrine to an action under the Abduction Convention,[140] subsequent rulings have been more cautious. *Walsh v. Walsh* concluded that the fugitive disentitlement doctrine was generally inappropriate in cases involving parental rights in light of parents' constitutionally protected interest in their relationships with their children.[141] *Walsh* is consistent with the Supreme Court's general approach to this doctrine, which suggests that it must be used with restraint and that the sanction of dismissal must be justified by some practical necessity, such as preventing prejudice, delay, frustration, or unenforceability of the court's judgment.[142]

Return Orders and Undertakings

In case of a successful application under the Convention, a child will ordinarily be returned to the State where the child was habitually resident before the removal or retention. This is not required, however. According to the Explanatory Report, language requiring return to the prior habitual residence was rejected during the negotiation of the Convention in order to preserve its flexibility in situations such as those in which the applicant no longer lives in the place that was the child's habitual residence.[143]

If return is ordered, the court should "carefully tailor an order designed to ameliorate, as much as possible, any risk to [the child's] well-being."[144] A return order does not of itself change the parties' rights of custody, and the Convention does not require that the child be turned over to a successful applicant. The court may allow the taking party to return with the child, particularly when that party is the child's primary carer. If returning with the child would place the taking party in a difficult situation for financial or other reasons, the court may order that return must take place subject to certain conditions.[145] In some cases, an applicant offers undertakings in order to facilitate the child's return or to persuade the court that return will be safe for the child and the child's primary carer.[146] These may address financial matters, such as paying travel and housing expenses, or legal matters, such as reopening custody proceedings or dropping criminal or contempt proceedings against the taking parent.

The Convention does not provide expressly for undertakings, but they are permissible under the "non-exclusivity" principle reflected in Article 18 and Article 34.[147] Whether the undertakings are voluntary or court-imposed, however, cross-border enforcement is difficult. The U.S. State Department recommends that undertakings should be "limited in scope" and particularly discourages undertakings "that address in great detail issues of custody, visitation, and maintenance." As already noted, courts in the United States sometimes exercise their discretion to order a child's return despite clear and convincing evidence of a grave risk of harm, if an applicant establishes that the risk can be sufficiently mitigated through the use of undertakings.[148] This is a controversial approach, however; it is not required by ICARA or the text of the Convention and has been squarely rejected in several circuits.[149]

Within the Hague Conference, there is ongoing discussion of means to facilitate return, including "safe harbor" or "mirror" orders, and direct communication between judges in different countries.[150] Ratification by the United States of the 1996 Hague Child Protection Convention would provide a framework for this type of cross-border cooperation.[151] Under the Child Protection Convention, measures for the protection of children entered within the parameters of the Convention must be recognized by operation of law in other Contracting States.[152]

Enforcement and Recognition of Return Orders

Enforcement of return orders under the Abduction Convention has sometimes been difficult to accomplish, and some countries have a discouraging record in this area.[153] In the United States, state courts may enforce Hague return orders using all of the remedies available for enforcing custody orders under the UCCJEA.[154] When a return order is entered, the respondent often requests a stay pending appeal to prevent the child's departure and protect the right to appeal. Without a stay or other order from the trial court, the return order may be effective immediately.[155] If the trial court denies a stay, the respondent may file an emergency motion for a stay pending appeal with the appellate court. There is authority to suggest that stays should not be granted routinely, in light of the Convention's purpose of securing the child's prompt return.[156] When there is a risk of a further abduction of the child, the court may take appropriate provisional measures to prevent the child's removal or concealment until return is accomplished.[157]

Within the United States, ICARA mandates that state and federal courts give full faith and credit to the judgment of any other state or federal court ordering or denying return of a child pursuant to the Convention.[158] The courts are not obligated to recognize and give effect to judgments of courts in other countries, however, and in determining whether to extend comity to a foreign country's judgment in a Hague abduction matter, courts in the United States have "looked closely at the merits of the foreign court's decision" denying a child's return.[159] Thus, in *Avesta v. Petroutsas*, the court concluded that comity should not be extended to a foreign court's determination "if it clearly misinterprets the Hague Convention, contravenes the Convention's fundamental premises or objectives, or fails to meet a minimum standard of reasonableness."[160]

Rights of Access

The return remedy under Article 12 is not available to remedy a breach of access rights, but Article 21 of the Convention provides a more limited set of protections for rights of access. Applications may be presented to a Central Authority, which has general obligations to cooperate under Article 7.[161] In addition, Article 21 describes the responsibilities of Central Authorities when they are presented with "[a]n application to make arrangements for organizing or securing the effective exercise of access rights." The Central Authority "shall take steps to remove, as far as possible, all obstacles to the exercise of such rights"[162] and may "initiate or assist in the initiation of legal proceedings with a view to organizing or protecting these rights and securing respect for the conditions to which the exercise of these rights may be subject." As described in the Explanatory Report, this might include seeking undertakings from the holder of access rights to assure that the child will not be abducted during the period of access.[163]

In the United States, ICARA allows judicial proceedings "for arrangements for organizing or securing the effective exercise of rights of access to a child."[164] As with proceedings for return, there is concurrent jurisdiction in state and federal courts, and the proceeding may be brought in a court authorized to exercise its jurisdiction in the place where the child is located when the petition is filed. In this type of proceeding, the petitioner must establish by a preponderance of evidence that he or she has such rights of access. With no return remedy, however, and no other substantive basis in either the Convention or ICARA to resolve access claims, the federal courts have declined to take jurisdiction in these cases.[165] Proceedings to secure access rights should be commenced in state court under the UCCJEA.

Special Procedural and Evidentiary Issues

Several articles in the Convention address procedural matters. Article 11 requires judicial and administrative authorities to act expeditiously in return proceedings and gives applicants the right to request "a statement of the reasons for the delay" if a decision is not reached within six weeks. To resolve these cases quickly, courts may proceed by way of summary judgment, without holding an evidentiary hearing, unless there are genuine issues of material fact.[166] The obligation to act expeditiously in these cases also extends to appellate courts.[167]

Neither the Convention nor ICARA specifies the procedures a court should use in hearing a return petition. As noted by the court in *Zajaczkowski v. Zajaczkowska*, the timelines associated with "ordinary civil cases would seem to be at odds with the Convention and ICARA's premium on expedited decision-making." Concluding that a petition under ICARA was more closely analogous to an application for a writ of habeas corpus,

---

Resources: Access Rights

The application of the Abduction Convention and the Child Protection Convention to claims involving access rights is discussed in HAGUE CONFERENCE ON PRIVATE INTERNATIONAL LAW, TRANSFRONTIER CONTACT CONCERNING CHILDREN: GENERAL PRINCIPLES AND A GUIDE TO GOOD PRACTICE (2008).

the court followed the procedures applicable to a habeas case.[168] This involved issuing an order directed to the respondent to appear before the court on a specific date with the child and show cause why the petition should not be granted and the child returned.

Under Article 23 and Article 30, incorporated into ICARA, applications and documents or other information relating to those applications need not be legalized or authenticated to be admissible in court.[169] Under Article 24, documents in incoming cases must be submitted in the original language accompanied by a translation into "the official language or one of the official languages of the requested State or, where that is not feasible, a translation into English or French." By reservation, a Contracting State may object to the use of either English or French, but not both; for the United States, incoming applications and documents should be translated into English. Article 14 allows the court to "take notice directly" of the law and judicial and administrative decisions of a child's habitual residence, "without recourse to the specific procedures for the proof of that law or for the recognition of foreign decisions which would otherwise be applicable."[170]

The International Hague Network of Judges was created to facilitate direct communication between judges on issues arising under the Child Abduction Convention. Members of the network are available to assist judicial colleagues in obtaining general information about the Convention, subject to whatever substantive and procedural requirements may apply in each jurisdiction. Judges do not communicate about the merits of specific cases, but the network can be a useful and efficient means of obtaining jurisdictional or other information about the legal or judicial system in another country.[171]

Provisional Measures

As contemplated by Article 7b of the Convention, ICARA authorizes temporary or provisional measures "to protect the well-being of the child involved or to prevent the child's further removal or concealment before the final disposition of the petition."[172] This may require courts to involve state child welfare authorities, issue restraining orders, or set bond requirements. Under ICARA, the court in a Convention case may not "order a child removed from a person having physical control of the child unless the applicable requirements of State law . . . are satisfied"[173] and notice must be given "in accordance with the applicable law governing notice in interstate child custody proceedings."[174] An applicant with primary custody rights may be able to use the procedures under the UCCJEA for registration and expedited enforcement of a foreign custody order. These procedures include the possibility of obtaining an emergency warrant on an ex parte basis if the child "is immediately likely to suffer serious physical harm or be removed from this State."[175] Courts and public officials should act cautiously in these cases so that the right to a hearing is not unfairly preempted.[176]

Hague Judicial Network

The International Hague Network of Judges includes members designated in more than 45 different countries, including the United States. A list of the member judges is available at http://www.hcch.net/upload/haguenetwork.pdf.

Interaction of Convention Proceedings and Custody Litigation

The terms of the Convention clearly mark its role as separate from the determination of rights of custody. Article 16 requires that custody proceedings in the requested state must not proceed until the return issue is resolved:

> After receiving notice of a wrongful removal or retention of a child . . . the judicial or administrative authorities of the contracting State to which the child has been removed or in which it has been retained shall not decide on the merits of rights of custody until it has been determined that the child is not to be returned under the Convention or unless an application under this Convention is not received within a reasonable time following receipt of notice.

The Convention does not restrict the authorities in the child's place of habitual residence from considering claims regarding custody or access during the pendency of a Hague return proceeding in another Contracting State. Under Article 15, authorities in the requested state may ask a return applicant to obtain a ruling from authorities in the habitual residence as to whether the child's removal or retention was wrongful within the meaning of Article 3. Typically, this determination would address whether the requesting party has "rights of custody" under the law of the habitual residence.[177]

When notified of a Hague abduction claim, state courts should suspend custody proceedings until the Hague issues are resolved.[178] If the return petition is denied, custody proceedings may resume, and Article 19 provides that "[a] decision under this Convention concerning the return of the child shall not be taken to be a determination on the merits of any custody issue."[179]

Regarding custody orders entered before the return proceeding is commenced, Article 17 specifies that the "sole fact" that a custody decision "has been given in or is entitled to recognition in the requested State shall not be a ground for refusing to return a child."[180] As described in the State Department's Legal Analysis, the effect of Article 17 is that an alleged abductor "cannot insulate the child from the Convention's return provisions merely by obtaining a custody order in the country of new residence," and cannot "rely upon a stale decree . . ., the provisions of which have been derogated from subsequently by agreement or acquiescence of the parties."[181]

In the United States, the interaction of custody proceedings and Convention proceedings is complicated by the traditional responsibility of state courts for family law matters and the concurrent jurisdiction of state and federal courts under ICARA. State and federal courts have had to address problems of parallel proceedings, within the framework of a few clear ground rules. A petition under the Abduction Convention may be filed in either state or federal court, but once a state or federal court rules on the Hague issues, all other state and federal courts must extend full faith and credit to that ruling.[182] Federal courts with jurisdiction under ICARA will not hear any related family law claims under state law.[183] In theory, a Hague petition filed in the state courts may be removed to federal court under 28 U.S.C. § 1441(a), but removal jurisdiction is rarely invoked in practice.[184]

Federal appellate courts have considered and largely rejected arguments for abstention in Abduction Convention cases. This includes abstention in favor of ongoing state court custody proceedings under the *Younger* doctrine,[185] the *Colorado River* doctrine,[186] and the *Rooker-Feldman* doctrine.[187] A petitioner does not waive potential federal remedies under the Abduction Convention by filing a custody proceeding in state court,[188] but federal abstention may be appropriate when the petitioner has already brought a claim under ICARA in state court.[189] One unusual case allowed a federal Hague case to proceed even though the petitioner had previously filed in state court when the state court indicated that it would not be able to hear the case for two months.[190]

Stays and Appeals

An appellate court reviews the lower court's "findings of fact for clear error and . . . its conclusions about American, foreign, and international law *de novo*."[191] Determination of intent is a question of fact, and the appellate court defers to the lower court's findings unless they are clearly erroneous.[192] Where the courts have taken different approaches to defining a key term, such as "rights of custody" or "habitual residence," the question of which standard should be applied is a question of law subject to de novo appellate review.[193] The determination of habitual residence has been characterized as a mixed question of fact and law, also subject to de novo review.[194] Whether there is a grave risk of harm under Article 13b is also a mixed question of law and fact.[195]

A petitioner who obtains a return order will ordinarily seek immediate enforcement, while a respondent who plans to appeal will seek an immediate stay, either from the trial court or on an emergency basis with the appellate court.[196] There is some authority holding that once the child leaves the court's jurisdiction, any appeal would be moot.[197] Because prompt resolution of abduction cases is important under the Convention, there are indications in the case law that stays are disfavored. At the same time, given the risk that an appeal will be mooted by denial of a stay and the difficulties for a child of being shuttled back and forth between countries, a stay may be appropriate when there are serious grounds for appeal. To accommodate these competing interests, the court in *Kijowska v. Haines* indicated that any stay granted by an appellate court should be accompanied by an accelerated schedule for briefing, argument, and decision.[198]

Mediation

Mediation may be useful to prevent child abduction, by assisting the parties in coming to agreement on terms for the child's relocation and ongoing access with the left-behind party. After a removal or retention has occurred, mediation may facilitate the child's return. Ideally, the mediation process can be faster and less expensive than litigation,

---

Resources: Mediation

The U.S. State Department information circular on Mediation is available at http://www.travel.state.gov/abduction/solutions/mediation/mediation_3853.html.

The Hague Conference is developing a Guide to Good Practice on Mediation, which will be available on its website at http://www.hcch.net (under "Child Abduction Section" and "Guides to Good Practice").

See also SARAH VIGERS, MEDIATING INTERNATIONAL CHILD ABDUCTION CASES (2011).

International Custody Mediation

Organizations with specialized programs for mediating international cases involving custody, relocation, access, and child abduction include the following:

- Reunite International Child Abduction Centre, PO Box 7124, Leicester LE1 7XX United Kingdom, http://www.reunite.org.

- International Social Service—USA, 200 E. Lexington St., Suite 1700, Baltimore, MD 21202—3533 phone: (443) 451-1200; fax: (443) 451-1220; website: http://www.iss-usa.org (under "Services" and "Other").
- International Child Abduction Centre (Netherlands), http://www.kinderontvoering.org/en/.
- European Parliament Mediator for International Parental Child Abduction (Belgium), http://www.europarl.europa.eu/parliament/public/staticDisplay.do?id=154.

but there is a risk in child abduction cases that it may be used strategically to delay return proceedings. To be enforceable, a mediated settlement of custody, relocation, or abduction issues should be incorporated in a written agreement filed with and approved by a court with appropriate jurisdiction.[199] This is another circumstance in which the rules on cross-border recognition of judgments in Hague Child Protection Convention are a useful counterpart to the Abduction Convention.

International family mediation requires specialized knowledge and experience, in light of the complex legal setting as well as cross-cultural or language considerations and domestic violence issues.[200] Mediation projects focused on resolution of international child abduction disputes have been instituted in a number of countries.[201] Central Authorities make referrals to these organizations, reflecting their obligation under Article 10 to "take all appropriate measures in order to obtain the voluntary return of the child." In the United States, a growing number of nonprofit organizations and private firms provide international family mediation services.[202]

Lawyer's Fees

Under Article 26, the Central Authorities bear their own costs in Convention cases, but may require applicants to pay expenses for the child's return. Contracting States may enter a reservation to the Convention declaring that they will not assume the costs arising from court proceedings or the participation of legal counsel, except insofar as those costs may be covered by a system of legal aid. The United States is one of many contracting states that have made this reservation.[203] To assist applicants in incoming Hague abduction or access cases in bringing proceedings, the U.S. Central Authority maintains a referral network of lawyers who may be available to take Convention cases on a pro bono or reduced-fee basis; it also provides various resources and services. Legal fees and expenses may be recovered at the conclusion of the litigation.

Hague Attorney Network

A flyer describing the U.S. State Department's Attorney Network with a form that can be used to join the Network is available at http://www.travel.state.gov/pdf/AttorneyNetworkFlyer.pdf.

Article 26 provides that when authorities enter return orders or orders concerning access rights under the Convention, they may also order the respondent "to pay necessary expenses incurred by or on behalf of the applicant, including travel expenses, any costs incurred or payments made for locating the child, the costs of legal representation of the applicant, and those of returning the child." Counsel sometimes handle these cases with the understanding that their fees will be paid only to the extent they can be recovered from the taking party.[204] According to the State Department's Legal Analysis, the purposes of awarding fees and costs under the Convention "are to restore the applicant to the financial position he or she would have been in had there been no removal or retention, as well as to deter such conduct from happening in the first place."[205] In the United States, this is implemented in 42 U.S.C. § 11607, which provides that a court ordering return shall order the respondent to pay the full range of these expenses, "unless the respondent establishes that such order would be clearly inappropriate."[206] Applying this statute, courts have generally employed a "lodestar" method, based on determination of a reasonable number of hours and a reasonable hourly rate.[207] The fee order may also be appealed; *Rydder v. Rydder* reduced the fees awarded by the lower court, concluding that the award was "so excessive as to constitute an abuse of discretion" in light of the taking parent's financial circumstances.[208]

Litigating Hague Abductions in Other Countries

The provisions of the Abduction Convention described here are equally applicable when a child habitually resident in the United States has been wrongfully removed to or retained in any of the other countries with which the United States has established a relationship under the Convention.[209] A left-behind parent or other party with rights of custody concerning a child who was habitually resident in the United States may request assistance in finding the child and making a return application from the Office of Children's Issues (OCI) in the State Department.[210]

A left-behind parent may work through the Central Authority system under the Abduction Convention, or work directly with local counsel in the country where the child has been removed or retained. In some countries, the Central Authority pays the costs of legal counsel in Hague return proceedings under Article 26 of the Convention.[211] Special-

---

Resources: Child Abduction Law in Other Countries

- The U.S. State Department website includes detailed country-specific information on international child abduction for more than 55 countries at http://www.travel.state.gov/abduction/country/country_3781.html.
- The Hague Conference website includes Country Profiles for many of the members of the Abduction Convention at http://www.hcch.net (under "Child Abduction Section" and "Country Profiles").
- The Hague Conference's International Child Abduction Database (INCADAT) includes summaries of decisions under the Abduction Convention from many Hague countries at http://www.incadat.com.
- See also LAW LIBRARY OF CONGRESS, HAGUE CONVENTION ON INTERNATIONAL CHILD ABDUCTION: AN ANALYSIS OF THE APPLICABLE LAW AND INSTITUTIONAL FRAMEWORK OF FIFTY-ONE JURISDICTIONS AND THE EUROPEAN UNION, LL File No. 2004-92 (Report for Congress, June 2004) (available from the Library of Congress Global Legal Information Network at http://www.glin.gov).

ized legal advice is extremely important because a complex range of strategic decisions have to be made in this situation, depending on the specific circumstances and the provisions of local law. For example, a parent with a custody order may be advised to pursue enforcement of that order in the appropriate tribunal, as an alternative or in addition to pursing a return claim under the Abduction Convention.

Within the Hague Conference, there are efforts to coordinate implementation of the Convention in Contracting States, including a searchable online database called INCADAT that collects case law from different jurisdictions. The Hague Conference web page includes an extensive bibliography on the Abduction Convention as well as Country Profiles with useful country-specific information. Each year, the U.S. State Department submits a Compliance Report to Congress with statistics and information on countries that have demonstrated a "pattern of noncompliance" with the Convention.[212]

To bring a claim under the Abduction Convention, the left-behind party will have to establish that the child was habitually resident in the United States. In addition, the claimant will need to show that he or she had "rights of custody" under the law of the United States within the definition of the Convention. As noted by the State Department, the general rule in the United States is that "both parents have equal rights of custody of their children prior to the issuance of a court order allocating rights between them." Therefore, "[i]f one parent interferes with the other's equal rights by unilaterally removing or retaining the child abroad . . . such interference could constitute wrongful conduct within the meaning of the Convention."[213] Because custody rights are defined by state law in the United States, however, the determination should be made with reference to the law of the particular state where the child was habitually resident. This may be complicated in some circumstances, particularly if the parents are unmarried and there has

---

Further Reading: Litigating Hague Abduction Cases

PAUL R. BEAUMONT & PETER E. MCELEAVY, THE HAGUE CONVENTION ON INTERNATIONAL CHILD ABDUCTION (1999).

STEVEN J. CULLEN ET AL, LITIGATING HAGUE CONVENTION CHILD ABDUCTION CASES IN THE U.S. — A TREATISE AND PRACTICE GUIDE (forthcoming 2012).

GLORIA F. DEHART, ED., INTERNATIONAL CHILD ABDUCTIONS: A GUIDE TO APPLYING THE HAGUE CONVENTION, WITH FORMS (2d ed. 1993).

JAMES D. GARBOLINO, INTERNATIONAL CHILD CUSTODY: HANDLING HAGUE CONVENTION CASES IN U.S. COURTS (3d ed. 2000).

NATIONAL CENTER FOR MISSING AND EXPLOITED CHILDREN (NCMEC) & KILPATRICK STOCKTON LLP, LITIGATING INTERNATIONAL CHILD ABDUCTION CASES UNDER THE HAGUE CONVENTION (2007).

NIGEL LOWE ET AL., INTERNATIONAL MOVEMENT OF CHILDREN: LAW PRACTICE AND PROCEDURE (2004); and NIGEL LOWE ET AL., THE NEW BRUSSELS II REGULATION: A SUPPLEMENT TO INTERNATIONAL MOVEMENT OF CHILDREN (2005).

Australia: NYGH'S CONFLICT OF LAWS IN AUSTRALIA 590–612 (Martin Davies et al. eds., 8th ed. 2010).

Canada: CASTEL & WALKER, CANADIAN CONFLICT OF LAWS § 18.3 (Janet Walker ed., 6th ed. 2008).

United Kingdom: DAVID HODSON, A PRACTICAL GUIDE TO INTERNATIONAL FAMILY LAW 247–301 (2008).

been no determination of the child's paternity.[214] Where there is a question, it may be useful for the left-behind parent in the United States to obtain an order that confirms his or her rights of custody as of the date of wrongful removal or retention in a form that can be provided to authorities in the requested state under Article 15.[215]

Using Criminal and Tort Law Remedies

In the United States, parental child abduction may give rise to liability under state and federal criminal and tort laws. While the specifics of these laws vary, all states have felony criminal statutes for child abduction or custodial interference, and some states have a range of related misdemeanor statutes.[216] Criminal liability may extend to relatives or other individuals who assist in an abduction.[217] Some statutes have defenses that may apply, for example, in cases of flight from domestic violence.[218] If an abductor flees from the state to avoid prosecution, the federal Fugitive Felon Act[219] may be applicable to assist state prosecutors in locating and returning an abductor. International extradition may be available in parental kidnapping cases under the Extradition Treaties Interpretation Act.[220]

In addition to criminal statutes, state laws include a range of possible tort law claims for child abduction under common law theories such as civil conspiracy, intentional infliction of emotional distress, or outrageous conduct.[221] The cause of action in *Restatement (Second) of Torts* § 700 for a custodial interference has been accepted in some but not all states.[222] State statutes may expressly authorize a tort claim for interference with custody or visitation. When abduction occurs before a formal custody decree is entered, the availability of criminal and tort law remedies under state law may help establish that the left-behind parent had rights of custody within the meaning of the Abduction Convention.

International Parental Kidnapping Crime Act

The International Parental Kidnapping Crime Act (IPKCA) provides a federal criminal remedy for international child abduction.[223] The statute allows for criminal prosecution of anyone who "removes a child from the United States, or attempts to do so, or retains a child (who has been in the United States) outside the United States with intent to obstruct the lawful exercise of parental rights."[224] The statute includes several affirmative defenses that are available (1) if a defendant "acted within the provisions of a valid court order" obtained pursuant to the Uniform Child Custody Jurisdiction Act or the Uniform Child Custody Jurisdiction and Enforcement Act, (2) if a defendant "was fleeing an incidence or pattern of domestic violence," or (3) if a defendant failed to return the child at the end of a period of custody or visitation due to circumstances beyond the defendant's control, provided that the defendant made reasonable attempts to notify the other custodian and returned the child as soon as possible.[225] The statute has no geographic limitations, but it includes a provision giving the "sense of Congress" that the procedures under the Abduction Convention, when applicable, "should be the option of first choice for a parent who seeks return of a child."[226] *United States v. Cummings* held that an unsuccessful Hague return action against a taking parent in another country did not bar a subsequent prosecution in the United States under the IPKCA.[227]

Immigration Sanctions

An additional sanction for international child abduction is incorporated into the federal immigration laws, which provide that certain classes of aliens are ineligible for visas or admission to the United States, including individuals who withhold custody of a U.S. citizen child outside of the United States.[228] In addition, individuals who assist an abductor, or provide "material support or safe haven," and certain relatives of such an abductor may also be inadmissible under this section.[229] The sanction has a clear remedial purpose since the bar on admission is removed once the child is surrendered to the legal custodian. It is targeted specifically at abductions to non-Hague countries; the sanction does not apply "so long as the child is located in a foreign state that is a party" to the Abduction Convention.[230]

Preventing Child Abduction

Measures to reduce the risk that a child will be wrongfully removed or retained in another jurisdiction are often incorporated into custody orders in an international case.[231] This may be accomplished in the United States pursuant to the court's general authority over custody matters, or under the Uniform Child Abduction Prevention Act (UCAPA).[232] Although courts frequently enter orders that prohibit either parent from removing a child from the jurisdiction without the permission of the court or the other parent, these exit restrictions should not be entered automatically. For many international cases, it may serve the child's best interests to allow the primary custodial parent to relocate with a child, with appropriate protections for access between the child and the left-behind parent.[233]

To secure compliance with its custody orders, a court may require either that the orders be registered in a foreign country before the child is taken there or that a party seeking permission to travel abroad post bond or provide other security. A detailed list of potential measures to prevent abduction is included in UCAPA § 8. In the State Department, OCI offers advice for prevention of abduction on its web page.[234]

Because the United States does not have a system of exit controls at its borders, a valid passport is generally sufficient to allow a parent to leave the country with a child. To reduce the risk of abduction, the United States has laws that require signatures of both of the child's legal parents or guardians before a passport will be issued for a child under age 16.[235] A parent or custodian may ask that the child's name be included in the State Department's Children's Passport Issuance Alert Program, which will alert the parent if an application is made for a U.S. passport. When there is a court order granting sole or joint legal custody to a parent, or prohibiting the child from traveling without permission of the parent or the court, the State Department may refuse to issue or renew a passport

---

Resources: Abduction Prevention

See National Center for Missing and Exploited Children (NCMEC), Family Abduction: Prevention and Response (Patricia M. Hoff ed., 6th ed. 2009), *available at* http://www.missingkids.com (under "Resources for Attorneys" and "Family Abduction").

for the child. These measures may not prevent a parent from taking the child out of the country, however, if the parent has or obtains a non-U.S. passport for the child. When there is an abduction risk for a child who has already been issued a U.S. or foreign passport, the parties may ask that any passports be held by the lawyers or the court.

Hague Abduction Convention Countries (as of November 15, 2011)

*(Accessions of countries marked with * had not yet been accepted by the United States.)*

Albania*	France	Peru
Argentina	Georgia*	Poland
Armenia*	Germany	Portugal
Australia	Greece	Romania
Austria	Guatemala	Saint Kitts and Nevis
Bahamas	Honduras	San Marino
Belarus*	Hungary	Serbia
Belgium	Iceland	Seychelles*
Belize	Ireland	Slovakia
Bosnia and Herzegovina	Israel	Slovenia
Brazil	Italy	South Africa
Bulgaria	Latvia	Spain
Burkina Faso	Lithuania	Sri Lanka
Canada	Luxembourg	Sweden
Chile	Macedonia	Switzerland
China (Hong Kong & Macau)	Malta	Thailand*
Colombia	Mauritius	Trinidad and Tobago*
Costa Rica	Mexico	Turkey
Croatia	Moldova*	Turkmenistan*
Cyprus	Monaco	Ukraine
Czech Republic	Montenegro	United Kingdom
Denmark	Morocco*	United States
Dominican Republic	Netherlands	Uruguay
Ecuador	New Zealand	Uzbekistan*
El Salvador	Nicaragua*	Venezuela
Estonia	Norway	Zimbabwe
Fiji*	Panama	
Finland	Paraguay	

Notes

1. Hague Convention on the Civil Aspects of International Child Abduction, October 25, 1980 T.I.A.S. No. 11,670, *reprinted at* 19 I.L.M. 1501.
2. International Child Abduction Remedies Act (ICARA), 42 U.S.C. §§ 11601–11610 (2010).

3. The Convention only operates between certain countries. *See infra* notes 29-30 and accompanying text. A list of these countries is included at the end of this chapter.
4. International Parental Kidnapping Crime Act (IPKCA), 18 U.S.C. § 1204 (2010).
5. The comprehensive manual from the National Center for Missing and Exploited Children is an outstanding practical resource; *see* NAT'L CTR. FOR MISSING & EXPLOITED CHILDREN & KILPATRICK STOCKTON LLP, LITIGATING INTERNATIONAL CHILD ABDUCTION CASES UNDER THE HAGUE CONVENTION (2007) [hereinafter NCMEC]. Another useful reference is HON. JAMES D. GARBOLINO, INTERNATIONAL CUSTODY CASES: HANDLING HAGUE CONVENTION CASES IN U.S. COURTS (3d ed. 2000). See also Stephen J. Cullen et al., Litigation Hague Convention Child Abduction Cases in the U.S.—A Treatise and Practice Guide (forthcoming 2012).
6. 560 U.S. __, 130 S. Ct. 1983, 1991 (2010); *see also* 42 U.S.C. § 11601(b)(3)(B) (2010).
7. Hague Conference on Private International Law, Concerning the Convention on the Civil Aspects of International Child Abduction, Child Abduction, The Hague, Neth., Oct. 25, 1980, Explanatory Report, at 445, III ACTES ET DOCUMENTS DE LA QUARTORZIÈME SESSION [hereinafter Explanatory Report]. The Explanatory Report and other resources are available on the Hague Conference website.
8. U.S. Dep't. of State, Pub. Notice 957, Legal Analysis of the Hague Convention on the Civil Aspects of International Child Abduction Public Notice 957, 51 Fed. Reg. 10,494 (1986) [hereinafter Legal Analysis].
9. See the child abduction web page maintained by OCI at http://www.travel.state.gov. Contact information for the Central Authorities of other countries is given on the Hague Conference website; *see infra* note 30. OCI statistics indicate that in 2010 the agency was notified of 1,022 outgoing cases involving 1,492 children. The Convention partner countries represented most often were Mexico (329 cases), Canada (47), the United Kingdom (35), Germany (27), Brazil (24), and Colombia (21); the most commonly represented non-Hague countries were India (36) and Japan (23). In the same year, the State Department received 290 applications in incoming abduction cases involving 389 children. The largest numbers came from Mexico (67 cases), Canada (28), Germany (18), the United Kingdom (17), and the Dominican Republic (14).
10. *See* 42 U.S.C. §§ 5771-5780.
11. Instructions on how to request a welfare and whereabouts visit are available by calling the Office of Children's Issues or by visiting the website at http://www.travel.state.gov/abduction/solutions/locatechildren/locatechildren_3850.html.
12. *See* art. 21, discussed *infra* at notes 161-63 and accompanying text.
13. Hague Convention on Jurisdiction, Applicable Law, Recognition, Enforcement and Co-Operation in Respect of Parental Responsibility and Measures for the Protection of Children, Oct, 19, 1996, *reprinted in* 35 I.L.M. 1391 (Child Protection Convention). The Child Protection Convention is discussed in Chapter 5.
14. A parent who succeeds in returning his or her child to the United States in violation of foreign law may also be faced with new Hague proceedings. *See, e.g.*, Karpenko v. Leendertz, 619 F.3d 259 (3d Cir. 2010).
15. *See* 22 C.F.R. §§ 94.1-94.8 (2010).
16. *See infra* notes 199-202 and accompanying text.
17. Mezo v. Elmergawi, 855 F. Supp. 59 (E.D.N.Y. 1994), rejected a plaintiff's claim that the State Department should be obligated to obtain return of her children from Egypt and Libya, which do not participate in the Convention. *See also* de Silva v. Pitts, 481 F.3d 1279, 1284 (10th Cir. 2007).
18. These are as follows:

Egypt: Memorandum of Understanding between the United States and Egypt Concerning Parental Access to Children (2003), http://www.state.gov/s/l/2003/44396.htm.

Lebanon: Memorandum of Understanding on Consular Cooperation in Cases Concerning Parental Access to Children (2004), http://www.state.gov/s/l/2005/87381.htm.

Jordan: Memorandum of Understanding on Consular Cooperation in Cases Concerning Parental Access to Children (2006), http://www.state.gov/documents/organization/101710.pdf.

19. *See infra* notes 216–20 and 223–30 and accompanying text. *See generally* JEREMY D. MORLEY, INTERNATIONAL FAMILY LAW PRACTICE 353–59 (2009); Patricia E. Apy, *Managing Child Custody Cases Involving Non-Hague Contracting States*, 14 J. AM. ACAD. MATRIM. LAW. 77 (1997).

20. The U.S. State Department information circular on "Using a Foreign Country's Civil Justice System" is available at http://www.travel.state.gov/abduction/solutions/solutions_3855.html.

21. *See infra* notes 221–22 and accompanying text.

22. This is permitted under Article 26 of the Convention; many other countries have made a similar reservation regarding legal fees and costs; Details are available on the Hague Conference website.

23. *See* CAL. FAM. CODE §§ 3455–3457 (2010).

24. *See* Chapter 5.

25. *E.g.*, Matter of Moshen, 715 F. Supp. 1063 (D. Wyo. 1989).

26. Taveras v. Taveraz, 477 F.3d 767 (6th Cir. 2007), *aff'g* 397 F. Supp. 2d 908 (S.D. Ohio 2005). *See also* Sosa v. Alvarez-Machain, 542 U.S. 692 (2004) (construing Alien Tort Statute).

27. 42 U.S.C. § 1603(a) (2010). *See infra* notes 182–90 and accompanying text.

28. Central Authorities including OCI offer services to help locate children who have been wrongfully removed or retained here or abroad. *See supra* notes 15–24 and accompanying text.

29. *E.g., Taveras*, 397 F. Supp. 2d at 912–13. Viteri v. Pflucker, 550 F. Supp. 2d 829, 833–36 (N.D. Ill. 2008), rejected a petitioner's "continuing removal or retention" theory, concluding that the Convention did not apply to a child who was removed from Peru to the United States after Peru acceded to the Convention but before the United States accepted Peru's accession, even though the child was retained in the United States after the Convention came into force between the United States and Peru. *See also* Mezo v. Elmergawi, 855 F. Supp. 59, 62 (E.D.N.Y. 1992) (convention inapplicable to children taken from United States to Egypt and then Libya).

30. Current information on ratifications, accessions, and acceptance of accessions is available on the website of the Hague Conference at http://www.hcch.net (under "Child Abduction Section" and then "Contracting States" or "Acceptances of Accessions").

31. 42 U.S.C. § 11603(e) (2010).

32. *See id.; see also* Friedrich v. Friedrich (*Friedrich I*), 983 F.2d 1396, 1400 (6th Cir. 1993). Much of the state and federal case law is collected in Scott M. Smith, Annotation, *Construction and Application of International Child Abduction Remedies Act*, 125 A.L.R. Fed. 217 (1995 & Supp.).

33. 560 U.S. __, 130 S. Ct. 1983, 1991 (2010); *see also* 42 U.S.C. § 11601(b)(3)(B) (2010).

34. *See* Abbott v. Abbott, 560 U.S. ___, 130 S. Ct. 1983, 1993–95 (2010).

35. *See* Explanatory Report, *supra* note 7.

36. *See Abbott*, 560 U.S. at ___; 130 S. Ct. at 1993.

37. *See* Legal Analysis, *supra* note 8.

38. Mozes v. Mozes, 239 F.3d 1067, 1070 (9th Cir. 2001), described Article 3 as posing these four questions:

(1) When did the removal or retention at issue take place? (2) Immediately prior to the removal or retention, in which state was the child habitually resident? (3) Did the removal or retention breach the rights of custody attributed to the petitioner under the law of the habitual residence? (4) Was the petitioner exercising those rights at the time of the removal or retention?

39. *See also* MORLEY, *supra* note 19, at 294–306.

40. *See, e.g.*, Silverman v. Silverman (*Silverman II*), 338 F.3d 886, 891 (8th Cir. 2003). *See also infra* note 73 and accompanying text. Under Article 15, the Central Authorities "so far as practicable" should assist applicants in obtaining this type of determination.

41. *See, e.g.*, Muhlenkamp v. Blizzard, 521 F. Supp. 2d 1140 (E.D. Wash. 2007).

42. Explanatory Report, *supra* note 7, at para. 66. *See, e.g.*, Friedrich v. Friedrich (*Friedrich I*), 983 F.2d 1396, 1401 (6th Cir. 1993). *See also* E. M. Clive, *The Concept of Habitual Residence*, (1997) JURIDICAL REV. 137.

43. *See, e.g.,* PAUL R. BEAUMONT & PETER E. MCELEAVY, THE HAGUE CONVENTION ON INTERNATIONAL CHILD ABDUCTION 88-113 (1999); MORLEY, *supra* note 19, at 306-15; Rhona Schuz, *Policy Considerations in Determining the Habitual Residence of a Child and the Relevance of Context,* 11 J. TRANSNAT'L L. & POL'Y 101 (2001). The term is intended to have an autonomous definition under the Abduction Convention, but it is also used in the 1996 Hague Child Protection Convention and in domestic custody legislation in Canada and the United Kingdom. *See id.* at 109-13 and 117-20.

44. *See* 42 U.S.C. § 11601(b)(3)(B) (2010) (recognizing "the need for uniform international interpretation"); *see also* Linda Silberman, *Interpreting the Hague Abduction Convention: In Search of a Global Jurisprudence,* 38 U.C. DAVIS L. REV. 1049, 1057-62 (2005).

45. *E.g.,* Feder v. Evans-Feder, 63 F.3d 217 (3d Cir. 1995) (finding that child of two American citizens had habitual residence in Australia); Kijowska v. Haines, 463 F.3d 583, 585 (7th Cir. 2006) (concluding that ex parte custody order obtained in the United States was irrelevant to determination of habitual residence).

46. *Friedrich I,* 983 F.2d at 1401; *see also* Robert v. Tesson, 507 F.3d 981, 988-93 (6th Cir. 2007).

47. *Feder,* 63 F.3d at 224. *See also Kijowska,* 463 F.3d at 588; Silverman v. Silverman (*Silverman II*), 338 F.3d 886, 898 (8th Cir. 2003).

48. Explanatory Report, *supra* note 7, at para. 72 ("In other words, the convention protects the right of children not to have the emotional, social, etc. aspects of their lives altered, unless legal arguments exist which would guarantee their stability in a new situation.").

49. *E.g., Robert,* 507 F.3d at 997-98; Yang v. Tsui, 499 F.3d 259, 271-72 (3d Cir. 2007); *but see* Karkkainen v. Kovalchuk, 445 F.3d 280, 293-96 (concluding that 11-year-old child had acclimatized over the summer; parents had agreed she could choose her residence).

50. *See* Clive, *supra* note 42, at 141.

51. Article 7 provides that even after a wrongful removal or retention the jurisdiction to take measures for the protection of children generally shifts to the new habitual residence after a year. *See* Schuz, *supra* note 43, at 117 and 153-56.

52. As discussed in Chapter 5, this is the rule under the Uniform Child Custody Jurisdiction and Enforcement Act, which is in effect in nearly all the states. *See also* BEAUMONT & MCELEAVY, *supra* note 43, at 105 and 109 (suggesting that "ordinarily a period of six months residence should be required before a residence may be classified as being habitual.")

53. *E.g.,* Delvoye v. Lee, 329 F.3d 330 (3d Cir. 2003); Kijowska v. Haines, 463 F.3d 583, 587 (7th Cir. 2006). *Cf.* Nunez-Escudero v. Tice-Menley, 58 F.3d 374 (8th Cir. 1995) (remanding for determination of habitual residence of child removed from Mexico at age of six weeks). *See also* Simcox v. Simcox, 511 F.3d 594, 602 (6th Cir. 2007) ("That they may have moved around to different communities within Mexico, had a 'nomadic lifestyle,' or often traveled internationally, does not change the fact that Mexico was the country in which the family principally resided during the period in question.") *See generally* Clive, *supra* note 42, at 146.

54. *See, e.g.,* Friedrich v. Friedrich (*Friedrich I*), 983 F.2d 1396, 1401 (6th Cir. 1993) ("A person can have only one habitual residence."); Silverman v. Silverman (*Silverman II*), 338 F.3d 886, 898 (8th Cir. 2003). *Cf.* Mozes v. Mozes, 239 F.3d 1067, 1075 n.17 (9th Cir. 2001). *But see* BEAUMONT & MCELEAVY, *supra* note 43, at 91 and 110-11; Clive, *supra* note 42, at 144; Schuz, *supra* note 43, at 152 (suggesting the possibility of dual habitual residence).

55. *See Mozes,* 239 F.3d at 1076-77. Rhona Schuz has identified competing policy considerations in the relocation decisions, including protecting children from abduction at all times, not rewarding abductors, not discouraging parents from beneficial foreign travel or trying to save a marriage, that agreements should be honored, and that disputes should be decided in the more convenient forum. Schuz, *supra* note 43, at 120-42.

56. *E.g.,* Baxter v. Baxter, 423 F.3d 363, 368-69 (3d Cir. 2005) (family had not decided whether to relocate when mother and child came from Australia to the United States). On the "temporary absence of long or short duration," *see Mozes,* 239 F.3d at 1075 and 1077.

57. *E.g., Baxter,* 423 F.3d at 366; *Silverman II,* 338 F.3d at 898-900.

58. *E.g., Silverman II,* 338 F.3d 898-99; Feder v. Evans-Feder, 63 F.3d 217, 220, 224 (3d Cir. 1995). *See also Mozes,* 239 F.3d at 1076-77 ("When courts find that a family has jointly taken all the

steps associated with abandoning habitual residence in one country to take it up in another, they are generally unwilling to let one parent's alleged reservations about the move stand in the way of finding a shared and settled purpose.").

59. *Mozes*, 239 F.3d at 1082–84 (concluding that "the appropriate inquiry . . . is whether the United States had supplanted Israel as the locus of the children's family and social development" and remanding case).

60. *E.g.*, Ruiz v. Tenorio, 392 F.3d 1247 (11th Cir. 2004); Gitter v. Gitter, 396 F.3d 124 (2d Cir. 2005).

61. *Ruiz*, 392 F.3d at 1247. *See also* Papakosmas v. Papakosmas, 483 F.3d 617, 623–26 (9th Cir. 2007) (four-month stay in Greece did not establish habitual residence); *Gitter*, 396 F.3d at 124 (no habitual residence established during 15 months in Israel; family's move there deemed conditional); Silberman, *supra* note 44, at 1065–68.

62. *E.g.*, Robert v. Tesson, 507 F.3d 981, 990–92 (6th Cir. 2007) ("Such a rule turns the Hague Convention on its head and it cannot be followed by the Sixth Circuit.") *See also* Stern v. Stern, 639 F.3d 449, 452 (8th Cir. 2011); *cf.* Karkkainen v. Kovalchuk, 445 F.3d 280, 296–97 (3d Cir. 2006). *See generally* MORLEY, *supra* note 19, at 310–15; Tai Vivatvaraphol, *Back to Basics: Determining a Child's Habitual Residence in International Child Abduction Cases Under the Hague Convention*, 77 FORDHAM L. REV. 3325, 3354–60 (2009) (discussing case law from other countries).

    Mozes acknowledges that "given enough time and positive experience, a child's life may become so firmly embedded in the new country as to make it habitually resident even though there be lingering parental intentions to the contrary." *Mozes*, 239 F.3d at 1078–79. But, given its emphasis on parental intentions, the decision suggested that a court should be slow to conclude that a child's habitual residence had changed based on objective indications of acclimatization. *Id.*

63. Delvoye v. Lee, 329 F.3d 330, 334 (3d Cir. 2003); *see also* Whiting v. Krassner, 391 F.3d 540, 549–51 (3d Cir. 2004).

64. Silverman v. Silverman (*Silverman II*), 338 F.3d 886, 898 (8th Cir. 2003); *Mozes*, 239 F.3d at 1078.

65. *See* Barzilay v. Barzilay, 600 F.3d 912, 919–21 (8th Cir. 2010) ("The notion that parents can contractually determine their children's habitual residence without regard to the actual circumstances of the children is thus entirely incompatible with our precedent.").

66. *Whiting*, 391 F.3d at 551.

67. *E.g.*, Zuker v. Andrews, 2 F. Supp. 2d 134, 139–40 (D. Mass. 1998), *aff'd*, 181 F.3d 81 (1st Cir. 1999); *but see* Falk v. Sinclair, 692 F. Supp. 2d 147 (D. Me. 2010) (holding that wrongful retention did not occur until date when child was supposed to return).

68. *See, e.g.*, Toren v. Toren, 191 F.3d 23, 27–28 (1st Cir. 1999).

69. Stern v. Stern, 639 F.3d 449, 452–53 (8th Cir. 2011).

70. Whallon v. Lynn, 230 F.3d 450 (1st Cir. 2000). On *patria potestad*, see also *Altamiranda Vale v. Avila*, 538 F.3d 581 (7th Cir. 2008), and *Gonzalez v. Gutierrez*, 311 F.3d 942 (9th Cir. 2002).

71. Furnes v. Reeves, 362 F.3d 702, 712–16 (11th Cir. 2004).

72. Explanatory Report, *supra* note 7, at para. 68. *See, e.g.*, Application of Adan, 437 F.3d 381 (3d Cir. 2006); Shalit v. Coppe, 182 F.3d 1124, 1128–31 (9th Cir. 1999). On the renvoi issue, *see, e.g.*, Van Driessche v. Ohio-Esezeoboh, 466 F. Supp. 2d 828, 844–45 (S.D. Tex. 2006); *see generally* BEAUMONT & MCELEAVY, *supra* note 43, at 46–48.

73. Because this is time consuming, it is less useful than the provisions in Article 8(f) and Article 14 allowing for certificates or judicial notice concerning the law of the habitual residence. *See also supra* note 39 and *infra* note 170 and accompanying text; BEAUMONT & MCELEAVY, *supra* note 43, at 63–65. Central authorities may transmit information about their custody laws together with an application under Article 7e, but the ultimate conclusion about whether an applicant has rights of custody under the Convention is the responsibility of the court and not the Central Authorities. *See, e.g.*, Giampaolo v. Erneta, 390 F. Supp. 2d 1269, 1277–79 (N.D. Ga. 2004).

74. *E.g.*, Adams *ex rel.* Naik v. Naik, 363 F. Supp. 2d 1025, 1026–30 (N.D. Ill. 2005).

75. *See* Chapter 5 for discussion of U.S. law regarding establishment of custody rights.

76. *E.g.*, Friedrich v. Friedrich, 78 F.3d 1060, 1064 (6th Cir. 1996).

77. *E.g.*, Yang v. Tsui, 499 F.3d 259, 275-77 (3d Cir. 2007); *Adan*, 437 F.3d at 392-94; *Shalit*, 182 F.3d at 1131. *See also* BEAUMONT & MCELEAVY, *supra* note 43, at 57-61.

78. *E.g.*, Hanley v. Roy, 485 F.3d 641, 645 (11th Cir. 1985) (grandparents had rights of custody as joint testamentary guardians under Irish law).

79. *See* art. 3a, which states that a removal or retention is to be considered wrongful where "it is in breach of rights of custody attributed to a person, an institution or any other body . . . ."

80. *E.g.*, C. v. S. (A Minor) (Abduction) [1990] 2 AC 562 (England, House of Lords), *discussed in* BEAUMONT & MCELEAVY, *supra* note 43, at 52-57. *See also* GARBOLINO, *supra* note 5, at § 4.13.

81. Abbott v. Abbott, 560 U.S. ___ , 130 S. Ct. 1983, 1990 (2010). This is subject to a court override if authorization cannot be granted or is denied without good reason. *See id.*

82. A ne exeat order with no parental consent provision might not be construed as a joint right of custody; *see id.* at 1992. Three justices dissented from this ruling, writing that: "A reading as broad and flexible as the Court's eviscerates the distinction the Convention draws between rights of custody and rights of access." *Id.* at 2005 (Stevens, J., dissenting).

83. *Id.* at 1993 (citing 42 U.S.C. § 11601(b)(3)(B)).

84. Explanatory Report, *supra* note 7, at para. 73. The Report contrasts this with the burden placed on a respondent resisting return under Article 13a to prove that the petitioner had not actually exercised his rights of custody, commenting: "Thus, we may conclude that the convention, taken as a whole, is built on the tacit presumption that the person who has care of the child actually exercises custody over it." *Id.*

85. Friedrich v. Friedrich, 78 F.3d 1060, 1064-66 (6th Cir. 1996).

86. *See id.*; Yang v. Tsui, 499 F.3d 259, 277-78 (3d Cir. 2007); Bader v. Kramer, 484 F.3d 666, 670-72 (4th Cir. 2007); Sealed Appellant v. Sealed Appellee, 394 F.3d 338, 344-45 (5th Cir. 2004). *See also* BEAUMONT & MCELEAVY, *supra* note 43, at 83-86.

87. Explanatory Report, *supra* note 7, at para. 34.

88. According to Article 18, "The provisions of this Chapter do not limit the power of a judicial or administrative authority to order the return of the child at any time." *See also* Explanatory Report, *supra* note 7, at paras. 112-113.

89. Explanatory Report, *supra* note 7, at paras. 107-109 ("[I]n so far as the return of the child is regarded as being in its interests, it is clear that after a child has become settled in its new environment, its return should take place only after an examination of the merits of the custody rights exercised over it—something which is outside the scope of the Convention.").

90. *See supra* notes 67-69 and accompanying text.

91. *See infra* notes 102-06 and accompanying text.

92. *E.g.*, *In re* B. Del C.S.B., 559 F.3d 999, 1009 (9th Cir. 2009); Castillo v. Castillo, 597 F. Supp. 2d 432, 437-41 (D. Del. 2009); *In re* Koc, 181 F. Supp. 2d 136, 152-55 (E.D.N.Y. 2001). *See also* BEAUMONT & MCELEAVY, *supra* note 43, at 206-08.

93. *E.g.*, Whiting v. Krassner, 391 F.3d 540, 550-51 (3d Cir. 2004).

94. *E.g.*, *Koc*, 181 F. Supp. 2d at 154; Bocquet v. Ouzid, 225 F. Supp. 2d 1337, 1349 (S.D. Fla. 2002); *but see B. Del C.S.B.*, 559 F.3d at 1010. *See generally* Catherine Norris, Comment, *Immigration and Abduction: The Relevance of U.S. Immigration Status to Defenses Under the Hague Convention on International Child Abduction*, 98 CAL. L. REV. 159 (2010).

95. 140 F.3d 927 (11th Cir. 1998).

96. *E.g.*, Duarte v. Bardales, 526 F.3d 563, 569-70 (9th Cir. 2008) (collecting cases); *B. Del C.S.B.*, 559 F.3d at 1014.

97. 362 F.3d 702, 723-24 (11th Cir. 2004).

98. *Duarte*, 526 F.3d at 570; *see also* Legal Analysis, *supra* note 8, at 10, 509; GARBOLINO, *supra* note 5, at 150-53.

99. *E.g.*, Toren v. Toren, 26 F. Supp. 2d 240, 244 (D. Mass. 1998), *vacated on other grounds*, Toren v. Toren, 191 F.3d 23 (1st Cir. 1999); *see generally* NCMEC, *supra* note 5, at 34-38.

100. *E.g.*, Antunez-Fernandes v. Connors-Fernandes, 259 F. Supp. 2d 800, 814-15 (N.D. Iowa 2003); *but see* BEAUMONT & MCELEAVY, *supra* note 43, at 203-04 and 208-09 (suggesting that there is no discretionary element in Article 12 and that Article 18 should not be used in this context). In *Lops*, which presented strong facts to support equitable tolling, the court concluded that

it did not need to reach that issue because the evidence supported the lower court's factual finding that the children were not well settled.

101. Explanatory Report, *supra* note 7, at para. 115.

102. 423 F.3d 363, 371 (3d Cir. 2005).

103. 251 F.3d 789, 793–95 (9th Cir. 2001); *cf. Baxter*, 423 F.3d at 371–73.

104. Friedrich v. Friedrich (*Friedrich II*), 78 F.3d 1060, 1069 (6th Cir. 1996); *see also Antunez-Fernandes*, 259 F. Supp. 2d at 812–14.

105. *Friedrich II*, 78 F.3d at 1070. *See also* BEAUMONT & MCELEAVY, *supra* note 43, at 115–30.

106. *See* Nicholson v. Pappalardo, 605 F.3d 100 (1st Cir. 2010).

107. Explanatory Report, *supra* note 7, at paras. 29 & 116.

108. Legal Analysis, *supra* note 8, at 10,510.

109. 596 F.3d 505, 509 (9th Cir. 2010) ("If that amounted to a grave risk of harm, parents in more developed countries would have unchecked power to abduct children from countries with a lower standard of living.") The court also rejected the father's argument that the legal system in Panama was too unfair or corrupt to decide the issue of custody fairly. *Id.* at 510.

110. *Friedrich II*, 78 F.3d at 1067–68. The court also wrote: "A removing parent must not be allowed to abduct a child and then—when brought to court—complain that the child has grown used to the surroundings to which they were abducted." *Id.*

111. *Id.* The "war zone" defense has been rejected in cases involving Israel and Argentina. *See* Silverman v. Silverman (*Silverman II*), 338 F.3d 886, 900–01 (8th Cir. 2003); Mendez Lynch v. Mendez Lynch, 220 F. Supp. 2d 1347, 1364–66 (M.D. Fla. 2002). *See also* Escaf v. Rodriguez, 200 F. Supp. 2d 603, 614 (E.D. Va. 2002) (circumstances in Colombia do not establish grave risk of harm).

112. The *Friedrich II* dicta are criticized in *Van de Sande v. Van de Sande*, 431 F.3d 567, 570–72 (7th Cir. 2005), *Baran v. Beaty*, 526 F.3d 1340, 1346–48 (11th Cir. 2008), and *Wigley v. Hares*, ___ So. 3d ___ , 2011 WL 3111898 (Fla. Dist. Ct. App. 2011). A case repeating the *Friedrich II* dicta is *Application of Adan*, 437 F.3d 381, 395 (3d Cir. 2006).

113. *See* Explanatory Report, *supra* note 7, at para. 113; BEAUMONT & MCELEAVY, *supra* note 43, at 155. This discretion may be exercised by requiring undertakings from the applicant to protect the children on return; *see id.* at 156–72 and *infra* notes 144–49 and accompanying text. In addition to *Friedrich II*, 78 F.3d at 1067, see *Walsh v. Walsh*, 221 F.3d 204, 221 n. 17 (1st Cir. 2000).

114. United Nations Convention on the Rights of the Child, art. 3(1), Nov. 20, 1989, 1577 U.N.T.S. 3. *See generally* Rhona Schuz, *The Hague Child Abduction Convention and Children's Rights*, 12 TRANSNAT'L L. & CONTEMP. PROBS. 393, 435–49 (2002).

115. Neulinger & Shuruk v. Switzerland [GC], no. 41615/07, ECHR 2010. Compare the earlier decision in *Maumousseau & Washington v. France*, no. 39388/05, ECHR 2007 XIII.

116. *See* Re E (Children) (FC) [2011] UKSC 27, on appeal from [2011] EWCA Civ. 361 (noting at para. 25 that the President of the European Court of Human Rights has rejected the broad reading of *Neulinger*). In *Re E*, the United Kingdom Supreme Court concluded that human rights principles do not "trump" the provisions of the Convention, but indicated that the best interests of the child are a primary consideration when Article 13b is properly applied.

117. *See* BEAUMONT & MCELEAVY, *supra* note 43, at 138–39.

118. *E.g., Friedrich II*, England v. England, 234 F.3d 268, 271–72 (5th Cir. 2000); Nunez-Escudero v. Tice Menley, 58 F.3d 374, 377 (8th Cir. 1995). To facilitate a caregiver's return with a child, courts sometimes may impose conditions on return, known as undertakings. *See infra* notes 144–49 and accompanying text.

119. *See, e.g.,* Carol S. Bruch, *The Unmet Needs of Domestic Violence Victims and Their Children in Hague Child Abduction Convention Cases*, 38 FAM. L.Q. 529 (2004); Merle H. Weiner, *International Child Abduction and the Escape from Domestic Violence*, 69 FORDHAM L. REV. 593 (2000).

120. *E.g., Nunez-Escudero*, 58 F.3d at 376–77; Whallon v. Lynn, 230 F.3d 450, 460 (1st Cir. 2000).

121. Van de Sande v. Van de Sande, 431 F.3d 567, 570 (7th Cir. 2005); *see also* Baran v. Beaty, 526 F.3d 1340, 1346 (11th Cir. 2008). *Miltiadous v. Tetervak*, 686 F. Supp. 2d 544 (E.D. Pa. 2010), refused return in a case in which the respondent had been granted asylum in the United States on the basis of serious domestic violence.

122. Blondin v. Dubois (*Blondin I*),189 F.3d 240, 242 (2d Cir. 1999). *See also id.* at 248-49 ("In the exercise of comity that is at the heart of the Convention . . . we are required to place our trust in the court of the home country to issue whatever orders may be necessary to safeguard children who come before it.") On remand, the trial court concluded that the proposed arrangements were not sufficient to mitigate the grave risk of harm, and this determination was upheld on appeal. Blondin v. Dubois (*Blondin II*), 238 F.3d 153 (2d Cir. 2001).

123. 221 F.3d 204, 218 (1st Cir. 2000).

124. *Id.* at 221. *See also Van de Sande*, 431 F.3d at 570-72; Danaipour v. McLarey (*Danaipour I*), 286 F.3d 1 (1st Cir. 2002); Danaipour v. McLarey (*Danaipour II*), 386 F.3d 289 (1st Cir. 2004).

125. Charalambous v. Charalambous, 627 F.3d 462, 469 (1st Cir. 2010). *See also Whallon*, 230 F.3d at 460.

126. *See* BEAUMONT & MCELEAVY, *supra* note 43, at 151-54; *see also* Merle H. Weiner, *Intolerable Situations and Counsel for Children: Following Switzerland's Example in Hague Abduction Cases*, 58 AM. U. L. REV. 335, 352-56 (2008).

127. Legal Analysis, *supra* note 8, at 10,510. The State Department Legal Analysis goes on to say that "An example of an 'intolerable situation' is one in which a custodial parent sexually abuses a child." *Id.* at 10,505. This example collapses the intolerable situation language into the grave risk of physical or psychological harm component in Article 13(b), and the history and syntax of the provision suggest that something distinct was intended by "intolerable situation." *See* BEAUMONT & MCELEAVY, *supra* note 43, at 136; Weiner, *supra* note 126, at 345-52.

128. For this reason, even after interviewing a child, a judge may decide to rule on different grounds. *E.g.*, Application of Robinson, 983 F. Supp. 1339, 1343-44 (D. Colo. 1997).

129. *See* Schuz, *supra* note 114, at 417-35.

130. 42 U.S.C. § 11603(e)(2)(B) (2010); *see* England v. England, 234 F.3d 268, 272 (5th Cir. 2000) (concluding that child's maturity was not established by a preponderance of the evidence).

131. *See* De Silva v. Pitts, 481 F.3d 1279, 1286-88 (10th Cir. 2007) (affirming ruling based on wishes of 13-year-old); Simcox v. Simcox, 511 F.3d 594, 603-04 (6th Cir. 2007) (affirming ruling that 8-year-old was not sufficiently mature). *Cf.* Yang v. Tsui, 499 F.3d 259, 278-80 (3d Cir. 2007) (affirming conclusion that 10-year-old was not sufficiently mature).

132. *E.g.*, Haimdas v. Haimdas, 720 F. Supp. 2d 183 (E.D.N.Y. 2010).

133. *E.g.*, McManus v. McManus, 354 F. Supp. 2d 62, 70-72 (D. Mass. 2005) (considering objections of four siblings aged 11 to 14 years).

134. *See, e.g., Haimdas*, 720 F. Supp. 2d at 204-09 (noting difference between a preference to remain and an objection to return); *see also* Falk v. Sinclair, 692 F. Supp. 2d 147 (D. Me. 2010); Trudrung v. Trudrung, 686 F. Supp. 2d 570 (M.D.N.C. 2010).

135. Explanatory Report, *supra* note 7, at para. 118. The Report also suggests that reference to general principles of international human rights is not sufficient; the defense requires a showing that the principles cited have been accepted in the law of the requested State and that the same principles are equally applicable in internal cases. *Id.*

136. Escaf v. Rodriguez, 200 F. Supp. 2d 603, 614 (E.D. Va. 2002); *but see* Mohamud v. Guuleed, 2009 WL 1229986 (E.D. Wis. 2009) (unpublished) (suggesting in dicta that Article 20 might provide basis to refuse return order that would transfer child from parent to a nonparent). *See generally* Merle H. Weiner, *Using Article 20*, 38 FAM. L.Q. 583 (2004); Merle H. Weiner, *Strengthening Article 20*, 38 U.S.F. L. REV. 701 (2004).

137. Karpenko v. Leendertz, 619 F.3d 259 (3d Cir. 2010).

138. *Id.* at 265.

139. *Id.* at 266-73 (Aldisert, J., dissenting).

140. *See In re* Prevot, 59 F.3d 556, 561-67 (6th Cir. 1995) (denying relief to a Hague petitioner who had fled the United States to avoid tax obligations and the consequences of a felony conviction for theft).

141. Walsh v. Walsh, 221 F.3d 204, 214-16 (1st Cir. 2000) ("To bar a parent who has lost a child from even arguing that the child was wrongfully removed to another country is too harsh. It is too harsh particularly in the absence of any showing that the fugitive status has impaired the rights of the other parent."). *See also* March v. Levine, 249 F.3d 462, 469-70 (6th Cir. 2001) (rejecting doctrine based on facts of the case).

142. *See* Degen v. United States, 517 U.S. 820 (1996) (discussed in *Walsh*, 221 F.3d at 214–16.)
143. Explanatory Report, *supra* note 7, at para. 110. *See, e.g.*, Rydder v. Rydder, 49 F.3d 369, 373 (8th Cir. 1995) (pleading in the alternative for return to either Sweden or Poland). Courts have refused return orders when the party seeking return has relocated to the same country where the child is located. *See* Von Kennel Gaudin v. Remis, 282 F.3d 1178, 1183 (9th Cir. 2002).
144. Application of Adan, 437 F.3d 381, 398 (3d Cir. 2006).
145. *E.g.*, Krefter v. Wills, 623 F. Supp. 2d 125, 137–38 (D. Mass. 2009).
146. Beaumont and McEleavy define undertakings as promises offered or imposed upon an applicant to overcome obstacles to the child's return. BEAUMONT & MCELEAVY, *supra* note 43, at 158.
147. *See* BEAUMONT & MCELEAVY, *supra* note 43, at 160.
148. *See* Simcox v. Simcox, 511 F.3d at 594, 604–10 (6th Cir. 2007). (remanding "to determine what undertakings, if any, will be sufficient to ensure the safety of the Simcox children upon their return to Mexico pending the outcome of custody proceedings.").
149. *See* Danaipour v. McLarey (*Danaipour I*), 286 F.3d 1, 21–26 (1st Cir. 2002); Baran v. Beaty, 526 F.3d 1340, 1349–52 (11th Cir. 2008); Van de Sande v. Van de Sande, 431 F.3d 567, 571–72 (7th Cir. 2005).
150. Silberman, *supra* note 44, at 1076–77.
151. Child Protection Convention, *supra* note 13. *See generally* Linda Silberman, *The Hague Child Abduction Convention Turns Twenty: Gender Politics and Other Issues*, 33 N.Y.U. J. INT'L L. & POL. 221, 233–34 (2000).
152. Child Protection Convention, *supra* note 13, at art. 23(1). Orders entered in the context of return proceedings under the Abduction Convention would fall within the scope of the jurisdiction in cases of urgency recognized by Article 11 of the Child Protection Convention.
153. *See* Jan Rewers McMillan, *Getting Them Back: The Disappointing Reality of Return Orders Under the Hague Convention on the Civil Aspects of International Child Abduction*, 14 J. AM. ACAD. MATRIMONIAL LAW. 99 (1997).
154. UCCJEA § 302, 9 (1A) U.L.A. 690 (1999). ("[A] court of this State may enforce an order for the return of the child made under the Hague Convention on the Civil Aspects of International Child Abduction as if it were a child-custody determination."). *See* Chapter 5.
155. NCMEC, *supra* note 5, at 81–82.
156. *See* Friedrich v. Friedrich, 78 F.3d 1060, 1063 (6th Cir. 1996).
157. *See* 42 U.S.C. § 11604 (2010).
158. 42 U.S.C. § 11603(g) (2010).
159. *See* Avesta v. Petroutsas, 580 F.3d 1000, 1011–14 (9th Cir. 2009), *on remand*, 2010 WL 1576463 (N.D. Cal. 2010) (concluding that trial court had abused its discretion by extending comity and remanding to lower court to determine merits of petition). *See also* Carrascosa v. McGuire, 520 F.3d 249 (3d Cir. 2008) (declining to extend comity to Spanish Hague order); Diorinou v. Mezitis, 237 F.3d 133 (2d Cir. 2001) (affirming extension of comity to Greek Hague order).
160. *Avesta*, 580 F.3d at 1014.
161. *See* HAGUE CONFERENCE ON PRIVATE INTERNATIONAL LAW, TRANSFRONTIER CONTACT CONCERNING CHILDREN: GENERAL PRINCIPLES AND A GUIDE TO GOOD PRACTICE (2008). *See also supra* note 12 and accompanying text.
162. These may be legal obstacles or the possibility of criminal liability, *see* Explanatory Report, *supra* note 7, at para. 127.
163. Explanatory Report, *supra* note 7, at para. 128.
164. 42 U.S.C. § 1160 3(b) (2010).
165. *See* Cantor v. Cohen, 442 F.3d 196 (4th Cir. 2006) (citing cases).
166. *E.g.*, Habrzyk v. Habrzyk, 759 F. Supp. 2d 1014 (N.D. Ill. 2011). *See* March v. Levine, 249 F.3d 462, 473–75 (6th Cir. 2001), *aff'g* 136 F. Supp. 2d 831 (M.D. Tenn. 2001). Any discovery permitted should also be completed on an expedited basis. *See* Norinder v. Fuentes, 657 F.3d 526 (7th Cir. 2011); *cf.* Vasquez v. Colores, 648 F.3d 648 (8th Cir. 2011).
167. *See* Robert v. Tesson, 507 F.3d 981, 995 (6th Cir. 2007); Kijowska v. Haines, 463 F.3d 583, 589–90 (7th Cir. 2006).

168. 932 F. Supp. 128 (D. Md. 1996) (applying federal habeas statute, 28 U.S.C. § 2243); *see also* Miller v. Miller, 240 F.3d 392, 397-98 (4th Cir. 2001).
169. 42 U.S.C. § 11605 (2010).
170. Article 8f provides that an application to a Central Authority may be accompanied by a certificate or an affidavit concerning the relevant law of the habitual residence "emanating from a Central Authority, or other competent authority of the State of the child's habitual residence, or from a qualified person."
171. *See* Hague Conference on Private International Law, Emerging Rules Regarding the Development of the International Hague Network of Judges and Draft General Principles for Judicial Communications, Prel. Doc. 3A (Mar. 2011), http://www.hcch.net/upload/wop/abduct2011pd03ae.pdf.
172. 42 U.S.C § 11604 (2010). *E.g.*, Etienne v. Zuniga, 2010 WL 1050290 (W.D. Wash. 2010) (granting ex parte temporary restraining order).
173. *E.g.*, Morgan v. Morgan, 289 F. Supp. 2d 1067, 1069 (N.D. Iowa 2003) (entering temporary restraining order). *See generally* GARBOLINO, *supra* note 5, at 59-63.
174. 42 U.S.C. § 11603(c) (2010). The notice required in interstate custody proceedings is defined in UCCJEA § 205, discussed in Chapter 5.
175. UCCJEA § 311, discussed in Chapter 5. *See also* GARBOLINO, *supra* note 5, at 60-63; MORLEY, *supra* note 19, at 298-300.
176. *See* Egervary v. Young, 366 F.3d 238 (3d Cir. 2004). Public officials may be held liable for acting to take a child from a parent's custody without a court order; *see* Suboh v. Dist. Att'y's Office, 298 F.3d 81 (1st Cir. 2002); *cf. Egervary*, 366 F.3d at 246-51 (no basis for *Bivens* action against officials who acted pursuant to erroneous court order under ICARA).
177. *E.g.*, *In re* Vernor, 94 S.W.3d 201, 209 (Tex. App. 2002).
178. *See* NCMEC, *supra* note 5, at 77-79. Filing of a Hague petition may not stop child protection proceedings, however. *See* Witherspoon v. Orange Cnty. Dep't of Soc. Servs., 646 F. Supp. 2d 1176, 1179-82 (C.D. Cal. 2009).
179. *See also* ICARA, 42 U.S.C. § 11601(b)(4) (2010).
180. *See, e.g.*, De Silva v. Pitts, 481 F.3d 1279, 1284-85 (10th Cir. 2007); Miller v. Miller, 240 F.3d 392, 399 (4th Cir. 2001); Shalit v. Coppe, 182 F.3d 1124, 1130-31 (9th Cir. 1999). Article 17 permits the authorities to take account of the reasons for a custody decision in applying the Convention.
181. Legal Analysis, *supra* note 8, at 10,504. *See also* Explanatory Report, *supra* note 7, at paras. 122-123.
182. *See* 42 U.S.C. § 11603(g) (2010).
183. This may be understood as an extension of the domestic relations exception to federal diversity jurisdiction, discussed in Chapter 1.
184. *See* GARBOLINO, *supra* note 5, at 42-43.
185. Younger v. Harris, 401 U.S. 37 (1971). *See* Barzilay v. Barzilay, 536 F.3d 844, 849-53 (8th Cir. 2008); Silverman v. Silverman, 267 F.3d 788, 792 (8th Cir. 2001); Yang v. Tsui (*Yang I*), 416 F.3d 199, 201-04 (3d Cir. 2005). In *Grieve v. Tamerin*, 269 F.3d 149 (2d Cir. 2001), the court concluded that *Younger* abstention was not appropriate, but held that plaintiff was barred from raising the issue as a matter of collateral estoppel. *See generally* Linda Silberman, *Patching Up the Abduction Convention: A Call for a New International Protocol and a Suggestion for Amendments to ICARA*, 38 TEX. INT'L L.J. 41, 56-60 (2003).
186. Colo. River Conservation Dist. v. U.S., 424 U.S. 800 (1976). *See* Holder v. Holder, 305 F.3d 854, 867-72 (9th Cir. 2002); Lops v. Lops, 140 F.3d 927, 935-36 (11th Cir. 1998).
187. This begins with the premise that the lower federal courts have no jurisdiction to review a state court's final judicial determination; the doctrine extends to cases in which the federal claim is "inextricably intertwined" with the claim decided by a state court. *See* Silverman v. Silverman (*Silverman II*), 338 F.3d 886, 893-96 (8th Cir. 2003); Mozes v. Mozes, 239 F.3d 1067, 1085 n. 55 (9th Cir. 2001) (holding that doctrine does not apply when Congress has specifically granted jurisdiction to the federal courts).
188. *Holder*, 305 F.3d at 872-73.
189. *See Holder*, 305 F.3d at 869 (noting in dicta that if "left-behind parent chose the state court as the forum for his or her Hague Convention petition, . . . it is more reasonable to confine the

left-behind parent to their choice and to be concerned about the forum-shopping implications of failing to do so") *See also* Witherspoon v. Orange Cnty. Dep't of Soc. Servs., 646 F. Supp. 2d 1176, 1179–82 (C.D. Cal. 2009); Cerit v. Cerit, 188 F. Supp. 2d 1239, 1244–51 (D. Haw. 2002).

190. *Lops,* 140 F.3d at 942–45 (district court did not abuse discretion in declining to abstain when state court could not act expeditiously).

191. Friedrich v. Friedrich (*Friedrich II*), 78 F.3d 1060, 1064 (6th Cir. 1996).

192. Koch v. Koch, 450 F.3d 703, 710 (7th Cir. 2006).

193. Robert v. Tesson, 507 F.3d 981, 987 (6th Cir. 2007).

194. *See* Ruiz v. Tenorio, 392 F.3d 1247, 1251 (11th Cir. 2004) (citing cases). Early decisions include *Mozes v. Mozes,* 239 F.3d 1067, 1073 (9th Cir. 2001), and *Feder v. Evans-Feder,* 63 F.3d 217, 222 n. 9 (3d Cir. 1995). *See also* Delvoye v. Lee, 329 F.3d 330, 332 (3d Cir. 2003) (appellate court should review the underlying "findings of historical and narrative fact for clear error, but exercise plenary review over the court's application of legal precepts to the facts").

195. Silverman v. Silverman (*Silverman II*), 338 F.3d 886, 896 (8th Cir. 2003); Blondin v. Dubois (*Blondin II*), 238 F.3d 158, 158 (2d Cir. 2001).

196. *E.g.,* Charalambous v. Charalambous, 744 F. Supp. 2d 375 (D. Me. 2010) (denying stay but extending return deadline by two weeks to allow respondent to seek stay from appellate court). *See* NCMEC, *supra* note 5, at 81–82. For cases pending in the federal courts, these issues are governed by federal procedural rules.

197. *Compare* Bekier v. Bekier, 248 F.3d 1051 (11th Cir. 2001), *and* Brown v. Orange Cnty. Dep't of Soc. Servs., 91 F.3d 150 (9th Cir. 1996) (appeal moot once child has returned to habitual residence), *with* Fawcett v. McRoberts, 326 F.3d 491, 497 (4th Cir. 2003), *and* Whiting v. Krassner, 391 F.3d 540, 542 (3d Cir. 2004) (appeal is not mooted by return). In *Navani v. Shahani,* 496 F.3d 1121 (10th Cir. 2007) the court held that an appeal had been mooted by the child's return and a new custody order issued in the child's habitual residence.

198. Kijowska v. Haines, 463 F.3d 583, 589–90 (7th Cir. 2006).

199. In *Altamiranda Vale v. Avila,* 538 F.3d 581 (7th Cir. 2008), the parties settled their dispute and agreed that the father could reopen the Hague proceeding if the mother failed to comply with the settlement. When the mother failed to comply, the federal courts resumed jurisdiction over the father's petition.

200. *See* HAGUE CONFERENCE ON PRIVATE INTERNATIONAL LAW, DRAFT GUIDE TO GOOD PRACTICE ON MEDIATION, Prel. Doc. No. 5 (May 2011), http://www.hcch.net/upload/wop/abduct2011pd05e.pdf. *See also* Melissa A. Kucinski, *Culture in Parental Kidnapping Mediations,* 9 PEPP. DISP. RESOL. L.J. 555 (2009); Julia Alanen, *When Human Rights Conflict: Mediating International Parental Kidnapping Disputes Involving the Domestic Violence Defense,* 40 U. MIAMI INTER-AM. L. REV. 49 (2008).

201. For discussion of a mediation model developed in the United Kingdom, see REUNITE CHILD ABDUCTION CENTRE, MEDIATION IN INTERNATIONAL PARENTAL CHILD ABDUCTION: THE REUNITE MEDIATION PILOT SCHEME (2006), http://www.reunite.org/edit/files/Library%20-%20reunite%20Publications/Mediation%20Report.pdf. *See also* Jennifer Zawid, *Practical and Ethical Implications of Mediating International Child Abduction Cases: A New Frontier for Mediators,* 40 U. MIAMI INTER-AM. L. REV. 1 (2008); Radoslaw Pawlowski, Note, *Alternative Dispute Resolution for Hague Convention Child Custody Disputes,* 45 FAM. CT. REV. 302 (2007).

202. Zawid, *supra* note 201, at 16–18.

203. At least 40 of the countries that have ratified or acceded to the Abduction Convention have made this declaration; details are available on the Hague Conference website. *See also* BEAUMONT & MCELEAVY, *supra* note 43, at 247, 249, 251–53. The current Attorney Referral Network is operated by the Office of Children's Issues.

204. Representation is carried out on a pro bono basis, but this does not preclude a fee award under the statute. *See* Cuellar v. Joyce, 603 F.3d 1142 (9th Cir. 2010).

205. Legal Analysis, *supra* note 8, at 10,511.

206. Section 11607 requires payment of "[N]ecessary expenses incurred by or on behalf of the petitioner, including court costs, legal fees, foster home or other care during the course of proceedings in the action, and transportation costs related to the return of the child . . . ."

207. *E.g.*, Blanc v. Morgan, 721 F. Supp. 2d 749 (W. D. Tenn. 2010); Neves v. Neves, 637 F. Supp. 2d 322, 339-47 (W.D.N.C. 2009); Distler v. Distler, 26 F. Supp. 2d 723, 727 (D.N.J. 1998); *see also* Antunez-Fernandes v. Connors-Fernandes, 259 F. Supp. 2d 800, 817 (N.D. Iowa 2003).
208. Rydder v. Rydder, 49 F.3d 369, 373-74 (8th Cir. 1995) (affirming award of $9,667.40 in expenses, and reducing award of legal fees and costs from $18,487.42 to $10,000).
209. *See supra* notes 29-30 and accompanying text. The State Department publishes an annual Report on Compliance with the Hague Convention, available on the OCI website, providing statistics and indicating which countries have demonstrated patterns of noncompliance with requests from the United States.
210. *See supra* notes 9-16 and accompanying text; *see also* NAT'L CTR. FOR MISSING & EXPLOITED CHILDREN, FAMILY ABDUCTION: PREVENTION AND RESPONSE (Patricia M. Hoff ed., 6th ed. 2009) [hereinafter FAMILY ABDUCTION].
211. *See supra* note 203 and accompanying text.
212. This information may be useful in structuring abduction prevention orders. *See* Chapter 5; *see also infra* notes 231-35 and accompanying text.
213. Legal Analysis, *supra* note 8, at 10,506.
214. This is discussed in Chapter 5. *See* Linda Silberman, *Hague International Child Abduction Convention: A Progress Report*, 57 LAW & CONTEMP. PROBS. 209, 222-24 (1994).
215. *Cf. In re* Vernor, 94 S.W.3d 201 (Tex. Ct. App. 2002) (concluding that unmarried father did not have rights of custody under Texas law at the time child was removed to Australia). *See generally* GARBOLINO, *supra* note 5, at 209-17; *see also* Legal Analysis, *supra* note 8, at 10,506.
216. *See* FAMILY ABDUCTION, *supra* note 210, at 49-51, 199-258 (Directory of Family-Abduction Laws and Resources).
217. *E.g.*, State v. Vakilzaden, 865 A.2d 1155 (Conn. 2005).
218. *E.g.*, FLA. STAT. § 787.03(4) (2010).
219. *See* 18 U.S.C. § 1073 (2010).
220. Extradition is governed by 18 U.S.C. §§ 3181-3196 (2010). Under § 203 the Extradition Treaties Interpretation Act, Pub. L. No. 105-323, 112 Stat. 3029, 34 (1998), kidnapping should be interpreted to include parental kidnapping for purposes of any extradition treaty. *See generally* FAMILY ABDUCTION, *supra* note 210, at 59.
221. *E.g.*, Stone v. Wall, 734 So. 2d 1038 (Fla. 1999) (intentional interference in parent-child relationship); Sheltra v. Smith, 392 A.2d 431 (Vt. 1978) (intentional infliction of emotional distress). Case law is collected in FAMILY ABDUCTION, *supra* note 210, at 199-258.
222. *Compare* Wood v. Wood, 338 N.W.2d 123 (Iowa 1983), *with* Larson v. Dunn, 460 N.W.2d 39 (Minn. 1990). Dicta in *Kessel v. Leavitt*, 511 S.E.2d 720 (W. Va. 1998), indicate that a parent may not make this claim against another parent with substantially equal custody rights.
223. 18 U.S.C. § 1204 (2010). Decisions sustaining the IPKCA in the face of constitutional and other challenges include United States v. Cummings, 281 F.3d 1046 (9th Cir. 2002), *cert. denied*, 537 U.S. 895 (2002); United States v. Alahmad, 211 F.3d 538 (10th Cir. 2000), *cert. denied*, 531 U.S. 1080 (2001); United States v. Amer, 110 F.3d 873 (2d Cir. 1997) *cert. denied*, 522 U.S. 904 (1997). *See also* United States v. Newman, 614 F.3d 1232 (11th Cir. 2010) (addressing federal sentencing guidelines under IPKCA).
224. Under § 1204(b)(1), "the term 'child' means a person who has not attained the age of 16 years." Parental rights means "the right to physical custody of the child (b)(2)(A) whether joint or sole (and includes visiting rights); and (b)(2)(B) whether arising by operation of law, court order, or legally binding agreement of the parties." Under this broad definition, "parental rights" may be exercised by someone other than a parent. *See, e.g., Alahmad*, 211 F.3d at 541 (maternal grandmother had parental rights within meaning of IPKCA).
225. 18 U.S.C. § 1204(c) (2010).
226. Pub. L. No. 103-173, 107 Stat. 1998, 1999 (1993) (codified at 18 U.S.C. § 1204(b)).
227. *See, e.g., Cummings*, 281 F.3d at 1051 (affirming conviction of father who removed and retained children in Germany after German court denied mother's petition for return under the Convention).

228. Under 8 U.S.C. § 1182(a)(10)(C)(i) (2010):

> [A]ny alien who, after entry of an order by a court in the United States granting custody to a person of a United States citizen child who detains or retains the child, or withholds custody of the child, outside the United States from the person granted custody by that order, is inadmissible until the child is surrendered to the person granted custody by that order.

229. *See* 8 U.S.C. § 1182(a)(10)(C)(ii).
230. Exceptions are set forth in 8 U.S.C. § 1182(a)(10)(C)(iii).
231. *See* Chapter 5. Research has indicated that certain factors signal a heightened risk of international abduction; *see, e.g.,* Janet R. Johnston & Linda K. Girdner, *Early Identification of Parents at Risk for Custody Violations and Prevention of Child Abductions,* 36 FAM. & CONCILIATION CTS. REV. 392, 401–03 (1998).
232. UNIF. CHILD ABDUCTION PREVENTION ACT 9 (1A) U.L.A. 41 (Supp. 2010), *reprinted in* 41 FAM. L.Q. 23 (2007).
233. *See, e.g.,* Mackinnon v. Mackinnon, 922 A.2d 1252 (N.J. 2007). These relocation issues are also addressed in Chapter 5.
234. *See* U.S. Dep't of State, Prevention: Guarding Against International Parental Child Abduction, http://www.travel.state.gov/abduction/prevention/prevention_560.html. The website includes information for judges and attorneys and links to other materials. *See also* FAMILY ABDUCTION, *supra* note 210.
235. Regulations concerning children's passports are at 22 C.F.R. 51.28 (2010). Under 22 C.F.R. § 51.60(e) (2010), the State Department:

> may refuse to issue a passport, except a passport for direct return to the United States, in any case in which the Department determines or is informed by a competent authority that the applicant is a minor who has been abducted, wrongfully removed or retained in violation of a court order or decree and return to his or her home state or habitual residence is necessary to permit a court of competent jurisdiction to determine custody matters.

7

Child
Support

The child-support system in the United States combines state and federal law: State laws set the substantive terms of family support obligations, and Title IV-D of the federal Social Security Act provides a template for child-support enforcement programs. Within the IV-D system, funded and administered by the Office of Child Support Enforcement (OCSE) in the Department of Health and Human Services (HHS), state and local child-support agencies provide services free of charge for determining parentage, establishing child-support obligations, and enforcing support orders. The state IV-D agencies also handle interstate and international cases, using the Uniform Interstate Family Support Act (UIFSA) to obtain enforcement or foreign support orders in the United States.[1]

International law recognizes parents' primary responsibility to provide for their children's financial support, and the Convention on the Rights of the Child encourages countries to take measures to secure the recovery of maintenance for a child from within the country and abroad.[2] Under a series of bilateral agreements with "foreign reciprocating nations," state IV-D offices provide services to establish and enforce child support for children living in those countries, and receive similar services abroad on behalf of children in the United States.[3] All of the states have also concluded state-level agreements with other foreign nations.[4] The United States is working toward ratification of the 2007 Hague Convention on the International Recovery of Child Support and Other Forms of Family Maintenance ("Maintenance Convention"),[5] which will be implemented by OCSE through the IV-D program. UIFSA was amended in 2008 to facilitate implementation of the new Maintenance Convention, and all states will be required to enact the 2008 amended version of UIFSA.[6] The analysis in this chapter is based on UIFSA 2008.

Working with State Child-Support Enforcement Offices

State child-support agencies offer services for establishing and enforcing child-support orders through the federal IV-D program; they provide assistance in locating noncustodial parents and establishing paternity as well as establishing and collecting child-support orders.[7] In addition, local offices assist with enforcement of a spousal support order for a child's custodial parent that is entered in combination with a child-support order.[8] Services are also available to noncustodial parents seeking to establish paternity, establish a wage-withholding order, or request a review of an existing order when their financial circumstances have changed. The IV-D agencies have a wide range of enforcement tools, including access to the Federal Parent Locator Service, which is also available to locate the whereabouts of a child who has been hidden in violation of a custody or visitation order.[9]

When state support enforcement agencies provide services, they take the steps necessary to enable the appropriate tribunal to obtain jurisdiction, requesting that the tribunal set a hearing, and make a reasonable effort to obtain information concerning the parties' income and property.[10] Establishment and enforcement of child-support orders may be handled either by a court or an administrative tribunal, depending on the states involved. In all states, courts and agencies work within the legal framework of UIFSA.

Although other family relationships may also give rise to duties of support, the procedures established in UIFSA and the federal IV-D system apply only to child-support and, with some qualifications, to spousal support.[11] UIFSA § 102(1) defines "child" broadly to include an individual "whether over or under the age of majority, who is or is alleged to be owed a duty of support by the individual's parent or who is alleged to be the beneficiary of a support order directed to the parent."

An individual seeking to establish or enforce a child-support order may choose to retain private counsel rather than using the IV-D agency for representation in parentage or support proceedings.[12] All states permit petitioners living within the state or beyond its borders to file an action to establish or enforce support directly with the appropriate state tribunal.[13]

When the Hague Maintenance Convention comes into effect, the U.S. Central Authority will be located in the federal OCSE. Under the implementing legislation, state IV-D offices will be required to provide services to individuals residing within the United States with a claim under the Convention and also to individuals residing in foreign countries that have ratified the Maintenance Convention or entered into a state or federal bilateral child-support agreement.[14] In cases brought under the Convention, states may require that individuals living in another country request services through the Central Authority in that country. Under new legislation, states may have discretion to deter-

The U.S. State Department information circular on Child Support Payments and Getting a U.S. Passport is available at http://travel.state.gov/passport/ppi/family/family_863.html.

mine whether to provide child-support enforcement services to petitioners residing in nations that do not have a treaty relationship with the United States.[15]

State courts and agencies have a wide range of devices for enforcing support obligations, including automatic wage withholding, garnishment of bank accounts or other assets, and interception of income tax refunds and lottery winnings.[16] Delinquent support obligors may have their professional, recreational, or occupational licenses revoked; their driver's licenses suspended; or be denied a U.S. passport.[17] In addition, support debtors with significant accumulated arrearages may face state or federal criminal prosecution for willful violation of support orders.[18] The OCSE also operates the Federal Parent Locator Service (FPLS), which is available to assist in locating an individual or that person's income or assets in order to establish parentage or to establish, modify, or enforce child support.[19] The FPLS is also available to assist authorities in locating a parent or child to enforce or determine child custody in cases of parental kidnapping.[20]

Establishing Parentage and Child Support

The parent's duty to support his or her children, recognized at common law, is now codified in an extensive series of statutes.[21] Today, the obligation to support children extends equally to marital and nonmarital children.[22] Determining parentage is a necessary first step, and all states have adopted procedures to simplify this process. Parent-child relationships may be recognized under state law based on the parent giving birth to a child, a marital tie to the child's birth parent, a written acknowledgment of parentage, biological parentage established by genetic testing, or, in some circumstances, living with and holding out the child as one's own.[23] When an administrative or judicial proceeding is necessary to determine parentage, UIFSA provides a basis for obtaining jurisdiction.

Defining Support Obligations

Most state statutes continue the parent's duty of support until the child reaches the age of 18, and a few states extend the obligation to age 19 or 21.[24] Some states allow courts to enter support orders for older children who are enrolled in college or other postsecondary education.[25] Many states have statutes or case law that obligate parents to support adult children who are incapacitated, particularly if the disability began before the child reached the age of majority.[26] Adults with no legally recognized parental role are generally not obligated to provide financial support.[27]

In every state, determination of child support begins with a guideline or formula that produces a presumptive support figure based on the parents' income and taking various other factors into account.[28] A court or other tribunal may deviate from this presumptive support award based on economic factors that are not reflected in the guidelines. Cases in several jurisdictions have considered whether a lower cost of living in the place where the child lives should be treated as grounds for deviation from the support guidelines and entry of a lower support award. Although the courts have reached different conclusions, many have refused to allow a deviation on this basis, suggesting that the child should be entitled to share in the noncustodial parent's standard of living.[29] Similarly, when a non-custodial parent lives in a place where wages are lower, courts take this fact into account in determining the parent's earning potential.[30]

Foreign currency conversion and exchange rate fluctuations significantly complicate some international child-support cases. In *Hixson v. Sarkesian*, a court in Alaska computed the support obligation of a father who was paid in Swiss francs by converting his income to dollars and then applying the Alaska child-support guidelines. After a significant change in the exchange rate, the court agreed to modify support, which had been set in dollars.[31]

Obtaining Jurisdiction under the Uniform Interstate Family Support Act

Jurisdiction in parentage and child-support cases is governed by UIFSA. As a matter of constitutional due process, a state tribunal must have personal jurisdiction over a potential obligor in order to adjudicate family support obligations. Personal jurisdiction may be based on consent, on residence within the forum state, on service with process in the forum state (also known as tag jurisdiction), or on service outside the forum on a respondent who has constitutionally sufficient "minimum contacts" with the state.[32] As described by the U.S. Supreme Court in *Kulko v. Superior Court*, long-arm jurisdiction based on minimum contacts requires "a sufficient connection between the defendant and the forum State to make it fair to require defense of the action in the forum."[33] In *Kulko*, the Court concluded that the presence of defendant's former wife and children in the state of California was not a sufficient connection to the state to allow the California courts to exercise personal jurisdiction to determine his child-support obligations. In *Burnham v. Superior Court*,[34] however, the Supreme Court upheld tag jurisdiction for purposes of child-support litigation without regard to the defendant's connections to the state.

Based on *Kulko* and *Burnham*, lawyers and judges in the United States accept tag jurisdiction and minimum contacts jurisdiction as routine, but orders entered on these jurisdictional grounds are not acceptable in many other jurisdictions. Conversely, courts in other countries typically consider that the residence of the child or the child-support creditor within the forum provides an appropriate basis for personal jurisdiction over the potential obligor, an approach that was squarely rejected by the U.S. Supreme Court in *Kulko*.[35]

A party seeking to obtain a support order in a case that spans multiple jurisdictions has three alternatives. The long-arm provision in UIFSA § 201 extends personal jurisdiction to the maximum extent permitted by the Constitution. This will often permit a court in the petitioner's state of residence to assert jurisdiction over a nonresident respondent. As an alternative, UIFSA allows a petitioner to initiate a two-state proceeding in which the petition is transmitted from a tribunal in the petitioner's state to a tribunal in the respondent's state of residence. In international cases, a similar two-state approach may be available under a state or federal bilateral child-support agreement or the Maintenance Convention. Finally, a petitioner may file directly with a tribunal in the state where the other party resides.[36] Given the substantive variations among the child-support laws of different jurisdictions, and the likelihood that the tribunal asked to decide the case will apply the law of the forum, the choice between these alternatives may involve important strategic considerations.[37]

Extended Personal Jurisdiction

UIFSA § 201(a) defines eight bases on which a state tribunal may exercise personal jurisdiction over a nonresident individual in a proceeding to establish or enforce a support order or determine parentage. A tribunal may not take jurisdiction under § 201 when a tribunal in another state or foreign country has previously entered a child-support order unless there is either a basis for modification jurisdiction under the statute, as described below, or no controlling child-support order under § 207.[38]

The provisions of UIFSA § 201(a) allow state tribunals to take jurisdiction in a significant number of international cases. For example, *In re Gonzalez* sustained the jurisdiction of a Texas court to establish paternity and enter a child-support order under § 201(a)(1) against a respondent who was a Mexican citizen, living in Mexico. Respondent was served in the state "when his plane touched down in Texas to refuel while en route to Colorado from Mexico"; in addition, he had business and personal ties to the state, and the child was conceived while petitioner and respondent were staying in San Antonio, Texas.[39] Conversely, *Bergaust v. Flaherty* concluded that a Virginia trial court did not properly exercise jurisdiction over a child's father who lived in France when the child

---

Personal Jurisdiction

Under UIFSA § 201(a), a state tribunal may exercise personal jurisdiction over a nonresident when

- the individual was personally served within the state;
- the individual has submitted to the tribunal's jurisdiction by consent, by entering a general appearance, or by waiver;
- the individual resided with the child in the state;
- the individual resided in the state and provided prenatal expenses or support for the child;
- the child resides in the state as a result of the individual's acts or directives;
- the individual engaged in sexual intercourse in the state that may have led to the child's conception;
- the individual asserted parentage of a child in the state's putative father registry; or
- there is any other basis consistent with the state and federal constitutions for the exercise of personal jurisdiction.

had been conceived in France and born in Virginia, and the father's only contact with the state was a brief visit when the child was seven months old.[40]

The jurisdictional grounds in § 201(a) based on prior residence within the state will often be sufficient for international cases. In *Marriage of Abu-Dalbouh*, husband and wife were married in Minnesota and lived there when their first child was born. They moved to Jordan and had two more children; the wife and children returned to Minnesota after the marriage deteriorated. Based on the statute, the Minnesota court concluded that it could exercise jurisdiction over the husband's support obligation for the oldest child, but concluded that it could not award support for the other two children.[41] In *Constance P. v. Avraam G.*, a New York court sustained jurisdiction in a paternity proceeding under § 201(a)(6) based on the child's conception within the state, even though the putative father was a resident of Greece.[42]

The grounds based on an individual's "acts and directives" under § 201(a)(5) have proven to be more difficult to apply, particularly within the constitutional constraints imposed by *Kulko*. For example, *Franklin v. Virginia* involved a couple who lived together in California and briefly in Virginia before moving to Africa with their two children. The marriage ended after "several physical altercations" when the "husband ordered [his] wife and children to leave their home."[43] She obtained emergency assistance from the U.S. embassy, and the husband's employer, and returned to Virginia with the children. On these facts, the Virginia courts held that the husband's actions provided a basis for jurisdiction under § 201(a)(5), concluding that the children were residing in the state "as a result of [his] acts or directives."[44] A number of interstate cases have considered whether there is a sufficient basis for jurisdiction under this provision when one parent has moved into the state with a child to escape from the other parent's acts of domestic violence. These decisions have gone both ways; however, courts are more likely to find a basis for exercising jurisdiction in cases involving more serious violence.[45]

A state tribunal exercising jurisdiction over a nonresident in a parentage or support proceeding applies its own procedural and substantive law.[46] UIFSA includes procedures for receiving evidence outside the state, communicating with another tribunal outside the state, or obtaining discovery through a tribunal outside the state.[47] If the respondent lives in another country, there are special requirements for international service of process and taking of evidence that must be observed.[48]

Two-State Proceedings

If local authorities cannot obtain personal jurisdiction over a respondent, UIFSA provides for cooperation between tribunals in different states or in a state and a foreign country. Under § 203, a court may act as an initiating tribunal to forward the proceedings to authorities in another state, or as a responding tribunal for proceedings initiated in another state or foreign country. A petitioner may participate in a proceeding in another state under UIFSA without being subject to personal jurisdiction in the state for any purpose other than the support proceeding.[49] UIFSA does not authorize state courts to transmit proceedings directly to a foreign tribunal, but a party seeking support may work with the local child-support enforcement office to initiate international proceedings under the terms of state or federal bilateral agreements or the Hague Maintenance Convention.

When the two-state procedure is used, the initiating tribunal is responsible for forwarding the petition and accompanying documents to the responding tribunal or support enforcement agency in the responding state. The initiating tribunal may be asked to issue certificates or other documents or make findings that are required in the responding state, and in international cases may be required to "specify the amount of support sought, convert that amount into the equivalent amount in the foreign currency . . . and provide any other documents necessary to satisfy the requirements of the responding foreign tribunal."[50]

When a responding tribunal in the United States receives a petition, it may establish a support order, determine parentage of a child, or order an obligor to comply with a support order.[51] Under § 303, a responding tribunal applies the "procedural and substantive law generally applicable to similar proceedings originating in this state" and determines the duty of support and the amount payable in accordance with its own law and support guidelines. Depending on the law of the state involved, the tribunal may take measures such as ordering income withholding, enforcing orders by civil or criminal contempt, setting aside property for satisfaction of the order or placing liens and ordering execution of the obligor's property, determining the amount of arrearages and specifying a method of payment, ordering the obligor to seek appropriate employment, and awarding fees and costs including reasonable attorneys' fees.[52]

Direct Filing

If no support order has been issued that is entitled to recognition under UIFSA, an individual or a support enforcement agency may file directly with a state tribunal that has personal jurisdiction over the parties to request that the court issue a support order. For this purpose, it does not matter where the individual resides or where the support enforcement agency is located.[53] Jurisdiction over the respondent may be established under § 201(a), and by making a direct filing, the petitioner consents to the court's jurisdiction for purposes of the support proceeding only.[54] A petitioner may also file directly without invoking UIFSA. For example, the court in *Edwards v. Dominick* sustained an adjudication of paternity and child support in Louisiana in an action brought by a plaintiff who was living in South Africa against a defendant who lived in Louisiana.[55]

Over time, UIFSA's two-state judicial procedure has been largely replaced by the IV-D system of cooperation between state agencies and direct filing by local authorities in the state where jurisdiction can be obtained over a respondent. Similarly, in international cases governed by a state or federal bilateral child-support agreement, agencies transmit case information so that proceedings can be commenced in the forum where the respondent is located.

Example:

M is the unmarried mother of a young child born in Country X, which has a reciprocal child-support enforcement agreement with the United States. The child's father, F, has never been present in Country X and is now living in State A in the United States. M may retain private counsel in State A to commence a paternity and support proceeding against F. Alternatively, M may apply to the authorities in Country X, which will transmit her request to the IV-D agency in State A to commence proceedings to establish paternity and obtain support.

Simultaneous Proceedings

When multiple support proceedings are commenced in different jurisdictions, UIFSA gives priority to the first action filed unless jurisdiction is challenged promptly. Under § 204, a state court may not exercise jurisdiction in a case commenced after pleadings have been filed in another state or foreign country, unless the party filing the second action brings a timely challenge to the jurisdiction of the first forum and establishes that the second action was filed in the child's home state. The "home state" is "the state or foreign country in which the child lived with a parent or a person acting as a parent for at least six consecutive months" immediately preceding the filing of the petition or comparable pleading.[56] The rule in § 204 gives the respondent a brief opportunity to shift the litigation to the child's home state if that tribunal can exercise jurisdiction over the other party under § 201. In international cases, a state court applying § 204 could similarly be required to defer to subsequent proceedings commenced in a foreign forum. Conversely, when the child's home state is in the United States, a tribunal in that state would not be required to defer to child-support litigation that was previously commenced in another country if § 204 is satisfied.[57] Beyond the requirements of § 204, UIFSA does not require deference to the child's home state.[58]

Continuing Jurisdiction

Once a tribunal acquires jurisdiction under UIFSA § 201 and issues a child-support order, it retains jurisdiction to modify the order under § 205 and to enforce the order under § 206.[59] Section 205 provides that a state tribunal has continuing, exclusive jurisdiction to modify if, when the request for modification is filed, the state is the residence of the obligor, the obligee, or the child for whose benefit the order was issued.[60] The tribunal also retains continuing exclusive jurisdiction to modify if the parties have given their written consent to continuing jurisdiction.[61] Conversely, continuing exclusive jurisdiction to modify terminates if the parties file their consent to another tribunal's jurisdiction. Once a new tribunal has modified a support order consistently with the principles in UIFSA, that tribunal acquires continuing exclusive jurisdiction under the statute.[62] A tribunal that lacks continuing exclusive jurisdiction to modify its order may continue to exercise jurisdiction to enforce arrears and any interest that accrued before the order was modified,[63] and it may act as an initiating tribunal to request that another state tribunal modify or enforce it.[64]

In international cases, state courts follow the same rules, retaining jurisdiction if any of the parties remains in the state. If the support creditor and the child have moved abroad, however, a foreign court may assume jurisdiction under its own law to enter a new order or modify the previous one. In this situation, if the obligor resides in the state where the original order was entered at the time modification proceedings are initiated,

---

Caution: UIFSA versus UCCJEA Jurisdiction

Jurisdictional rules are different for state court child-support proceedings under the Uniform Interstate Family Support Act (UIFSA) and custody and access proceeding under the Uniform Child Custody Jurisdiction and Enforcement Act (UCCJEA).

> ### Example: Continuing Jurisdiction under UIFSA
>
> Mother and Father are foreign citizens living in State A in the United States when their child is born. Father acknowledges paternity, and Mother obtains child-support and custody orders from the authorities in State A. Two years later, Mother and the child return to her home country.
>
> - Father remains in State A and obtains a new position with a much larger salary. Under UIFSA, the court in State A has continuing exclusive jurisdiction to modify the original support order.
>
> - If, instead, Father relocates to a different country and obtains a new position with a larger salary, State A will lose its continuing jurisdiction to modify the original support order.

courts in the United States treat the original forum as having continuing exclusive jurisdiction under UIFSA, and the foreign court order would not be enforceable in the United States.[65] This rule was applied in *Baars v. Freeman*, in which the initial support decree was entered by a court in Georgia in connection with the parents' divorce. After the divorce, the father moved to the United Kingdom, and the mother relocated with the child to the Netherlands for four years before returning to Georgia. After her return, she filed a petition for contempt sanctions in the Georgia court. Given the rule of continuing exclusive jurisdiction under UIFSA, the court concluded that the trial court "unquestionably possesses authority to enforce the child support provisions of the decree prospectively and as to past violations."[66]

Special Procedures in International Parentage and Support Cases

For the most part, state tribunals apply the same laws and procedures to international parentage or support cases that they apply in interstate proceedings. International litigation presents some significant differences, however. State laws define what types of service a state tribunal will authorize, but service beyond the court's jurisdiction must also comply with the requirements of local law in the place where service is made. As a matter of constitutional due process, the respondent in a support or parentage proceeding must be given notice that is "reasonably calculated under all of the circumstances" to inform the respondent of the action and afford an opportunity for a hearing.[67] Ideally, this will be accomplished by personal service, although state laws may permit substituted forms of service, including service by publication, when the respondent's location cannot be determined.[68] Personal service outside the state where the tribunal is located does not confer jurisdiction on the court; but if there are constitutionally sufficient minimum contacts, it may be the basis for exercising extended personal jurisdiction under UIFSA § 201(a). Under UIFSA, the physical presence of a nonresident party is not required for "establishment, enforcement or modification of a support order or rendition of a judgment determining parentage."[69]

Basic pleading requirements are addressed in UIFSA § 311, in terms designed to coordinate with the federal requirements governing interstate and international cases. If a party alleges in an affidavit or sworn pleading that disclosure of identifying

> **Caution:** Service of process in international cases must comply with local law in the place where service is made. In many countries, service may be accomplished using the Hague Service Convention, discussed in Chapter 1.[70]

information would jeopardize "the health, safety, or liberty of a party or child," the information must not be disclosed under § 312. A petitioner may not be required to pay filing fees or other costs. If a support creditor prevails, the tribunal may assess fees and costs against the obligor under § 313.[71] In some circumstances, a state tribunal may enter a temporary order to govern child support during the pendency of the proceedings.[72]

The statute includes specialized rules of evidence and procedure designed to facilitate interstate and international cases, including the requirement that a tribunal must permit a party or witness residing outside the state to be deposed or to testify by telephone, audiovisual means, or other electronic means at a designated tribunal or other location.[73] A state tribunal may communicate with a tribunal outside the state to obtain or provide "information concerning the laws, the legal effect of a judgment, decree or order of that tribunal, and the status of a proceeding."[74] The tribunal may also request that another tribunal assist in obtaining discovery, or, "upon request, compel a person over which it has jurisdiction to respond to a discovery order issued by a tribunal outside this state."

If discovery is carried out abroad, counsel must be careful to respect the local laws in the jurisdiction where the evidence is sought.[75] Litigants may use traditional procedures for obtaining evidence abroad, such as letters rogatory, or Letters of Request under the 1970 Hague Convention on the Taking of Evidence Abroad in Civil and Commercial Matters.[76] In the child-support context, these procedures may be used to obtain samples for genetic testing in parentage cases. Authorities in the United States also assist in obtaining this type of evidence for use in foreign proceedings.[77]

Recognizing and Enforcing Child-Support Orders

Child-support orders entered in other countries are often directly enforceable in the United States pursuant to UIFSA. Enforcement of a "foreign child support order" as defined by UIFSA 2008 may be handled either by the state child-support enforcement office or by a direct filing in the appropriate tribunal. When this procedure is not available, a state court may recognize and enforce a foreign order on the basis of comity. Although other types of foreign judgments may be enforced under the Uniform Foreign

> **Caution:** The analysis in this chapter is based on the 2008 amended version of the UIFSA. Because substantial changes have been made to the statute over time, case law decided in different states or under older versions of UIFSA should be evaluated carefully before being used, particularly in international cases.

Further information and resources for caseworkers in international child-support cases are available from the International Resources web page of the U.S. Office of Child Support Enforcement at http://www.acf.hhs.gov/programs/cse/international/ and on the web page of the National Child Support Enforcement Association (NCSEA) at http://www.ncsea.org (under "International").

Money Judgments Recognition Act (UFMJRA), this statute does not apply to judgments for support "in matrimonial or family matters."[78]

The procedures for registration and enforcement of orders in UIFSA Article 6 extend to child-support orders entered in a country that meets the definition of "foreign country" in § 102(5). Child-support orders from a non-U.S. jurisdiction that does not qualify as a "foreign country" may be recognized and enforced on the basis of comity. Recognition based on comity is discretionary, however, while recognition and enforcement of "foreign support orders" from countries within the definition of § 102(5) is mandatory. Note that under UIFSA the term "State" includes the District of Columbia, Puerto Rico, "any territory or insular possession under the jurisdiction of the United States," and an Indian nation or tribe.[79]

Defining "Foreign Country" Support Orders

A foreign child or spousal support order is eligible for registration and enforcement under UIFSA if it was entered by a tribunal in a "foreign country" as that term is defined in § 102(5).[80] The definition includes four specific groups of countries: countries that have been declared under the law of the United States to be foreign reciprocating countries (§ 102(5)(A)); countries that have established a reciprocal arrangement for child support at the state level (§ 102(5)(B)); countries that have enacted laws or established procedures for issuing and enforcing support orders substantially similar to the procedures under UIFSA (§ 102(5)(C)); and countries in which the Maintenance Convention is in force for the United States (§ 102(5)(D)).[81] This definition is new to UIFSA 2008; previous versions of the statute addressed international cases by defining the term "State" to include some foreign countries.[82] Understanding the new definition of "foreign country" is centrally important to working with UIFSA in international cases, since the definition is incorporated into the definition of other key terms, including "foreign support order" in § 102(6), "foreign tribunal" in § 102(7), and "home state" in § 102(8).

Foreign Reciprocating Countries

The term "foreign reciprocating country" in § 102(5)(A) refers to a country, or a political subdivision of a country, with which the United States has entered a bilateral child-support agreement. The federal government has designated 25 entities as reciprocating countries for the purpose of enforcing family support obligations as defined by 42 U.S.C. § 659(a).[83]

Foreign Reciprocating Countries

These jurisdictions have been designated as foreign reciprocating countries by the United States

Australia	Hungary	Norway	Switzerland
Czech Republic	Ireland	Poland	United Kingdom
El Salvador	Israel	Portugal	
Finland	Netherlands	Slovak Republic	

Canadian Provinces or Territories:

Alberta	New Brunswick	Newfoundland/ Labrador	Saskatchewan
British Columbia	Northwest Territories	Nova Scotia	Yukon
Manitoba	Nunavut	Ontario	

Further information is available from the International Resources web page of the U.S. Office of Child Support Enforcement at http://www.acf.hhs.gov/programs/cse/international/.

Countries with State-Level Reciprocal Arrangements

Each state in the United States has entered into reciprocal arrangements for child-support establishment and enforcement, as referenced in § 102(5)(B), with some number of foreign jurisdictions. Although the specific list is different in every state, countries including Austria, France, Germany, Ireland, South Africa, and Sweden and a number of Canadian provinces and Mexican states have agreements with many states.[84] Current information for each state is available from the state's Child Support Recovery Unit or from the federal Office of Child Support Enforcement.[85]

Countries with Substantially Similar Procedures

The reference in § 102(5)(C) to countries that have "procedures for the issuance and enforcement of support orders which are substantially similar to the procedures" under UIFSA brings forward language used in the original 1993 version of the statute. As elaborated in official comments and the case law under successive versions of the statute, the touchstone of this inquiry is reciprocity. For example, *Foreman v. Foreman* approved registration and enforcement of an English spousal support order after concluding that various statutory instruments in England had established a procedure that would allow similar enforcement of North Carolina maintenance orders.[86] In contrast, *Kalia v. Kalia* concluded that the Indian Code of Civil Procedure, which provides for recognition of

---

State-Level Agreements

State profiles with detailed information on child-support laws, including listings of the foreign countries with which each state has reciprocal child-support agreements, are available through the OCSE Intergovernmental Referral Guide Public Map Page at https://extranet.acf.hhs.gov/irgps/stateMap.do.

Convention Countries

Current information on ratifications and accessions to the Maintenance Convention is available on the website of the Hague Conference on Private International Law at http://www.hcch.net (under "Conventions," "38," and "Status table").

---

foreign judgments but does not address issuance and enforcement of support orders, did not provide procedures that were substantially similar to the procedures under UIFSA.[87]

Convention Countries

Finally, the reference in § 102(5)(D) to countries in which the Family Maintenance Convention is in force for the United States will apply once the Convention takes effect. At the outset, this list will include the countries of the European Union, including many that now fall into other categories of the definition in § 102(5). In cases involving Convention Countries, the special rules in UIFSA Article 7 are also applicable.[88]

Registration and Enforcement

"Foreign country" support orders, including spousal support orders, may be registered for enforcement under UIFSA § 601.[89] The statute provides for filing a petition "seeking a remedy that must be affirmatively sought under other law of this state" and defines the specific information that must be sent to the appropriate tribunal.[90] Once a foreign country support order is registered with a state tribunal pursuant to UIFSA, § 603(b) provides that it "is enforceable in the same manner and is subject to the same procedures as an order issued by a tribunal of this state." Under § 603(c), the state tribunal must "recognize and enforce, but may not modify, a registered order if the issuing tribunal had jurisdiction." The choice-of-law language in § 604 stipulates that the law of the issuing tribunal governs most questions, including the "nature, extent, amount, and duration of current payments" under a registered order, and the computation and payment of arrearages and interest. To the extent that the law of the issuing tribunal is different from the law of the responding tribunal, a party intending to rely on the law of the issuing tribunal should be careful to follow the appropriate procedures in the responding tribunal govern pleading and proof of foreign law.[91] The responding tribunal applies its own procedures and remedies to enforce support and collect arrears, and it applies either its own statute of limitations or the statute of limitations of the issuing state, whichever is longer.

Contesting Registration

UIFSA § 605 provides that the nonregistering party must receive notice of registration and have an opportunity to request a hearing to contest the validity or enforcement of the registered order. The nonregistering party may seek to vacate the registration, assert a defense to the order, or contest the remedies being sought or the amount of any alleged arrearages. If the nonregistering party fails to contest the validity or enforcement of the registered order in a timely manner, "the order is confirmed by operation of law."[92] If the nonregistering party chooses to contest registration or enforcement, that party has the burden of proving one or more of the defenses specified in § 607. If the contesting party does not establish one of these defenses, the registering tribunal must confirm the registered order. Section 608 provides that confirmation of a registered support order precludes any further contest of the order with respect to any matter that could have been asserted at the time of registration.[93]

Controlling Order

If multiple orders regarding the same obligor and child have been issued by different state or foreign tribunals, UIFSA § 207 provides a rule for determination of which order controls and must be recognized.[94] This determination must be made by a tribunal with personal jurisdiction over all litigants to assure that its decision will be binding. Under § 207(b), if only one tribunal would have continuing, exclusive jurisdiction as defined in § 205, that tribunal's order controls. If more than one of the tribunals would have continuing, exclusive jurisdiction, the controlling order is the one issued in the child's current home state or, if no order has been issued in the current home state, the most recent order. If none of the tribunals would have continuing, exclusive jurisdiction, the tribunal hearing the action "shall issue a child support order, which controls." Once the controlling order is determined, the tribunal that issued the order must be recognized as having continuing, exclusive jurisdiction, and its order fixes the support obligation and its duration.[95]

Defending against Registration or Enforcement

UIFSA § 607 provides eight defenses that are available to either party in interstate or international cases to contest the validity of a registered order. These first of these is that "the issuing tribunal lacked personal jurisdiction over the contesting party," § 607(a)(1), and this is discussed further below. In addition to making a jurisdictional challenge, either party may argue that the order was obtained by fraud, § 607(a)(2); that the order has been vacated, suspended, or modified by a later order, § 607(a)(3); that the issuing tribunal has stayed the order pending appeal, § 607(a)(4); that there is a defense under the law of the registering state to the remedy sought, § 607(a)(5); that full or partial payment has been made, § 607(a)(6); that the statute of limitations precludes enforcement of some or all of the arrearages claimed, § 607(a)(7); or that the alleged controlling order is not the controlling order, § 607(a)(8).[96] The defenses on this list are the only ones that can be raised in an action to register and enforce a child or spousal support order. Courts will not recognize equitable defenses based on laches, waiver, estoppel, or a custodial parent's concealment of the child in proceedings under UIFSA.[97]

The jurisdictional defense in UIFSA § 607(a)(1) may lead to the conclusion that some foreign-country support orders are not enforceable in the United States, because the issuing tribunal did not have personal jurisdiction on a basis that conforms with constitutional due process requirements.[98] For example, it is common in other parts of the world for courts to assert jurisdiction in family support cases based on the residence of the family members who need support, but jurisdiction based solely on this ground would not be sufficient in the United States.[99]

A state court asked to register and enforce a foreign-country order will apply the same standards for personal jurisdiction used in domestic cases, considering whether the nonregistering party had sufficient minimum contacts with the forum where the order was entered. In *Willmer v. Willmer*, a divorced father contested a German child-support order registered for enforcement in North Carolina, arguing that German court did not have a basis for personal jurisdiction consistent with "traditional notions of fair play and substantial justice" as required under cases such as *Kulko*.[100] The court rejected this argument, noting that the couple lived together in Germany when the child was born and had their last common residence in Germany.[101] In contrast, the court in *Luxembourg ex rel. Ribeiro v. Canderas* vacated registration of a support order entered by a court in Luxembourg when the defendant had never been in the country.[102] Similarly, *Marriage of Kohl* refused to confirm registration of an Israeli support order when there was insufficient proof that support obligor had been served with notice of the Israeli proceeding.[103]

Recognizing Support Orders Based on Comity

Before the enactment of UIFSA, child-support orders from other countries could be recognized and enforced on the basis of comity, and § 104(a) expressly preserves this possibility.[104] In addition, § 105(b) states that in a comity case, courts may apply the procedural and substantive provisions of UIFSA. The primary distinction, then, is that recognition and enforcement of orders from "foreign countries" is often mandatory under UIFSA, while recognition and enforcement of orders from nations that fall outside of UIFSA's definition of "foreign country" is discretionary.[105] Because the list of "foreign countries" is somewhat different in each state, the comity approach will be applied to a different range of support orders in each state.[106] The argument for recognition based on comity is particularly strong in child-support cases, where the basic policies are widely shared among nations and the failure to extend comity could result in some support obligations being practically unenforceable.[107] For example, the court in *Kalia v. Kalia* concluded that a support order from India was not subject to registration under UIFSA, but it enforced the order in Ohio as a matter of comity.[108]

In determining whether to extend comity to a foreign judgment, a court typically begins by considering the proceeding in which it was rendered. As articulated in *Hilton v. Guyot*, comity is "the recognition which one nation allows within its territory to the legislative, executive, or judicial acts of another nation, having due regard both to international duty and convenience, and to the rights of its own citizens, or of other persons under the protection of its laws."[109] Courts implement this norm by applying broad standards of due process, and a judgment entered without jurisdiction, without notice or an opportunity for a hearing, or in circumstances that suggest fraud or other unfairness will not be recognized.[110] Foreign decrees are generally presumed valid, however, unless evidence is presented to the contrary.[111] Before a support order is presented for recognition and enforcement based on comity, any arrearages should be reduced to judgment in the country where the order was entered.[112] Once a foreign decree has been recognized, it may be enforced by the tribunal. If the decree was modifiable in the foreign jurisdiction where it was entered, it may be modified by the tribunal that is extending comity.[113]

In deciding whether to extend comity to a support judgment from a foreign nation, courts generally consider the range of defenses listed in UIFSA § 607(a). Thus, an order entered by a court that does not have an adequate basis for exercising personal jurisdiction over the support obligor will not be subject to comity, just as it cannot be registered and enforced under UIFSA.[114] A wider range of defenses may be available in an action based on comity, however, including equitable defenses and arguments based on public policy.[115]

Although a court may decline to extend comity to a foreign judgment based on public policy, this requires more than proof of substantive differences between the support laws of the country where the order was entered and the law of the state where comity is requested.[116] Thus, *Rains v. State* enforced an Italian order that extended support obligations well beyond the age of majority.[117] Similarly, *Kalia v. Kalia* rejected the argument that an Indian support order violated public policy because it was entered under a religious divorce law and also rejected the argument that the order violated public policy because Indian law requires financial support for a female child for a longer period of time than a male child.[118] In *Pfeifer v. Cutshall*, however, the court declined to extend comity to a German support order that included more than ten years of retroactive support.[119]

State courts are divided on the question whether recognition based on comity should be limited to orders from those nations that would enforce a comparable order from the United States. Most states now reject the reciprocity requirement, as do the *Restatement (Second) of Conflict of Laws* and the *Restatement (Third) of Foreign Relations Law.*[120] For states that require reciprocity, recognition based on comity is not likely to extend beyond the group of countries within § 102(5)(c) that "have enacted a law or established procedures for issuance and enforcement of support orders which are substantially similar to the procedures under" UIFSA.

Other Family Support Obligations

Under the common law, parents had a duty to support their minor children, and husbands had an obligation to support their wives. In some jurisdictions, support obligations also extended to other relatives, particularly if those family members would otherwise require public support.[121] For example, laws in some states require adult children to support their indigent parents.[122] Parents may also have a legal obligation to support a disabled adult child.[123]

Support for individuals other than minor children generally falls outside the IV-D support enforcement system, except for spousal support orders that are combined with a child-support order.[124] Spousal support orders are also covered by UIFSA and the recognition and enforcement provisions of the Hague Maintenance Convention.[125] When UIFSA is not available, family support orders from another state or country may be enforced on the basis of full faith and credit or comity. For example, in *Rains v. State*, the court extended comity to an Italian order and enforced a father's post-majority support obligation that continued under Italian law until the children were capable of supporting themselves in an "appropriate" manner.[126]

Modifying Child-Support Orders

In the system established by the UIFSA, a state court's jurisdiction is strictly limited if a child-support order has previously been entered in another state or foreign country. The state court may register and enforce the previous order, but it may not take jurisdiction to modify or enter a new order unless the prior tribunal has lost continuing, exclusive jurisdiction and additional requirements are met, as described below. As a substantive matter, child-support orders are modifiable under state law based on a substantial change in the parties' financial circumstances.[127] In *Hixson v. Sarkesian*, the court considered fluctuations in the exchange rate between U.S. dollars and Swiss francs and agreed to modify support on this basis when the changes met the statutory threshold for support modification.[128]

Determining Jurisdiction to Modify

UIFSA § 205 generally provides that a state tribunal has continuing, exclusive jurisdiction to modify child-support orders if the individual support debtor or creditor or the child for whose benefit the support order was issued resides in that state at the time the request for modification is filed.[129] If the individual parties are both residing in the same new state, a tribunal in that state can exercise jurisdiction under § 613 to enforce and to modify the child-support order.[130] If the individual parties have moved from the issuing state to different states, a tribunal in either one of these new states may take jurisdiction to modify under § 611.

To address the potential for jurisdictional conflict in cases where the parties have moved to different states, § 611(a)(1) requires that the party seeking modification go out of state to file the petition for modification. This is sometimes referred to as "playing an away game." Specifically, a petitioner who files a motion for modification of child support in a new tribunal must establish under § 611(a)(1) that "(A) neither the child, nor the obligee who is an individual, nor the obligor resides in the issuing state; (B) a [petitioner] who is a nonresident of this state seeks modification; and (C) the [respondent] is subject to the personal jurisdiction of the tribunal of this state." Alternatively, § 611(a)(2) allows a tribunal in a new state to modify the support order if the individual parties give their consent. Once a tribunal issues an order modifying a child-support order issued in another state, the new tribunal takes on continuing, exclusive jurisdiction.[131]

In international cases, the rules for modification of child support are slightly different. When the controlling child-support order was entered in a foreign country, UIFSA treats the foreign tribunal as having continuing, exclusive jurisdiction to modify, if either party is residing in that country at the time the petition for modification is filed.[132] If, however, the foreign tribunal lacks or refuses to exercise jurisdiction to modify its child-support order under its own law, § 615 permits a state tribunal with personal jurisdiction over both parties to take jurisdiction to modify the foreign support order.[133] The Comment to § 615 suggests that this may be an important occasion for communication between the state and foreign tribunals.[134] In cases that fall within the scope of the Maintenance Convention, there are slightly different modification rules.[135]

If the controlling child-support order was issued by a tribunal in the United States, and one party resides in another country, § 611(f) provides that the tribunal in the issuing state retains jurisdiction to modify even if the other party and the child have left the issuing state. The drafters concluded that extending the modification jurisdiction of the initial forum was appropriate so that the party who remained in the United States would not be obligated to "play away" in a foreign court.[136] A party residing outside the United

States in this situation has the option of seeking modification in the issuing state under § 611(f), or in the state where the other party or child currently reside under § 611(a)(1).[137]

The operation of these provisions is illustrated by *State v. Beasley,* which began with a child-support order entered by a court in the state of Georgia. After the father moved to Louisiana and the mother and child relocated to Germany, the order was registered for enforcement in Louisiana. Under the "play away" rule in § 611(a)(1), the court in Louisiana had no jurisdiction to entertain the father's request for modification of the order.[138] The father could return to the court in Georgia, however, under § 611(f).[139] Similarly, in *Grumme v. Grumme,* after an initial child-support order was entered in Guam, the mother moved to the United Kingdom with the child and the father moved to Mississippi. UIFSA would permit the mother to seek modification in either Guam, under § 611(f), or Mississippi, under § 611(a)(1).[140] If the father were to seek modification, UIFSA would allow him to file in Guam, under § 611(f), but not in Mississippi, based on § 611(a)(1).

UIFSA does not address directly the situation in which an order is entered by a foreign tribunal and the parties' subsequent relocation brings one to the United States and the other to a different foreign country. The foreign order can be registered and enforced in the United States under UIFSA, and it can be modified in the United States if the requirements of § 615 are satisfied. This will ordinarily allow a party residing outside the United States to register the order in the state where the other party resides and initiate modification proceedings there. A party living in the United States in a state where there is no basis to exercise personal jurisdiction over the other party may need to pursue a modification claim in the foreign country where the other party resides.

Modification Procedures

A party seeking to modify, or modify and enforce, a child-support order from another state or a foreign country should begin by registering the order if it is not already registered, along with or followed by a petition that specifies the grounds for the modification

---

Examples: Jurisdiction to Modify

- Mother and Father live in Country X when an administrative tribunal there enters a child-support order against Mother. Father later moves with the child to State A in the United States. Mother remains in Country X, which is a "foreign country" for purposes of UIFSA.

  1. If Father seeks a modification to increase child support in State A, the court must decline to hear the case on the basis that the tribunal in Country X has continuing exclusive jurisdiction. If the tribunal in Country X lacks or refuses to exercise jurisdiction to modify the order under its own law, UIFSA § 615 permits the court in State A to modify the order if it can obtain personal jurisdiction over Mother.

  2. If Mother seeks a modification to decrease support, she can proceed in Country X; or, if Country X lacks or refuses to exercise jurisdiction to modify the order, she can consent to jurisdiction in State A to have the order modified.

- Mother and Father are living in State A in the United States when a state court in A enters a child-support order against Father. Father later moves to State B, and Mother moves with the child to Country X. In this situation, the court in State A will retain jurisdiction to modify the original support order under UIFSA § 611(f). Mother also has the alternative of seeking modification in State B.

request.[141] With a child-support order from another state, this procedure is governed by UIFSA §§ 609–614; and with child-support orders from a foreign country, the procedure is governed by §§ 615–616. Special procedures for orders that fall under the Hague Convention are addressed below.

For interstate cases, UIFSA provides in § 611(c) that a state a tribunal "may not modify any aspect of a child-support order that may not be modified under the law of the issuing state, including the duration of the obligation of support."[142] Section 611(d) states that the duration of a child-support obligation is determined by the law of the state that issued the initial controlling child-support order. Thus, the age when child support terminates as a matter of law is controlled by the law of the original forum. Although the language in § 611(c) and (d) does not encompass orders from foreign countries, the broad policy of extending comparable treatment to foreign-country support orders suggests that courts should generally apply the same approach in international cases.

Establishing and Enforcing Child Support in Another Country

In many circumstances, individuals in the United States seeking to establish or enforce a support order against an individual living in another country will find it best to work with their local state child-support enforcement agency. For cases involving countries designated as foreign reciprocating countries at the federal level or those with which the state has established reciprocity, the state IV-D agencies have access to tools and relationships to facilitate establishment of paternity or child support for U.S. residents.[143] The same will be true for countries that participate in the Hague Maintenance Convention, once it comes into effect in the United States.

As an alternative, or when there is no reciprocity at the federal or state level, individuals may choose to retain foreign counsel to seek support in a country where it is possible to obtain jurisdiction over the support obligor. The Maintenance Convention preserves whatever rights may exist under local law to make this type of direct request to local authorities.[144] Whether or not individuals in the United States choose to work though the IV-D agencies, however, foreign law may provide a simplified process for the recognition and enforcement of U.S. support orders. All countries participating in the Hague Maintenance Convention will be obligated to recognize and enforce support orders within the terms of the Convention.[145]

Child-support laws of other countries are often quite different from the system in place in the United States. In some countries, determinations are made by courts vested with broad discretion to set an appropriate award; in others, the process is largely administrative and based on a formula or guideline. Many systems focus on assuring support at a basic subsistence level, rather than increasing awards as parental income increases.[146] The 2007 Maintenance Convention does not extend to choice-of-law questions, which are addressed in a separate Protocol on the Law Applicable to Maintenance Obligations.[147] Contracting States that do not join the Protocol are free to apply their own law in establishing support obligations, which is also the approach taken under the current U.S. bilateral child-support agreements. Under both the Maintenance Convention and the Protocol, the obligation of support applies to all children "regardless of the marital status of the parents."[148]

> **Resources: Comparative Child-Support Laws**
>
> These sources provide an introduction to child-support laws of other countries:
>
> Australia: GEOFF MONAHAN & LISA YOUNG, FAMILY LAW IN AUSTRALIA 389–474 (6th ed. 2006).
>
> Canada: JULIEN D. PAYNE & MARILYN A. PAYNE, CANADIAN FAMILY LAW 281–372 (2d ed. 2006).
>
> New Zealand: 1 FAMILY LAW IN NEW ZEALAND 259–370 (Dick Webb et al. eds., 13th ed. 2007).
>
> United Kingdom: NIGEL LOWE & GILLIAN DOUGLAS, BROMLEY'S FAMILY LAW (10th ed. 2007).
>
> When the Hague Maintenance Convention comes into force, "Country Profiles" with information about child-support laws in Contracting States will be available on the Hague Conference website at http://www.hcch.net (under "Conventions," "38," and "Country Profiles").

Additional remedies are available to obtain family support from an individual who is employed abroad by the U.S. government or a company based in the United States. The salary of a federal government employee may be garnished for purposes of enforcing a child or spousal support order.[149] For an individual on active military duty, it is also possible to obtain an involuntary allotment from military pay.[150] These remedies are subject to detailed federal regulations; information and assistance are available from the state child-support enforcement offices.[151] If the whereabouts of a U.S. citizen parent are unknown, child-support agencies may be able to obtain assistance in locating the parent from a U.S. embassy or consulate.[152] Lawyers initiating litigation against an individual living in another country should be careful to comply with the special requirements for serving process and taking evidence abroad, even if the respondent is a U.S. citizen, is serving in the U.S. military, or is employed by the U.S. government.

Bilateral Agreements

In those jurisdictions designated as "foreign reciprocating countries," establishment or enforcement of state child-support orders may be accomplished under a bilateral agreement or a declaration of reciprocity with the United States.[153] The federal statute permits the Secretary of State to declare any foreign country or political subdivision (such as a state or province) to be a foreign reciprocating country if it "has established, or undertakes to establish, procedures for the establishment and enforcement of duties of support owed to obligees who are residents of the United States."[154] These must include procedures "(i) for establishment of paternity, and for establishment of orders of support for children and custodial parents; and (ii) for enforcement of orders to provide support to children and custodial parents, including procedures for collection and appropriate distribution of support payments under such orders."[155] The procedures must be provided to residents of the United States at no cost, and there must be an agency of the foreign country designated as a Central Authority responsible for "(i) facilitating support enforcement in cases involving residents of the foreign country and residents of the United States; and (ii) ensuring compliance with the standards established pursuant to this subsection."[156] These agreements take a variety of forms; some include details on the logistics of administrative cooperation, and others contain a single paragraph declaring reciprocity.[157] Some include general provisions for recognizing and enforcing maintenance decisions that may also be useful in actions filed outside the administrative cooperation system.[158]

In addition to federal bilateral agreements, a state may enter into reciprocal arrangements with foreign jurisdictions that have not entered into a federal bilateral agreement with the United States. Originally framed by states as "parallel unilateral policy declarations" (or PUPDs) rather than treaties, these state declarations are now expressly authorized by federal law.[159] A number of foreign jurisdictions have entered into reciprocal arrangements with a large number of U.S. states; information on current state-level arrangements should be obtained from the child-support enforcement agency in the state where the support obligor resides.[160]

Multilateral Treaties and the 2007 Maintenance Convention

The United States is not a party to the 1956 United Nations Convention on the Recovery Abroad of Maintenance, also known as the New York Convention, which provided an early framework for cooperation in child-support cases. The United States also has not ratified a series of Hague maintenance conventions, concluded between 1956 and 1973, that address recognition and enforcement of child-support judgments and choice-of-law questions. These agreements remain in force in many jurisdictions, along with several important regional conventions. Although they are not applicable to cases involving parties in the United States, they may be useful in cases that involve two foreign countries.[161]

Negotiations carried out in The Hague from 2003 through 2007 produced the new Maintenance Convention, which builds on the prior international experience with multilateral and bilateral child-support agreements. The United States was actively involved in the negotiations and is proceeding toward ratification.[162] The negotiations also produced a separate Protocol on the Law Applicable to Maintenance Obligations, which the United States does not intend to ratify.[163]

Working with the Hague Maintenance Convention

The 2007 Maintenance Convention establishes a system of administrative cooperation for international child-support cases similar to the interstate support enforcement program in the United States. The OCSE will be the U.S. Central Authority for the Convention.[164] In addition to its administrative cooperation scheme, the Maintenance Convention mandates recognition and enforcement of child and spousal support orders from Contracting States. This may be accomplished either through the Central Authority system or by

---

Hague Maintenance Convention

Hague Convention of 23 November 2007 on the International Recovery of Child Support and Other Forms of Family Maintenance, *reprinted in* 47 I.L.M. 257 (2008).

See also ALEGRIA BORRÁS & JENNIFER DEGELING, EXPLANATORY REPORT, CONVENTION OF 23 NOVEMBER 2007 ON THE INTERNATIONAL RECOVERY OF CHILD SUPPORT AND OTHER FORMS OF FAMILY MAINTENANCE (2009).

The full text and current information for the Maintenace Convention are available from the Hague Conference web site at http://www.hcch.net (under "Conventions" and "38").

means of a direct request to the appropriate tribunal or other competent authority in the jurisdiction where enforcement is sought. Typically, a direct request will involve a lawsuit filed by private counsel.[165] The recognition and enforcement provisions of the Convention also apply to spousal support orders.

The administrative cooperation provisions of the Convention apply to "maintenance obligations arising from a parent-child relationship towards a person under the age of 21 years" and to recognition and enforcement of any spousal support order that is tied to a child-support obligation.[166] By reservation, Contracting States may limit application of the Convention to persons under age 18; and by declaration, States may extend its application to maintenance obligations arising from other family relationships.[167]

Administrative Cooperation

Under Article 6, Central Authorities transmit and receive applications under the Maintenance Convention and initiate or facilitate the institution of proceedings in respect of these applications. In addition, the Central Authority must take "all appropriate measures" to provide other assistance, such as help in finding legal assistance, locating the creditor or debtor, and obtaining information about the parties' financial circumstances as well as in encouraging amicable solutions, facilitating ongoing enforcement of support payments including arrears, facilitating the collection and transfer of maintenance payments, facilitating obtaining of documentary or other evidence, assisting with establishing parentage where necessary for the establishment of maintenance, instituting or facilitating provisional measures to secure the outcome of a pending application, and facilitating service of documents. Some of these measures, such as help in locating the debtor or creditor or establishing paternity, may be requested by the Central Authority or another Contracting State even when no application is pending.[168]

Applications Available under the Maintenance Convention

Under Article 10 of the Convention, a support creditor in a requesting state may apply for

- recognition or recognition and enforcement of a child support order;

- enforcement of a support order made or recognized in the requested state;

- establishment of a new support order in the requested State where there is no existing order, including where necessary an order establishing parentage;

- establishment of a new support order when recognition and enforcement of an order is not possible, or is refused, under the Convention in the requested state;

- modification of a support order made in the requested state;

- modification of a support order made in a country other than the requested state.[170]

A support debtor in a requesting state against whom there is an existing maintenance decision may apply for

- recognition of a decision, or an equivalent procedure leading to the suspension, or limiting the enforcement, of a previous decision in the requested state;

- modification of a decision made in the requested state;

- modification of a decision made in a country other than the requested state.[171]

Applications begin with the Central Authority in the Contracting State where the applicant resides, referred to as the "state of origin" or the "requesting state," and are sent to the Central Authority of the requested State.[169] Article 10 identifies the range of applications that may be made through the Central Authorities and specifies that these applications "shall be determined under the law of the requested state."[172] Support creditors and support debtors are both able to make applications through the Central Authority system.

Article 14 provides that the authorities in the state where services are requested "shall provide applicants with effective access to procedures, including enforcement and appeal procedures," including free legal assistance. The obligation to provide free legal assistance extends to all child-support applications made through the Central Authorities, with a few narrow exceptions.[173] Each Central Authority is responsible for bearing its own costs.

Recognition and Enforcement under the Convention

The Convention rules regarding recognition and enforcement of child-support decisions apply to cases filed directly through private counsel as well as cases handled through the Central Authority system. According to Article 19(1), the obligation of recognition and enforcement extends to all decisions "rendered by a judicial or administrative authority in respect of a maintenance obligation," including a "settlement or agreement concluded before or approved by such an authority." The decision "may include automatic adjustment by indexation and a requirement to pay arrears, retroactive maintenance or interest and a determination of costs or expenses." The same obligation extends to recognition and enforcement of private "maintenance arrangements" as defined in the Convention.[174]

A child-support decision made in one Contracting State must be recognized and enforced in other Contracting States pursuant to Article 20 if the respondent was habitually resident in the State of origin at the time proceedings were instituted, or if the respondent submitted to the tribunal's jurisdiction, or if the child for whom maintenance was ordered was habitually resident in the state of origin at the time proceedings were instituted, provided that the respondent lived with the child in that state or resided in that state and provided support for the child there. In addition, Article 20 provides several bases for recognition and enforcement of support orders that are optional, in the sense that Contracting States may make a reservation declining to recognize and enforce decrees on these grounds.[175] The United States intends to make this reservation, since jurisdiction on these other grounds would be inconsistent with our norms of due process.[176] Under Article 20(3), a Contracting State that has made this reservation must nevertheless recognize and enforce a maintenance decision "if its law would in similar factual circumstances" have conferred jurisdiction to make the decision.[177]

Article 22 enumerates the grounds on which recognition and enforcement of a maintenance decision may be refused. These include a lack of notice,[178] fraud "in connection with a matter of procedure,"[179] grounds that address the possibility of multiple proceedings or inconsistent determinations,[180] and a more general provision that recognition and enforcement may be refused if it is "manifestly incompatible with the public policy ("ordre public") of the State addressed."[181] In addition, recognition and enforcement may be refused if the decision violates the limits in Article 18 on modification of an earlier decision.[182]

Examples: Articles 20 and 22

- M is the unmarried mother of a young child, who was born in Country X and is habitually resident there. The child's father, F, has never been present in Country X and now lives in Country Y. Both countries have ratified or acceded to the Maintenance Convention. If M obtains a paternity and child-support order in Country X, that order may be recognized and enforced in Country Y under Article 20, unless Country Y has made the reservation permitted under Article 20.

- Father lives together with Mother and her child in Country X for several years. Mother and Father then separate, and Father moves to Country Y. Both countries have ratified or acceded to the Maintenance Convention. Mother obtains an administrative determination of paternity and child support in Country X, which is then sent to Country Y. The authorities in Country Y may refuse recognition and enforcement under Article 22 if Father did not receive notice of the proceedings in Country X.

Under the Maintenance Convention, recognition and enforcement of a support order is governed by the law of the State addressed, subject to the Convention's specific requirements as to notice, the documents that may be required from an applicant, grounds on which registration may be refused, and opportunity for challenge and appeal.[183] Authorities in the requested state are bound by the findings of fact on which the authorities in the state of origin based its jurisdiction,[184] and the Convention stipulates that there shall be no review of the merits of a decision.[185] The physical presence of the child or the applicant may not be required in a proceeding for recognition and enforcement,[186] and the State addressed must provide at least the same range of enforcement methods for cases under the Convention as are available in domestic cases.[187] One advantage of proceeding under the Convention is that authorities may not require formalities such as legalization.[188] A Contracting State may require that an application and related documents must be translated into one of its official languages or another language it has indicated it will accept in a declaration made pursuant to the Convention.[189]

One goal of the Convention was to streamline the procedures for recognition and enforcement of child-support orders that have imposed serious burdens and delays in some countries. Article 23 addresses this concern with a set of common procedural requirements designed to assure that cases are handled expeditiously. Contracting States are permitted, however, to declare that they will apply an alternative procedure for recognition and enforcement.[190]

Support Modification under the Convention

When a maintenance decision has been made in a Contracting State where the creditor is habitually resident, Article 18 provides that proceedings to modify the decision generally cannot be brought by the debtor in any other Contracting State as long as the creditor remains habitually resident in the nation where the decision was made, subject to several exceptions.[191] This is partially consistent with the UIFSA approach, which recognizes the continuing exclusive jurisdiction to modify of the court that entered the order when either party remains a resident of the issuing state.[192] In contrast to the UIFSA approach, however, Article 18 would not recognize continuing exclusive jurisdiction over an order entered in the United States when an obligor/debtor remains in the United States but the obligee/creditor has moved to another Convention country. Under Article 18, jurisdic-

---

Examples: Article 18

Mother and Father are habitual residents of Country X when Mother obtains a child-support determination against Father in Country X. Mother and Father are originally from Country Y, and both countries have ratified or acceded to the Maintenance Convention.

- If Mother relocates to Country Y with the child, and Father remains in Country X, Article 18 permits the Mother to obtain a modification of the prior support determination from a tribunal in Country Y.

- If Mother and the child remain in Country X, and Father relocates to Country Y, Article 18 prohibits the Father from obtaining a new order or a modification of the prior determination from a tribunal in Country Y, unless one of the Article 18 exceptions applies.

---

tion to modify an order entered in the United States would continue in the United States even if the creditor moves to a different U.S. state, and UIFSA § 611(f) helps assure that a forum will be available in the United States in this situation.[193]

Handling Convention Cases in the United States

The Maintenance Convention will be implemented in the United States through UIFSA 2008. The new UIFSA Article 7 includes specialized rules and definitions for Convention cases.[194] Article 7 builds on the other provisions of UIFSA, but in the event of a conflict between the UIFSA's general provisions and Article 7, the terms of Article 7 control.[195] The Article 7 provisions for recognition and enforcement apply to cases handled through the

---

Grounds for Refusing Recognition and Enforcement under the Convention

Under UIFSA § 708(b), state authorities may refuse recognition and enforcement of a support order presented under the Maintenance Convention if

- recognition and enforcement of the order is manifestly incompatible with public policy, including minimum standards of due process, which include notice and an opportunity to be heard;

- the issuing tribunal lacked personal jurisdiction consistent with UIFSA § 201;

- the order is not enforceable in the issuing country;

- the order was obtained by fraud in connection with a matter of procedure;

- a record transmitted in accordance with UIFSA § 706 lacks authenticity or integrity;

- a proceeding between the same parties and having the same purpose is pending in the state and that proceeding was the first to be filed;

- the order is incompatible with a more recent support order involving the same parties, if the more recent support order is entitled to recognition and enforcement under UIFSA;

- payment, to the extent alleged arrears have been paid in whole or in part;

- in a case of a default judgment, the respondent did not have proper notice of the proceedings and an opportunity to be heard; or proper notice of the order and an opportunity to challenge or appeal the order before a tribunal; or

- the order was made in violation of the modification rules in UIFSA § 711.[196]

Example: Obtaining a New Order

M is the unmarried mother of a young child, who was born in Country X and is habitually resident there. The child's father, F, has never been present in Country X and now lives in State A in the United States. M obtains a paternity and child-support order from a tribunal in Country X, which has no basis for exercising personal jurisdiction over F. Assuming that both Country X and the United States have ratified or acceded to the Maintenance Convention, and that the United States has made the reservation permitted under Article 20, the order from Country X need not be enforced under UIFSA § 708 and Article 20 of the Maintenance Convention. The court in State A must allow M time to request establishment of a new child-support order.

Central Authority system and also to cases initiated by a petitioner who chooses to file a direct request with the state court or other tribunal.[197] Section 705(a) clarifies that a petitioner may also seek establishment or modification of a support order or determination of parentage of a child by filing directly with the tribunal and proceeding under state law.

Generally, the procedures for recognition and enforcement of child-support orders under the Maintenance Convention are the same as the UIFSA procedures for any out-of-state child-support orders, beginning with registration of the order. In cases under the Convention, the documents required and the timelines for contesting registration are slightly different. In addition, § 708(b) provides an exclusive list of grounds on which a state tribunal may refuse recognition and enforcement of a registered Convention support order, tracking the provisions of Article 22.

If a state tribunal does not recognize the order for reasons of personal jurisdiction, fraud, or a lack of notice and opportunity for a hearing, UIFSA and the Convention provide an important protection: The tribunal may not dismiss the proceeding without allowing a reasonable time for a party to request establishment of a new support order.[198] If the application to the tribunal for recognition and enforcement was made by a state agency, the agency must take "all appropriate measures" to request a new child-support order.[199] These provisions help address the problems that arise when foreign support orders are based on jurisdictional grounds that are not recognized in the United States. Even if the foreign order cannot be enforced, a new order may be entered to ensure that child support will be paid prospectively.

Hague Maintenance Convention Contracting States (Table indicates signing of Convention as of November 15, 2011.)

(Countries marked with * are covered by the signature of the European Union, and countries in italics had not yet completed ratification or accession)

Albania	Germany*	*Poland**
Austria*	Greece*	*Portugal**
Belgium*	Hungary*	Romania*
Bosnia and Herzegovina	Ireland*	Slovakia*
Bulgaria*	Italy*	Slovenia*
Burkina Faso	Latvia*	Spain*
Cyprus*	Lithuania*	Sweden*
Czech Republic*	Luxembourg*	Ukraine
Estonia*	Malta*	United Kingdom*
Finland*	Netherlands*	United States
France*	Norway	

Notes

1. Unif. Interstate Family Support Act (UIFSA) (amended 2008), 9 U.L.A. (pt. 1B) 72 (Supp. 2011). Enacting UIFSA is a requirement of participation in the federal IV-D program. *See* 42 U.S.C. § 666(f) (2010); *see generally* 42 U.S.C. § 654 (2010).
2. United Nations Convention on the Rights of the Child (CRC), art. 27, G.A. Res. 44/25 (Annex), U.N. GAOR, 44th Sess., Supp. No. 49, at 166, U.N. Doc. A/RES/44/49 (1990), *reprinted in* 30 I.L.M. 1448 (1989).
3. *See* 42 U.S.C. § 659a (2010). Information on international child support is available from the websites listed above for the Department of State and the Department of Health and Human Resources.
4. Authority for state bilateral agreements is provided in 42 U.S.C. § 659a(d): "States may enter into reciprocal arrangements for the establishment and enforcement of support obligations with foreign countries that are not the subject of a declaration pursuant to subsection (a) of this section, to the extent consistent with Federal law." *See generally* Office of Child Support v. Sholan, 782 A.2d 1199 (Vt. 2001).
5. Hague Convention on the International Recovery of Child Support and Other Forms of Family Maintenance, Nov. 23, 2007, *reprinted in* 47 I.L.M. 257 (2008) [hereinafter Maintenance Convention]. *See also* Hague Convention on the International Recovery of Child Support and Family Maintenance, S. Treaty Doc. No. 110-21 (2008).
6. *See generally* Battle Rankin Robinson, *Integrating an International Convention into State Law: The UIFSA Experience*, 43 Fam. L.Q. 61, 73 (2009).

    Previous versions of UIFSA were adopted by the National Conference of Commissioners on Uniform State Laws (NCCUSL) in 1992, 1996, and 2001. States were required to enact the 1996 version and were permitted but not required to enact the 2001 version. Each set of amendments introduced significant changes to the statute. For an explanation of the evolution in UIFSA and its treatment of foreign support orders, see the Prefatory Note and Comments published with UIFSA 2008, *available at* 43 Fam. L.Q. 75, 81–86 (2009) [hereinafter *Comments*].
7. The Office of Child Support Enforcement in the Department of Health and Human Services makes detailed information available about the program and the state offices on its website, http://www.acf.hhs.gov/programs/cse/. There is only a nominal fee for these services.

8. *E.g.*, Office of Child Support Enforcement v. Gauvey, 241 S.W.3d 771 (Ark. Ct. App. 2006) (Office of Child Support Enforcement can enforce spousal support order included in German divorce decree). *See* 42 U.S.C. § 654(4)(B) (2010) (state plan for child and spousal support must provide that state will enforce any support obligation established with respect to a child and the child's custodial parent).

9. *See* 42 U.S.C. § 663 (2010) (making services of Federal Parent Locator Service established under 42 U.S.C. § 653 available to determine whereabouts of parent or child to make or enforce custody or visitation determination or enforce state or federal law with respect to the unlawful taking or restraint of a child).

10. UIFSA § 307(b). If a support order has already been established, an agency in the state where registration of the order is requested for enforcement or modification will have additional obligations described in § 307(c) and (d).

11. *See* UIFSA § 102(4) (amended 2008), 9 U.L.A. (pt. 1B) 76 (Supp. 2010): "'Duty of support' means an obligation imposed or imposable by law to provide support for a child, spouse, or former spouse, including an unsatisfied obligation to provide support." *See also supra* note 8 and accompanying text.

12. UIFSA § 309.

13. *See* UIFSA §§ 105(a), 301(b). *See, e.g.*, Edwards v. Dominick, 815 So. 2d 236 (La. Ct. App. 2002).

14. *See* UIFSA § 307(a) Alternative B; *see also* 42 U.S.C. § 654 (32) (2010).

15. *E.g., In re* A.K., 72 P.3d 402 (Colo. App. 2003) (approving child-support agency's provision of services under state statute to mother and child who lived in Russia). Some authorities interpreted the prior wording of the federal statute to require that state IV-D services be available to any applicant without regard to residency or citizenship. *See, e.g.*, State v. Villasenor del Castillo, No. A04-1528, 2005 WL 1331220 (Minn. Ct. App. 2005) (unpublished opinion). Cf. Lajennesse v. Mo. Dep't Soc. Servs., 350 S.W.3d 842 (Mo. Ct. App. 2011).

16. *See* 42 U.S.C. § 666(a).

17. *See id.; see also* 42 U.S.C. § 652(k) and 22 C.F.R. § 51.60(a)(2) (authority to deny passports for child-support arrearages of $2,500 or more).

18. *See* 18 U.S.C. § 228, *applied in* United States v. Kerley, 544 F.3d 172 (2d Cir. 2008).

19. *See* 42 U.S.C. § 652.

20. *See* 42 U.S.C. § 663.

21. *See* 1 HOMER H. CLARK, JR., THE LAW OF DOMESTIC RELATIONS IN THE UNITED STATES § 7.2 (2d ed. 1987).

22. *See* Gomez v. Perez, 409 U.S. 535 (1973).

23. Determination of Parentage is discussed in Chapter 5.

24. Support continues to age 21 in a handful of states. *See* ALA. CODE § 26-1-1 (2010); CAL. FAM. CODE § 3901 (2010); IND. CODE ANN. § 31-16-6-6 (2010); MASS. GEN. LAWS ch. 208, § 28 (2010); N.Y. FAM. CT. LAW § 413 (2010).

25. Annotation, *Responsibility of Noncustodial Divorced Parent to Pay for, or Contribute to, Costs of Child's College Education*, 99 A.L.R.3d 322 (1980 & Supp.).

26. *E.g.*, CAL. FAM. CODE § 3910 (2010), IOWA CODE § 598.1(9) (2010); MASS. GEN. LAWS ch. 123B, § 16 (2010). *See generally* Sande L. Buhai, *Parental Support of Adult Children with Disabilities*, 91 MINN. L. REV. 710 (2007).

27. *Cf.* Stein v. Stein, 831 S.W.2d 684 (Mo. Ct. App. 1992) (holding that husband was not liable for support of Korean child adopted by wife alone; nonbiological and non-adoptive parent may be obligated to support a child based on contract or estoppel theories).

28. State child-support guidelines are required under 42 U.S.C. § 667 (2010).

29. *See* Gladis v. Gladisova, 856 A.2d 703, 708–14 (Md. 2004) (citing cases). *See also In re* A.K., 72 P.3d 402, 404–05 (Colo. App. 2003) (outlining factors that trial court must consider in determining whether to deviate from guidelines based on different cost of living in another country); Nicholson v. Nicholson, 747 A.2d 588, 591 (Me. 2000) (concluding that higher cost of living in England was offset by cost of visits between Maine and England).

30. *See* Ibrahim v. Aziz, 953 A.2d 508, 509 (N.J. Super. Ct. App. Div. 2008) ("Given the differences between wages in Egypt and wages in New Jersey, the trial court erred in imputing to defendant income that he could have earned in New Jersey.").

31. 123 P.3d 1072 (Alaska 2005). *See also* RESTATEMENT (THIRD) OF FOREIGN RELATIONS LAW § 823 cmt. e (1987).
32. *See, e.g.*, Harris v. Harris, 922 N.E.2d 626, 635–38 (Ind. Ct. App. 2010). *Kulko v. Superior Court of California*, 436 U.S. 84, 91 (1978).
33. *Kulko*, 436 U.S. at 91. The constitutional standards for personal jurisdiction are discussed in more detail in Chapter 1 and Chapter 4.
34. *Burnham v. Superior Court*, 495 U.S. 604 (1990).
35. *See, e.g.*, Luxembourg *ex rel.* Ribeiro v. Canderas, 768 A.2d 283 (N.J. Super. Ct. Ch. Div. 2000); *Kulko*, 436 U.S. at 93. *See also* Kevin N. Clermont and John R.B. Palmer Exorbitant Jurisdiction, 58 ME. L. REV. 474 (2006).
36. *See* UIFSA § 301(b):

    An individual [petitioner] or a support enforcement agency may initiate a proceeding authorized under this [act] by filing a [petition] in an initiating tribunal for forwarding to a responding tribunal or by filing a [petition] or a comparable pleading directly in a tribunal of another state or a foreign country which has or can obtain personal jurisdiction over the [respondent].

    See also Marriage of Richardson, 102 Cal. Rptr. 3d 391 (Cal. Ct. App. 2009) (holding that a wife living in Japan could pursue custody and child-support orders in California, where her husband lived, when he initiated divorce proceedings there); *In re* A.K., 72 P.3d 402, 404 (Colo. App. 2003) (approving action filed by state child-support agency on behalf of mother and child living in Russia); Ratner v. Ratner, 342 N.Y.S.2d 58 (N.Y. Fam. Ct. 1973) (finding court has jurisdiction over support petition filed on behalf of children living in Israel).
37. *See infra* notes 56–58 and accompanying text.
38. UIFSA § 207. UIFSA § 201(b) prohibits a court from taking jurisdiction to modify a child-support order of another state or foreign country unless the requirements of Section 611 or 615 are met. *See infra* notes 132–40 and accompanying text.
39. 993 S.W.2d 147, 151 (Tex. App. 1999). The opinion suggested that respondent also had "significant, purposeful and direct contacts with Texas related to this suit," including the fact that the child was conceived in the state, and that exercising jurisdiction "comports with fair play and substantial justice." *Id.* at 153. *See also* Flores v. Melo-Palacios, 921 S.W.2d 399 (Tex. Ct. App. 1996).
40. 703 S.E.2d 248 (Va. Ct. App. 2011).
41. 547 N.W.2d 700, 702–03 (Minn. Ct. App. 1996).
42. 813 N.Y.S.2d 463 (N.Y. App. Div. 2006). Because the putative father died before commencement of the proceeding, service was effected on his father, mother, and brother in Greece as personal representatives of his estate. *Id.* at 755.
43. 497 S.E.2d 881, 885–86 (Va. Ct. App. 1998).
44. *Id.* at 886.
45. *Compare* Sneed v. Sneed, 842 N.E.2d 1095 (Ohio Ct. App. 2005) (exercising jurisdiction over child-support claim where petitioner testified to a pattern of abuse), *and* Marriage of Malwitz, 99 P.3d 56, 61 (Colo. 2004) (court had jurisdiction in light of "course of conduct designed to terrorize [mother] and her family"), *with* McNabb *ex rel.* Foshee v. McNabb, 65 P.3d 1068 (Kan. Ct. App. 2003) (no jurisdiction when mother relocated to Kansas a year after an episode of physical abuse), *and* Windsor v. Windsor, 700 N.E.2d 838 (Mass. App. Ct. 1998) (no basis for long-arm jurisdiction where complaint offered no specific facts to support claim of abusive treatment).
46. UIFSA § 210 (amended 2008), 9 U.L.A. (pt. 1B) 95 (Supp. 2010).
47. *Id.; see* UIFSA §§ 316–318.
48. *See infra* notes 67–77 and accompanying text.
49. *See* UIFSA § 14:

    (a) Participation by a [petitioner] in a proceeding under this [act] before a responding tribunal, whether in person, by private attorney, or through services provided by the support enforcement agency, does not confer personal jurisdiction over the [petitioner] in another proceeding.

(b) A [petitioner] is not amenable to service of civil process while physically present in this state to participate in a proceeding under this [act].

(c) The immunity granted by this section does not extend to civil litigation based on acts unrelated to a proceeding under this [act] committed by a party while physically present in this state to participate in the proceeding.

        Note that "responding state" is defined in § 102(23) to include a tribunal in either a state in which a petition for support or parentage is filed or a state to which a petition has been forwarded for filing from another state. *See also* § 305(d), which states that "A responding tribunal of this state may not condition the payment of a support order issued under this act upon compliance by a party with provisions for visitation."

50. UIFSA § 304. A similar procedure was available under the prior uniform law. *See* Halina V. v. Juan P.V., 578 N.Y.S.2d 98 (N.Y. Fam. Ct. 1991); Poland *ex rel.* Bieniek v. Wegrzyn, 517 N.W.2d 81 (Minn. Ct. App. 1994); Bieniek v. Wegrzyn, No. C2-95-2272, 1996 WL 146735 (Minn. Ct. App. 1996) (unpublished).

51. *E.g.*, H.M. v. E.T., 930 N.E.2d 206 (N.Y. 2010) (ordering determination of parentage on request of Canadian authorities).

52. UIFSA § 305(b).

53. UIFSA § 401(a).

54. UIFSA § 201(a). *See supra* note 49. Direct filing is also available for proceedings to determine parentage. *See* UIFSA § 402.

55. 815 So. 2d 236 (La. Ct. App. 2002).

56. "Home state" is defined in UIFSA § 102(8) as:

the state or foreign country in which a child lived with a parent or a person acting as parent for at least six consecutive months immediately preceding the time of filing of a [petition] or comparable pleading for support and, if a child is less than six months old, state or foreign country in which the child lived from birth with any of them. A period of temporary absence of any of them is counted as part of the six-month or other period.

See also Comments, *supra* note 6, at 101.

57. *Cf.* Cahen-Vorburger v. Vorburger, 725 N.Y.S.2d 343 (N.Y. App. Div. 2001). Although *Prizzia v. Prizzia*, 707 S.E.2d 461 (Va. Ct. App. 2011), does not consider UIFSA, the facts of the case describe a situation in which § 204 would be applicable. Instead, the court concluded that the trial court had jurisdiction to award child support "as an equitable concomitant to its jurisdiction over child custody."

58. *See, e.g.*, Marriage of Richardson, 102 Cal. Rptr. 3d 391, 393 (Cal. Ct. App. 2009).

59. UIFSA § 202.

60. UIFSA § 205(a)(1). In addition, the tribunal's order must be the controlling order under § 207.

61. UIFSA § 205(a)(2). Conversely, a court may not exercise continuing exclusive jurisdiction if the parties have consented to modification in another tribunal or if its order is not the controlling order. § 205(b).

62. UIFSA § 205(c).

63. UIFSA § 612(1), (2). In earlier versions of UIFSA, this rule was located in § 205(c). *See, e.g.*, Bouquety v. Bouquety, 933 So. 2d 610 (Fla. Dist. Ct. App. 2006) (concluding that Florida court retained jurisdiction to enforce order as to amounts accruing before modification by another tribunal); Youssefi v. Youssefi, 744 A.2d 662, 667–70 (N.J. Super. Ct. App. Div. 2000) (state tribunal retained jurisdiction to enforce child-support order after all parties left the state).

64. UIFSA §§ 205(d), 206(a).

65. On the UIFSA approach to modification jurisdiction, see *infra* notes 129–40 and accompanying text.

66. 708 S.E.2d 273 (Ga. 2011). This was true even though she had lived out of the country for a period of time and had commenced an action for reciprocal enforcement of the support arrearages in the United Kingdom.

67. Mullane v. Cent. Hanover Bank & Trust Co., 339 U.S. 306, 314 (1950).

68. *See* Willmer v. Willmer, 51 Cal. Rptr. 3d 10, 15–18 (Cal. Ct. App. 2006) (enforcing German support order based on service by publication).

69. UIFSA § 316(a).

70. *E.g.*, Youssefi v. Youssefi, 744 A.2d 662, 667–67 (N.J. Super. Ct. App. Div. 2000) (service by mail on respondent in child-support enforcement action permitted under Article 10(a) of the Hague Service Convention).

71. This may include "filing fees, reasonable attorney's fees, other costs, and necessary travel and other reasonable expenses incurred by the obligee and the obligee's witnesses." § 313.

72. *See* UIFSA § 401(b). A temporary order may be entered against an individual who is a presumed father of the child, petitioning to have his paternity adjudicated, identified as the father of the child through genetic testing, an alleged father who has declined to submit to genetic testing, shown by clear and convincing evidence to be the father of the child, an acknowledged father of the child under state law, the mother of the child, or an individual who has been previously ordered to pay support if the order has not been reversed or vacated. *Id.*

73. UIFSA § 316(f). *See also* Ratner v. Ratner, 342 N.Y.S.2d 58 (N.Y. Fam. Ct. 1973) (allowing testimony of petitioner in Israel to be presented by deposition); Sandra S. v. Glenn M.S., 506 N.Y.S.2d 259, 263 (N.Y. Fam. Ct. 1986) (same).

74. UIFSA § 317.

75. *See generally* Chapter 1.

76. Hague Convention of 18 March 1970 on the Taking of Evidence Abroad in Civil and Commercial Matters, 25 U.S.T. 2555, T.I.A.S. 7444, 847 U.N.T.S. 231, *appended to* 28 U.S.C. § 1781, *reprinted in* 18 I.L.M. 37 (1969).

77. *E.g.*, *In re* Letter of Request from Amstgericht Ingolstadt, Fed. Republic of Ger., 82 F.3d 590 (4th Cir. 1996); *In re* Letter Rogatory from the Nedenes Dist. Court, Nor., 216 F.R.D. 277 (S.D.N.Y. 2003).

78. Unif. Foreign Money-Judgments Recognition 1962 Act § 1(2), 13 U.L.A. (pt. 2) 49–73 (2002)(UFMJRA). This is also true under Unif. Foreign-Country Money Judgments Recognition Act § 3(b)(3), 13 U.L.A. (pt. 2) 12 (Supp. 2010) (UFCMJRA). Some states apply the UFMJRA to family support obligations; *see, e.g.*, Mich. Comp. Laws § 691.1151 & Mich. Stat. Ann. § 27.955(1), *applied in* Dart v. Dart, 568 N.W.2d 353 (Mich. Ct. App. 1997). The statute is discussed in Chapter 1 and Chapter 4.

79. UIFSA § 102(26). This definition includes the Northern Mariana Islands, American Samoa, and Guam, but the Northern Marianas and American Samoa do not currently participate in the IV-D program. Previous versions of UIFSA included some foreign countries within the definition of "state," but this is no longer the case with UIFSA 2008.

80. UIFSA § 105 provides that the statute applies to "a support proceeding involving: (1) a foreign support order; (2) a foreign tribunal; or (3) an obligee, obligor, or child residing in a foreign country." This provision was introduced with the 2008 revision of the statute, but the 1996 and 2001 versions of UIFSA also applied to cases with foreign elements. *See infra* note 86.

81. The definitions of "foreign support order" in section 102(6) and of "foreign tribunal" in section 102(7) incorporate the definition of "foreign country."

82. *See, e.g.*, Kalia v. Kalia, 783 N.E.2d 623, 632–33 (Ohio Ct. App. 2002) (holding that India was not a "state" for purposes of UIFSA and enforcing spousal and child-support orders based on comity).

83. *See* 42 U.S.C. § 659a (2010); U.S. Dep't of State, Notice of Declaration of Foreign Countries as Reciprocating Countries for the Enforcement of Family Support (Maintenance) Obligations, 73 Fed. Reg. 72,555–601 (Nov. 28, 2008). *See, e.g.*, Gladis v. Gladisova, 856 A.2d 703, 706 n. 1 (Md. 2004) (affirming support award to foreign petitioner represented by local support enforcement agency and noting that Slovak Republic is a foreign reciprocating jurisdiction under federal law).

84. *E.g.*, Willmer v. Willmer, 51 Cal. Rptr. 3d 10 (Cal. Ct. App. 2006) (enforcing German child and spousal support based on reciprocal relationship between Germany and California).

85. The web page of the National Child Support Enforcement Association (NCSEA) includes contact information and forms and procedures for a number of these countries at http://www.ncsea.org (under "International" and "U.S. Website Visitors").

86. 550 S.E.2d 792, 794–95 (N.C. Ct. App. 2001). *See also* Dep't of Human Servs. v. Shelnut (*Shelnut I*), 772 So. 2d 1041, 1044–45 (Miss. 2000) (citing Canada's Reciprocal Enforcement of Maintenance Orders Act, 1996). As originally adopted, UIFSA included within its definition of the term "state" any foreign jurisdiction that "has enacted a law or established procedures for issuance and enforcement of support orders which are substantially similar" to the procedures in effect under UIFSA or the prior uniform reciprocal support enforcement acts. § 102(21) 9 U.L.A. (pt. 1B) 177 (2005).

87. 783 N.E.2d 623, 632–33 (Ohio Ct. App. 2002). *See also In re* V.L.C., 225 S.W.3d 221, 227–28 (Tex. App. 2006) (no evidence presented that state of Sinaloa, Mexico, had reciprocal child-support agreement at the federal or state level or substantially similar procedures). Haker-Volkening v. Haker, 547 S.E.2d 127 (N.C. Ct. App. 2001) (petitioner failed to establish that procedures in Switzerland were substantially similar to those under UIFSA). Many similar cases were decided under the prior uniform laws; *see, e.g.,* cases cited *supra* note 50.

88. *See infra* notes 194–99 and accompanying text.

89. State law may also provide other procedures for domesticating and enforcing a foreign support judgment. *See, e.g.,* Salles v. Salles, 928 So. 2d 1 (La. Ct. App. 2004) (entering Louisiana judgment to enforce German child-support deeds).

90. UIFSA § 602.

91. *See, e.g.,* Ugochukwu v. Ugochukwu, 627 S.E.2d 625 (N.C. Ct. App. 2006) (holding that submission of foreign support order is not sufficient to raise conflict-of-laws issue concerning law of that country and North Carolina).

92. UIFSA § 606 (b). Section 605 prescribes the information that must be included in the notice of registration of order, and if the notice does not include all of the required information, § 606 will not have this effect. *See, e.g.,* Marriage of Kohl, 778 N.E.2d 1169, 1176–77 (Ill. App. Ct. 2002) (§ 606 was not triggered when notice of registration for Israeli support order did not include time limit for requesting hearing).

93. *See, e.g.,* Dia v. Oakley, 217 P.3d 1010 (Kan. Ct. App. 2009) (registration of order confirmed when father failed to attend hearing he requested); Campbell v. Campbell, 917 A.2d 302 (N.J. Super. Ct. App. Div. 2007) (denying motion to vacate registration of Australian support order); Liuksila v. Stoll, 887 A.2d 501, 506–07 (D.C. 2005).

94. Because the definition of "foreign tribunal" in § 102(7) refers to a court, administrative agency, or quasi-judicial entity of a foreign country, it should be read as limited by the definition of "foreign country" in § 102(6). *See supra* notes 80–88 and accompanying text. Thus, an order issued by a tribunal in a nation that does not meet the test in § 102(6) would not be eligible for treatment as the controlling order under § 207.

95. UIFSA treats the duration of support as a nonmodifiable aspect of the controlling support order. *See* §§ 604, 611(c), discussed *infra* at note 142 and accompanying text.

96. *E.g.,* Foreman v. Foreman, 550 S.E.2d 792, 795 (N.C. Ct. App. 2001) (approving registration of English spousal support order); *see also Campbell,* 917 A.2d at 302 (denying motion to vacate registration of Australian child-support order).

97. *E.g.,* Schmitz v. Engstrom, 13 P.3d 38, 41–42 (Mont. 2000) (laches or equitable estoppel defenses not available); *cf.* Shelnut v. Dep't of Human Servs., 9 So. 3d 359, 364 (Miss. 2009) (no basis for concealment defense).

98. *See also* § 603(c).

99. *See* the discussion of *Kulko* at *supra* text accompanying note 33. *See generally* Robert G. Spector, *Toward an Accommodation of Divergent Standards for the Determination of Maintenance Obligations in Private International Law,* 36 Fam. L.Q. 273, 274–76 (2002).

100. 51 Cal. Rptr. 3d 10, 14–15 (Cal. Ct. App. 2006). *See also* Dep't of Healthcare and Family Servs. *ex rel.* Heard v. Heard, 916 N.E.2d 61 (Ill. App. Ct. 2009) (holding that German support order should not have been registered where German court did not have personal jurisdiction over support obligor under the *Kulko* test); Claire Lucia D. v. Russell Morris D., Jr., 842 N.Y.S.2d

361 (N.Y. App. Div. 2007) (service of process in England on respondent's appointed counsel was not sufficient to give English court in personam jurisdiction over respondent in support proceeding).

101. The court in *Willmer* also rejected the argument that service by publication in Germany was inadequate in the circumstances of the case; *see id.* at 15–18. *See also* Dep't of Human Servs. v. Shelnut (*Shelnut I*), 772 So. 2d 1041, 1044–47 (Miss. 2000) (respondent who did not appeal jurisdictional ruling of Canadian court barred by res judicata from subsequent challenge).

102. 768 A.2d 283 (N.J. Super. Ch. Div. 2000). Defendant had lived for six years with the plaintiff and their child in Portugal, where the child was conceived and born, before he moved to New Jersey. The court found that none of the bases of jurisdiction under UIFSA were satisfied, pointing out that the residence of the plaintiff and the child in Luxembourg were not a sufficient basis for jurisdiction under *Kulko* and other precedents. *Id.* at 287–88.

103. Marriage of Kohl, 778 N.E.2d 1169, 1177–81 (Ill. App. Ct. 2002); *cf.* State *ex rel.* Desselberg v. Peele, 523 S.E.2d 125 (N.C. Ct. App. 1999) (concluding that German decree was based on adequate service of process in the United States).

104. *See also* Office of Child Support v. Sholan, 782 A.2d 1199, 1203 (Vt. 2001) (holding that language of 42 U.S.C. § 659(a) "does not reflect in any way an intent by Congress to preempt state-level efforts at enforcement of foreign support orders"). As noted above, family support orders are expressly excluded from the UFMJRA. *See supra* note 78 and accompanying text.

Comity is not available in every state for enforcement of a foreign support judgment. *See, e.g.*, Nardi v. Segal, 234 N.E.2d 805 (Ill. App. Ct. 1967) (holding that Illinois state courts have no general powers of equity to enforce foreign decrees absent statutory authorization); *cf.* Wolff v. Wolff, 389 A.2d 413, 415–19 (Md. Ct. Spec. App. 1978).

105. *See supra* notes 80–88 and accompanying text.

106. Over time, these lists have been fluid, subject to change as more countries enter into federal-level bilateral agreements or move to join the Maintenance Convention.

107. *E.g.*, Sandra S. v. Glenn M.S., 506 N.Y.S.2d 259, 263–64 (N.Y. Fam. Ct. 1986).

108. 783 N.E.2d 623, 632–33 (Ohio Ct. App. 2002).

109. 159 U.S. 113, 143 (1895). Comity is discussed at greater length in Chapter 1 and Chapter 4.

110. If there was reasonable notice and a basis for jurisdiction, even a default judgment may be recognized based on comity. *See* Nicol v. Tanner, 256 N.W.2d 796, 801–03 (Minn. 1976).

111. *Cf.* Wolff v. Wolff, 389 A.2d 413, 415–19 (Md. Ct. Spec. App. 1978).

112. *E.g.*, M.H. v. M.G., 658 N.Y.S.2d 551 (N.Y. Fam. Ct. 1996).

113. *See id.* at 554; *see also* Manor v. Manor, 811 S.W.2d 497 (Mo. Ct. App. 1991); Sandra S. v. Glenn M.S., 506 N.Y.S.2d 259 (N.Y. Fam. Ct. 1986).

114. *E.g.*, Luxembourg *ex rel.* Ribeiro v. Canderas, 768 A.2d 283, 288–89 (N.J. Super. Ch. Div. 2000); Marriage of Kohl, 778 N.E.2d 1169, 1181 (Ill. App. Ct. 2002), Aranoff v. Aranoff, 642 N.Y.S.2d 49 (N.Y. App. Div. 1996).

115. Note, however, that a custodial parent's interference with the other parent's visitation is not generally regarded as a defense to the obligation to pay support. *See, e.g.*, Hambleton v. Palmer, 283 N.Y.S.2d 404 (N.Y. Fam. Ct. 1967).

116. *See* RESTATEMENT (THIRD) OF FOREIGN RELATIONS LAW § 482 cmt. f (1987) (scope of public policy defense).

117. 989 P.2d 558 (Wash. Ct. App. 1999). *See also In re* Purviance, No. 04-20665-TLM, 2005 WL 2178802, 55 Collier Bankr. Cas. 2d (MB) 692 (June 9, 2005) (unpublished). *Cf.* Dart v. Dart, 568 N.W.2d 353 (Mich. Ct. App. 1997) (English property division law is not repugnant to state's public policy).

118. Kalia v. Kalia, 783 N.E.2d 623, 630–32. *See also* Marriage of Lam, No. B139303, 2001 WL 1464507 (Cal. Ct. App. 2001) (unpublished) (declining to enforce Hong Kong consent order based on showing that wife's consent was product of duress).

119. 851 A.2d 983 (Pa. Super. Ct. 2004). *Pfeifer* is not clear on whether the German order was registered under UIFSA, but modification of arrearages would not be permissible under UIFSA unless there are grounds within § 607. *See supra* notes 96–103 and accompanying text.

120. RESTATEMENT (SECOND) OF CONFLICT OF LAWS § 98 cmt. f (1971, 1986 revision); RESTATEMENT (THIRD) OF FOREIGN RELATIONS LAW §§ 481–482 (1987). *See* Nicol v. Tanner, 256 N.W.2d 796, 796–801 (Minn. 1976) (rejecting reciprocity requirement in case involving German paternity and child-support judgment); Office of Child Support v. Sholan, 782 A.2d 1199 (Vt. 2001) (same).

121. *See also* CLARK, *supra* note 21, § 7.7 (citing statutes imposing support duties on grandparents and grandchildren or brothers and sisters).

122. *E.g.*, CAL. FAM. CODE § 4400 (2010); IOWA CODE §§ 252.2, 252.5 (2010). *See generally* Shannon Frank Edelstone, *Filial Responsibility: Can the Legal Duty to Support Our Parents Be Effectively Enforced?* 36 FAM. L.Q. 501 (2002).

123. This duty may be imposed by case law or statute. *See, e.g.*, Feinberg v. Diamant, 389 N.E.2d 998 (Mass. 1979); CAL. FAM. CODE § 3910 (2010) ("The father and mother have an equal responsibility to maintain, to the extent of their ability, a child of whatever age who is incapacitated from earning a living and without sufficient means."). *See generally* Sande L. Buhai, *Parental Support of Adult Children with Disabilities*, 91 MINN. L. REV. 710 (2007).

124. *See supra* note 8 and accompanying text.

125. International enforcement of support orders is discussed in Chapter 4.

126. 989 P.2d 558, 562–64 (Wash. Ct. App. 1999). The children had both graduated from college and were working; the father argued unsuccessfully that enforcing the obligation would violate Washington's public policy.

127. *See generally* 2 CLARK, *supra* note 21, § 18.2.

128. 123 P.3d 1072 (Alaska 2005). Under the Alaska statute, a material change in circumstances is presumed if the recalculated support obligation is more than 15 percent above or below the amount of the existing support order. *Id.* at 1073.

129. If all of these individuals have left the state, the issuing tribunal does not have jurisdiction to modify, unless the parties consent to a continuation of that jurisdiction.

130. In this situation, the new tribunal applies its own procedural and substantive law to the enforcement or modification proceeding. In a modification under § 613, which is no longer an interstate matter, § 613(b) states that UIFSA Articles 1, 2 and 6 apply but that Articles 3, 4, 5, 7, and 8 do not.

131. UIFSA § 611(e).

132. *E.g.*, Marriage of Beeson, No. 92,673, 2005 WL 2347788 (Kan. Ct. App. 2005) (unpublished) (concluding that Dutch court had continuing exclusive jurisdiction under UIFSA).

133. This is an alternative to the jurisdictional requirements of § 611 and § 613, and the tribunal may take jurisdiction to modify under § 615 without regard to where the party seeking modification resides or whether the parties have consented to modification jurisdiction.

134. *See* Comments, *supra* note 6.

135. *See infra* notes 191–93 and accompanying text.

136. *See* Comments, *supra* note 6.

137. *See* Comments, *supra* note 6.

138. State v. Beasley, 801 So. 2d 515, 519–20 (La. Ct. App. 2001).

139. Note that this alternative was not discussed in *Beasley*, because § 611(f) was not added to UIFSA until the 2008 revision.

140. 871 So. 2d 1288 (Miss. 2004). Because Guam is a U.S. territory, it falls within the definition of a "state" for purposes of UIFSA; *see supra* note 79 and accompanying text.

141. UIFSA § 616; the registration provisions in UIFSA §§ 601–608 are described above.

142. Note that if there are competing child-support orders, the controlling order under UIFSA § 207 "establishes the aspects of the support order which are nonmodifiable." *See supra* notes 94–95 and accompanying text.

143. *See supra* notes 83–85 and accompanying text. *See also* 7 U.S. DEP'T OF STATE, FOREIGN AFFAIRS MANUAL (FAM) §§ 1754–1756, http://www.state.gov/m/a/dir/regs/fam/.

144. Maintenance Convention, *supra* note 5, at art. 37.

145. *Id.* at art. 19. This is also true in requests for recognition and enforcement presented directly to local authorities. *See id.* at art. 19(5).

146. *See* Hague Conference on Private International Law, *Towards a New Global Instrument on the International Recovery of Child Support and Other Forms of Family Maintenance*, Prel. Doc. No. 3 (Apr. 3, 2003), http://www.hcch.net/upload/wop/maint_pd03e.pdf. *See also* CHILD SUPPORT: THE NEXT FRONTIER (J. Thomas Oldham & Marygold S. Melli eds., 2000); JEREMY D. MORLEY, INTERNATIONAL FAMILY LAW PRACTICE 213-16 (2009).

147. Protocol of 23 November 2007 on the Law Applicable to Maintenance Obligations, http://www.hcch.net/index_en.php?act=conventions.text&cid=133. Although the United States does not plan to ratify the Protocol, all EU Member States except for Denmark and the United Kingdom are bound by it. *See* Council Regulation (EC) No. 4/2009 (Dec. 18, 2009) on jurisdiction, applicable law, recognition, and enforcement of decisions and cooperation in matters relating to maintenance obligations.

148. Maintenance Convention, *supra* note 5, at art. 2(4).

149. *See* 42 U.S.C. § 659 (2010); 5 C.F.R. § 581 (2010) (garnishment for child-support and alimony orders). For cases involving State Department employees, *see* 7 FAM § 1758.

150. *See* 42 U.S.C. § 665 (2010). OCSE's "Working with the Military as an Employer—A Quick Guide" is available at http://www.acf.hhs.gov/programs/cse/newhire/employer/publication/military_quick_guide.htm. For other useful information, see the Defense Finance and Accounting Service website at http://www.dfas.mil under "Find Garnishment Information" and "Child Support and Alimony." *See also* MARK E. SULLIVAN, THE MILITARY DIVORCE HANDBOOK 237-97 (2d ed. 2011).

151. Links to the state child-support agency web pages are included on the OCSE website at http://www.acf.hhs.gov/programs/cse/.

152. U.S. consular and embassy officials cannot provide this information to individuals, but may be able to assist state IV-D agencies; *see* 7 FAM § 1751.1.

153. *See supra* note 83 and accompanying text. Information including copies of these agreements is available on the OCSE website at http://www.acf.hhs.gov/programs/cse/international/ (last visited July 21, 2010).

154. 42 U.S.C. § 659a(a)(1).

155. 42 U.S.C. § 659a(b)(1)(A).

156. 42 U.S.C. § 659a(b)(1)(C).

157. *E.g.*, U.K., Poland.

158. *E.g.*, Finland, Australia.

159. *See supra* note 4.

160. *See supra* notes 84-85 and accompanying text.

161. Convention on the Law Applicable to Maintenance Obligations Towards Children, Oct. 24, 1956, 510 U.N.T.S. 161. Convention on the Recognition and Enforcement of Decisions Relating to Maintenance Obligations, Oct. 2, 1973, 1021 U.N.T.S. 209. Convention on the Law Applicable to Maintenance Obligations, Oct. 2, 1973, 1056 U.N.T.S. 199.

162. The U.S. Senate gave its advice and consent to ratification in September 2010; *see* S. TREATY DOC. No. 110-21 (2008). For the proposed implementing legislation, *see* Strengthen and Vitalize Enforcement of Child Support (SAVE Child Support) Act, S. 1383, 112th Cong. (2011).

163. *See supra* note 5. *See also* William Duncan, *The New Hague Child Support Convention: Goals and Outcomes of the Negotiations*, 43 FAM. L.Q. 1 (2009); Mary Helen Carlson, *United States Perspective on the New Hague Convention on the International Recovery of Child Support and Other Forms of Family Maintenance*, 43 FAM. L.Q. 21 (2009).

164. This is the current practice under federal bilateral child-support enforcement agreements. *See supra* notes 83 and 153-58 and accompanying text. On the designation of Central Authorities, see Article 4. Information on these Authorities will be available on the website of the Hague Conference at http://www.hcch.net.

165. The Convention does not appear to require states to make this type of procedure available. Article 37 (1) provides:

The Convention shall not exclude the possibility of recourse to such procedures as may be available under the internal law of a Contracting State allowing a person (an applicant) to seise directly a competent authority of that State in a matter governed by the Convention including, subject to Article 18, for the purpose of having a maintenance decisions established or modified.

166. Art. 2(1). Under Article 2(4), the Convention applies to children "regardless of the marital status of the parents."
167. Arts. 2(2), 2(3). The United States has not proposed to limit application of the Convention to children under 18 or extend its scope to other family maintenance obligations. *See* S. Treaty Doc. No. 110-21 (2008), at XXVI.
168. Art. 6(2).
169. Art. 9. The Convention addresses the mechanics of this process in Articles 11-13.
170. Art. 10(1).
171. Art. 10(2).
172. Art. 10(3). Except for applications for recognition or recognition and enforcement, the applications under Article 10 are also subject to the jurisdictional rules of the requested state. *Id.*
173. *See* arts. 15-17.
174. Articles 19(4) and 30 extend the Convention's recognition and enforcement provisions to maintenance arrangements. Article 3(e) defines "maintenance arrangement" as:
an agreement in writing relating to the payment of maintenance which—

Has been formally drawn up or registered as an authentic instrument by a competent authority; or

has been authenticated by, or concluded, registered or filed with a competent authority, and may be the subject of review and modification by a competent authority.

175. Art. 20(2). These optional grounds are that the creditor was habitually resident in the State of origin at the time proceedings were instituted, *see* art. 20(1)(c); that there has been agreement to the jurisdiction in writing by the parties, *see* art. 20(1)(e); and that the decision was made by an authority exercising jurisdiction on a matter of personal status or parental responsibility, *see* art. 20(1)(f).
176. *See* S. Treaty Doc. No. 110-21 (2008), at XXVI; *see also* S. Comm. on Foreign Relations, 111th Cong. 2d Sess., Report on Hague Convention on the International Recovery of Child Support and Other Forms of Family Maintenance (2010). *See generally* Spector, *supra* note 99, at 277-78.
177. *See also* Spector, *supra* note 99, at 278-81. Articles 20(4) and 20(5) provide additional requirements for Contracting States in circumstances where recognition of a child-support decision is not possible because of this reservation.
178. Art. 22(e).
179. Art. 22(b).
180. Arts. 22(c), (d).
181. Art. 22(a).
182. Art. 22(f); *see infra* notes 191-93 and accompanying text.
183. *See* art. 23(1): "Subject to the provisions of the Convention, the procedures for recognition and enforcement shall be governed by the law of the State addressed." Article 32(1) provides: "Subject to the provisions of this chapter, enforcement shall take place in accordance with the law of the State addressed."
184. Art. 27.
185. Art. 28.
186. Art. 29.
187. Art. 33.
188. Art. 41; the process of legalization is discussed generally in Chapter 1 of this book.
189. Art. 44.
190. *See* art. 24; *see generally* Carlson, *supra* note 163, at 32 & 34.

191. The exceptions in Article 18(2) include an agreement in writing between the parties to the jurisdiction of another Contracting State (except in disputes relating to maintenance obligations in respect of children); where a creditor submits to the jurisdiction of another Contracting State; where the competent authority in the State of origin cannot or refuses to exercise jurisdiction to modify the decision or make a new decision, or where the decision made in the State of origin "cannot be recognized or declared enforceable in the Contracting State where proceedings to modify the decision or make a new decision are contemplated."

192. *See supra* notes 59–64 and accompanying text.

193. *See supra* notes 136–37 and accompanying text.

194. *See* Robinson, *supra* note 6. UIFSA § 704 enumerates the types of support proceedings available to an obligee or obligor under the Convention, tracking the categories listed in Article 10 and quoted in *supra* text accompanying notes 171–72.

195. UIFSA § 702.

196. UIFSA § 711 restricts the circumstances in which convention child-support orders may be modified.

197. UIFSA § 705(b). A petitioner making a direct filing is not entitled to assistance from the child-support enforcement office. *See* UIFSA § 705(d).

198. UIFSA § 708(c)(1).

199. *See* art. 20(4); UIFSA § 708(c)(2). Section 709 states that if a tribunal cannot recognize and enforce a support order in its entirety, "it shall enforce any severable part of the order."

8

Adoption

American families adopt thousands of children every year from about 100 different countries. Federal immigration law shapes the practice of international adoption,[1] and U.S. Citizenship and Immigration Services (USCIS) has a significant role in all incoming international cases. Since 2008, when the Hague Intercountry Adoption Convention came into force in the United States, there have been two distinct procedures for intercountry adoption, depending on whether the other country involved has ratified or acceded to the Adoption Convention. Adoptions within the scope of the Convention are subject to the federal Intercountry Adoption Act (IAA)[2] and fall within the jurisdiction of the Office of Children's Issues in the U.S. State Department (OCI), which serves as the U.S. Central Authority under the Convention.

International adoption also raises questions under state adoption laws. State court proceedings may be necessary to finalize an adoption that was begun in another country, and many states provide for readoption under state law after foreign adoption proceedings are completed. The validity of a foreign adoption may be questioned in family or inheritance disputes. The Adoption Convention may apply when a foreign citizen child is the subject of adoption proceedings in the United States, and state courts and agencies have responsibilities under the Adoption Convention when children who are habitually resident in the United States are placed for adoption with parents in another Hague country.

As a matter of international human rights law, the United Nations Convention on the Rights of the Child (CRC) sets parameters for intercountry adoption, mandating that the child's best interests must be the paramount consideration and that countries must ensure that the process involves safeguards and standards equivalent to those applied to domestic adoption. An intercountry adoption must be authorized by competent authorities, who determine that adoption is permissible in accordance with applicable laws and procedures and that parents, relatives or legal guardians have given their informed consent.[3] The CRC also encourages countries to enter into international agreements to ensure that placement of a child across national borders is carried out according to these principles.

Adopting in the United States

Adoption, which was not part of the common law tradition, is regulated by a confusing tangle of state statutes. Uniform laws in this area have not been widely enacted, and adoption laws and procedures of different states vary significantly.[4] Federal law establishes the basic parameters of state child welfare systems, including a system of subsidies to support the adoption of hard-to-place children from the foster care system.[5] Although federal law generally prohibits the use of race as a factor in making an adoptive placement,[6] the Indian Child Welfare Act establishes particular rules governing adoption of Native American children.[7]

Before a child is eligible for adoption, any existing parental rights must be properly terminated under state law. This occurs either by a voluntary consent or relinquishment process, or when parents abandon a child, or by an involuntary termination of the rights of the child's existing parents.[8] Jurisdiction in child welfare or termination of parental rights proceedings is based on the child's presence or residence in the state as set out in the Uniform Child Custody Jurisdiction and Enforcement Act (UCCJEA).[9] Although state laws vary on the specific grounds for involuntary termination of parental rights, the U.S. Constitution requires that parents must be afforded notice and an opportunity for a hearing, and that the state prove the case for termination by clear and convincing evidence.[10]

Children who are present in the United States but who are not U.S. citizens may be subject to child protection, guardianship, or adoption proceedings in state courts.[11] In most respects, state courts hearing child welfare cases with an international dimension follow the same procedures that apply to purely domestic cases.[12] They apply their own laws to determine the scope of their jurisdiction and address such questions as whether the child is free for adoption and whether the adoption is in the child's best interests.[13] Lawyers and judges should be aware that two groups of adoption cases in state court may fall within the scope of the Hague Adoption Convention: cases involving foreign-born children from Convention countries being adopted by U.S. citizens,[14] and cases in which children born in the United States are being adopted by parents who are habitually resident in another Convention country.[15]

Adoption agencies are licensed at the state level and may be either public or private. When an adoption agency is involved, it typically takes legal custody of the child after the child is freed for adoption. Most states also permit private or independent adoptions, arranged by an intermediary or directly between a child's birth parents and the prospective adoptive parents.[16] If an adoption proceeding in the United States involves a child who will become a habitual resident of another Hague adoption country, however, there must be an agency involved with Hague accreditation in the United States, and the pro-

---

Resources: State Adoption Laws

Detailed information on state adoption laws can be found on the Child Welfare Information Gateway website of the Administration for Children & Families in the U.S. Department of Health and Human Services. Go to http://www.childwelfare.gov and then "Systemwide," "Laws & Policies," and "State Laws on Adoption."

cedures must comply with the Hague Convention and the Intercountry Adoption Act.[17] State courts and agencies also play an important role in intercountry adoptions that have not been finalized when the child enters the United States. These adoptions must satisfy the requirements of state law as well as federal immigration law, and states may impose special licensing requirements for agencies handling intercountry adoptions.[18]

Adoption Proceedings

In all states, children who become available for adoption, based on either a voluntary consent or relinquishment by their parents or an involuntary termination of parental rights, may be placed with prospective adoptive parents by a licensed adoption agency. In many states, a child may also be placed privately, either directly by the child's parent or guardian or through unlicensed intermediaries. Laws regulating these placements vary widely among the states.[19] Placements made by an agency are generally preceded by counseling, a home study, and an evaluation of the child, followed by post-placement visits with the adoptive family. Some state statutes limit adoptive placements based on factors such as age, marital status, or sexual orientation.[20] Adoption cannot be finalized until the prospective parents have filed a petition to adopt and the court determines that all applicable statutory requirements are met and that adoption is in the best interests of the child.

In some intercountry adoptions, children are placed in their adoptive parents' custody and admitted to the United States before the adoption has been finalized. Federal immigration laws require that the adoptive parents complete the adoption under state law in their state of residence.[21] In unusual cases, children may be allowed to enter the United States based on a temporary humanitarian parole, with the possibility of adjusting their immigration status after adoption proceedings are completed.[22]

Determining Jurisdiction

Given the significant differences among state adoption laws, and the rule that state courts usually apply their own law to these proceedings,[23] complex jurisdictional questions and forum shopping are common. A pregnant birth mother may be living away from her usual home when she gives birth, adoptive parents may live in a different state or country than the one where the child is born, or the parties may choose a state that they have no other connections with if it appears to offer a favorable set of legal rules. These jurisdictional difficulties are compounded in surrogate parenting cases, where an adoption may be necessary to establish rights in the intended parents after the child is born.[24] Different questions arise when an adoption involves modification of prior custody or visitation orders. In this situation, adoption proceedings are subject to the requirements of the federal Parental Kidnapping Prevention Act (PKPA).[25]

The Restatement (Second) of Conflict of Laws § 78 articulates broad principles of adoption jurisdiction, but every state applies different rules.[26] The 1994 Uniform Adoption Act (UAA) includes carefully considered jurisdictional provisions, but has only been enacted in Vermont.[27] Some states have applied the Uniform Child Custody Jurisdiction Act (UCCJA) to adoption cases, although it was not originally designed for adoption and it is not well adapted to many adoption cases.[28] The UCCJEA, which has replaced the

> ### Surrogacy and Adoption
>
> Although domestic and international surrogacy practices often make use of adoption laws to confirm or establish a legal relationship between the child and the intended parents, surrogacy lies beyond the scope of current intercountry adoption laws. The Hague Adoption Convention does not apply to international surrogacy cases, and the citizenship and immigration status of children born from surrogacy arrangements presents numerous difficult problems.[29] For more information, see the U.S. State Department information circular on "Important Information for U.S. Citizens Considering the Use of Assisted Reproductive Technology (ART) Abroad" at http://travel.state.gov/law/citizenship/citizenship_5177.html.

UCCJA in almost every state, applies to proceedings for termination of parental rights but excludes adoption from its scope.[30] Adding to this complexity, an adoption in which a child will be placed across state lines must also comply with the Interstate Compact on the Placement of Children.[31]

Recognizing Adoption Decrees

A final state court adoption decree is entitled to recognition in every state under the constitutional Full Faith and Credit Clause, provided that it is consistent with the requirements of due process.[32] This is true even if the adoption is one that would otherwise violate the public policy of the state in which recognition is sought.[33] Under *Restatement (Second) of Conflict of Laws* § 290, an adoption rendered in a state with appropriate jurisdiction "will usually be given the same effect in another state as is given by the other state to a decree of adoption rendered by its own courts." Thus, an adoption ordered in another state will be effective to establish a parent-child relationship for purposes such as child support, eligibility for public benefits, or inheritance.[34]

An adoption decree granted by a state court does not confer immigration rights or citizenship status, but the adopted child may be eligible to adjust status after a decree has been entered.[35] This procedure cannot be used to bypass the immigration and adoption procedures under federal law. In *Guadarrama-Garcia v. Acosta*, a federal court refused to order immigration authorities to release a child into the custody of parents who had attempted to adopt him in Texas after bringing the child and his birth mother into the country illegally. The court noted:

> [T]he state court correctly focused on the best interest of the child based upon the evidence and record before it as a state family court may only deal with the adoption matter brought within its statutory purview. The immigration status of Guadarrama and Aldo, however, is a separate and overriding federal issue.[36]

Foreign-Country Adoption Decrees

As matter of common law, state courts recognize foreign-country adoption decrees on the basis of comity. This is true even if the adoption laws and procedures of the foreign country are different from those in the state where recognition is sought.[37] This rule of comity is an extension of the recognition principle in *Restatement (Second) of Conflict of Laws* § 290.[38] Courts may decline to extend comity to a foreign adoption decree on procedural grounds, as when the decree was not final, or if it had an inadequate jurisdictional basis,[39] or if the birth parents did not consent or were not given notice and an opportunity for a hearing before their rights were terminated.[40] In these cases, as in other types of international litigation, translation and legalization, or authentication of foreign documents may be necessary.[41] Numerous state statutes address recognition of foreign adoption decrees,[42] and these may in turn depend on whether the parties have complied with federal immigration laws.[43] One important benefit of the Hague Adoption Convention is that an adoption carried out under the Convention must be recognized as valid for all purposes in all Convention countries, and in every U.S. state under the Intercountry Adoption Act (IAA).

Once recognized, a foreign adoption is given the same legal effect as a domestic adoption, even if the adoption would have different consequences under the law of the place where it occurred. Thus, a child adopted in a jurisdiction that does not permit adopted children to inherit by intestate succession may be permitted to inherit if that would be the effect of an adoption in the state where the estate is administered.[44] In *Adoption of Doe*, involving a father who obtained an adoption decree in Cambodia before his former partner obtained a competing Cambodian order for the same child, the court concluded that the first order was entitled to comity and that the father had a right to consent before his partner could readopt the child in New York.[45] Holding that New York law governed the dispute between the parents, the court noted, "When New York parents have acquired, by virtue of a foreign country adoption, parental rights that are recognized in New York, those rights can no longer depend upon the vagaries of a foreign country's law."[46]

When a foreign country recognizes informal or customary adoption as legally binding, this may also be given effect for purposes of state or federal law in the United States. For example, *Kaho v. Ilchert* concluded that a customary adoption in Tonga should be recognized for immigration purposes where the evidence established that such adoptions "have the effect of creating a parent/child relationship recognized under Tongan law" even though the law of Tonga did not permit all adopted children to inherit from their adoptive parents.[47] Conversely, a Minnesota court concluded that a cultural adoption carried out by Hmong refugees in Thailand did not give rise to a parent-child relationship and a corresponding child support obligation because it was not a legally valid adoption under Thai law.[48] Courts considering cases in which parties obtained a false birth certificate for a child, usually to facilitate the child's immigration to the United States, have consistently ruled that this cannot be given effect as an adoption.[49]

A few cases have taken the position that a state may refuse to extend comity to a foreign adoption if doing so would be contrary to its strong public policy.[50] Such cases are extremely rare, however, and any public policy applied in this context must also take into account the best interests of the adopted child.[51] *Doulgeris v. Bambacus* declined to recognize a Greek adoption decree that was not based on a consideration of the child's best interests.[52] In contrast, *Estate of Christoff* extended recognition to a Greek adoption decree for inheritance purposes, despite evidence that the decedent had carried out the adoption in order to allow his great-nephew to immigrate to the United States.[53]

Under Article 23 of the Adoption Convention, adoptions completed under the Convention must be recognized by operation of law in all contracting states. Article 24 further specifies that recognition may be refused "only if the adoption is manifestly contrary to public policy, taking into account the best interests of the child."[54] In the United States, this question is controlled by federal law, since an adoption that has been certified by the U.S. Central Authority under the Convention must be recognized under the IAA.[55]

Readoption in the United States

After a final adoption in a foreign country, many states provide procedures for valida-tion of the foreign decree or readoption under state law, which has the benefit of provid-ing a new birth certificate for the child and a state court adoption decree entitled to full faith and credit in every state.[56] In deciding whether to grant a readoption, state courts may consider the same factors relevant to a comity determination.[57] Although statutes in some states mandate readoption proceedings after a foreign adoption, this requirement cannot be applied to Hague adoptions, which must be recognized in every state under 42 U.S.C. § 14951, or to other circumstances in which recognition is mandated by inter-national treaties.[58] Moreover, as noted by the court in *Marriage of Lunina & Pozdnyakov*, readoption should not be necessary in cases of "foreign adoptions where both the child and the parents were residents of the foreign country" at the time of the adoption.[59] As an alternative to readoption, many states provide a simplified procedure for obtaining a new or amended U.S. birth certificate after a foreign adoption.[60]

Handling Post-Adoption Issues

Once it is final, an adoption creates a permanent parent-child relationship. A breakdown in that relationship is subject to state laws and procedure that govern child protection and termination of parental rights. Parents who have difficulty caring for a child may seek state services and support, and in extreme circumstances may surrender care of the child to the state, but they will ordinarily continue to be responsible for the child's financial support.[61] State laws may allow a court to revoke or annul an adoption decree based on fraud or other procedural defects.[62] This type of remedy is almost always contrary to the interests of the adopted child, however, and is particularly inappropriate in intercountry adoption cases.[63]

Courts in a number of states have allowed tort claims for wrongful adoption based on an agency's negligent or intentional misrepresentation or nondisclosure of facts con-cerning the child's history before an adoption.[64] This type of recovery has been more diffi-cult in the setting of intercountry adoption, where agencies typically require prospective adoptive parents to sign agreements in advance releasing the agencies from liability for negligence.[65] In *Dresser v. Cradle of Hope Adoption Center*, the court dismissed the adop-tive parents' claims but ruled that their contractual waiver of liability did not preclude

See the U.S. Administration for Children & Families pamphlet "State Recognition of Intercountry Adoptions Finalized Abroad: Summary of State Laws" at http://www.childwelfare.gov/systemwide/laws_policies/statutes/intercountry.pdf.

Further Reading: Adoption Law in the United States

JENNIFER FAIRFAX, THE ADOPTION LAW HANDBOOK: PRACTICE, RESOURCES AND FORMS FOR FAMILY LAW PROFESSIONALS (2011).

ADOPTION LAW AND PRACTICE (3 vols.) (Joan Heifetz Hollinger ed., 2010).

a claim against the agency by the adopted child, on the theory that the agency's failure to furnish his medical records to his adoptive parents within a reasonable time had an adverse effect on his subsequent medical treatment.[66]

For adoptions within the scope of the Adoption Convention, the enforcement provisions of the IAA extend civil and criminal penalties to any person who makes "a false or fraudulent statement, or misrepresentation, with respect to a material fact."[67] Although there is no private right of action under the IAA,[68] the statute and regulations institute a procedure for filing complaints against accredited or approved agencies or adoption service providers.[69] Accredited and approved bodies are subject to an oversight process, which includes the possibility that accreditation or approval may be suspended or canceled, or that an agency or person may be temporarily or permanently debarred based on a pattern of serious, willful, or grossly negligent failures to comply with the regulations.[70]

Citizenship of Adopted Children

Children adopted abroad and brought into the United States by U.S.-citizen parents after the adoption is final obtain automatic U.S. citizenship under the Child Citizenship Act of 2000.[71] Children whose adoption is not yet final when they arrive in the United States enter as lawful permanent residents and obtain citizenship automatically once the adoption is granted or recognized by state authorities.[72] A foreign-born adopted child who does not qualify for automatic U.S. citizenship may be eligible for naturalization on the application of his or her adoptive parent. Once the adopted person reaches age 18, he or she may apply for naturalization as an adult.[73]

Working with the Hague Intercountry Adoption Convention

More than 80 nations have joined the 1993 Hague Convention on Protection of Children and Co-Operation in Respect of Intercountry Adoption, which has been in force in the United States since 2008.[74] The Adoption Convention applies whenever a child who is habitually resident in one Convention country "has been, is being, or will be moved to another Contracting State" for purposes of adoption, whether the relocation occurs before or after the adoption is finalized.[75] The Convention applies regardless of the nationality of the child and the prospective adoptive parents, and it does not address issues of the child's citizenship after adoption.[76] Each Contracting State must designate a Central Authority to carry out various duties under the Convention. Current information on the Adoption Convention and its Contracting States is available on the website maintained by the Hague Conference.

Hague Adoption Convention

Hague Convention on Protection of Children and Co-Operation in Respect of Intercountry
  Adoption, May 29, 1993, *reprinted in* 32 I.L.M. 1134–46 (1993). The full text and current
  information for the Adoption Convention is available from the Hague Conference web site at
  www.hcch.net (under "Conventions" and "33").

See also G. PARRA-ARANGUREN, EXPLANATORY REPORT, CONVENTION ON PROTECTION OF CHILDREN AND CO-
  OPERATION IN RESPECT OF INTERCOUNTRY ADOPTION, HAGUE CONFERENCE ON PRIVATE INTERNATIONAL LAW,
  II ACTES ET DOCUMENTS DE LA DIX-SEPTIÈME SESSION 537 (1993).

In the cooperative regime of the Adoption Convention, Article 4 assigns to the competent authorities of the child's state of origin the responsibility to assure that the child is adoptable, that appropriate counseling has been provided and consents given, and that the consent "has not been induced by payment or compensation of any kind." Article 5 provides that the competent authorities of the receiving state must determine that the prospective parents are "eligible and suited to adopt," that they have been counseled as may be necessary, and that the child will be authorized "to enter and reside permanently" in the receiving state. Under Article 17, the child may not be entrusted to prospective adoptive parents until the Central Authorities of both the state of origin and the receiving state agree that the adoption may proceed;[77] and under Article 19, the child may not be transferred to the receiving state until the requirements of Article 17 have been satisfied.

The Preamble to the Adoption Convention establishes a principle known as subsidiarity; its language recommends that States should take, "as a matter of priority, appropriate measures to enable the child to remain in the care of his or her family of origin," and suggests that "intercountry adoption may offer the advantage of a permanent family to a child for whom a suitable family cannot be found in his or her state of origin." The Preamble also affirms the importance of finding families for children, noting that "for the full and harmonious development of his or her personality," a child should "grow up in a family environment, in an atmosphere of happiness, love and understanding."

Central Authorities have a range of different responsibilities under the Convention, some of which may be carried out through other public authorities "or other bodies duly accredited in the State." Articles 10 and 11 address the broad requirements for this accreditation. Typically, accreditation of agencies occurs in receiving States, and these accredited agencies must then seek authorization to act in particular States of origin under Article 12, which states that "[a] body accredited in one Contracting State may act in another Contracting State only if the competent authorities of both States have authorized it to do so."[78] Information on Central Authorities and accredited bodies in each Contracting State is reported to the Hague Conference and available on its website.

Extensive adoption information is available on the Hague Conference website at http://www
.hcch.net under "Intercountry Adoption Section." This includes Country Profiles with details on
Central Authorities and information on adoption laws for many of the Contracting States.

Caution: Only Hague-accredited agencies and approved persons may provide intercountry adoption services in cases covered by the Adoption Convention.

Besides delegating functions to accredited bodies, Article 22(2) allows Contracting States to declare that some adoption services may be performed in that State by other approved bodies or persons, "to the extent permitted by law and subject to the supervision of competent authorities of that State."[79] To be approved under Article 22(2), an adoption service provider must "meet the requirements of integrity, professional competence, experience and accountability of that State," and must be "qualified by their ethical standards and by training or experience to work in the field of intercountry adoption." If a Contracting State disagrees with this approach, it may declare under Article 22(4) "that adoptions of children habitually resident in its territory may only take place" if the Central Authority functions are performed by public authorities or accredited bodies. A significant group of countries have made this declaration, including Australia, Brazil, several Canadian provinces, and many European nations. Even without making this declaration, a country of origin may decline to authorize accredited bodies or approved persons to work within their country under Article 12. Whether or not private adoption service providers are permitted to perform Convention functions, all entities and individuals involved must comply with the rule in Article 32(1) that states: "No one shall derive improper financial or other gain from an activity related to an intercountry adoption." More specifically, "[o]nly costs and expenses, including reasonable professional fees of persons involved in the adoption, may be charged or paid."[80]

Convention Procedures

Under the Convention, persons habitually resident in one Contracting State who wish to adopt a child habitually resident in another begin by applying to the Central Authority in their country of residence, which will become the receiving State.[81] Authorities in the receiving State are responsible for evaluating prospective adoptive parents, making a determination under Article 5 that they "are eligible and suited to adopt" and that they have been appropriately counseled.[82] Authorities in the child's country of habitual residence are charged with determining under Article 4 that a particular child is adoptable and that intercountry adoption is in that child's best interests. Under the subsidiarity principle, this requires those authorities to give "due consideration" to possibilities for placement of the child within the State of origin.

States of origin must ensure that appropriate counseling is provided and consent obtained from those "persons, institutions and authorities" whose consent may be required for adoption. Consent must not "be induced by payment or compensation of any kind," and it may not be given before the child is born. It must be expressed or evidenced in writing, and it must not have been withdrawn. Parties must be informed of the effects of their consent, "in particular whether or not the adoption will result in the termination of the legal relationship between the child and his or her country of origin."[83] Children must also be counseled, "having regard to their age and maturity," and must have an opportunity to consent as determined by the law of the State of origin.[84]

Exchange of Reports and Matching Process

After determining that the applicants are suitable, the Central Authority in the receiving state (or another public authority or accredited body) prepares and transmits a report under Article 15 to the authorities in the child's country of habitual residence. The Article 15 report must address the prospective parents' "identity, eligibility and suitability to adopt, background, family and medical history, social environment, reasons for adoption, ability to undertake an intercountry adoption, as well as the characteristics of the children for whom they would be qualified to care." On receipt of the report, the authorities in the child's country prepare a report under Article 16 and transmit this to the Central Authority in the receiving state. The Article 16 report addresses the child's "identity, adoptability, background, social environment, family history, medical history including that of the child's family, and any special needs of the child."

Under Article 16, the child's State of origin has the major responsibility to approve the match of a child with adoptive parents. The authorities are directed to "determine on the basis in particular of the reports relating to the child and the prospective adoptive parents whether the envisaged placement is in the best interests of the child," giving "due consideration to the child's upbringing and to his or her ethnic, religious and cultural background." After making this determination, the authorities in the State of origin must transmit their report to the Central Authority of the receiving State, along with "proof that the necessary consents have been obtained and the reasons for its determination on the placement."

Hague Adoption within Families

The Adoption Convention procedures apply, with minor modifications, to adoptions by family members of a child who is habitually resident in another Convention country. This includes the preparation and exchange of reports between the Central Authorities of the two countries involved.[85] In this situation, however, there is no prohibition on contact between the prospective adoptive parents and the child's parents or other care providers under Article 29.[86] The subsidiarity principle gives way in this situation, although the authorities in the child's habitual residence must consider whether the proposed adoption by a family member abroad would be in the child's best interest.[87] In some countries, including the United States, intercountry adoption legislation permits a "domestic" adoption in the child's country of origin by a citizen of that country living abroad, but the Hague Conference has noted that this approach is not consistent with the terms of the Convention.[88]

Formal Adoption and Transfer of Child

Article 17 stipulates that authorities in the State of origin may not entrust a child to prospective adoptive parents until the process of counseling and consent has occurred, the exchange of information between authorities has been completed, and the authorities in both states have agreed that the adoption may proceed. Before accepting custody, the prospective parents must give their consent to the adoption. Significantly, Article 29 prohibits any contact between the prospective adoptive parents and the child's parents (or other person having care of the child) until the process of counseling and consent have been completed, "unless the adoption takes place within a family or unless the contact is in compliance with the conditions established by the competent authority of the State of origin." The Convention does not restrict contact between the prospective adoptive parents and the child.[89]

Adoptions under the Convention may be finalized in either the State of origin or the receiving State. The requirements of Article 17 must be carried out before a child may be transferred to the receiving State, and a State of origin may require that the adoption must be completed before the child moves.[90] If the adoption is not finalized before the child's transfer, the Central Authority of the receiving State has special responsibilities to protect the child if it appears that the continued placement with the prospective parents is not in the child's best interests, including consulting with the Central Authority in the State of origin.[91]

Once an adoption is certified under Article 23 as having been made in accordance with the Convention, it must be recognized as a matter of law in other Contracting States. A state may refuse this recognition "only if the adoption is manifestly contrary to its public policy, taking into account the best interests of the child."[92] Specifically, this includes recognition of the legal parent-child relationship between the child and his or her adoptive parents, and the parental responsibility of the adoptive parents for the child. This will also include recognition of the termination of the preexisting legal relationship between the child and his or her mother or father, if the adoption had this effect in the country where it took place.[93]

Post-Adoption Responsibilities

Article 30 of the Adoption Convention requires authorities to "ensure that information held by them concerning the child's origin, in particular information concerning the identity of his or her parents, as well as the medical history, is preserved."[94] The applicable regulations in the United States require that records must be preserved for at least 75 years.[95] The Convention also provides that the child or the child's representative should have access to this information, "under appropriate guidance, in so far as is permitted by the law of that State."[96]

Although the Convention does not require follow-up reports, many countries of origin impose reporting requirements for periods that range from two to 18 years. The Convention also does not address the range of problems that may come up after an intercountry adoption is finalized. Both of these issues have been extensively discussed within the Hague Conference in the years since the Convention was negotiated, and are addressed in the Good Practice Guides. Those sources suggest the importance of post-adoption services to support adoptive families that may encounter adjustment difficulties and for older adoptees who may seek information and support for exploring their identity and heritage.[97]

Under Article 9 of the Convention, Central Authorities must "promote the development of adoption counseling and post-adoption services in their States." Post-adoption services are particularly important for adoptions involving older children and children with special needs, but they also extend to measures to assist adopted children in preserving cultural ties to their countries of origin.[98] Depending on the law of the child's country of origin, a child adopted internationally may retain his or her original citizenship even after acquiring a new nationality.[99]

Further Reading: Hague Adoption Convention

HAGUE CONFERENCE ON PRIVATE INTERNATIONAL LAW, THE IMPLEMENTATION AND OPERATION OF THE 1993 HAGUE INTERCOUNTRY ADOPTION CONVENTION: GUIDE TO GOOD PRACTICE No. 1 (2008).

HAGUE CONFERENCE ON PRIVATE INTERNATIONAL LAW, ACCREDITATION AND ADOPTION ACCREDITED BODIES: GENERAL PRINCIPLES AND GUIDE TO GOOD PRACTICE No. 2 (Draft 2010).

In some countries of origin, placement of a child for intercountry adoption is subject to obligations to cooperate with post-placement follow-up and reporting back to authorities in the child's country of origin.[100] Under the Convention, Central Authorities are obligated to "reply, in so far as permitted by the law of their State, to justified requests from other Central Authorities or public authorities for information about a particular adoption situation."

Article 21 of the Convention addresses the possibility that a placement for adoption may break down after the child is transferred to the receiving country and before the final adoption is ordered. In this situation, the Central Authority of the receiving State must take steps to protect the child, including withdrawing the child from the prospective adoptive parents and consulting with the Central Authority of the country of origin concerning a new placement for the child. As a last resort, if necessary to protect the child's best interests, the authorities may arrange the return of the child.[101]

Intercountry Adoption Procedures in the United States

Intercountry adoption in the United States follows two distinct tracks. Incoming and outgoing cases within the scope of the Hague Adoption Convention are subject to the IAA, 42 U.S.C. § 14901 *et seq.*, and the regulations promulgated pursuant to the act. Intercountry adoptions from non-Hague countries are regulated by state law and federal immigration laws. USCIS has a significant role in all incoming intercountry adoption cases, but the procedures are different in Hague and non-Hague cases. Both the State Department and USCIS have developed websites that provide extensive information about these procedures.

For prospective adoptive parents, the starting point should be selection of a reputable, licensed agency to assist with navigating the intercountry adoption process. For adoption from any of the more than 80 Hague Convention countries, parents must work

---

Where to Begin

For detailed and useful information concerning intercountry adoption in the United States, refer to the excellent website of the State Department's Office of Children's Issues at http://adoption.state .gov and the website of the USCIS, http://www.uscis.gov.

To contact the OCI, write to: U.S. State Department, Office of Children's Issues SA-29, 2201 C Street, NW, Washington DC 20520 or AskCI@state.gov (for general adoption questions) or AdoptionUSCA@state.gov (for Hague adoption questions)—phone: 888-407-4747 (from the U.S. or Canada) or (202) 501-4444 (from outside the U.S. or Canada); fax: (202) 736-9080.

To contact USCIS, call (800) 375-5283 (Customer Service) or (877) 424-8374.

> **Caution:** Under the U.S. regulations implementing the Adoption Convention, the two-year rule is not available for adoptions by U.S. citizens of children who were habitually resident in a Hague Adoption Convention country immediately before coming to the United States.[103]

with an agency that is accredited or approved under federal law and authorized to work in the country where adoption is sought.[102] The expenses of adoption across borders are substantial, the risks of fraud and exploitation are real, and the children available for placement are increasingly older children who may have significant medical or other needs. In this context, agencies bear extremely important responsibilities for counseling and preparing prospective parents before an intercountry adoption and providing support after the adoption is complete.[104]

In addition to the Hague and non-Hague adoption procedures, used by U.S.-citizen parents to bring an adopted child into the United States immediately after the child is placed in their custody, federal immigration laws allow both U.S. citizens and lawful permanent residents to obtain a visa for an adopted child under the "two-year rule" in 8 U.S.C. § 1101 (b)(1)(E). This rule applies to "a child adopted while under the age of sixteen years if the child has been in the legal custody of, and has resided with, the adopting parent or parents for at least two years."[105] In some circumstances a child who meets this definition with an adoptive parent who is a U.S. citizen is eligible to enter as an immediate relative,[106] and a child who meets the definition with an adopted parent who is a lawful permanent resident of the United States is eligible for family preference status.[107] In some circumstances child living in the United States who meets the requirements of the two-year rule while living in the United States may apply for adjustment of immigration status.

In non-Hague cases, a U.S. citizen may petition to bring an adopted child into the country as an immediate relative under 8 U.S.C. § 1101(b)(1)(F) (the "Orphan Rule"). Alternatively, for adoption of a child who is habitually resident in a Hague Adoption Convention country, a U.S.-citizen parent may petition to bring the child into the country under the Hague rules and 8 U.S.C. § 1101(b)(1)(G). In either of these categories, the adoption may be finalized in the child's country of origin or in a state court after the child arrives in the United States. For a child to enter as an immediate relative under either the orphan rules or the Hague rules, the petition must be filed before the child reaches the age of 16, unless the child is between 16 and 18 and is also the natural sibling of a child under age 16 who is also being adopted.[108]

Who Can Adopt?

To adopt a foreign-born child and bring that child into the United States, an adoptive parent must

- hold U.S. citizenship;
- be unmarried and at least 25 years old *or* be married and adopt the child jointly with a spouse who has U.S. citizenship or legal status in the United States; and
- satisfy requirements including a home study, criminal background checks, and fingerprinting.

See U.S. Dep't of State, *Who Can Adopt?*, http://adoption.state.gov/adoption_process/who.php.

Caution: There is no visa category that would allow immigration of a child who is placed in the care or guardianship of a U.S. citizen or lawful permanent resident, unless the placement is for purposes of a full adoption. This means that a simple or limited adoption, or a placement for *kafalah* under Islamic law, does not qualify as an adoption under these rules.[110]

Immigration laws impose significant constraints on intercountry adoption for prospective adoptive parents living in the United States who are not U.S. citizens. These individuals are not eligible to bring adopted children into the United States under the Orphan Rule or the Hague rules. For this reason, lawful permanent residents who are eligible for naturalization may consider becoming U.S. citizens before adopting.[111] Non-immigrant visa holders may need to return to their home countries before adopting.[112] A new immigrant coming to the United States with an adopted child is generally able to bring that child to the United States on the same basis as any other children.[113]

Adopting from Non-Convention Countries (Orphan Visa Process)

Intercountry adoption from countries that have not joined the Adoption Convention is regulated through the procedures for obtaining an immigrant visa. To enter the United States, the adopted child must meet the statutory definition of "orphan" in 8 U.S.C. § 1101(b)(1)(F). In addition, the child must also be under age 16 at the time the visa petition is filed.[114] The adoptive parents must be either a U.S. citizen and spouse adopting jointly, or an unmarried U.S. citizen at least 25 years of age. If the final adoption occurs abroad, the adoptive parents must have "personally [seen] and observed the child prior to or during the adoption proceedings"; and if the adoption will be finalized in the United States, the adoptive parents must "have complied with the preadoption requirements, if any, of the child's proposed residence." Finally, the Attorney General "must be satisfied that proper care will be furnished the child if admitted to the United States."

Definition of "Orphan"

Under § 1101(b)(1)(F), a child may be an orphan "because of the death or disappearance of, abandonment or desertion by, or separation or loss from, both parents," or if "the sole

Adoption Visa Categories

Immigrant Visas for Children Adopted by U.S. Citizens[109]	If adoption has been completed abroad before child enters the United States:	If adoption is not yet complete when child enters the United States:
Adopted Child (Two-Year Rule) 8 U.S.C. § 1101(b)(1)(E)	IR-2	(No immigrant visa available in this situation.)
Non-Hague Adoption (Orphan Rule) 8 U.S.C. § 1101(b)(1)(F)	IR-3	IR-4
Hague Adoption 8 U.S.C. § 1101(b)(1)(G)	IH-3	IH-4

or surviving parent is incapable of providing the proper care and has in writing irrevocably released the child for emigration and adoption." These terms are further defined in the regulations at 8 C.F.R. § 204.3(b), which specify that the parents' relinquishment of a child for purposes of adoption does not constitute abandonment for purposes of the statute.[115] This means that many children who would be adoptable under state law following a relinquishment of parental rights by both birth parents are not eligible for intercountry adoption under the orphan rules. The determination of orphan status must be made by a U.S. visa officer, based on the record submitted with the visa application and an independent investigation. Although this question is sometimes litigated, the determination generally falls within the broad discretion of the immigration authorities.[116]

Case law adheres to the strict definition of orphan in the statute and regulations. For example, *Rogan v. Reno* upheld the agency's determination that a child adopted in the Philippines was not an orphan under the statute, in circumstances in which the child's mother had consented to her sister's petition to adopt within a few weeks after the child's birth. Evidence also indicated that the child's father was living with and supporting the child's birth mother and siblings.[117] There may be an abandonment under the statute even when a child's legal parents can both be identified, however. *Matter of Del Conte* concluded that twin girls, born to a married woman after an adulterous relationship and relinquished by the woman because her husband refused to accept responsibility for them, were orphaned by abandonment for purposes of the statute.[118]

Foreign Adoption Proceedings

In a non-Hague intercountry adoption, prospective adoptive parents adopt or obtain legal custody of a child in the child's country of origin before applying for a visa to allow the child to enter the United States. These proceedings are governed by foreign law, which may require multiple trips or an extended stay in the child's country.[119] Under that law, there may be either a full and final adoption, or the child may be placed in the custody of the adoptive parents for purposes of emigration and adoption in the United States. Parents who wish to return to the United States with their adopted child will obviously want to be sure that the foreign proceedings meet the requirements for obtaining an orphan visa as well as any requirements for preadoption approval or readoption under the law of their state of residence.[120] If the child does not meet the definition of "orphan" in federal law, the parent's only alternative may be to live for two years with the child in the foreign country and then apply for a visa under the two-year rule.[121]

Orphan Visa Procedures

As a matter of United States law, adoptive parents typically begin by filing Form I-600A (Application for Advance Processing of Orphan Petition) with USCIS in order to establish their suitability as parents and eligibility to adopt under U.S. law. With the Form

I-600A, parents must file proof of U.S. citizenship and a home study that complies with USCIS regulations.[122] The I-600A is optional, but there are strong advantages to having this approval in advance, both for expediting the process of obtaining a visa for the child after the adoption is complete and protecting the adoptive parents against the risk that approval might be denied after they have already adopted the child.[123]

After the foreign court enters its adoption or custody order, the adoptive parents file Form I-600 (Petition to Classify Orphan as Immediate Relative). The Form I-600 must be accompanied by documentation including the child's birth certificate, the final adoption or custody decree, and proof of orphan status.[124] In determining whether to approve the Form I-600, particularly in circumstances that suggest the possibility of fraud or child buying, U.S. authorities may conduct a further investigation into whether the adopted child is an orphan.[125] An orphan petition must be denied if the prospective adoptive parents or anyone working on their behalf have or will give money or other consideration directly or indirectly to the child's parents or any other individual "as payment for the child or as an inducement to release the child."[126]

Once their Form I-600 is approved, the adoptive parents may apply for an immigrant visa from the U.S. Embassy to allow the child to enter the United States. At this stage, parents must prove that the child meets the statutory age requirements[127] and the medical and other conditions of entry into the United States.[128] After the child is admitted to the United States, the parents will be required to complete the adoption in their state of residence if it was not already finalized in the child's country of origin.[129] Even if the adoption was finalized abroad, parents may wish to readopt the child or obtain a new birth certificate under state law.[130]

The United States has sometimes entered into bilateral adoption agreements with other countries. In July 2011, the United States and the Russian Federation signed a broad agreement including elements drawn from the Hague Adoption Convention in order to strengthen adoption safeguards.[131] Periodically, the United States has stopped processing adoption petitions and visa requests from particular countries based on concerns of fraud or a lack of sufficient protection for children's best interests. This type of suspension has been imposed for both Convention and non-Convention countries, including Cambodia in 2001 and Guatemala in 2008. A suspension in Nepal in 2010 applies to cases of children alleged to have been abandoned by their parents. When a suspension is put in place, it applies to new cases and not adoptions that were already in process at the time the new policy was announced. Information on these developments is posted regularly on the State Department's adoption web page.

Foreign Adoption Laws

For detailed country-specific information on adoption laws and procedures, including notices regarding current conditions, see the State Department's adoption web page at http://adoption .state.gov (under "Country Information").

See also INTERNAL AND INTERCOUNTRY ADOPTION LAWS (4 vols.) (International Social Service ed., 2003 & Supp. 2005).

Adopting from Hague Convention Countries

Intercountry adoption from countries that have joined the Adoption Convention is goverend by the Intercoutry Adoption Act and 8 U.S.C. § 1101(b)(1)(G). Although the Adoption Convention is in effect in more than 80 contracting states, it does not impose any obligation to participate in intercountry adoption, and each contracting state may determine whether to allow intercountry adoption and which countries it will cooperate with. The United States has indicated that it will not approve adoptions from contracting states that do not have Hague-compliant adoption procedures in place.[132] The Hague process is mandatory for intercountry adoptions from Convention countries; children from these countries are not eligible for an orphan visa under § 1101(b)(1)(F) or adjustment of status in the United States under 8 U.S.C. § 1101(b)(1)(E) and 8 U.S.C. § 1255.[133] Many of the requirements of the non-Hague and Hague adoption procedures are the same, including the basic rule that a child must be under age 16 at the time the visa petition is filed—with an exception to allow the same parents to adopt that child's older siblings up to age 18.[134]

Habitual Residence

The Convention applies when the child and the prospective adoptive parents are habitually resident in different countries. Although this term is not defined in the Convention, the U.S. implementing regulations address the question. Under the definition in 8 C.F.R. § 204.303, a U.S. citizen seeking to adopt under the Convention is generally deemed to be habitually resident in the United States based on his or her domicile,[135] and a child "whose classification is sought as a Convention adoptee" is "generally, deemed . . . to be habitually resident in the country of the child's citizenship."[136] Under the regulation, if the child resides in another country, that other country will be deemed to be the child's habitual residence if the Central Authority in the other country has "determined that the child's status in that country is sufficiently stable for that country properly to exercise jurisdiction over the child's adoption or custody."

Although these definitions are not fully congruent with the treaty, their effect is to extend the Convention procedures to a wider range of cases, including foreign country adoptions of foreign-citizen children by U.S. citizens living abroad in Hague countries but not domiciled there, and adoptions in the United States of children who are not U.S. citizens.[137] Because the U.S. definition of habitual residence contains elements that are not included in the Convention, there may be differences in interpretation on this point.

Accredited and Approved Agencies and Persons

In the United States, many Central Authority functions within the framework of the Convention have been delegated to accredited agencies and approved adoption service

Caution: In circumstances where there is any question as to whether a particular adoption falls within the scope of the Convention, parents should attempt to work with the appropriate Central Authorities of both countries and follow the Convention procedures to assure cross-border recognition of the adoption.

Finding a Hague-Approved Adoption Agency

Information on how to locate and work with Hague-accredited or approved adoption service providers, and the process for registering complaints, is available on the State Department's adoption website at http://adoption.state.gov/adoption_process/how_to_adopt/agencies.php.

providers.[138] In both incoming and outgoing Hague cases, six types of adoption services may be performed only by an accredited or approved agency or person.[139] These are (1) identifying a child for adoption and arranging an adoption, (2) securing necessary consents and termination of parental rights, (3) completing a background study on a child or home study on prospective adoptive parents, (4) making a placement determination, (5) monitoring a placement until the final adoption occurs, and (6) assuming custody and arranging alternate care in case of a disruption in the placement before the final adoption.[140] Standards for accreditation and approval address requirements for licensing and corporate governance; financial and risk management; ethical practices and responsibilities; professional qualifications and training for employees; information disclosure, fee practices, and quality control practices; responding to complaints and records and reports management; and service planning and delivery in incoming and outgoing cases.[141] In addition to providing for accreditation, the regulations address oversight of adoption service providers and procedures for processing complaints against accredited agencies and approved persons.[142]

Hague Adoption Procedures

Parents who wish to adopt a child from another Convention country must begin by working with an accredited or approved adoption service provider. In addition to identifying an accredited or approved agency, prospective parents should consider whether the agency has been approved to work in the country from which the parents would like to adopt a child. In working with the adoption service provider, the first step is to complete a home study consistent with the federal guidelines.[143]

After completion of the home study, prospective adoptive parents initiate the legal process by filing the home study and Form I-800A (Application for Determination of Suitability to Adopt a Child from a Convention Country) with USCIS.[144] If USCIS approves the Form I-800A, it may be forwarded to the Central Authority in the country where the prospective parents seek to adopt. Under the Convention, those authorities then determine whether the parents are eligible to adopt in that country, and whether the parents

Hague Regulations: Incoming Adoptions

Incoming Hague adoptions are governed by the IAA, 42 U.S.C. § 14901 *et seq.*, and three sets of regulations developed by the U.S State Department: 22 C.F.R. § 42.24 (Visas for Convention Adoptees); 22 C.F.R. § 96 (Accreditation Standards); 22 C.F.R. § 98 (Convention Records). In addition, these USCIS regulations apply specifically to Hague adoptions: 8 C.F.R. § 204.300 *et seq.* (Intercountry Adoption of a Convention Adoptee).

can be matched with a suitable child. This may be a long process; in many countries, the number of prospective adoptive parents is much larger than the number of children who have been found to be eligible for intercountry adoption.

When and if a match is made, the authorities in the child's country of origin provide the agency and the prospective parents with a report, under Article 16 of the Convention, providing background information on the child. If the prospective parents accept the referral of the child, their next step is to file the Article 16 report and a Form I-800 (Petition to Classify Convention Adoptee as an Immediate Relative) with USCIS.[145] Once the I-800 is provisionally approved, it may be submitted to the U.S. consular post with the application for a U.S. visa for the child. If the visa official determines that the child meets the medical and other requirements for entry to the United States, the official issues a letter under Article 5 of the Convention, indicating that the child is eligible to immigrate.

In contrast with the non-Hague adoption process, all of these approvals must be completed before an adoption or guardianship decree is entered.[146] Moreover, under Article 29 of the Convention, the petitioner may not meet or have any other form of contact with the child's parents, legal custodian, or any other individual or entity responsible for the child's care except within strict parameters.[147] This bar on contact does not apply if the prospective parent has a family relationship to the child's parent,[148] and the Convention does not limit contact between the prospective parents and the child.

In a Hague case, the order for adoption or legal custody for purpose of emigration and adoption may be entered by the competent authorities in the child's country of origin after the exchange of reports under Article 16 and Article 5. Depending on the law of the country involved, one or both of the adoptive parents may need to be present for this proceeding. Once this order is entered, the adoptive parents must obtain a new birth certificate and a passport from the child's country of origin and submit these documents to the U.S. consular officials for final approval of the child's visa to enter the United States. Consular officials are also responsible for issuing a certificate under Article 23 that the adoption was carried out in compliance with the Convention.

If a final adoption is decreed in the child's country of origin, there is no need for further proceedings in the United States, and the adopted child will acquire U.S. citizenship upon entry into the United States. If adoptive parents obtain legal custody for purposes of emigration and adoption but the adoption is not finalized in the country of origin, the process will need to be concluded with final adoption proceedings in the state where the parents and child reside.[149] Under the IAA, a state court may not enter an order declaring the adoption to be final unless the State Department has certified that the adoption or legal custody order was entered pursuant to the Convention.[150] Once the adoption is finalized in the United States, the child acquires automatic U.S. citizenship.[151] If the adoption is not finalized for some reason, the child will retain lawful permanent resident (LPR) status.[152]

Beyond the procedural differences, there are other important distinctions between Hague and non-Hague adoptions. The definition for immigration purposes of who may be adopted under the Convention is wider than the orphan definition that governs non-Hague adoptions.[153] In a Hague adoption, parents are not required to comply with preadoption or readoption requirements under state law, and it may be possible for a couple to complete the adoption without the necessity of both parents traveling to the child's country.[154] By statute, records in Convention cases must be preserved for at least 75 years.[155]

> **Resources: Post-Adoption Services**
>
> For information and pre- and post-adoption assistance with the specialized medical needs of adopted children, contact the Center for Adoption Medicine at the University of Washington: http://www.adoptmed.org.
>
> For nutrition resources, go to http://www.adoptionnutrition.org, a project of the Joint Council on International Children's Services and the SPOON Foundation.

Just as state adoption laws may include post-adoption requirements, many countries of origin require adoptive parents or the agencies involved to send periodic post-adoption reports, sometimes for many years. Agencies should also provide post-adoption services and counseling for children and parents, particularly following adoptions of older children and those with special needs. Adoption disruption is not uncommon in these cases.[156] Some adopted children will benefit from specialized medical attention addressing their unique nutrition and developmental issues.

Domestic Hague Adoptions

Under the definition of habitual residence used for purposes of intercountry adoption in the United States, a child who is present in the United States but not a U.S. citizen is generally deemed to be habitually resident in the country of his or her citizenship.[157] If that child is a citizen of a country in which the Adoption Convention is in effect, adoption proceedings in the United States must follow the procedures applicable to incoming Hague adoptions in order for the child to acquire immigration status as the child of a U.S. citizen. This includes filing the I-800A and I-800, and obtaining an adoption or custody order in the child's country of citizenship. If an adoption has already been granted without observing these procedures, it must be set aside.[158] Once the procedure is completed, the child will be immediately eligible to adjust status and obtain U.S. citizenship.

As an alternative, the Central Authority of the child's country of citizenship may be asked to file a written statement with the court in the United States, before issuance of an adoption order, indicating that "the Central Authority is aware of the child's presence in the United States, and of the proposed adoption, and that the Central Authority has determined that the child is not habitually resident in that country." If the state court's adoption order states that the Central Authority has filed this statement, the parents may submit the order and the statement from the Central Authority to USCIS with a petition to adjust the child's status.[159] In this situation, however, the petition must be filed under the two-year rule, which may involve a significant delay.

Adopting under the Two-Year Rule

In addition to the Hague and non-Hague procedures, children adopted by either U.S. citizens or lawful permanent residents may be eligible to enter the United States as immediate relatives under 8 U.S.C. § 1101(b)(1)(E), which applies to "a child adopted while under the age of sixteen years if the child has been in the legal custody of, and has resided with, the adopting parent or parents for at least two years."[160] A child who meets this definition with an adoptive parent who is a U.S. citizen is eligible to enter as an immediate relative with an IR-2 visa,[161] and a child who meets the definition with an adopted parent who is a lawful permanent resident is eligible for family preference status.[162]

For a child to obtain a visa under the two-year rule, the adoption must have been legally valid in the jurisdiction where it took place,[163] but the more detailed requirements applied to orphan cases and Hague adoptions do not apply. Both legal custody and residence are required,[164] and custody must have been formalized by a court order or similar document granting custody, guardianship, or adoption.[165] Although the statute is limited to children adopted before the age of 16, a child adopted while under the age of 18 is also eligible if that child is the natural sibling of a child adopted before age 16.[166] A U.S. citizen who seeks to sponsor the immigration of an adopted child as an immediate relative under the two-year rule must file an I-130 visa petition before the child's 21st birthday. [167]

There is a great deal of flexibility under the two-year rule. The two years of custody and residence do not have to be continuous, and they may occur either before or after the adoption was finalized. When the child's adoptive parents are a U.S. citizen and a noncitizen, residence with the noncitizen adoptive parent is sufficient.[168]

In the case of children already living in the United States, the adoption and the period of custody may take place in the United States. Once the requirements are satisfied, the child may adjust his or her status to that of lawful permanent resident.[169] Moreover, adjustment of status is permitted even if the adopted child entered the United States illegally or if the child was legally admitted and overstayed.[170]

Adoption Following Humanitarian Parole

In unusual circumstances, parents who have adopted or wish to adopt a child residing outside the United States who does not qualify for a visa under the usual rules may be able to obtain a temporary immigration parole for "urgent humanitarian reasons" under 8 U.S.C. § 1182(d)(5), which would allow the child to enter the United States without a visa.[172] Parole is granted for a limited time period, on a case-by-case basis, within the discretionary authority of USCIS. For example, a large group of Haitian children, who had been adopted by or matched with U.S.-citizen parents at the time of the January 2010 earthquake, were admitted into the United States on this basis. An individual admitted by parole may be eligible to adjust status after arriving in the United States. In adoption situations, this may require that parents complete adoption proceedings in the United States and then file a petition under the two-year rule. To accomplish this, it may be necessary to apply for an extension of the child's humanitarian parole.[173]

Handling Outgoing Intercountry Adoptions

The Adoption Convention also applies to cases in state courts in which a child habitually resident in the United States is adopted or placed for adoption with parents whose habitual residence is in another Hague Convention country.[174] Under the definition of

Caution: Adjustment of status as an adopted child is generally not permitted for adoptions involving children who were habitually resident in a country that participates in the Adoption Convention immediately before coming to the United States.[171]

Hague Regulations: Outgoing Adoptions

Outgoing Hague adoptions are subject to the IAA, 42 U.S.C. § 14901 *et seq.*, and the U.S. State Department regulations at 22 C.F.R. § 96 (Accreditation Standards), 22 C.F.R. § 97 (Outgoing Cases), 22 C.F.R. § 98 (Convention Records), and 22 C.F.R. § 99 (Reporting Requirements for Outgoing Cases).

habitual residence applied in the United States, however, the Convention may not apply when U.S.-citizen parents living abroad adopt U.S.-citizen children residing in the United States.[175] Adoption services in outgoing Hague adoption cases must be performed either by agencies or providers who have been accredited or approved under federal law or by public domestic authorities as defined in the regulations.[176] In these cases, adoption service providers must comply with Convention standards.[177]

Agency Responsibilities in Outgoing Hague Cases

Outgoing Hague adoption cases begin when a child is determined to be in need of placement. An accredited or approved adoption service provider or public domestic authority must complete a background study on the child and obtain the appropriate consents for adoption and emigration.[178] In most cases, the provider must also make "reasonable efforts to actively recruit and . . . a diligent search for prospective adoptive parents to adopt the child in the United States."[179] Efforts to find a domestic placement are not required if the child will be adopted by relatives, or if the birth parents have identified specific adoptive parents, unless an adoption service provider or its agents have assisted a birth parent in identifying prospective adoptive parents.[180]

Prospective adoptive parents resident in another Convention country must file an application to adopt with the Central Authority or accredited body in their country, and they must have a home study completed that complies with the U.S. regulations as well as the requirements of the state with jurisdiction over the adoption.[181] Once the appropriate authority in the prospective parents' home country approves their application to adopt, a proposed placement may be presented to the foreign authority and then the prospective parents.[182] Before this point, unless the child is being adopted by a relative, there may be no contact between the prospective adoptive parents and the child's birth parents or any other person who has care of the child.[183] If the placement is accepted, the prospective parents will need to obtain authorization for the child to enter the receiving country and remain there permanently or on the same basis as the adopting parents.[184]

Adoption or Custody Decree and Hague Certificate

Adoption proceedings or an order granting custody for purposes of an intercountry adoption are governed by state law. In addition to meeting the requirements of state law, the

See "A Guide to Outgoing Cases from the United States," on the State Department website at http://adoption.state.gov/content/pdf/OutgoingCasesFAQs.pdf, and "A Web-Guide for State Authorities on Outgoing Adoption Cases from the United States to Another Convention Country," at http://adoption.state.gov/content/pdf/web_guide_state_authorities.pdf.

Further Reading: International Adoption in the United States

THE INTERNATIONAL ADOPTION SOURCEBOOK (Dan H. Berger, ed. 2008).

SARAH IGNATIUS & ELISABETH STICKNEY, IMMIGRATION LAW AND THE FAMILY § 6.02 (Susan Compernolle updating ed., 2010).

Elizabeth Bartholet, *International Adoption: Overview, in* 2 ADOPTION LAW AND PRACTICE 10–1 (Joan Heifetz Hollinger ed., 2010).

Joan Heifetz Hollinger, *International Adoption: Legal Requirements and Practical Considerations, in* 2 ADOPTION LAW AND PRACTICE 11–1 (Joan Heifetz Hollinger ed., 2010).

adoption must satisfy additional requirements before the adoptive parents can obtain a Hague Adoption Certificate (or Hague Custody Declaration). The state court must verify that the necessary steps under the Convention were completed, and that the adoptive placement is in the best interests of the child.[185] An official copy of the adoption court's findings and its final order must then be submitted to the State Department with a Form DS5509 ("Application for a U.S. Hague Adoption Certificate or Custody Declaration").[186] The Hague Adoption Certificate ensures that the adoption will be recognized under the Convention in all contracting States.

Non-Hague Outgoing Adoption Cases

Procedures for outgoing intercountry adoption cases that do not fall within the scope of the Adoption Convention are defined almost entirely by state law. The United States has no border exit controls, and an adopted U.S.-citizen child does not need permission to leave the country with his or her legal custodian. There are now reporting requirements for these cases under the IAA, which established a federal registry for all adoptions involving children immigrating into or emigrating from the United States, whether or not they fall within the scope of the Convention.[187] The IAA requires that all "[a]ccredited agencies, approved persons, and other persons, including governmental authorities, providing adoption services in an intercountry adoption not subject to the Convention that involves the emigration of a child from the United States" must report information on the adoption to the registry.[188]

Hague Adoption Convention Countries (as of November 15, 2011)

Albania	Estonia	Mongolia
Andorra	Finland	Netherlands
Armenia	France	New Zealand
Australia	Georgia	Norway
Austria	Germany	Panama
Azerbaijan	Greece	Paraguay
Belarus	Guatemala	Peru
Belgium	Guinea	Philippines
Belize	Hungary	Poland
Bolivia	Iceland	Portugal

Hague Adoption Convention Countries — continued

Brazil	India	Romania
Bulgaria	Ireland	San Marino
Burkina Faso	Israel	Seychelles
Burundi	Italy	Slovakia
Cambodia	Kazakhstan	Slovenia
Canada	Kenya	South Africa
Cape Verde	Latvia	Spain
Chile	Liechtenstein	Sri Lanka
China (and Hong Kong)	Lithuania	Sweden
Colombia	Luxembourg	Switzerland
Costa Rica	Macedonia	Thailand
Cuba	Madagascar	Togo
Cyprus	Mali	Turkey
Czech Republic	Malta	United Kingdom
Denmark	Mauritius	United States
Dominican Republic	Mexico	Uruguay
Ecuador	Moldova	Venezuela
El Salvador	Monaco	Vietnam

Notes

1. Children adopted abroad must obtain an immigrant visa to enter the United States. *See infra* note 113 and accompanying text.
2. Intercountry Adoption Act (IAA), 42 U.S.C. §§ 14901–14954 (2010). *See infra* notes 132–59 and accompanying text.
3. Convention on the Rights of the Child (CRC), art. 21, G.A. Res. 44/25 (Annex), U.N. GAOR, 44th Sess., Supp. No. 49, at 166, U.N. Doc. A/RES/44/49 (1990), *reprinted in* 30 I.L.M. 1448 (1989). *See* SYLVAIN VITÉ & HERVÉ BOÉCHAT, A COMMENTARY ON THE UNITED NATIONS CONVENTION ON THE RIGHTS OF THE CHILD, ARTICLE 21: ADOPTION (2008).
4. The 1994 Uniform Adoption Act (UAA), 9 (1A) U.L.A. 11 (1999), was enacted only in Vermont.
5. Federal legislation in this area is tied to the child welfare system established and funded under Title IV-B and IV-E of the Social Security Act. *See* 42 U.S.C. §§ 621–628b, 670–679b (2010).
6. *See* 42 U.S.C. § 5115a (2010).
7. Indian Child Welfare Act, 25 U.S.C. § 1901–1963 (2010). *See also infra* note 179.
8. *See generally* JENNIFER FAIRFAX, THE ADOPTION LAW HANDBOOK: PRACTICE, RESOURCES AND FORMS FOR FAMILY LAW PROFESSIONALS 127–40 (2011); Joan Heifetz Hollinger, *Consent to Adoption, in* 1 ADOPTION LAW AND PRACTICE ch. 2 (Joan Heifetz Hollinger ed., 2010).
9. *See* Chapter 5.
10. *See* Chapter 5; *see generally* HOMER H. CLARK, JR., THE LAW OF DOMESTIC RELATIONS IN THE UNITED STATES § 20.2 (2d Student ed., 1988).
11. If the child concerned is not a U.S. citizen, the appropriate foreign consulate should be notified early in the proceedings. *See* Vienna Convention on Consular Relations, art. 37, Apr. 24, 1963, 596 U.N.T.S. 261, 21 U.S.T. 77, T.I.A.S. No. 6820, which provides that "if the relevant information is available" to state and local authorities, they have a duty "to inform the competent consular post without delay of any case where the appointment of a guardian or trustee appears to be

in the interests of a minor or other person lacking full capacity who is a national of the sending State."

12. *See, e.g.,* J.B. v. DeKalb Cnty., 12 So. 3d 100 (Ala. Civ. App. 2008); Adoption of D.J.F.M., 643 S.E.2d 879 (Ga. Ct. App. 2007); Adoption of Peggy, 767 N.E.2d 29 (Mass. 2002). *Cf.* Adoption of Doe, 923 N.E.2d 1129 (N.Y. 2010). *See* Chapter 5.

13. *Id.; see also* Huynh Thi Anh v. Levi, 586 F.2d 625 (6th Cir. 1978).

14. *See infra* notes 157-59 and accompanying text.

15. *See infra* notes 174-86 and accompanying text.

16. *See generally* FAIRFAX, *supra* note 8, at 77-100; James B. Boskey & Joan Heifetz Hollinger, *Placing Children for Adoption, in* 1 ADOPTION LAW AND PRACTICE § 3.04 (Joan Heifetz Hollinger ed., 2010). Colorado, Connecticut, Delaware, and Massachusetts prohibit direct private placement of children with unrelated prospective adoptive parents. *Id.*

17. *See infra* notes 138-42 and accompanying text.

18. *E.g.,* CAL. FAM. CODE §§ 8901-8919; N.Y. DOM. REL. LAW § 115-a (2010); WIS. STAT. § 48.839 (2010).

19. *See generally* FAIRFAX, *supra* note 8, at 77-100; Boskey & Hollinger, *supra* note 16.

20. *Id.* § 3.06.

21. *See generally* FAIRFAX, *supra* note 8; SARAH IGNATIUS & ELISABETH STICKNEY, IMMIGRATION LAW AND THE FAMILY § 13:22 (Susan Compernolle updating ed., 2010); Joan Heifetz Hollinger, *Intercountry Adoption: Legal Requirements and Practical Considerations, in* 2 ADOPTION LAW AND PRACTICE § 11.04[7][b] (2010).

22. *See infra* notes 172-73 and accompanying text.

23. RESTATEMENT (SECOND) OF CONFLICT OF LAWS § 289.

24. Assisted reproduction is discussed in Chapter 5.

25. 28 U.S.C. § 1738A. *See, e.g.,* Baby Girl Clausen, 502 N.W.2d 649 (Mich. 1993).

26. RESTATEMENT (SECOND) OF CONFLICT OF LAWS § 78 (1971). *E.g.,* Barry E. v. Ingraham, 371 N.E.2d 492 (1977). Under section 78, a state court has power to exercise jurisdiction to grant an adoption if it is in the state of domicile of either the adopted child or the adoptive parent, and the adoptive parent and either the adopted child or the child's legal custodian is subject to the court's personal jurisdiction.

27. UAA, *supra* note 4, § 3-101.

28. *See* Adoption of Asente, 734 N.E.2d 1224 (Ohio 2000). *See generally* CLARK, *supra* note 10, § 20.3; EUGENE F. SCOLES ET AL., CONFLICT OF LAWS § 16.5 (4th ed. 2004). *See also* Herma Hill Kay, *Adoption in the Conflict of Laws: The UAA, Not the UCCJA, Is the Answer,* 84 CAL. L. REV. 703 (1996).

29. Jurisdiction under the UCCJEA is discussed in Chapter 5.

30. 9 (1A) U.L.A. 649 (1999). *Compare* UCCJEA § 102 (4) (defining "child custody determination"), *with* UCCJEA § 103 (stating that the act "does not govern an adoption proceeding"). The Comment to § 103 explains that adoptions were excluded from the UCCJEA to prevent a conflict with the jurisdictional provisions of the 1994 Uniform Adoption Act. *See* 32 FAM. L.Q. 301, 320-22 (1998).

31. *See generally* Robert G. Spector & Cara N. Rodriguez, *Jurisdiction Over Children in Interstate Placement: The UCCJEA, Not the ICPC, Is the Answer,* 41 FAM. L.Q. 145 (2007). *See also* FAIRFAX, *supra* note 8, at 101-14.

32. *Cf.* Armstrong v. Manzo, 380 U.S. 545 (1965). Note that this standard brings the jurisdictional problems of adoption law into the recognition question.

33. *See* Finstuen v. Crutcher, 496 F.3d 1139, 1156 (10th Cir. 2007); Adar v. Smith, 597 F.3d 697 (5th Cir. 2010) (mandating recognition of out-of-state adoptions by same-sex couples that would not be permitted under the local law of the jurisdiction where recognition was sought); *see also* Adoption of Sebastian, 879 N.Y.S.2d 677 (N.Y. Surr. Ct. 2009) (entering adoption decree to assure that parental rights of same-sex couple will be recognized in all states).

34. *See* RESTATEMENT (SECOND) OF CONFLICT OF LAWS § 290; SCOLES ET AL., *supra* note 28, § 16.6.

35. In child protection cases, a child who becomes eligible for long-term foster care as a result of abuse, neglect, or abandonment may be classified as a special immigrant under 8 U.S.C.

§ 1101(a)(27)(J) and may petition for adjustment of status under 8 U.S.C. § 1255(h). *See also* 8 C.F.R. § 204.12. On the application of the orphan immigration rules in this setting, see IGNATIUS & STICKNEY, *supra* note 21, § 13:33.

36. Guadarrama-Garcia v. Acosta, 217 F. Supp. 2d 802, 805 (S.D. Tex. 2002).

37. *E.g.*, Corbett v. Stergios, 137 N.W.2d 266, 269–70 (Iowa 1965); Zanzonico v. Neeld, 111 A.2d 772 (N.J. 1955); Martinez v. Gutierrez, 66 S.W.2d 678 (Tex. Comm'n App. 1933). For a comparison of domestic and foreign adoption rules, see SCOLES ET AL., *supra* note 28, § 16.7.

38. *See also* RESTATEMENT (THIRD) OF FOREIGN RELATIONS LAW § 481(1) (1987) ("Except as provided in § 482, a final judgment of a court of a foreign state . . . establishing or confirming the status of a person, . . . is entitled to recognition in courts in the United States.").

39. *E.g.*, Barry E. v. Ingraham, 371 N.E.2d 492 (N.Y. 1977) (declining to recognize adoption in Mexico by a New York couple of a child born in New York to a New York mother).

40. *E.g.*, State *ex rel.* Smith v. Smith, 662 N.E.2d 366 (Ohio 1996) (foreign adoption decree was not res judicata in subsequent parentage action where birth father had no notice or opportunity for a hearing); Doulgeris v. Bambacus, 127 S.E.2d 145 (Va. 1962) (adoptive child's birth mother did not consent or participate in foreign adoption proceeding). *Cf.* Adoption of Francesca M., 506 N.Y.S.2d 642 (N.Y. Surr. Ct. 1986) (no readoption allowed in New York where child had not been freed for adoption under Italian law).

41. *Cf.* Adoption of Dafina T.G., 613 N.Y.S.2d 329 (N.Y. Surr. Ct. 1994) (dispensing with legalization requirement in readoption case). Where required, this may be accomplished by use of the Hague Apostille Convention, discussed in Chapter 1.

42. *E.g.*, ALASKA STAT. § 25.23.160 (2010); FLA. STAT. § 63.192 (2010); IOWA CODE § 600.15 (2010); TEX. FAM. CODE § 162.023(a) (2010). *See generally* Malinda L. Seymore, *International Adoption and International Comity: When Is Adoption "Repugnant"?* 10 TEX. WESLEYAN L. REV. 381 (2004) (citing statutes).

43. *E.g.*, MINN. STAT. § 259.60 (2010); N.J. STAT. § 9:3-43.2 (2010); N.Y. DOM. REL. LAW § 111-c (2010); OHIO REV. CODE § 3107.18 (*applied in* Walsh v. Walsh, 764 N.E.2d 1103 (Ohio Ct. App. 2001)).

44. *E.g.*, *In re* Patrick's Will, 106 N.W.2d 888 (Minn. 1960). *See generally* SCOLES ET AL., *supra* note 28, § 16.6. Local succession law will also govern the question whether an adopted child has the right to inherit from his or her natural parents; see *id.*

45. 923 N.E.2d 1129 (N.Y. 2010).

46. *Id.* at 1135–36.

47. 765 F.2d 877, 884 (9th Cir. 1985). The court also declined to defer to immigration authorities on this issue, ruling that the question whether customary adoptions were legally recognized in Tonga was a matter of law, subject to Federal Rule of Civil Procedure 44.1 and de novo review in the federal courts. *Id.* at 881. *Cf.* Mila v. Dist. Dir. of Denver Colo. Dist. of Immigration & Naturalization Serv., 678 F.2d 123 (10th Cir. 1982).

48. Ramsey Cnty. v. Yee Lee, 770 N.W.2d 572 (Minn. Ct. App. 2009); *see also* Rasmussen v. Wisconsin, 69 N.W.2d 467 (Wis. 1955). *Cf. Patrick's Will*, 106 N.W.2d at 892 (recognizing common law adoption under Scottish law); Comstock v. Johnson, 223 P.2d 105 (Cal. Ct. App. 1950) (recognizing customary adoption under Norwegian law).

For a brief summary of the current laws and procedures relating to adoption in various foreign countries, see IGNATIUS & STICKNEY, *supra* note 21, at app. G.

49. *See* Kupec v. Cooper, 593 So. 2d 1176 (Fla. Dist. Ct. App. 1992); Walsh v. Walsh, 764 N.E.2d 1103 (Ohio Ct. App. 2001); Taylor v. Taylor, 364 P.2d 444 (Wash. 1961).

50. RESTATEMENT (SECOND) OF CONFLICT OF LAWS § 290, cmt. c.

51. *See generally* Seymore, *supra* note 42, at 388–91.

52. 127 S.E.2d 145 (Va. 1962). *See also* Tsilidis v. Pedakis, 132 So. 2d 9 (Fla. Dist. Ct. App. 1961) (adult adoption in Greece by unmarried Florida resident violated Florida's public policy).

53. 192 A.2d 737 (Pa. 1963). *But see* Guarantee Bank & Trust Co. v. Gillies, 83 A.2d 889 (N.J. 1951).

54. *See also* G. PARRA-ARANGUREN, EXPLANATORY REPORT, CONVENTION ON PROTECTION OF CHILDREN AND CO-OPERATION IN RESPECT OF INTERCOUNTRY ADOPTION, paras. 421–428, Hague Conference on Private International Law, 2 ACTES ET DOCUMENTS DE LA DIX-SEPTIÈME SESSION 537 (1993).

55. *See* 42 U.S.C. § 14951.
56. *E.g.*, CAL. FAM. CODE § 8919 (2010); COLO. REV. STAT. § 19-5-205 (2010); MINN. STAT. § 259.60 (2010); N.Y. DOM. REL. LAW § 115-a(8) (applied in Adoption of Dafina T.G., 613 N.Y.S.2d 321, 329 (Sur. Ct. 1994)). *See also* FAIRFAX, *supra* note 8, at 97–99; Hollinger, *supra* note 21, § 11.04[7] [a].
57. *See, e.g.*, Adoption of W.J., 942 P.2d 37 (Kan. 1997) (upholding Chinese adoption in readoption proceeding); Barry E. v. Ingraham, 371 N.E.2d 492, 493–94 (N.Y. 1977) (denying readoption in New York following adoption decree in Mexico when the child and all other parties had been "domiciled, resident, and present in New York").
58. *See, e.g.*, Corbett v. Stergios, 381 U.S. 124 (1965) (per curiam) (mandating recognition of Greek adoption based on terms of treaty between the United States and Greece).
59. 584 N.W.2d 564, 566 (Iowa 1998).
60. *E.g.*, OHIO REV. CODE § 3107.18(C) (2010); 23 PA. STAT. § 2908 (2010); TEX. FAM. CODE § 162.023(b). *See also* Hollinger, *supra* note 21, § 11.04[7][c].
61. *See, e.g.*, *In re* Greene Cnty. Dep't of Soc. Servs., 870 N.E.2d 1132 (N.Y. 2007). *See generally* FAIRFAX, *supra* note 8 at 225–31.
62. *See generally* Margaret M. Mahoney, *Permanence and Parenthood: The Case for Abolishing the Adoption Annulment Doctrine*, 42 IND. L. REV. 639 (2009).
63. *See* Adoption of M.S., 103 Cal. Rptr. 3d 715 (Cal. Ct. App. 2010) (construing CAL. FAM. CODE § 9100).
64. *E.g.*, Mohr v. Commonwealth, 653 N.E.2d 1104 (Mass. 1995) (collecting cases). *See generally* D. Marianne Blair, *Liability of Adoption Agencies and Attorneys for Misconduct in the Disclosure of Health-Related Information, in* 3 ADOPTION LAW AND PRACTICE ch. 16 (Joan Heifetz Hollinger ed., 2002); Harriet Dinegar Milks, *"Wrongful Adoption" Causes of Action Against Adoption Agencies Where Children Have or Develop Mental or Physical Problems That Are Misrepresented or Not Disclosed to Adoptive Parents*, 74 A.L.R.5th 1 (1999 & Supp.) *See also* FAIRFAX, *supra* note 8 at 233–41.
65. *See* Regensburger v. China Adoption Consultants, Ltd., 138 F.3d 1201 (7th Cir. 1998); Dresser v. Cradle of Hope Adoption Ctr., Inc., 358 F. Supp. 2d 620 (E.D. Mich. 2005); Ferenc v. World Child, 977 F. Supp. 56 (D.D.C. 1997); *cf.* Sherman v. Adoption Ctr. of Wash., Inc., 741 A.2d 1031 (D.C. 1999). *See generally* Hollinger, *supra* note 21, § 11.02[1][b]; Donovan M. Stelzner, *Intercountry Adoption: Toward a Regime That Recognizes the "Best Interests" of Adoptive Parents*, 35 CASE W. RES. J. INT'L L. 113 (2003).
    See also Harshaw v. Bethany Christian Servs., 714 F. Supp. 2d 751 (W.D. Mich. 2010) (addressing choice of law in tort action following adoption in Russia); Prince v. Illien Adoptions Int'l, 806 F. Supp. 1225 (D. Md. 1992) (addressing long-arm jurisdiction in tort action following adoption in India).
66. *Dresser*, 358 F. Supp. 2d at 638–42.
67. 42 U.S.C. § 14944; 22 C.F.R. § 96.72 (2010). Note, however, that the U.S. regulations allow agencies to require clients to sign liability waivers within the limits of applicable state law. *See* 22 C.F.R. § 96.39 (D.). *See also infra* note 142 and accompanying text.
68. 42 U.S.C. § 14954.
69. 42 U.S.C. § 14922(b)(2); 22 C.F.R. §§ 96.68–.72.
70. *See* 8 C.F.R. §§ 96.81–.88.
71. *See* 8 U.S.C. § 1431; 8 C.F.R. pts. 320, 322. *See generally* IGNATIUS & STICKNEY, *supra* note 21, § 15.31; Hollinger, *supra* note 21, § 11.05.
72. Automatic citizenship may also be available to children adopted under the two-year rule. *See id.*, § 11.05.
73. *See* IGNATIUS & STICKNEY, *supra* note 21, § 15.31–.33; Hollinger, *supra* note 21, § 11.05[6].
74. A list of Contracting States is listed at the end of this chapter; current information is available from the Hague Conference website at http://www.hcch.net.
75. The scope is established in Article 2(1):

> The Convention shall apply where a child habitually resident in one Contracting State ("the State of origin") has been, is being, or is to be moved to another Contracting State

("the receiving State") either after his or her adoption in the State of origin by spouses or a person habitually resident in the receiving State, or for the purposes of such an adoption in the receiving State or in the State of origin.

Under Article 2(2), the Convention covers only adoptions that create a permanent parent-child relationship. *See* Explanatory Report, *supra* note 54, at paras. 87–94. Note that in the United States, regulations define habitual residence for purposes of the Convention with reference to both the citizenship and residence of the adoptive parents and child. *See infra* notes 135–37 and accompanying text.

76. *See* Hague Conference, The Implementation and Operation of the 1993 Intercountry Adoption Convention: Guide to Good Practice No. 1106–11 (2008) [hereinafter Good Practice Guide No. 1]. *See also* William Duncan, *Nationality and the Protection of Children Across Frontiers, and the Example of Intercountry Adoption*, 8 Y.B. Priv. Int'l L. 75–86 (2006).

77. *See infra* notes 81–89 and 143–152 and accompanying text.

78. *See generally* Hague Conference on Private International Law, Accreditation and Adoption Accredited Bodies: General Principles and Guide to Good Practice No. 2 (Draft 2010) [hereinafter Draft Good Practice Guide No. 2].

79. If a state makes this declaration, Article 22(3) requires that it keep the Permanent Bureau of the Hague Conference informed of the names and addresses of approved bodies and persons. Not all functions may be delegated in this manner. Under Article 22(5), the reports required by Articles 14 and 15 must be prepared under the authority of the Central Authority or other public authorities or accredited bodies. Article 22 reflects a careful compromise between the delegates who drafted the Convention after extensive discussion of "private" or "independent" adoptions. *See* Explanatory Report, *supra* note 54, at paras. 373–98.

80. Note also that Article 32(3) limits the remuneration that "directors, administrators and employees of bodies involved in an adoption" may receive to amounts that are not "unreasonably high in relation to services rendered." *See* Explanatory Report, *supra* note 54, at paras. 526–34.

81. Art. 14. The U.S. definition of habitual residence is discussed *infra* at notes 135–37 and accompanying text.

82. The receiving State must also determine that the child "is or will be authorized to enter and reside permanently" in the receiving State under Article 5(c).

83. *See* arts. 4(c), 16(1)(c).

84. *See* art. 4(d).

85. *See* Good Practice Guide No. 1, *supra* note 76, at 113–15.

86. *See also infra* note 148 and accompanying text. There is also the possibility under Article 26(1) (c) that the adoption may be treated as terminating the legal relationship between the child and his or her mother and father but not the child's relationship with other family members. *See* Explanatory Report, *supra* note 54, at para. 92.

87. *See* Good Practice Guide No. 1, *supra* note 76, at 114–15. In the United States, relative adoptions are accommodated under the Intercountry Adoption Act at 42 U.S.C. § 14952(a) and 22 C.F.R. § 96.54. *See infra* notes 180 and accompanying text.

88. *See* art. 2; *see also* Good Practice Guide No. 1, *supra* note 76, at 114.

89. Explanatory Report, *supra* note 54, at para. 499.

90. *See* art. 19. The Convention does not affect any law in a State of origin requiring that adoption be formalized in that State or prohibiting transfer to the receiving State before adoption. *See* art. 28. Under Article 18, the Central Authorities of both states must "take all necessary steps" to obtain permission for the child to leave the State of origin and enter and reside permanently in the receiving State." The transfer must take place "in secure and appropriate circumstances and, if possible, in the company of the adoptive or prospective adoptive parents."

91. *See* art. 21.

92. *See* art. 24.

93. *See* art. 26(1). Articles 26 and 27 address the special questions involved with a "simple adoption" that does not terminate preexisting parent-child relationships. *See also* the EXPLANATORY REPORT, *supra* note 54, at paras. 436-86.

94. This obligation implements the child's identity rights under Articles 7 and 8 of the Convention on the Rights of the Child, *supra* note 3.

95. *See* 42 U.S.C. § 14941(a); 22 C.F.R. pt. 98.

96. Art. 30 (1). Article 31 protects the privacy of information, requiring that personal data "'shall be used only for the purposes for which they were gathered or transmitted." *See generally* GOOD PRACTICE GUIDE NO. 1, *supra* note 76, at 123-25.

97. *See* GOOD PRACTICE GUIDE NO. 1, *supra* note 76, at 123-30; DRAFT GOOD PRACTICE GUIDE NO. 2, *supra* note 78, at paras. 619-22.

98. *See* GOOD PRACTICE GUIDE NO. 1, *supra* note 76, at 125-27.

99. *See id.* at 108-11; Duncan, *supra* note 76.

100. *See* GOOD PRACTICE GUIDE NO. 1, *supra* note 76, at 127-29.

101. *See id.* at 129-30. Depending on the child's age and degree of maturity, the child must also be consulted concerning measures taken following a disruption in placement.

102. *See infra* notes 138-42 and accompanying text.

103. *See infra* notes 157-59 and accompanying text.

104. *See generally* Hollinger, *supra* note 21, § 11:02; DRAFT GOOD PRACTICE GUIDE NO. 2, *supra* note 78, at paras. 573-622.

105. *See generally* IGNATIUS & STICKNEY, *supra* note 21, § 13.3. This section also allows immigration of a child "adopted while under the age of sixteen years . . . if the child has been battered or subject to extreme cruelty by the adopting parent or by a family member of the adopting parent residing in the same household." The requirement of two years of legal custody and residence do not apply in cases of battering or extreme cruelty. *See id.*, § 6.29.

106. *See* 8 U.S.C. § 1151(b)(2)(A)(i).

107. *See generally* Cynthia Hemphill et al., *Intercountry Adoption: The Three Categories of Immigrant Visas*, *in* THE INTERNATIONAL ADOPTION SOURCEBOOK 18 (Dan H. Berger ed., 2008). *See also* IGNATIUS & STICKNEY, *supra* note 21, §§ 3:3, 13:8, 13:34.

108. *See* 8 U.S.C. § 1101(b)(1)(F)(ii), (G)(iii).

109. *See generally* IGNATIUS & STICKNEY, *supra* note 21, at ch. 13.

110. *Cf. In re* Khatoon, 19 I. & N. Dec. 153, 1984 WL 48596 (BIA 1984) (adoption not recognized under personal law applicable to Muslims in India).

111. *See* U.S. Dep't of State, *Advisory Opinion on Adopted Children of LPRs and NIV Holders*, *reprinted at* 73 INTERPRETER RELEASES 869 (1996). *See also* IGNATIUS & STICKNEY, *supra* note 21, § 13:34; Hollinger, *supra* note 21, § 11.03[2][a]. A lawful permanent resident may obtain a family preference visa under 8 U.S.C. § 1153(a)(2)(A) for an adopted minor child, but this typically involves a significant waiting period and a risk of aging out.

112. Similarly, U.S. citizens living abroad may return to the United States to adopt, but they will need to consult the law of their place of residence to determine whether their adopted child will be eligible to enter and reside with them.

113. *See* 8 U.S.C. § 1153(d); 8 U.S.C. § 1101(b)(1)(E).

114. *See* 8 U.S.C. § 1101(b)(1)(E)(ii).

115. *See generally* IGNATIUS & STICKNEY, *supra* note 21, §§ 13:15-:22; Hollinger, *supra* note 21, § 11.03[2][c]. *See also* Hemphill et al., *supra* note 106, at 19-20.

116. *E.g.*, Rogan v. Reno, 75 F. Supp. 2d 63 (E.D.N.Y. 1999).

117. *Id.*

118. 10 I. & N. Dec. 761, 1964 WL 12135 (BIA 1964).

119. *See* IGNATIUS & STICKNEY, *supra* note 21, § 13:23; Hollinger *supra* note 21, § 11.04[4]. The State Department provides detailed information on adoption procedures in different countries on its website at http://www.adoption.state.gov.

120. *See* 8 C.F.R. § 204.3(f).

121. *See infra* notes 160-71 and accompanying text.

122. *See* 8 C.F.R. § 204.3(e); IGNATIUS & STICKNEY, *supra* note 21, §§ 13:24–:27; Hollinger, *supra* note 21, § 11.04[2]–[3].

123. The parents' alternatives would be either to attempt to set the adoption aside or to reside with the child in the foreign country for two years and then petition for a visa under the two-year rule.

124. *See* IGNATIUS & STICKNEY, *supra* note 21, §§ 13:28–:29; Hollinger, *supra* note 21, § 11.04[5]. If the adoptive parents were not previously approved to adopt on the basis of a Form I-600A, additional documents and processing are required with the Form I-600.

125. *See* 8 C.F.R. § 204.3(k); *see also* Hollinger, *supra* note 21, § 11.04[6].

126. 8 C.F.R. § 204.3(i). Reasonable payment for "administrative, court, legal, translation and/or medical services related to the adoption proceedings" are permitted.

127. The filing date of the Form I-600 determines whether the child meets the age limits for entry as an adopted child.

128. *See generally* IGNATIUS & STICKNEY, *supra* note 21, § 13:30; Hollinger, *supra* note 21, § 11.04[6].

129. *See* Hollinger, *supra* note 21, § 11.04[7]. An IR-4 visa is also issued, and readoption required, unless one or both of the adoptive parents "personally saw and observed the child prior to or during the adoption proceedings."

130. *See supra* notes 56–60 and accompanying text.

131. *See* U.S. Dep't of State, FAQs: Bilateral Adoption Agreement with Russia (July 13, 2011), http://adoption.state.gov/content/pdf/FAQs_re_Agreement_07_13_2011_FINAL2.pdf.

132. Guatemala and Cambodia have been in this category; current information is available from the State Department's adoption web page at http://adoption.state.gov under "Country Information."

133. *See infra* notes 157–59 and accompanying text. Adopted children habitually resident in Hague Convention countries who meet the requirements of the two-year rule in 8 U.S.C. § 1101 (b)(1)(E) are eligible for an IR-2 visa without following the Hague adoption process.

134. *See* 8 U.S.C. § 1101(b)(1)(G)(i), (iii).

135. Under 8 C.F.R. § 204.303(a), a U.S. citizen seeking to bring an adopted child into the country under § 1101(b)(1)(G) is deemed to be habitually resident in the United States if he or she:

> (1) Has his or her domicile in the United States, even if he or she is living temporarily abroad; or
>
> (2) Is not domiciled in the United States but establishes by a preponderance of the evidence that:
>
>> (i) The citizen will have established a domicile in the United States on or before the date of the child's admission to the United States for permanent residence as a Convention adoptee; or
>>
>> (ii) The citizen indicates on the Form I-800 that the citizen intends to bring the child to the United States after adopting the child abroad, and before the child's 18th birthday, at which time the child will be eligible for, and will apply for, naturalization under section 322 of the Act and 8 C.F.R. pt. 322. This option is not available if the child will be adopted in the United States.

136. 8 C.F.R. § 204.303(b) provides that "A child whose classification is sought as a Convention adoptee is, generally, deemed for purposes of [the Adoption Convention] to be habitually resident in the country of the child's citizenship." The rule goes on to state:

> If the child's actual residence is outside the country of the child's citizenship, the child will be deemed habitually resident in that other country, rather than in the country of citizenship, if the Central Authority (or another competent authority of the country in which the child has his or her actual residence) has determined that the child's status in that country is sufficiently stable for that country properly to exercise jurisdiction over the child's adoption or custody. This determination must be made by the Central Authority itself, or by another competent authority of the country of the child's habitual

residence, but may not be made by a nongovernmental individual or entity authorized by delegation to perform Central Authority functions. The child will not be considered to be habitually resident in any country to which the child travels temporarily, or to which he or she travels either as a prelude to, or in conjunction with, his or her adoption and/or immigration to the United States.

137. *See generally* Carine Rosalia-Marion et al., *Determining Habitual Residency, in* THE INTERNATIONAL ADOPTION SOURCEBOOK (Dan. H. Berger ed., 2008); IGNATIUS & STICKNEY, *supra* note 21, §§ 13:39–:41. *See infra* notes 157–59 and accompanying text.

138. *See* 42 U.S.C. §§ 14921–14924 (2010); 22 C.F.R. pt. 96. *See generally* DRAFT GOOD PRACTICE GUIDE NO. 2, *supra* note 78; Hollinger, *supra* note 21, § 11.07[2]–[4].

139. *See* 42 U.S.C. § 14921; 22 C.F.R. §§ 96.12–.17. The regulations permit some providers to work under the supervision of an accredited agency or approved person acting as the primary provider.

140. *See* 42 U.S.C. § 14902(3); 22 C.F.R. § 96.2; 8 C.F.R. § 204.302.

141. *See* 8 C.F.R. §§ 96.29–.55; *see also* 42 U.S.C. §§ 14921–14923.

142. *See* 42 U.S.C. § 14924. *See also* notes 67–70 and accompanying text.

143. *See* 8 C.F.R. § 204.311.

144. *See* 8 C.F.R. § 204.310. *See generally* IGNATIUS & STICKNEY, *supra* note 21, §§ 13:49–:54.

145. *See* 8 C.F.R. § 204.313. *See generally* IGNATIUS & STICKNEY, *supra* note 21, §§ 13:55–:59.

146. *See* 8 C.F.R. § 204.309(b)(1). This restriction does not apply if the adoption or grant of custody is subsequently annulled and the petitioner files a new form I-800.

147. *See* 8 C.F.R. § 204.309(b)(2). *See generally* IGNATIUS & STICKNEY, *supra* note 21, § 13:48.

148. *See* 42 U.S.C. § 14952(a). Contact is permitted under 8 C.F.R. § 204.309(b)(2)(iii) if:

The petitioner was already, before the adoption, the father, mother, son, daughter, brother, sister, uncle, aunt, first cousin (that is, the petitioner, or either spouse, in the case of a married petitioner had at least one grandparent in common with the child's parent), second cousin (that is, the petitioner, or either spouse, in the case of a married petitioner, had at least one great-grandparent in common with the child's parent) nephew, niece, husband, former husband, wife, former wife, father-in-law, mother-in-law, son-in-law, daughter-in-law, brother-in-law, sister-in-law, stepfather, stepmother, stepson, stepdaughter, stepbrother, stepsister, half brother, or half sister of the child's parent(s).

See also supra notes 85–88 and accompanying text.

149. *See* 8 C.F.R. § 204.305.

150. *See* 42 U.S.C. § 14931(c); *see also* 22 C.F.R. § 97.5.

151. *See supra* notes 71–73 and accompanying text.

152. For a discussion of unresolved issues in this area, see Hollinger, *supra* note 21, § 11.07[8].

153. 8 U.S.C. § 1101(b)(1)(G)(i) allows a child to enter the United States after an adoption under the Convention if, among other requirements:

the child's natural parents (or parent, in the case of a child who has one sole or surviving parent because of the death or disappearance of, abandonment or desertion by, the other parent) or other persons or institutions that retain legal custody of the child, have freely given their written irrevocable consent to the termination of their legal relationship with the child, and to the child's emigration and adoption;

and, "in the case of a child having two living parents, the natural parents are incapable of providing proper care for the child."

154. *See* Hemphill et al., *supra* note 106, at 28.

155. *See* 42 U.S.C. § 14941; 22 C.F.R. § 98.2.

156. *See supra* notes 61–70 and accompanying text.

157. *See* 8 C.F.R. § 204.303.

158. *See* 8 U.S.C. § 1154(d)(2); 8 C.F.R. § 204.2(d)(2)(vii)(D), (F); 8 C.F.R. § 204.309(b)(1), (b)(4). *See also* USCIS, *Frequently Asked Questions: Intercountry Adoptions* 7 (Sept. 29, 2008), *reprinted at* 85 INTERPRETER RELEASES 2630, 2673–82 (2008). *See generally* IGNATIUS & STICKNEY, *supra* note 21, § 13:41; Hemphill et al., *supra* note 106, at 13, 29–30.

159. *See id.; see also* USCIS, *Q & A Regarding Intercountry Adoptions Following Implementation of the Hague Convention*, 85 INTERPRETER RELEASES 2630 (2008).

160. *See generally* IGNATIUS & STICKNEY, *supra* note 21, § 13:3. This section also allows immigration of a child "adopted while under the age of sixteen years . . . if the child has been battered or subject to extreme cruelty by the adopting parent or by a family member of the adopting parent residing in the same household." The requirement of two years of legal custody and residence do not apply in cases of battering or extreme cruelty. *See id.* § 6.29.

161. *See* 8 U.S.C. § 1151(b)(2)(A)(i).

162. In addition to "immediate relatives," who may enter the United States outside the immigration quota system, citizens and lawful permanent residents may sponsor the immigration of family members through the family preference visa system established in 8 U.S.C. § 1153(a). In general, an adopted child who is part of a principal immigrant's household before the immigrant enters the United States is eligible to enter on the same basis as any other children would be. *See generally* Hemphill et al., *supra* note 106, at 18. *See also* IGNATIUS & STICKNEY, *supra* note 21, §§ 13:8–:3, 13:8, 13:34.

163. A substantial body of case law addresses the question whether a foreign adoption was valid for this purpose. These cases indicate that a legally valid customary adoption may be the basis for admission of an adopted child; *see* Kaho v. Ilchert, 765 F.2d 877 (9th Cir. 1985). *See also* Pascual v. O'Shea, 421 F. Supp. 80 (D. Haw. 1976) (Hawaiian adoptions valid based on adoptive parents' residence there even though children lived in the Philippines). *See* IGNATIUS & STICKNEY, *supra* note 21, §§ 13:3–:6.

164. *See* 8 C.F.R. § 204.2(d)(2)(vii). *E.g.*, Moge v. Morris, 470 F. Supp. 556 (E.D. Pa. 1979) (adopted Jordanian children not entitled to adjust status after adoption by U.S. citizens where children continued to reside with their natural parents). *See generally* IGNATIUS & STICKNEY, *supra* note 21, §§ 13:8–13:9.

165. *See generally* IGNATIUS & STICKNEY, *supra* note 21, § 13:11; Hollinger, *supra* note 21, § 11.03[2][b].

166. 8 U.S.C. § 1101(b)(1)(E)(ii). *See generally* IGNATIUS & STICKNEY, *supra* note 21, § 13:7.

167. *See* IGNATIUS & STICKNEY, *supra* note 21, §§ 6:29–:34, 13:10–:12.

168. *See* Ng Fun Yin v. Esperdy, 187 F. Supp. 51 (S.D.N.Y. 1960).

169. 8 U.S.C. § 1255. *See* IGNATIUS & STICKNEY, *supra* note 21, § 8:22.

170. *See* IGNATIUS & STICKNEY, *supra* note 21, §§ 13:33–:34; *but see* Guadarrama-Garcia v. Acosta, 217 F. Supp. 2d 802 (S.D. Tex. 2002).

171. *See* 8 C.F.R. § 204.2(d)(2)(vii)(D), (F); U.S. CIS Adjudicators Field Manual § 21.4 (d)(5)(F). *See generally* IGNATIUS & STICKNEY, *supra* note 21, §§ 13:40–:41; Hemphill et al., *supra* note 106, at 13, 29–30.

172. *See* 8 C.F.R. § 212.5. Information is available on the USCIS website at http://www.uscis.gov (under "Humanitarian" and "Humanitarian Parole").

173. Parole was granted to a small group of Cambodian and Vietnamese children whose adoptions were subject to dispute at the time the United States suspended processing of adoption visas in those countries. *See* News Release, U.S. Dep't of Justice, INS Announces Suspension of Cambodian Adoptions and Offer of Parole in Certain Pending Cases (Dec. 21, 2001), http://www.uscis.gov/files/pressrelease/CambAdop_122101.pdf.

174. *See* U.S. Dep't of State, A Guide to Outgoing Cases from the United States (last updated Jan. 6, 2009), http://adoption.state.gov/content/pdf/OutgoingCasesFAQs.pdf; U.S. Dep't of State, A Web-Guide for State Authorities on Outgoing Adoption Cases from the United States to Another Convention Country (last updated Apr. 2008), http://adoption.state.gov/content/pdf/web_guide_state_authorities.pdf.

175. *See* 8 C.F.R. § 204.303, discussed *supra* at notes 135–37 and accompanying text.

176. *See supra* notes 138–42 and accompanying text. Under 22 C.F.R. § 96.2, "Public domestic authority means an authority operated by a State, local, or tribal government within the United States." 22 C.F.R. § 96.12(b) allows a public domestic authority to "offer, provide, or facilitate the provision of any such adoption service."

177. *See* 42 U.S.C. § 14932(a); 22 C.F.R. §§ 96.53–.55.

178. *See generally* 42 U.S.C. § 14932(a). Counseling is also required; *see* 22 C.F.R. § 97.3(g), (h).

179. 42 U.S.C. § 14932(a)(1)(B). Intercountry adoptions must also comply with the federal Indian Child Welfare Act, if applicable. *See* 42 U.S.C. § 14953(b).

180. *See* 22 C.F.R. §§ 97.3(c), 96.54; and Guide to Outgoing Cases, *supra* note 174. Efforts to find a domestic placement are also not required "in other special circumstances accepted by the State court with jurisdiction over the case." 22 C.F.R. § 96.54. For a critique of these rules as implemented in the United States, see Galit Avitan, Note, *Protecting Our Children or Our Pride? Regulating the Intercountry Adoption of American Children*, 40 CORNELL INT'L L.J. 489 (2007).

181. *See* 22 C.F.R. § 97.3(d). Under U.S. law, U.S. citizens need not begin with the Central Authority in the country where they reside if they wish to adopt a U.S.-citizen child in the United States. *See supra* note 175 and accompanying text.

182. *See* 22 C.F.R. § 97.3(b) (transmission of child data); 97.3(f) (consent by foreign authorized entity); 97.3(i)(1), (2).

183. *See* 22 C.F.R. § 97.3(j).

184. *See* 22 C.F.R. § 97.3(e).

185. *See* 42 U.S.C. § 14932(b). *See* Hollinger, *supra* note 21, § 11.07[10].

186. *See* 42 U.S.C. § 14932(c); 22 C.F.R. §§ 97.1–.4.

187. The purpose is "to permit tracking of pending cases and retrieval of information on both pending and closed cases." *See* 42 U.S.C. § 14912(e).

188. *See* 42 U.S.C. § 14932(d); 22 C.F.R. §§ 99.1–.2.

Index